D0478301

to my children

contemporary adolescence: readings

**edited
by
hershel d. thornburg
the university of arizona**

brooks/cole publishing company
belmont, california
a division of wadsworth publishing company, inc.

L. C. Cat. Card No.: 79-141368
ISBN 0-8185-0007-7
Printed in the United States of America

1 2 3 4 5 6 7 8 9 10—75 74 73 72 71

preface

A book of readings has a different function than a textbook. Although a text may provide a good overview and an excellent summary of a topic, it typically does not include primary source materials. In contrast, a book of readings exposes the student to a broad range of research that has not been interpreted by the author. A book of readings also presents more points of view than a textbook does. As various aspects of social life and values shift, the book of readings can assist the reader in formulating his own position on a topic.

I wrote this book for the undergraduate student majoring in the behavioral sciences. For many students it will be their initial experience in adolescent psychology. The diversity of this book makes it a useful companion to most current adolescent psychology texts, but it can also

serve as the primary source for a class in adolescent psychology.

I have organized the book into 11 chapters on 11 important aspects of adolescent psychology. Each chapter begins with an introduction and contains from three to five articles. The introductions are designed to give the reader some background information on each topic, to acquaint him with the current status of that topic, and to show the interrelatedness of the articles to one another. The annotated bibliographies at the end of each chapter will give the student suggestions for additional reading.

Chapter One is designed to provide an overview of current thinking in adolescent psychology. The chapter introduction is a reinterpretation of Robert Havighurst's developmental tasks theory. In a sense, this introduction sets the tone for the rest of the book, although no other chapter is dependent on this one for clarity or understanding.

Two criteria affected my choice of articles. First, I chose only those that are related to a topic's current emphasis, which is stressed in each introduction. Thus I have bypassed the so-called classic articles in order to present the most recent research in adolescent psychology. Second, for the highly controversial or multi-faceted topics, I selected articles that will represent conflicting positions.

For their critical but helpful comments on the manuscript, I would like to thank Professors Henry Angelino, of The Ohio State University; Elizabeth Douvan, of The University of Michigan; Frank B. W. Harper, of The University of Western Ontario; and the late Norma E. Werner, of San Jose State College. I would also like to thank Terry Hendrix, Bonnie Fitzwater, and Micky Stay, of Brooks/Cole Publishing Company, for their editorial assistance. I am especially grateful to Glen Nicholson, of The University of Arizona, for his criticisms on the chapter introductions, and to Alice Schoenberger for her untiring efforts in typing the manuscript. My final word of appreciation is to my wife, Ellen, without whose enduring patience and timely support this book might not have become a reality.

Hershel D. Thornburg

contents

five

the adolescent and school 145

six

adolescence: peers and values 181

seven

adolescent delinquency   219

eight

the adolescent and drugs   267

nine

the adolescent and activism   307

contemporary adolescence: readings

one

adolescence today

We live in a changing society—one in which today's adolescent wants action. As he grows physically and mentally, he searches for the emotional and social experiences that will lead him to adulthood. Although we no longer accept Hall's (1904) storm-and-stress *(Sturm and Drang)* theory that adolescence is an inevitable period of emotional conflict, we cannot deny that today's youths are highly conflict oriented. These conflicts stem from a rapidly evolving culture that offers ambiguous, changing, and often contradictory privileges to its youth.

Today's adolescents are no different from those of previous generations; the difference lies within our society. The media bombard us with accounts of the restlessness, nonconformity, and rebelliousness of our youth. Yet these characteristics can apply to older individuals as well. An advancing technology, rapid social change, affluence,

unrest, and violence have created a social dilemma that challenges the previously accepted life styles of all people.

Each of these social phenomena helps perpetuate a growing conflict between the generations and positively reinforces adolescent dissatisfaction with the adult culture. As a result, many youths either alienate themselves or become activists and strike out at the established way of life. They blame society for not allowing them to become a vital part of the adult world. Yet this accusation may not be valid. Gottlieb (1968, p. 13) has made the following point on this issue:

> The middle class Hippie, Teeny Bopper, Beat, or adolescent who is not readily identifiable by some group association but adopts a life style which we label as deviant, is not usually the product of an unjust economic system. He is not the victim of a social order which blocks entry into the

3

dominant culture. The middle class adolescent has other alternatives. No matter how painful or absurd is the business of growing up in America he can stay with it, if he chooses to do so. External pressures do not force the withdrawal. He most often has sufficient referents who have both the desire and the ability to help him attain the good life if and when he so chooses.

Certainly there is nothing wrong with differences between the generations' social and political views or even with many of the expressive tastes and fashions of youth today. Often what is deemed unacceptable behavior is only the activity of atypical youth. Adolescents are generally no different from adults in their beliefs—only in the behavioral forms those beliefs take.

Many of today's problems stem from the progress made in the past 20 to 30 years. The adolescents who make up our youth culture are the post-World-War-II babies who have been constantly exposed to industrialization, technology, automation, television, urbanization, affluence, advanced scientific discoveries, the space age, the atomic age, increasing leisure, greater communication and mobility, a sexual liberalization, and increasingly stricter prerequisites for educational and occupational realizations.

The impact of social advancement may be analyzed by looking at the biological, psychological, and cultural factors that may contribute to changing adolescent behavior. If any new factors exist in these three areas, then it seems only fair to evaluate youth in view of *contemporary advancements* rather than those of previous ages. Although many psychologists have observed different developmental behaviors in the adolescent, the most thorough and systematic categorization of adolescent developmental tasks was advanced in Havighurst's *Developmental Tasks and Education* (1952).

Developmental Tasks in Adolescence

Developmental tasks may be defined as skills, knowledge, functions, or attitudes that an individual should acquire during a specific period of his life. Havighurst sees these tasks as being acquired through (1) physical maturation, (2) cultural expectations, and (3) personal aspirations. These forces "set for the

individual a series of developmental tasks which must be mastered if he is to be a successful human being" (1952, p. 4). Referring specifically to the adolescent, Havighurst advances the following developmental tasks (1952, pp. 33-71) as necessary accomplishments to move successfully into adulthood.

1. Forming new and more mature relationships with agemates of both sexes.
2. Achieving a masculine or feminine social role.
3. Accepting one's physique and using the body effectively.
4. Achieving emotional independence from parents and other adults.
5. Achieving assurance of economic independence.
6. Selecting and preparing for an occupation.
7. Preparing for marriage and family life.
8. Developing intellectual skills necessary for civic competence.
9. Acquiring a set of ethics as a guide to behavior.

Tasks 1, 2, and 3, which accompany the onset of puberty, have a strong biological base. Other competencies, such as emotional maturity (Task 4), occupational selection (Task 6), and developing intellectual skills (Task 8), are also strongly influenced by physical maturation. Some tasks are resolved by the adolescent through personal and cultural expectations. Striving for economic independence (Task 5), marriage (Task 7), and gaining social responsibility and acquiring values (Task 9) are characteristic of identity striving.

Most tasks, even those with a strong biological basis, are affected by social approval and disapproval. Furthermore, society has set appropriate times for adolescents to work out their tasks. The inability to accomplish a task within the allotted interval often results in nonresolution within the individual. Therefore, in light of (1) society's attempt to help the individual learn tasks, (2) rapid social and technological changes that have been made since World War II, and (3) continuing change within our contemporary society, it seems necessary to reevaluate several adolescent developmental tasks in respect to our contemporary society.

1. Forming new and more mature relationships with agemates of both sexes. Heterosexual involvements are instrumental in learning proper sex roles, and our culture sets a pattern for expected adolescent social behaviors. As groups of adolescents move into their own subcultures, these patterns may vary from those designated by the larger society. By high school, boys and girls should be socializing with the opposite sex—an expectation that is not out of line with the accomplishment of Task 1.

Havighurst (1952) notes that, from the age of 13 or 14, most boys and girls are preoccupied with social activities and experimentation. He suggests that from their own sex they learn to behave as adults among adults and with the opposite sex they learn adult social skills. At about 14 to 16, a more intimate type of companionship develops.

Yet there is increasing evidence that heterosexual roles are developing at about 11 or 12, and single and double dating is quite common among 13- to 14-year-old youths. Martinson's (1968) research indicates that children feel pressures from their parents to date and to attend heterosexual functions by the sixth grade. *Esquire's* (Braun, 1968) "Micro-Boppers" provided a descriptive but somewhat overexaggerated discussion on adultlike behaviors (business investments, television commercial-making, martinis, and sexual candidness) of the 9–13 age group and illustrated how merchandising is capitalizing on the psychosexual conflicts of youth.

Boys initially experience growth in the testes and penis at about 12, and pigmented pubic hair appears at about 13. Their growth spurt reaches its peak by about 14 (Meredith, 1967). The average girl has her adolescent growth spurt shortly after 10, with the peak being reached at about 12. During this time two significant events occur: breast enlargement and the menarche. Breast enlargement begins at about 10-1/2, and full breast development usually occurs within three years. Approximately 80 percent of all girls reach menarche between 11-1/2 and 14-1/2 (Meredith, 1967). These body changes, combined with business' appeal to 10- and 11-year-old femininity, have thrown many girls into a social-sexual role earlier than they have been in previous generations.

One additional factor contributes to an earlier adolescent socialization: the new junior high or "middle-school" movement. Many schools have been reorganized to include only grade five or six through grade eight. A 1967–68 survey has shown that in the 1960s more than 1100 school districts adopted this organizational plan (Alexander, 1968). It is highly probable that having 10- to 13-year-old students in one school will greatly increase the earlier socialization of youth.

2. Achieving a masculine or feminine social role. Havighurst feels it is necessary for the boy to accept the idea of becoming a man and the girl to accept the idea of becoming a woman. The traditional roles he suggests in his book (1952) are work roles for men and wife-mother roles for women. However, social changes have given today's woman more freedom than was permitted in earlier generations. Thus there are alternative roles in our society that place less emphasis on male-masculine/female-feminine traits. Boys still find it easy to fit into the traditional role, but that role has become more competitive as females have begun to reject the wife-mother role for acceptable alternatives. Two factors contribute to the shift from clearly distinct to less definitive sex roles: (1) movement of the female from the home to many roles outside the home, and (2) dress modes that are considered asexual rather than either masculine or feminine.

The growth of industrial centers with the concentration of population around the cities and the shift from extended to nuclear families have resulted in an increasing individualism and less definite masculine and feminine roles within and outside the home. In 1890, 4.5 percent of the married women in the United States worked. By 1940 this figure had risen to 16.7 percent. A 1962 government report stated that the number of women 14 years of age and older who were gainfully employed had risen steadily from 25 percent in 1940 to 35 percent in 1960 *(The impact of urbanization,* 1962). These statistics reveal that females are placing less emphasis on the traditional wife-mother role.

Changing dress modes have probably had a more significant effect on men than on women. Our society has become more tolerant of the in-between types of appearance, which Winick (1968) refers to as sexual crisscrossing. He points out that since World War II clothing and appearance have become increasingly unisexual. Regarding men, Winick states (p. 20):

> Men are wearing colorful and rakishly epauleted sports jackets, iridescent fabrics, dickies, and bibbed and pleated shirts of fabrics like batiste and voile.
>
> Men's trousers are slimmer and in many instances are worn over girdles of rubber and nylon. Ties are slender and often feminine. The old reliable gray fedora has given way to softer shapes and shades, sometimes topped by gay feathers. Sweaters are less likely to have the traditional V-neck than a boat neck adopted from women's fashions. Padded shoulders on a suit are as out of date as wide lapels and a tucked-in waist. The new look is the soft, slender, straight-line silhouette that also characterizes the shift, which has been the major woman's dress style of the 1960's.

Clearly, masculinity is not so obvious as it once was. Several studies indicate that boys' long hair and dress are major sources of conflict with parents *(Phi Delta Kappan,* 1969; *Generations Apart,* 1969), which implies that observable male-masculinity/female-femininity is still desired by many adults.

3. Accepting one's physique and using the body effectively. A major problem for adolescents during this period is learning how to channel sexual energy and drive into socially acceptable behaviors. This problem is often compounded by (1) physical attractiveness, (2) accelerated physical growth, and (3) parental overprotectiveness.

Many attitudes toward one's body derive from comparison between oneself and other adolescents; differences typically cause anxiety. Adolescents are particularly concerned with height, weight, facial blemishes, size of hips and breasts in girls, and size of genitals in boys (Angelino & Mech, 1955). Our society emphasizes physical appearance and maturation. The closer a person's body fits the "norm," the greater the social reinforcement. Youths whose bodies do not fit this norm suffer anxiety and negative self-feelings and question their own normality.

Society prefers girls to look feminine and be attractive to boys. It wants boys to be masculine, to gain recognition among other boys, and to be popular with girls. Adolescent anxiety about personal appearance can be reduced if youth can learn to accept themselves. To be proud and satisfied with oneself is an important developmental task.

4. Achieving emotional independence from parents and other adults. Achieving independence has always been difficult for American adolescents. As they develop peer relationships, they exercise behavioral independence; but in doing so, they often run into conflicts with parents and the adult world. Such conflicts are often generated by the adolescent's need to relinquish childhood ties with his parents and to find sufficient independent behaviors that are not overpowering to him. Physical maturation causes the adolescent to want fewer controls and inhibitions from parents. Increased social skills learned through peer interaction facilitate self-responsibility and create a degree of emotional as well as behavioral independence. Yet, occasionally, rapid and drastic behavioral change only intensifies adolescent conflict. Therefore, although youth should learn to throw off habits of dependency on adults, the goal is often best accomplished with a degree of parental guidance.

Parents should have an awareness of their child's need to become autonomous. They should allow him, in his early childhood, to exercise initiative and responsibility that will later permit him to make his own way with minimal dependency on them. Such families are usually characterized by warmth, concern, and democratic household procedures. Today's changing society and an increasing confrontation with the Generation Gap have made the problems of behavioral autonomy blatant.

5. Achieving assurance of economic independence. Achieving economic independence is obviously related to occupational opportunity. Automation has reduced the number of unskilled jobs to 5 percent of all available positions (Wolfbein, 1964), and numerous semiskilled and skilled jobs are becoming obsolete. Slightly more than a million youths between 16 and 21 are out of school and unemployed *(The impact of urbanization,* 1962). Affluence has convinced another group of youths that a job is not necessary. Therefore, there is limited, if any, opportunity for these adolescents to gain the assurance of personal capability to be economically independent; both economics and occupations become either distant or unrealistic goals. In some cases this task is not resolved until the individual makes an occupational choice or completes some type of post-high-school training or education.

6. Selecting and preparing for an occupation. As Gold and Douvan have stated, adolescence is the time when "the child presumably becomes critically aware of the work life—of the need to choose a vocation toward which he can gear education, and the other instrumental activities, of the variety of work roles, of the relationship that binds adulthood, economic independence, and vocational responsibility into a tight nexus" (1969, p. 225).

Slocum and Empey (1956) found that meaningful work experiences affect occupational choice. Moreover, studies on aspirational levels of students indicate that they generally aspire to high occupational goals (Garrison, 1955), probably because of the underlying cultural pressure that relates a man's worth to his occupation and success. Aspirations are also affected by a person's immediate needs. To discern one's needs and goals during adolescence is difficult, especially since most youths are exhorted to go to college or to take some post-high-school training before they enter the job market.

In 1952, Havighurst stated "Employers want workers who can read and write, and when the labor supply is plentiful, employers like to insist on a high school diploma as a prerequisite. This is a convenient way of selecting people who can learn a new job fairly rapidly" (pp. 47-48). This description is no longer accurate. Employers are considerably more selective, and occupational requirements are more stringent. As a result, adolescents are prolonging the time spent in selecting, preparing for, and actually becoming involved in the occupational world.

The developmental task of selecting a career is becoming increasingly vital for adolescent girls. Many jobs once awarded only to males are now given to qualified females. Yet two factors make the task more complex for females than for males: (1) many occupations are still not accessible to them, so they must discern which choices are most realistic; and (2) their choices may be tentative,

depending on when and whom they marry.

Thus occupational mobility, job obsolescence, and stricter job requirements point out the importance of adolescent awareness of the changing occupational world. Indeed, perhaps the most successful career prototype hinges around the adolescent who acquires transferable occupational skills.

7. Preparing for marriage and family life. Adolescents must experience the naturalness of sexual attraction to the opposite sex. As attachments become deeper, attitudes toward sexual involvement, marriage, and rearing a family emerge. The more the individual is aware of the involvement and commitment required of him, the more realistic these attitudes will be.

Marriage is considered the core of social life. Because each social class influences the way the individual will regard the marital relationship, varying patterns of marriage can be seen within a society. This situation creates a great need for family-life education.

Learning an appropriate sex role in marriage involves the acceptance and understanding of socially approved male and female roles. This problem often focuses on expressing the sex drive in socially acceptable ways. In our society there is no single code of sexual morality. When dating problems arise over petting and premarital intercourse, different standards are suggested by one's peers, parents, and church. This situation often results in intense conflict within the individual. Sex education and family-life information from a reliable source can prevent misinformation and ignorance from causing much confusion over the adult sex role (Thornburg, 1969b).

Youths must learn to view marriage in a variety of dimensions other than sex. The more broadly based a marriage, the greater the chances of putting all dimensions into a wholesome perspective.

8. Developing intellectual skills necessary for civic competence. Because the learning of social and civic skills usually follows the learning of academic skills, this task is usually not accomplished before late adolescence. The young person acquires civic intelligence through understanding what society gives to him and, in turn, what he may give to society. However, not all individuals are capable of achieving this understanding to the same degree.

In today's complex society, social order often becomes confused and civic responsibility is lost in the apparent inconsistencies of our political structure. As a result, we must learn new coping skills. One such skill includes the ability to tolerate ambiguity. Not all things are black or white; not every question can be answered. Social and civic matters require a tolerant citizenship. Another skill needed by today's youth is the ability to delay gratification (Hollister, 1966). We hear demands and ultimata from our adolescents and confuse the democratic process with the necessity of immediately satisfying those demands. They must understand that some things take time, whether they like it or not. A third social skill is the ability to tolerate seemingly insoluble problems within our society, such as civil rights and the Vietnam War. The individual's ability to cope with them can strengthen his personal frame of reference.

9. Acquiring a set of ethics as a guide to behavior. An individual's value system begins to form through the social-psychological influences of the family. During adolescence his values are tested by experiences outside the home, and he discovers how closely his values resemble those of his parents or how much value autonomy he is experiencing. Associated with values is a person's basic philosophy of life. Through parents, peers, religion, philosophy, and ideals, a value hierarchy emerges and serves as a reference point for adolescent and subsequent adult behavior.

Since the 1940s there has been a decrease in religious interest in this country. Individuals have developed new ethical codes and practices that do not center around any religious dogma. Although recent research indicates that there is an increasing concern for religion by today's youth (Thornburg, 1969a), many adolescents consider it meaningless and find no help within its framework.

Subsequently, many enduring values no longer have much significance. Rather than modify parental values, many adolescents label them traditional, conservative, or stifling and reject them outright. Yet adolescents need a personal reference point. Although they may be disenchanted with the beliefs that their parents or society holds, they must find replacements. Through a personal value system an individual can resolve indefinite and ambiguous questions and learn to be himself—morally, ethically, and philosophically.

Contemporary Issues

In the first article in this chapter, Chickering presents a candid analysis of today's society and how it got that way. He pulls his ideas about today's problems from the experiences of youth and observes that "The new environment makes us an experience-oriented generation; the prevailing culture makes us experience-starved."

Schmuck, drawing on his research with several hundred teen-agers, lists adolescents' major concerns in relating to parents, teachers, and peers. Despite widespread reports of adolescent rebellion, parents play the most instrumental role in shaping adolescent interests, and 65 percent of all adolescent concerns involve parents. Teen-agers must learn to integrate parental influences with those of teachers and peers.

The third article in this chapter discusses various aspects of extended adolescence. Goldberg coins a new word, *juvenatrics,* to describe the study of prolonged adolescence. He notes changes in our society that prevent the adolescent from achieving full adult status for roughly ten years after puberty.

The College Student

In his article, Wrenn describes two basic modes of expression on today's campus: one is characterized by the hippie individual who withdraws into his inner world and the second by the activist who makes a direct attack on existing problems. Wrenn suggests that conflict with authority is a natural process. Yet he urges college personnel to discuss the issues raised by students.

The adolescent does not automatically

resolve his developmental tasks by entering college. Many of the protests we hear are merely the pleas of youths trying to work out directions in their lives. Neither restrictiveness nor irresponsibility will help them solve their problems. A better balance of emphasis between college students and noncollege adolescents could help all young people discover their identities as individuals.

Understanding the Research

Often a student may lose interest in what he is reading or miss the significance of an article because he does not understand statistical terms. Karabinus' article will provide a background to help the student interpret the tables, graphs, correlations, and levels of confidence that appear throughout this text.

sherman b. chickering

how we got that way

We have our own America, our own bag. We all participate to a greater or lesser extent in a common youth culture. The culture is homogeneous, integral and pervasive. We are part of it because we were born into it. We differ only in how much we identify with it, not whether. We are the other side of the Generation Gap.

Just as the term "Other America" became workable in the sixties, so did the term "Generation Gap." History set forth the Poor in the sixties. And Youth: When the war babies came of age, the Gap appeared.

The Generation Gap began when the war babies could articulate their response to the new environment. We who were born after, say, 1940 grew up in an environment radically different from that of our parents. We were able to see the environment, and our parents couldn't. Our parents could see only that we were different, not why we were different.

Some scholars have gotten close to the why of the matter. The ones I find most congenial are: Reuel Denney, Edgar Z. Friedenberg, Paul Goodman, Nevitt Sanford, Harold Taylor, Harris Wofford, Margaret Mead, David Riesman, Laurence Wylie, Kenneth Keniston and, as will be clear enough, Marshall McLuhan. The scholars have written about some of the forces operating on modern youth, but, understandably, they do not represent the experience of youth in meeting those forces. Naturally enough, they do not try to "tell it like it is." That's what people like me are supposed to do.

Youth culture is the way we affirm the existence of a totally new environment; it is our response to it. The religion of the youth culture is the cult of experience; campus chaplains tailor their ministry to helping students become involved in "meaningful human relationships." The sex is not so much a revolution as it is a relationship; it is a ritual, a shared experience consecrated by the engagement of the whole person. The education is action-oriented; it makes of society a laboratory for the humanities and breaks down the walls between disciplines and classrooms. The politics is crisis-oriented, a "participatory democracy" founded on confrontations between youth and the leaders of the prevailing culture. The arts are "action arts," notably folk singing, jazz and abstract films. Leisure activity is kinesthetic, characterized by discotheques, "happenings," psychedelia, and the omnipresent motorcycle. The economics is self-imposed poverty, the hallmark of which is exploitation of the consumer economy (for example, theft, "borrowing," living off the land, "scarfing" of leftovers). The hero of the culture is the man of "sincerity," whether he be the hedonistic Jean-Paul Belmondo, the strident Fidel Castro, the scrofulous Bobby Dylan, or the David Merrick who said, *"Holly Golightly* was my Bay of Pigs."

The culture is of a piece. All the elements reflect a central thrust, which is why the New

Reprinted with permission of the author and publisher from *The American Scholar*, 1967, **36,** 602-07.

Left radical and the seemingly traditional fraternity "jock" are on common ground. Although some young people express most of
the manifestations of the culture, and others
very few, all express at least some elements
of the common culture. Youth culture cannot
be dismissed as the handiwork of the dissident minority or of the campus health service
habitues.

In fact, a case can be made for considering the sick students the ones who participate only somewhat in youth culture. Those
who participate *most* in youth culture, the
ones who are not "well-adjusted" to society,
are often the ones who are the most at peace
with themselves. As John Leo reported in the
New York *Times* of June 19, 1967, "Psychologists and social scientists, operating independently on various campuses and with
varying research methods, agree [that] . . .
activists as a group are . . . psychologically
more stable than nonactivists."

The activists are not the only true believers within youth culture. The other prevalent
type is the "hippie," the complete dropout
from organized society. The two types differ
in origin: the activist is most likely to be the
child of liberal Democratic parents; the hippie is most likely to be the child of conservative Republicans. The one considers his
father a New Deal sellout, but adopts his father's Constitutional ideals; the other considers his father irrelevant, and rejects the
prevailing culture entirely. Nevertheless, the
common ground between the activist and the
hippie is considerable. Professor Richard
Flacks of the University of Chicago singles
out at least three common traits: "romanti-
cism," "moral purity," and rejection of conventional career opportunities. All are
characteristic of youth culture generally, and
all are logical responses to the postwar environment.

Youth culture seems to provide the
necessary matrix within which a young person can find an entire, well-integrated identity. Those young people who do not partake
of the entire culture because they are attracted to the traditional culture (for example, parental values, career patterns) are the
ones who appear to suffer the most acute
and prolonged identity crises.

At one extreme there are those who accept the traditional culture completely, and
are somehow able to resist the psychic im-

plications of the new environment. In the
middle is a vast and growing group of young
people who are torn between the starkly different alternatives posed by the two cultures.
At the other extreme are a growing number
of young people who identify themselves in
the way Stokely Carmichael does, embracing
"blackness" rather than trying to become
"white."

This celebration of youth culture as a
complete answer to every human need undoubtedly appears bizarre to anyone over
the age of thirty. In the past, youth culture
such as it was could never have been a complete answer. Younger generations in times
past seem to have latched onto experiences
they called their own, such as goldfish swal-
lowing, only to find more lasting satisfaction
within the prevailing culture. The difference
today is that the new experiences of the
young are no longer confined to a response
to new *fragments* of reality. For the first
time, in recent history at least, youth culture
is a response to a *totally new environment*.
The postwar generation has grown up in an
environment radically different in degree and
kind from past environments. Their culture is
an appropriate and total response to the demands of the new environment, which is why
they can be at peace with themselves and at
war with the world.

There are four elements, or forces, which
I find most crucial to a definition of the new
environment, and most responsible for the
new youth culture. In describing them I am
extrapolating in part from my own experience, which under other circumstances
might have produced either an activist or a
hippie.

The first element was our peculiar parents. Ours was an Oedipal childhood, especially if we were war babies. Father was away,
or dead. Mother was independent, working,
worried, and looked to us for affection. A
sense of perpetual siege was built into us,
and hence a sensitivity to potential or actual
human loss. While the experience was probably similar to that of a World War I or Depression baby in this respect, the enormity of the
conflict and yet the state of relative economic
abundance fostered in us a sensibility peculiar to the times. We absorbed the impression
that economic security could not replace or
compensate for emotional insecurity.

If we were postwar babies, we absorbed

much the same impression, although for somewhat different reasons. Some of the reasons are those documented by Kenneth Keniston in *The Uncommitted*. Our mothers were the dominant figures in our lives because our fathers were so involved in "making it" with the drive, and sense of time lost, left over from the war. This situation deepened and exacerbated the split already evident between the educated, emancipated woman frustrated in her attempts at role definition and her somewhat shadowy, elusive husband whose energies were spent somewhere off in the anonymous void of the economy. Our mothers often felt insecure about their self-fulfillment in marriage and so invested an inordinate amount of emotional capital in their children. (See Nevitt Sanford's study of guilt-ridden Vassar graduates.) The parents set the stage. Their children, especially the boys, became uprooted. Boys tended to identify more with the "emotional" qualities of their mothers rather than the principles and practices of their fathers.

The most important, and most multidimensional, of the forces shaping youth culture was mass communications—the second crucial element of the new environment.

The postwar child was surrounded, as no other generation before, by messages. Signs, billboards, store displays, supermarkets, the traditional media, and finally the new, all-consuming, substitute environment, television, enveloped us in a cocoon of sensory information. I think it is doubtful that anyone who did *not* grow up in this postwar period can appreciate how much the senses of the young were bombarded, as they are today, by messages. Indeed, the media—in the broadest sense of the word—provided a new environment. To those who grew up in the new urban complexes, it virtually *was* the environment. (For example, I learned more to read from signs and store displays than I did from books and teachers.)

The effects of this new media-envelope on us seem to have been twofold, each with many ramifications.

We felt like members of global village; indeed we were exposed to instant news, the Top Ten and Westerns with a worldwide audience of two hundred million. Our common experience was our media experience. So, to set Marshall McLuhan aside for the time be-

ing, the *content* of the media made us feel at home in a world of jingles, jungles and juggernauts. In turn, this environment impressed upon us the presence, and the all-consuming importance, of *people*. Our ideas had arms and legs. (Especially when we figured out our chances of winning a trip to the Howdy Doody Show—about one in ten million?) Hence, unlike our parents, we thought of principles, programs and power in terms of personalities and clever phrases.

We were also massaged. McLuhan has it right. Sights, sounds, bombardments—the little boxes tuned in on our aural and tactile senses, and activated them the way print never did, or could. Sensory "information" seemed to go through our *bodies* to our brains, or central nervous systems, rather than almost directly into cognitive perception. Our perceptions were throbbing, pulsating. Ours were participant perceptions. Experience rather than knowledge became the wellspring of our motivation. And the only permanent feature of our affluent, static society that provided us regularly with stimulating experience was television, and the related aural/tactile media. No wonder I have difficulty with the word "media"; I can't consider television and the media environment generally as an intermediary; I consider it— feel it, perceive it—as a beginning and end, a constitutive feature of everyday experience.

Both content and medium conspired to make us more sophisticated than any amount of heritage, tutelage or erudition could have. The world as a global village taught us to see people in the nakedness of deeds that contradicted words. The message of the media taught us to leap into life with all five senses. The result was that we learned to see right through to the quick; we learned to distinguish thought from action in others, and learned to mesh thought and action in our own lives. We learned that Ipana toothpaste was better than Crest if it felt better, not if it claimed to be, and learned that Captain Video was sometimes more for real than toothpaste.

The media made hypocrites, squares, finks and fnerds of the world's big shots, and made hippies and swingers of us little boys. Which is why General Sarnoff will be to this age what Lenin was to the last, and Marshall McLuhan will be the ex post facto Marx.

The news media is one reason, the main

one, why we took so well to social criticism, especially in its comic-book form. *Mad* comics became our Word. As Laurence Wylie writes, *"Mad's* symbol, the insipidly smiling Alfred E. Neuman, who maintains his ghoulishly cheerful expression while the most appalling things go on around him, stands for American culture itself as the adolescent experiences it." He also stands for the adolescent who says, "What, Me Worry?—I've got it all figured out." Which he did: when we read the serious literature of social criticism we knew all about it already.

Mad comics and their ilk became for us the most true, valuable, relevant, enlightening and uplifting form of literature. *Mad* became the reflective part of our youth culture, the gloss on our substitute environment, the trot for our television retentions.

Our first environment was our peculiar parents. Our second was the synthetic one, the new, all-pervasive media and the primers for it such as *Mad.* Our third was the affluent, populous, classless society and, with it, the absence of tomorrow.

Most of us either grew up in sizeable cities or were at least exposed to them regularly. (Seventy percent of Americans now live in "metropolitan areas.") We knew instinctively what a "behavioral sink" was before Tom Wolfe applied the term to New York. We became used to fighting for our classroom, transport or theater seats. We were no longer a people brought up with the luxury of a fence separating us from our "good neighbors." We had to face up to interpersonal confrontations. Like our Swiss counterparts, we grew up majoring in "international relations" without benefit of a tea-and-crumpets, arm's-length People-to-People program.

We were members of the first classless society. Whether we were the sons of union organizers or corporation presidents or civil servants, we had relatively equal chances for survival in the new postwar technocracy. We no longer felt predestined to a place high or low in the social hierarchy. By the same token, we no longer felt so deeply the internal compulsion to fulfill the promise of that high or low place. We were aided and abetted in this lack of the traditional drive by the new economic facts of life.

We were the first generation born into widespread affluence. Eighty percent of the nation's families could afford to buy—on or off time—almost anything mass-produced, including a higher education. And there were grants, loans, government handouts, fringe benefits, and pensions available to carry us seemingly from cradle to grave. Furthermore, all white-collar occupations offered relatively equal financial promise, save for the uppermost reaches of a few of them. For us the economic incentive, as well as the class/status incentive, had largely disappeared.

This condition was fostered considerably by our peculiar fathers (not to be confused necessarily with my own). Children of the Depression, our fathers did not wish to see their own children go through similar deprivation. Thus we were weaned on "the good things in life," all of which were costly. In this frame of reference, the habit of solving sibling problems with money was, of course, congenial to shadowy Depression-bred Dad. His parental responsibilities could be discharged financially rather than paternally. Hence, when son came to father with a "How do the stars work?" question, Dad could feel confident, or at least complacent, in saying, "Here, kid, take five bucks and go see a movie." As it were.

So, What, Me Worry? The question of tomorrow became considerably less pressing. Money was at hand. And father was not to be listened to for advice on the big questions later on because he didn't bother with our little questions earlier. The rewards available through playing the Tomorrow game—Dad's game—were evaporating. This situation was fine by us, for we were more tuned in on Today anyway by our electronic media, and the manifold seductions of the new environment. The old secular eschatology had been shattered.

The fourth element, aside from the new home, media and marketplace, was provided by The Bomb. This was the extra-terrestrial dimension, the symbolic Armageddon. The Bomb was never right on top of us, of course. None of us had ever felt the impact of a bomb. We were, in one respect, the most unravaged generation that has ever lived. Yet, almost by contrast, we felt deeply the ghoulish presence of the mushroom cloud. As young writer Sheldon Renan says, "We were the Ground Zero Generation."

The Bomb became for us the equivalent of knowing at night that Boris Karloff really *was* hiding under the bed. After all, we saw the documentaries of the Bikini blasts, and we had to wear name tags around our necks back there in the late forties. And we had to lie under our desks during air raid drills, wondering whether the wooden top of our desk was strong enough to keep out the blast. For kids this is not a game or a functional necessity; it is a reality. It is a tangible fear. It is a nightmare. (Some of us have, every month like clockwork, what might be called a "nuclear dream.")

In a way, an ironic way, The Bomb is even more real for us than for the man who survived the first-wave landing at Anzio. We feel in our bones what total destruction means, whereas the Anzio survivor doesn't simply because he survived. We feel the absurdity represented by The Bomb, and react in at least two observable ways: We have one more reason to live for Today rather than Tomorrow, and the fact that The Bomb exists becomes an absolute gauge, an ultimate proof, by which to consider our leaders misguided at best, and, at worst, sick. *(Mad* magazine once carried a sequence that showed two land masses on the planet hurling I.C.B.M.'s at each other until the missiles were finally being launched from tiny fragments of orbiting terra firma.)

The generation gap again: There are evidently those who can read Herman Kahn and take him seriously. We can't take Kahn seriously because we *can* take The Bomb seriously. Hence the popularity among us of sick jokes, horror film revivals, the theater of the absurd, Hobbits, trivia games, *Dr. Strangelove,* the *Realist* magazine, *Marvel* comics, and C-grade movie heroics.

Our peculiar parents, our new media, our marketplace, our Bomb: They bring us face-to-face with a prevailing culture that does not respond to the new environment. So we become alienated, and take up exclusively with each other.

Youth culture gains its hold over us through our confrontation with institutional America as well as through our response to the new environment. The confrontation becomes most acute when we reach college, for college is the gateway through which we are invited to participate fully in the major institutions of society.

We discover after we settle into college that we are not really there to learn but to get good grades and acquire a passport into the economy. To a generation raised on person-to-person peer group experience and heightened sensitivities (if not sensibilities), this sort of higher Pavlovian encampment is frustrating. We chafe for less grading and more individualized professorial attention not out of a desire for license but out of a need for the chemistry of interpersonal confrontation. We consider the old education a sybaritic appurtenance of the Industrial Revolution, class privilege and a hardship-oriented society. It does not answer to our needs.

The ultimate frustration for the college man, prior to freak-out or sellout, comes from the sizeable time span between vocational choice and actual application. A virtual galaxy of forces conspires to keep young men, as Harold Taylor puts it, huffing and puffing on the sidings of higher and higher education: the specialized requirements of the "knowledge explosion"; an antiquated, book-oriented curriculum rather than an experience-oriented one involving work-study programs; the convenience offered recruiters by the designation "Ph.D.," over "M.A.," over "B.A."; and, until recently amended to eliminate loopholes, the Draft that feeds an Alfred E. Neuman war.

We are not allowed to go to work in a job that uses our education until we have had too much education for our own good. We lose our executive drive drying up over economics textbooks. When we finally enter the economy, if we haven't fallen out of it first, we have become too old to take chances. We have moved from farm club to clubhouse without our turn at the plate. The massive institutions into which we move are generally too big to offer us our turn at bat while we're in our twenties anyway—even if we still had enough stuff to handle it.

No wonder an increasing number of young people embrace youth culture not only as a logical response to the environment but also as an alternative preferable to waiting for action until it's too late to act.

The new environment creates a new response, and the response bears a striking resemblance to the culture of Negro youth in the ghetto. Parents: In the ghetto, children often grow up with a mother but no father. Media: The truncated ghetto family has a television set and a transistor radio if it has anything. Marketplace: The psychological function of enforced deprivation is strikingly similar to that of affluence in eliminating the success drive. The Bomb: For the ghetto child, "Whitey," or The Man, is The Bomb. Because the ghetto child's environment in many ways functions like the middle-class youth's new environment, the two youth cultures resemble each other. As a result many middle-class youths find it easier to identify with ghetto children than with their own parents. The student insurrection at Berkeley in 1964 was motivated by many of the same emotions as was the Watts rebellion of 1965 and subsequent ghetto uprisings.

We are made in America, a hundred percent American. Yet we are a foreign country on American soil. Older Americans are just beginning to realize we are something else. Some of them sound as Nasser would if he discovered that his kids were raised by an Israeli nanny. They call us Commies. Which makes the subject a bit more complicated than it really is. It's really quite simple:

The new environment makes us an ex-perience-oriented generation; the prevailing culture makes us experience-starved.

The radicals and youth cultists deserve a hearing. The outspoken and outrageous few are saying a great deal about the relatively quiescent multitude. The vast majority of young people shares the experience, if not the logical response. The majority is simply unprepared to respond logically and integrally to the new environment. They perceive existing institutional patterns, and try to fit in. They are governed by the objectives of getting a job and raising a family. Which is as it has always been and, I imagine, ever will be. But this majority, like the militants and dropouts, has been conditioned by forces that deny the logic of the existing institutional environment. As a result, the majority is troubled. It is a susceptible majority, open to the suasions of the motivated minority.

Out of a logical response to the new environment, the majority is susceptible to the seductions of a minority. Leadership responsive to the new environment is available. Vast institutional change is inevitable, and will be forthcoming.

richard schmuck

concerns of contemporary adolescents

In this paper, I will emphasize problems as seen by working and middle-class adolescents with considerable economic security, little anxiety about survival, and generally healthy personalities. Youngsters of the working and middle-classes, though generally contented, healthy, and competent, do have realistic concerns which often keep them from fully realizing themselves intellectually and socially. These concerns are not focused on the tangible and the concrete, as they are for the impoverished youth of our inner cities and barren countryside. In contrast, working and middle-class youngsters are bothered by the complexities and conflicts in the interpersonal demands of the present and future—they are concerned with making sense out of the multiple demands of parents, teachers, and peers while trying to become an autonomous and integrated individual.

Each of the adolescent concerns presented below was derived from questionnaires systematically collected from three groups of teenagers, 30 participants in a weekend human relations laboratory sponsored by the Institute for Social Research and YWCA (Hawkinshire, 1962), about 200 youth of the Episcopalian church, and 15 Unitarian teenagers. The specific responses are grouped into more general categories of concern. In every case the listed concerns

Reprinted with permission of the author and publisher from the *National Association of Secondary School Principals Bulletin*, 1965, **49**, 19-28.

come directly from adolescents; they are not derived from a psychological theory. In the main, the concerns involve parents, teachers, and peers. Let us begin a description of the most common concerns with parents as viewed by the adolescent boy or girl.

Concerns with Parents

Adolescents view parents as the most significant figures in their lives. They usually refer to them whenever decisions they feel are important have to be made. Of all the concerns which the youngsters reported, over sixty-five per cent involved their parents. Although several hundred statements of problems with parents were collected, it was possible to organize almost all of them into four categories.

1. Parents not discussing with the adolescent what he or she considers important. Some examples of statements about parents are: "They won't listen to me," "They think many of my wishes and fears are silly," "I often feel that I am not trusted and listened to by them," and "They treat me like a child, never listen to me." The adolescent who makes statements like these means that his parents and he are unable to communicate successfully; that the different generations cannot bridge the psychological gulf between them. These comments are seldom based on the youth's perceptions that his parents do not have enough time for him. Accurate communication and genuine empathy, not time spent, concern the adolescent.

Even a cursory analysis suggests that responsibility for unclear communication and an absence of empathy lies with both generations. On the one hand, parents often do not appreciate the importance to the adolescent of his own thoughts, feelings, and terminology; conversely adolescents have difficulty in perceiving the limits of their parents' knowledge about youth culture and become impatient with them too quickly. Often parents increase the gulf by failing to talk with the adolescent about values and personal controls. Because parents are looked to for guidance concerning important decisions, communication difficulties with them heighten the youth's anxieties about his autonomy. Adolescent anxieties over autonomy, as well as related fears of the parents concerning controls, complicate the youth's attempts to achieve individuality.

2. Parents demanding that the adolescent's thoughts and activities be public. Some of the youth interviewed, mostly girls, were distressed about a lack of privacy. They said such things as, "My parents always want to know what I'm doing and thinking," "My mother sometimes picks up the extension phone and listens to my telephone conversations with boys," and "My father asks my girl friends about what I do on dates." Here the concern primarily is with clandestine parental observations of activities with peers. Often, of course, the youngster suspects his parents of doing more of this than is actually the case. Nevertheless, this fairly typical perception, represented by about twenty per cent of the youth interviewed, eighty-five per cent of whom were girls, is representative of a basic problem of trust.

Parents and teenagers find difficulty in achieving a comfortable balance in sharing their public and private lives. This difficulty in sharing often leads to distrust between the generations. Some parents try to develop trust by imitating the behaviors of their adolescent son or daughter. These parents feel that trust can be established by using teenage jargon, by joining the screaming over the latest theatrical or musical rage, or by dressing as though they were seventeen. In attempting to establish trust by imitating

youth, parents forfeit their status leaving the adolescent without clarity in his search for attractive and reachable adult models. Without active parental guidance, the adolescent has little sense of where he is headed, experiences disorganization and discouragement, and is easily manipulated by the fads and fancies of the day. Parents tend to establish trust when they respect adolescent privacy while showing an honest and sincere adult interest in what the adolescent believes and feels.

3. Parents restricting dating patterns. Many of the girls (sixty per cent), but only a few of the boys (five per cent), discussed dating as a focus of conflict with parents. The girls mentioned such things as, "My mother doesn't allow me to date even though most of the other girls in my class date often" (a tenth grade girl), "My Dad gives me a hard time when I want to date a boy older than me," and "My father is always checking up on me when I'm out on a date." Comments like these demonstrate the importance of the adolescent girl's attempts to relate effectively to boys. In contrast to boys, for whom success in adult life depends largely on occupational adjustment, a satisfactory adulthood for girls depends much more on a healthy marriage. For adolescent girls, dating serves as a barometer of later happiness.

Although there is some pressure on girls to date early, the demands of the 1960's for specialized skills and advanced education increase the waiting period before marriage. One major consequence of this bind is that both parents and adolescent girls worry about the consequences of dating. The girl must date as a preparation for adulthood, but she must not go too far too soon with her dates. The anxieties raised by this dilemma manifest themselves often in a lessening of effective communication between the generations about romance and marriage.

Some parents unconsciously aggravate these adolescent concerns about dating and marriage. They dread the girl's eventual severance from home and respond by smothering her with affection and rigid controls. Fathers often react this way out of a fear that their daughter may be "ruined" by the "evil men" in the world. Some mothers fear that their child, male or female, will not be able to solve personal problems without parental guidance. In other families, the presence of an adolescent keeps the parents together. Such parents, out of anxiety over a loss of marital stability, work to keep the adolescent dependent on them. Parental over-control restrains the adolescent from doing what teachers and peers indirectly tell him to do—become an individual, rely on himself, become autonomous from his family, become competent on his own.

4. Adolescents lacking respect for, and trust in, their parents. The most frequent concern for adolescent boys involves the integrity, trustworthiness, and forthrightness of their parents. Some boys say of their parents, "They say one thing and do another," "They are real phonies," and "They do not agree often on what they want me to do." Although comments like these occurred in only about twenty-five per cent of the boys interviewed, they were laden with feeling and must be considered as significant. The perceptions that parents are sometimes "phonies" leads to an alienation from adult modeling and often a destructive, extrapunitive outpouring against adult society.

Some parents evoke such feelings through their own inconsistencies in decision-making about child-rearing. When one parent plays a minor role in the family *vis-a-vis* the youth, the adolescent becomes confused about parent expectations concerning his behavior. The adolescent learns about this power discrepancy and plays one parent against the other. The family without a united front and shared responsibility in deciding important matters with the youth tend to be manipulated by him. Moreover, given these family experiences, the youth often has difficulty in adjusting to others, especially teachers and peers who are not so easily manipulated.

Concerns with Teachers

Teachers were the second most common group of people with whom adolescents had major concerns. At least forty per cent of the youth remarked about problems they have had with their teachers. Some of these were:

1. Teachers not getting to know the students.

The most frequent concern with teachers (about 20 per cent of the sample) had to do with a lack of intimacy and personal contact between the generations. Examples of comments which typified this concern were, "We get too little personal attention from our teachers," "Teachers don't care if they know you very well or not," and "Our teachers are like machines—you go to class and they 'spiel' out information." Adolescents making such statements are asking for some consideration and respect as persons.

Some teachers seemingly do not realize that an adolescent's perceptions of his own competence and effectiveness make up an integral part of his school motivation. Even where teachers are aware of this, they sometimes fail to appreciate that these self-perceptions can change from day to day, depending on the reflected appraisals received by the adolescent from important others. Since competence and achievement are valued so highly in contemporary society, the adolescent is especially sensitive to others' evaluations of his school performance. The teacher plays a special role in defining how competent or incompetent the adolescent is. Some teachers unknowingly deprive youth of their self-respect, confidence, and esteem. The more an adolescent is treated as incompetent, the more he will come to exhibit this prophecy; and, of course, conversely when he is given support and respect, he develops a more positive view of himself. The adolescent's concept of himself, especially in the areas of expertness and personal efficacy, is built up through the accumulated reflected appraisals of teachers with whom he comes in contact. A positive view of self facilitates high academic performance, while a negative view inhibits it.

2. Teachers lacking interest in teaching and youth. About ten per cent of the adolescent boys and girls interviewed pointed to their teachers' lack of interest in teaching, and to their ineffectiveness in relating to students in the classroom. They said, "He always comes to class unprepared," "He doesn't seem to care if we learn," and "He isn't even interested in what he is teaching." Adolescent perceptions that the teacher does not care either about getting to know the student or about his subject matter encourage a lack of classroom involvement on the part of the student.

Moreover, some teachers treat adolescents as objects of manipulation rather than as human beings with whom to relate honestly and sincerely. Such teachers are concerned that the adolescent not view their "seamy sides." For instance, the adolescent should not know that teachers smoke in the furnace room, that they drive cars rapidly, and that they enjoy sensational movies. The irony is that adolescents usually know these things about the teachers, and the teachers' inconsistencies lead to a feeling among youth that teachers are phony, distrustful, and not interested in youth. Teachers establish more respect from youth when they behave as adults and confront the adolescent directly with what their prerogatives are as adults and what the limitations are for the adolescent because he is young. To live by such a double standard, so long as both parties are aware of it, may be better than glaring inconsistencies between verbal platitudes and actual behaviors.

3. Teachers showing partiality for other students. Here about five per cent of the interviewees, mostly boys, said about their teachers, "They have their pets," "Many girls get away with murder—simply because they are girls," and "You have to 'brown-up' the teacher to do well." Teachers, sometimes, are not cognizant of the role they play in influencing a student's relationships with his peers. The teacher's own behaviors and feelings toward a student contribute toward the acceptance of that student by his peers. If the teacher himself accepts each student as an individual—understanding his limitations and giving him support to expand his strong points and help overcome his shortcomings —members of the peer group often will tend to follow a similar pattern. If, on the other hand, the teacher supports primarily the highly competent adolescents and shows rejecting or disapproving behavior to those who are not so successful, a competitive, nonsupportive peer climate is likely to emerge in the classroom. Such atmospheres do not facilitate adolescent self-development. Adolescents who experience successful and secure relationships with their peers achieve more highly on academic tasks, have higher self-esteem, and more positive attitudes toward school than adolescents with poor peer relations (Schmuck, 1963).

Concerns with Peers

Specific concerns over relationships with peers were brought up by about thirty per cent of the entire sample. Even though parents and teachers were mentioned more often, concerns with peers evoked a similar amount of strong feeling. Many different concerns were expressed but only two categories of responses occurred very frequently.

1. Personal values clashing with those of friends. The most typical concern dealt with discontinuities between one's own values and those of others. Comments expressing this problem were, "I don't always agree with them and it bothers me," "Sometimes you can't convince kids that they're wrong," and "I don't agree with what some of the girls do on dates." These concerns demonstrate the tension which adolescents experience as they attempt to develop their own values and self-concepts.

2. Difficulty in retaining friends and popularity. Statements which were about as frequent as those on value conflicts had to do with friendship and popularity. Examples of statements in this category were, "It's hard to know what you have to do to be popular," "I'm very nervous about losing friends," and "I'm afraid that I won't be respected by other kids."

These two categories of concerns are closely interrelated. The adolescent begins to find out who he is and what his values are by intimately relating with others. Peers are the most available persons for intimate relationships. They have similar needs, conflicts, terminology, and interests. At the same time, conflicts naturally arise between peers as to the "right values and beliefs for me." Only through intimate sharing and introspection can the adolescent solve these conflicts for himself. His concern about being detached from friends stems from his fear that he will not be able to figure out who he is without assistance. Provided the adolescent has given up on adults in this regard, peers are the only relevant and available figures who remain.

Adolescent Concerns as the Social Psychologist Sees Them

My experiences with the working and middle-class adolescent of today indicate that he is not extremely rebellious and intransigent. His stated concerns involve relationships with other people, primarily parents, teachers, and peers. His problems center on integrating the simultaneous, and often inconsistent, demands of these three groups of people. The most basic issue for the adolescent is the attempt to achieve a sense of autonomy and individuality. Both this end of shaping an individuality and the means of reaching it, interacting with important others, are sources of concern.

In the junior and senior high school years, youngsters move through a developmental period of transition between childhood and adulthood. During this time, the adolescent structures his sense of who he is and how valuable he is; his self-concept and self-esteem take on a unique form. As the adolescent experiences this transition, the impressions he has of himself are tractable and his anxieties about how valuable he is are heightened. He is at the crossroads of developing an identity. At this point, he can become several selves, he can cherish several different goals for himself. The demands of parents, teachers, and peers somehow have to be joined and integrated to help in the development of a coherent self-picture.

The interpersonal concerns of this period are heightened by the adolescent's physical development—biologically he is an adult during the high school years. He looks to parents and teachers as models for expectations about and ways of expressing his maturing urges. Adults often respond by being aloof and unsympathetic to these feelings. The adolescent then looks to peers as "safe objects" for trying out these new awarenesses. Perhaps the most outstanding feature which is easily visible during this period is the adolescent's self-consciousness about his clothing. If he does not feel properly dressed, or more importantly if he does not feel personally attractive, the adolescent feels inadequate. In fact, the conformity in dress, which is also widespread in adult culture, appears to stem in part from a fear of public criticism and loss of support and affection from others.

While the adolescent seeks security in his relations with peers, he also searches for a sense of competence and self-efficacy. The achievement of competence and personal effectiveness becomes more difficult as the complexity of contemporary times increases. Indeed, in part at least, the adolescent's problems of becoming an integrated individual can be understood as a function of contemporary social changes. The most obvious change involves increased bureaucratization and the complexity of face to face relationships with various individuals and occupants of roles. One method of coping with the ever increasing sphere of interpersonal relationships that occur in the bureaucratic setting is psychological distance or impersonality. The adolescent who is trying to find intimacy and human affect with teachers and peers often finds superficiality and phoniness instead. Learning to be intimate with someone outside the family is a critical part of self-development. If satisfactory contacts are not available, the adolescent either withdraws or, more commonly, takes on the defensive aloofness and superficiality of his models.

While relationships with parents are very important for the adolescent, more and more I have come to the conclusion that relationships with teachers and peers also play a major part. In a recent study of junior and senior high school students, Van Egmond and I found that the perception of teacher emotional support was by far the most potent facilitator of academic performance in both sexes (Schmuck & Van Egmond, in press). In fact, a high school pupil's relationship with his teacher was the most significant indicator of his school adjustment. The perception that one is respected by the peer group was the second most important facilitating variable. The perception that one's parents felt positive toward school was least important among these three variables, especially for boys. For girls, the perception of parental attitudinal support of school was, however, still significantly related to academic performance.

The most concise way of summing up the psychological basis of adolescent concerns with parents, teachers, and peers is to point to the incessant attempt of the adolescent to establish a consistent picture of himself and to achieve a sense of self-esteem. Every adolescent makes use of the reactions of these other people in formulating his opinion of himself. He relies on them for the gratifications and rewards which make him feel worthwhile and esteemed, or for the punishments and disapproval which make him feel inadequate and worthless. It is primarily parents, teachers, and peers—in person or in the images the adolescent holds of them—who are able to make him feel secure and happy or lost and alienated. The adolescent strives to see himself as competent, respected, and effective in intimate interpersonal relations. If he sees himself this way—if he thinks others see him this way—he can continue the process of self-development and move toward a healthy level of personal esteem.

Conclusions

Observations and interviews collected over the last five years indicate that working and middle-class adolescents are not alienated from adults. They are not retreating from, or rebelling against, adult society; they are not against school achievement and the core values of the society. Adolescents are, however, struggling with the integration of interpersonal messages and appraisals from parents, teachers, and peers. They are attempting to pull these diverse inputs together into an autonomous and consistent picture of themselves.

The adolescent works out this integration through his intimacies with important others, most often peers in contemporary society. Teachers and peers can play a special part during this transitional period in assisting the adolescent in moving beyond the family. At the same time, the adolescent requires guidance from parental models. Parents and youth need to work more creatively to find ways of sharing their most meaningful and personal thoughts and experiences. The adolescent is in need of discussion with what he perceives to be trustworthy and forthright adults, whether they be teachers or parents. Moreover, the adolescent needs to be supported in his intimate sharing with peers and personal introspection about self. The contemporary adolescent builds a coherent picture of self with least pain and most satisfaction when he is allowed intimacy with peers within the context of mature and honest guidelines from both parents and teachers.

arthur goldberg

juvenatrics: study of prolonged adolescence

Much is made of increased longevity. This is dramatic. It brings to focus earlier retirement, medicare, pension funds, housing for the aged, social security. It has brought to the fore a new branch of medicine (geriatrics) and a new study in sociology (gerontology). For all that, there is another, almost a compensatory, development which is at least equally worthy of our attention. For lack of a better phrase, let us call it "prolonged adolescence." We may yet see such a word as "juvenology" in current use—and, perhaps, "juvenatrics."

Let us take as a point of departure Arthur T. Jersild's definition of the adolescent period, in *The Psychology of Education* (1963):

> The term "adolescence" is used in this book to denote a period during which the growing person makes the transition from childhood to adulthood. While it is not linked to any precise span of years, adolescence may be viewed as beginning roughly when young people begin to show signs of puberty and continuing until most of them are sexually mature, have reached their maximum growth in height, and have approximately reached their full mental growth as measured by intelligence tests. The period as covered in this book includes the years from about the age of twelve to the early twenties (p. 5).

It seems that the word "denote" in the first sentence of the definition might more

Reprinted with permission of the author and publisher from *Clearing House*, 1964, **41**, 218-22.

appropriately have been "connote." Whatever the case, three factors are specified in the definition for the attainment of adulthood: sexual maturity, maximum physical growth, and full mental growth (by I.Q.). Only the last factor projects adolescence into the "early twenties." The attainment of "full mental growth" as a condition for making the transition to adulthood is a fairly recent prerequisite.

There was a time in the not too distant past when physical growth ("He's big enough to do a man's job"), which coincides fairly closely in time to sexual maturity, was the one most significant criterion of adulthood. It had, in addition, these virtues: (1) physical growth is clearly recognizable, (2) there were jobs for "men" to do. Indeed, in accepting Jersild's definition, one may argue only that the early twenties is too soon, and that intellectual maturity dependent upon education rather than I.Q. should be the criterion.

Industrialization and its concomitant urbanization have combined forces to postpone youth's arrival at adulthood. Industrialization, in a negative sense, has delayed adulthood for youth, if for no other reason than to keep the labor market tight. The productivity of technological advances has made it possible for adults to retire earlier and live longer. It has, too, freed youth from being chained to the machines. It is, indeed, desirable not only to retire the aged earlier but to delay the entrance of youth into the act of production, so that unemployment figures may be kept as low as possible.

In a positive sense, technology has prolonged adolescence simply because the skills required for productivity call for longer periods of training and study; thus Jersild must add "mental growth" as a condition for adulthood. To this add technological unemployment and the relocation of workers, whether geographically or industrially, and it becomes even more desirable to keep youth in school.

With advanced technology has come an ever greater reliance on research. Research requires ever more scientists and technicians. It feeds on itself and grows ever bigger as it consumes itself. It spreads over the nonindustrial areas. Note, if you will, the rise of the drug industry, hospitals, and other such service areas whose growth can be traced to research and from research to the technology and industrialization that preceded it.

Urbanization has contributed its bit to the prolongation of adolescence. Urban living is packaged, mechanized living, a long cry from a self-sufficient agricultural society. (Even the word "rural" no longer applies, for there is a new rural, non-farm ecology.) The city today offers its youth adult status largely in the one phase of "social" living: parties, dates, night-clubbing, and the like. This, if anything, comes at an earlier age. The key is that youth is no longer an important factor in the productive processes, but *is* an increasingly important factor in the consuming sector of modern Western society. If children in a rural economy were once an economic asset, they are today, in an industrialized urban society, an economic liability.

An interesting and pertinent sidelight to this urbanization is the effect it has had on the family structure. The larger kinship group that included grandparents is no longer the norm. That larger family group afforded the child and adolescent a model for parent-child relationships. His own mother and father stood in somewhat the same relationship to his grandparents as he, himself, stood to his parents. This model for adolescent behavior has been lost.

What is obvious, but not recognized by school and society, is that youth is denied full adult status for roughly ten years from puberty. Adult status is still predicated upon economic self-sufficiency. This is implicit in at least two of Jersild's criteria. What is even more obvious is that puberty still follows physiological laws, not economic laws. If anything, puberty seems to be arriving at an earlier age. Economically and sociologically (but not socially) adult status, with all its adult responsibilities and obligations, is delayed.

Primitive societies narrowed this transition period to a matter of months, even days. In their native wisdoms they avoided the "youth problem." Margaret Mead's studies in Samoan youth are so well known that it is unnecessary to labor over the proof of this thesis. But even before Mead we were aware of primitive puberty rites: how a pubescent youth was taken into the forest by an aged member of the tribe and initiated into the mysteries of adulthood; how the ceremony of initiation was performed and, presto, the youth was an adult, possibly by no further act than the cutting of the hair in the accepted adult style. If this is an oversimplification, it nonetheless illustrates validly the contrast with modern society.

Vestiges of these puberty rites remain in the confirmation at pubescence of the youth of the various churches. In the "Bar Mitzvah" services of the synagogue, the "acceptance speech" of the confirmant has achieved renown through the efforts of TV comedians. "Today I am a man" is a phrase certain to invoke a hilarious response from the cognescenti in the audience. But even this, for all its ritual, is without sociological or economic meaning and has been moved from the churches to the schools—to the graduation exercises.

At one time a person could be graduated from elementary school and proudly proclaim, "Today I am a man." Within memory this changed to "One can't even be a ditchdigger (let alone a man) without a high school diploma." And now the trend is to move "manhood" to college graduation. The number of high school graduates going on to "higher" education is fast exceeding the 50 per cent mark. Does this prolong adolescence? Does it help to explain early marriages? Does it help to explain what is glibly called the irresponsibility of youth? Certainly marriage is an assumption of responsibility (even if that is not the motivating cause), but the assumption of this full responsibility is impossible if the "man" of the family is still in school.

But there are further complications in the role youth must play. In less complicated societies, youth's progress to adulthood required adjustment to a fairly homogeneous, single-standard society. If social class differences prevailed, the youth knew the social class he was destined for by birth. A mark of a democratic society today is its vertical social mobility. And it may hastily be added that school has become the best (if not the last) avenue for this rise (and fall) of the individual in a modern democratic society.

One more point is to be made in discussing the prolonging of adolescence. This is the too easy, too rapid, and perhaps too uninformed acceptance of the new study of psychology over the last half-century. The prospective mother buys a copy of "Spock" practically at the moment of conception. The child is carefully guarded against "frustrations." The "whole child" concept has confused the role of the school and prevented its development as a social institution with a defined character. Youth is the time for "fun," while the physical development of youth says, "Fun, yes, but I am a full grown man, too." Children are born with a copy of *Psychology Made Easy* in their hands. At the slightest provocation they disarm the parent with "You don't love me."

U.S. culture has always been youth centered, perhaps because the U.S. itself is a young country (or was and still thinks it is). Note, if you will, the sum spent on cosmetics and hairdressers in an effort to maintain a youthful appearance. Note the octogenarian sport car enthusiast. And note the accent on youth in daily advertisements. Adults would prolong their own youth. This is in marked contrast to societies where maturity is more respected. This focus on youth has caused adults to encourage the prolongation of adolescence.

Youth occupies a peculiar position in the law as well. The legal status of the adolescent was—and still is—designed to protect him against exploitation; against child labor, against adult punishment for adolescent misdemeanors. But the conditions against which these laws were passed no longer obtain. Youth today occupies a most favored position. Where there is not merely hedonism, there is a conscious and deliberate taunting of law enforcement officers and agencies for their inability to enforce societal standards. As adolescence is prolonged, this, too, becomes an increasingly dangerous factor in the achievement of adult status. Wild oats were not unknown or unsown in an earlier age. But the sower was conscious of the extralegal nature of the harvest.

The forces driving at the prolongation of adolescence are clear. They converge upon the adolescent to create for him, from 12 to 22, a time not so much of transition as of limbo. As this becomes more true, the school becomes the "receiver in bankruptcy" of adolescent youth.

Prolonged schooling is the handmaiden of prolonged adolescence. Which is cause and which effect is unimportant. Each feeds upon the other. What is important is what the institutional character of the school should be if it is to be the one reality for adolescents in this long period before adulthood. Unfortunately, all the school has to offer (other than social functions which may just as well be offered by home, community center, or even church) is of the nature of deferred gratifications: study now so that you may be a more adequate adult later. Learning is a preparation. No amount of experience curricula, or industrial arts, or homemaking alters this fundamentally. Building a book rack, or cooking a meal, or studying family living may have some aspects of immediate gratifications; yet, in essence, they remain preparatory—skill building for the real thing later.

There are those for whom there is no "later." Their desire to play the adult role that their bodies or social class orientation assure them they can play is immediate. Their social values predispose them to gratifications *now*. After all, buying on credit is a socially approved scheme (and in respect to our economy, highly desirable) for immediate gratification. "Forced savings" through credit has replaced "A penny saved is a penny earned" as a maxim for Poor Richard. For today's adolescents, delayed gratifications through learning has little appeal.

One of the fables in American education is that graduation is at the age of 18. Earlier graduation is acceptable as a mark of genius. Later graduation is to be abhorred as a mark of dullness or irresponsibleness, or both. For those who would not postpone adulthood to "full mental growth," 18 is too long to wait. Twenty-two is entirely impossible. Although it means legal and cultural rethinking, it is suggested here that adolescents be encouraged to leave school as close to sexual and physical maturity as possible. The postwar G.I. experience would suggest that many of these "dropouts" might well return to take much greater advantage of their educational opportunities. For those who would not return, extension or continuous education services as in the Scandinavian countries might well reduce the tendency toward "prolonged adolescence."

For those who would be doctors, engineers, teachers, lawyers, *et al.,* there is no reversal of the trend to prolonged adolescence. Their problem is no less acute, but they do have the strength of deferred goals and, if successful in attaining them, social and financial rewards. Where formerly the adolescent won his independence—i.e., his adulthood—in work, he must now win his independence in school, or at least through school. Education should be harnessed to the purpose of making adolescence a period of life in itself, not a transition to an adulthood which is ever more postponed. School is for learning—for preparation. This we should proclaim without apologies. This does not still the physical growth of youth, but it may sublimate it.

There may be other schemes for providing status for adolescents: perhaps pay for school achievement, perhaps a greater respect for unskilled labor, perhaps government subsidies of early marriages, perhaps something like the CCC camps of the 30's oriented more to study, perhaps a turning away from technology and automation to craftsmanship and its apprenticeship (not likely to occur), perhaps lowering the compulsory school age attendance laws. Whatever the scheme, for the school itself (and this means for society's image of the school) "study" needs somehow to acquire the dignity and the importance in the winning of personal independence that "work" once enjoyed.

Youth once contributed to production and to the family's welfare through their labors. They were then vitally involved in adult responsibilities. Can "study" do this? Of course families do now recognize that their children's marks in school afford status to the parents. But this is more in the nature of exploitation of the child than an active participation of the child in the welfare of the family.

This much follows logically: if school is the world of adolescents, then school has a right to and must demand of youth a more complete dedication. This is not a plea for monasticism. It is to ask that we frankly see school as a place for learning. What else is left to adolescents but a long period of waiting, even a restlessness that often has overt antisocial manifestations? Even young adolescents are impatient to play the "big man." This may be their way of recognizing the long period of waiting ahead of them.

For the potential scholar or professional man, prolonged adolescence affords some difficulties in his personal life, but with these he can usually cope in a fashion more or less approved by society. For him the prolonged adolescence is not without its advantages. He needs the time for study and preparation. He is sustained by a deferred goal. For a few, scholarship is an end in itself and is its own reward. It is unlikely that this can ever be true of all youth. But school and society can afford dignity to study if they insist upon and give dignity to the school. In so much as the school gains in dignity, so will youth. In so much as youth has dignity, so will the period of adolescence be more than an awkward age between childhood and adulthood, its awkwardness more pronounced in that it takes longer and longer for youth to "grow out of it."

robert l. wrenn

the authority controversy and today's student

College and high school personnel workers sometimes nurture irrational thoughts concerning the motives of students, particularly those motives that appear to question the authority of the establishment. Student-administration conflicts noted in history indicate close resemblance in kind to the Berkeley riots. Empirical descriptions of student activists and of the expectations of "normal" students reveal that there are conditions within the college experience that deserve closer scrutiny. Parents and college officials are often concerned about different moral issues than are the students. The student, in turn, often feels more a means in the educational process than an end. Future trends in personnel administration are suggested as a partial remedy.

A psychiatrist at the Student Health Center at the University of Colorado was asked by a journalist what sort of embarrassing questions students are asking these days. He replied, "They're asking what are the rules for being alive." It is likely that a university official, if asked this question, would reply, "They're asking what are the rules for controlling the university." While only a vocal minority of students are active and on the front line, a surprisingly large number of students are becoming more interested in what the multiversity, or any university for that matter, can offer and what it cannot.

This paper considers the topic of today's college student's attitudes and expectations and the potential these expectations may

Reprinted with permission of the author and publisher from *Personnel and Guidance Journal,* 1968, **46,** 949-953.

have on the operation of institutions of higher education. The primary concern of the paper is to convey the thought that there is some reasonableness to the behavior and expectations students have of their academic and social existence.

Two basic modes of feeling expression are being dramatically characterized by today's student. The withdrawal or retreat into an inner world typifies the Hippie or Beat individual, at least to the degree that he is more preoccupied with a love-in than a peace march. The students who make a direct attack on the problem (or pseudo-problem) are the activists, as typified by Mario Savio. Both types are upsetting to the older generation partly because it never occurred to people in previous generations to seriously challenge the academic system.

Some Perspectives from Recent History

Suspicion and outright attack on school authority, however, is not new with our generation. One description (Solberg, 1966, p. 305) of student behavior dating back to pre-Civil War time is as follows:

Students gained revenge on the authoritarianism of the colleges by resistance and insubordination. They defied faculty judgments, underscored their dissent with gunpowder explosions in college buildings, physically assaulted professors and presidents, and even whipped, shot and stabbed them.

Both Princeton and Yale had student uprisings or internal conflicts bordering on anarchy during the first quarter of the 1800's. In 1889 the President of the Illinois Industrial University denied a request to dedicate the new armory building with a dance. The students went ahead anyway with the dedication and the dance. When the President appeared at the doors of the armory building to assert his authority he was received by a welcoming committee of students who washed him out of the building with a fire hose (Solberg, 1966). G. Stanley Hall, a college president and psychologist at the turn of the century, wrote an article on student customs in which he worried some about the overindulgence of college students and the lack of their ability to take responsibility (Hall, 1900).

Of interest here is not so much the fact that insubordination can be noted throughout recent educational history, but that with history in mind, the 1964 riots at Berkeley still seem to many to be something new. "Bigger and better," perhaps, but certainly not new.

Student Activists

In an address to the parents of Stanford's Class of '65, Robert McAfee Brown raised questions commonly asked by parents about their college children. "Why don't these students stick to getting an education, instead of getting involved in activities outside of school? Why don't they study harder, instead of raising money to send students to Mississippi, or worse yet, going to Mississippi themselves? Why don't students study political science instead of holding protest meetings on Vietnam?" The rebuttal is in the form of a value statement, felt by many of the student generation: *Thought without action is sterile.* Brown felt that parents should be urged,

> ... to believe that the revolts of the present generation represent the right kinds of *basic* concerns, and that moral indignation expressing itself in action (even if the action may seem occasionally misguided) is a far healthier and more encouraging index of the

success of the educational venture, than is the moral apathy, exemplified in lack of concern.

This statement is a truism for mental health, generally.

Certainly the active rebels are a small minority. The majority of students rebel only in the traditional sense of the conflict between the generations. According to Buell Gallagher, President of the City College of New York, students

> ... are irritated, amused, disgusted or disinterested in the face of what they interpret to be contempt, condescension or indifference in their elders; but they merely hang the losing coach in effigy in the fall, strike against institutional food in the winter, and stage a panty raid in the spring. Some miracle of the human spirit prevents widespread alienation.

When it does occur, however, what distinguishes these students from the majority? In one study (Golden & Rosen, 1966), students on the campuses of three up-state New York colleges were assessed prior to the Berkeley riots. Students with the most liberal attitudes regarding student participation in college decision-making were more likely to hold better than average academic records and were less likely to be authoritarian as measured by the California *F* scale. Heist (1965) reminds us that colleges or universities that witness frequent student activity and unrest draw a student body measurably different from the mass of institutions. In one study described by Heist, student leaders were assessed on three widely separated campuses. Across the three colleges, the key leaders comprised no more than eleven people. These eleven were significantly brighter than the average student. They came from homes where religious affiliations were liberal or non-existent. From the standpoint of observable activity, dress, and style of life, only three or four could be classified as practicing nonconformists. After graduating from college (and up to Heist's publication date) nine had gone on to graduate study. Six had finished or were completing their doctorate. Two were entering their last year of medical school. These data jibe nicely with other data he gathered on the Free Speech Movement leaders at Berkeley. These students were described as more autonomous and brighter than the average Berkeley student, and a larger proportion were transfer students coming from selective colleges and universities.

The College Experience

Mervin B. Freedman, in his book, *The College Experience* (1967), reminds us that the expectation that college will exert a marked impact on large numbers of students is completely unreasonable. He points to a variety of myths we hold concerning the college experience. To counteract myths such as "mental ability is fixed by the time a student enrolls in college" or "primary socialization efforts are achieved toward the end of one's college work," he points optimistically to evidence that social and intellectual changes do occur in college, early in college, and they tend to last.

Studies comparing freshmen with seniors often find seniors to be more flexible, less censorious of people, more critical of institutional authority, more introspective. In research reported by Stern (1966) 3,075 incoming freshmen at four different institutions were asked to describe what their university would be likely to offer them. More than three-quarters of the students felt the college experience would develop a strong sense of responsibility, would bring them in contact with politically active professors who would encourage them to take an active part in social reforms and political programs. They felt they could express extreme or unpopular viewpoints because of the school's excellent reputation for academic freedom, and so on. Barely half of the college seniors at these schools consider any of these statements to be valid. It was Stern's feeling that college administrators share more the view of the freshmen than of the seniors. Perhaps it is expedient for them to do so—as well as naive. Some of the research to come from the Center for the Study of Higher Education at Berkeley indicates a mean personality profile spread for entering freshmen of as much as two standard deviations between schools. This demonstrates gross individual differences not only within a given college but between schools as well.

In May, 1967, the National Educational Television network produced an hourly program entitled *University Power: A Conversation with Clark Kerr.* Kerr indicated that alumni leaders and campus leaders often do not agree in their attitudes toward education. While this is not a new idea, he did go on to indicate a less obvious fact. Parents, alumni, and college personnel are often concerned about *different* moral issues than are the students. While parents and school officials are talking about the sex and drug problems on campus, students are concerned about the war in Vietnam and the riots in Detroit. Sex and drugs, somehow, are less an issue to most students than the possibility of being sent to war. According to Max Ways (1965), the parents of today's college student are more permissive and less authoritarian than was the case for previous generations. Presumably this is one reason for the authority conflict between students and the university establishment. Whether the American family is becoming more personal and less institutional or vice versa is a moot point. What does seem more likely is that authority as a basis for decision-making is being put in perspective by students—as a "blind" to the real issues at hand. Many of the more active students are interested in social reform. They react quite negatively to rules handed down in an arbitrary way, especially after a course or two in American Government. During his television interview, Kerr further argued that, within legal bounds, students should be allowed to be a part of what is traditionally thought of as a main function of a university —a critic of society. For that matter, the public does seem more accepting of student protest than of faculty protest. Another cue to the student that we have sold out.

A predominant reason for students' dissatisfaction in college is their belief that neither the means nor the ends of the college experience, as organized, is valid. This is sometimes summed up in the phrase, "I am a human being; do not fold, bend, or mutilate." They resent not only the ever-present sense of being evaluated and processed, but also the grim, humorless, competitive classroom battle, which they feel does not give them a functional background for the world of the future.

As part of this feeling of being a means rather than an end is the loneliness, the anomie. According to one professor, students able to corner a professor in his office these days "have won at hide-and-seek against heavy odds." This was particularly true at Berkeley (Selection Committee, 1966), where a professor's rewards centered less on student contact than is true at a number of smaller institutions.

After listing some of the reasons college students pursue drugs, Blum (1966) indicated that student personnel workers have an attitude toward students that goes something like this:

> I don't mind if you look at nature critically and you can tear hell out of Shakespeare, Lysenko, Reagan and L.B.J. Still I don't think you should publicly advocate drug use, and I don't believe in beards; indeed it offends me personally that you wear such outlandish clothing.

The fact that people say these things bothers a number of students. They find it logically inconsistent and hypocritical. It's like condoning alcohol and eschewing pot. At any rate, it becomes ammunition for use with anyone over 30 who, by definition of age, has sold out—to the establishment.

Time for a Change

The time seems ripe for college personnel to put their expectations and attitudes more in line with those of the student—at least in regard to educational matters. Much of our thinking is not realistic and feeds on the myths of yesteryear. We hear that the suicide rate for students is 50 per cent above that for the general population and that there will be a hundredfold increase in consciousness-altering drugs in the next 10 years, and we panic. Sometimes we act by tightening school regulations. We miss the cues from history and from the daily complaints of our students.

If we continue to do so, we will have more action taken by the student. A student leader at Michigan (Rapoport, 1967) relates that several years ago the campus paper ran an article about a dean of women who was notifying parents of students dating interracially. The article prompted her resignation. A university regent was also forced to resign when the matter of his conflict of interest between business and university was uncovered in the school paper. The President of Chatham College, Edward Eddy, Jr., was quoted in the Washington *Post,* October 7, 1965, as saying, "Every college and university committee ought to include voting student members." The only reason for not doing so is the fear of "student power." Anyone aware of the psychology of group behavior, or of the individual in a group, would understand how groundless this fear is.

The Future of Our Enterprise

The National Student Association, the American Association of University Professors, the Association of American Colleges, the National Association of Student Personnel Administrators, and the National Association of Women Deans and Counselors have all informally endorsed (in principle) a statement on rights and freedoms of students that centers on many of the complaints students harbor. For example, it describes recommended conduct in the matter of: (1) searching of rooms, (2) disclosure of grades, (3) off-campus speakers, (4) off-campus protests, (5) taking reasoned exception to professors' views, (6) censorship of campus papers, (7) financing campus papers, and (8) the student's right to participate in the formulation and application of institutional policy affecting academic and student affairs.

Certainly more attention will be given to this document. Stern (1966, p. 414) makes a general prediction, worthy of note:

> The elimination of grades as a coercive device, joint participation in curriculum change and administration, the withdrawal of custodial supervision in the name of the family that would itself no longer attempt to exercise such prerogatives, are all pointing towards the future of the college community.

Other trends, some based on present example at a few schools, include more team teaching at the college level, more broadly conceived academic programs, giving students a "grade free" semester to find themselves, programming routine information with teachers functioning more as discussion leaders, and the like.

Some schools have also found new ways to handle old problems. At Kansas State University, a halfway-house dormitory program was begun in 1966, wherein 25 highly disturbed, but ambulatory, students are given special attention while going through the regular college program. In a different sphere, two or three schools have found a fairly satisfactory answer for the demand for grades by local draft boards. The University of Washington withholds class rank from the local draft board on the student's request. Yale and Wisconsin send class rank IBM cards to each male student for him to dispose of as he sees fit.

Authority conflicts will occur between the generations as a natural process of law, order, and civilized social living. The fear that students are getting away with something, and are duping us in the process, is a little too paranoid for me. The evidence we have at this point is that both student and college personnel are striving for closer agreement and understanding. The student, frequently, is taking the initiative.

I am reminded of a quote from Robert Nixon's book, *The Art of Growing* (1962, p. 150):

> It may help us to remember that the years of youth are characterized by a high degree of toughness and resilience, by a fast rate of recuperation, by great stamina.

Looking at the pressures youth face in order to receive an education, I feel myself thinking, in terms of Nixon's statement, "Thank God!"

robert a. karabinus

how we know what we know about psychological measurement

Even though the title of this article might suggest a treatise about knowledge that would require some sophistication in the discipline of epistemology (the study of knowledge), let me quickly reassure you that this is not the intention. Rather, the primary purpose is to explore the kinds of information usually found in adolescent psychology textbooks, some ways this information is presented, the problem of data reliability, and the somewhat obscure language that is customarily used to express it, so that there might be a better understanding of the problems and procedures involved in acquiring knowledge of human behavior.

Many students have begun reading in a general, educational or adolescent psychology text and have been disturbed or even frustrated when trying to grasp meanings and principles from the material because nearly every other paragraph referred to some study or experiment, and the qualifying statements surrounding each of the findings were confusing. How often has this state of confusion and lack of understanding led to a distaste for the subject matter and course? Since a situation like this does not offer or lead to a positive learning situation in the classroom, it might be well to examine more closely the usual method of acquiring knowledge about education.

Probably most of you have had some ex-

posure to general psychology or introductory philosophy where scientific method or inductive logic has been discussed. However, learning about this method is quite different from learning other disciplines by using it. This may be part of the problem then. Many just have not learned how to apply the techniques learned, at least not in disciplines dealing with human behavior. Even though there may be a great deal of folklore and tradition in psychology, any related discipline that has human behavior as its core has an especially difficult task in organizing a body of knowledge. Adolescent psychology is a relatively new discipline, and psychologists have only recently begun to find out how to learn about human behavior, how to measure it, how to control it, and to some extent how to predict it. So, as with any new science, there is very likely to be not only contradictory findings from many different scientists but also very laboriously qualified conclusions reported. Therefore, as you read the literature you may receive the impression that we really do not know very much yet, and what we do think we know is not definitely known. Even though this may be an unsettling realization, it is nevertheless a true picture of the state of affairs.

A review of the basic procedure (scientific method) used in educational research may help. Basically it involves the following:

1. A problem exists that needs solving, or

1. a situation is present that needs to be understood.
2. Relevant data are gathered and placed in some sensible order.
3. Solutions, concepts or theories, or hypotheses are suggested and stated formally.
4. These solutions, concepts, or hypotheses are tried or tested.
5. They are "not rejected" if they are shown to be possible solutions or explanations, and they are "rejected" if they are shown to be inadequate solutions or explanations.
6. Other solutions, concepts, or hypotheses may be tried and tested.
7. Solutions, concepts, or hypotheses that hold up when tested are then after much replication and consideration accepted as part of knowledge in that subject.

This method is also called the inductive method in logic, where one proceeds from specific information to a general conclusion. Notice, however, that a conclusion is inferred —it is not absolute. It is accepted as true or part of knowledge only after other rival solutions, concepts, or hypotheses have been shown to be inadequate or false. This statement is a key to comprehending the method of educational research. To repeat, there is always some degree of doubt in the conclusion accepted as truth.

A reference to the *Perry Mason* television series might be helpful at this juncture. The problem presented in the hour-long show is usually to find the murderer. The district attorney has evidence that seems to point toward one person (Mason's client) as the murderer and uses it to support his case (hypothesis). On the other hand, Mason attempts to show that the evidence does not necessarily support the statement that his client is guilty. In fact, he shows how others might also be guilty, which then reduces the tenability of the district attorney's case. The court trial often ends with the real murderer confessing, and Mason's client is freed—an event that just does not occur in educational research. So at this point the parallel breaks down, but up until then the search for a solution to the problem (finding the murderer) is identical in principle to the search for knowledge about psychological principles of human behavior. It is just that in the latter case, we are left with tenable hypotheses that are only probably true. No one tells us we are right or wrong, even though many do try by

replicating the experiment or study or by doing further research to support or reject the previous findings.

The fact that knowledge in adolescent psychology is based on probability may not be appreciated by the nonscientifically oriented student. Even when this fact is accepted, though, understanding the language used by the researchers and textbook writers in stating their conclusions may be another matter. For example, here is a very common statement found in the literature: "The achievement scores of the experimental group were significantly higher than the scores of the control group." The word *experimental* is used to describe the group given special attention, training, or treatment, and the word *control* is used to describe the untreated or other group. To illustrate, an experimental group might be taught via programed instruction techniques while the control group via regular lecture-discussion methods. A comparison of achievement between these two groups would obviously be necessary before coming to any conclusion about the hypothesized superiority of programed instruction techniques.

The word that is responsible for most of the confusion, however, is *significantly*. In research, the word *significant* generally means meaningful, probably true, or not easily or likely to be explained or accounted for by chance. Since almost anything might happen by chance, educational researchers have generally agreed upon the degree or level of nonchance (confidence) that can be labeled as significant. The confidence level commonly used is the 95% level. This means that a chance or error level of 5% is present. Therefore, to say that a group of scores is significantly higher than another group simply means that the difference between the two groups is so large that chance could account for it only 5% (or less) of the time. Chance is not accepted as an explanation for the difference in this case. Sometimes researchers will use a more conservative error level, and then a statement given might be that a difference was found to be significant at the 1% (.01) level. The interpretation of this statement is identical to that with the 5% level, except of course for the change of percent. If the statement was that no significant difference between the sets of scores was found, that would mean that chance could explain the difference more than 5% of the time. Therefore, the difference found would be accepted as a chance event. To repeat, then, when significance is affirmed it is assumed that chance probably was not the explanation for the difference between the scores of the two groups, but that other circumstances were responsible, specifically the differences in treatment or attention given the groups.

This leads to another very crucial problem in interpreting the findings from research. The burden of proof is still on the researcher's shoulders to rule out not only chance but any other rival hypotheses that could possibly account for the differences found. Such rival hypotheses might include IQ level of the subjects, sex or age, personality factors, etc. You see, to conclude that it was a treatment difference that was responsible is like naming the murderer when only circumstantial evidence is available. There may be other explanations equally as good or better, so one must be careful to have ruled out as possible explanations all but the variables of interest (variables that were controlled, and supposedly the only factors that made the experimental and control groups different).

These are some of the reasons why good researchers are especially careful in the way they state their conclusions. Not only must there be a careful statement about chance error that might be involved in the conclusion (significance at the 5% level means that chance could explain the conclusion only 5%, or less, of the time), but also present must be a qualified statement about what probably was responsible. No wonder the wording in the texts often sounds vague and obscure. Some of this just must be—some of it certainly could be—stated more clearly, but, in any case, this further understanding of the terminology and related problems should help the student profit more from the readings than before. For further and more detailed explanation of probability, "significance" statements, and rival hypotheses, read a good beginning text in statistics or research design. Of special help might be the first part of Campbell and Stanley (1963).

Unfortunately, comprehending the scientific method and learning the language of educational researchers are not the only

problems. The very nature of the subject matter, human behavior, has its own complex of difficulties. Life does not stand still long enough for one to obtain an accurate measure of anything. Even standardized achievement tests, which have been moderately successful in measuring understandings in certain disciplines, are limited in that they are usually paper-pencil tests, objective in nature, and heavily dependent on the student's perception ability, especially his reading skill. Knowledge can be demonstrated on paper, certainly, but there are other ways that may be better in measuring what is intended, e.g., application, oral demonstration, etc. This becomes even more obvious when other measurement devices are used, e.g., attitude and personality inventories. Is telling someone else on paper what your attitude is toward a particular object the most reliable method of collecting attitude data? Might not a person not really know his true attitude, or put down what sounds "right" according to society's mores and then behave in an entirely different way?

Human behavior is complex, and it is a very difficult task to isolate any part of it for measurement so that data can be collected and used in research. Needless to say, the research conclusions will not be—in fact, cannot be—better or more accurate than the data used in the research. That refers directly to the measurement of the concept or construct (achievement, ability, perception, attitude, etc.) that is being studied. An expression heard frequently in computer and data processing centers is *GIGO,* which, simply translated, means "Garbage In, Garbage Out." Why is it possible to find in education research many contradictory findings when measuring essentially the same concepts? Changes of circumstances, differences in people, and inaccuracy in measurement devices can certainly account for many of them.

As one reads more and more about attempts to learn about human behavior, one can easily become discouraged. When it is not possible to measure behavior accurately, how can we possibly do any kind of respectable research? Well, rather than give up completely, our only hope is to keep searching for knowledge in spite of the obstacles. Knowing what the limitations of our research are, we can then be more honest in the statement of our findings. There is a challenge in this also, and that is to keep improving our measuring instruments and controlling the variables operating in our research so that when and if we do find something that is significant (see above explanation), we can be reasonably sure that we have added to our knowledge about that aspect of human behavior.

Assuming that our measurement of human behavior can be reasonably reliable (accurate and consistent), what are some of the ways we describe these data so that we can use them in our research? Most beginning statistics books discuss this topic in detail, so only brief mention will be made here.

It is customary to describe a set of scores in terms of an average. This might be an arithmetic average (the mean), the midscore of the set (the median), or that score that occurs most frequently in the set (the mode). The first two of these are most frequently used as measures of central tendency for groups of data. But knowing just the average or central tendency of a group of data does not describe it sufficiently to distinguish it from other groups of data. For example, two groups of students may have the same mean on a test and yet not be much alike at all. The students in the first group might all have earned very similar scores, whereas those in the second might have earned a wide variety of scores, but the overall average in both groups might have been the same. Therefore, to describe adequately a set of data, in addition to a measure of central tendency, a measure of dispersion must be used. This could be a simple measure of the total range or spread of scores, a range of scores for the middle 90%, 50%, or 25% of the students, or a relatively sophisticated measure called a standard deviation. Although the former techniques tell us only how far it is from the top to the bottom score for whatever percentage of the group being considered, the latter measure tells us something about how the scores deviate from the mean. It is calculated by taking the square root of the average squared deviation and is described as a score interval above and below the mean that encompasses about 68% of all the scores. For example, if the mean of a set of scores is 78 and the standard deviation is 6, about 68% of all scores will fall between 72 and 84 (6 score units below and above the mean). We could also say that

about 96% of all the scores will fall between 66 and 90 (2 standard deviations below and above the mean).

In research studies, even though comparisons are usually made between the means of sets of scores, the appropriate statistical tests always measure the significance of difference between the means in terms of the dispersion of the scores in each group compared to mean and dispersion differences that could be explained by chance. The standard deviation unit, and various forms of it, is the primary measure of dispersion used in educational research.

In addition to being able to compare sets of data by studying their means and standard deviations, we often want to know if there is a relation between the scores. For example, is there a relation between the extroverted personality and high achievement in school? Here we would have one group of students and for each student two sets of information, a measure on extroversion and a measure on grades. The statistic used is called a "product moment coefficient of correlation." Coefficient values range from −1.00 to +1.00, and 0.00 indicates no relation at all. If we find that many extroverts have high grades and many introverts have low grades, then the coefficient might be calculated to be .80. By squaring this coefficient, we can learn something about the extent of relation that exists. We might say that there is about 64% agreement between the two sets of paired scores; that is, there is only that much in common between this personality trait and high grades. In most situations a correlation coefficient as high as .80 would be rather meaningful, especially if a large number of scores were involved. In no circumstances should the correlation itself be considered a percentage. Only the square of the coefficient can be so interpreted. Furthermore, it must be emphasized that a correlation coefficient is not a measure of cause and effect. Just because we are hearing today that smoking and lung cancer are related does not mean that one causes the other. Of course, one may be the cause of the other, but the correlation does not prove it. If there is cause and effect present, however, and this could be inferred after many replications of the study and the careful elimination of all other rival hypotheses, it would be there only to the extent of the square of the correlation coefficient.

Data are described basically in the three methods presented above: measures of central tendency, dispersion, and relation. They are then subjected to appropriate statistical analyses to test for significance. These data may be incorporated in sentences and paragraphs or may be presented in more graphic form, i.e., tables or charts. Whichever way is used, effective communication to the reader is the objective. Many times charts and tables can depict the data much more adequately than can prose. Many scholars in the past have sneered at the use of graphics because of the belief that there was no substitute for good literary style. Often the charts were relegated to the appendix for those who could not understand the prose. Fortunately, today charts and tables have gained respectability among the scholars and are being used effectively to express findings that can be expressed very awkwardly at best through prose. For an explanation of the various graphic devices available, you are encouraged to refer to a beginning descriptive statistics text.

To conclude this discussion about "How we know what we know . . . ," let me refer to a familiar dictum many of us heard from our parents and teachers not too many years ago: "Practice makes perfect." This is similar to Thorndike's famous law of practice effect, which in essence said that learning takes place through practice. Is this dictum a true statement? Is it part of our knowledge about human behavior? If you were to attend a debate on this subject by competent scholars, or read the vast amount of literature on the subject, you would be made aware of many modifications, explanations, and definitions of the principle (statement) and the words used in it, all of which reflect more recent research. The principle does not stand up today unqualified. Why? Not only have research techniques improved greatly recently, but the measurement of human behavior has become much more precise than before. It is through constant exploration and examination of concepts, theories, and practice (using the scientific method) that we have been able to add to our knowledge about human behavior and thus give the discipline of educational·psychology a body of knowledge that

is defensible and respectable. The fact that our texts often refer to many studies and experiments is truly a healthy sign of a young and dynamic discipline.

References

Alexander, W. M. The middle school movement. *Theory into Practice,* 1968, **7**, 114-117.

Angelino, H., & Mech, E. V. "Fears and worries" concerning physical changes: A preliminary survey of 32 females. *Journal of Psychology,* 1955, **39**, 195-198.

Blum, R. H. Drugs and personal values. Paper presented at the National Association of Student Personnel Administrators Drug Education Conference, Washington, D.C., November 1966.

Braun, S. Life-styles: The micro-bopper. *Esquire,* 1968, **69** (3), 22-24, 103-106.

Campbell, D. T., & Stanley, J. C. Experimental and quasi-experimental designs for research on teaching. In N. L. Gage (Ed.), *Handbook of research on teaching.* Chicago: Rand-McNally, 1963. Pp. 171-246.

Freedman, M. B. *The college experience.* San Francisco: Jossey-Bass, 1967.

Garrison, K. C. Developmental tasks and problems of the late adolescent period. *Education,* 1955, **76**, 232-235.

Garrison, K. C. *Psychology of adolescence.* Englewood Cliffs, N.J.: Prentice-Hall, 1966.

Generations apart. New York: Columbia Broadcasting System, 1969.

Gold, M., & Douvan, E. (Eds.) *Adolescent development.* Boston: Allyn and Bacon, 1969.

Golden, M. P., & Rosen, N. A. Student attitudes toward participation in university administration: An empirical study related to managerial prerogatives. *Journal of College Student Personnel,* 1966, **7**, 323-330.

Gottlieb, D. Activist youth today. *Research Resume No.38.* Burlingame, Calif.: California Advisory Council on Educational Research, 1968, **38**, 3-16.

Hall, G. S. Student customs. *Proceedings of the American Antiquarian Society,* 1900, New Series XIV, 83.

Hall, G. S. *Adolescence,* Vol. 1. New York: Appleton, 1904.

Havighurst, R. L. *Developmental tasks and education.* New York: McKay, 1952.

Hawkinshire, F. (Ed.), *Parents, teachers, and youth: A teenage weekend laboratory.* Ann Arbor: Institute of Social Research, University of Michigan, 1962.

Heist, P. Intellect and commitment: The faces of discontent. In *Order and freedom on the campus.* Western Interstate Commission for Higher Education and the Center for the Study of Higher Education, 1965.

Hollister, W.G. Preparing the minds of the future. *National Association of Secondary School*

Principals Bulletin, 1966, **50**, 30-50.

The impact of urbanization on education. Washington, D.C.: Government Printing Office, 1962.

Jersild, A. The psychology of education. New York: Macmillan, 1963.

Keniston, K. The uncommitted. New York: Harcourt, 1965.

Martinson, F. M. Sexual knowledge, values and behavior patterns of adolescents. Child Welfare, 1968, **48**, 405-410, 426.

Meredith, H. V. A synopsis of pubertal changes in youth. Journal of School Health, 1967, **37**, 171-176.

Nixon, R. E. The art of growing. New York: Random House, 1962.

Phi Delta Kappan, 1969, **48** (7), 354.

Rapoport, R. Viewpoint. The Atlantic, 1967, **219** (6), 73-74.

Schmuck, R. Some relationships of peer liking patterns in the classroom to pupil attitude and achievement. School Review, 1963, **71**, 337-359.

Schmuck, R., & Van Egmond, E. Sex differences in the relationship of interpersonal perceptions to academic performance. Psychology in the Schools, in press.

Selection Committee on Education. Education at Berkeley. University of California, Berkeley, March 1966.

Slocum, W. L., & Empey, L. T. Occupational planning by young women. Pullman, Wash.: Agricultural Experimental Station, State College of Washington, 1956.

Solberg, W. U. The University of Illinois and the reform of discipline in the modern university, 1868–1891. AAUP Bulletin, 1966, **52**, 305-314.

Stern, G. G. Myth and reality in the American college. AAUP Bulletin, 1966, **52**, 408-414.

Thornburg, H. D. Student assessment of contemporary issues. College Student Survey, 1969a, **3**(1), 1-5,22.

Thornburg, H. D. Sex education in the public schools. Phoenix: Arizona Education Association, 1969b.

Ways, M. On the campus: A troubled reflection of the U.S. Fortune, September 1965, pp. 131ff.

Winick, C. The beige epoch: Depolarization of sex roles in America. The Annals of the American Academy of Political and Social Science, 1968, **376**, 18-24.

Winter, G. D. Physical changes during adolescence. In G. D. Winter, & E. M. Nuss, (Eds.), The young adult. New York: Scott, Foresman, 1969, Pp. 85-89.

Wolfbein, S. L. Labor trends, manpower, and automation. In H. Borow (Ed.), Man in a world at work. Boston: Houghton Mifflin, 1964.

Annotations

Demos, J., & Demos, V. Adolescence in historical perspective. Journal of Marriage and the Family, 1969, **31**, 632-638. This article reviews the literature on adolescence from the time of G. Stanley Hall (1900) to the present. The authors suggest that the concept of adolescence is related to changes in American life, especially the change in the structure of the family as part of the new urban and industrial order. This synthesis article shows the cumulative effects of the study of adolescence.

Herzog, E., & Sudia, C. E. The generation gap in the eyes of youth. Children, 1970, **17**, 53-58. A sample of 251 high school students in different parts of the United States were asked several questions that focused on the generation gap. Most gaps were thought to be communication linked. Youths charged parents with a failure to give the teen-ager respect and trust and full status as a person. About one-third of the students felt their values differed from those of their parents. The youths also tended to deplore world conditions and blamed adults for the existing problems. About 10 percent of the youths had no criticisms of the adult generation.

Horrocks, J. E., & Weinberg, S. A. Psychological needs and their development during adolescence. Journal of Psychology, 1970, **72**. An adolescent-needs questionnaire was administered to 330 boys and 324 girls, from grades seven through twelve. The authors found that both sexes indicated work success, affection, and conformity to external authority to be the most enduring needs during adolescence. Social status was also important to the girls. The study indicates a gradual self-assertiveness during late adolescence.

Kelly, H. Adolescents: A suppressed minority group. Personnel and Guidance Journal, 1969, **47**, 634-640. Kelly considers adolescents a subculture and suggests that they as a group have some of the same characteristics as other minority groups. He maintains that a general feeling of alienation among adolescents has been manifested in rebellious and nonrebellious activity that indicates continued resistance to the system. In conclusion, he suggests several steps that can be taken to reduce such alienation.

Lail, S. Developmental task achievement of disadvantaged adolescents. High School Journal, 1968, **52** (2), 89-97. This article reports the results of a study among 240 middle- and lower-class adolescents on their achievement of several of Havighurst's developmental tasks. The study indicates that disadvantaged adolescents differ from middle-class adolescents in developmental task achievement. Lail suggests that the inability of lower-class youths to achieve the developmental tasks may have a close relationship with dropping out of high school.

Mead, M. Early adolescence in the United States. National Association of Secondary School Principals Bulletin, 1965, **49** (300), 5-10. Mead's article, written about the junior high school student, discusses the idea that today's society has killed the ability to experience for most youths. Youths are bored because of the slight and superficial communication they have received. She suggests that greater maturation, more media focus on "teen-ages," and an acting out against conformity are pertinent phases of adolescent growth. It is an interesting and concise look at early adolescence.

Murphy, G. What youth can tell us about its potentialities. *National Association of Secondary School Principals Bulletin,* 1966, **50**, 10-34. Murphy focuses on the need for listening to youth. He discusses their language and stresses the need to understand what they are trying to say. Murphy suggests that youths have much creativity potential to solve existing teen-age problems. He maintains that they want a balance of guidance, along with respect and independence, from adults.

Nakashima, I. I. Adolescence: Rebellion and resolution. *Journal of School Health,* 1965, **35**, 402-406. Nakashima views adolescence as a time when youths are struggling with a strange and unfamiliar body characterized by awkwardness and clumsiness during an early adaptation period. After discussing adolescent hypochondriasis, he reviews the effects of dependence-independence needs, peer groups, and psychosexual conflicts on resolving many adolescent problems.

Sexton, P. How the American boy is feminized. *Psychology Today,* 1970, **3** (8), 66-67. This article discusses the feminized or "sissy" male and suggests that such a youth is not so retiring and quiet as he appears to be. Sexton suggests that the female-dominated school is the strongest influence on males. Women set the standards for adult behavior and favor students who conform to their own behavioral norms. The author researched 12,000 high school students. She found that highly masculine boys made lower grades than less masculine boys. She also attributes body build, peers, and conflict as masculine-identity processes. She suggests that we need to place more emphasis on boylike, masculine behavior.

Werkman, S. L. Adolescence: A twentieth century predicament. *American Association of University Women Journal,* 1966, **59**, 185-187. This article is an overview of various social and psychological forces affecting the adolescent. Werkman reviews such needs as emancipation, independence, self-identity, and career seeking. He deplores the existing demands for immediate gratification. The plea is for some restoration of past social rituals that tend to be ignored today. Werkman suggests that parents are excluded from adolescent life and feels that it would be well if the youth were reminded that he lives in his father's house.

adolescence: intellectual behavior

Controversy and confusion have surrounded the term *intelligence.* Intellectual development appears to be a potentiality, the achievement of which depends on both genetic endowment and quality of the environment. Intelligence is not a static condition; it is not a mere reservoir of force or energy waiting to be exercised. On the contrary, it denotes degrees of competence in behavior as they are expressed during the various developmental stages.

Perhaps the most plausible theory of intelligence is that advanced by Jean Piaget. He suggests that an individual passes through stages of intellectual growth during which he develops increasing intellectual capacities (1951). In Piaget's theory both heredity and environment play a role in intellectual development, but primary emphasis is on the interrelationship of these two factors.

Ginsburg and Opper (1969) have summarily discussed Piaget's definitions of intelligence, such as "intelligence is a particular instance of biological adaptation," "intelligence is the form of equilibrium toward which all the (cognitive) structures . . . tend," and "intelligence is a system of living and acting operations." Essentially these definitions have a biological basis, but they assume that mental activity involves interaction with the environment. As an individual functions, heredity affects intelligence in two ways: (1) "Inherited physical structures set broad limits on intellectual functioning," and (2) "Inherited behavioral reactions have an influence during the first few days of human life but afterward are extensively modified as the infant interacts with his environment" (Ginsburg & Opper, 1969, p. 17). Thus individuals inherit organization and adaptation tendencies.

Organization refers to the "tendency for all species to systematize or organize their processes into coherent systems which may be either physical or psychological" (Ginsburg & Opper, 1969, p. 17). As a person interacts with knowledge, he organizes it into a logical order, which makes it coherent and useful.

Adaptation is also essential because it allows a person to adjust to his environment. When an individual interrelates with knowledge in his environment, he does so with his existing mental structure. Piaget maintains that a person adapts through the processes of assimilation and accommodation. *Assimilation* involves interpreting new experiences by relating them to existing knowledge. *Accommodation* refers to changing existing knowledge in response to one's environment. Piaget sees these processes as complementary and present in every intellectual act.

According to Piaget, organization and adaptation aid in processing information or knowledge. Therefore he claims that the individual "does not inherit particular intellectual reactions; rather, he does inherit a tendency to organize his intellectual processes, and to adapt to his environment, in some way" (Ginsburg & Opper, 1969, p.19).

Hunt (1961) has outlined Piaget's developmental stages of intelligence from infancy through adolescence:

I.	Sensorimotor Period	0-2
II.	Concrete Operations Period	2-11
	A. Preoperational subperiod	(2-4)
	B. Intuitive subperiod	(4-7)
	C. Concrete operations subperiod	(7-11)
III.	Formal Operations Period	11-15

Elkind (1967b) suggests that the major cognitive task during the *sensorimotor period* is the conquest of the object (see his article on p. 50). The child changes from a completely egocentric individual who cannot differentiate between self and external reality to an object-oriented individual capable of distinguishing self from other people and objects in the environment. The child's reactions are reflexive—that is, based on the physical nature of the objects within his environment. He is limited to nonsymbolic activity. Lovell (1968) contends that at 18–21 months the child finds new ways to approach objects and thus learns symbolic activity.

In the *preoperational subperiod* people and objects in the child's environment begin to have some meaning to him. Elkind (1967b) characterizes this stage by conquest of the symbol, which occurs through the acquisition of language and the internalization of persons and objects. The 4-year-old focuses on a specific aspect of the symbol and subsequently fails to account for all the factors involved. The result may be faulty reasoning.

During the *intuitive subperiod* the child begins to think perceptually. Although he has advanced beyond thinking of environmental objects as permanent, no logical explanations are forthcoming as to why certain objects are as they are. Through perception, the child focuses on what he sees; he is not yet ready to base his decisions on reasoning.

At about 6 or 7 the child moves from the intuitive to the *concrete operations subperiod.* The 8-year-old child becomes less rigid and self-oriented in his thinking, which is broader and more flexible. Elkind (1967b) sees the child's major cognitive task at this period as mastering classes, relations, and objects. As the child's thoughts become more systematized, they conform to certain rules and appear more logical. Although the child's attention is still focused on concrete objects, his internal cognitive behavior is distinguished by increasingly complex systems of action (Waller, 1969). He reaches the awareness that not everything can be explained in concrete, logical terms and begins his search for more plausible answers.

In the final developmental stage of intelligence, the *formal operations period*, adolescent intelligence realizes its full growth potential. The adolescent begins to function with an adult intellect and deals in abstract terms. No longer relying on concrete experiences, he can formulate hypotheses to explain the phenomena in his environment. His thinking has become clearer, differentiated, more logical, and more combinational. The acquired ability to think abstractly indicates that his intelligence is fully developed, although he will continue to learn throughout his life.

Cognitive Growth

The first two articles in this chapter reflect the Piagetian point of view. The Ausubels' discussion of cognitive development in adolescence focuses on the transition from the concrete to the formal (abstract) operations stages. The greatest distinction between the two periods is the decreasing need for props to assist intellectual functioning in the abstract stage. The Ausubels describe the characteristics of the formal operational period, especially as they affect abstract cognitive functioning in school.

Elkind enlarges on the formal operations problem by discussing *adolescent egocentrism.* Simply stated, egocentrism is the inability to differentiate between the real and the ideal. It ceases to be a problem for the adolescent at about 15 or 16, when his intelligence becomes fully developed. Through a series of reality-testing behaviors he learns to recognize the difference between his own preoccupations and the ways others relate to him. As egocentrism is reduced, adolescent cognitive structure becomes firmly established.

Intellectual Function

Hollister proposes that we can prepare the adolescent to function intellectually by helping him to develop ego strength. By *ego strength,* he is not referring to the traditional egotistical sense—!—but to the technical sense—as a collective term covering the numerous functions of the mind, such as decision-making and thinking. This article maintains that the mind, when properly stimulated, is highly able to differentiate. Thus adolescents can be challenged, through problem-solving activities and the development of a social intelligence, to extend their capacities for living with and adjusting to human behaviors. It becomes a process of integrating the self. Educators can achieve this end by designing classroom experiences that will foster emotional, motivational, and intellectual strengths.

david p. ausubel

pearl ausubel*

cognitive development in adolescence

During the six-year interval since the appearance of the last issue on adolescence, theoretical and research activity with respect to cognitive development has increased tremendously. Unfortunately for our purposes, however, most of this activity has been directed toward the preschool and elementary school periods. The few research studies and theoretical papers that did concern themselves with cognitive development during adolescence were stimulated by the pioneering work of Inhelder and Piaget (1958). During this same interval, interest in adolescent intelligence declined markedly.

The Transition from Concrete to Formal Operations

Inhelder and Piaget presented considerable evidence indicating that "formal" (abstract) operations appear slightly before the onset of adolescence. On the whole their findings were corroborated by other investigators (Goldman, 1965; Jackson, 1965; Lovell, 1961; Yudin and Kates, 1963). Lovell's subjects attained this stage of devel-

opment somewhat later than Inhelder and Piaget's, and Case and Collinson's (1962) somewhat earlier. Both Goldman and Jackson reported greater age variability, and Jackson less intertask generality, than did Inhelder and Piaget in the development of formal thinking. None of these findings, however, detracted from the essential validity of Piaget's conclusion that for the first time the child entering this stage of cognitive development thinks in terms of all-inclusive hypothetical possibilities (instead of "the here and now") or in terms of propositional logic ("second-degree operations" or "operations on operations"). "Instead of just coordinating facts about the actual world," Piaget (1957) stated, "hypothetico-deductive reasoning draws out the implications of the possible and the necessary."

The elementary school child, according to Inhelder and Piaget (1958), is by no means dependent on *immediate* concrete-empirical experience in understanding and manipulating simple abstractions or ideas about objects and phenomena. It is true, of course, that the emergence of such ideas must always be preceded by an adequate background of direct, nonverbal experience with the empirical data from which they are abstracted. But once their meaning becomes firmly established as a result of this background of past experience, the child can meaningfully comprehend and use them

Ausubel, D. P., and Ausubel, P., "Cognitive Development in Adolescence," *American Educational Research Journal,* 1966, pp. 403-413. Copyright by American Educational Research Association.

*The writers acknowledge the bibliographic assistance of Edward S. Wood in preparing this chapter.

without any *current* reference to concrete-empirical data.

The meaningful understanding or manipulation of *relationships* between abstractions or of *ideas about ideas,* on the other hand, is quite another matter. In this kind of operation the elementary school pupil is still dependent upon current or recently prior concrete-empirical experience; when such experience is not available, he finds abstract relational propositions unrelatable to cognitive structure and hence devoid of meaning. This dependence upon concrete-empirical props self-evidently limits his ability meaningfully to grasp and manipulate relationships between abstractions, since he can only acquire those understandings and perform those logical operations which do not go beyond the concrete and particularized representation of reality implicit in his use of props. Thus, where complex relational propositions are involved, he is largely restricted to a subverbal, concrete, or intuitive level of cognitive functioning, a level that falls far short of the clarity, precision, explicitness, and generality associated with the more advanced abstract stage of intellectual development.

Beginning with the adolescent period, however, children become increasingly less dependent upon the availability of concrete-empirical experience in meaningfully relating complex abstract propositions to cognitive structure. Eventually, after sufficient gradual change in this direction, a qualitatively new capacity emerges: the intellectually mature individual becomes capable of understanding and manipulating relationships between abstractions *directly,* that is, without any reference whatsoever to concrete, empirical reality. Instead of reasoning directly from a particular set of data, he uses indirect, second-order, logical operations for structuring the data; and instead of merely grouping data into classes or arranging them serially in terms of a given variable, he formulates and tests hypotheses based on all possible combinations of variables. Since his logical operations are performed on verbal propositions, he can go beyond the operations that follow immediately from empirical reality (equivalence, distinctiveness, reversibility, and seriation) and can deal with all possible or hypothetical relations between ideas. He can now transcend the previously achieved level of intuitive thought and understanding and formulate general laws relating general categories of variables that are divorced from the concrete-empirical data at hand. His concepts and generalizations, therefore, tend more to be second-order constructs derived from relationships between previously established verbal abstractions already one step removed from the data.

Careful analysis of the experiments performed by Inhelder and Piaget and by the other investigators cited above does not substantiate their view, as well as Lunzer's (1965), that the *distinctive* feature of formal or abstract (as opposed to concrete) operations is that the older child is able to deal operationally and verbally with ideas about ideas, to perform "second-order operations," or to go "beyond the framework of transformations bearing directly on empirical reality." The younger ("concrete operational") child can also do these things, as shown by the studies of Case and Collinson (1962) and Hill (1961). The latter demonstrated, for example, that most children ages six to eight can easily draw correct inferences from hypothetical premises involving second-order operations. It is rather the preadolescent's and adolescent's ability verbally to manipulate relationships between ideas ("second-order relations") *in the absence of recently prior or concurrently available concrete-empirical props* that is the distinctive attribute of formal operations. (Hill's subjects, after all, were given logical problems that were invariably stated in terms of particular instances.) This new capability emerging at age 11 and beyond invests propositional thought with a genuinely abstract and nonintuitive quality. Ideas about ideas now achieve a truly general status that is freed from any dependence whatsoever on particular instances and concrete experience. It is for this reason that thinking becomes hypothetico-deductive in nature, that is, refers to all possible relationships between variables rather than to relationships delineated by concrete manifestations of particular instances.

Validity of the Stage Concept

Many American psychologists and educators have been sharply critical of Piaget's designation of concrete and formal stages of cognitive development. They argue that the transition between these stages occurs gradually rather than abruptly or discontinuously; that variability exists both between different cultures and within a given culture with respect to the age at which the transition takes place; that fluctuations occur over time in the level of cognitive functioning manifested by a given child; that the transition to the formal stage occurs at different ages both for different subject matter fields and for component subareas within a particular field; and that environmental as well as endogenous factors have a demonstrable influence on the rate of cognitive development. But although much more rigorous empirical data than have been presented to date are required to substantiate Piaget's conclusions with respect to the existence of these two *particular* stages of cognitive development, the aforementioned criticisms reflect many gratuitous and unwarranted assumptions regarding the criteria that *any* designated stage of development must meet.

Actually, developmental stages imply nothing more than identifiable sequential phases in an orderly progression of development that are *qualitatively* discriminable from adjacent phases and generally characteristic of most members of a broadly defined age range. As long as a given stage occupies the same sequential position in all individuals and cultures whenever it occurs, and must reach equilibrium before the next stage can develop (Case and Collinson, 1962), it is perfectly compatible with the existence of intraindividual, interindividual, and intercultural differences in age level of incidence and in subject matter field. It reflects the influence of both genic and environmental determinants and can occur either gradually or abruptly. Hence, all of the aforementioned arguments disputing the legitimacy of Piaget's stages of intellectual development seem quite irrelevant.

Although stages of development are qualitatively discontinuous in *process* from preceding and succeeding stages, there is no reason why their *manner of achievement* must necessarily be abrupt or saltatory. This is particularly true when the factors that bring them into being are operative over many years and are cumulative in their impact. Unlike the situation in physical, emotional, and personality development,

cognitive development is not marked by the sudden, dramatic appearance of discontinuously new determinants.

It is also unreasonable to insist that a given stage must always occur at the same age in every culture. Since rate of development is at least in part a function of environmental stimulation, the age range in which a stage occurs tends to vary from one culture to another. Thus, considering, for example, the marked differences between the Swiss and American school systems, it would be remarkable indeed if comparable stages of development occurred at the same ages (Case and Collinson, 1962; Lovell, 1961).

Similarly, within a given culture, a particular stage cannot be expected to occur at the same age for all individuals. When a particular age level is designated for a given stage, it obviously refers to a mean value and implies that a normal range of variability prevails around the mean. This intra-age variability (Case and Collinson, 1962; Goldman, 1965; Jackson, 1965; Lovell, 1961) reflects differences in intellectual endowment, experiential background, education, and personality. It is hardly surprising, therefore, that a population of mentally retarded children never did reach the formal stage of logical operations (Jackson, 1965); that mental age correlated more highly than chronological age with attained stage of cognitive development (Goldman, 1965); and that characteristic sex differences (e.g., in mathematical thinking), reflective of differences in cultural expectations and experiential background, were found in degree of cognitive development in different areas of subject matter (Elkind, 1962b). As in any developmental process where experiential factors are crucial, however, age per se and brightness level are generally less important than degree of relevant experience (Dodwell, 1960, 1961; Elkind, 1961b).

It follows, then, that a certain amount of overlapping among age groups is inevitable. A particular stage may be generally characteristic of five- and six-year-olds but also typically include some four- and seven-year-olds and even some three- and eight-year-olds. Piaget's age levels, like Gesell's, are nothing more than average approximations set for purposes of convenience. Hence, to attack the concept of developmental stages on the grounds that a given stage includes children of varying ages, instead of taking place at the precise age designated by Piaget, is simply to demolish a straw man.

One also cannot expect complete consistency and generality of stage behavior within an individual from one week or month to another, and from one subject matter or level of difficulty to another. Some overlapping and specificity are inevitable whenever development is determined by multiple-variable factors. A particular 12-year-old may use abstract logical operations in his science course in October, but may revert for no apparent reason to a concrete level of cognitive functioning in November, or even several years later when confronted with an extremely difficult and unfamiliar problem in the same field. Furthermore, he may characteristically continue to function at a concrete level for another year or two in social studies and literature. Since transitions to new stages do not occur instantaneously but over a period of time, fluctuations between stages are common until the newly emerging stage is consolidated. In addition, because of intrinsic differences in level of subject matter difficulty, and because of intra- and interindividual differences in ability profiles and experiential background, it is small wonder that transitions from one stage to another do not occur simultaneously in all subject matter areas and subareas. Abstract thinking, for example, generally emerges earlier in science than in social studies because children have more experience manipulating ideas about mass, time, and space than about government, social institutions, and historical events. However, in some children, depending on their special abilities and experience, the reverse may be true. Finally, stages of development are always referable to a given range of difficulty and familiarity of the problem area. Beyond this range, individuals commonly revert (regress) to a former stage of development (Case and Collinson, 1962).

Neither is the concept of developmental stages invalidated by the demonstration that they are susceptible to environmental influence. It is erroneous to believe that stages of intellectual development are exclusively the products of "internal ripening," and hence that they reflect primarily the influence of endogenous factors. Gesell's embryological model of development has little applicability to human development beyond the first year of life when environmental factors become increasingly more important determinants of variability in developmental outcomes. In fact, as the educational system improves we can confidently look forward to earlier mean emergence of the various stages of cognitive development.

General and Specific Aspects of the Transition

It is apparent from the previous discussion that the transition from concrete to abstract cognitive functioning takes place specifically in each separate subject matter area and invariably presupposes a certain necessary amount of sophistication in each of the areas involved. This state of affairs follows directly from intraindividual differences in experience and component intellectual abilities. Inhelder and Piaget (1958) explicitly recognized that complete intersituational generality cannot be expected at any stage of development, referring to this phenomenon as "horizontal decalage." This prediction has been confirmed by many other investigators (Dodwell, 1960, 1961, 1962, 1963; Elkind, 1961c; Jackson, 1965; Lovell and Slater, 1960).

In the more general sense of the term, however, it is possible to designate the individual's *overall* developmental status as "concrete" or "abstract" on the basis of an estimate of his characteristic or predominant mode of cognitive functioning. This distinction is important for two reasons: (a) the individual necessarily continues to undergo the same transition from concrete to abstract cognitive functioning in each *new* subject matter area he encounters—even *after* he reaches the abstract stage of development on an overall basis; (b) once he attains this latter general stage, however, the transition to abstract cognitive functioning in unfamiliar new subject matter areas takes place much more readily.

Thus, even though an individual characteristically functions at the abstract level of cognitive development, when he is first introduced to a wholly unfamiliar subject matter field he tends initially to function at a concrete-intuitive level. But since he is able to draw on various transferable elements of his more *general* ability to function abstractly, he passes through the concrete stage of functioning in this particular subject matter area much more rapidly than would be the case were he still generally in the concrete stage of cognitive development. These facilitating transferable elements presumably include transactional terms, higher-order concepts, and experience in *directly* understanding and manipulating relationships between abstractions (i.e., without the benefit of props) which, although acquired in specific subject matter contexts, are generally applicable to other learning situations.

Determinants of the Transition

It appears that the combined influence of three concomitant and mutually supportive developmental trends accounts for the transition from concrete to abstract cognitive functioning (Ausubel, 1963). In the first place, the developing individual gradually acquires a working vocabulary of transactional or mediating terms that makes possible the more efficient juxtaposition and combination of different relatable abstractions into potentially meaningful propositions. Second, he can relate these latter propositions more readily to cognitive structure and hence render them more meaningful, in view of his growing fund of stable, higher-order concepts and principles encompassed by and made available within that structure. A sufficient body of abstract ideas that are clear and stable is obviously necessary before he can hope efficiently to manipulate relationships between them so as to develop meaningful general propositions. The possession of a working body of inclusive concepts also makes possible the formulation of more general statements of relationship that are less tied to specific instances; greater integration of related ideas and different aspects of the same problem; the elaboration of more precise distinctions and finer differentiations; and less dependence on complete concrete-empirical data in reaching warranted inferences. Finally, it seems reasonable to suppose that after many years of practice in meaningfully understanding and manipulating relationships *with* the aid of concrete-empirical props, he gradually develops greater facility in performing these operations, so that eventually (after acquiring the necessary transactional and higher-order concepts) he can perform the same operations just as effectively *without* relying on props. The same sequence of events is seen in acquiring many other neuromuscular and cognitive skills, e.g., walking without "holding on," bicycling "without hands," speaking a foreign language without internal translation from one's mother tongue, transmitting Morse code in sentences rather than in word or letter units.

Inhelder and Piaget (1958) have advanced a motivational explanation to account for the transition from concrete to abstract cognitive functioning, namely, cultural pressure and adolescent desire to assume adult roles, which in turn presuppose adult modes of thought. But even though motivation may conceivably energize and facilitate cognitive change, it cannot possibly explain either its occurrence or direction. No amount of motivation would suffice to effect the change in question in the absence of both the necessary genic potentialities and the supportive experience. Whatever facilitative influence motivational factors have is undoubtedly mediated through greater effort to seek out and participate in the kind of cognitive experiences that promote a shift from concrete to abstract functioning. It is also unconvincing to attribute the shift to "maturation of cerebral structures," by invoking the patently circular Gestalt argument that "lattice and group structures are probably isomorphic with neurological structures" (Inhelder and Piaget, 1958). No independent evidence of significant neuroanatomical or neurophysiological change at adolescence has yet been adduced.

Braham (1965) suggests that the negative sanctioning of intellectual achievement in adolescent peer groups, particularly among lower class and culturally deprived youth, has a deterrent effect on cognitive development during adolescence. Such negative sanctioning of intellectual achievement has been reported for Maori adolescents (Ausubel, 1965).

Educational Implications of the Transition from Concrete to Abstract Cognitive Functioning

From the standpoint of the secondary school teacher, the most significant development in cognitive functioning that occurs during the preadolescent and early adolescent years is the gradual transition from a predominantly concrete to a predominantly abstract mode of understanding and manipulating complex relational propositions. This developmental shift, in turn, has far-reaching implications for teaching methods and curricular practices in the secondary school.

Once the developing individual reaches the abstract stage of cognitive functioning, he becomes in large measure an abstract verbal learner. He now acquires most new concepts and learns most new propositions by *directly* apprehending verbally or symbolically stated relationships between previously learned abstractions. To do so meaningfully, he need no longer refer to firsthand, nonrepresentational experience, nor actually perform any of the abstracting or generalizing operations on the underlying empirical data. With his developmental dependence on concrete-empirical props removed, the only condition necessary for the meaningful understanding and manipulation of higher-order concepts and relational propositions is that their substantive import be nonarbitrarily relatable to his particular cognitive structure and that he adopt a set to learn them in this fashion. Hence, on developmental grounds, he is ready at the secondary school level for a new type of verbal expository teaching that uses concrete-empirical experience primarily for *illustrative* purposes, i.e., to clarify or dramatize truly abstract meanings rather than to generate intuitive meanings.

Many features of the activity program were based on the quite defensible premise that the elementary school child perceives the world in relatively specific and concrete terms and requires considerable firsthand experience with diverse concrete instances of a given set of relationships before he can abstract genuinely meaningful concepts and relate them meaningfully to cognitive structure. Thus, an attempt was made to teach factual information and intellectual skills in the "real-life" functional contexts in which they are customarily encountered, rather than through the medium of verbal exposition supplemented by artificially contrived drills and exercises. This approach has real merit provided that a fetish is not made of naturalism and incidental learning; that ade-

quate use is made of appropriate expository teaching; that drills and exercises are provided in instances where opportunities for acquiring skills do not occur frequently and repetitively enough in more natural settings; and that deliberate or guided effort in most learning situations is not regarded as incompatible with incidental learning in others. Even more important, however, is the realization that in older children, once a sufficient number of basic concepts is consolidated, new concepts are primarily acquired from verbal rather than from concrete experience. Hence, in secondary school it may be desirable to reverse both the sequence and the relative balance between abstract concepts and supportive data. There is a good reason for believing, therefore, that much of the time presently spent in cookbook laboratory exercises in the sciences could be much more advantageously employed in formulating precise definitions, making explicit verbal distinctions between concepts, generalizing from hypothetical situations, etc.

It would be very misleading, however, to assert that secondary school students and even older students can *never* profit either from the use of concrete-empirical props to generate intuitive meanings, or from the use of inductive discovery and deductive problem-solving techniques to enhance such meanings. As previously suggested, generally mature students tend to function at a relatively concrete level when confronted with a particularly *new* subject matter area in which they are as yet totally unsophisticated. But since abstract cognitive functioning in this new area is achieved with the attainment of a minimal degree of subject matter sophistication, these special auxiliary techniques should be employed only for the aforementioned purposes during the early stages of instruction. Continued use for other purposes, however, (i.e., to improve problem-solving skills, to foster appreciation of scientific method, or to test verbal understanding) is quite another matter. It is one thing occasionally to use examples and analogies to clarify meanings of particularly difficult or unfamiliar concepts, but it is quite another to use them routinely as an invariably necessary prop for the acquisition of all relational meanings.

The transition from concrete to abstract cognitive functioning also enables the secondary school student to master a much greater volume of subject matter knowledge. To begin with, the logistics of the learning situation become more favorable. His ability to understand abstract relational propositions directly (i.e., to dispense with the time-consuming operations of using both concrete-empirical props and discovery and problem-solving experience to generate and enhance intuitive insights) permits one to present much more subject matter in the same period of time. In addition, his qualitatively higher level of abstract understanding makes possible a more efficient means of organizing and integrating the materials that are presented. Because his higher-order concepts and relational propositions are no longer intuitive, but are meaningfully formulated in truly abstract and general terms, they become clearer, more stable, more precise, and sufficiently inclusive to subsume a wider array of differentiated facts and subconcepts.

In view of these latter developments and of the greater differentiation of his abilities and interests, the secondary school student is prepared to cope with a greater depth as well as with a greater volume of subject matter. He is ready for more intensive and differentiated coverage of smaller areas of knowledge as opposed to more global and superficial coverage of larger areas. "Depth" in this context, however, implies greater substantive density of knowledge rather than greater degree of autonomy in discovering the principles and obtaining the information to be learned. If the secondary school student is required to discover most principles autonomously, to obtain most subject matter content from primary sources, and to design his own experiments, he only has time to acquire methodological sophistication. In terms of *substantive* depth, he has simply moved from previously superficial coverage of broad areas to comparably superficial coverage of more circumscribed areas. The aim of secondary school and undergraduate education is not to produce substantively ignorant junior scholars and scientists, but to produce students who are knowledgeable both in breadth and depth of subject matter.

Intelligence in Adolescence

By intelligence we simply mean a measurement construct designating level of ability in performing a graded series of tasks implicating the component aspects of cognitive functioning at any given stage of intellectual development. For the most part, it is representative at adolescence and beyond of a general capacity for processing information and for utilizing abstract symbols in the solution of abstract problems. Intelligence tests, therefore, are valid to the extent that they measure this capacity. An intellectual ability, in other words, is really nothing more nor less than a functional manifestation of a distinct and identifiable cognitive process as expressed in a range of individual performance or capacity differences.

Ljung (1965) has recently described an "adolescent growth spurt" in mental development that is more marked in girls than in boys. This spurt undoubtedly reflects the adolescent's greater ability to process information and solve abstract problems more efficiently that results from the shift to abstract cognitive functioning. It is not typically reflected in conventional intelligence tests but was in Ljung's tests because the measures he used were more comparable to academic achievement tests. Both Meyer (1960) and Bradway and Thompson (1962) confirmed the fact that the predictive power of total intelligence test scales, as well as of primary ability scales, increases with age.

Cattell (1963) has reported the isolation of "fluid" and "crystallized" components of intelligence. As might be anticipated, the crystallized factor consists largely of process functions, presumably not much influenced by learning or educational experience, and reaches maturity at a relatively early age. The fluid factor, in contrast, consists more of product functions which are appreciably influenced by education and experience and therefore reach maturity later in life. So-called culturally deprived adolescents are naturally more deficient in the fluid than in the crystallized components of intelligence.

Evidence continues to accumulate that intellectual ability becomes more highly differentiated with increasing age (Green and Berkowitz, 1964; Guilford, 1966; Heinonen, 1963; Ljung, 1965; Meyer, 1960). This trend exists despite the fact that the older individual, who has presumably undergone the shift from concrete to abstract logical operations in more subject matter areas, is probably more homogeneous in his mode of cognitive functioning. Increased integration also occurs *within* the various component subabilities. Thus the more established differential aptitude batteries probably have greater predictive value for the *particular* kinds of subject matter achievement for which they are relevant than do composite scores on tests of general intelligence or of general scholastic aptitude. However, the latter tests, as McNemar (1964) points out, are more useful for predicting complex criteria of academic achievement, involving the interaction among several abilities.

Bradway and Thompson (1962) confirmed the well established fact that males show more IQ gain from adolescence to adulthood than do females. Differences in favor of girls were found in word fluency, rote memory, and reasoning, but boys were superior in spatial and quantitative ability (Carlsmith, 1964).

david elkind

egocentrism in adolescence

This paper describes the different forms of egocentrism characteristic of each of the major stages of cognitive growth outlined by Piaget. Particular attention is paid to the egocentrism of adolescence which is here described as the failure to differentiate between the cognitive concerns of others and those of the self. This adolescent egocentrism is said to give rise to 2 mental constructions, the imaginary audience and the personal fable, which help to account for certain forms of adolescent behavior and experience. These considerations suggest, it is concluded, that the cognitive structures peculiar to a given age period can provide insights with respect to the personality characteristics of that age level.

Within the Piagetian theory of intellectual growth, the concept of egocentrism generally refers to a lack of differentiation in some area of subject-object interaction (Piaget, 1962). At each stage of mental development, this lack of differentiation takes a unique form and is manifested in a unique set of behaviors. The transition from one form of egocentrism to another takes place in a dialectic fashion such that the mental structures which free the child from a lower form of egocentrism are the same structures which ensnare him in a higher form of egocentrism. From the developmental point of view, therefore, egocentrism can be regarded as a negative by-product of any emergent mental

Reprinted with permission of the author and publisher from *Child Development*, 1967, **38**, 1025-1034.

system in the sense that it corresponds to the fresh cognitive problems engendered by that system.

Although in recent years Piaget has focused his attention more on the positive than on the negative products of mental structures, egocentrism continues to be of interest because of its relation to the affective aspects of child thought and behavior. Indeed, it is possible that the study of egocentrism may provide a bridge between the study of cognitive structure, on the one hand, and the exploration of personality dynamics, on the other (Cowan, 1966; Gourevitch & Feffer, 1962). The purpose of the present paper is to describe, in greater detail than Inhelder and Piaget (1958), what seems to me to be the nature of egocentrism in adolescence and some of its behavioral and experiential correlates. Before doing that, however, it might be well to set the stage for the discussion with a brief review of the forms of egocentrism which precede this mode of thought in adolescence.

Forms of Egocentrism in Infancy and Childhood

In presenting the childhood forms of egocentrism, it is useful to treat each of Piaget's major stages as if it were primarily concerned with resolving one major cognitive task. The egocentrism of a particular stage can then be described with reference to this special problem of cognition. It must be stressed, however, that while the cognitive task characteristic of a particular stage seems to attract the major share of the child's mental energies, it is not the only cognitive problem with which the child is attempting to cope. In mental development there are major battles and minor skirmishes, and if I here ignore the lesser engagements it is for purposes of economy of presentation rather than because I assume that such engagements are insignificant.

Sensori-motor Egocentrism (0–2 Years)

The major cognitive task of infancy might be regarded as *the conquest of the object.* In the early months of life, the infant deals with objects as if their existence were dependent upon their being present in immediate perception (Charlesworth, 1966; Piaget, 1954). The egocentrism of this stage corresponds, therefore, to a lack of differentiation between the object and the sense impressions occasioned by it. Toward the end of the first year, however, the infant begins to seek the object even when it is hidden, and thus shows that he can now differentiate between the object and the "experience of the object." This breakdown of egocentrism with respect to objects is brought about by mental representation of the absent object.[1] An internal representation of the absent object is the earliest manifestation of the symbolic function which develops gradually during the second year of life and whose activities dominate the next stage of mental growth.

Pre-operational Egocentrism (2–6 Years)

During the preschool period, the child's major cognitive task can be regarded as *the conquest of the symbol.* It is during the preschool period that the symbolic function becomes fully active, as evidenced by the rapid growth in the acquisition and utilization

[1] It is characteristic of the dialectic of mental growth that the capacity to represent internally the absent object also enables the infant to cognize the object as externally existent.

of language, by the appearance of symbolic play, and by the first reports of dreams. Yet this new capacity for representation, which loosed the infant from his egocentrism with respect to objects, now ensnares the preschool children in a new egocentrism with regard to symbols. At the beginning of this period, the child fails to differentiate between words and their referents (Piaget, 1952b) and between his self-created play and dream symbols and reality (Kohlberg, 1966; Piaget, 1951). Children at this stage believe that the name inheres in the thing and that an object cannot have more than one name (Elkind, 1961a, 1962b, 1963).

The egocentrism of this period is particularly evident in children's linguistic behavior. When explaining a piece of apparatus to another child, for example, the youngster at this stage uses many indefinite terms and leaves out important information (Piaget, 1952b). Although this observation is sometimes explained by saying that the child fails to take the other person's point of view, it can also be explained by saying that the child assumes words carry much more information than they actually do. This results from his belief that even the indefinite "thing" somehow conveys the properties of the object which it is used to represent. In short, the egocentrism of this period consists in a lack of clear differentiation between symbols and their referents.

Toward the end of the pre-operational period, the differentiation between symbols and their referents is gradually brought about by the emergence of concrete operations (internalized actions which are roughly comparable in their activity to the elementary operations of arithmetic). One consequence of concrete operational thought is that it enables the child to deal with two elements, properties, or relations at the same time. A child with concrete operations can, for example, take account of both the height and width of a glass of colored liquid and recognize that, when the liquid is poured into a differently shaped container, the changes in height and width of the liquid compensate one another so that the total quantity of liquid is conserved (Elkind, 1961b; Piaget, 1952a). This ability, to hold two dimensions in mind at the same time, also enables the child to hold both symbol and referent in mind simultaneously, and thus distinguish between them. Concrete operations are, therefore, instrumental in overcoming the egocentrism of the pre-operational stage.

Concrete Operational Egocentrism (7–11 Years)

With the emergence of concrete operations, the major cognitive task of the school-age child becomes that of *mastering classes, relations, and quantities.* While the preschool child forms global notions of classes, relations, and quantities, such notions are imprecise and cannot be combined one with the other. The child with concrete operations, on the other hand, can nest classes, seriate relations, and conserve quantities. In addition, concrete operations enable the school-age child to perform elementary syllogistic reasoning and to formulate hypotheses and explanations about concrete matters. This system of concrete operations, however, which lifts the school-age child to new heights of thought, nonetheless lowers him to new depths of egocentrism.

Operations are essentially mental tools whose products, series, class hierarchies, conservations, etc., are not directly derived from experience. At this stage, however, the child nonetheless regards these mental products as being on a par with perceptual phenomena. It is the inability to differentiate clearly between mental constructions and perceptual givens which constitutes the egocentrism of the school-age child. An example may help to clarify the form which egocentrism takes during the concrete operational stage.

In a study reported by Peel (1960), children and adolescents were read a passage about Stonehenge and then asked questions about it. One of the questions had to do with whether Stonehenge was a place for religious worship or a fort. The children (ages 7–10) answered the question with flat statements, as if they were stating a fact. When they were given evidence that contradicted their statements, they rationalized the evidence to make it conform with their initial position. Adolescents, on the other hand, phrased their replies in probabilistic terms and supported their judgments with material gleaned from the passage. Similar differences be-

tween children and adolescents have been found by Elkind (1966) and Weir (1964).

What these studies show is that, when a child constructs a hypothesis or formulates a strategy, he assumes that this product is imposed by the data rather than derived from his own mental activity. When his position is challenged, he does not change his stance but, on the contrary, reinterprets the data to fit with his assumption. This observation, however, raises a puzzling question. Why, if the child regards both his thought products and the givens of perception as coming from the environment, does he nonetheless give preference to his own mental constructions? The answer probably lies in the fact that the child's mental constructions are the product of reasoning, and hence are experienced as imbued with a (logical) necessity. This "felt" necessity is absent when the child experiences the products of perception. It is not surprising, then, that the child should give priority to what seems permanent and necessary in perception (the products of his own thought, such as conservation) rather than to what seems transitory and arbitrary in perception (products of environmental stimulation). Only in adolescence do young people differentiate between their own mental constructions and the givens of perception. For the child, there are no problems of epistemology.

Toward the end of childhood, the emergence of formal operational thought (which is analogous to propositional logic) gradually frees the child from his egocentrism with respect to his own mental constructions. As Inhelder and Piaget (1958) have shown, formal operational thought enables the young person to deal with all of the possible combinations and permutations of elements within a given set. Provided with four differently colored pieces of plastic, for example, the adolescent can work out all the possible combinations of colors by taking the pieces one, two, three and four, and none, at a time. Children, on the other hand, cannot formulate these combinations in any systematic way. The ability to conceptualize all of the possible combinations in a system allows the adolescent to construct contrary-to-fact hypotheses and to reason about such propositions "as if" they were true. The adolescent, for example, can accept the statement, "Let's suppose coal is white," whereas the child would reply, "But coal is black." This ability to formulate contrary-to-fact hypotheses is crucial to the overcoming of the egocentrism of the concrete operational period. Through the formulation of such contrary-to-fact hypotheses, the young person discovers the arbitrariness of his own mental constructions and learns to differentiate them from perceptual reality.

Adolescent Egocentrism

From the strictly cognitive point of view (as opposed to the psychoanalytic point of view as represented by Blos [1962] and A. Freud [1946] or the ego psychological point of view as represented by Erikson [1959]), the major task of early adolescence can be regarded as having to do with *the conquest of thought.* Formal operations not only permit the young person to construct all the possibilities in a system and construct contrary-to-fact propositions (Inhelder & Piaget, 1958); they also enable him to conceptualize his own thought, to take his mental constructions as objects and reason about them. Only at about the ages of 11–12, for example, do children spontaneously introduce concepts of belief, intelligence, and faith into their definitions of their religious denomination (Elkind, 1961a; 1962b; 1963). Once more, however, this new mental system which frees the young person from the egocentrism of childhood entangles him in a new form of egocentrism characteristic of adolescence.

Formal operational thought not only enables the adolescent to conceptualize his thought, it also permits him to conceptualize the thought of other people. It is this capacity to take account of other people's thought, however, which is the crux of adolescent egocentrism. This egocentrism emerges because, while the adolescent can now cognize the thoughts of others, he fails to differentiate between the objects toward which the thoughts of others are directed and those which are the focus of his own concern. Now, it is well known that the young adolescent, because of the physiological metamorphosis he is undergoing, is primarily concerned with himself. Accordingly, since he fails to differentiate between what others are thinking about and his own mental preoccupations, he

assumes that other people are as obsessed with his behavior and appearance as he is himself. *It is this belief that others are preoccupied with his appearance and behavior that constitutes the egocentrism of the adolescent.*

One consequence of adolescent egocentrism is that, in actual or impending social situations, the young person anticipates the reactions of other people to himself. These anticipations, however, are based on the premise that others are as admiring or as critical of him as he is of himself. In a sense, then, the adolescent is continually constructing, or reacting to, *an imaginary audience.* It is an audience because the adolescent believes that he will be the focus of attention; and it is imaginary because, in actual social situations, this is not usually the case (unless he contrives to make it so). The construction of imaginary audiences would seem to account, in part at least, for a wide variety of typical adolescent behaviors and experiences.

The imaginary audience, for example, probably plays a role in the self-consciousness which is so characteristic of early adolescence. When the young person is feeling critical of himself, he anticipates that the audience—of which he is necessarily a part—will be critical too. And, since the audience is his own construction and privy to his own knowledge of himself, it knows just what to look for in the way of cosmetic and behavioral sensitivities. The adolescent's wish for privacy and his reluctance to reveal himself may, to some extent, be a reaction to the feeling of being under the constant critical scrutiny of other people. The notion of an imaginary audience also helps to explain the observation that the affect which most concerns adolescents is not guilt but, rather, shame, that is, the reaction to an audience (Lynd, 1961).

While the adolescent is often self-critical, he is frequently self-admiring too. At such times, the audience takes on the same affective coloration. A good deal of adolescent boorishness, loudness, and faddish dress is probably provoked, partially in any case, by a failure to differentiate between what the young person believes to be attractive and what others admire. It is for this reason that the young person frequently fails to understand why adults disapprove of the way he dresses and behaves. The same sort of ego-centrism is often seen in behavior directed toward the opposite sex. The boy who stands in front of the mirror for 2 hours combing his hair is probably imagining the swooning reactions he will produce in the girls. Likewise, the girl applying her makeup is more likely than not imagining the admiring glances that will come her way. When these young people actually meet, each is more concerned with being the observed than with being the observer. Gatherings of young adolescents are unique in the sense that each young person is simultaneously an actor to himself and an audience to others.

One of the most common admiring audience constructions, in the adolescent, is the anticipation of how others will react to his own demise. A certain bittersweet pleasure is derived from anticipating the belated recognition by others of his positive qualities. As often happens with such universal fantasies, the imaginary anticipation of one's own demise has been realized in fiction. Below, for example, is the passage in *Tom Sawyer* where Tom sneaks back to his home, after having run away with Joe and Huck, to discover that he and his friends are thought to have been drowned:

> But this memory was too much for the old lady, and she broke entirely down. Tom was snuffling, now, himself—and more in pity of himself than anybody else. He could hear Mary crying and putting in a kindly word for him from time to time. He began to have a nobler opinion of himself than ever before. Still, he was sufficiently touched by his aunt's grief to long to rush out from under the bed and overwhelm her with joy—and the theatrical gorgeousness of the thing appealed strongly to his nature too—but he resisted and lay still.

Corresponding to the imaginary audience is another mental construction which is its complement. While the adolescent fails to differentiate the concerns of his own thought from those of others, he at the same time overdifferentiates his feelings. Perhaps because he believes he is of importance to so many people, the imaginary audience, he comes to regard himself, and particularly his feelings, as something special and unique. Only he can suffer with such agonized intensity, or experience such exquisite rapture. How many parents have been confronted with the typically adolescent phrase, "But

you don't know how it feels. . . . " The emotional torments undergone by Goethe's young Werther and by Salinger's Holden Caulfield exemplify the adolescent's belief in the uniqueness of his own emotional experience. At a somewhat different level, this belief in personal uniqueness becomes a conviction that he will not die, that death will happen to others but not to him. This complex of beliefs in the uniqueness of his feelings and of his immortality might be called *a personal fable,* a story which he tells himself and which is not true.

Evidences of the personal fable are particularly prominent in adolescent diaries. Such diaries are often written for posterity in the conviction that the young person's experiences, crushes, and frustrations are of universal significance and importance. Another kind of evidence for the personal fable during this period is the tendency to confide in a personal God. The search for privacy and the belief in personal uniqueness lead to the establishment of an I-Thou relationship with God as a personal confidant to whom one no longer looks for gifts but rather for guidance and support (Long, Elkind, & Spilka, 1967).

The concepts of an imaginary audience and a personal fable have proved useful, at least to the writer, in the understanding and treatment of troubled adolescents. The imaginary audience, for example, seems often to play a role in middle-class delinquency (Elkind, 1967a). As a case in point, one young man took $1,000 from a golf tournament purse, hid the money, and then promptly revealed himself. It turned out that much of the motivation for this act was derived from the anticipated response of "the audience" to the guttiness of his action. In a similar vein, many young girls become pregnant because, in part at least, their personal fable convinces them that pregnancy will happen to others but never to them and so they need not take precautions. Such examples could be multiplied but will perhaps suffice to illustrate how adolescent egocentrism, as manifested in the imaginary audience and in the personal fable, can help provide a rationale for some adolescent behavior. These concepts can, moreover, be utilized in the treatment of adolescent offenders. It is often helpful to these young people if they can learn to differentiate between the real and the imaginary audience, which often boils down to a discrimination between the real and the imaginary parents.

The Passing of Adolescent Egocentrism

After the appearance of formal operational thought, no new mental systems develop and the mental structures of adolescence must serve for the rest of the life span. The egocentrism of early adolescence nonetheless tends to diminish by the age of 15 or 16, the age at which formal operations become firmly established. What appears to happen is that the imaginary audience, which is primarily an anticipatory audience, is progressively modified in the direction of the reactions of the real audience. In a way, the imaginary audience can be regarded as hypothesis—or better, as a series of hypotheses—which the young person tests against reality. As a consequence of this testing, he gradually comes to recognize the difference between his own preoccupations and the interests and concerns of others.

The personal fable, on the other hand, is probably overcome (although probably never in its entirety) by the gradual establishment of what Erikson (1959) has called "intimacy." Once the young person sees himself in a more realistic light as a function of having adjusted his imaginary audience to the real one, he can establish true rather than self-interested interpersonal relations. Once relations of mutuality are established and confidences are shared, the young person discovers that others have feelings similar to his own and have suffered and been enraptured in the same way.

Adolescent egocentrism is thus overcome by a twofold transformation. On the cognitive plane, it is overcome by the gradual differentiation between his own preoccupations and the thoughts of others; while on the plane of affectivity, it is overcome by a gradual integration of the feelings of others with his own emotions.

Summary and Conclusions

In this paper I have tried to describe the forms which egocentrism takes and the mechanisms by which it is overcome, in the course of mental development. In infancy, egocentrism corresponds to the impression that objects are identical with the perception of them, and this form of egocentrism is overcome with the appearance of representation. During the preschool period, egocentrism appears in the guise of a belief that symbols contain the same information as is provided by the objects which they represent. With the emergence of concrete operations, the child is able to discriminate between symbol and referent, and so overcome this type of egocentrism. The egocentrism of the school-age period can be characterized as the belief that one's own mental constructions correspond to a superior form of perceptual reality. With the advent of formal operations and the ability to construct contrary-to-fact hypotheses, this kind of egocentrism is dissolved because the young person can now recognize the arbitrariness of his own mental constructions. Finally, during early adolescence, egocentrism appears as the belief that the thoughts of others are directed toward the self. This variety of egocentrism is overcome as a consequence of the conflict between the reactions which the young person anticipates and those which actually occur.

Although egocentrism corresponds to a negative product of mental growth, its usefulness would seem to lie in the light which it throws upon the affective reactions characteristic of any particular stage of mental development. In this paper I have dealt primarily with the affective reactions associated with the egocentrism of adolescence. Much of the material, particularly the discussion of the *imaginary audience* and the *personal fable,* is speculative in the sense that it is based as much upon my clinical experience with young people as it is upon research data. These constructs are offered, not as the final word on adolescent egocentrism, but rather to illustrate how the cognitive structures peculiar to a particular level of development can be related to the affective experience and behavior characteristic of that stage. Although I have here only considered the correspondence between mental structure and affect in adolescence, it is possible that similar correspondences can be found at the earlier levels of development as well. A consideration of egocentrism, then, would seem to be a useful starting point for any attempt to reconcile cognitive structure and the dynamics of personality.

william g. hollister

preparing the minds of the future

Through this paper I am going to share with you some growing intellectual excitement in the field of education. The excitement is about some streams of behavioral research —research that is opening up, with increasing clarity, the possibilities of an educational technology for potentiating minds.

It has long been a dream in education that some day we might find a way of potentiating the thinking abilities of the mind, of bringing them to their highest development. For years we believed that certain subjects ought to be taken by children because they did something to stir up the ability to think. Many of you probably studied Latin. Probably it was placed in your curriculum not only on the ground that you needed to know something about Latin as a language, but even more in the hope that it would stimulate your thinking capacity. At least we had the dream that that was so.

Now what I want to share with you is my conclusion that this dream of being able to potentiate specific capacities of thinking and of the mind is coming to be realized. Research points to the possibility of preparing the kinds of minds that are likely to survive and to be creative in the much tougher, more stressful intellectual and social living of the future. This research does not point to the value of certain subjects, but rather to a general mode which needs to characterize all

Reprinted with permission of the author and publisher from *National Association of Secondary School Principals Bulletin*, 1966, **50**, 30-50.

teaching and learning, in fact the very life and growth of the learner. But that is getting ahead of the story. The significant thing is that we are beginning to get research evidence that really offers new horizons in curriculum development.

Ego as a Collective Term

Since I am going to use the term "ego" over and over again in this presentation, I had better explain that I shall not be using it in the old-fashioned egotistical sense—the "I" sense—but in the technical sense, as it is used in my own field of psychiatry. The term "ego" is a concept of rising importance, not just in the field of mental health but also in the field of education. It is a collective term. It covers the numerous executive functions of the mind, the decision-making and thinking functions. You may be more accustomed to using the term in the "I" sense, but I hope you can accept it in this technical sense, so that we can communicate.

Eli Bower (Bower & Hollister, in press) has amusingly described the ego as the "dark, mysterious tunnel between the input of perceptions into the mind and the output of thoughts and behaviors." Increasingly, people who are interested in these functions —ego-analysts, and ego-psychologists, and now the curriculum developers—are becoming fascinated with what goes on inside that tunnel. You put something in; but what are the various patterns by which it is processed so that it comes out in certain kinds of behaviors, and certain kinds of talents and certain kinds of emotions? What mysteriously different mental processes go on inside the mind? How do they develop? And what are the processes of the ego that are instrumental in producing what we are all striving for, an integrated personality that is competent and effective?

Now let me briefly trace for you, in a very selective fashion, some of the emerging ideas that are converging to open up greater possibilities for us in education. Back in 1939 a German psychiatrist by the name of Heinz Hartmann provided the stimulus for a major breakthrough in the field of behavioral sciences in his book *Ego Psychology and the Problem of Adaptation (1958)*. Apparently he had got fed up with the Freudian concept that everything produced in our minds was a product of the interaction or the conflict between our impulses inside and our attempts to calm them down and shape them so that we wouldn't get out of control. Freud conceived of the human mind mainly as a battleground of conflict between impulses and what we would call the ego. Hartmann felt that it was time to move beyond the concept that every pattern of behavior could be traced and described as based on internal conflict. He was convinced that everything that happens in the human mind is not just a defense against some impulse or a way to control ourselves.

Growth Potential of the Mind

Hartmann claimed, further, that there were many functions of the mind that grew by themselves (a view, by the way, to which many educators had held for a long time). He said that the functions of the ego to create man's competencies, creativity, and his unitary self were produced not out of conflict but out of capacities that grew and developed in the mind. He did a big service to the behavioral sciences by getting us out of a pathological rut—out of the idea of looking only at the difficulties that people get into and the conflicts inside people, and moving toward the idea of looking at the positive growth potential of mental capacities.

From this point, Hartmann moved on

very rapidly. He was one of those "great-leap" thinkers, and he began to classify the various executive functions of the mind into three major classes.

He called the first class the *assimilation* functions. These are the taking-in functions with which we all are so well acquainted because they have been the major preoccupation of education. In connection with this class of functions we raise all the old questions of how content gets into a learner's mind and how it is processed and stored in memory.

But the second major group of functions, which Hartmann described as the "executive control tower" of the ego, are not so familiar. He called them the *differentiation* functions. These have to do with the capacities to break things down into their parts and to separate them out. He used as his model for this a basic gradient in human growth. Those of you who have studied child growth and development know that the human arm, for instance, develops as a massive function. Babies first can wave each arm as a whole; then they begin to operate the forearm separately. Gradually they differentiate out of the total gross movement finer and finer movements until they can wiggle their fingers in various ways and pick up articles they want, until they have differentiated many kinds of movements out of one gross movement.

Different Kinds of Mental Abilities

This phenomenon seems to illustrate a biological law. Hartmann theorized that the law holds for the mind, too: that the mind has some general functional capacities, but as it is stimulated and educated and reacts to the environment it begins to differentiate out individual abilities. The more we stimulate and educate it, the more different kinds of abilities we can differentiate. Thus just as a man whose fingers have learned many differentiated skills can play the piano with many different movements, so a well-differentiated mind has many different kinds of capacities. This idea sparked a great deal of thinking.

Hartmann went on to still another seminal conception, that when differentiation has been accomplished, the various separated, differentiated functions of the mind can be recombined into new abilities. Let me again go back to the model of the arm. The baby's arm, which is capable only of gross movement at first, gradually becomes differentiated so that it can make many different and refined movements. Once the baby has all these separated and developed, he can begin to put together new combinations. He can oppose the thumb to the finger. Later he can learn all kinds of combinations of movements which would not have been possible if the differentiation had not taken place first. This recombining of differentiated capacities Hartmann called the *integration* process. He applied this concept to the mind also. The more we can differentiate kinds of abilities out of the general capacities of the mind, the more combinations can be put together to create new kinds of mental abilities.

These have turned out to be what I call germinative ideas, ideas that are just like germ plasm. They reproduce themselves; they hit various minds; they move through the scientific world and a lot of people react to them. The concepts of *assimilation, differentiation,* and *integration* gave psychologists three basic classes of ego-functions of the mind. Theory and research and practice in education have long concentrated on the assimilation function, on how learners take in and assimilate knowledge, so I am not going to spend much time on that. But I should like to talk a little bit about some of the things that have emerged out of the idea of the differentiation of abilities and the integration of these differentiated parts into ever-new combinations and new capacities of the ego.

What Can Educators Do?

As educators let's ask ourselves, What kinds of specific functions of the mind or ego functions could we nurture? What could we separate out, to blow on like embers and fan into flame? How can we prepare minds for the future that are more differentiated, that have more capacities, more different kinds of abilities? Certainly the future, with all of the stresses of the kind of life we are evolving, is going to call for more capable and effective minds. Some of us have already had the experience of finding that we do not have some of the abilities that are required of young people today; they were not nurtured in us. The need for well-developed minds is going to accelerate.

Men and women in the future will have to cope with a floodtide of knowledge that could engulf them in what Jerome Bruner calls "cognitive overload." Intellectual survival is going to depend more and more on the growth of our students' abilities to group and encode information so that what is known is grouped in simpler, more useful forms—so that it is categorized in ways that make it usable. We need to organize what we learn so that we can maximize every combination of knowledge to make new breakthroughs and new social inventions.

Therefore, let's first look at what might be done to build the mental capacities to take this terrible floodtide of information and break it down into usable form, so that we can master it and not be engulfed by it. The need here is for mental abilities in the area of *conceptualization of categories.* How can this key mental strength be built? Well, the ability to conceptualize categories is surely one that we could foster while teaching grammar, vocabulary, biology, mathematics, and other subjects. Let me give you a few illustrations. Already we teach the classification of biological phenomena into various categories. We classify biological phenomena by homologous structure or analogous function. Certainly we can teach—and intellectualize—the conceptualization of categories while we do this.

Likewise, chemistry is loaded with opportunities to teach the categorization of data by common elements or by common derivation or by the qualities of relationships or by the consequences of interaction. As we use these several styles of categorization in teaching chemistry, we can teach categorization itself. Mathematics is another royal road for teaching some of the techniques for categorization. The mathematician studies various kinds of relationships; for instance, linear relationships, reciprocal relationships, parallel relationships, geometric relationships, algebraic relationships. We already present the basic principles of grouping data in much of what we teach.

Building Students' "Coping Capacities"

We teach categorization at many widely divergent points in our present curriculum. But, I wonder, do we identify the important tool processes involved, processes that are so vital in the area of data analysis and re-search, and even in the understanding of hu-man behavior? Do we demonstrate concretely to students the transferability of various ways of grouping and analyzing data? Do we teach explicitly how these ways can be transferred to other kinds of data and prob-lem-solving situations, so that our students will not simply have been unconsciously ex-posed to all these things by the teaching of mathematics and chemistry? Can we not make these various techniques of analyzing and codifying data visible, so that students can then see them as tool processes to use in problem-solving in all aspects of life? A little attention, a little more practice applied to data-grouping abilities would provide some important "coping capacities" for these minds of the future.

Let me give you an illustration of what I propose. I shall never forget one high school literature class I visited. It was one of those Silas Marner days which we have all gone through—Silas Marner and his life compan-ions were being analyzed. But this teacher had ideas about what the experience could mean. Here in English class she was analyz-ing and categorizing various kinds of behav-ior and teaching some coping techniques the students would need in human relationships. First, the class had listed on the board its own criteria of maturity—about 30 of them. Then, day by day, as they read, they would stop and ask themselves: "How does this kind of behavior match our criteria of maturity?" Two things had begun to happen. First, the students began to discover that people go up and down in the maturity of their behavior and that this is a normal thing; that we all aren't mature all the time. The second thing they began to learn was that their criteria were inadequate, that some-times they were quite unfair to particular in-dividuals. They saw, too, that some criteria had to be flexible and had to be thought about in different ways. In other words, they were learning that, from episode to episode, both maturity and the criteria of maturity might change. They were beginning to experi-ment with classifying relationships and behaviors in books.

Then the teacher did a very interesting thing. She told the students to go home and listen to some of the old soap operas that were coming over the radio and to analyze them. They did, and their analysis was roughly like this: In terms of the maturity of

the people in it, every soap opera deterio-rates in the last five minutes so that there will be a reason for another episode. Then she said to them, "You're all dating and going to movies. I want you to analyze the behavior and the maturity of the people in the movies you see." As they came back with their analyses of the relative maturity of some of the characters in the movies they went to, it was devastatingly clear that these kids were getting beyond the unsophisticated splash of experience. They were beginning to differen-tiate out some new capacities which, I would guess, served them well in choosing a wife or husband, in selecting business partners, and in guiding their own children in later years.

"Silas Marner" and Social Intelligence

I hope I have made clear what I am talk-ing about. I am talking about using a medium like *Silas Marner* to identify different kinds of human behaviors—using it deliberately to awaken a whole area in the mind which we call social intelligence.

I know that we cannot continue to do more and more in our schools; we are over-loaded now. But we could do more to use what we are already teaching to train explic-itly the thinking capacities needed to cope with cognitive overload and with the human relationship tasks of the future.

We need to provide learning experiences that range over many ways of approaching problems. Not all the data that come to us are of one kind, and we don't use the same analytical or understanding approach for all styles of data. Some of the data we get are what we call *figural*—like sensations that come through our fingers or the sensations that are in your ears right now. You have to learn how to encode and grasp and manipu-late and analyze these data to make meaning out of them. Then there is another group of data call *symbolic*—like words or like figures in mathematics. We do a lot of teaching of how to manipulate, encode, and handle this kind of data.

But we keep forgetting two other major kinds of data, one of which involves *semantic* data—where you don't look at just the sym-bol but rather at the meaning behind it. A great deal of the input that people have to understand is semantic, not just symbolic. For instance, the other night my daughter went to the telephone and said, "Yes, yes, well that's all right; I'm sorry." The person evidently hung up and she slammed the phone back on the hook and said, "I *hate* boys!" What had happened was that she had got turned down on a date. Now, you see, if you just read the words "I hate boys" you would have been reading the symbols; but if you understand the situation, you know that the meaning of "I hate boys" was really deep disappointment because she loved boys or wanted to be with boys.

The Meaning behind the Symbols

In much of the data that come to us these days, the symbols are not the thing to read. The meaning is the thing to read, and it is often very different from the verbal symbols. My point is that there is a whole world of semantic data input which people need to be trained to be sensitive to. They need to know how to reach for it and perceive it and put it to work.

Finally, there's a fourth kind of data—the *meaning of behaviors*. The behavior of a given boy in school might mean a dozen different things. If you really get behind it, you may find it quite different from what you first assumed. One of the things we must do in sensitizing teachers to create a better emotional climate in their classrooms is to make them aware of the drama of their own behavior. The teacher who walks around with a grade book and pen in hand may have all the rational ideas in the world. But if he doesn't understand the emotional impact of his behavior he is going to miss what he is doing to his students by assuming this particular academic posture.

What I want to emphasize is that there are various kinds of data which we need to be able to handle, and handling them calls for varied skills. The data are coming in all the time in our classrooms, and students are getting practice in using them. But we have not made the different ways of thinking of problems *visible*. And we could do it so easily, while we are teaching the subject matter we want to teach anyway. Let's take history as an example.

History as a Teaching Tool

History is a marvelous way of teaching people how to cope with one of the most horrendous realities in our future; namely, that most of the input of knowledge and information that will come to us is not going to be clean scientific data. Much of the time the input will be subjective, heavily biased, and full of irrelevancies. The task of the thinking man—especially in the fields of social and human relationships, but even in science as well—is to sort out the irrelevant from the relevant and, having made this differentiation, to reassemble the more nearly clean data in some meaningful way. History provides a magnificent means of teaching how to read cues—about man's behavior, for instance. It is an excellent tool for teaching some differentiations and inference-making abilities that are vital to a world of better human relations.

Any group of events in history—let's use those of World War II—can be read in many different ways. *First*, World War II data could be read inductively as items in an incomplete puzzle or in an unfolding phenomenon. Practice in this type of analysis leads to the nurturance of predictive ability, an intellectual ability which Guilford emphasizes. *Second*, the same data could be read deductively, as descriptions of a whole phenomenon which require factor analysis to understand. *Third*, in addition to these usual angles of approach, history could be read as a distorted whole filled with hidden values requiring thoughtful elimination of the irrelevant elements, followed by resynthesis of the relevant. *Fourth*, an historical event could be viewed as an exception or an illustration of negative evidence which must be reversed in order to make any sense. Or, *fifth*, an historical event could be viewed as a product of conflict in which one must detect the biases involved, in order to place the data in perspective.

Even this rapid listing of five different ways to analyze the same body of data does not exhaust the analytical differentiation techniques that can be taught with history. But I have illustrated how a social science curriculum can serve explicitly in preparing students for a future in which the major inputs of information are likely to be subjective, incomplete, distorted, and full of irrelevant data.

Other Ego Strengths Needed

Now let me move into another group of capacities we can differentiate in the minds of our students right in the courses we are teaching, another set of ego strengths needed in the minds of the future. These include the *ability to tolerate ambiguity, the ability to delay gratification,* and *the ability to live with problems and processes that require long-continued uncertainty and effort in their solution*. As our culture grows more complex, we find that many of our problems will not respond to simple black-and-white solutions. Some social problems are so complex and our human variability is so great that oversimplified solutions only create program failures and more unmet needs. We cannot take our complex human problems and reduce them to simple formulas which will work in every town in America; you know that through bitter experience.

I believe we can foster intellectual and emotional strengths that will prepare people for the frustrations, the nonresolution of problems, and the constant ambiguity of modern life. We can add learning experiences with graded series of simple and then more complex problems to solve. During this process we can gradually increase the number of factors to consider, slip in irrelevant data to be detected and eliminated, and then call for the tailoring of solutions to fit different kinds of consumers and different kinds of publics. We can create tolerance of ambiguity and of nonresolution by introducing these elements into our curriculum in graded sequences.

"Process Problem-Solving"

Beyond all this we must go on to what is called "process problem-solving." We must if we are to move our business and social planning beyond the oversimplified package solutions that impede social and political action today. We can help by making visible the concept that most problem-solving in physics and chemistry and human affairs is a process requiring a chain of related responses to a sequence of cues. This will begin to prepare minds for the coping techniques and the emotional stability required in modern living.

It has already been demonstrated that process-oriented thinkers (as opposed to those who think in terms of formulas or unitary facts or classes of things) use an entirely different approach in solving their problems and tend to come out with more variable answers, which fit the situation more aptly. The major problems of the future will not be solved by pat formulas or simple little solutions. The answers will come only through continuous, sequential, thoughtful analysis of a whole process or chain of forces at work over a long period of time. Getting answers will require people to "stick with it," to tolerate ambiguity and nonresolution. And when finally answers do emerge, these will often be multiple answers to fit different situations.

Developing competence in this kind of process-thinking is already being explored in 14 school systems by the Commission on Science Education of the American Association for the Advancement of Science. Perhaps some of you have read the recent reports of Robert Gagne (1966) on processes and content used to train students in the observation and ordering of data. He has developed curricula that provide opportunities in predicting, making inferences, formulating hypotheses, producing operational definitions, and learning to change and control variables in a process. These elements are being taught as part of a general school program to develop thinking ability and creativity. Recognizing the interactions of various kinds of intellectual and emotional factors, the curricula deliberately reward novel ideas, definitions, and solutions. To me this would appear to fulfill Jerome Bruner's (1966) idea that we ought to encourage youth to invent answers rather than search the literature for formulas or solutions previously found by others.

The 14 schools are doing this on the assumption that such problem-solving instruction will impart something that will be transferable and usable in many other situations over the years to come. Again, you see, we are talking about ways of differentiating

61

out some key capacities of the mind that may make the difference in how we are going to solve problems of the future. This is not just something for the gifted; it is for all children. I am talking about building a school program that not only teaches content but also potentiates minds.

Nonintellectual Capacities

Up to this point I have been trying to show that certain kinds of mental functioning can be fostered, nurtured, and strengthened while we are teaching the subjects we are already teaching. I hope you have noticed that not all of the strengths I have mentioned are intellectual capacities; some are emotional or motivational strengths, such as the ability to tolerate ambiguity, to tolerate nonresolution, and the ability to delay immediate gratification and to persist at a long-term process of thinking and problem-solving. Many ego strengths are a blend of emotional and intellectual ability. We should heed Barbara Biber's statement that standards of educational excellence must include operational and instructional awareness of the emotional processes associated with learning.

If you have been following the recent writings of Sanford and Bowers and others, you know that the split we have made between the intellectual and emotional is a dichotomy that is trapping us. The strong mind is the mind that has the motivational, the emotional, and the intellectual interlocked. We must not overlook the high importance of emotional strength if we seek to build strong individuals. There are ego strengths which are blends of the intellectual and the emotional, such as tension tolerance, the capacity to take stress, the tolerance of a moderate amount of guilt—we all feel guilty about some things. Another extremely important factor—which involves a blend of the emotional and the intellectual—is the capacity for empathy. So is the ability to enter into mutually enhancing and constructive relationships with other people. The capacity of an individual to obtain reasonable enjoyment, to enforce reasonable prohibitions of his own conscience, to formulate and pursue aspirations, and to forge and maintain a favorable self-image—these all are blended emotional and intellectual strengths.

Certain investigators are searching for childhood and educational experiences that will build emotional and intellectual strengths in children. Slater, for instance, reports that rigid, intolerant parents—and this might apply to teachers as well—cripple ego development, while warm-hearted, supportive parents tend to produce buoyant, spontaneous, and gregarious children. Dr. Elizabeth Drews (1966) has been conducting curricular experiments using the identification mechanism. She uses leading Americans as models and gets her students to identify with them for a while, to act like them, think like them, and feel like them, as a way of widening their choices of who they themselves might become. She uses a mental mechanism—identification—to build emotional and intellectual capacities to identify with other people and to understand them, and then out of these wider choices to select a kind of a goal person they would like to become.

Need for Emotional Base

Pauline Sears (1963), in her studies of the influence of classroom conditions on the strengths and achievement of children, has shown that, for average children, a situation in which they like their teacher and peers and the teacher and peers like them is a key ingredient in the ego process of developing a positive self-image. This same factor correlates with average children's achievement in the classroom and the development of what she calls an industrious pattern of classroom working. Such an emotional-relationship base for learning and behaving was found to be less important, at least outwardly, in the achievement and work patterns of superior children. In other words, the emotional foundation was very very important for the average child, but superior children seemed to be relatively independent of the need for this "liking business." They could be loners and go off and do many things on their own without the need for constant emotional feedback and support. Thus, Sears' findings will support the experiences we have all had in schools, that there are children who depend on the emotional and social climate of the school for resources essential to their happiness and ability to learn.

Here again we are faced with a challenge: How can we design classroom experiences that will simultaneously foster emotional, motivational, and intellectual strengths in children? Better yet, how can we find and actuate teachers whose personal ego styles and method of relating to people are of the kind that catalyze children's ego development?

To reinforce this portrayal of the rising potential at our command, I call your attention to work coming out of Switzerland, England, Russia, as well as that going on in this country which helps us understand the separated-out, discrete, specific intellectual abilities of the mind. Out of the studies of men like Piaget (1926), Guilford (1959), Vygotsky, and Cattell (1963) is emerging evidence of the existence of certain discrete abilities and evidence on the time when they emerge in the personality and on the manner in which they can be matured and strengthened. For instance, through widespread curricular experimentation for the benefit of gifted children, we are learning how to foster divergent thinking, innovation, and creativity. Men like Calvin Taylor (1964) and Paul Torrance (1965) are depicting ways to nurture various integrative ego capacities.

New Integrations of Self

In addition to these endeavors aimed at understanding when and how various mental abilities separate out and what we can do about stimulating them and nurturing them, we are learning from the works of Piaget (1926) and Erikson (1963) and Havighurst (1952) that there are certain times when people put various separated abilities together and emerge with something new inside themselves. We call these the key developmental tasks. Furthermore, experimentation has been going on as to the kinds of interpersonal relationships or classroom learning experiences that expedite the process of putting together these new integrations of self.

One of the important personality integrations is a sense of basic trust of other people. This requires a blending of emotional and intellectual experiences. The person who has a sense of basic trust in other people can eventually rise to leadership and have people work gladly for him. By contrast, persons who have not been able to synthesize in their personality a sense of basic trust in other

people constantly undermine the people under them.

Another personality integration is autonomy. Many persons really have no self-autonomy. They have not been able to integrate this concept in themselves. They are still dependent. As students they are always coming into class trying to figure out, "Now what's his angle, so I can play back the right things in order to get a grade?" They lack the sense of autonomy that would enable them to engage in an intellectual effort for what it will do for them. They are always trying to read the other person. They are other-person centered. High school students often work very hard to integrate a self-identity and a valid self-image.

You probably know how Piaget has watched the emergence of these various integrations of self and has virtually arrived at a timetable as to when they occur. He has suggested that our educational efforts should be timed to stimulate them at the time when they emerge.

Research in Russia

But from our colleagues over in Russia comes an almost entirely opposite stream of research, under the leadership of a man named Vygotsky. They believe they are finding that sometimes a mental ability can be ripened even before it appears by exposing the person to certain education experiences. They feel that instruction does not have to wait until development is complete, that it can sometimes precede development and thus actually increase its progress. Certain kinds of instruction seem to activate large areas of the consciousness. What Vygotsky is trying to say is that you actually can *wake up* new areas of consciousness by exposing children to certain instructional experiences. This is not a new idea. Many of our friends in education have held it before. (They were beaten down during the 1930's and 1940's.) Vygotsky says, "Good instruction is that which marches ahead of development and leads it. It must be aimed not so much at the ripe as at the ripening function." These findings may completely revise our timetables of instruction and ideas of gradation of material.

When many of us studied chemistry, not all of the spots in the periodic chart were filled in. Yet somebody had predicted that there were 93 different elements, and he could predict it on certain logical laws. (Now the scientists have found not only all of the 93, but have run the known list up to 106.) Somewhat similarly, J. P. Guilford (1956) of UCLA went through studies of intellectual capacities, looked at principles involved, and developed a three-dimensional model of the human intellect predicting that there are 120 different intellectual capacities. He decided there were five thinking functions: a memory function, a knowing function, convergent thinking (where you add up things and come out with one answer), divergent thinking (where you brainstorm and develop many ideas and associations from one idea), and evaluative thinking. He then added a four-way classification of the data the mind might process: figural or sensory data, symbolic (words and arithmetic data), semantic (meaning data), and behavioral data. He believed the mind might deal with these data by classifying them into units, classifying them into classes, understanding systems of things like processes, understanding things by relationships, understanding the process of change, and making inferences about future predictions from implications.

120 Possible Mental Functions

By organizing this way Guilford came out with 120 different intellectual functions that might be discovered in the human mind. When he first came out with this predictive list, he had to admit that only 37 of the possible functions had actually been identified by developed tests. Today there are over 65 for which we have tests.

Better than anything else I know of, this analysis carries the very important message to us of how we were fooled by the first intellectual functions we discovered. IQ tests measure only that small part of human intellectual capacity. Now you can see why the IQ test is not enough to guide our educational efforts to prepare minds for the future.

We are beginning to see we have barely scratched the surface in learning to develop the mind. The fact that we might differentiate out 120 individual capacities is complicating enough by itself. But we are also beginning to realize that there are many possible *clusters*

of abilities. There is the cluster that makes up the research mind, the psychotherapeutic mind, or the good mind for any purpose you care to mention.

Cattell (1963) and his colleagues are identifying, assessing, and following the lifetime development of certain clusters that really are ego styles. These are basic patterns of behavior produced by the integrative functions of the ego. Cattell has identified and labeled a number of ego styles; for instance, "critical practicality," "social willingness," "nervous alert reactivity," "wary-realism," "exuberance," and "dour pessimism." Perhaps more exciting are the research efforts to ascertain what kinds of family and experiential settings produce these styles of ego-functioning. Already Cattell has evidence that the capacities and noncapacities that make up what he calls "hypomanic smartness" emerge from homes that stress success with little moral restraint as to how it is attained. There is also a high level of competition and mutual criticism in such homes. These people seem to be "smart-smart" but they are not "deep-deep." They show a high pressure to complete tasks and make decisions.

On the Practical Level

What does all this mean to you who operate schools? It can mean this: With further development of behavioral research the teacher of the future may be provided with much more specific profiles of the capacities and strengths—intellectual, emotional, and motivational—of the boys and girls he is teaching. He will have more information about learning styles, ego styles, and the kinds of potential that can be developed. Education will be deeply involved in fostering the integration of new kinds of mental and behavioral abilities.

If you review the writings of Cattell, Guilford, Taylor, and others who are studying the capacities individuals can develop, you will stand face to face with a tremendously wide range of strengths that we might choose to foster. Imagine yourself on a curriculum committee of the future that is challenged to design learning experiences to build such specific abilities as: problem-penetration, practicality-testing, associational fluency,

persistence, reflective capacity, nondistracti-
bility, relational skill, computational ability,
or sensitivity to feelings. These are actual
behaviors that have been analyzed and differentiated into testable factors, and there is
growing evidence that they have been influenced if not catalyzed by educational experiences. That is, they can be "taught for,"
if we choose to do so.

For a long time, liberal education has
pursued the goal of a double curriculum—
one that not only imparts knowledge but also
potentiates a mind and a personality. What I
have tried to explain is that we are now closer
than we have ever been to having the technical ability to do so. But we have only begun.
It is time to elevate the goal of potentiating
minds to equal status with the job of impart-
ing content. It is time to integrate this goal
into a 12-grade concerted and interlocked
curriculum effort which will add up to the
planned potentiation of the whole range of
possible mental abilities.

I am not trying to say that the story is all
told, that the research is finished and conclu-
sive. Much, much needs to be done. But the
evidence we already have is enough to justify
genuine excitement and a faith that we have
it almost in our grasp not only to impart content, but also to potentiate minds.

I am a psychiatrist, but I say that the
building of the mentally healthy mind, the
mind with effectiveness and competence and
capacity to deal with life, is going to be the
privilege and responsibility of educators, not
of psychiatrists.

References

Ausubel, D. P. *The psychology of meaningful verbal learning.* New York: Grune and Stratton,
1963.

Ausubel, D. P. *Maori youth: A psychoethnological
study of cultural deprivation.* New York: Holt,
1965.

Blos, P. *On adolescence.* New York: Free Press,
1962.

Bower, E. M., & Hollister, W. G. (Eds.) *Behavioral
science frontiers in education.* New York: Wiley, in press.

Bradway, K. P., & Thompson C. W. Intelligence at
adulthood: A twenty-five year follow-up. *Journal of Educational Psychology,* 1962, **53,** 1-
14.

Braham, M. Peer group deterrents to intellectual
development during adolescence. *Educational Theory,* 1965, **15,** 248-258.

Bruner, J. S. *Toward a theory of instruction.* Cambridge, Mass.: Harvard University Press,
1966.

Carlsmith, L. Effect of early father absence on
scholastic aptitude. *Harvard Educational Review,* 1964, **34,** 3-21.

Case, D., & Collinson, J. M. The development of
formal thinking in verbal comprehension.
British Journal of Educational Psychology,
1962, **32,** 103-111.

Cattell, R. B. Theory of fluid and crystallized intelligence. *Journal of Educational Psychology,*
1963, **54,** 1-22.

Charlesworth, W. R. Development of the object
concept in infancy: Methodological study.
American Psychologist, 1966, **21,** 623. (Abstract)

Cowan, P. A. Cognitive egocentrism and social interaction in children. *American Psychologist,*
1966, **21,** 623. (Abstract)

Dodwell, P. C. Children's understanding of number and related concepts. *Canadian Journal
of Psychology,* 1960, **14,** 191-205.

Dodwell, P. C. Children's understanding of number concepts: Characteristics of an individual
and a group test. *Canadian Journal of Psychology,* 1961, **15,** 29-36.

Dodwell, P. C. Relations between the understanding of the logic of classes and of cardinal
numbers in children. *Canadian Journal of
Psychology,* 1962, **16,** 152-160.

Dodwell, P. C. Children's understanding of spatial
concepts. *Canadian Journal of Psychology,*
1963, **17,** 141-161.

Drews, E. M. Self actualization: A new focus for
education. In W. B. Waetjen & R. R. Leeper,
(Eds.), *Learning and mental health in the
school.* Washington, D.C.: Association for
Supervision and Curriculum Development,
National Education Association, 1966.

Elkind, D. The child's conception of his religious
denomination. I: The Jewish child. *Journal of
Genetic Psychology,* 1961a, **99,** 209-225.

Elkind, D. Quantity conceptions in junior and senior high school students. *Child Development,* 1961b, **32,** 550-560.

Elkind, D. The development of quantitative thinking. *Journal of Genetic Psychology,* 1961c,
98, 37-46.

Elkind, D. Quantity conceptions in college students. *Journal of Social Psychology,* 1962a,
57, 459-465.

Elkind, D. The child's conception of his religious
denomination. II: The Catholic child. *Journal
of Genetic Psychology,* 1962b, **101,** 185-
193.

Elkind, D. The child's conception of his religious
denomination. III: The Protestant child. *Journal of Genetic Psychology,* 1963, **103,** 291-
304.

Elkind, D. Conceptual orientation shifts in children
and adolescents. *Child Development,* 1966,
37, 493-498.

Elkind, D. Middle-class delinquency. *Mental Hygiene,* 1967a, **51,** 80-84.

Elkind, D. Egocentrism in adolescence. *Child
Development,* 1967b, **38,** 1025-1034.

Erikson, E. H. Identity and the life cycle. *Psychological issues,* Vol. 1, No. 1. New York: International Universities Press, 1959.

Erikson, E. *Childhood and society.* New York: Norton, 1963.

Flavell, J. H. *The developmental psychology of Jean Piaget.* New York: Van Nostrand, 1963.

Freud, A. *The ego and the mechanisms of defense.* New York: International Universities Press, 1946.

Gagne, R. M. Elementary science: A new scheme of instruction. *Science,* 1966, **151,** 49-56.

Ginsburg, H., & Opper, S. *Piaget's theory of intellectual development.* Englewood Cliffs, N.J.: Prentice-Hall, 1969.

Goldman, R. J. The application of Piaget's scheme of operational thinking to religious story data by means of the Guttman Scalogram. *British Journal of Educational Psychology,* 1965, **35,** 158-170.

Gourevitch, V. & Feffer, M. H. A study of motivational development. *Journal of Genetic Psychology,* 1962, **100,** 361-375.

Green, R. F., & Berkowitz, B. Changes in intellect with age: II. Factorial analysis of Wechsler-Bellevue scores. *Journal of Genetic Psychology,* 1964, **104,** 3-18.

Guilford, J. P. The structure of intellect. *Psychological Bulletin,* 1956, **53,** 267-298.

Guilford, J.P. Three faces of intellect. *American Psychologist,* 1959, **14,** 469-479.

Guilford, J.'P. Intelligence: 1965 model. *American Psychologist,* 1966, **21,** 20-26.

Hartmann, H. *Ego psychology and the problem of adaptation.* (Translated by David Rapaport). London: Imago Publishing Company, 1958.

Havighurst, R. J. *Developmental tasks and education.* New York: McKay, 1952.

Heinonen, V. *Differentiation of primary mental abilities.* Jyvaskyla, Finland: Kustantajat Publishers, 1963.

Hill, S. A. A study of the logical abilities of children. Unpublished doctoral dissertation, Stanford University, 1961.

Hunt, J. McV. *Intelligence and experience.* New York: Ronald Press, 1961.

Inhelder, B., & Piaget, J. *The growth of logical thinking from childhood to adolescence.* New York: Basic Books, 1958.

Inhelder, B., & Piaget, J. *The early growth of logic in the child: Classification and seriation.* New York: Harper, 1964.

Jackson, S. The growth of logical thinking in normal and subnormal children. *British Journal of Educational Psychology,* 1965, **35,** 255-258.

Kohlberg, L. Cognitive stages and preschool education. *Human Development,* 1966, **9,** 5-17.

Ljung, B.-O. *The adolescent spurt in mental growth.* Stockholm Studies in Educational Psychology 8. Uppsala, Sweden: Almquist and Wiksell, 1965.

Long, D., Elkind, D., & Spilka, B. The child's conception of prayer. *Journal of the Scientific Study of Religion,* 1967, **6,** 101-109.

Lovell, K. A follow-up study of Inhelder and Piaget's "The growth of logical thinking." *British Journal of Psychology,* 1961, **52,** 143-153.

Lovell, K. Developmental processes in thought. *Journal of Experimental Education,* 1968, **37,** 14-21.

Lovell, K. & Slater, A. The growth of the concept of time: A comparative study. *Journal of Child Psychology and Psychiatry,* 1960, **1,** 179-190.

Lunzer, E. Problems of formal reasoning in test situations. *Monographs of the Society for Research in Child Development,* 1965, **30,** 19-46.

Lynd, H. M. *On shame and the search for identity.* New York: Science Edition, 1961.

McNemar, Q. Lost: Our intelligence? Why? *American Psychologist,* 1964, **19,** 871-882.

Meyer, W. J. The stability of patterns of primary mental abilities among junior high and senior high school students. *Educational and Psychological Measurement,* 1960, **20,** 795-800.

Mischel, W. Preference for delayed reinforcement and social responsibility, *Journal of Abnormal Social Psychology,* 1961, **62,** 1-7.

Peel, E. A. *The pupil's thinking.* London: Oldbourne, 1960.

Phillips, J. L., Jr. *The origins of intellect: Piaget's theory.* San Francisco: Freeman, 1969.

Piaget, J. *The moral judgment of the child.* New York: Harcourt, 1926.

Piaget, J. In D. Rapaport, (Ed.), *The organization and pathology of thought.* New York: Columbia University Press, 1950.

Piaget, J. *The child's conception of the world.* London: Routledge and Kegan Paul, 1951.

Piaget, J. *The child's conception of number.* New York: Humanities Press, 1952a.

Piaget, J. *The language and thought of the child.* London: Routledge and Kegan Paul, 1952b.

Piaget, J. *The construction of reality in the child.* New York: Basic Books, 1954.

Piaget, J. *Logic and philosophy.* New York: Basic Books, 1957.

Piaget, J. *Comments on Vygotsky's critical remarks concerning "The language and thought of the child."* Cambridge, Mass.: MIT Press, 1962.

Sears, P. *The effect of classroom conditions in the strength of achievement motive and work output on elementary school children.* Washington, D.C.: Cooperative Research Project OE–873 of the U.S. Office of Education, 1963.

Taylor, C. W. (Ed.) *Creativity: Progress and potential.* New York: McGraw-Hill, 1964.

Torrance, E. P. *Mental health and constructive behavior.* Belmont, Calif.: Wadsworth, 1965.

Waller, P. F. Intellectual skills. *National Association of Secondary School Principals Bulletin,* 1969, **53** (336), 65-96.

Weir, M. W. Development changes in problem solving strategies. *Psychological Review,* 1964, **71,** 473-490.

Yudin, L., & Kates, S. L. Concept attainment and adolescent development. *Journal of Educational Psychology,* 1963, **54,** 117-182.

Annotations

Cartwright, W. J., & Buetis, T. R. Race and intelligence: Changing opinions in social science. *Social Science Quarterly,* 1968, **49,** 603-618. This study provides a historical, changing, and contemporary viewpoint of the issue of race and intelligence. The authors become entangled in the heredity-environment controversy, and they disallow that race is a significant factor in intelligence. The article contains some substantive conclusions for the heredity-environment student.

Ebel, R. L. Cognitive development of personal potential. *National Association of Secondary School Principals Bulletin,* 1966, **50,** 115-130. Ebel emphasizes that mental capacity must be educationally developed. He asserts that, since all learning is built on prior learning, deficiencies in educational opportunities or efforts at any stage will tend to restrict development of potential. Ebel feels that misplaced faith in the power of native genius and its inevitable fruition has caused some educators to underestimate the importance of basic education.

Jensen, A. R. How much can we boost IQ and scholastic achievement? *Harvard Educational Review,* 1969, **39,** 1-123. Jensen's article reexamines intelligence and achievement in light of the failure of compensatory education to produce lasting effects on intellectual growth. In looking at heredity and environment, Jensen concludes that genetic factors are more important in determining IQ. In analyzing environment, he suggests that social-class and racial variations in intelligence cannot be accounted for by differences in environment but rather, in part, by genetic differences. He discusses educational attempts at raising intelligence and concludes that much activity has been misdirected.

Krech, D. Psychoneurobiochemeducation. *Phi Delta Kappan,* 1969, **50,** 370-375. In this article Krech sees biochemists, neurologists, psychologists, and educators all combining forces and contributing to the intellectual stature of man. He proposes a new basis for understanding human intelligence. He suggests that for every separate memory in the mind, we will eventually find a differentiated chemical in the brain. He accentuates the importance of language development and suggests it may provide an insight into the mental basis for life.

Lovell, K. Developmental processes in thought. *Journal of Experimental Education,* 1968, **37,** 14-21. This article reports on the stages of human intellectual growth hypothesized by Piaget. Lovell suggests that children are constantly modifying existing schemata, and he considers this modification the basis for learning.

Neimark, E. D., & Lewis, N. The development of logical problem-solving strategies. *Child Development,* 1967, **38,** 107-117. This article reports research on the age and intelligence of children when they begin problem-solving activities. It was found that those activities begin at 11 or 12. Another finding was that brighter children are more able to formulate a rule and verbalize it. One characteristic of logical thinking is the control of self-generated stimuli, in contrast to the environmental stimuli experienced at earlier stages.

Waller, P. F. Intellectual skills. *National Association of Secondary School Principals Bulletin,* 1969, **53,** 63-89. This article focuses on the various current approaches to assessing intellectual skills. The author discusses (1) the factor-analytic approach, (2) Guilford's operational categories, (3) Piaget's developmental approach, (4) Bruner's analytic approach, and (5) learning-theory explanations of intelligence.

Wilhelms, F. T. The influence of environment and education. *National Association of Secondary School Principals Bulletin,* 1969, **53,** (336), 1-36. This article considers the basic variables within environment and education that may affect intellectual growth. After establishing heredity's role in intellectual capacity, Wilhelms looks at variables-research studies that reflect different ways in which intellectual growth is facilitated. He also discusses the contributions of institutional programs.

three

the adolescent and sex

Currently one of the most vital topics in the behavioral sciences is sexual behavior. Throughout history man's sexuality was generally either condemned or ignored. However, since the beginning of the 20th century, attitudes have changed and some writers have proposed that we are living in a "sex age" or sexual renaissance. Undoubtedly the works of Freud and Kinsey have played a major role in catapulting our society into a new awareness of the individual and his sex life.

Freud demonstrated that man is a sexual being throughout his lifetime—that is, that sexuality begins in early childhood and does not suddenly emerge within the confines of a monogamous marriage. Society could no longer ignore this aspect of man's existence, and the study of sexual behavior became a science.

The Kinsey Reports (Kinsey, Pomeroy, & Martin, 1948, 1953) shattered the illusion that sexual behavior was consistent with moral standards. Using a sample of 5300 males and 5940 females, the Reports analyzed the incidence and frequency of orgasm through six sexual outlets: masturbation, intercourse, nocturnal emissions, heterosexual petting, homosexuality, and animal contacts. Kinsey's research revealed three major conclusions: (1) sexual power reached its peak during adolescence, (2) sexual urges and activity could not be sublimated until marriage, and (3) a new morality was emerging.

Yet the traditional sexual codes have not disappeared. As a result, the adolescent in contemporary society is confused and frustrated by the ambiguity that surrounds him. He has strong physical urges that he cannot deny; his peers espouse liberal views about premarital and extramarital sexual relationships, masturbation, homosexuality, abortion, and birth control; he sees the sex drive exploited openly in movies, advertising, art, and literature. At the same time his parents, his church, and society at large maintain that he should repress his sexuality until he is married. He does not know what to believe.

What courses of action do our adolescents take in seeking an answer to their personal dilemma? Many of them choose sexual involvement, which is spurred by rebellion, by the desire for pleasure or conquest, by ego bolstering, and by pressures to be up-to-date. However, in many cases sexual activity results in more frustration rather than in fulfillment.

A Mythical Revolution?

The first article in this chapter, by Reiss, suggests that the sexual revolution is rather an evolution in that our youths are beginning to assume responsibility for their own sexual standards and behavior. He surveyed 1500 young adults and 1200 adolescents and found that (1) there are cultural differences in sexual behavior, (2) guilt is not a deterrent to sexual activity, and (3) the majority of the respondents felt that their sex standards were similar to those of their parents (although they were closer still to those of their peers, especially close friends).

The second article, by Smigel and Seiden, concerns the double standard. They illustrate its decline by comparing today's sexual behavior with that of the 1920s and attribute the new permissiveness to industrialization, the automobile, affluence, birth-control methods, and urbanization.

Sources of Information

Martinson's article criticizes society for expecting a high degree of maturity in adolescents' sexual behavior without providing them any direct sexual outlet. He discusses dating patterns, methods of birth control, and sources of sex education. Most of the adolescents in his study felt that they were poorly informed and had negative, un-

wholesome attitudes about sexuality. Their peers, rather than home, school, or church, represented the basic influencing force on their ideas.

Research by Thornburg (1970a, 1970b) revealed the same statistics. In Thornburg's study peers provided more basic sex information for the student than any other source. Almost all information about petting, intercourse, and homosexuality came from agemates. Only in the nonbehavioral aspects of sex information did sources other than peers contribute significantly. For instance, schools provide much information about venereal disease, and menstruation and the origin of babies are generally explained by mothers.

TABLE 1. A COMPARATIVE ANALYSIS OF SEX INFORMATION SOURCES

	Arizona (N = 191)	Oklahoma (N = 190)	Total	Percent
Mother	382	406	788	19.3
Father	23	20	43	1.8
Peers	688	829	1517	37.9
Literature	461	360	821	20.6
School	377	213	590	14.8
Minister	20	13	33	.8
Physician	12	9	21	.5
Street talk/experience	62	107	169	4.3
Unanswered	76	133	209	—
Total	2101	2090	4191	100.0

From H.D. Thornburg, "A Comparative Study of Sex Information Sources." *Journal of School Health,* 1970b, in press. Reprinted with permission of the publisher.

Adolescents in our society need to develop a healthier attitude toward their sex roles; they need help in building within themselves a better frame of reference to adjust to societal norms. Much of the adolescent's unrest stems from a lack of basic and adequate information concerning sexuality. It is difficult because youths view teacher-offered, stereotyped analyses of human sexuality skeptically, even though they are receiving highly informal and inaccurate information elsewhere. Educators must find a way to approach the topic without appearing to be superimposing adults out of step with the times.

The adolescent is more concerned with peer approval than with that of his parents or teachers (Thornburg, 1968). It is among his peers that life continues. To be excluded or to become unacceptable to them can be such a traumatic experience that he appears to intuitively fight against it. The adolescent finds it easier to bend or stretch adult expectations regarding his attitudes and values than those of his peers. Thus he is concerned that the school's teachings about sexuality will influence his patterns of conduct.

Most adolescents maintain that, when the home, school, or church does provide sex information, it is presented in a negative, unwholesome way. Since adolescents obviously gain so much of their knowledge about sexuality from peers, it seems vitally important that the home and the school become involved in the task of disseminating accurate information about sexual behavior in a positive, wholesome way. The selection in this chapter by Thornburg is an analysis of what can and should be done to help our young people in their search for a reasonable and acceptable code of sexual behavior.

Subcultures

Sex roles differ according to socioeconomic class and ethnic subcultures. Rosenberg and Bensman's article deals with the sexual patterns of poverty-stricken adolescents within three specific ethnic subcultures in Chicago, New York City, and Washington, D.C. The patterns that emerge clearly do not reflect middle-class standards of love and sex. Moreover, the three subcultures differ from one another in their sexual mores. Rosenberg and Bensman suggest that sexual practices among ghetto youths are highly associated with nonsexual aspects of life-style. That is, slum sex codes are consistent with overall slum codes. Nevertheless, the adolescent in the ghetto experiences something of the behavioral dilemma that plagues the middle-class adolescent.

ira l. reiss

how and why america's sex standards
are changing

The popular notion that America is undergoing a sexual "revolution" is a myth. The belief
that our more permissive sexual code is a
sign of a general breakdown of morality is
also a myth. These two myths have arisen in
part because we have so little reliable information about American sexual behavior. The
enormous public interest in sex seems to
have been matched by moralizing and reticence in scholarly research—a situation that
has only recently begun to be corrected.

What *has* been happening recently is
that our young people have been assuming
more responsibility for their own sexual
standards and behavior. The influence of
their parents has been progressively declining. The greater independence given to the
young has long been evident in other fields—
employment, spending, and prestige, to
name three. The parallel change in sexual-
behavior patterns would have been evident if
similar research had been made in this area.
One also could have foreseen that those
groups least subject to the demands of old
orthodoxies, like religion, would emerge as
the most sexually permissive of all—men in
general, liberals, non-churchgoers, Negroes,
the highly educated.

In short, today's more permissive sexual

standards represent not revolution but evolution, not anomie but normality.

My own research into current sexual
behavior was directed primarily to the question, Why are some groups of people more
sexually permissive than other groups? My
study involved a representative sample of
about 1500 people, 21 and older, from all
over the country; and about 1200 high-
school and college students, 16 to 22 years
old, from three different states. On the pages
that follow, I will first discuss some of the
more important of my findings; then suggest
seven general propositions that can be induced from these findings; and, finally, present a comprehensive theory about modern
American sexual behavior.

Are Race Differences Rooted in
Class?

A good many sociologists believe that
most of the real differences between
Negroes and whites are class differences—
that if Negroes and whites from the same
class were compared, any apparent differences would vanish. Thus, some critics of the
Moynihan Report accused Daniel P. Moynihan of ignoring how much lower-class whites
may resemble lower-class Negroes.

But my findings show that there are large
variations in the way whites and Negroes *of*

precisely the same class view premarital sexual permissiveness. Among the poor, for instance, only 32 percent of white males approve of intercourse before marriage under some circumstances—compared with 70 percent of Negro males. The variation is even more dramatic among lower-class females: 5 percent of whites compared with 33 percent of Negroes. Generally, high-school and college students of all classes were found to be more permissive than those in the adult sample. But even among students there were variations associated with race. (See Table 1.)

TABLE 1. PERCENT ACCEPTING PREMARITAL SEX

	Lower-class adults*	Lower-class students**
White men	32% of 202	56% of 96
Negro men	70% of 49	86% of 88
White women	5% of 221	17% of 109
Negro women	33% of 63	42% of 90

*From National Adult Sample
**From Five-School Student Sample

The difference between Negro and white acceptance of premarital intercourse is not due to any racial superiority or inferiority. All that this finding suggests is that we should be much more subtle in studying Negro-white differences, and not assume that variations in education, income, or occupation are enough to account for all these differences. The history of slavery, the depressing effects of discrimination and low status—all indicate that the Negro's entire cultural base may be different from the white's.

Another response to this finding on sexual attitudes can, of course, be disbelief. Do people really tell the truth about their sex lives? National studies have revealed that they do—women will actually talk more freely about their sex lives than about their husbands' incomes. And various validity checks indicate that they did in this case.

But people are not always consistent: They may not practice what they preach. So

TABLE 2. SEXUAL STANDARDS AND ACTUAL BEHAVIOR

Current Standard	Most Extreme Current Behavior			Number of Respondents
	Kissing	Petting	Coitus	
Kissing	64%	32%	4%	25
Petting	15%	78%	7%	139
Coitus	5%	31%	64%	84

I decided to compare people's sexual attitudes with their actual sexual behavior. Table 2 indicates the degree of correspondence between attitudes and behavior in a sample of 248 unmarried, white, junior and senior college-students.

Obviously, the students do not *always* act as they believe. But in the great majority of cases belief and action do coincide. For example, 64 percent of those who consider coitus acceptable are actually having coitus; only 7 percent of those who accept nothing beyond petting, and 4 percent of those who accept nothing beyond kissing, are having coitus. So it is fairly safe to conclude that, in this case, attitudes are good clues to behavior.

Guilt Is No Inhibitor

What about guilt feelings? Don't they block any transition toward more permissive sexual attitudes and behavior? Here the findings are quite unexpected. *Guilt feelings do not generally inhibit sexual behavior.* Eighty-seven percent of the women and 58 percent of the men said they had eventually come to accept sexual activities that had once made them feel guilty. (Some—largely males—had never felt guilty.) Seventy-eight percent had *never* desisted from any sexual activity that had made them feel guilty. Typically, a person will feel some guilt about his sexual behavior, but will continue his conduct until the guilt diminishes. Then he will move on to more advanced behavior—and new guilt feelings—until over that; and so on. People differed, mainly, in the sexual behavior they were willing to start, and in how quickly they moved on to more advanced forms.

The factor that most decisively motivated women to engage in coitus and to approve of coitus was the belief that they were in love. Of those who accepted coitus, 78 percent said they had been in love—compared with 60 percent of those who accepted only petting, and 40 percent of those who accepted only kissing. (Thus, parents who don't want their children to have sexual experiences but do want them to have "love" experiences are indirectly encouraging what they are trying to prevent.)

How do parents' beliefs influence their children's sexual attitudes and conduct?

Curiously enough, almost two-thirds of the students felt that their sexual standards were at least similar to those of their parents. This was as true for Negro males as for white females—although about 80 percent of the former accept premarital intercourse as against only about 20 percent of the latter. Perhaps these students are deluded, but perhaps they see through the "chastity" facade of their parents to the underlying similarities in attitude. It may be that the parents' views on independence, love, pleasure, responsibility, deferred gratification, conformity, and adventurousness are linked with the sexual attitudes of their children; that a similarity in these values implies a similarity in sexual beliefs. Probably these parental values, like religiousness, help determine which youngsters move quickly and with relatively little guilt through the various stages of sexual behavior. Religiousness, for the group of white students, is a particularly good index: Youngsters who rank high on church attendance rank low on premarital coitus, and are generally conservative.

Despite the fact that 63 to 68 percent of the students felt that their sexual standards were close to their parents' standards, a larger percentage felt that their standards were even closer to those of peers (77 percent) and to those of very close friends (89 percent). Thus, the conflict in views between peers and parents is not so sharp as might be expected. Then too, perhaps parents' values have a greater influence on their children's choice of friends than we usually acknowledge.

The Importance of Responsibility

This brings us to another key question. Are differences in sexual standards between parents and children due to changing cultural standards? Or are they due to their different roles in life—that is, to the difference between being young, and being parents responsible for the young? Were the parents of today that different when they courted?

My findings do show that older people tend to be less permissive about sex—but this difference is not very marked. What is significant is that childless couples—similar to couples with children of courtship age in every other respect, including age—are much more willing to accept premarital intercourse as standard (23 to 13 percent). Furthermore, parents tend to be *less* sexually permissive the *more* responsibility they have for young people. Now, if the primary cause of parent-child divergences in sexual standards is that cultural standards in general have been changing, then older people should, by and large, be strikingly more conservative about sex. They aren't. But since parents are more conservative about sex than nonparents of the same age, it would seem that the primary cause of parent-child divergences over sex is role and responsibility—the parents of today were *not* that different when courting.

Being responsible for others, incidentally, inhibits permissiveness even when the dependents are siblings. The first-born are far less likely to approve of premarital intercourse (39 percent) than are the youngest children (58 percent).

Another intriguing question is, How do parents feel about the sexual activities of their boy children—as opposed to their girl children? The answer depends upon the sex of the parent. The more daughters a white father has, the more strongly he feels about his standards—although his standards are no stricter than average. The more sons he has, the less strongly he feels about his beliefs. White mothers showed the reverse tendency, but much more weakly—the more sons, the stronger the mothers' insistence upon whatever standards they believed in. Perhaps white parents feel this way because of their unfamiliarity with the special sexual problems of a child of the opposite sex—combined with an increasing awareness of these problems.

What explains these differences in attitude between groups—differences between men and women as well as between Negroes and whites? Women are more committed to marriage than men, so girls become more committed to marriage too, and to low-permissive parental values. The economic pressures on Negroes work to break up their families, and weaken commitment to marital values, so Negroes tend to be more permissive. Then too, whites have a greater stake in the orthodox institution of marriage: More white married people than unmarried people reported that they were happy. Among Negroes, the pattern was reversed. But in discussing weak commitments to marriage we are dealing with one of the "older" sources of sexual permissiveness.

The sources of the new American permissiveness are somewhat different. They include access to contraception; ways to combat venereal infection; and—quite as important—an intellectualized philosophy about the desirability of sex accompanying affection. "Respectable," college-educated people have integrated this new philosophy with their generally liberal attitudes about the family, politics, and religion. And this represents a new and more lasting support for sexual permissiveness, since it is based on a positive philosophy rather than hedonism, despair, or desperation.

In my own study, I found that among the more permissive groups were those in which the fathers were professional men. This finding is important: It shows that the upper segments of our society, like the lower, have a highly permissive group in their midst—despite the neat picture described by some people of permissiveness steadily declining as one raises one's gaze toward the upper classes.

Patterns of Permissiveness

All these findings, though seemingly diverse, actually fall into definite patterns, or clusters of relationships. These patterns can be expressed in seven basic propositions:

1. The *less* sexually permissive a group is, traditionally, the *greater* the likelihood that new social forces will cause its members to become more permissive.

Traditionally high-permissive groups, such as Negro men, were the least likely to have their sexual standards changed by social forces like church-attendance, love affairs, and romantic love. Traditionally low-permissive groups, such as white females, showed the greatest sensitivity to these social forces. In addition, the lower social classes are reported to have a tradition of greater sexual permissiveness, so the finding that their permissiveness is less sensitive to certain social forces also fits this proposition.

2. The more liberal the group, the more likely that social forces will help maintain high sexual permissiveness.

There was diverse support for this proposition. Students, upper-class females in liberal settings, and urban dwellers have by and large accepted more permissiveness than those in more conservative settings.

Indeed, liberalism in general seems to be yet another cause of the new permissiveness in America. Thus, a group that was traditionally low-permissive regarding sex (the upper class), but that is liberal in such fields as religion and politics, would be very likely to shift toward greater premarital permissiveness.

3. According to their ties to marital and family institutions, people will differ in their sensitivity to social forces that affect permissiveness.

This proposition emphasizes, mainly, male-female differences in courting. Women have a stronger attachment to and investment in marriage, childbearing, and family ties. This affects their courtship roles. There are fundamental male-female differences in acceptance of permissiveness, therefore, in line with differences in courtship role.

Romantic love led more women than men to become permissive (this finding was particularly true if the woman was a faithful churchgoer). Having a steady date affected women predominantly, and exclusiveness was linked with permissiveness. Early dating, and its link with permissiveness, varied by race, but was far more commonly linked with permissiveness in men than in women. The number of steadies, and the number of times in love, was associated with permissiveness for females, but was curvilinear for males— that is, a man with no steadies, or a number of steadies, tended to be more permissive than a man who had gone steady only once.

Such male-female differences, however, are significant only for whites. Among Negroes, male-female patterns in these areas are quite similar.

4. The higher the overall level of permissiveness in a group, the greater the extent of equalitarianism within abstinence and double-standard subgroups.

Permissiveness is a measure not only of what a person will accept for himself and his own sex, but of what behavior he is willing to allow the opposite sex. Permissiveness, I found, tends to be associated with sexual equalitarianism in one particular fashion: I found, strangely enough, that a good way to measure the *general* permissiveness of a group is to measure the equalitarianism of two subgroups—the abstinent, and believers in the double-standard. (Nonequalitarianism in abstinence means, usually, petting is acceptable for men, but only kissing for women. Equalitarianism within the double-standard means that intercourse is acceptable for women when in love, for men anytime. The nonequalitarian double-standard considers all unmarried women's coitus wrong.) In a generally high-permissive group (such as men), those adherents who do accept abstinence or the double-standard will be more equalitarian than will their counterparts in low-permissive groups (such as women). The implication is that the ethos of a high-permissive group encourages female sexuality and thereby also encourages equalitarianism throughout the group.

5. The potential for permissiveness derived from parents' values is a key determinant as to how rapidly, how much, and in what direction a person's premarital sexual standards and behavior change.

What distinguishes an individual's sexual behavior is not its starting point—white college-educated females, for instance, almost always start only with kissing—but how far, how fast, and in what direction the individual is willing to go. The fact is that almost all sexual behavior is eventually repeated, and comes to be accepted. And a person's basic values encourage or discourage his willingness to try something new and possibly guilt-producing. Therefore, these basic values—derived, in large part, from parental teaching, direct or implicit—are keys to permissiveness.

Since the young often feel that their sex standards are similar to their parents', we can conclude that, consciously or not, high-permissive parents intellectually and emotionally breed high-permissive children.

6. A youth tends to see permissiveness as a continuous scale with his parents' standards at the low point, his peers' at the high point, and himself between but closer to his peers—and closest to those he considers his most intimate friends.

The findings indicate that those who consider their standards closer to parents' than to peers' are less permissive than the others. The most permissive within one group generally reported the greatest distance from parents, and greatest similarity to peers and friends. This does not contradict the previous proposition, since parents are on the continuum and exert enough influence so that their children don't go all the way to the opposite end. But it does indicate, and the data bear out, that parents are associated with relatively low permissiveness; that the courtship group is associated with relatively high permissiveness; and that the respondents felt closer to the latter. Older, more permissive students were less likely to give "parental guidance" as a reason for their standards.

7. Greater responsibility for other members of the family, and lesser participation in courtship, are both associated with low-permissiveness.

The only child, it was found, had the most permissive attitudes. Older children, generally, were less permissive than their younger brothers and sisters. The older children usually have greater responsibility for the young siblings; children without siblings have no such responsibilities at all.

The findings also showed that as the number of children, and their ages, increased, the parents' permissiveness decreased. Here again, apparently, parental responsibility grew, and the decline in permissiveness supports the proposition above.

On the other hand, as a young person gets more and more caught up in courtship, he is progressively freed from parental domination. He has less responsibility for others, and he becomes more permissive. The fact that students are more sexually liberal than many other groups must be due partly to their involvement in courtship, and to their distance from the family.

Thus a generational clash of some sort is almost inevitable. When children reach their late teens or early 20's, they also reach the peak of their permissiveness; their parents, at the same time, reach the nadir of theirs.

These findings show that both the family and courtship institutions are key determinants of whether a person accepts or rejects premarital sexuality. Even when young people have almost full independence in courtship, as they do in our system, they do not copulate at random. They display parental and family values by the association of sex with affection, by choice of partners, by equalitarianism, and so on.

However, parental influence must inevitably, to some extent, conflict with the pressures of courting, and the standards of the courting group. Young people are tempted by close association with attractive members of the opposite sex, usually without having any regular heterosexual outlet. Also, youth is a time for taking risks and having adventures. Therefore, the greater the freedom to react autonomously within the courtship group, the greater the tendency toward liberalized sexual behavior.

This autonomy has always been strong in America. Visitors in the 19th century were amazed at freedom of mate choice here, and the equalitarianism between sexes, at least as compared with Europe. The trend has grown.

Now, families are oriented toward the bearing and rearing of children—and for this, premarital sex is largely irrelevant. It becomes relevant only if it encourages marriages the parents want—but relevant negatively if it encourages births out of wedlock, or the "wrong," or no, marriages. Most societies tolerate intercourse between an engaged couple, for this doesn't seriously threaten the marital institution; and even prostitution gains some acceptance because it does not promote unacceptable marital unions. The conflict between the family and courtship systems depends on the extent to which each perceives the other as threatening its interests. My own findings indicate that this conflict is present, but not always as sharply as the popular press would have us believe.

Courtship pressures tend toward high-permissiveness; family pressures toward low-permissiveness. It follows that whatever promotes the child's independence from the family promotes high-permissiveness. For example, independence is an important element in the liberal position; a liberal setting, therefore, generally encourages sexual as well as other independence.

A Comprehensive Theory

To summarize all these findings into one comprehensive theory runs the risk of oversimplifying—if the findings and thought that went into the theory are not kept clearly in mind. With this *caveat,* I think a fair theoretical summary of the meaning of the foregoing material would be: How much premarital sexual permissiveness is considered acceptable in a courtship group varies directly with the independence of that group, and with the general permissiveness in the adult cultural environment.

In other words, when the social and cultural forces working on two groups are approximately the same, the differences in permissiveness are caused by differences in independence. But when independence is equal, differences come from differences in the socio-cultural setting.

There is, therefore, to repeat, no sexual revolution today. Increased premarital sexuality is not usually a result of breakdown of standards, but a particular, and different, type of organized system. To parents, more firmly identified with tradition—that is, with older systems—and with greater responsibilities toward the young, toward the family, and toward marriage, greater premarital sexuality seems deviant. But it is, nevertheless, an integral part of society—their society.

In short, there has been a gradually increasing acceptance of and overtness about sexuality. The basic change is toward greater equalitarianism, greater female acceptance of permissiveness, and more open discussion. In the next decade, we can expect a step-up in the pace of this change.

The greater change, actually, is in sexual attitude, rather than in behavior. If behavior has not altered in the last century as much as we might think, attitudes *have*—and attitudes and behavior seem closer today than for many generations. Judging by my findings, and the statements of my respondents, we can expect them to become closer still, and to proceed in tandem into a period of greater permissiveness, and even greater frankness. I do not, however, foresee extreme change in the years to come—such as full male-female equality. This is not possible unless male and female roles in the family are also equal, and men and women share equal responsibility for child-rearing and family support.

erwin o. smigel

rita seiden*

the decline and fall of the double standard

Abstract: The limited available information on premarital, heterosexual behavior of young people in the United States reveals that the changes in sexual behavior which took place in the 1920's have changed only slightly in the 1960's, and that this slow change is continuing. The belief that a gradual transformation is taking place (except in overtness) rests on a comparison of the early studies on sexual behavior, the data from attitudinal studies, researched from 1940 to 1963, and observations of the current scene. Conclusion: the double standard is declining but has not yet fallen.

To find meaningful correlations,[1] especially in a pluralistic society, between the multitude of social forces and sexual behavior is difficult; to determine these correlations accurately, when appropriate data on sexual behavior are not available, is impossible. Nonetheless, it is our assignment to examine these social forces in order to see what effect they have had on sexual behavior and attitudes—specifically on sexual behavior and attitudes of unmarried heterosexuals of college age and younger in the United States.

Reprinted with permission of the authors and publisher from the *Annals of the American Academy of Political and Social Sciences*, 1968, **376**, 6-17.

*The authors wish to acknowledge gratefully the criticisms and suggestions of Martha Crossen Gillmor, Irwin Goffman, and Edward Sagarin.

[1]It is understood that even if it were possible to determine these correlations accurately, we would not have an explanation of causality.

Most recent examinations of sexual behavior still cite Kinsey's data [1948, 1953] (1938-1949) and/or Terman's [1938] (1934-1935). No one has published a Kinsey-type study for the United States in the 1960's. However, a few limited studies (Gilbert Youth Research, 1951; Burgess & Wallin, 1953; Landis & Landis, 1957; Ehrmann, 1959; Freedman, 1965; Reiss, 1967) on premarital sexual behavior have been completed since Kinsey published *The Human Male* in 1948. The various studies of college students show percentages of premarital coitus for males and females which range from 54:35 in 1929 (Hamilton, 1929); 51:25 in 1938 (Bromley & Britten, 1938); to 56:25 in 1951 (Gilbert Youth Research, 1951); and, in 1953, 68:47, 41:9, or 63:14, depending on whose figures are accepted (Burgess & Wallin, 1953; Landis & Landis, 1957; Ehrmann, 1959). The most recent examination of sexual behavior puts the rate of college female premarital experience at 22 per cent (Freedman, 1965). This is consistent with Kinsey's findings that 20 per cent of all college women had had premarital intercourse (Kinsey, 1953).

Most of the studies of sex completed after Kinsey's main works appeared have been limited to collecting statistics on attitudes. The most extensive of these studies, for which data were collected through 1963, was conducted by Ira Reiss,[2] on sexual permissiveness. Reiss's findings point to a coming together of sexual practices, and, for the young at least, of attitudes about sex. He found definite movement away from the orthodox double standard toward a standard of permissiveness with affection (shorthand for "premarital sex is acceptable when there is mutual affection between the partners").

The earlier statistics of Kinsey and Terman point up important differences in sexual behavior between the generation of women born before 1900 and the generation born in the following decade. Kinsey found that 73.4 per cent of women born before 1900 had had no premarital intercourse, but among those born between 1900 and 1909, only 48.7 per cent had been virgins at marriage. The figures for those born in the 1920–1929 generation are the same—48.8 per cent (Reiss, 1961).[3] Terman's findings are essentially in agreement. The statistics for both the Kinsey and Terman studies referred to here are for women of all ages, and not just for college women (Davis, 1929).[4] Terman found that 74 per cent of the females born between 1890 and 1899 had had no premarital intercourse, whereas among those born between 1900 and 1909, the percentage of virgin brides had dropped to 51.2. His figures reveal that this trend also held for men: of those interviewees born between 1890 and 1899, 41.9 per cent had had no premarital coitus, whereas of the interviewees born in the next generation, 32.6 per cent had had no such premarital

experience (Terman, 1938; Kinsey, 1948).[5] Clearly, the major change in sex practices occurred in the generation born in the decade 1900–1909, which came to sexual age during or immediately after World War I, a period characterized by marked social change and innovation.

It may well be true that changes in sexual behavior and attitudes are related to the social changes which began in the late nineteenth century and accelerated rapidly over the past 67 years. It is not as clear, except perhaps for the post-World War I years, exactly what the effects of these social changes have been on sexual behavior. Reiss argues that, despite popular belief to the contrary, "the sexual revolution [is] a myth and the only basic change [is] a trend toward more equality between the sexes. . . . There has been less change than [is] popularly believed between modern American males and their Victorian grandfathers" (Iowa Sociologist, 1967).

It is generally thought, however, that the late-nineteenth-century break with Victorian morality was a tangential result of the Industrial Revolution, urban migration, war, the feminist movement, and the scientific study of once-taboo topics. Wilbert Moore, a leading authority on social change, credited industrialization with certain effects on the social structure (1963); and it is our opinion that industrialization affected sex attitudes and behavior as well. He specified increased social and geographic mobility; growth of industrial centers with concomitant concentration of population in urban areas; emphasis on rationality as a necessary part of an industrialized society (for example, a lessening of the influence of religion); transition from extended (rurally located) families to nuclear (urban) families; emphasis on individualism resulting from the breakdown (Burch, 1967)

---

[2]Ira L. Reiss, *The Social Context of Premarital Sexual Permissiveness* (New York: Holt, Rinehart and Winston, 1967), chap. vii. Reiss's primary purpose was not to examine behavior (at least not in this latest presentation); he was interested in attitudes. He asked 268 students (42 of them males) in an Iowa college about their behavior. What he did was to correlate expressed feelings of guilt with behavior, and found relationships with age and behavior and relationships between expressed standards and behavior. The Institute for Sex Research at Indiana University conducted a 1967 study of sex behavior among college students, but the final results have not as yet been published.

[3]These data were based on Kinsey (1953), but were especially prepared for [Reiss's] paper . . . [by] Drs. Gebhard and Martin of the Institute of Sex Research. These were based on 2,479 women who either were or had been married by the time of the interview.

[4]Of those women who attended college in the early 1900's (that is, were born before 1900), only 7 per cent had premarital intercourse. According to Bromley and Britten (1938), 25 per cent of the college women of the 1930's had premarital intercourse. And according to Freedman (1965, p. 45): "The rate of premarital nonvirginity tripled from 1900 to 1930."

[5]Kinsey noted generational differences within his male sample; but the "generations" were formed by dividing his subjects into "younger" (under 33 years of age at the time of the interview) and "older" (over 33 years of age at the time interviewed) groups. He did not compare them by decade of birth as he did the women. The median age of the younger group was 21.2 years, that is, born approximately between 1917 and 1926. The median age of the older group was 43.1 years, that is, born approximately between 1895 and 1904 (Kinsey, *The Human Female*, chap. vii). Information is provided here that premarital petting had increased with each generation since 1920 even though incidence of premarital coitus had not. One of the possible explanations for the continued relatively high number of virgins is that heavy petting is now very common, so that there are a large number of "technical" virgins who engage in almost everything except coitus.

of the extended kinship system; decreased family size accompanied by a decline in the economic significance of the family unit as the unit of survival; and, finally, increased education.

Each of these general effects of social change can be shown, at least theoretically, to have potential impact on sexual behavior and attitudes. As the population moves from small towns and intimate personal relationships to urban centers, old forms of social control break down. This disintegration and the accompanying anonymity is speeded by new and faster forms of transportation which further increase the possibilities of anonymity and independence. A rational society affects the individual's world view, and he tends to see his own life in terms of more rational standards. As the extended kinship system dissolves or loses its importance, mate-selection processes become a more personal responsibility, and increase the importance of peer group norms, which take precedence over family norms. In the evolving industrial society, women take a new and larger part in the working world, thereby securing greater independence for themselves and increased equality in male-female relationships. The general increase in education has made possible widespread dissemination of sex information to the public.

In sum, the family has declined in importance as the unit upon which or around which society is organized, and individualism, in relationship to the family, is in the ascendency. As individualism has grown, sexual behavior has become more a personal matter and is less exclusively influenced by family and procreational considerations.

The complex social changes discussed have been gradual, but the impact of war can be immediate and abrupt. This is clearly indicated in the data on sexual behavior during and immediately after World War I. In any war, the mores governing family life tend to decay. Removed from some of the responsibilities, restrictions, and supports of the family, removed from the all-seeing eye of the small town or the neighborhood, soldiers are suddenly subject only to the mostly approving observations of their fellow soldiers. In the face of death or the possibility of being severely wounded, hedonism becomes the prevailing attitude. This attitude appears to be contagious and spreads to the civilian population. In World War I, it particularly affected the young women who were working in factories, taking on roles and responsibilities that had once belonged exclusively to men, often for the first time living alone in relative anonymity, and in many instances emotionally involved with men who were scheduled to be sent overseas. (This same hedonistic philosophy may be held by contemporary young people who are faced with the dangers of limited wars and the always present possibility of extinction by nuclear explosion.)

Many soldiers had contact with prostitutes and contracted venereal diseases. The United States Interdepartmental Social Hygiene Board reports: "Between September, 1917, and February 14, 1919, there were over 222,000 cases of venereal disease in the army and there were over 60,000 in the navy" (Storey, 1920). Venereal disease and the prostitute taught the soldier more about sex in his relatively short career in the armed services than he might normally have learned. The incidence of venereal disease was so high that it became a matter of both private and official army talk. The consequence was that most soldiers left the service knowing not only the protective effects but also the birth control uses of prophylactic sheaths. This kind of sex education became a standard part of the army curriculum.

The soldier who went abroad had new sexual experiences and came in contact with women whose behavior derived from different and more permissive sex norms; the returned veteran brought back with him sexual attitudes shaped by these new norms. Although they were not consciously intended for his mother, sister, wife, or wife-to-be, they tended to affect them as well.

War also tends to spread industrialization and to extend the need for women in industry, and, in turn, to increase their economic independence. The war and wartime experiences intensified the gradual way in which industrialization was changing the social structure.

War, industrialization, and an increase in political democracy seem to have led to the struggle for equal rights for women. The nineteenth-century feminists, who fought for financial and social rights and by 1920 had been enfranchised, were now also demanding more sexual freedom. Margaret Sanger, an American housewife, was a leader in this war. She waged a courageous battle for the control of pregnancy, and she was brought to trial for making birth control information available to interested persons. It was the trial, the wide publicity she received, and her persistence which helped to acquaint the public with the possibilities of birth control. She and other fighters for female sexual freedom were supported by a backdrop of the new norms of the returning soldiers, the effects of economic gains for women, and an increase in the scientific study of sex.

Although Krafft-Ebing (1886), Havelock Ellis (1910), and others were writing about sex pathology and sexuality, Freud's writings about the unconscious and the effect of sex on personality had the most influence upon American behavior and attitudes. Although *Studies in Hysteria,* written by Freud and Breuer, which made these ideas available to the public, was published in 1895, "it was not until after the war that the Freudian gospel began to circulate to a marked extent among the American reading public" (Allen, 1932). No one can estimate what popularization of psychoanalytic theory has done to free individuals—particularly women—from the puritan anxieties about sex. The fact of its influence, however, cannot be doubted. These studies by the sexologists and those by the sociologists, anthropologists, and psychologists studying and writing in the late 1920's and early 1930's provided the setting for the public acceptance of Kinsey's impressive work—which may in turn have had great influence on a society already impatient with Victorian sex mores. In any event, studies of sex were being undertaken, and

they provided information about taboo topics which helped to free the average individual from the restraint against serious discussion of sexual behavior. Each generation of sex researchers has extended the study and broadened the understanding of sex, from Kinsey's counting of sexual outlets in the 1940's to Masters and Johnson's detailed study of human sexual response (1966) in the early 1960's.

In addition to those factors already described, which have affected so many aspects of the social structure, other elements, although less powerful forces for general change, have also contributed to the alteration of sexual mores in a more immediate sense. Cultural interchange resulting from wartime contact since World War I and from the great increase in travel has led to a broadened participation with other societies. Furthermore, the disappearance of the chaperon undoubtedly created opportunities for sexual freedom which are not subject to the social sanctions of one's own society. The availability of the automobile, the affluent society which permits young people to live apart from their parents, and the growth of community size made privacy much more accessible. There has been a virtual removal of "fear-evoking" deterrents with the development of effective contraceptive devices.

All of these factors seem to be related to the change in sexual practices and to the apparent liberalization of sexual standards reflected in Reiss's data (1960). Since these social forces are still operating in the same direction, we should also expect to see changes in the direction of permissive sexual attitudes and behavior to continue.

TABLE 1. ATTITUDES TOWARD PREMARITAL INTERCOURSE (IN PERCENTAGES)

Approve of	1940 Cornell[a]			1947 Michigan State University[b]			1952–1955 11 Colleges[b]			1958 University of Florida[c]		
	M	F	Total	M	F	Total	M	F	Total	M	F	Total
1. Sex relations for both	15	6	9	16	2		20	5		42	7	25
2. Abstinence	49	76	65	59	76		52	65		20	86	52
3. Sex relations for men only	23	11	16	10	15		12	23		33	0	17
4. Sex relations for engaged/in love	11	6	8	15	7		16	7		5	7	6
(N)	(73)	(100)	(173)		(2000)			(3000)		(45)	(42)	(87)

[a] Percentages are based on N of 173, but 3 per cent (1 per cent male, 2 per cent female) did not answer the question. The total per cent appearing in Reiss is 101; therefore, ours totals 98.

[b] Separate N's for the male and female samples were not given; therefore, it was not possible to compute total percentage advocating each standard.

[c] Total percentages were not shown by Reiss and were computed by the authors of this article.

81

The data we have on sexual behavior are limited; but more data are available on attitudes.

The research statistics are analyzed in Tables 1, 2, 3, and 4 (Rockwood & Ford, 1945; Landis & Landis, 1957; Ehrmann, 1959).

Reiss's later data, collected in 1959 and 1963 (1967),[6] confirm the trends evidenced in the findings of the earlier studies (see Table 2).

TABLE 2. PERCENTAGE[a] ACCEPTING EACH STANDARD

Standard	1959[c]		
	Male	Female	Total
Permissiveness with affection	24	15	19
Permissiveness without affection	13	2	7
Abstinence	28	55	42
Orthodox double standard	9	13	11
Transitional double standard[b]	18	10	14
$N =$	(386)	(435)	(821)

[a]Percentages of adherents to the reversed double standard have been omitted. Therefore, totals do not equal 100 per cent.

[b]Transitional double standard means that sex relations are considered all right for men under any condition, but are acceptable for women only if they are in love.

[c]The 1959 sample was drawn from the student populations of five schools: two Virginia colleges (one Negro, one white); two Virginia high schools (one Negro, one white); and one New York college.

We can probably safely conclude from these data:

(1) Abstinence and permissiveness with affection are the favored standards for both males and females.

(2) There has been a rise in female approval of permissiveness with affection and a decline in approval of the abstinence standard.

(3) Permissiveness without affection, if we consider it comparable to a blanket endorsement of casual sex relations for both, is apparently on the decline—even more sharply for men than for women.

(4) The orthodox double standard is also on the decline if we compare the Table 1 data (sex relations for men only) with the Table 2 data (orthodox double standard).

(5) The percentage of men who favor permissiveness with affection has increased markedly while the female endorsement remains about the same. The redistribution of women's attitudes seems to be away from abstinence and the orthodox double standard toward greater endorsement of the transitional double standard—coitus is all right for men under any condition, but is acceptable for women only if they are in love. Therefore, while women still endorse abstinence more highly than other standards, they are coming to favor sexual relations in the context of affection. Reiss's 1963 data support the 1959 evidence which indicates an increasingly favorable attitude on the part of females[7] toward sex with affection. Eighteen per cent favor permissiveness with affection; one per cent endorse permissiveness without affection; 56 per cent support abstinence. The percentage endorsing the transitional double standard was not given.[8]

(6) Succinctly: The percentage of both men and women who accept increased permissiveness with affection as their standard has increased (see Table 3).

Since the 1947, 1952–1955, and 1959 studies used the largest number of subjects and employed somewhat more rigorous sampling techniques, they are probably more reliable indicators of the trend in these attitudes. They strongly support the assumption that there has been an important

TABLE 3. PERCENTAGE ACCEPTING THE STANDARD

	1940		1947		1952–1955		1958		1959[a]		1963[a]	
	M	F	M	F	M	F	M	F	M	F	M	F
Sex relations for engaged/in love	11	6	15	7	16	7	5	7	24	15	[b]	18

[a]We are considering Reiss's "permissiveness with affection" as equivalent to "sex relations for engaged/in love."

[b]Figure for men has been omitted as total number of male interviews is a small proportion of the total sample.

[6]The reverse double standard category has been omitted, for Reiss says that this "response is almost certainly an error." (For his discussion of this point, see Reiss, 1960). Reverse double standard adherents are understood to believe that women should have greater sexual freedom than men. Percentage accepting this standard were: 1959—9 per cent male, 6 per cent female, 7 per cent total; 1963—0 per cent male, 5 per cent female, 4 per cent total.

[7]The data for males have not been utilized because the men represent only a small percentage of the total number of cases in the sample (Reiss, 1967).

[8]Reiss reported 20 per cent of the females endorsing the double standard, but did not break down the figure to show the percentage accepting the orthodox standard nor the percentage accepting the traditional standard.

change in attitudes toward sex in the direction of permissiveness.

In explaining the differences between statistics on sexual behavior and statistics on attitudes (namely, that behavior seems to have changed little since the 1920's, but attitudes have become more liberal), Reiss suggests that we are seeing a "consolidation process" taking place, that is, "a change in attitudes to match the change in behavior" is occurring (1967). Nelson Foote cites a variety of evidence which, he claims, indicates the decline of the double standard: decline in prostitution, increasingly equal sexual opportunities and experiences for women, increase in orgasm in marital sex relations, "the steady approach to equivalence of male and female premarital petting and marital sex play techniques," the increase of extramarital coitus, decreasing insistence on virginity in females at marriage, and "some decline in frequency of marital coitus implying more mutual consent and less unilateral demand (1964, p. 161).

Finally, in line with both Reiss's and Foote's arguments that there is a trend toward a new single standard of permissiveness with affection, Robert Bell suggests that for young adults, sex becomes acceptable today when the couple feels they are in love. Peer group members accept and approve of sex without marriage, but not of sex without love (1966).

For the unmarried, there is an increasing tendency to reject marriage as the arbitrary dividing line between "socially approved and socially disapproved sexual intimacy" (Bell, 1966). And in the same way that male and female roles have become more equal in other areas of life, greater equality has come to the area of sexual relations: "fair play has been replacing chastity as the badge of honor in the interpersonal relations of the sexes" (Foote, 1964).

The results of the various studies of attitudes show two particularly interesting and possibly related findings:

First, there has been an increase in permissive attitudes toward sex since the 1940's. This may be due to the accumulating reforming influence of those social factors which were operating in the twentieth century. Certainly, the changed attitude shows itself sharply in the increase in sexual content of movies, the candid use of sexual lures in advertising, an increasing social sanctioning (if not precisely approval) of sexual material in popular literature, and a generally freer atmosphere which permits open talk about sex. But the new standard for coital involvement insists on permissiveness with affection.

Second, the parent generation (sampled in 1963 by Reiss) is far more conservative than the younger generation—and is apparently more conservative than it was when it was the younger generation. In Reiss's 1963 adult sample, only 17 per cent endorsed permissiveness with affection for males and only 5 per cent endorsed this standard for females (Reiss, 1967).

Apparently, the conservative parent generation refuse to endorse for their children standards of behavior in which members of their generation, and perhaps they themselves, engaged. What appears to be a "generation gap," however, is probably a manifestation of a change in role (Reiss, 1967; Bell, 1966). Reiss's data on his adult sample give a concise picture of the relationship between role position and attitudes.

TABLE 4. "MARITAL AND FAMILY STATUS AND PERMISSIVENESS IN THE ADULT SAMPLE" [a]

Marital and Family Status	Per Cent Permissive	N
Single	44	(108)
Married		
No children	23	(124)
All preteen	22	(384)
Preteen and older	17	(218)
All teen and older	13	(376)

[a] Reiss, The Social Context of Premarital Sexual Permissiveness, p. 142, Table 9.2 (some data omitted).

Permissiveness evidently reaches its highest point on one curve (for the college student) while it reaches its lowest point on another curve (for the parents of the college student). What the data describe, then, are changes which occur as individuals come to occupy parental role positions, and they are not descriptive of differences between individuals of the post-World War II generation and their parents' generation.

In part, this information suggests that parents try to modify behavior in their children in which they themselves participated as young adults. This reaction may portend how the current young adult generation will feel when they are parents themselves. However, the qualification to be noted here is that the generation which came to maturity in the 1920's broke with previous generations in terms of behavior. The following generations continued in the same kind of practices but gradually came to express more liberal attitudes. The new liberalism of the younger generation may very well contribute to a shift in expressed adult values for the parent generations of the late 1960's and 1970's.

We know that sexual attitudes have changed and that sexual standards appear to be in a period of transition. "What was done by a female in 1925 acting as a rebel and a deviant can be done by a female in 1965 as a conformist" (Reiss, 1966).

Data based on a large sample are available on sex behavior up to 1949 and on attitudes up to 1963. We do not know what has happened during the last five years or what is happening now. The general public impression is that there has been a very recent sexual revolution and that it is still going on. Most researchers do not believe that this is the case. The authors of this article, as social observers and recent reviewers of the literature on sexual behavior and attitudes toward sex, will attempt to "crystal ball" what has occurred during the last five years and what is occurring now. What follows, then, is not fact, but guess.

Past trends in social change, in behavior, and in attitudes toward sex are continuing. What seems to be taking place (except for pockets of our society) is a growing tendency toward more sexual permissiveness among the young unmarried. Sex with affection appears to be increasingly accepted. More and more this norm is based on personal choice, and it manifests itself for middle-class college youth in the form of trial marriage, for the girl, and for the boy at least as a stable, monogamous relationship, to the point of setting up housekeeping. Increasingly, this happens with parental knowledge though not necessarily with parental approval. If Kinsey repeated his study today, he would probably find premarital virginity slightly lower and figures for those who have had premarital intercourse only with their spouse, a circumstance which was already on the increase in 1947 (born before 1900, 10.4 per cent; born 1920–1929, 27.3 per cent) (Reiss, 1961), somewhat higher.

Promiscuity, a word objected to by many

young people, probably has lessened. Certainly the use of prostitutes has diminished. If we are correct in believing that more young people are living monogamously together, and if marriage for both men and women [the figures are: median age of first marriages in 1890 for brides was 22.0 and for grooms was 26.1 (Vital Statistics, 1959); for 1966, the median age for brides was 20.5 and for grooms 22.8 (Statistical Abstracts, 1967)] is occurring at earlier ages, then the statistical probabilities of premarital promiscuity have lessened, except when it is a reflection of mental illness. Today, except for the "hippies," who, according to the press, indulge in group sex, promiscuity as a form of rebellion is significantly on the decline.

We are living in a much more permissive society, and we are much more vocal about sex. As Walter Lippman put it, even as early as 1929: "It was impossible to know whether increased openness about sex reflected more promiscuity or less hypocrisy" (1939). While we do not have much new evidence concerning sexual behavior, we do have non-systematic overt indications about attitudes. It is seen in advertisements which are much more suggestive than they used to be. At one time, an advertiser would indicate to a male reader that, if he used a certain product, a pretty girl would kiss him. Now the ads suggest that she will have intercourse with him: "When an Avis girl winks at you she means business," and as Chateau Martin asks, leering only slightly, "Had any lately?" Movies have become less suggestive and more obvious; nudity as well as intercourse have become not uncommon sights. The Scandinavian picture, *I, A Woman,* for example, consists of a number of seductions with a number of different men. Perhaps what is more significant is that censorship boards, the courts, and power groups in this country have sharply amended their definitions of obscenity. The theater has, for some time, been more open about sex and its various ramifications, and four-letter words are becoming a theatrical cliche.

Another indicator of this generation's expressed attitudes toward sex are the omnipresent buttons, which express not only political, but also sexual opinions. The buttons are designed for fun and shock, and for public declaration for sexual freedom. Sold in large cities all over this country, they range from simple position-statements such as

"Make Love Not War," "I'm For Sexual Freedom," or "Equality for Homosexuals," to invitations which read "Roommate Wanted," "Join the Sexual Revolution—Come Home With Me Tonight," to such shock jokes as "Phallic Symbols Arise," "Stand Up For S-X," and "Come Together."

More sophisticated young people feel that the dirty-word movements or the shock words no longer have any impact. In the October 26, 1967, *Washington Square Journal,* a New York University publication, the student reviewer of an off-Broadway production, *The Beard,* which freely uses four-letter words and ends with an act of cunnilingus on stage, says: "Unfortunately the force of the play rests on the anticipated violation of social taboo, and violating social taboos just isn't what it used to be."

Except for the rediscovered poor, the United States is a society of unprecedented abundance. Upper- and middle-class white Americans pamper their children, give them cars and money, send them to college and abroad, and set them up in their own apartments while they are going to school. These young people have leisure and the wherewithal to use it in amusing themselves—only the war is real, which gives a special significance to college as a way of avoiding the war. This abundance means that college-age men and women can travel together, live together, and have a sex life encouraged by their peers, whose opinions they have now come to value more than those of their elders.

Abundance for the young unmarrieds in the city has made it possible to meet other young unmarrieds in new ways. Apartment houses are being built for them; clubs are formed for them, but perhaps the most significant of all the developments is the use of bars, now often called pubs, which serve as meeting places where singles can meet without prejudice. A girl who visits the pub is under no obligation to "go to bed" with the man whom she meets and with whom she may leave. These pubs (and they begin to specialize in different kinds of singles), in a sense, institutionalize a system of bringing together like-minded people; they speed the dating and the trial-and-error process, for they offer this particular group of affluent young people a wide variety of partners to choose from, and they can choose quickly, independently, and frequently (The Pleasures, 1967).

Many observers of the current scene consider the "pill" the most significant single force for increased sexual freedom. A count of the articles listed in the *Reader's Guide to Periodical Literature* reveals that more articles were published about birth control in the period March 1965 to February 1966 than were listed in any ten-year sampling starting with 1925 and ending with 1957. The sampling yielded 89 titles. But we doubt that the pill has added materially to the increase in the numbers of young adults or adolescents who have had premarital sex. Effective techniques of birth control existed, and were used, before the pill. True, the pill makes birth control easier to manage (except for the memory requirement), but romantic love is still important; it makes taking the pill, when no definite partner is available, undesirable. What the pill does is to give sexual freedom to those who are having steady sexual relationships, for then the use of the pill adds to romantic love by making elaborate preparations unnecessary.

According to our crystal ball, which, of course, may be clouded, we have not had a recent or current sexual revolution in terms of behavior. However, there probably has been some increase in the proportion of women who have had premarital intercourse. It is our guess that the increase has occurred largely among women who have had premarital sex only with their spouses-to-be. If there has been a sexual revolution [similar to the 1920's but ideologically different (Berger, 1967)], it is in terms of frankness about sex and the freedom to discuss it. Women have demanded and have achieved more education, more independence, and more social rights; one of these is the right to choose a partner for sex. Men are accepting many of these changes in the status of women and are tempering their insistence on what have generally been considered male prerogatives, for example, the right to demand that a bride be a virgin. Young men today are probably less promiscuous and more monogamous, and their relationships tend to be more stable. Both sexes are approaching a single standard based on sex with affection. We are still in a stage of transition. Despite the title of this article, the only indisputable conclusion which we can draw from the current scene is that we are witnessing the decline, but not yet the fall, of the double standard.

floyd m. martinson

sexual knowledge, values, and behavior
patterns of adolescents

This paper will present the findings of a recent study in Minnesota of sexual behavior patterns of a number of unmarried adolescents. During the 15-month duration of the study, we spent a month apiece in each of four communities—two rural, one suburban, and one inner-city—observing and interviewing around the general theme: What is it like to grow up in a Minnesota community? Or, more specifically: What is it like to grow up *sexually* in a Minnesota community? We were primarily interested in learning of the sources, the extent, and the quality of both sex and family life education. We also analyzed dating histories of 500 Minnesota high school students from throughout the state. These were youth in the leadership group, youth who upon graduation from high school enrolled in college. We also interviewed nearly 200 unwed mothers who received services offered by the Unwed Mother Unit of Lutheran Social Service of Minnesota.

Our study did not cover a complete cross section of the unmarried in Minnesota, but concentrated on that part of the youth population which comes within the middle class. This report does not deal to any degree with the "Gold Coast" or the slums. In some states the high rate of illegitimacy can be traced in large part to the presence in the state of large numbers of culturally-deprived members of some minority group. We have no such convenient scapegoat for the incidence of illegitimacy in Minnesota.

Sexual Behavior and Values

In Minnesota the number of illegitimate births increased tenfold during the last decade and can be expected to increase tenfold in the next decade. The question being asked by Lutheran Social Service of Minnesota, sponsors of the research in question, and its board of directors is this: Are we only to take care of the results of nonmarital sexual activity—unwed parents and their offspring—or do we have a responsibility for influencing, more directly than we are doing at present, the conditions leading to the ever-increasing problem of illegitimacy?

Assuming for the moment that we want to do something about the present situation, it is necessary to understand the situation in some depth. To do so, we must look at the dating practices of these young people and try to understand why they pattern their behavior in the ways they do.

Even these dating practices, however, are conditioned by certain imperatives. First, we must bear in mind that man is a sexual being, without season to his sexual desire. Sexual desire and capability are at their

Reprinted with permission of the author and publisher from *Child Welfare*, Vol. XLVII, No. 7 (1968), 405–410, 426.

height during the years following pubescence. There is little evidence that a healthy adolescent boy does not need regular sexual outlet, through nocturnal emission (wet dreams), masturbation, or some other means. Sexual drive and interest are ever-present factors in the life of a healthy human being. Second, the age period of man's fertility is lengthening with earlier onset of pubescence (perhaps because of better nourishment and care) and later onset of menopause. The age at which people enter marriage is not decreasing. Hence the period calling for continence on the part of the unmarried (according to our traditional morality) is lengthened. Third, man does not live primarily by instinct, but by chosen values. Man is not born with the knowledge of how best to use his sexual powers for his own good or for the good of others. He must be taught. He can learn from responsible adults, through such agencies as the home, the church, and the school. If adults are unwilling or unable to teach, he will still learn, but he will learn from other sources, sources that do not share the reticence on this subject that has characterized home, church, and school. Some of these sources are popular magazines, the movies, and peers. A number of studies of young people show that youth prefer to get their values for important life decisions from responsible adults, primarily their parents, rather than from their peers and the mass media (Bernard, 1961; Brittain, 1963; Smith, 1962). It is when responsible adults fail them that they turn to their peers and other sources.

Claims on Adolescence

Society to date has not provided any direct sexual outlet for the unmarried to which it unequivocally gives its blessing. Sublimation of the sex drive may be what our society ideally recommends for the unmarried, but this requires a degree of maturity that cannot be expected of adolescents. All that is left according to our mores is for the sex drive to be repressed. This is hardly a positive prescription.

Just as the period of adolescence is a time when young people are supposed to be preparing for responsible adulthood in areas of vocation and social adaptation, so is it even more fundamentally a time when sexual nature and identity become central concerns of the maturing individual. The establishment of a comfortable sense of sexual identity and of understanding about the implications of human sexuality for healthy personality development are crucial tasks of adolescence.

In their attempt to understand and relate to persons of the opposite sex youth develop patterns of their own. One of the main patterns is to band together in groups—groups of boys and groups of girls—and to relate to each other within the safety of numbers. In sixth or seventh grade or earlier, often with the assistance or at least the consent of parents, young people plan parties in their homes. They get together and eat potato chips and drink coke, they listen to music, they talk, and they dance. At the same time they are subject to myriad suggestions from the mass media, older youth, and publicized behavior of some adults that there is more to relating to the opposite sex than these things. So they not uncommonly play suggestive games and turn out the lights and "make out." "Making out" at this age usually refers to kissing, necking, and perhaps some degree of petting. As one girl reflects:

> Eighth grade was when I began kissing a boy with some affection. Parties used to be just "make out" parties. It all seems so silly now: the parents would take us to the party; we would go to the basement and neck; and then our parents would take us home again.

Children do not always want such sexual involvement at this early age:

> I shall never forget one Christmas party I attended when I was in seventh grade. There were only couples there. We ate and danced for a while and then everyone sat on the couch with the lights out and kissed. I was so embarrassed and confused at such activity that I left the party early, went home, and cried. I hated that boy from then on and refused to go any place with him.

If the parents are away from home when a party is held, as our subjects reported was often the case, young people may use not only the living or recreation room, but also the bedrooms for "making out." Many high school youths attested from experience that "making out" on a bed is better than "making out" in a car or on a davenport. If father has left the liquor cabinet unlocked, this can help to liven up the party. Drinking is prevalent among Minnesota high school youth. According to a student from a suburb:

> I never went to a party, school or private, where there wasn't some drinking, and usually a lot of it.

The relationship between drinking and sexual activity is indicated in the report of one girl about an outdoor party:

> Accompanied by a case of beer and sleeping bags, we proceeded on an evening canoe trip. We paddled across the lake and set up camp. We drank and proceeded to our sleeping bags. I had never felt so comfortable in a boy's arms.

Dating Patterns

Besides group parties, which continue on into senior high school, some adolescents in Minnesota begin paired dating in junior high school, with parental approval or support. Parents sometimes encourage early dating.

> In the selection of my friends my mother did let me make my own decisions. One time, though, she was quite perturbed when, in sixth grade, I turned down my first date offer because I felt I was too young to accept.

Paired dating develops into going steadily or going steady (they are not the same thing). "Going steadily" means that neither person is dating anyone else. "Going steady" commonly involves the exchange of expressions of love, promises to be faithful, and some outward ritual and symbols, such as the wearing of matching clothing or the giving or exchanging of rings or pins. Judging from our study, few Minnesota high school students "play the field" once they begin dating. They go steadily or steady. They explain that they find it difficult to "play the field." Boys find the idea of a regular date to be satisfying and convenient. Girls find that if they do not agree to go steady, no other boy may ask them out and they may end up with no dates at all.

In dealing with illegitimacy, we have learned that promiscuity is not part of the problem among the young people with whom we work. We find, rather, the problem of paired, unchaperoned dating of high school students who lack the required sophistication to handle intimate involvement.

Intimate dating is greatly facilitated by the availability of family cars. Raising the age requirement for a driver's license could in itself affect the illicit sex problem, especially in rural areas. After a date, that often consists of going to a movie and having a snack, there is usually some time left before the girl's curfew, and many parents set a very late curfew or none at all. For example:

> My mother never set a curfew for me to be home; it was left up to me to be in at a decent hour. As a result we would park or sit in my yard for an hour before going in. This made petting happen very often, whereas if we had to be in earlier, I don't think it would have happened frequently.

This parking time is "free" time. A couple may only sit and talk, but there is tremendous personal and peer pressure to use the parking period for "making out." Some of the more astute young people, and those who want to remain unattached, say that it is in this period before curfew that there are few alternatives to parking and petting. If a boy and girl are going steadily, they need not "make out," but if they are going steady, it is generally understood in the peer group that they will be together a great deal and will "make out" when they are together.

> . . . By the beginning of my junior year, we carried on an enjoyable intimate relationship. I loved our physical relationship. We would park for hours at a time and never tire of necking and petting. We petted heavily until there was nothing left but sexual intercourse. His parents went to church every Sunday night and we usually occupied the house while they were gone. He had seen me without clothes and neither of us felt especially guilty.

"Making out" among high school students is progressive. It begins on first dates with kissing and the light embrace and progresses to deep kissing, body fondling, petting to orgasm, simulated intercourse ("humping"), mutual masturbation, and in some cases sexual intercourse.

Sex played an important part in our life, and though we never did have intercourse, we would pet to orgasm four or five times a week and maybe even more.

Nudity or seminudity is not at all uncommon among Minnesota high school daters. One reported:

... we progressed rapidly from one stage to the next. ... We were alone quite a lot of the time, either at his home or mine, and our involvement became quite serious. Many times we would be in bed with no clothes on. We got so completely caught up in this sexual exploration, however, that all other aspects of our relationship suffered.

Yet, I repeat, Minnesota young people are not promiscuous. This kind of behavior does not occur unless the two like each other very much or think that they are in love. They do not know how to cope with their feelings. They think that it is love rather than sex and that it should not be denied. The more sophisticated may feign love in order to establish grounds for sexual involvement.

I discovered that one does not simply "go steady" in high school. One *must* be in love and admit it. This was just pushing things a little too far for my comfort, but to me this "love" was just a game that brought me an abundance of attention so I played. Little did I realize what I was letting myself in for.

Love makes sexual behavior right. This teenage morality has been labeled "permissiveness with affection." If you have strong affection for the other person, you will be permissive.

Petting to sexual climax is widely utilized by couples who do not want to engage in coitus. Petting is their way of forestalling coitus, which they have been taught to avoid by the parent generation.

We neck and pet a lot and are both able to achieve orgasm without intercourse. We practice mutual masturbation most of the time. We find it to be a very workable technique for letting off tensions that are built up by extensive necking and petting.

Methods of Birth Control

Those who do have sexual intercourse are quite successful in preventing conception. Adolescents as a group are relatively sterile. They utilize the withdrawal method of conception control quite extensively; they use condoms and rhythm to some extent. Girls not uncommonly expect the boy to be responsible for contraception. But, out of ignorance and for other reasons, they do not necessarily insist. In general, it appears that they use contraceptives in a hit or miss fashion—sometimes yes, sometimes no.

The lack of a consistent and reliable source of supply of contraceptives to teenagers in the state, coupled with the lack of sex education, is no doubt a deterrent to their use.

We didn't use any contraceptives, as I was too bashful to buy condoms.

Condom vending machines did appear in service station restrooms in the southern part of the state within the last year. However, the attorney general ruled that they are illegal in Minnesota. The vending machine is a source of supply in many other states. In doing research in an eastern state last summer, we noted that there were as many as three brands of condoms available in vending machines in a single filling station.

These patterns of youth behavior that I have described are not carried out with confidence, with arrogance, or with much assurance that the behavior is right or proper. But youth have not found many adults, or any adults, who appear to understand or care enough about their situation to be helpful.

Available Sex Education

In evaluating the sex education they receive from childhood up until graduation from high school, the majority of Minnesota youth whom we studied are dissatisfied. Too often they feel themselves to be poorly informed and to have formed impressions about sex and sexual behavior that are negative and unwholesome. All of the institutions stand under their indictment—the home, the school, and the church, as well as other media of sex information such as peer group, dates, and the mass media. It is from the mass media and peers that they have learned that sex is fun, and that it is a proper expression of one's feeling for another person. This confuses them. Why have adults let them understand that sex is dirty, shameful, secretive, wrong, or so sacred that it is completely out of reach, while they and their peers have found much about it that is fun, exciting, enjoyable, and meaningful? And why is there this discrepancy between adult and youth experience?

In some homes parents give no sex instruction at all, and in many homes sex is regarded as a taboo subject never to be brought up.

> My parents never came out and actually told me about the facts of life. . . . But indirectly they told me plenty. They made me feel that sex was dirty and something to be ashamed of or embarrassed about. Yet they joked about it and my father always had some "girly" magazines lying around the house. At first I got a big kick out of looking at them, but later they just disgusted me and made me hate being a girl if all that men did was look at our bodies and make jokes about us.

Some Minnesota parents actually refuse to give their children information when asked for it.

> When I asked my mother where the kittens came from in the first place and why they couldn't go back again, she scolded me and said that nice girls don't ask things like this. . . . How I made it through my adolescent years I will never know. My parents, like so many parents, didn't take advantage of the opportunities to explain love and sex expression. They were neither sympathetic nor helpful to my adolescent needs.

Some parents emphasize only the negative, telling only what should not be done. Some of the confusion develops because parents teach rules of behavior without giving the factual information needed to appreciate the rules.

> My parents attempted with all their ability to hide the facts of life from me. . . . I feel that this is why I have always been afraid of sex. . . . Strict dating rules were laid down for me partly because "something" might happen. That something was always left up to my imagination. I was never told what it was. I put myself on a pedestal (as my parents directed), and inwardly scoffed at those who were teasing the boys with their flirting and

suggestive ways. In a way I considered myself better because I knew something that they didn't know. Yet did I? I only knew what I wasn't supposed to do, but not why. I guess my mother never thought that a little knowledge could do more than the strictest set of rules. . . . I sought information by reading romance magazines. My feelings of horror and repulsion grew as I read of the ugly thoughts that boys had in their heads about sleeping with girls and wanting to fondle and caress them. I saw the pain caused by illegitimate babies and out-of-wedlock mothers. I also saw the filthy ways people made love in dirty motels and cabins, in back seats of cars, and lying in the weeds. I could see no beauty in sex. It was hateful and repulsive, and I wanted no part of it.

On the other hand, there are Minnesota youth who are appreciative of relationships with their parents and the sex education received in the home.

> . . . I think that I know more about sex than most of the students my age. Anything that the other students knew about sex was mostly what they had heard and learned from each other. My mother had informed me at an early age about where babies come from, etc. She always told me things about sex in advance so that I never heard anything from the other students that I didn't know or hadn't already heard. As a result . . . I never believed any of the perverted and misleading ideas about sex. I have always respected my mother a great deal for the free and honest way that she spoke to me about sex.

Sex and family life educating can be done in the home, but most parents are not doing it, and I am not hopeful that it will be well done in the home in the foreseeable future. Good sex education in the home, when it does occur, often is a part of an open and affectionate relationship between parent and child. Expecting the child to take the initiative in parent-child discussions on sex is not realistic. The child early becomes embarrassed about sex and may be as unable to bring up the subject with parents as parents are with the child. Good sex education is more than instruction in the physical aspects of love. The few Minnesota students we encountered who have been well taught show their appreciation by wholesome attitudes and values, proper etiquette, and respect for other persons, especially the person being dated.

In speaking about major sources of sex education, a minority of Minnesota high school students mention the school. Whatever Minnesota schools have offered to date in sex education seems to have made little impact on students. I have not made a systematic survey, but I have not run across a single school in Minnesota that in my estimation is doing an adequate job of sex and family life education.

As with the school, so also with the church; the majority of our group of Minnesota youth do not mention the church as a major source of sex and family life education.

> I felt that my church beat around the bush and whatever was said about it was a paraphrase of the idea that "you should keep your body pure and holy because it is a temple of God." I certainly maintain that the sex act is holy. . . . But I believe that my church should not stop with this idea, but go on [to] a more liberal and full explanation about sex, with the unabashed use of technical terms.

An occasional person will mention the sex education he has received under religious auspices with appreciation. More characteristically, however, young people appear to be critical of sex education received under religious auspices. The concept of body-soul dualism and the lower nature of the body is a common impression left by religious instructors.

A commonly mentioned source of sex information is peers. Sex is a major topic of conversation among both sexes. The person one is dating often becomes a source of sex instruction especially in those cases where responsible educational agencies in the community have not done a satisfactory job. Occasionally, a young person will look back with satisfaction to the high school boy friend or girl friend as a source of sex education.

> I know now that if I ever marry I will always consider my years with him as a

healthy experience and one to be cherished and never ashamed of. I value our relationship as one that helped both of us in our attitude toward goals and ideals to try to attain. I have never experienced any other sexual partners besides him. . . . I am not condemning my relationship with him, but only wish that we had used more discretion and that it had happened when we were both more mature, for I feel that it would have brought less conflict.

But persons whose primary source of sex education has been the date often give the date a low rating as source of information.

Conclusion

We conclude our report with the general observation that many Minnesota high school graduates look back upon going steady in high school as having been a mistake. The following case is not atypical:

> It is a pity that we had such a strong association when we were so young. Had we been older, we probably would have known much more about sex and about life in general. . . . I am sure that if we had been older we would have realized the extreme seriousness of the results of sexual intercourse. To us, then, a pregnancy seemed so impossible. Now we know how very possible it was and how it could have ruined both of our lives. When I have children of my own, I do not think I will let them go steady.

These are some of the facts we learned about the sexual behavior and attitudes of the young people we studied. We believe that these behavior patterns and these confused, searching attitudes are typical of today's middle-class adolescent. It is our firm conclusion that if young people are to develop a healthy and mature sexuality, they need help.

hershel d. thornburg

sex education: an uncertain quest

Most literature on family life and sex education focuses on (1) objectives of a sex education program, (2) student needs for sex education (Thornburg, 1968), (3) problems in the implementation and administration of a sex program, and (4) evaluating sex education. Cognizant of these issues, the following comments are written to consider necessary problems to be encountered in helping youth in their search for finding a code of practiced sexuality.

The problem is that adolescents are physically adult, yet mentally unprepared for adult life. Growth, as we usually study it, involves not only change in form but also change in function and status. After boys and girls reach puberty and have gained the physical ability to have sexual relations, they are thrown into many heterosexual social experiences. Building an increasing dependence on peer groups and increasing an awareness of one's own physical capabilities throw most adolescents into a dilemma about sex. The social pressures combined with basic biological urges precipitate most adolescent sexual behavior. There is simply no denying that adolescents are physically ready for sexual activity.

The dilemma heightens when adolescents encounter mental and emotional blockades to sexual expression. The mores built

Reprinted by permission of the author and the Arizona Education Association from H. D. Thornburg, *Sex Education in the Public Schools*. Phoenix: Arizona Education Association, 1969, Chap. 5.

into our society still treat sexual activity between unmarried persons ambiguously. Most adolescents find difficulty in fitting the so widely acclaimed relaxed attitude about sex into their behavioral patterns. This lack of social definition combined with the limited emotional experiences of most adolescents intensifies their dilemma.

Naivete demands a toll from the adolescent. With the upsurge in changing social and moral definition, we cannot afford to let our youth ride the crest of popular sexual behavior at great mental and emotional expense. They must be assisted in learning the consequences of engaging in differing sexual expressions. Many adolescents experience sex with a natural, simple candor. The well-known emotional binds so frequently associated with sexuality often do not accompany the adolescent's sexual behavior. Yet, because of all the popular verbiage about sex our youth are exposed to, and because of the many delusions they have, some systematic, enlightening approach to human sexuality must be attempted. Without it the cost of naivete may be too much.

Who is to educate? Most people feel that the desirable place for sex education is within the home. While the family could do a better job than other units in providing children with sex knowledge and information, there are other forces that have an impact on sex education: the school, the church, mass media, and peer groups.

Most parents believe that discussions

about human sexuality should be approached guardedly. Through their embarrassment, lack of knowledge, or simple neglect, many parents never get around to discussing sex with their children. When it is discussed, most adolescents feel they are being preached to concerning negative aspects of sex. Only limited discussion about the positive features of human sexuality is heard. Rarely is it put within the framework of family life. The result has been a reluctance on the part of adolescents to discuss sexual matters with their parents.

Realizing the dilemma of the adolescent quest for sex information, educators have become concerned about the insufficient knowledge and the social problems that arise from a lack of definition of human sexuality. Therefore, numerous school districts are planning, or have already incorporated a program in family life and sex education into the curriculum to give our youth accurate and complete information in hopes of reducing their naivete. We must remember—the school is not trying to usurp the authority of the home or church. It is simply trying to focus on sexual dilemmas of youth so that a reasonable code of practical sexuality can emerge.

The influence of mass media must also be considered. Motion pictures, television, and many magazines all allude to sexual conduct. The excitement, thrills, and naturalness of sex are vividly portrayed. Most sexual behaviors are presented in a way that lures or entices sexual play without consequence. While the effects of these visual barrages have not been fully ascertained, they are obviously powerful sources for adolescents to pick up notions about sex, although they often see only a partial picture of what sex is all about.

The most profound factor of sexual behavior among youth is the social impact of the peer group. As was reported earlier, more information about sex comes from peers than any other source. Off-the-cuff conversations, assessment of what the "in-crowd" is doing, and actual sexual experiences serve to educate our youth, though they do not insure them as to the accuracy of information received.

Youth share common problems and experiences. Youth also share attitudes that make sense. Sex is no exception. Adolescents share the accuracies of sexuality as well as its inaccuracies. The challenge of providing youth with factual information is a great one. It is a topic about which they themselves invite discussion. And it is a topic to which they will listen in a responsible manner. Today's challenge is to understand. The challenge is to our adults. We need to understand and provide understanding for our youth. We should provide guidelines which will encourage youth to develop attitudes and values conducive to mature and responsible sexuality. Beyond that we must provide an appreciation of the positive satisfactions that wholesome human relations can bring in family life.

The challenge is to our schools and community. The need is interaction over new curricula. The pursuit is in behalf of our youth. The community must support the school and the teacher who is teaching sex education. The school must consider the community in developing its program. The school and its responsible teachers must reassure the community. Both must continually interact so roles do not become ambiguous and bruising conflicts develop. Above all, school and community must agree on this: Our youth need adequate, consistent, and formative information. They need our help to emerge eventually with a practical code of human sexuality. After all, they are *our* youth.

bernard rosenberg

joseph bensman

sexual patterns in three ethnic subcultures
of an american underclass

Abstract: Three American ethnic subcultures, all consisting of transmigrated
groups living in poverty, were studied and
the sexual patterns of the youth described.
The groups consisted of white Appalachians
living in Chicago, Negroes in Washington,
D.C., and Puerto Ricans in New York.
Sharply differentiated patterns of sexual
behavior, involving conquest, sex education,
sex misinformation, attitudes toward
females, responsibility, and affect were discovered, and these patterns are reflected in
the language of the subcultures, particularly
in their argot. The underclass sexual mores
differ from those of the American middle
class, but not more than they differ from
each other among the three ethnic groups.
Sexual practices are related to general life
styles, and reflect ghettoization, subcultural
isolation, and short-range hedonism in
groups only recently transplanted from
their rural areas of origin.

No American who wishes to discuss love and
sex can avoid the long Western tradition from
within which we, knowingly or unknowingly,
come by all our perspectives. Jerusalem,
Athens, Rome, and their several sequelae
constitute, or symbolize, that tradition. From
it, that is to say, from the Hellenic and
Judaeo-Christian past, Western man derives

Reprinted with permission of the authors and publisher
from the Annals of the American Academy of Political and Social
Sciences, 1968, 376, 61-75.

not only certain prescriptions and prohibitions, but a whole framework of ideas, concepts, and theories that are his heavy
cultural burden. Diffusion and dilution notwithstanding, the sexual analyst and those he
discusses share that burden. To be sure, neither need recognize or acknowledge the connection that binds them together in an
inescapable matrix.

We have come to our present sexual pass
through devious and tangled paths, still
strewn with innumerable laws, parables, images, aftereffects, and reflections. In this
brief statement, we can do no more than
touch upon a few highlights which may illumi-
nate part of our rich and varied background.

For example, the poems of Sappho and
those of Ovid, like a score of other such
sources—including philosophical schools,
and religious cults—have in common that
they celebrate erotic joy. All of them say to us
that love (as in the story of Ruth) and sex (as
in the mythopoeic figure of Priapus) should
involve deep feeling or great pleasure. This
notion is currently fashionable among many
otherwise disenchanted, proudly "rational,"
and highly sophisticated people. At the same
time, they are affected by those provisions of
the Decalogue, as interpreted by Talmudic
and Scholastic commentators, that set
severe limits upon love and sexuality while

emphasizing the responsibilities inherent in sacramental and indissoluble relationships whose purpose is solely reproductive.

With *eros* and *agape,* Plato spiritualized sex. St. Augustine, and, later on, many of the Schoolmen who introduced Aristotelian modifications, took over these Platonic ideas. In various guises, they became essential to both the Catholic and Protestant world view. The Christian churches also fashioned sexual codes of their own which, even when they were systematically violated, produced discrete and historically specialized sexual behavior. In Europe and America, sexual renunciation, with deep intellectual and religious roots, always seems to have had an obverse side, or to have proceeded in dialectical sequence to eroticism. Thus, to condemn the pleasures of the flesh may itself entail, or simply lead to, precisely those pleasures. The medieval denial of sex was in no way incompatible with chivalry and romantic love as practiced at the courts of Aquitaine and Provence. Here, if anywhere, as Denis de Rougemont has shown, are the beginnings of a romantic conception made universally familiar in our time by way of Hollywood films. Dante and Beatrice, Tristan and Iseult, or Romeo and Juliet are prototypic cases in which sexual desire feeds upon the loved one's permanent inaccessibility.

Seventeenth-century Puritanism and nineteenth-century Victorianism, each in its complex and contradictory manner, left us with a dualistic dogma whose force is not yet fully spent. Mind and body (therefore, love and sex) were pitted against each other. As the underside of Victorian life is subjected to increasing exposure, one beholds not only the sexually etherealized woman of virtue, but her fallen sister, whether given to prostitution or not, who is cynically and mercilessly exploited. As hitherto unpublishable memoirs reach the contemporary reader, he comes to know the moralistic upper-class gentleman who collects pornography, indulges in exotic, probably inverted and polymorphous, perverse sexual tastes while practicing hypocrisy, if not perfecting it to a high art.

Victorianism and the revolt against it are our immediate antecedents. And that revolt is largely ideological. The exaltation of eroticism tends to be academic. Proponents of "sexual freedom" contrast it favorably with artificial and hypocritical Victorian conventions. Beginning with feminism as a political movement, proceeding in the 1920's under banners like companionate or trial marriage, through a strident call for emancipation and liberation, to the present "sexual revolution," learned men have set forth their ideas. Hedonists and rationalists, champions of homosexuality, of a return to infantile gratification with "love's body" and no mere fixation on genital pleasure: here is a peculiar gamut from Bertrand Russell to Albert Ellis, Herbert Marcuse, and Norman O. Brown. None of them, the logician, the psychotherapist, the Hegelian, or the Classical scholar, is primarily interested in the restoration of "natural" sexuality. All of them are passionately interested in proving or disproving theories.

Even Sigmund Freud, who did more than anyone else to free Western thought from the straightjacket of Victorianism, was himself a puritan—in perhaps the best Biblical sense of the term. Furthermore, Freud, in his sexual speculations and investigations, drew heavily upon Greek philosophy, specifically the ideas of *agape, eros,* and *caritas.* Freud's "scientific" attitude toward sex is actually permeated with several of the oldest concepts of antiquity—with which they are perfectly continuous. Insofar as Freudian psychology fuels the sexual revolution, it is directed not at the demolition of Western norms, but only at one narrow version of a complicated social heritage.

Like speech, dress, manners, and a score of other visible stigmata, conduct in the sexual sphere has always been class-bound. To speak of the mores dominant in any period is necessarily to be elliptical. For example, the Victorian double standard was, in its own time, mainly an upper-middle-class phenomenon, rarely affecting higher and lower social strata. Similarly, the revolt against it seems to have liberated segments of the middle class at least from the idea of sexual repression. For some time now, as Theodore Dreiser noted over and over in his early novels, the relatively stable blue-collar working class has best exemplified puritanical prudery and sexual hypocrisy.

All the while, romantic writers, artists, and social scientists have been searching for "genuine" or "natural" sexuality, embodied in an eroticized and newly ennobled savage, uncontaminated by that odious sophistication which reduces the physical expression of love to *le contact de deux epidermes.* Thus occurs the idealization of peasants, "earthmen," primitives, those sexually spontaneous and unalienated humans who—when viewed from a safe distance—look so free and easy in all their ways. Are there such groups of people within the underclass of our own society? Does their alleged culture of poverty so far remove them from Western civilization that research in their midst will reveal what love and sex are really like when they are emancipated from history and intellectuality?

The Three Ethnic Subcultures

These are some of the questions implicit in the material that follows.[1] Three miserably, and more or less equally, impoverished areas in New York, Chicago, and Washington, D.C., were selected for prolonged study. Lander and his associates held poverty constant and introduced ethnicity as the variable. They concentrated on all the inhabitants of one social block (with dwellings that face each other) in each of the three cities. In New York, most of the subjects were Puerto Ricans, in Chicago, Appalachian whites, and in Washington, Negroes. Intensive nondirected "tandem interviews" (with two interviewers and one respondent) yielded the qualitative data about adolescent youth that we cite and sift in our analysis.

All three of these ethnic groups are composed largely of recent migrants, who had come to the urban centers from other parts of the United States (including Puerto Rico), and who had brought with them many of their ways of life, perhaps even accentuated by contrast with their new environment and their new neighbors.

A common culture presupposes that those who belong to it speak the same language. There is such a language for all Americans as there is an overarching culture that unifies urban dwellers and farmers, the

[1] This essay stems from a much larger study conceived and directed by Bernard Lander under multiple sponsorship, including the President's Committee on Juvenile Delinquency and Youth Crime, Notre Dame University, and the Lavanburg Corner House Foundation.

young and the old, the privileged and the underprivileged. Subcultural segmentation produces "special languages" within the larger linguistic community, and they are intelligible only to initiates, that is, members of ethnic, occupational, regional, and religious groups. That the broadly conceptualized culture (or subculture) of poverty is somewhat illusory can be demonstrated by the variegated speech patterns characteristic of poor Appalachian whites, Negroes, and Puerto Ricans. Indeed, for each of our populations, it would be possible to assemble a glossary of terms widely used by insiders but meaningless to most outsiders. How luxuriant local variation takes place (in meaning, accent, and value) is the proper subject matter of a highly technical discipline called ethnolinguistics. It is not our intention to turn that discipline loose on data gathered for other purposes. Nevertheless, this much must be said: each group living in its own slum moves towards a certain linguistic homogeneity, bringing ancestral speech ways, borrowing symbols from the larger society, and synthesizing them into distinctive configurations. Peculiarities of speech are a rough index of differential association and cultural isolation. Unique idioms emerge from intense in-group living, and disappear at the opposite pole of full acculturation. In between, we find a complex mixture reflecting uneven exposure to the wider institutional order, which is itself in constant flux. A few illustrations from the heterosexual sphere may be in order.

Chicago

In our sample, the adolescent males among the New York Puerto Ricans and Washington Negroes are unresponsive to questions about dating. The word does not appear in their lexicon, and, as it turns out, this fact points to a substantive difference in behavior between these boys and those in Chicago. Every respondent among the Chicago Appalachian whites knows what a date is. One at first defines it as "goin' out with a fox," then adds, "You just go out driving, make some love, catch a crib—and that's all." Here, indeed, are the cadences, the inflections, and the semantics of a special language in which "fox" means girl and "crib" stands for house or apartment, which, in turn, signifies a trysting place that one "catches" along with the "fox." Such expressions may have their origin in the hill country of Kentucky and Alabama, whence they were transplanted to the Midwest and, merged with much else, produced a dynamic amalgam that cannot be duplicated elsewhere.

There are fuzzy edges around every word that is variously defined not only at different levels of the social hierarchy, but within any one level. For those who generalize in the grand manner, dating is understood to be "an American" phenomenon; the more sophisticated family sociologists (who prepare textbooks for college students) see it as a peculiar ritual, a courtship pattern, practiced by middle-class youth in the United States. In our samplings of the underclass, only the poor white teen-agers date, and they do so in ways similar to and dissimilar from those of their middle-class counterparts. The telephone, for instance, plays no great part in their activities, as it does among more privileged adolescents, but the automobile is central. Neither matters much with Puerto Ricans and Negroes.

The Chicago boys, who will sometimes commit crimes to get a car, and need it to commit other crimes, and whose vocabulary is rich with the knowledge they have of car parts, may be said to live in a car complex. This circumstance provides them with a degree of physical mobility far greater than that of any other economically deprived group we have studied. In a crisis, occasioned, say, by the impregnation of a girl friend (scarcely a rare occurrence), they can always take to the road, ranging widely over Illinois and adjacent states. The automobile liberates them, up to a point, not only from their constricted neighborhood, but from the metropolis itself. And, given the car, they are able to date girls in a more or less conventional manner. The "portable bedroom" can be used for preliminary sex play most conveniently at drive-in movies, where two or three couples commonly occupy one car. Asked what he usually does on a date, a fifteen-year-old Chicago boy replies, in part:

If your friend's got a girl he's taking to the drive-in, you take her with him. And you take your girl to the show, go out to eat, dance, stuff like that.

On the average, what does a date cost?

Well, if you go to a show, you won't have to spend but about, at the most, five, maybe six dollars. . . . If you go to the drive-in, you spend a dollar and a half for each one to get in. That's three dollars. Give the kid who's driving the car a buck, split the gas bill, you know, help to pay for some of the gas—and you eat. Oh, it costs you about six dollars.

Bowling and roller-skating are other diversions deemed to be suitable on dates in our Chicago sample. Neither is a popular boy-girl pastime in the other cities—where boys like sports that they play with other boys. Pickups are made on the street from a car, in neighborhood movie houses, and in teen-age bars which are frequented with great regularity only by the Appalachians.

All of this sounds a great deal like the textbook account, even to a general preference for double-dating. Yet, the reasons behind that preference give us a clue to something different, and specific to the Chicago group, namely, that a heavy streak of violence is woven into the texture of their heterosexual behavior. Hence: "I like to go out with other couples because it's better when you travel together. When you're alone, there's always other guys trying to start trouble." You date, but you appear alone with a girl at your own peril, as this little vignette makes clear:

I saw her walking down the hall with another boy, and I got pretty jealous. I started saying, "If you like that guy so much, go ahead and go out with him," and he walked up and started smartin' off to me. So I hit him, and then I beat him up. She turned around and slapped me. She called me a brute or something. . . . So that didn't hit me just right, and I said, "Forget it."

If a date culminates in sexual intercourse, it is also useful to have someone else along:

I was going with a girl. She was sixteen. She squealed on me, and they tried to get me on statutory rape. And, oh, she gave 'em a big long story, trying to get me into a lot of trouble. But there was another kid along with me on that date. And she claimed that he held her down and that I held her down. But this boy's stories matched and hers didn't. Otherwise, I would have been sunk.

With dating, there go the lineaments of a rating-dating complex, which does not precisely parallel Willard Waller's famous description of a widespread campus phenomenon, but does imply a measure of respect for the girls one dates, by contrast with the disrespect accorded girls and older women who are nothing but sexual objects. The following example is somewhat extreme but highly indicative:

> I consider a girl you go out with and a girl you have intercourse with two different kinds of girls. There's a girl I date. I like to hold hands with her and make out with her, kiss her, but that's as far as I want to go with any girl I take out. If I like the girl, I don't want to mess her up. But then, there is the other girls I just don't care about because they give it to the other guys—which means they don't care too much for theirselves.

The type of boy who makes this provisionally puritanical division between good girls (with lovers who hold back from final consummation) and bad girls who "give it to the other guys," is yet capable of treating "good girls" with even greater harshness. This double standard means that there are separate norms; less is expected of the promiscuous girl, much more of the girl you date who may, after all, become your wife. If so, unquestioning submission to male authority is expected:

> What if you married a girl who talked back to you? What would you do?
> Shut her up.
> How?
> Well, I'd fix her where she wasn't able to talk too much.

The specter of violence is omnipresent. It may issue from association with either type of girl, and although there are always two types, criteria for establishing them vary. (Asked whether he still considers girls decent if they go to bed with him, a Chicago boy answers, "It's a matter of how hard I have to work. If I have to work real hard I think a lot of them. If they give it to me right off I think they're pigs.") Infidelity in a girl friend will ordinarily provoke a physical assault of some sort. What to do if the woman you marry is unfaithful? "Beat the shit out of her" is the semiautomatic response.

Acts of aggression connected with sex are, no doubt, intensified by heavy consumption of alcohol. Sex, liquor, and violence form

a *Gestalt* in Chicago not nearly so discernible in New York or Washington. In another context, whiskey and beer act as a catalyst for serious fighting, possibly with recourse to knives and firearms. In the sexual context, alcohol is also believed to be useful as a means of emboldening the boy and rendering the girl more compliant to his advances:

> Do the girls get pretty wild when they've had a few drinks?
> Yes.
> Do most of the guys try to get the girls loaded?
> Yes.
> How often are you successful?
> We're not very successful at getting them loaded. I mean that takes a little money.

Beer is cheaper than whiskey and favored for that reason; a low alcohol content notwithstanding, it is believed to serve the purpose. Girls plied with beer are considered "better," that is, more available, than those who remain unlubricated. They can more easily be "cut"—which is typical and revealing Chicago argot for the sex act.

New York City

In the New York sample, there is no "cutting." The first few interviews with Puerto Rican youth revealed little about sex, a topic concerning which we had not anticipated that there would be unusual reticence. The breakdown in communication turned out to be no more than terminological. Once in possession of key words and phrases, the interviewers encountered no serious resistance to the free discussion of plain and fancy sex. There are taboo topics, notably religion as it shades off into magic, but sex is not one of them. The linguistic breakthrough occurred in this matter when a resident observer advised us to ask about "scheming." We did so, causing faces to light up that had remained blank as long as we struggled vainly to find the right conventional or unconventional sexual expression. "Scheming" was that expression. Equivalent, in a way, to "cutting" which suggests sex-and-sadism, "scheming" has mildly conspiratorial overtones. It stands for kissing, necking, petting, and full sexual consummation, everything from prepubertal exploration to real coitus, which is secret, exploitative, and pleasurable, but seldom brutal. With appropriate language, much information can be elicited, and comic misunderstandings are left behind. (To the question, "Did you ever have a girl sexually?" the young Puerto Rican respondent answers by asking, "Did I ever have a girl *sectionally?*" And some minutes are consumed, to no avail, in disentangling the adverbs. We want to know from another boy whether he goes to bed with girls, whether he sleeps with them, and he takes us literally: "No. I sleep by myself, in my own bed.")

Scheming is initiated at parties, and parties are called sets. They function as substitutes for going out, picking up, and dating. Young people at or around twenty may have apartments of their own which, like any of many vacant apartments on the block, can be used for sets, as they can be and are used for private or collective sexual adventures. At sets, boys and girls meet, play records, dance, drink beer or whiskey more or less moderately, smoke cigarettes and take pot more or less immoderately, and, under dim colored lights, engage in uninhibited foreplay. With twenty or more in attendance, sets seem to be fairly large affairs, and while some are organized during the week by hedonistic truants, there are sure to be others around the clock on week-ends. Since the youngsters use stimulants and depressants that are costly, and Saturday is the traditional day for pilfering small objects whose sale produces money with which to buy supplies, the best sets are most likely to occur on Saturday nights. You drink a little, you smoke a lot, you are high, a girl offers to dance with you, and by and by, when the dim lights go out altogether, you fondle her. Presently, you step outside with your girl and scheme in the hallway, at her place if no one is at home, on a rooftop—this one, or another at the nearby housing project. And:

> If you got a really good friend, and the girl is willing if she's really bad off or somethin', you know what she will do? *She'll pull the train.*
> Pull the train?
> Yes, that's what we call it: pulling the train. You take one chance. Then another guy takes a chance. You know.
> Usually, how many guys are there?
> Two.
> Not like ten guys with one girl?
> Oh, depends like on what kind of a girl.
> . . . I been in a situation with about six guys.

"Pulling the train" is by no means an everyday occurrence. Sets are. They may be regarded as a spontaneous expression of youth culture, an informal device contrived by teen-agers for their own pleasure, a technique for circumventing official and established organizations, an escape from uplift sponsored by benevolent adults. Sets provide an arena—or constitute a preparation—for scheming, which, in most cases, means private and secret sexual activity. Boys do boast, with a probable admixture of phantasy and exaggeration, about sexual conquests, but they are loath to name names and thus cause "trouble" for themselves or their girl friends. The set in which they begin to participate at about age fifteen is understood to be somewhat illicit. It may become a pot party or a sex party (our respondents are ambivalent and divided among themselves about which they like best)—and either one, if publicized, can lead to unpleasant sanctions.

Washington, D.C.

Boy-girl relations in the Washington poor Negro community are neither as car- and show-centered as in the Chicago white group nor as party-centered as in the New York Puerto Rican group. In Washington, the school, despite all its deficiencies, is much more pivotal than we would have supposed. Young people attend school dances now and then, meet classmates formally and informally, and, while ungoverned by any particular protocol, they begin to "go out" with one another. Soon there is sex play, and, in many cases, real sexual involvement. Things tend to begin in school, and there, too, the "facts of life" are transmitted most frequently and most effectively. Only in our Washington Negro sample do high school children use technical (now and then garbled) scientific terms for the sex act and the sex organs. They describe human reproduction as it has been explained to them by their biology teachers:

> We had it in school. I know how the sperms come down, when a boy is having sex relations with a girl; they meet the egg, go up through the vagina, stay in the womb and grow month after month. And then after a period of time, the woman have a baby.
> We're supposed to do that next half, after we finish with music (find out where babies come from and things like that).

Well, I know the process of starting—I mean, you have to have two unions, I mean a fusion of, uh, male and female, between the two organs. I mean the vulva and the, um, penis. The vulva and the penis. And, um, it takes a union of sperm and meeting with the egg. And after that, I know the situation of—what do you call it?—the embry—yeah, embry—and that's the first stage of the child. . . . And the food which the child receives comes from the navel of the mother. It's connected to the child, I believe mouth-to-navel, something like that. And after a nine month period, the child's supposed to be born.

A boy whose parents told him "all about it" at age twelve, says:

They explained it to me, that it was the entrance of the penis into the woman's vulva. I mean, they used other terms, but that's the terms I would use because, let's say, I'm more up on it now, on this education.

Again:

Well, uh, let's see, when the sperm, I think goes into the vagina, something like that, then, it meets the other sperm I think, and it starts doing something.

However imperfectly they may have absorbed their biology lessons, these teenagers show a degree of sophistication unavailable to their counterparts among the New York Puerto Ricans and in Chicago, where sexual knowledge is more likely to be associated with the street—and its earthy language—than with the classroom. (With the Puerto Ricans, a self-taught, semi-demi-social worker has helpfully taken it upon himself to provide some sex instruction in yet another linguistic style—largely Spanish, partly English argot.) For children to seek or parents to offer information, even when it is urgently needed, seems to be a rare occurrence. (We suspect that parent-youth embarrassment on this score is a class phenomenon. There is reason to believe that the middle-class parent now speaks freely to his children about the facts of life while evading questions about the facts of death.) The young mother of two illegitimate children in Washington tells us that she developed early: "At the age of twelve I was as developed as any girl of fourteen or fifteen. Being young, I never paid too much attention to it, but older people in the community noticed." As she recounts it, men got fresh; some began to follow her home, and she took to making "smart" remarks. Then, after awhile, "I had one man run me home from school." She ran and found sanctuary on a neighbor's porch, and "the man started to come after me till he looked up and spotted a lady and another man on the porch. After that my mother came over, and we told her about it, and the three of them walked around, but they didn't see him." This incident was but the first of several, including one "proposition" from a preacher, about which the mother was informed. She still divulged nothing to her daughter, and the daughter observes, "I just could not bring myself to look up at my mother and ask her what was happening."

The whole story, "the nitty gritty," came from experience with "fellows," who, however, were judged to be stupid, as well as girls on the street and an older sister. From her own account, but never officially, she was a sexual delinquent by age thirteen.

On the other hand, in Washington, a Negro boy may experience sexual initiation under his father's auspices. If there is an older woman who wishes to "come some," that is, who wishes to have a sex partner, the father sometimes encourages his son to co-operate. We have one such case on record:

She (the older woman) came down to see my sister, and she started liking me. She started paying my way to the movies and all that. So my father told me to go on and do it. So I did. . . . He say, "I know you going to do it when I ain't around." So he gave me a protector, and I go on and do it. . . . He say we were going to do it behind his back anyhow, and that he just wanted to help me along. I ain't never used the protection, though.

Attitude Comparisons

Although he tends to confuse protection against venereal disease with protection against pregnancy, the Negro teen-ager is generally more knowledgeable about this, too, than his Puerto Rican or poor white age mate. He more often recognizes and applies terms like contraceptive, diaphragm, coil, prophylactic, or rubber—for one reason, because he more often knows what they mean. Not that he or his girl friend is much inclined to use any of these objects, for their interposition threatens the individual with loss of his "cool"—an important but amorphous quality which must be maintained at all times. Although among all three ethnic samples, only a minority favor contraception, the Negro youth understand best, and Puerto Rican youth least, just what it is that they habitually decline to use. And, while amorality or *anomie* tends to prevail in sexual matters, it assumes a degree of egocentricity among the poor white boys unequalled elsewhere. In this exchange, we have an extreme but not atypical expression of the Chicago attitude:

> Do you ever use contraceptives?
> Nope.
> How about women? Do they ever use anything?
> Nope.
> Do you ever think about it?
> Nope.
> Are you afraid of what might happen?
> Nope. *They can't touch me. I'm under age.*

Seeing it exclusively from his own standpoint, and then only insofar as his conduct may lead to legal jeopardy, he is not afraid of making girls pregnant. Later on, when he does come of age, in order to avoid possible charges of statutory rape, such a boy will prefer sexual relations with older women. Even then, this respondent insists, he "ain't gonna use anything." Told by the interviewer about diaphragms and how they work, he vehemently protests against their use. They would interfere with his pleasure: "Might get in my way." To be sure, without contraception, it is possible to spawn an illegitimate child, something he at first claims to have done at least once—before second thoughts cause him to cast doubt on the "mother's" veracity. This is his complete verbatim statement on the matter:

> She told me we were gonna have a kid. I said "Tough." She said, "Ain't it though?" I said, "What you gonna do about it?" She said, "I ain't gonna do nothin' about it. How about you?" I said nothin'. She said, "That's good." I said goodbye and she said goodbye. And that's the last I saw of her. I mean I *saw* her in school. She's still goin' to school. I don't believe that we had a kid, though. She just said we did.

Risk or no risk, boys are generally hostile to the idea of prophylaxis. One objection is phrased purely in terms of the pleasure principle, most colorfully by a Chicago boy who explains why he never uses anything like a rubber, "I tried it once. It's like riding a horse with a saddle instead of bareback." Is he afraid of "knocking a girl up"? Answer: "Sure. *I worry about it afterwards.* I guess I'm lucky so far. That's all." The cost factor appears again in Chicago where the poor-white boys are markedly more reluctant than the Negroes and Puerto Ricans in Washington and New York, respectively, to spend money on contraceptive frills. At the climactic moment, their impecuniosity can be frustrating. As a rule, in the white population, girls are no more eager than boys to insure against pregnancy, but once in awhile they are:

> Oh, I've used them a couple of times. Like one time, a broad got all worried, and she told us to lay off. . . . We had her pants off and everything. She ask me if I didn't have some rubbers. Uh-uh. "Get off." I had to wait a little longer. I didn't have any money either.

In the Chicago underclass, there is, then, a minimum of anxiety about the consequences of sexual intercourse, a strong disinclination to take any responsibility for what happens. Most boys are poorly informed and unconcerned about measures taken or not taken by their sex partners. "I wouldn't know if they did or not [use anything to prevent pregnancy]. I don't care if they do or not." Does he know what girls might do to protect themselves? "Well, there's with the hot water, like that. Then, there's, they press on their stomachs someplace . . . on some cords, usually when you get done, the girl has to go to the bathroom. She goes in, she presses here and there, and it all comes out. They claim that's one of the best ways." Ignorance of the facts should not be discounted, but knowledge may or may not be correlative with action. Even if a girl asks for restraint, so that she will not have to cope with unwed motherhood, the boy is likely to refuse:

> Do many girls ask you to stop before you come?
> Most don't. Some do.
> They don't want to get pregnant?
> That's right.
> Do you usually oblige them?
> Well, not usually, no.

Biologists like Ashley-Montagu have established the existence of adolescent sterility, a period after the onset of puberty during which reproduction presumably cannot take place. Widespread premarital sexual experimentation, not always related to courtship, among "primitive peoples" to whom puritanism is unknown, has been noted for over a century. Adolescent sterility helps anthropologists to account for the smoothness with which such relations occur. In ever larger sectors of our own society, birth control has "sterilized" teen-agers, thereby insuring them against the many complications of illegitimacy. Neither of these mechanisms seems to be significantly operative in any of our cities. Adolescent *fertility* is high, and respondents (males only slightly more so than females) express a very nearly uniform distaste for every kind of contraceptive device. Significant differences are, in the first instance, more attitudinal than behavioral. How much responsibility does a boy who has got his girl with child feel? Some in the Puerto Ricans and Negroes of New York and Washington; virtually none in the whites of Chicago. That unimpeded sexual contact can and does lead to babies is something a transplanted Appalachian white boy is likely to know only too well. For the most part, he "couldn't care less"; the interviewer asks such a boy: "What's stopping you from knocking up girls?" Answer: "Nothin'. I've got four kids, maybe five. Two here in Chicago, two in Wisconsin, and when I left Wisconsin, I heard there was one more." Does he support any of them? "Shit no." After getting a girl pregnant, "I just take off."

Less able to "take off," as careless but more likely to be "trapped," hemmed in on every side, the New York Puerto Rican boy generally finds insemination of his girl friends a worrisome matter. It is seldom a question of direct responsibility to the "victim"—which would presuppose a kind of socialization or internalization of standards evident neither among "good boys" nor among "bad boys." What if the girl has a baby? "Maybe the parents might make him marry her." Coercion under these circumstances into unwanted matrimony is a nightmare in the New York group to the like of which no one in Chicago ever alludes. We pursue the issue one step farther: "Suppose they didn't make you. Would you marry her

anyhow?" The response is a derisive, "Nah!" But then we want to know whether he would support the baby, and to this the answer is a subculturally typical *yes.* Even if, in order to do so, he would have to quit school (and this respondent values school)? Yes, even so, although, "that would be pretty bad."

The qualitative difference we wish to point up is more than a matter of nuance. Lloyd Warner and his associates were able to rank people, whom they interviewed in Yankee City, by class-typed responses to interview questions. We, in turn, can situate boys and girls (and could do so "blind," that is, without any accompanying data) in one of three impoverished subcultures, by their responses to a variety of straightforward, nondirective, and projective questions. Thus, a Puerto Rican boy who presents a tougher "front" than the one just quoted above is still unmistakably a Puerto Rican, and not an Appalachian or Negro boy:

> Do you try to avoid getting a girl pregnant or don't you care?
> I try to avoid it.
> Suppose you did, and she found out where you lived?
> I'd have to marry the broad.
> Would you like that?
> No, that's a hell of a mess.

The less insouciant type, a boy, for instance, whose presentation of self is somewhat gentler, simply says of the hypothetical girl he has impregnated: "You've got to marry her," leaving implicit why you have got to.

Since precautions to avert childbirth are unpopular, and pregnancy takes place willy-nilly, abortions should be common. If so, boys in Chicago tend to feel that it is no business of theirs. How different is the attitude that emerges in New York where, to select one of many examples, an advanced adolescent remarks apropos a girl friend who might get pregnant, "If I liked the girl enough I would marry her, or something." Suppose he didn't like her all that much, would he still feel obligated? "Yeah." In what way, we wonder. Would he arrange for an abortion? "No. That would mess her up too much. . . . Cause some ladies, they just do it to get money out of it; they don't really do it to help a person at all." Nonmedical abortionists, charging about eighty dollars a job, are said to abound on the street. Nevertheless, the white boys recoil from availing themselves of these services, obviously not for financial reasons, which are important in Chicago, since the stated alternative, assuming marital or non-marital responsibility for support, would be so much costlier than disposition of an undesired fetus.

The differential warmth, involvement, and concern for "the other" in sexual affairs, while significant, should not be exaggerated. It is nonetheless present whatever tack we take. The myth of *machismo,* incorporating an alleged need for constant dramatic assertions of masculinity, notwithstanding, our Puerto Rican teen-age boys do not preen themselves on their virility. Most of them accept the code which prohibits tattling "to other guys about girls they have schemed with." Some do engage in invidious talk about "street girls" whose well-known promiscuity makes it impossible to take pride in having "scored" with them. Similarly, the reaction to betrayal is a mild one. Violent assault on a girl may occur if she is suspected of having squealed to the police about stealing or fighting—not so about sexual defections. When they occur, New York boys say, "I walk away," "I tell her not to do that again," "I call it quits." The gorge does not rise very high, one's manhood is not called into question, and violence flares up but rarely. Likewise, the readiness to spare a girl friend undue embarrassment—or to share it with her by prematurely shouldering the parental responsibility—is quite exceptional. Commenting on the large number of unmarried girls with babies that boys refuse to support, a respondent explains, "Maybe one guy has her, then another, and then another. She doesn't know who the father is." Then what? "The last guy gets the blame." And getting the blame, more often than not, seems to mean accepting the blame, which, in turn (age permitting), means marriage. In this realm, as elsewhere, *fatalismo* apparently counts for more than *machismo.*

Sexual experience, which begins early and mounts in frequency, if not intensity, should not be equated with sexual sophistication. Indeed, the manifest naivete is sometimes monumental. So:

> How do you avoid getting girls pregnant? (Long pause)
> I don't really know.
> Nobody ever told you about that?

Nobody ever told me.
> Well, how do you keep the girl from having a baby?
> I guess you kill the baby.
> Do you know about killing babies?
> I don't know, but . . .
> Is that what they do around the block?
> If they gonna kill the babies, they gonna kill theirself.
> So you never heard about protection? Like a rubber?
> What did you say? Girdle? Maybe that's the only way. I know a girl lives in my neighborhood. She had a baby, but you couldn't tell, and after awhile they found out she had a girdle on. But she still had a baby. I don't really know how you could stop it. The only way, I suppose, is wearing a girdle.

Another boy reports making a girl pregnant, but there was no baby, "because she took it out." How he does not know or will not say. Yet another, asked what he would do if he got his girl friend pregnant, replies, "There's nothing I could do," and, for lack of options, lets it go at that.

Early marriage ensues, in a spirit best described as resignation. This "solution" becomes all the more irrational whenever boys protest, as they do with great vehemence, that it is the one thing that they wish, above all, to avoid. They speak of no marriage or late marriage, drawing the lesson of delay and circumvention from their own experience in unsatisfactory family relations. And, pointing to others all around them, they declaim against too many people marrying too soon, having too many children. It is on this basis that they diagnose most of their own trouble and most of the ills that others encounter in a slum environment. It all starts, they say, when a young man fathers a child he does not want—whose conception he will do nothing to prevent. Here, indeed, for one part of the underclass is the way of all flesh: fully aware of the danger, our young man tumbles headlong into it, doing exactly what he had sworn not to do, classically entering a scene he had resolved to sidestep, with some, no doubt, unconscious, propulsion into a trap he professes to abhor.

A finer distinction must be made among Appalachians in Chicago. There, group-affiliated males show a consistent unwillingness to marry, holding out for very long, while, among the unaffiliated, there is a noticeably higher incidence of early marriage. When it takes place, males tend to be several years older than females, even if both are still in their teens. In the majority of cases, delay is secured through reinforcement of a powerful male peer group that seemingly functions much like the one analyzed by William Foote Whyte in *Street Corner Society* (1943). It is the opinion of two long-time resident observers in Chicago that "most of the males find it impossible to maintain regular and satisfying experiences with a girl and quickly withdraw their attention and return to the male peer group." They also indicate that despite a well-nigh-universal claim to early sexual experience, many of the male youths admit to prolonged periods of disengagement both from overt heterosexual activity and coed sociability. Much of the sexual play that does take place involves a group of boys who exploit one or two females, many of them "young runaways" or disillusioned young wives, viewed as "easy scores" for all. After a week or so of intensified sexuality with one such female, she usually disappears. Then the males resume their involuntary celibacy. Later, they embark once again on the same cycle. All of this is absolutely affectless.

Appalachian girls in Chicago stress early marriage as a female adjustment. They hope for husbands who "won't be unfaithful," "won't drink," "will be nice," and "will work hard." Demographic findings and intimate observation make it clear that, personal preference apart, a girl often marries the first young male adult with whom she has a steady relationship. Our resident observers also tell us that their "noncodified observations yield another interesting pattern of marital relationship in the next older group," which they feel may have a bearing on "the essentially brittle relations of the teen-agers." During our study, a number of marriages have been observed to dissolve into a peculiar pattern of realignment, such that: Male A, aged thirty-five, establishes a liaison with Female X, his own age or older; wife of A establishes a liaison with unmarried Male B, aged twenty-five or thirty or with a formerly married male, aged twenty-five to thirty who, in turn, has separated from his younger wife. Consequently, for the second marriage, or for sexual adventures after a first marriage, the male is ordinarily younger than the female. We find, in short, that, parallel to the traditional form (older husband, younger wife), there is a deviant form that leaves separated,

divorced, and unfaithful women with younger husbands and lovers. There is a certain distinctiveness in this duality.

Cultural Values Compared

We suspected at the outset of our inquiry that the rhetoric and the activity of impoverished American subcultures would be far removed from traditional Western ideas of love and sex. They are. Middle-class standards, in all their present disarray, carry those ideas (or reactions against them) in a confusing melange that can only bewilder young people who are their residuary legatees. Not so in the underclass, where, with all its diversity, these ideas appear—if at all —only in mutilated form.

With a mixture of envy and indignation, middle-class people often impute pure sensual pleasure to their social inferiors, who are thought to pursue this objective heedlessly, if not monomaniacally. There is no warrant for this judgment. Puerto Rican youth in New York seem, somewhat more than the other groups, to stress sensual pleasure, but even they are manifestly more interested in *collective* fun, in "the set" itself, than in pure hedonism. All the same, insofar as "scheming" is an act of rebellion against authority, it does not much differ from taking pot or ingesting alcohol. In any class, youthful manifestations of defiance are a tacit acknowledgement of that coercive culture which some choose to resist. On the face of it, a Puerto Rican boy willing to "accept the responsibility" of marriage to, or help for, the girl he has impregnated, responds in accordance with one element of the Western Catholic tradition. For him, heterosexual dalliance imposes an obligation, but only if "the worst should happen," and then only when he is actuated by a sense of fatality rather than by love or duty. Chance has dealt him a heavy blow, rendered him powerless to fight back, left him a plaything of mysterious forces, destroyed his capacity to act as a free agent.

That culturally induced responsibility for one's sex acts cannot be taken for granted is clear enough in the other two groups, whose members refuse to do what the New York Puerto Rican boy feels that he must do. In this milieu, a residue of the declining tradition may still be observed. Not so in the

Washington and Chicago samples of Negroes and Appalachian whites.

Given time, any group encapsulated in a constricted ghetto can be severed, not just from the mainstream of a larger culture but from its ancestral subculture as well. The unique circumstances of isolation and contact, impoverishment and opportunity, continuity and rupture with the past, will produce new codes, new standards, new articulations, and new behavior patterns. The Appalachian whites and the Washington Negroes are in most ways slightly less "Westernized" (that is, made into middle-class people) than Puerto Rican youth in New York. All, however, have rural, but by no means identical, origins. And all have moved into hideous urban ghettos where, to varying degrees, they are shut off from the major values of Western society. For people from the Southern hill country or the Southern plantation, lack of contact with outsiders is an old story. Urbanization, even in ghettos, reduces their isolation. The Appalachian white may have been culturally on his own since the pre-Revolutionary settlement of this country. For lower-class Negroes, isolation may have begun with the capture of their ancestors in Africa, and continued through Southern slavery to Northern segregation. The Negro subclass has had practically no exposure to Western sexual ideals, and the Appalachian white's exposure occurred so long ago that its effects are virtually inoperative.

For these submerged peoples, our dominant sexual ideologies have little relevance. Neither emotional and material responsibilities, nor their opposite, pure joy in unrestrained sexuality, is much in evidence. Sexual fulfillment is experienced merely as a physical release—the "friction of two membranes"—in which the female is the necessary but unequal partner. Otherwise, sexual conquest provides a trophy calculated to enhance one's prestige in peer-group competition. Masculinity is affirmed as part of a game whose competitors must incessantly prove themselves before an audience of others engaged in the same pastime. Since it is a competitive game, the boy who plays cannot expect to earn points for scoring over an easy mark, a "pig." Victory consists in overcoming the largest possible number of inaccessible girls. The conversion of females into trophies reduces them to nonpersons. Their personal, sexual, or simply human, needs do not matter. They exist to be tricked, deceived, manipulated—and abandoned. Skill in all these techniques is a sign of stylistic virtuosity. For a boy to abuse his sexual partner in many ingenious ways makes him a big winner. To all this, the lush rhetoric and varied responses elicited from our interviews are ample testimony. Customary allusions to Western concepts of love and sex are "foreign" to people who cannot express them verbally or in terms of their actual conduct. They are historically and personally alienated from the amorous and sexual context that Western idealism, with all its twists and turns, has to offer. That condition, for which no single urban ghetto is a carbon copy, can only deepen as subcultural segregation runs its course.

Investigation of ethnic underclass sexual mores in our own society, while it points to important differences, certainly does not provide us with examples of "natural," spontaneous, unrepressed, and nonneurotic sensual pleasure. Sexual practices are indissolubly linked to nonsexual aspects of life-style. For this reason, it would in any case be impossible to transfer the really illusory freedom of slum sex codes to an academic and bureaucratic world. If in that world, "intellectualized," "artificial," and "abstract" standards prevail, they cannot be banished by sexual personalism. No more than primitive or peasant society do subcultures of poverty offer us solutions to our sexual dilemma.

References

Allen, F. L. *Only yesterday: An informal history of the nineteen-twenties.* New York: Blue Ribbon Books, 1932.

Bell, R. R. Parent-child conflict in sexual values. *Journal of Social Issues,* 1966, **22,** 34-44.

Berger, B. M. The new morality. Unpublished paper read at the Plenary Session of the Society for the Study of Social Problems, 1967.

Bernard, J. Teen-age culture. *Annals of the American Academy of Political and Social Science,* 1961, **338.**

Brittain, C. V. Adolescent choices and parent-peer cross pressures. *American Sociological Review,* 1963, **28,** 385-391.

Bromley, D. D., & Britten, F. H. *Youth and sex.* New York: Harper, 1938.

Burch, T. K. The size and structure of families: A comparative analysis of census data. *American Sociological Review,* 1967, **32,** 347-363.

Burgess, E. W., & Wallin, P. *Engagement and marriage.* Philadelphia: Lippincott, 1953.

Davis, K. B. *Factors in the sex life of twenty-two hundred women.* New York: Harper, 1929.

Ehrmann, W. *Premarital dating behavior.* New York: Holt, 1959.

Ellis, H. *The psychology of sex.* Philadelphia: F.A. Davis, 1910.

Foote, N. N. Sex as play. *Social Problems,* 1964, **1,** 161.

Freedman, M. E. The sexual behavior of American college women: An empirical study and an historical study. *Merrill-Palmer Quarterly,* 1965, **2,** 33-48.

Gilbert Youth Research. How wild are college students? *Pageant,* 1951, **7,** 10-21.

Hamilton, G. V. *A research in marriage.* New York: Albert and Charles Boni, 1929.

Iowa sociologist calls sex revolution a myth. *New York Times,* Oct. 22, 1967, p. 80.

Kinsey, A. C., Pomeroy, W. B., & Martin, C. E. *Sexual behavior in the human male.* Philadelphia: Saunders, 1948.

Kinsey, A. C., Pomeroy, W. B., & Martin, C. E. *Sexual behavior in the human female.* Philadelphia: Saunders, 1953.

Kirkendall, L. A. Sexual revolution—myth or actuality? *Religious Education,* 1966, **61,** 411-418.

Krafft-Ebing, R. von. *Psychopathia sexualis,* 1886. (Translated by Franklin S. Klaf.) New York: Dell, 1965.

Landis, J. T., & Landis, M. *Building a successful marriage* (3rd ed.) Englewood Cliffs, N.J.: Prentice-Hall, 1957.

Lippman, W. *A preface to morals.* New York: Macmillan, 1939.

Masters, W. H., & Johnson, V. E. *Human sexual response.* Boston: Little, Brown, 1966.

Moore, W. E. *Social change.* Englewood Cliffs, N.J.: Prentice-Hall, 1963.

The pleasures and pain of the single life. *TIME,* Sept. 15, 1967, pp. 26-27.

Reiss, I. L. *Premarital sexual standards in America.* New York: Free Press, 1960.

Reiss, I. L. Standards of sexual behavior. In A. Ellis & A. Abarbanel, (Eds.), *Encyclopedia of sex.* New York: Hawthorne, 1961.

Reiss, I. L. The sexual renaissance: A summary and analysis. *Journal of Social Issues,* 1966, **22,** 126.

Reiss, I. L. *The social context of premarital sexual permissiveness.* New York: Holt, 1967.

Rockwood, L., & Ford, M. *Youth, marriage, and parenthood.* New York: Wiley, 1945.

Smith, E. A. *American youth culture: Group life in teen-age society.* New York: Free Press, 1962.

Statistical abstracts of the United States, 1967. Washington, D.C.: Government Printing Office, 88th ed.

Storey, T. A. *The work of the United States Interdepartmental Social Hygiene Board.* New York: United States Interdepartmental Social Hygiene Board, 1920.

Terman, L. M., et al. *Psychological factors in marital happiness.* New York: McGraw-Hill, 1938.

Thornburg, H. D. Sex education: Part II: The student. *Arizona Teacher,* 1968, **57,** 11, 27-28.

Thornburg, H. D. *Sex education in the public schools.* Phoenix: Arizona Education Association, 1969.

Thornburg, H. D. Ages and first sources of sex information as reported by 88 women. *Journal of School Health,* 1970a, **40,** 156-158.

Thornburg, H. D. A comparative study of sex information sources. *Journal of School Health,* 1970b, in press.

Vital statistics: National summaries. Washington, D.C.: U.S. Department of Health, Education, and Welfare, 1959, **50,** 28.

Whyte, W. F. *Street corner society.* Chicago: University of Chicago Press, 1943.

Annotations

Abortion—homosexual practices—marihuana. *Modern Medicine,* 1969, **37** (22), 18-25. A poll was conducted among 28,000 physicians on the three issues mentioned in the title. A majority favored legalizing abortion and homosexuality. On both issues psychiatrists were most in favor of the legalization and general practitioners were least in favor. In contrast, all physicians were strongly opposed to legalizing marihuana except anesthesiologists, 56 percent of whom favored it. The article presents an interesting breakdown of results according to speciality and geographical location.

Mirande, A. M. Reference group theory and adolescent sexual behavior. *Journal of Marriage and the Family,* 1968, **30,** 572-577. The author stresses that a reference group is useful among college students for understanding premarital sexual behavior. Data reveal that the sexual behavior of students seems to be consistent with the standards and behavior of the peer group.

Montagu, A. The pill, the sexual revolution, and the schools. *Phi Delta Kappan,* 1968, **49,** 480-484. Montagu discusses the pill and its consequences on our social norms. He focuses on (1) sexual emancipation, (2) social emancipation for women, (3) premarital sex, (4) sexual responsibility, and (5) love and marriage. The article challenges traditional positions about sexuality and suggests two or three major social changes that will put more order into our social structure.

Reiss, I. L. (Ed.) The sexual renaissance in America. *Journal of Social Issues,* 1966, **22,** entire issue. This issue analyzes the sexual renaissance through a discussion of such topics as teen-age unwed mothers, parent-child conflicts, lower-class sexual behavior, and Scandinavian and American sex norms.

Robinson, I. E., King, K., Dudley, C. J., & Clune, F. J. Change in sexual behavior and attitudes of college students. *Family Coordinator,* 1968,

17, 119-123. A survey of 244 college students in a major Southern university was conducted to ascertain the extent of change in sexual behavior and attitudes from data reported by Kinsey in 1948. It found no major changes in reported incidence of premarital coitus or petting. Attitudes toward certain aspects of sexual behavior were changed in the direction of placing responsibility on the individual rather than on the community. The students had a tolerant attitude about sexual promiscuity.

Sagarin, E. (Ed.) Sex and the contemporary American scene. *Annals of the American Academy of Political and Social Science,* 1968, **376,** entire issue. This journal issue is a comprehensive, 14-article analysis of human sexuality from several perspectives. Major issues discussed are (1) sex within our society; (2) the double standard; (3) the role of the family, school, and church in human sexuality; and (4) attitudes toward sex. Articles dealing with the sexual behavior of different groups and types of people are also presented. Special problems, such as deviance, prostitution, abortion, and sex offenses, are discussed.

Sex education, doctors, and the backlash. *Medical World News,* 1969, **10** (40), 25-28d. A group of psychoanalytically oriented psychiatrists raise some questions about sex education interfering with the normal sexual developmental pattern of youth. Other reactionaries cry out that sex education encourages sex participation. In contrast, several physicians, citing the early participation of youth in various forms of sex play, support the need for sex education.

Simon, W. Sex. *Psychology Today,* 1969, **3,** 23-27. The author briefly traces a shift in sexual concerns and patterns since 1900. Simon suggests that the changes in the public face of sexuality have been easier to discern since World War II. However, he emphasizes that few new patterns of sexual practice are likely to occur among today's adolescents, especially girls. He still sees most sexual behavior aimed at family formation and maintenance and suggests that much sexual activity is harnessed and amplified by social uses.

Thornburg, H. D. Ages and first sources of sex information as reported by 88 college women. *Journal of School Health,* 1970, **40,** 156-158. The survey indicates that most information is learned between 12 and 15 years of age. Female peers are the major sources of information, although much information is also learned from mothers and through literature.

Thornburg, H. D. *Sex education in the public schools.* Phoenix: Arizona Education Association, 1969. This five-chapter booklet focuses on family life and sex education in the public schools. The basic considerations are: (1) objectives for sex education, (2) the students' view of sex education, (3) the administration of a sex-education program, and (4) the evaluation of a sex-education program. The concluding chapter discusses the adolescent's uncertain quest of sexuality.

four

the adolescent and the family

The aim of child rearing is socialization, the process by which an individual learns and adapts to the ways, ideas, beliefs, and values of his particular culture. Since to a young child society is largely his family, his values and those of his parents are generally the same. As he approaches adolescence, other agencies, such as peers, the school, the church, and the mass media, become influential in the socialization process. Through them the adolescent is encouraged to develop values and behaviors that often exclude or conflict with those of the home.

The combined effect of family and non-family influences on the youth is that he strives for some privacy and independence. He wants the right to make personal decisions. Therefore he becomes more aware of and sensitive to the home and the behavioral characteristics of his family. He looks for the same opportunity for self-direction at home that he has begun to experience at school.

Of central concern to the adolescent, then, is autonomy, or independence from strong family ties and influences. Douvan and Adelson (1966) categorize this autonomy in three ways: (1) emotional autonomy, (2) behavioral autonomy, and (3) value autonomy.

Emotional autonomy is defined as "the degree to which the adolescent has managed to cast off infantile ties to the family" (Douvan & Adelson, 1966, p. 130). The adolescent must give up much of his childhood dependency. He must learn self-control and self-reliance and he should come to identify with his parents as friends or confidantes rather than as models. Parents can facilitate this process by encouraging adolescent independence. If they set up conditions for gradual emancipation, the adolescent will be able to work out his independence with minimal internal conflict or rebellion.

Behavioral autonomy centers around adolescent behaviors and decisions. According to Douvan and Adelson:

> Behavioral autonomy is, in short, a dependent variable. To give it meaning we have to know its antecedents, its sources. In the case of the adolescent we imagine that these are to be found in parental values. What the youngster is free or unfree to do and decide probably tells us less about him than it does his parents; it tells us about him directly, through what it may suggest about the family milieu and the parents' implicit ideology of socialization (p. 131).

The importance of adolescent-parent understanding cannot be minimized. The time interval between generations is brought into sharp focus over the matter of behavioral autonomy. Parents may view adolescents as rebellious, and adolescents see parents as old-fashioned. Many parents cannot condone behaviors that are commonplace today because those behaviors were inappropriate when they were young. This conflict of values may breed a lack of common understanding, since what parents often mean by independence is that the adolescent should take more initiative in doing what they want him to do. "They expect him to be 'grown up' in the sense of possessing all the virtues parents value, and yet to lack all the vices usually tolerated by adults in one another" (Josselyn, 1952, p. 188).

Without question there are marginal issues between a young person and his parents. But adolescents count on parents asserting themselves. They need limits, and generally they like them. To the adolescent "there is great comfort in knowing that those who love you love you enough to take the responsibility for marking out the permissible" (Wilder, 1948, p. 194).

Value autonomy, as defined by Douvan and Adelson, is "the capacity to manage a clarity of vision which permits one to transcend customary structurings of reality" (1966, p. 131). This level of autonomy usually develops during late adolescence, probably after such major issues as sexuality, educational decisions, vocational considerations, and self-identity have been at least partially resolved. The adolescent forms his system of values after he has considered those of his peers and parents. Typically, adolescents think that accepting parental values will put them out of step with peers. By adopting peer values, social acceptance is increased but parental conflict arises. However, through these experience-defining situations, the adolescent emerges with value autonomy.

Other family phenomena are relevant to a consideration of adolescent emancipation. Cultural changes and urbanization have produced significant structural shifts in the family, and today adolescent autonomy must often be achieved outside the home. Whereas the family was once the primary influence on adolescent behavior, peers, the schools, and other cultural institutions have now taken over many of the functions formerly performed by the homes.

In a technological society that emphasizes the role of the male provider, the ever-present possibility of a father's unemployment also has an impact on the family, and it holds potential hazards for the adolescent. Particularly affected are semi-skilled and unskilled workers. Adolescents who cannot meet increasing educational and occupational requirements face the threat of indefinite unemployment and a prolongation of their dependence on the family.

The working mother also influences the adolescent's search for emancipation. How much the shift of woman's interest from the home to community and career has affected the family is uncertain, because research has provided contradictory evidences (Clancy & Smitter, 1953; Moore & Holtzman, 1965; Whitmansh, 1965).

Family Structure and Dynamics

In the first article in this chapter, Larson and Myerhoff discuss the structure and organization of the family according to such variables as authority sources, goals, and modes of family interaction. They emphasize the role of both parents in the adolescent's socialization process. The mother is seen as the more personal, expressive, and emotional parent, and the father, whose authority is more positional and rational, tends to interact in a consistently more formal manner. Larson and Myerhoff also point out that adolescent socialization is more complex and less definitive in a one-parent family.

Parental interaction is an important factor in adolescent socialization. Meissner, in article two, reports on his survey of 1278 high school boys in the eastern United States. He asked questions pertaining to the boys' perceptions of their parents and their level of interaction. Only 12 percent of the boys in his sample were from broken homes.

One of Meissner's findings supports the Larson and Myerhoff distinction between father and mother. The students in Meissner's sample thought their fathers were colder, less understanding, more unreasonable, more indifferent, and more old-fashioned than their mothers. Mothers were viewed as more friendly and more nervous than fathers. Although there were distinguishable differences in the adolescents' perception of their parents, 74 percent of the boys sampled felt proud of their parents and said they like to have them meet their friends.

Meissner's study also analyzed positive and negative parent-child interaction. The younger boys felt they had adequate social opportunity and freedom, and they generally accepted parental authority and guidance. However, as they grew older, they expressed an increasing dissatisfaction with home life, with the imposition of parental ideas, and with the level of parental understanding of their problems and behaviors.

It is interesting that Meissner's results are similar to Moore and Holtzman's (1965), who studied the attitudes of 13,000 high school students toward their parents. They found that (1) 73 percent of the students valued their parents highly and felt responsibility to them throughout their lives; (2) 75 percent disagreed that parents should sacrifice everything for their children; (3) 80 percent felt that both parents should share family responsibilities equally; and (4) approximately 75 percent felt no urgency about getting married and leaving home. Thus available research indicates that positive parent-child interaction is widespread.

Most adolescents spend much time reaching beyond the home for satisfaction of their social needs. Nevertheless, Musgrove's article shows that 77 percent of the students he sampled felt their homes provided a sense of being needed, feeling secure, and having a chance to talk over personal problems with parents. Home emerged as a predominantly satisfying social institution for young people. Indeed, the home becomes both status-defining and experience-defining for the adolescent (Horrocks, 1962).

The Broken Home

Parents serve as transmitters of the cultural value system which has been previously internalized by the parents, and as the child's contact with and representative in the adult world. For the very small child the parent is virtually the sole means of communication. Whatever his interests, values, and opinions of the parent, the loss of a parent of one sex produces a structural distortion in the communications between the child and the adult world (Glasser & Navarre, 1965, p. 106).

Roughly 10 percent of all children in the United States are living with only one parent, usually the mother, in homes that have been broken by death, divorce, separation, or desertion. Moreover, almost 48 percent of these families are in the low-income group. "Non-whites are much more likely to live in such circumstances, with one-third of them living in one-parent families. By March, 1962, the mother-child families represented 8-1/2 percent of all families with their own children" (Glasser & Navarre, 1965, p. 99). Thus we see an emerging matriarchal structure, especially within the culturally disadvantaged home. The child from a broken home is likely to suffer stress and anxiety. "In place of continuity and sameness, he experiences instability and disruption of his environment" (Beiser, 1965).

Providing for the physical, emotional, and social needs of the family is the responsibility of two adults. In the one-parent family it is unlikely that one person can take over all the parental tasks on a long-term basis. Consequently, children are often forced into roles that they are not mature enough to handle. For example, if the mother must take on the role of provider, her household tasks are left almost entirely to her children.

In the last selection in this chapter Burchinal discusses characteristics of adolescents from unbroken, broken, and reconstituted families. In his study unbroken families were those with both biological parents present; broken families were those in which only the mother was present; and reconstituted families were of three types: mothers and stepfathers, fathers and step-mothers, and divorced parents who had both remarried. Burchinal found no significant differences in emerging personality characteristics or social relationships between adolescents from broken or reconstituted homes and those from unbroken homes.

william r. larson

barbara g. myerhoff

primary and formal family organization and
adolescent socialization*

Human collectivities are frequently characterized on the basis of the intimacy or impersonality of the members' interactions with one another. Groups whose members have strong emotional bonds, extensive face-to-face contacts and share a sense of similarity and identity have been called primary, and described in detail by Cooley, G. H. Mead and E. Faris to name but a few. The nuclear family has often been designated as the prototype of the primary group, for it offers the possibility of interactions as intimate and intense as people are ever likely to have. Status-differentiated, goal-oriented formal organizations are thought to exemplify an *opposite* kind of group, in which members' interactions are more impersonal, rational, and emotionally neutral. A bureaucratically-organized, economically-oriented collectivity such as the factory may be conceived of as a prototype of the formal group. Primary and formal groups are usually thought of as offer-

ing the members qualitatively different experiences and, indeed, are often treated as mutually exclusive. This means, for example, that the bases for interactions which take place in the family on the one hand and the factory on the other are considered to be diametrically opposed.

In the course of a study of family organization and adolescent behavior presently being conducted by the authors, it became apparent that the formal characteristics of family life were often as salient as the primary attributes, and, in fact, the dichotomy between these two kinds of groups began to appear as an over-simplification which masked similarities between them. The question raised by this observation is the subject of the present paper: What kinds of status-based, rational and unemotional interactions can be found in families? Or put another way: To what extent is the family in our society a formal organization as well as a primary group?

These questions do not originate with us. Several authors have been cognizant of the presence of formal attributes in primary groups and primary attributes in formal groups. Parsons (Parsons & Bales, 1955), in passing, has referred to the family as a kind of factory, whose product is the human personality, but he did not elaborate on this

Reprinted with permission of the authors and publisher from *Sociology and Social Research*, 1965, **50**, 63-71.

* The authors are indebted to the U.S. Office of Education for financial support, under Cooperative Research Project #1353, entitled "Critical Factors in Adolescence: Intra-Family Relations and Differential School Adjustment." This paper is one of the working papers developed within that project. A slightly shorter version of this paper was presented at the First International Congress of Social Psychiatry, London, England, August, 1954.

point. Blau (Blau & Scott, 1962) has indicated that in every formal organization, there arise informal, primary groups; however, he did not consider the converse, that primary groups may likewise manifest characteristics of formal organizations. Our paper is intended to explore the implications of these suggestions and to elaborate on what has thus far only been adumbrated.

This paper is, in actuality, a child of serendipity, for in the course of our research on the family, we observed what appeared to be an unexpectedly high degree of consensus on the goals held by families for their adolescent sons. Agreement on these goals seemed unrelated to the social-environmental influences exerted by class, race, and religion. Though specifically looking for manifestations of family disorganization and disruption, instead we were struck by the prevalence of organization, as indicated by high agreement on goals. If we were surprised to find this instance of formality of family organization on one dimension (agreement on goals), what other formal attributes in families might we be inclined to overlook? It occurred to us that a theoretical comparison of the family and the factory would perhaps sensitize us to the presence, in varying degrees, of features which might be found in both these kinds of groups. By focusing on the similarities between family and factory and discarding the summary and reductionist labels of "primary" and "formal," which emphasize contradictions between them, we felt we would be able to identify organizational dimensions usually neglected in family research.

In making this comparison we have concentrated on the family's influential function, that is, the family's ability to induce and sustain conformity by the child, who, in our present research is the adolescent boy.

Our comparison of ways in which families and factories induce conformity has led us to the identification of three continuous variables which are equally pertinent to and operative in both kinds of groups. The first of these variables defers to the *source or basis of the authority exerted.* We have used polar terms to define the continuum of authority source: *personal* at one end and *positional* at the other. Authority which is purely personal in origin is exemplified by the charismatic leader, whose followers voluntarily obey him

because of his unique, individual attributes, and because of the emotional bonds between him and his followers. Purely positional authority is exemplified by the army officer who, by virtue of his ability to apply coercive sanctions, can demand conformity. Personal authority ideally is an emotional appeal, presupposing close emotional ties, while positional authority is a rational, emotionally neutral command, presupposing the ability to enforce compliance, without regard for individual preferences.

How do these polar sources of authority operate in the family and factory? In the family, a father may request his son to conform to his wishes to please him, presupposing that his son's affection for him will motivate him to want to do so. Or, he may insist on conformity on the grounds that he is the father, he is older, he knows what's best, and so forth, treating as irrelevant any emotional bonds between him and his son, and implying that his requests can be enforced if necessary. Similarly, the factory foreman may induce compliance with his wishes by appealing to the worker's liking for him, by being a nice guy, or, he may merely indicate that as the superordinate, he has the right to demand compliance. Further, he has coercive sanctions at his disposal in case there is any question about the matter.

Our second variable refers to the intended outcome of the influence being exerted by the authority. What are the authority's *goals* for the individual over whom he has control? Toward what ends does he aspire in his attempts to induce conforming behavior?

Again, our contrast between family and factory is helpful, for we find that both kinds of organizations are oriented toward both these kinds of goals. The father's goals for his son may emphasize the *expressive,* but he must also concern himself with rearing a child who will be able to meet externally originating demands, such as passing his courses in school, and getting and holding a job. The factory foreman of necessity emphasizes *instrumental* goals, since matters such as output and productivity are involved with the explicit rationale of the institution, but he is also concerned with the workers' morale and the quality of the interpersonal relations between himself and the workers in situations that do not directly bear on work goals.

Finally, a variable has been identified which refers to the practices used by the authority figure in attaining his goals for the subordinate. To what extent are the *techniques* used by the authority figure *emotional* and to what extent *rational?* A technique may be described as emotional when it involves the *feelings* of the authority, for example, expressions of anger, affection, approval or disapproval. A rational technique typically involves the bestowal, removal or withholding of goods, services and privileges. Emotional techniques are usually less intentionally or self-consciously applied than are rational, which necessarily involve a minimum of spontaneity and a maximum of premeditation, and incidentally, are often more "appropriate" in the sense of being fair or proportionate.

The father may communicate his desires to his son in a myriad of ways. He may reward or punish him by a great range of emotional techniques, including subtle, nonverbal cues such as smiling, frowning, and touching. Inevitably, he must also deliberately apply sanctions which he considers appropriate and must formally assert his authority by rational techniques such as confinement of the son, restricting his use of family possessions and the like. The factory foreman, in addition to using rational techniques such as docking pay, giving bonuses and time off, influences and motivates the worker by subtle, interpersonal communications indicating his pleasures and displeasures.

These variables may be summarized thus:

1. Authority source: Personal
   Positional
2. Goals: Expressive
   Instrumental
3. Techniques: Emotional
   Rational

It is apparent that these variables are so closely intertwined as to be aspects of one another; all refer to the primary and formal attributes of interactions. By distinguishing between them, however, it becomes possible to locate any group at any point in time as possessing more or fewer primary and formal attributes on several dimensions rather than one. If this multidimensional view of the family's conformity-inducing function is to be of heuristic value to research, it must be integrated with other conceptualizations in the field. To illustrate the extent to which the viewpoint expressed here can be related to the finding of other writers, two frequently recurring problems of family studies—efficacy of child rearing techniques and effects of a broken home—will be examined using these variables.

Zelditch's (1955) consideration of the expressive and instrumental functions of the family in our society as sex-linked is particularly fruitful and relevant to our conceptualization. He has described the mother as being the expressive leader in the family and the father as the instrumental. This notion may be taken, in our scheme, as implying that the mother's interactions with the child should be consistently in the primary direction of the primary-formal continuum for all three variables. This would mean that it is appropriate for the mother's authority to be *personal,* her goals *expressive* and her techniques *emotional.* Correspondingly the father as instrumental leader should interact with the child in a consistently more formal manner. His authority should be positional, his goals instrumental and his techniques rational. Numerous questions which might be readily operationalized are raised by assuming consistency. To what extent is there such consistency on the part of mothers and fathers, so that mothers are more primary and fathers more formal in their relations with the child? What are the implications of consistency or lack of consistency among these dimensions for the effectiveness of the socialization process? What are the implications for personality development of such consistency or its absence?

Viewed in this light, it can be seen that Parsons' (1949) article on sources and patterns of aggression in the western world and Green's (1960) article on the middle class male child and neurosis refer to just such questions as these. Both authors describe the tendency of middle class mothers to use "personality-absorbing techniques" (highly emotional techniques) to promote instrumental goals in their children. The mother manipulates the child by using her personal authority, and gives or withholds her love on the basis of the child's successes and failures outside the family. Thus the child who fails in school feels he has failed to show he loves his mother, and that she in turn will withhold her love from him. This combination of personal authority, emotional technique and instrumental goal arouses great anxiety and guilt in the child, a situation which is unquestionably a powerful motivation to success. But as both Parsons and Green have suggested, the effectiveness of such a tactic is not the only consideration; the personality damage which may be sustained by the child as a result must also be taken into account. An everyday instance of an inappropriate combination of goals and techniques is found in the father who is in a rage because his son does not show him enough respect. He demands this respect as his filial prerogative and takes the son's car away to make sure he is respected in the future. Such a juxtaposition of a rational technique and an expressive goal (which is by no means uncommon) is considered ludicrous and ineffectual on face value. The investigation of the most desirable combinations of our three variables in terms of the relative balance of primary and formal characteristics, taking into account psychological consequences as well as efficiency, is an area which could be examined by direct research as well as by recasting extant studies and concepts into these terms.

The heuristic value of using these three variables is exemplified further by considering how they may operate in the much-discussed matter of the broken home, that is, a family in which one parent is missing. One of the most important issues of the broken home situation is the difficulties faced by the remaining parent in socializing the child without the assistance of an opposite sex partner. In our terms, a broken home is an instance of a critical position becoming vacant. One may then ask, what are the strategies open to the remaining parent in dealing with this lacuna? How, if at all, can the parent contrive to make up to the child for the missing incumbent?

To demonstrate the kinds of questions raised by this approach, we may consider an example of the child as an adolescent son and the position unfilled as that of father. The mother has six basic alternatives open to her. (1) She may do nothing, perhaps because she feels the position cannot and should not be filled, since no one else will have the personal attributes of the previous incumbent, and that position and personal parental duties are inextricable. (2) She may re-marry and let the step-father fill the posi-

tion as he sees fit. Alternatives three through six represent attempts by the remaining family members to cope with the situation through their own efforts, that is, without bringing in a new incumbent. (3) The mother may try to compensate for the missing parent by intensifying her role as expressive leader in relation to her son. This would involve making her techniques more emotional, her authority more personal and her goals more expressive. For example, she might go out of her way to spend time talking with her son about his attitudes and emotions; she might be more demonstrative of affection, reveal her intimate feelings to him, and in various ways strengthen and deepen the personal bonds between them. (4) She may attempt to compensate for the absent father by taking over his functions, that is, becoming the instrumental leader herself; thus she would base her authority on her parental position, use rational techniques in dealing with her son and encourage task-oriented behavioral goals for him. This would mean she would, so to speak, be a father to her son, perhaps by taking him camping and fishing, counseling him on vocational possibilities, tutoring him in his school work, and generally relating to him in terms less personal, more rational and formal, than was previously the case. (5) The mother may attempt to be both expressive and instrumental leader at the same time. She may spend time talking with her son, showing him how to fix the lawnmower, play ball with him, and tell him of her problems, attempting, as the familiar saying goes, "to be both father and mother to him." (6) The mother may manipulate the son himself into the missing position, by urging him to take on the responsibilities which are properly the father's. The son may be expected to bring money into the home for household expenses, help discipline younger children, offer emotional support to his mother, and in many ways, subtle and overt, become the "man of the family."

These six alternatives, incidentally, seem equally applicable to homes in which the father is physically present but is weak, ineffectual, perpetually absent or isolated from the mainstream of family life.

There are obvious hazards in all these alternatives, particularly the last four, which involve the mother's or son's attempt to fill the vacant position. In the first instance, the mother's intensification of expressive leadership may emotionally overwhelm the son. This situation is particularly dangerous at a time in the son's development when, as psychoanalysts have pointed out, oedipal conflicts resurge with great force. Further, the son's failure to be instructed in the achievement of instrumental tasks may damage his chances of success in society. In the second instance, wherein the mother assumes the role of instrumental leader, she may overlook the son's emotional needs and desires for primary interactions with her. In addition, because instrumental and expressive roles are sex-linked, her assumption of the instrumental role may confuse the son regarding what constitutes appropriate feminine and masculine behavior. Should he come to equate instrumental goals with femininity, he might find it necessary to reject both the goals and his mother, in his attempt to establish a masculine identity. As Parsons has pointed out, the boy raised exclusively by his mother may even be driven to antisocial behavior if he associates her urging him to be a "good boy" with feminine goals. The third case, in which the mother tries to fill both parental roles at once, may also interfere with the son's establishment of a satisfactory sexual identification. Further, it may maximize the son's dependence on his mother, thus impeding his desire and ability to move toward adulthood. Finally, when the *son* is thrust into the missing position, his adolescence is prematurely cut short so that instead of gradually discarding the status of a youth he is catapulted into an adult role and must assume responsibilities for which he is unprepared socially, emotionally, and physiologically. Such a situation also results in alienating the boy from his peers, whose adolescence is permitted to run its full course.

It has been the purpose of this paper to present some preliminary thoughts and questions growing out of a serendipitous development of the authors' current research on family organization and the socialization of adolescent boys.

By pointing out the often striking instances of similarities between family and factory, we have tried to call attention to the conceptual limitations imposed on the researcher by the use of such over-polarized terms as primary and formal. We have suggested that there are variables which might underlie these general labels, denoting continua upon which a collectivity might be evaluated, with the result that we have become aware of the existence of both formal and primary attributes in so called formal and primary groups.

Although we have concentrated upon the family for the most part, relating the source of authority, types of goals, and techniques of influence to the family socialization process, it is clear that a similar application of these concepts could be made with equal relevance to the factory or to any formal organization. The same problems which may occur in the family due to inconsistency of goals, techniques, and authority source, may have obvious analogues in the industrial organization. But this we shall leave for further papers, projects, or investigators.

Further research based on the conceptual outline developed here can be directed toward several major foci. Our own research deals with the successful or unsuccessful socialization of the adolescent by the family. We are concerned with the family's utilization of formal or primary procedures as outlined above, and the relative occurrence of each pattern in families whose children appear to be making satisfactory progress in school, peer and community affairs, as contrasted with families whose children are not making satisfactory progress.

Only one focus among many has been treated here; it can and should be followed by examinations of formal and primary behavior in the family over time, for example, to consider the changes which have occurred in the American family in its movement from a patriarchal economically based group to an emotionally based, democratic system. Different subcultures in our society—the Negro family, the suburban family, the immigrant family—all offer situations for analysis according to the balance of primary and formal goals, techniques and authority. In addition, crosscultural studies, utilizing family data covering a range of societies, from the preliterate to the urban industrial, may actually allow us to examine the roots and developmental processes of organizational authority, and its relation to personal influence.

Finally, it is possible that studies of the

family emphasizing its structure and organization can bring to the arena of family research the benefits of a greater number of theoretical systems and methodological devices. These are urgently needed, and if an extension of conceptual schemes can be effected such that organizational and family theory can be blended in mutual support, behavioral science in general and our knowledge of human social development in particular is certain to benefit.

w. w. meissner, s.j.

parental interaction of the adolescent boy

A. Introduction

In the last few years, the awareness of the importance of the home environment and the pattern of interaction between the parents and the child has become central in the search for a better understanding of personality development and adjustment. The adolescent years represent a crucial period in the formation of "identity" (Erikson, 1959) and in the formation of values, ideals, and attitudes; and the formation of values, ideals, and attitudes is profoundly influenced by the relations that obtain between the adolescent and his parents. Disturbances in the development of identity or the "identity diffusion" that has been thought to underlie the defective adjustment of so many adolescents (and, subsequently, adults) in American culture has been traced to the influence of inconsistencies in intrafamilial relationships and early deprivation (Beres, Gale, & Oppenheimer, 1960). Also, evidence has been provided that seems to link delinquency, which is a major symptom of identity diffusion, with a defect in parental identification and a lack of strong and open affection (Andry, 1960).

While the importance of the parent-child interaction has been widely accepted, no clear understanding has emerged as to what factors are crucial in the parent-child interaction. The importance of the mother's role has

Reprinted with permission of the author and publisher from the *Journal of Genetic Psychology*, 1965, **107**, 225-233.

been accepted ever since Sullivan's work (Sullivan, 1953), but more recently the father's influence on a child's development has received emphasis. Andry's investigations (1960) seem to imply that a child's failure to identify with his father and inadequate communication with his father are central elements in the etiology of delinquency. Further, current studies in family dynamics have focused on the importance of the father's role (Bowen, Dysinger, & Basamanis, 1959; Lidz et al., 1956, 1957). Undoubtedly, the significant environment within a family is compounded not only of the level of adjustment and functioning of each parent individually or not only of the pattern of the interaction of the parents with each other, but also of the manner in which both parents interact with the growing adolescent. This study is directed to the assessment of the frequency of occurrence of certain typical parent-child interactions in a population of normal adolescent boys.

B. Procedure

The results presented arise from a 217-item questionnaire that was given to 1278 high-school boys attending nine schools. The schools were private, denominational schools under Catholic direction and were located in the states of New York, Pennsylvania, New Jersey, and Maryland. The questionnaires were given with a standard set of instructions read to the subjects by the test administrator. The test forms were sent in a sealed envelope to each administrator, who opened the envelope in the presence of the subjects, and immediately after the questionnaires were completed resealed the forms in an envelope for delivery to the investigator.

The subjects were selected randomly according to classes in their respective schools and they represented the medium range in academic achievement in their schools. Three hundred thirty-one were freshmen; 313, sophomores; 343, juniors; and 291, seniors. Ages ranged from 13 to 18, with average ages as follows: freshmen, 14.3 years; sophomores, 15.2 years; juniors, 16.2 years; and seniors, 17.2 years.

Results from the questionnaire were tabulated, per cents were computed, and chi squares were determined (Hess, 1960).

C. Family Characteristics

The families from which the boys came can be described as average middle-class families, and the average family group consists of father, mother, and siblings. Only 13 per cent of the subjects reported any persons living in the home other than members of the immediate family group. In six per cent of the families the father was deceased; in two per cent of the families the mother was deceased. Eight of the subjects lost a parent before the subject reached the age of 2 years; 13, between the ages of 2 and 6; 28, between the ages of 6 and 10; and 41, after the age of 10. Only four per cent of the boys reported divorce or separation of parents, not an unexpected figure in a predominantly Catholic population.

The families, for the most part, appear to have been financially stable; but 21 per cent of the subjects reported that financial troubles were a source of difficulty at home, and 27 per cent of the subjects reported a mother engaged in some form of work outside the home. The parents were predominantly native-born Americans, with only 14 per cent of the fathers and 10 per cent of the mothers having been born outside the United States. The proportion of Catholics in this population is strong: 91 per cent of the fathers and 96 per cent of the mothers profess the Catholic faith.

The only significant difference between fathers and mothers is educational level (Anastasi & Foley, 1953). Seventy per cent of the fathers and 72 per cent of the mothers had progressed beyond the high-school level, but 37 per cent of the fathers and 54 per cent of the mothers failed to finish college. Thirty-three per cent of the fathers and only 17 per cent of the mothers had graduated from college or had received some postgraduate training.

Not quite 13 per cent of the boys indicated that illness is a source of frequent home difficulty.

D. Perception of Parents

Whatever may be the attitudes or behavior of parents toward their children, the effect on the children is mediated through the children's perception of them (Ausubel et al., 1954) and there seem to be detectable differences between the perceptions of parents and adolescents. Hess (1960), for example, has shown that (while the descriptions of teenagers of themselves tend to agree with descriptions of them by their parents) teenagers expect their parents to underrate them; and parents expect the teenagers to overestimate the maturity and ability of teenagers. Adolescents rate parents higher than parents rate themselves on every item on which adolescents were questioned. These findings can be explained easily on the basis of the high valuation put on adult status by the adolescent who is struggling to define his own identity; but, at the same time, the explanation raises the question of the relationship between the objective situation and the adolescent's perception of it. In other words, the adolescent's perception of his home and parents is colored to a certain extent by his own needs.

The questionnaire responses suggest that certain differences exist between the perceptions of fathers and mothers and that these differences may be meaningful for understanding the interactions between adolescents and their parents. The differential parental characteristics can be listed as follows:

Father
Colder and more indifferent.
More old-fashioned.
Less understanding.
More unreasonable.

Mother
More friendly and interested.
More nervous.
More understanding.
More reasonable.

Thirty-five per cent of the students felt that their fathers were cold or indifferent; only 13 per cent thought this of their mothers. Fifty-one per cent thought their fathers more or less old-fashioned; 41 per cent regarded their mothers that way. Thirty-nine per cent thought their fathers understood the subject's difficulties; 54 per cent thought their mothers did. Thirteen per cent thought their fathers "nervous"; 30 per cent perceived their mothers as "nervous."

The typical relationship that emerges is decidedly more positive in regard to the mother than it is in regard to the father. Although the configuration may or may not run counter to the presumptive identification of the male child with the father figure, it raises a question about the influence of typical parental perceptions on the course of child development. Apparently the father figure becomes fixed with the role of mediator of parental authority and restriction; while the mother is perceived as responding more to emotional needs for sympathy, acceptance, and understanding. Moreover, the trends in the data, while not always significant, suggest that the foregoing perceptions become more dominant as one moves from the first year to the senior year of high school.

In general, the attitudes toward parents tapped by our questions were positive. The majority thought their parents not overly careful or concerned about them (62 per cent) or overly strict (85 per cent). Most felt proud of their parents and liked to have them meet their friends (74 per cent).

E. Parent-Child Interaction

As the young boy proceeds through the adolescent period, the pattern of his interactions with his parents shifts in both positive and negative dimensions. The dimensions of interaction, in which the shifts are statistically significant ($p < .05$), can be listed as follows:

Positive
1. Increased feeling of adequate social opportunity.
2. Increased feeling of sufficient social freedom.
3. Increased acceptance of parental authority.
4. Increased valuation of father's guidance.

Negative
1. Increased dissatisfaction with home life.
2. Increased unhappiness in the home.
3. Decrease in amount of leisure time spent at home.
4. Increased conflict with parents over religion.
5. Decreased approval of parental guidance.
6. Increase in seeing friends disapproved by parents.
7. Increased feeling of the imposition of parents' ideas.
8. Decreased valuation of father's understanding of personal problems.
9. Increased feeling of being misunderstood by parents; more misunderstood by father than mother.

The overall picture is one of gradual alienation from parental influence and increasing rebelliousness against parental control. The shifts, however, are variable. As might be expected, reports of satisfaction and happiness in the home situation are high (80 per cent and 89 per cent respectively), and a large majority (84 per cent) report that half or more of their leisure time is spent at home. Dissatisfaction and unhappiness, however, increase significantly as the boy grows older.

Religious belief does not provide a singular source of conflict. Only seven per cent report that differences in the religious beliefs of their parents have ever caused them any difficulty, and only 16 per cent report that they have ever come into conflict with their parents on the question of religion. There is a trend, however, toward increasing conflict as the boy grows older. This pattern coincides with the previously reported finding (Meissner, 1961) that religious belief becomes a primary source of serious doubt for this same group in their junior and senior years. This increasing concern would be likely to express itself in conflict with the parents.

Most of the boys do not feel that their parents' demands are excessive, but 18 per cent feel that their parents expect more than they can ordinarily accomplish. The large majority, however, approve of the manner in which their parents guide them (73 per cent). These attitudes undergo a significant shift ($p < .01$) between the freshman year (79 per cent) and the junior year (68 per cent).

The adolescent period is one of increasing social and heterosexual contacts; consequently it is to be expected that the regulation of these activities provides a common source of friction between the adolescent and his parents. In general, the majority of our subjects report that their parents encourage them to bring their friends into the home (75 per cent) and, to a lesser extent, that their parents approve of all their friends (54 per cent). Parental approval is reported as increasing steadily until the junior year and dropping off sharply in the senior year ($p < .02$). However, when parents do not approve of particular friends, only 34 per cent stop going with those friends.

Most of the parents (75 per cent) have the practice of setting a time for their sons to be home at night, but the practice seems to be observed less frequently as the boys grow older (freshmen, 83 per cent; sophomores, 82 per cent; juniors, 76 per cent; and seniors, 60 per cent). The difference between seniors and each of the other groups is significant at the .01 level; that between juniors and freshmen is significant at the .05 level. Coincident with a relaxation of parental restriction, there is an increasing feeling that the boys are being treated as maturely as they should be (freshmen, 54 per cent; sophomores, 64 per cent; juniors, 73 per cent; and seniors, 77 per cent). A majority of the boys (66 per cent) feel that they are given as much social freedom as other boys, and the frequency of that feeling parallels closely their feelings of being maturely treated (freshmen, 55 per cent; sophomores, 65 per cent; juniors, 70 per cent; seniors, 74 per cent). One-half of the boys (50 per cent) claim that they argue for greater liberty when they feel they deserve it.

In a minority of cases, parents are listed as the first source of sex information. Fathers are given as the source of first sex information by 22 per cent of the boys; mothers, by 20 per cent. For the most part, parents seem to be successful in giving such information. Only 11 per cent of the boys report that they lost confidence in their parents because of the way the sex issue was handled. In the majority of cases (73 per cent), the parents are acquainted with the girls whom the boys date, and conflict with the parents over girl friends is not frequent (13 per cent).

A large majority of the boys (87 per cent) recognize that parents exercise legitimate authority over them, but the figure fluctuates significantly between class groups. The shift that occurs between the freshman and senior years may reflect a maturing acceptance of the intellectual awareness of the grounds of parental authority or it may reflect a greater degree of identification with adult figures and adult status. In any case, parents are selected as the persons whom the boys obey more frequently than they do any other authority figure (83 per cent). Ninety per cent of the boys report that they understand the reason why they should obey their parents.

Parental authority, however, is not accepted without resistance. A small minority of the boys feel that the discipline in the home is too severe (10 per cent), and 19 per cent express the feeling that they are not treated as young men of their age should be treated. The majority, however, feel that in the exercise of responsibility their parents give them sufficient opportunity (58 per cent). At the same time, 28 per cent are not satisfied with the opportunities made available to them for responsible activity. Some boys (32 per cent) report that they are frequently scolded by their parents, and an even larger number (42 per cent) express the feeling that parents tend to impose their own ideas and customs. This latter feeling grows more frequent as the boy matures, possibly because of the increasing influence on him of opinions and attitudes derived from his peer group and because of other influences external to the home. Finally, 14 per cent feel that parents exert too much authority over them.

Negative attitudes toward parental authority and discipline are damaging because the internalization of parental norms is an essential step in the development of a responsible person. The formation of a mature identity depends in part on the stable and mature use of authority on the part of the parents; so unless the adolescent maintains positive attitudes the developmental pattern is more likely to be one of rejection and rebellion than one of acceptance. More often than not the question of rebellion does not arise so much as does the question of the adolescent's need and desire to establish his independence. When parental norms are presented in an authoritarian manner there is a tendency to develop negative attitudes toward them, and this tendency becomes more noticeable as the child grows older or shows better verbal intelligence. When parental restrictions are presented with rational motivations there is a tendency for positive attitudes to assert themselves (Pikas, 1961).

Perhaps the most important area of interaction between the adolescent and his parents is that of communication. It is particularly during the period of adolescence that the maturing young man needs the counsel and advice of his elders to enable him to work his way through the conflicts and turmoil characteristic of that period of development. In the present study, 33 per cent of the boys claim that they do discuss difficulties and personal problems with their fathers. Almost 39 per cent feel that their fathers understand their difficulties, while the rest of the subjects are divided between those who feel their fathers do not understand them (30 per cent) and those who are still undecided (31 per cent). There is a definite trend between the freshmen and the seniors (freshmen, 45 per cent; seniors, 33 per cent) to call into question the father's understanding. Fifty-three per cent of the boys say that they discuss their problems with their mothers, and 54 per cent feel that the mother understands the difficulties.

The father's influence regarding guidance seems to become relatively more dominant as the boy grows older. This trend presents a pattern much different from the previously observed pattern of discussing problems and difficulties. Apparently, adolescent boys turn to the father when there is a question of working out the ordinary everyday affairs; but, when immediate problems and difficulties arise, they tend to turn to the mother.

A small per cent of the boys (nine per cent) report that they fear their fathers rather than love them. In all age groups, there is a consistent tendency to feel more often misunderstood by the father than by the mother. The fixation of the perception of the mother establishes an expectation of continued feminine responsiveness in the future marriage relationship. The more negative fixation of the perception of the father, however, may have the effect of inhibiting the acceptance of the more masculine characteristics that depend on internalization of norms of restrictive discipline. Internalization is essential to the development of a strong sense of masculine identity. At the same time, the positive aspect of the significantly increased valuation of the father's guidance must be kept in mind.

The results of this study imply that there is a pattern of increasing alienation from parental influence and control that can be traced through the critical years of adolescence. There is a growing acceptance of the principle of parental authority and increased respect for parental judgment, especially significant because the strong Catholic influence would have been expected to have reinforced parental authority and to have stressed the value of obedience.

It is not clear, however, that the independent indications justify an identification of the visible pattern as one of rebelliousness. Analysis in terms of "rebelliousness" may reflect a prejudice dictated by a vested interest. From the point of view of the adolescent, the growing indications of decreasing parental authority may represent nothing more than a critical phase of differentiation from parental influence: an essential part of development toward mature and independent functioning.

In conclusion, the author suggests that there is a relationship between identifiable perceptions of parental figures and patterns of interaction between the adolescent and his parents, and that there is a determinable shift in these perceptions reflected in shifting patterns of interaction.

F. Summary

A total of 1278 high-school boys were asked to answer 217 questions on areas of interaction between themselves and their parents. The results indicate that certain typical perceptions of father and mother can be identified, and that these perceptions are significantly different. Also identified were patterns of interaction that reveal significant shifts between the early and the late years of high school. The shifts, generally, are in the direction of parental alienation and increased rebelliousness. An attempt was made to relate the boys' perceptions of parental perceptions to the developing pattern of interaction with the parents.

f. musgrove

the social needs and satisfactions of some young people: part i—at home, in youth clubs and at work

Summary. Questionnaires completed by 367 young people between 14 and 20 in the industrial North indicated the range and nature of the needs which they thought should be met by home, school, club and work, respectively, and the needs which they thought were, in fact, met. Two-hundred-and-fifty subjects were members of mixed youth clubs (fifty were at work, 200 at school). Their responses on a sentence-completion test were compared with the responses of fifty non-club members who were at work and sixty-seven who were at school.

Boys and girls, club members and non-members, young workers and those still at school, all demanded predominantly "expressive" functions of their homes: feeling at ease, wanted, loved and secure. Approximately a quarter of their demand referred to "instrumental" functions: character training, instruction in domestic and other skills, preparation for getting ahead in the world. Their demands were broadly satisfied, although some 10 per cent of club-members' statements referred to frustrations and restrictions at home. Less than 2 per cent of non-club members' statements about home were negative; and it seems possible that club members may often come from comparatively restrictive homes.

The club was expected to provide mainly "expressive" satisfactions, and did so. Only 6 per cent of members' statements referred to frustrations. Both work and school were expected to be almost equally "expressive" and "instrumental." The instrumentality of work was seen mainly in terms of character/independence training. School massively failed to fulfill the expressive functions expected of it—particularly the grammar school. But club members were more frustrated by school than non-club members; and again, it seemed that the club might be an important source of "expressive" satisfactions denied elsewhere. The predominantly negative self-concepts of some grammar-school sixth-formers, who were independently investigated, were in line with the need-frustrations which grammar school pupils appeared to suffer.

I. Introduction

The needs of young people between 14 and 20 are met by a range of social institutions among which home, school, work and clubs have an obvious importance. The inquiry described below is an attempt to answer two main questions: What are the needs which young people think should be met by home, school, club and work? and, What are the needs which they think are actually met? In answering these questions it was hoped that some light would be shed on the interconnections between institutions, the extent to which one compensates for the deficiencies of another; and that frustrations might be judged by comparing expectations with satisfactions.

Reprinted with permission of the author and the *British Journal of Educational Psychology*, 1966 (Part I), **36**, 61-71. This article also constitutes Chapter VI of *The Family, Education and Society*, by Frank Musgrove. London: Routledge and Kegan Paul, 1966.

It seemed probable that the home might provide relatively trivial satisfactions and a large measure of frustration. Functionalist analyses of contemporary society have often suggested that major satisfactions provided by the home in the past are now provided by other institutions, notably the school (Wilson, 1962); and writing about "youth culture" often suggests that it originates in conflict with the values and authority of parents. Work was also expected to be a scene of considerable frustration. The mechanization and routinization of work and youthful impatience with authority might be expected to breed widespread resentment among young workers, particularly those in manual employment.

Schools and youth clubs, on the contrary, might be expected to provide important gratifications. The club is a voluntary association and would be unlikely to exist if expectations were widely frustrated. School for pupils over fifteen years of age is also a voluntary organization; and in any case schools, it is claimed, are today humane, interesting, "child-centred," geared with unprecedented psychological insight to pupils' needs; and they have an obvious value in a relatively open society in improving a young person's prospects in life.

The relationship between personal needs and the "press" of institutions has been systematically investigated in American colleges. Job-satisfaction in America has similarly been explored by comparing individual needs with the satisfactions provided by employment (Schaffer, 1953). On a self-rating questionnaire the subject indicates the importance he attaches to allegedly universal human needs such as "Dominance," "Recognition and Approbation," "Dependence" and "Independence." He also indicates the levels of satisfaction in these various areas which he derives from his work. Need-strength can be compared with need-satisfaction.

The congruence or incongruence between personal needs and the practices and provisions of American colleges have been explored by Stern (1962) and Pace and Stern (1958). Again the point of departure is supposed universal human needs such as "Achievement," "Affiliation," "Order," "Sex" and "Understanding." The psychological needs of subjects are inferred from their responses on an "Activities Index": they indicate their preferences "among verbal descriptions of various possible activities." There are descriptions of orderly behaviour, dominant behaviour, deferential behaviour and so on. On the College Characteristics Index subjects score true or false corresponding descriptions of the college environment. Needs can then be compared with the perceived satisfactions, pressures and demands of college life.

But needs are felt in relation to particular institutions. It is true that an institution which manifestly aims to satisfy a particular need may in fact satisfy others. But the boy who goes to a youth club is unlikely to expect satisfaction of the needs which are met through work, or to feel frustrated if these latter needs are not met by the club. He may have a great need for achievement which the club affords little chance to satisfy; but he will not feel disgruntled, because he never expected it to do so. The author decided to allow spontaneous statements of need in relation to home, club, school and work respectively. No prior assumptions about needs were made: their nature would be determined only after inspection of responses given in an open-ended questionnaire. Satisfactions would be established from corresponding (spontaneous) statements about actual experience of the institutions in question.

II. Methods

Two-hundred-and-fifty members of six mixed youth clubs in a northern conurbation completed usable questionnaires, sixty-seven secondary school children who were not members of youth clubs, and fifty young workers who were not club members. The needs for which subjects sought satisfaction at home were elicited by the following sentence openings:

"At home you *should* always have plenty of chance to . . ."
"First and foremost home *should* help you to . . ."
"At home you *should* always be able to feel that . . ."

The same three openings were applied to school, work and club respectively. Corresponding cues were then provided to elicit statements of actual satisfaction (or frustration):

"At home you always *have* plenty of chance to . . ."
"Above all else home *does* help you to . . ."
"At home you *do* feel that . . ."

Thus, six statements were made by each subject about his home, his club, his school if he was still at school, or work if he was at work —a total of eighteen statements. Questionnaires were completed anonymously, but classificatory information was obtained and attached to each questionnaire: age, sex, type of education, age of leaving school or proposed age of leaving, examinations taken and passed, professional qualifications, type of employment (for those at work), and father's occupation.

There is an apparent danger that statements of needs are in reality statements of frustration; that the boy who writes, "At home you should always have plenty of chance to express yourself" says this precisely because he is given no such opportunity. The same difficulty arises in the "need-press" analysis of Pace and Stern and the job-satisfaction inquiries of Schaffer. But the latter did not find a negative correlation between need-scores and satisfaction scores, and significant correlations have not been found between corresponding scores on the College Characteristics Index and the Activities Index (McFee, 1961). In the inquiry reported here there was no significant tendency for statements of need to re-appear in negative form in the second part of the questionnaire, as statements of dissatisfaction.

The type of projective test used in the present inquiry has the advantage that it does not present the subject with a perhaps arbitrary and possibly irrelevant list of "needs" and "satisfactions" which he is forced to reject or endorse. It has been fruitfully employed in America (e.g., Lindgren, 1954) and England (e.g., Bene, 1957); and Symonds (1947) found that a sentence-completion schedule not only supplemented personal data obtained in interviews, but was useful in correcting them. (Thus, a report

based on interview may describe a man as "energetic"; responses on a projective test may show that a more accurate description would be "nervous.") It has the disadvantage that the need categories to which responses are assigned cannot be established in advance of the inquiry.

A coarse two-fold classification of responses was made initially into "expressive" and "instrumental" categories. The distinction is taken from Talcott Parsons: "Action may be oriented to the achievement of a goal which is an anticipated future state of affairs, the attainment of which is felt to promise gratification." "There is a corresponding type on the adjustive side which may be called *expressive* orientation. Here the primary orientation is not to a goal anticipated in the future, but the organization of a 'flow' of gratifications (and of course the warding off of threatened deprivations)" (Parsons, 1964, pp. 48-49). "Problems of expressive interaction concern relationships with alters which ego engages in primarily for the immediate direct gratification they provide" (Parsons and Shills, 1962, p. 209). By extension we refer not only to expressive and instrumental actions and functions, but to expressive and instrumental needs and satisfactions.

After scrutinizing all the responses six subdivisions which appeared logically distinct were made of the instrumental category, and seven of the expressive category. Two judges working independently were able to assign statements to these thirteen subgroups with virtually complete agreement. The instrumental category (I) was subdivided thus: (1) Intellectual skills, understanding and enlightenment; (2) Physical skills (including competence at games and sports); (3) Manual skills (including competence in domestic tasks); (4) Social skills (including poise and self-assurance in relationship with others); (5) Moral development (including references to "forming a good character," "becoming a good citizen," "Learning to be self-reliant and stand on your own feet"); (6) Personal advancement (including passing examinations, obtaining promotion, getting on in life).

The expressive category (E) was subdivided into: (1) Ease/emotional security (feeling at ease, wanted, loved, welcome); (2) Freedom/self-direction (including the freedom to express your views, have your say, "be yourself"); (3) Friendship; (4) Sense of competence (including "having a chance to prove yourself"); (5) Support from adults (including "knowing that you can take your problems to parents/teachers/youth leaders"); (6) Sense of identity with the group ("feeling one of the crowd/a member of the family/as if you belong"); (7) Sense of purposeful activity.

When the subjects who took part in the inquiry stated not what their institutions should, but did, provide, statements could be either positive or negative ("At home you always have a chance to relax," "At home you always feel unwanted"). Statements referring to expressive satisfactions were divided into Expressive: Positive (E+) and Expressive: Negative (E−). The latter referred to (1) restrictions, constraints, humiliation, belittlement, rejection, and (2) boredom and demoralization.

The author first administered the questionnaire in six mixed youth clubs which were selected to represent different social areas within a large industrial conurbation. Two clubs were in well-to-do residential suburbs, two in working class districts, and two in socially mixed, transitional, areas. The clubs had a nominal membership of over 300. The clubs were given a week's notice of the author's visit. Club members co-operated well, and over 90 per cent of those present completed the questionnaire. Two-hundred-and-sixty-eight questionnaires were filled in; eighteen were incomplete, illegible, or otherwise unusable; 250 were used in the analysis.

There were 135 males and 115 females. The age range was 14 to 20; 129 (51.6 per cent) were 16 years of age or above. One-hundred-and-sixty-three (65.2 per cent) came from the homes of professional and white-collar workers. Two hundred were still at school, 130 at grammar schools and seventy at modern schools. Sixty-seven of the grammar school pupils were in the sixth form. Twenty-four boys and twenty-six girls were at work. Twenty-nine of the workers had attended grammar schools and were all in non-manual, white-collar employment; twenty-one had attended secondary modern schools: the eight boys were all in manual occupations, but ten of the thirteen girls were in routine non-manual employment, mainly as office workers.

For comparative purposes three classes of fourth-year pupils in three secondary schools in the areas served by the clubs were asked to complete the questionnaire. Sixty-seven of these boys and girls were not members of youth organizations. Fifty-seven (85.1 per cent) came from the homes of manual workers.

Fifty young workers between the age of 16 and 20 were approached in recreational centres. They were not members of youth clubs or formal youth organizations. They were matched for age, sex and type of occupation with the fifty youth club members who were at work. Twenty-two of the twenty-five girls were in white-collar employment, fifteen of the twenty-five boys. All fifty completed the questionnaire.

III. Results

Home

Both the expectations and satisfactions of home are predominantly "expressive." Two-hundred-and-fifty club members made 750 statements about the needs which they expected home to satisfy, and 77.2 per cent of their statements referred to expressive satisfactions: being needed, feeling secure, having a chance to talk over personal problems with parents, and the like. Seven-hundred-and-fifty statements were made about the actual satisfactions of home: 72.3 per cent referred to expressive satisfactions.

In summary, the need-statements were: Expressive (E) 77.2 per cent, Instrumental (I) 22.8 per cent. The statements of satisfaction were: Expressive positive (E+) 72.3 per cent, Expressive negative (E−) 9.7 per cent, and Instrumental (I) 18.0 per cent.

Boys of all ages and girls over 16 place more stress on the instrumental functions of home than do younger girls. 29.8 per cent of older girls' demands referred to instrumental needs, only 15.3 per cent, of the younger girls' demands (CR 3.9, $P < 0.001$). The younger girls also find more dissatisfaction at home: 15.3 per cent of their statements refer to restrictions and other grievances, only 6.4 per cent of the older girls' statements (CR 8.3, $P < 0.001$).

Although there is a broad correspondence between needs and satisfactions, there are some major shifts within sub-categories. While the greatest demand is for emotional security (approximately a third of all need-statements), this is closely followed by the demand for freedom and self-direction (approximately a quarter of all statements). The first demand is met in full, the second falls substantially short of satisfaction. Twenty-two point five per cent of the boys' demands and 23.9 per cent of the girls' referred to freedom and self-direction at home; only 13.3 per cent of the boys' stated satisfactions mentioned freedom and self-direction, and only 11.3 per cent of the girls' statements.

Nevertheless, home emerges on this sentence-completion schedule as a pre-eminently satisfying social institution for young people. This is in line with other inquiries into home life today. Inquiries among representative samples of English adolescents (Hancock and Wakeford, 1965), as well as comparative studies sponsored by UNESCO (Berge, 1964), indicate close bonds between young people and their parents and widespread appreciation of parents and reliance on them as guides and counsellors in times of trouble.

In the present inquiry tributes to parents were frequent at all social levels. Subjects often stated a desire to talk over problems with their parents, and as often stated that they were in fact able to do so. A 15-year-old daughter of a plumber wrote: "At home you always feel you can tell your troubles to your parents and not be laughed at"; a 15-year-old son of a labourer: "At home you always have a chance to tell someone your troubles"; a 16-year-old apprentice hair-dresser, daughter of a textile buyer: "At home you always have plenty of chance to talk sensibly to your parents"; a 17-year-old postman's daughter: "At home you always feel that your opinions matter"; the 15-year-old son of a tailor: "At home you always have plenty of chance to talk over matters with your parents"; the 15-year-old daughter of a fireman: "At home you always have plenty of chance to air your views."

Appreciation of home was expressed in more general, and often enthusiastic, terms. The 18-year-old daughter of a clerical worker wrote: "At home you always feel confident that you are needed by someone"; the 16-year-old son of a shop manager: "At home you always feel joyful"; the 14-year-old son

of a bus driver: "At home you always feel wanted and grateful to your mother." Home offers relaxation, emotional security, and freedom to "be yourself." The 14-year-old daughter of a shopkeeper wrote: "At home you always feel relaxed, unafraid, easygoing, and enjoying every minute of it." (The same girl says of her grammar school: "You always feel petrified of punishment and nervous of exams.") The 17-year-old son of a company director claimed that: "At home you always feel happily unconscious of life"; the 16-year-old daughter of an engineer: "Above all home helps you to have roots in a crazy world." An 18-year-old typist, daughter of a civil servant, said that: "At home you always have plenty of chance to relax after work and you do not feel that you have to put on an act."

At home you can be natural; individuality is recognized; a person is not an anonymous member of a larger social category. "At home," says the 14-year-old-son of a manufacturer, "you should be able to feel an individual in your own right." Home should be, and is a place where your opinions count. The 16-year-old son of a businessman was of the opinion that "At home you should have plenty of chance to take part in things and have a say in things—like interior decoration (the colour of the wallpaper), to take one of many examples." Such demands appear to be met. "At home," says the 17-year-old son of a salesman, "you do feel that it really is a home, and not just a house you happen to live in."

The instrumental purposes of home are overshadowed by the expressive; but more than 10 per cent of the expectations of home refer to moral training and character development, "learning to stand on your own feet," "becoming a responsible citizen," "having a more sympathetic outlook toward others." Table 1 shows the level of demand and satisfaction in this regard.

TABLE 1. STATEMENTS ABOUT MORAL DEVELOPMENT (BOYS AND GIRLS)

	Demand %	Satisfaction %
School (N = 600)	9.8	6.0
Club (N = 750)	4.0	4.4
Home (N = 750)	12.1	7.8

Social skills, manual skills and intellectual enlightenment are also sought at home, but to a smaller extent. About three per cent of the subjects looked for some form of intellectual understanding. "Above all," said a 17-year-old girl, "home helps you to understand about adult things." A 17-year-old boy thought that "First and foremost home should help you to secure knowledge of things not taught at school, such as sex." A general social competence is sometimes mentioned: "Above all home helps you to manage your money and look after yourself" (18-year-old typist). "Above all home helps you to learn how to live with people and how to be well-mannered" (18-year-old daughter of a clerical worker). The 14-year-old son of a bus driver claimed that "Above all home helps you to learn a lot about gardening." For girls the instrumentality of home lies mainly in learning domestic skills: "home helps you to learn about married life," and "home helps you to learn how to run a home."

9.7 per cent of statements about the actual experience of home expressed dissatisfaction or criticism (8.4 per cent of the boys' statements, 11.0 per cent of the girls'). Some references were made to being misunderstood (a 15-year-old girl, daughter of a Y.M.C.A. secretary, said: "At home you feel that you're always in the wrong," the 15-year-old son of a bingo hall manager said that at home "you always feel that everyone is against you"). In the main grievances referred to restrictions and an overload of chores. "At home you always feel that you must do a few jobs and bring home an unopened wage packet" said an 18-year-old laboratory assistant. An 18-year-old tripe dresser always has the urge, when at home, "to be off all the time on my motor-bike." A 16-year-old trainee draughtsman "always feels cooped up" at home; a 15-year-old engineer's daughter "always feels in the way"; the 16-year-old daughter of a civil servant "always feels helpless." A 15-year-old girl, daughter of an insurance agent, always "feels like an unpaid char." Some—by no means entirely from working class homes—complain of the lack of privacy at home. And the mass media are intrusive. Although some appreciate home as a place where television is constantly available (a 14-year-old boy appreciates the chance to "loll around all the time with a cup of tea watching television"), others are like the 17-year-old son of a tailor who feels, at home, that he is "televisionised, radioised, bookised, and newspaperised."

Home is an enclosed world, isolated from wider social contacts, and largely accepted as such. The girls make some demand that they should be able to meet their friends at home (3.8 per cent of responses), but only 2.1 per cent mention home as a place where they do in fact meet their friends and non-family persons. Only one per cent of the boys mention home as a place where friends should or can be met. It is pre-eminently the club that is expected to meet the need for non-family contacts; and the need appears to be met in full.

The Youth Club

Like home, the youth club is seen primarily in "expressive" terms. It is not valued for any training it may provide in intellectual or even physical skills; in so far as it is instrumental, it is required to provide social training.

The needs which subjects hoped the club would satisfy were: 82.9 per cent expressive, 17.1 per cent instrumental. The actual satisfactions were: E+ 78.3 per cent, E– 5.9 per cent, and I 15.8 per cent.

When the club was mentioned as a place to meet friends and be friendly with people, the statement was placed in the expressive category. ("Expressive action is not oriented to the attainment of a goal outside the immediate action situation and process itself in the same sense as is instrumental action" (Parsons, 1964).) When there was clearly a notion of learning to get on with people, developing one's social skills, the statement was placed in the instrumental class. In such statements the club was seen as a training situation, helping you to overcome shyness, gain social confidence and poise, learn how to mix and get on with people.

Above all club members demand from their clubs a sense of ease and emotional security. A quarter of their statements refer to feeling relaxed, at ease, wanted, welcome. A comparable number of statements refer to being friendly, meeting and making friends. Other statements refer specifically to a sense of group solidarity, feeling "part of it," being "one of the crowd."

The demand for friendship often makes explicit mention of the opposite sex. Demands for specifically sexual contact or experience were rare, made by half a dozen

TABLE 2. FRIENDSHIP AND THE SENSE OF BELONGING (BOYS AND GIRLS)

	Demand				Satisfaction			
	School (N = 600) %	Club (750) %	Home (750) %	Work (150) %	School (N = 600) %	Club (750) %	Home (750) %	Work (150) %
Group solidarity	2.0	7.6	7.7	10.0	2.3	5.3	7.1	9.0
Ease and security	8.0	24.9	34.3	6.9	1.5	28.4	33.8	8.3
Friendship	4.7	23.8	2.3	8.6	4.5	21.7	1.6	9.3
Totals . .	14.7	56.3	44.3	25.5	8.3	55.4	42.5	26.6

boys. A 16-year-old grammar school boy thought that "At the club you should have plenty of chance for sex"; another said that "At the club you always feel sexy"; and a third 16-year-old boy said that "At the club you always feel in a good and sexy mood." Other-sex references were usually in less specifically sexual terms. A 14-year-old boy always feels happy at the club "because of Valerie, Susan and Joan." Sex antagonism as well as attraction was mentioned by three boys, thus: "At the club you always feel opposed to the opposite sex" (a 16-year-old grammar school boy).

The club is expected to provide a place of refuge from the stress of life outside. Its main purpose is to offer compensation for the restrictions, anxieties and humiliations promoted by other institutions. It is an escape from the constraints of school and the surveillance of parents. "At the club," says the 14-year-old son of a solicitor, "you should be able to feel relaxed and forget the terrible turmoil and distress of the world." "Above all the club helps you to get out of the school routine" (14-year-old grammar school girl).

Club membership legitimizes absence from home. "Above all the club helps you to go out without my dad arguing" (14-year-old daughter of a lorry driver). It is an escape from parents: "Above all the club helps you to do something constructive without criticism from parents: it is completely separate from parents" (17-year-old daughter of a senior civil servant). "At the club you always feel that there is no-one there to snap at you" (14-year-old daughter of a lorry driver). "At the club you should always be able to feel relaxed, without grown-ups nagging on to do this and not to do that" (15-year-old labourer's son). "Above all the club helps you to get away from the washing up" (14-year-old architect's daughter).

At the club you should be able to express your views, have your say, put forward a point of view. Thirteen per cent of all demands were of this character; and 11 per cent of stated satisfactions were in these terms. Still greater demands of this nature are made of school and home, but satisfaction falls much further short of demand.

The club is expected to a greater extent than school or home to provide training in social skills. "First and foremost the club should help you not to be afraid of meeting people" (14-year-old modern school girl, daughter of a shopkeeper). "The club should help you to talk to people more easily than you would otherwise" (15-year-old son of a chemist). "First and foremost the club should help you to socialize" (17-year-old grammar school boy).

TABLE 3. STATEMENTS ABOUT SOCIAL SKILLS

	Demand %	Satisfaction %
School:		
Boys (N = 336)	2.9	1.8
Girls (N = 264)	7.2	3.4
Club:		
Boys (N = 405)	8.1	5.2
Girls (N = 345)	10.7	7.8
Home:		
Boys (N = 405)	2.7	1.0
Girls (N = 345)	2.0	1.5

Although the club is appreciated for the informal training in sociability which it affords, complaints are made of undue pressure from the leaders to "mix in" and conform. The 16-year-old daughter of an engineer says that at the club she feels "organised, frustrated, got-at, expected to conform, keep quiet, take part in ridiculous discussions, able to hike." The 15-year-old daughter of a fishmonger feels that "you're always expected to go along with everyone else"; the 15-year-old son of a bricklayer that "you're always expected to do what the others are doing."

Club leaders hope that the club will be far more instrumental than members want it to be. The questionnaire for members was modified for leaders. Twenty-seven leaders were asked to say what young people should have a chance to do at the club, in what ways the club should help them, and what, above all, they should feel when they were at the club. They were then asked what they thought, from their experience, young people did in fact look for in the club. They placed considerable stress on instrumental, mainly moral purposes; but when they considered reality, they recognised that "expressive" purposes were predominant. (No club leader made an adverse comment on reasons for attending the club.)

TABLE 4. FUNCTION OF THE YOUTH CLUB (STATEMENTS BY LEADERS AND MEMBERS)

	Should		Is		
	E %	I %	E+ %	E− %	I %
Leaders (*N* = 81)	53.1	46.9	74.0	nil	26.0
Members (*N* = 750)	82.9	17.1	78.3	5.9	15.8

The "instrumentality" that leaders hope for in the club is chiefly in the form of character training: teaching members to accept responsibility, to become useful citizens, to find a true sense of values, to achieve "maturity." They recognize that they come in the main to feel welcome, at ease, unconstrained and relaxed.

Of course some members valued the club in precisely the instrumental terms that leaders would approve. "Above all," said a 17-year-old grammar school boy, "the club helps you to develop your administrative powers." "Above all, the club helps you to learn self-discipline and human relations" (another 17-year-old grammar school boy). But the predominant demand was for current feelings rather than for future competence and personal development.

Statements expressing dissatisfaction with the club were few: 5.9 per cent of all statements made. Since the club is a voluntary association, this low proportion is not, perhaps, surprising. Dissatisfaction was almost wholly directed towards aimlessness and lack of clearly defined purpose: "At the club you feel that you never do anything out of the ordinary and it is often boring."

Work

In the sentence-completion schedule completed by the fifty youth club members who were in full-time employment, work appeared to be generally satisfying, and in unexpected directions. The number of subjects in this group is, of course, small; and sub-groups (white-collar female workers, ex-grammar school boys, etc.) are too small to make reliable comparisons possible.

As one would expect, work was seen in instrumental terms to a far greater extent than home or club. But work was an instrument for other than crudely material ends: in fact, it is referred to largely as a learning situation (in a broad sense) by both manual and non-manual employees.

Forty-eight per cent of subjects' statements referred to expressive needs, 52 per cent to instrumental needs. Stated satisfactions were: E+ 45.3 per cent, E− 7.3 per cent, and I 47.4 per cent.

Boys and girls are alike in placing great stress on the educative value of work: Understanding not only of techniques and processes, but of people and wider social problems should be promoted. Boys differ from girls in placing considerable stress on work as a means to "getting on in life." Girls look for friendship at work; but boys also place a high value on a sense of solidarity with the work group or organization.

"At work you always have plenty of chance to learn something new and to ask about things without being considered a nuisance," says a 17-year-old trainee nurse. But it is not only trainees who appreciate work as education; indeed, for a 16-year-old apprentice electrician, work seems to mean, above all, a place "where you are expected to put the kettle on at 9:55 sharp."

It is the wider education in human affairs and understanding that receives most frequent mention: "Above all work helps you to increase your knowledge of society" (16-year-old audit clerk); "At work you always have plenty of chance to see how people react under the same conditions" (18-year-old male clerk); "At work you always have plenty of chance to meet people and learn about different people" (15-year-old grocery assistant); "Above all work helps you to be able to listen to older people's ideas and views" (18-year-old typist). And work promotes skill in human relationships: "Above all work helps you to get on with other people" (18-year-old printing works operative).

Work is expected to develop "character." No less than 21 per cent of the demand is for moral training, in a broad sense. (On the other hand, only 11 per cent of subjects' statements about reality refer to satisfactions in this regard.) Work is expected to help you to become responsible, to learn to shoulder responsibility, to help you to "grow up" to learn to "stand on your own feet." And in large measure it is seen as promoting a sense of responsibility, independence and self-reliance. Work "helps you to prepare for responsibility later in life," says a 17-year-old office worker; "Above all work helps you to become a more mature person" (17-year-old fitter); "Above all work helps you to rely on yourself" (17-year-old male shop assistant); "Above all work helps you to have a life of your own, giving more independence than school did" (ex-grammar school clerical worker).

15 per cent of the boys' statements demanded a sense of corporate membership at work; 11 per cent of their statements of satisfaction indicated that they achieved this sense of identification. (Only 5 per cent of the girls' demands and satisfactions referred to this sense of belonging to an organization or group.) "At work you always feel part of the firm," said a 19-year-old articled clerk; "At work you always feel you are an essential part of the mechanism" (16-year-old bank clerk).

7.3 per cent of the statements describing actual experience of work referred to frustrations and dissatisfactions. In no case was there any complaint about pay (except an oblique reference by a Post Office maintenance engineer: "At work you always feel that it is a rich man's world").

A minority of statements referred to a sense of wasting time or being under undue pressure ("always feeling rushed off your feet"). A few statements referred to a sense of humiliation: "At work you feel that some adults do not treat young people with any kind of respect" (18-year-old ex-grammar school girl employed as a clerk). "At work you always feel you're being told what to do" (18-year-old operative in a printing works). But the broad picture which emerges is one of appreciation of work as an environment which fosters growth towards a self-confident and self-respecting maturity.

lee g. burchinal

characteristics of adolescents from unbroken, broken, and reconstituted families*

This study investigates the possible effects of divorce upon the behavior of adolescent children. A large sample of parents (N=1,566) completed usable questionnaires; the sample was then divided into the independent variables of family type and social class and the dependent variables of adolescent characteristics and school social relationships. Nonsignificant differences were found for the majority of relationships tested pertaining to the detrimental effects of divorce upon children.

Although the secular trend in divorce rates has become arrested in recent years, the secular trend in the increasing proportion of divorces affecting children under 18 years of age has continued. The proportion of divorces affecting children under 18 years of age increased from approximately 41 per cent in 1932 to 60 per cent in 1959. Another way of viewing the trend toward the increasing proportion of children affected by divorce is to examine the ratio of children per 100 divorces. In 1935, 68 children were involved in every 100 divorces; this figure became 74 in 1948 and 100 in 1957. The number of children affected by divorce has increased each year, from an estimated 330,000 in 1953 to an estimated 379,000 in 1957. In recent years, the number of children under 18 affected by divorce has been increasing by approximately 20,000 annually.[1]

Few parents divorce without considering the effects of divorce upon the children. Friends, relatives, clergymen, and judges reiterate their concern, reflecting the general agreement among most Americans that when children are involved, the decision to divorce should be made reluctantly. It is generally assumed that unless the behavior of one or both parents is already harming the children, the process of divorce itself and the withdrawal of one parent is damaging to the children. This view also predominates in most discussions of divorce in family textbooks (Kenkel, 1960).

On the other hand, recent research on the developmental characteristics of children from various types of unbroken and broken homes suggests that the widely held apprehension about the detrimental influences of divorce upon children is not well founded. The present study represents a further test of the relationship between divorce

Reprinted with permission of the author and publisher from the *Journal of Marriage and the Family,* 1964, **26**, 44-51.

*Project No. 1425, Journal Paper No. J-4617 of the Iowa Agricultural and Home Economics Experiment Station, Ames, Iowa. This project was supported by the Division of Child Welfare of the Iowa Department of Social Welfare.

[1]These data were adapted from statistics reported by the National Office of Vital Statistics, Public Health Service, U.S. Department of Health, Education, and Welfare. See particularly: *Summary of Marriage and Divorce Statistics: United States,* 1957, Vital Statistics—Special Reports, National Summaries, Vol. 50, No. 18; *Vital Statistics of United States, 1959,* Section 2, "Marriage and Divorce Statistics," and Section 10, "Detailed Divorce and Annulment for the Divorce-Registration Area."

characteristics of adolescents

and remarriage of parents and the developmental characteristics of children.

Review of the Literature

Paul H. Landis compared children from broken and unbroken homes. While some significant social-psychological differences existed between the two groups of youth, these differences were not as extreme as might have been expected in light of the credence given to the assumed detrimental influences of divorce. Moreover, in a few areas, adolescents from broken homes seemed better adjusted than those from unbroken homes. These adolescents participated more in family counsels, more frequently shared their parents problems, reported less prying into their affairs by their parents, and reported less criticism of dates and the persons they dated. Also, despite or perhaps because of their greater concern about the adequacy of their family incomes and levels of living, youths from broken homes seemed to achieve economic maturity earlier than youth from unbroken homes (Landis, 1953).

Goode has reported extensive data on the process of divorce as it relates to children, custody and visitation arrangements, and various aspects of the mothers' perceptions of the ways in which divorce and, for most, remarriage affected their children. These data also question the assumption that divorce leads to poorer adjustment of children. Although almost all mothers worried about the effects of divorce upon their children, almost all remarried mothers subsequently thought their children's lives had improved after divorce (Goode, 1956).

Nye compared selected characteristics of several groups of high-school-aged youth. These were youth from unhappy but unbroken families, happy and unbroken families, and several types of broken families—those families broken by separation or divorce, those broken by other causes, and those in which youths lived only with their mothers. Null differences were found between the adjustments of adolescents in unhappy, unbroken families and those in broken families in the areas of church or school relationships and in delinquency companionship. Adolescents from broken families showed significantly better adjustment

than those from unhappy, unbroken families in relation to psychosomatic illnesses, delinquency behavior, and parent-child adjustment. In general, children from families broken by divorce did not have poorer adjustment than children from families broken in other ways. Children living in mother-only households scored higher in parent-child relationships, but in other ways their adjustment levels generally were similar to those of the other youth (Nye, 1957).

The present investigation represents an attempt to contribute further to the study of the adjustment or developmental characteristics of youth from unbroken families, one type of broken families, and several types of reconstituted families.

Method

Data for the present analyses were obtained from a study originally designed to investigate relationships between maternal employment and developmental characteristics of children. Since details of the methodology used in this investigation are available elsewhere (Burchinal, 1961; Burchinal & Rossman, 1961), a brief comment will suffice here.

Approximately 98 per cent of all students in the seventh and the eleventh grades in Cedar Rapids, Iowa, completed the questionnaire from which most of the data for dependent variables were taken. Using information provided by the students, parents were mailed a three-page questionnaire. Among other items, this questionnaire asked about the marital histories, educational levels, and occupations of each parent. By supplementing the original mailing with follow-up letters and interviews, 91 per cent of the original 1,824 parental questionnaires were completed. However, the number of cases for which data are reported in this study is less than this number because of loss of cases through editing, use of white families only, and failure by students to respond to certain items.

Data for the independent variable, family type, were obtained from the responses of parents to the marital-history item included in their questionnaires. Separate items for fathers and mothers asked if they were married only once and living with their original spouse, divorced and remarried, widowed and remarried, or if they were living with their children as a separated, divorced, or widowed person. A sufficient number of cases was available for developing five family types; the unbroken family consists of both biological parents; families headed only by the mother represent the broken family type; and three family types are included as reconstituted families—those consisting of mothers and stepfathers, those in which both parents had divorced and were remarried, and those headed by fathers and stepmothers. The number of cases of each type are shown in the tables. The two family types that included one parent and one stepparent are separated from the type in which both parents are remarried to differentiate between cases in which the stepparents had married for the first time and cases in which the stepparents also were previously married. In the latter type, both parents frequently brought their own children into the new home.

Data were available for two sets of dependent variables: measurements of selected personality characteristics of the adolescents, and measurements of selected aspects of their social relationships at school and in the community. Details of the measurement of these variables are provided at appropriate places in the findings section.

Considerable research documents the greater divorce rates among lower status families. Other studies support the generalization of greater indications of personality disturbance among lower status children, their less active participation in organized activities at school or in the community, and their lower academic achievement. Therefore, in all analyses, the status of the families should be controlled. It was possible to control family status for continuous data by using co-variance analysis in which the Hollingshead family-status scores were used as the control variable. However, the small number of cases for certain family types precluded imposing socio-economic status controls on the analyses of discrete data.

The need for controlling status is obvious from Table 1. Significant differences in status occurred among the five family types. All status scores except those for "mothers only" were based on data for the male heads (Hollingshead, 1957). For the type including mothers only, scores were based on the edu-

cational levels and the occupations of mothers, including the weight for unemployment when the mother was not employed. The unbroken families had the highest status levels. Smaller variations in status levels occurred among the other four family types.

Other analyses in which the category including mothers only was deleted also were significant: for the occupational status of fathers by the four family types, $X^2 = 39.15$, df $= 18$, $P < .01$; for level of education of fathers by the four family types, $X^2 = 30.64$, df $= 15$, $P < .01$. Tests involving educational and occupational levels of fathers for four family types and those for mothers for one family type are not directly comparable. Therefore, the analyses were redone, using only the educational levels of mothers. As shown in Table 2, significant results were obtained when the educational levels of mothers were compared. In this analysis, however, women with the highest levels of education were stepmothers, followed by mothers in unbroken families, whereas smaller variations in educational levels among mothers existed for the remaining family types. Thus, whether analyses are based upon status characteristics derived from fathers or mothers, there is an obvious need for controlling status differences among the family types.

Hypotheses

In the present investigation, the usual dichotomy between broken and unbroken families is elaborated to include the five types of families previously described. Only the one type in which children were living with their mothers only represents a current broken home. Three other types represent previously broken homes that now include two parents, although one is a stepparent. Most discussions on the impact of divorce upon children involve comparisons between children from homes broken by divorce and children from unbroken homes. In this investigation, however, over-all tests are made among children from the five family types. Tests are made separately for each sex. Characteristics of boys and girls may differentially reflect impacts associated with a divorce or remarriage of their fathers as contrasted to mothers. To avoid unnecessary

TABLE 1. PERCENTAGE DISTRIBUTIONS OF FAMILY STATUS BY THE FIVE FAMILY TYPES

Hollingshead social status index[a]	Family types										
	Unbroken families		Mothers only		Mothers and stepfathers		Both parents remarried		Fathers and stepmothers		Total	
	No.	Per cent	No.	Per cent	No.	Per cent	No.	Per cent	No.	Per cent	No.	Per cent
High	267	21.7	10	7.9	10	11.2	5	6.1	5	13.2	297	18.9
Middle	389	31.6	40	31.7	20	22.2	25	30.5	10	26.3	484	30.9
Low	574	46.7	76	60.4	60	66.6	52	63.4	23	60.5	785	50.2
Total	1,230	100.0	126	100.0	90	100.0	82	100.0	38	100.0	1,566	100.0

$X^2 = 68.54$, df = 16, $P < .01$. Df equals 16 because each of the two extreme categories was subdivided, but for convenience the results are presented in trichotomous form.

[a]Based on the Hollingshead social status index. Cutting points were based on approximate natural breaks in the distribution.

TABLE 2. PERCENTAGE DISTRIBUTIONS FOR THE EDUCATIONAL LEVELS OF MOTHERS BY THE FIVE FAMILY TYPES

Educational levels of mothers	Family types										
	Unbroken families		Mothers only		Mothers and stepfathers		Both parents remarried		Fathers and stepmothers		Total	
	No.	Per cent	No.	Per cent	No.	Per cent	No.	Per cent	No.	Per cent	No.	Per cent
More than 12 years	447	36.4	31	24.7	15	16.6	15	18.3	15	39.5	523	33.3
12 years	473	38.4	50	39.6	28	31.2	33	40.3	17	44.7	601	38.4
Less than 12 years	310	25.2	45	35.7	47	52.2	34	41.4	6	15.8	442	28.3
Total	1,230	100.0	126	100.0	90	100.0	82	100.0	38	100.0	1,566	100.0

$X^2 = 41.576$, df = 8, $P < .01$.

repetition, separate hypotheses are not presented for each sex and for each variable. Instead, two general null hypotheses are used to guide the analyses for each sex:

1. There are nonsignificant differences among selected personality characteristics of adolescents from the five family types.
2. There are nonsignificant differences among selected measures of social relationships of adolescents from the five family types.

Findings

Selected Personality Characteristics of Adolescents

The data used to measure personality characteristics of children were derived from indices developed from questions similar to those included in several of the personality inventories and the emotionality scale of the Minnesota Test of Personality (Darley & McNamara, 1941). Each question was followed by three responses: "Yes," "No," and "Don't Know," which were scored as two for "Yes," one for "Don't Know," and zero for "No." Eleven scores were derived by sorting items into homogeneous pools on the basis of agreement among three judges. Details of the content and statistical properties of these scores are available elsewhere; for present purposes, only their descriptive titles are used (Burchinal, 1961).

The first step in the co-variance analysis involving control for family status was to test for common slope between the status variable and the 11 measures of personality characteristics. The resulting F ratios were significant for three variables: illness-proneness, nervousness, and anxiety and fright reactions. These significant differences precluded application of the co-variance test to these variables. The unadjusted means for these three scores are presented later. For the remaining eight personality scores, all F ratios for differences associated with family type were nonsignificant. These scores were each considered as a separate measurement of the personality development of the adolescents and included measurements of mood fluctuations, fatigue reactions, envy and withdrawal reactions, head and eye complaints, respiratory complaints (both viewed as psychosomatic tendencies), excessive introspection, over-sensitivity to others, and obsessive feelings. Since all results are non-significant, tables are omitted.

The means for the three personality characteristics not included in the co-variance tests are reported in Table 3. Means for participation in school activities are also included in Table 3, although these data are discussed later in relation to the social relationships of the adolescents.

Higher scores on personality characteristics represent greater indications of disturbance. Means for one score cannot be compared with those for another score because the means are based on a different number of items. Analyses must be limited to comparisons among the five means for each score. For those scores not included in co-variance tests, only small variations existed among the means for either boys or girls. There was no evidence of clear-cut superiority of adolescents from one family type in comparison with adolescents from other types of families.

When all data are considered, there is no basis for rejecting the first null hypothesis.

Scores for selected personality characteristics of adolescents from the five family types were not related to the present marital status of their parents.

Social Relationships

The school and community-participation scores are obvious measures of the degree of social participation in a variety of organizations available to the adolescents at school or in Cedar Rapids. Participation in community activities was included in the co-variance analyses, and the resulting mean differences among boys or girls were nonsignificant. Means for school-activity scores could not be included in the co-variance test because of the significant F ratio for the test for common slope. Therefore, the unadjusted means for the social-activity scores are presented in Table 3.

Scores for boys from unbroken families, boys from families where both parents were remarried, and boys living with fathers and stepmothers were relatively similar. Lower and similar school-activity scores were observed for boys who lived with their mothers only or with mothers and stepfathers. Girls from unbroken families clearly were more active in school activities than other girls. Girls living with their mothers only were next most

TABLE 3. MEANS FOR SCORES NOT INCLUDED IN THE CO-VARIANCE TESTS AND FOR THE SIGNIFICANT DIFFERENCES FOR DAYS ABSENT FROM SCHOOL BY THE SEX OF THE ADOLESCENTS AND THE FIVE FAMILY TYPES

Variables	Five family types				
	Unbroken families	Mothers only	Mothers and stepfathers	Both parents remarried	Fathers and stepmothers
Number of cases					
Boys	641	60	37	46	25
Girls	568	63	5	36	13
Scores not included in co-variance tests					
Illness-proneness					
Boys	3.8	4.3	4.5	3.6	3.8
Girls	3.8	3.9	4.2	4.0	3.8
Nervousness					
Boys	0.4	0.6	0.5	0.7	0.7
Girls	0.5	0.7	0.6	0.6	0.6
Anxiety and fright					
Boys	1.1	1.2	1.2	1.3	1.2
Girls	1.7	1.8	2.2	2.3	2.0
School activities					
Boys	5.8	4.7	4.5	5.9	5.4
Girls	5.3	4.6	3.7	3.2	3.4
Significant differences after co-variance test					
Number of days absent*					
Boys	5.3	10.0	6.3	6.6	5.9
Girls	5.8	8.1	8.6	6.2	6.5

*F (sex) = .152, df = 1, 1526, $P > .05$. F (family type) = 3.800, df = 4, 1526, $P < .05$. F (sex by family type) = 1.120, df = 4, 1526, $P > .05$.

TABLE 4. RESPONSES OF THE ADOLESCENTS TO SOCIAL RELATIONSHIP ITEMS HAVING SIGNIFICANT DIFFERENCES BY THE FAMILY TYPES

Sex of respondent and school-relationship question	Family types											
	Unbroken families		Mothers only		Mothers and stepfathers		Both parents remarried		Fathers and stepmothers		Total	
	No.	Per cent	No.	Per cent	No.	Per cent	No.	Per cent	No.	Per cent	No.	Per cent
Girls												
How well do you like school?												
Very well	217	34.3	31	38.8	21	35.6	12	33.3	5	35.8	286	34.8
Pretty well	350	55.4	36	45.0	31	52.5	14	38.9	8	57.1	439	53.5
Not very well and not at all	65	10.3	13	16.2	7	11.9	10	27.8	1	7.1	96	11.7
Total	632	100.0	80	100.0	59	100.0	36	100.0	14	100.0	821	100.0
X^2 = 15.87, df = 8, P < .05.												
Teachers give more attention to others.												
Much or somewhat more	238	38.0	34	42.5	34	58.6	20	55.6	3	21.4	329	40.4
Hardly ever or not at all	389	62.0	46	57.5	24	41.4	16	44.4	11	78.6	486	59.6
Total	627	100.0	80	100.0	58	100.0	36	100.0	14	100.0	815	100.0
X^2 = 15.90, df = 4, P < .05.												
Teachers harder on you than others.												
Much or somewhat more	102	16.1	17	21.2	20	33.9	5	13.9	1	7.1	145	17.7
Hardly ever or not at all	530	83.9	63	78.8	39	66.1	31	86.1	13	92.9	676	82.3
Total	632	100.0	80	100.0	59	100.0	36	100.0	14	100.0	821	100.0
X^2 = 14.69, df = 4, P < .05.												
Boys												
How many of your schoolmates do you like?												
One to three	68	9.5	9	12.2	9	18.0	7	15.2	6	23.1	99	10.9
Four	295	41.3	33	44.6	13	26.0	12	26.1	12	46.1	365	40.1
Five or more	351	49.2	32	43.2	28	56.0	27	58.7	8	30.8	446	49.0
Total	714	100.0	74	100.0	50	100.0	46	100.0	26	100.0	910	100.0
X^2 = 17.06, df = 8, P < .05.												

active, and still lower and relatively similar scores were observed for the girls in the remaining three family types. However, the inability to control for family status precludes interpretation of the differences among school-activity scores.

Absences from school, school grades, and responses to five attitude questions were also available for testing differences in social relationships among the five groups of adolescents. All of the school-related variables are considered as indicators of social relationships and developmental characteristics in the context of the school as an important social system for adolescents.

Nonsignificant results were found after the co-variance tests for the differences in grade-point means of the five groups of adolescents, although girls had significantly higher grade-point means than boys. Significant differences in frequency of absence from school, as shown in Table 3, remained after the co-variance test. Among both boys and girls, adolescents from unbroken families had been absent the fewest days from school, although the means for several other

groups closely approximated those for adolescents from unbroken families. The means for boys living with fathers and stepmothers were only about half a day greater than those for the boys from unbroken families. Means for boys living with mothers and stepfathers or with parents who both had remarried were approximately one day greater than those for the boys from unbroken homes. In contrast, the means for boys living with their mothers only were about twice those for boys from unbroken families and about two-thirds larger than the means for the other three groups of boys.

Less variation occurred among the means for days absent among girls. About a half day separated the lowest mean for girls from unbroken families from that for girls from families where both parents had remarried or that for girls living with their fathers and stepmothers. Means for girls living with their mothers only or with their mothers and stepfathers were about two days greater than the other means.

Additional data on the social relationships of adolescents were obtained from their responses to five attitude items: "Taking everything into consideration, how well do you like school?" "How often do you feel your teachers give more attention to other students than to you?" "How often do you feel your teachers are harder on you than on other students?" "How many of your schoolmates do you like?" "In comparison with other students in your school, how well do you think you are liked by your schoolmates?" The dichotomous or trichotomous responses obtained for these items were analyzed separately by the boys and girls in the five family types.

Nonsignificant chi squares were obtained for the responses of both boys and girls to the last question: "How well do you think you are liked by your schoolmates?" Of the remaining four sets of analyses, one significant difference was found for boys and three for girls. The responses for the four items having significant differences are given in Table 4.

The significant difference among the boys' responses for the number of schoolmates they liked formed three patterns: (1) boys from unbroken families and those who lived with mothers only; (2) boys who lived with their mothers and stepfathers and those whose present parents both had remarried; and (3) boys living with fathers and stepmothers. The first group less frequently reported three or fewer friendships and reported four or five or more friends with almost equal frequency. The second group more frequently reported three or more friendships than did the first group, but the second group of boys least frequently reported having four friends and most frequently reported having five or more friends. The third group of boys most frequently reported fewest friendships and least frequently reported the most friendships. The only clear-cut result of this test was the fewer number of friendships among boys living with their fathers and stepmothers. This one significant result does not appreciably alter the general interpretation of null differences among the responses of the boys to the attitude questions. Therefore, when all data are considered, the null hypothesis is not rejected for the relationships between family type and the measures of the boys' social relationships.

Responses to three of the five items were statistically significant for girls, but somewhat differing patterns of responses were found among the three sets of results, making clear interpretation of the data difficult. The only consistent result was the more favorable responses of girls living with their fathers and stepmothers, suggesting that these girls had more positive attitudes toward school and maintained better relationships with teachers than other students. Otherwise, there are no clear or consistent patterns among the girls' responses to the three items. It is clear, however, that girls from unbroken homes did not display uniformly more favorable attitudes toward school than girls from other types of homes, even though the girls from the unbroken homes were absent less frequently.

Summary and Discussion

Comparisons of personality and social relationship scores for five groups of adolescents from unbroken families, those living with mothers only, and adolescents from three types of reconstituted families support the following conclusions:

1. Among boys and girls, nonsignificant differences prevailed among the measures of personality characteristics of the adolescents from the five family types.
2. For both boys and girls, nonsignificant differences also were observed for the following measures of social relationships: participation in school or community activities, mean school-grade points, and the number of schoolmates the respondent thought liked him or her.
3. Nonsignificant differences existed among the responses of the five categories of boys to the three items related to their attitudes toward school.
4. In addition, nonsignificant differences occurred for the girls' responses to how many of their schoolmates they liked.
5. Significant differences were found for the number of days absent from school: adolescents from the unbroken homes were absent the fewest number of days.
6. Significant differences occurred among the girls' responses to the three school-related items and among the boys' responses to the item asking about how many of their schoolmates they liked.

While the null hypothesis was rejected for these four significant tests based on the attitude items, the data did not lend themselves to summarization by an alternative hypothesis that was theoretically meaningful. Moreover, the lack of control for differences in social status among the five family types precludes direct interpretation of the differences for these items.

Thus, the over-all conclusions of this investigation are that data are lacking to support rejection of either null hypothesis tested. Inimical effects associated with divorce or separation and, for some youth, with the remarriage of their parents with whom they were living, were almost uniformly absent in the populations studied. Acceptance of this conclusion requires the revision of widely held beliefs about the detrimental effects of divorce upon children. Many persons will quarrel with the results of this study—and similar results from other studies as well—by pointing to their obvious limitations. It is true that data were limited to the type collected by questionnaires or obtained from school records. It is also true that some children will suffer extreme trauma because of divorce or separation and consequent withdrawal of one parent, and, for some, their development will be affected deleteriously. However, even in these cases it is difficult to assess whether the difficulty occurs because of divorce or whether it reflects the conflict preceding the divorce and separation. Nevertheless, for the adolescents in the seventh and eleventh grades in one metropolitan area, there is no question that in terms of variables measured, family dissolution and, for some families, reconstitution, was not the overwhelming influential factor in the children's lives that many have thought it to be.

Instead of focusing on the possible negative influences of divorce upon the development of children—efforts that frequently may be more oriented toward preserving family stability than toward insuring the best development of children of the families in conflict—research and family-education specialists could do well by studying the processes whereby parents have minimized possible trauma for their children at the time of divorce and have best helped the children adapt to new family situations (Despert, 1962).

References

Anastasi, A. & Foley, J. P. *Differential psychology.* New York: Macmillan, 1953.

Andry, R. G. *Delinquency and parental pathology.* London: Methuen, 1960.

Ausubel, D. P., Balthazar, E. E., Rosenthal, I., Blackman, L. S., Schpoont, S. H., & Welkowitz, J. Perceived parental attitudes as determinants of children's ego structure. *Child Development,* 1954, **25,** 173-183.

Beiser, M. Poverty, social disintegration, and personality. *Journal of Social Issues,* 1965, **21,** 56-78.

Bene, E. The use of a projective technique, illustrated by a study of the differences in attitudes between pupils of grammar schools and secondary modern schools. *British Journal of Educational Psychology,* 1957, **27,** 89-100.

Beres, D., Gale, C., & Oppenheimer, L. Disturbance of identity function in childhood: Psychiatric and psychological observations. *American Journal of Orthopsychiatry,* 1960, **30,** 369-381.

Berge, A. Young people in the Orient and Occident. *International Journal of Adult and Youth Education,* 1964, **16.**

Blau, P., & Scott, W. R. *Formal organizations.* San Francisco: Chandler, 1962.

Bowen, M., Dysinger, R. H., & Basamanis, B. The role of the father in families with a schizophrenic patient. *American Journal of Psychiatry,* 1959, **115,** 117-120.

Burchinal, L. G. *Maternal employment, family relations, and selected personality school-related and social-development characteristics of children.* Iowa Agriculture and Home Economics Experimental Station Research Bulletin No. 497, 1961.

Burchinal, L. G., & Rossman, J. E. Relations among maternal employment indices and developmental characteristics of children. *Marriage and Family Living,* 1961, **23,** 334-340.

Clancy, N., & Smitter, F. A study of emotionally disturbed children in Santa Barbara county schools. *California Journal of Educational Research,* 1953, **4,** 209-222.

Darley, J. G., & McNamara, W. J. *Minnesota personality scale.* New York: Psychological Corporation, 1941.

Despert, J. L. *Children of divorce.* Garden City, N.Y.: Doubleday, 1962.

Douvan, E. & Adelson, J. *The adolescent experience.* New York: Wiley, 1966.

Erikson, E. H. *Identity and the life cycle.* New York: International Universities Press, 1959.

Glasser, P. & Navarre, E. Structural problems of the one-parent family. *Journal of Social Issues,* 1965, 98-109.

Goode, W. J. *After divorce.* New York: Free Press, 1956.

Green, A. Middle class male child and neurosis. In N. W. Bell, & E. F. Vogel (Eds.), *A modern* introduction to the family. New York: Free Press, 1960. Pp. 563-572.

Hancock, A., & Wakeford, J. The young technicians. *New Society,* 1965, **120**, 13-14.

Hess, R. D. Parents and teenagers: Differing perspectives. *Child Studies,* 1960, **37**, 21-23.

Hollingshead, A. B. Index of social position. Unpublished paper, Department of Sociology, Yale University, 1957.

Horrocks, J. E. *The psychology of adolescence.* (2nd ed.) Boston: Houghton Mifflin, 1962.

Josselyn, I. Social pressures of adolescence. *Social Casework,* 1952, **33**.

Kenkel, W. F. *Family in perspective.* New York: Appleton, 1960.

Landis, P. H. *The broken home in teenage adjustment.* Washington, D.C.: Washington Agriculture Experiment Stations Bulletin No. 542, 1953.

Lidz, T., Cornelison, A. R., Fleck. S., & Terry, D. The intrafamilial environment of the schizophrenic patient: I. The father. *Psychiatry,* 1957, **20**, 329-342.

Lidz, T., Parker, B., & Cornelison, A. R. The role of the father in the family environment of the schizophrenic patient. *American Journal of Psychiatry,* 1956, **113**, 126-132.

Lindgren, H. C. The use of a sentence completion test in measuring attitudinal change among college freshmen. *Journal of Social Psychology,* 1954, **40**, 79-92.

McFee, A. The relationship of students' needs to their perceptions of a college environment. *Journal of Educational Psychology,* 1961, **52**, 25-29.

Meissner, W. W. Some indications of the sources of anxiety in adolescent boys. *Journal of Genetic Psychology,* 1961, **99**, 65-73.

Moore, B. M., & Holtzman, W. H. *Tomorrow's parents.* Austin, Texas: Hogg Foundation for Mental Health, 1965.

Nye, F. I. Child adjustment in broken and unbroken homes. *Marriage and Family Living,* 1957, **19**, 356-361.

Pace, C. R., & Stern, G. G. An approach to the measurement of college environment. *Journal of Educational Psychology,* 1958, **49**, 269-277.

Parsons, T. Certain primary sources and patterns of aggression in the social structure of the Western world. In F. Mullahy (Ed.), *A study of interpersonal relations.* New York: Grove, 1949. Pp. 269-296.

Parsons, T. *The social system.* London: Routledge and Kegan Paul, 1964.

Parsons, T., & Bales, R. (Eds.) *Family, socialization and interaction process.* New York: Free Press, 1955.

Parsons, T., & Shills, E. *Toward a general theory of action.* New York: Harper, 1962.

Pikas, A. Children's attitudes toward rational versus inhibitory parental authority. *Journal of Abnormal and Social Psychology,* 1961, **62**, 315-321.

Schaffer, R. H. Job satisfaction as related to need satisfaction at work. *Psychological Monographs,* 1953, **67**, 14.

Stern, G. G. Environments for learning. In N. Sanford (Ed.), *The American college.* New York: Wiley, 1962.

Sullivan, H. S. *The interpersonal theory of psychiatry.* New York: Norton, 1953.

Symonds, P. M. The sentence completion test as a projective technique. *Journal of Abnormal and Social Psychology,* 1947, **42**, 320-329.

Whitmansh, R. E. Adjustment problems of adolescent daughters of employed mothers. *Journal of Home Economics,* 1965, **57**, 201-204.

Wilder, T. *The ides of March.* New York: Harper, 1948.

Wilson, B. R. The teacher's role—a sociological analysis. *British Journal of Sociology,* 1962, **13**, 15-32.

Zelditch, M. Role differentiations in the nuclear family. In T. Parsons & R. Bales (Eds.), *Family socialization and interaction process.* New York: Free Press, 1955.

Annotations

Bell, A. P. Role modeling of fathers in adolescence and young adulthood. *Journal of Counseling Psychology,* 1969, **16**, 30-35. Bell's study reveals that, although fathers are the most important role models for their sons in adolescence, nonparents emerge as increasingly significant models as the boys move into young adulthood. Also, the father-model role is predictive of the son's adult occupational choice.

Brantley, D. Family stress and academic failure. *Social Casework,* 1969, **30**, 287-290. The author investigates academic failure in youth. In evaluating family patterns, he concludes that there is a high correlation between family stress and adolescent social and family dysfunction. Forty percent of the homes studied were broken in some way. In the 60 percent intact, home stress was cited as arising from alcoholism, improper guidance, rigidity, rejection, unreasonable expectations, and inconsistent discipline. Brantley illustrates counseling programs that helped resolve some adolescent conflicts.

Bryan, J. H. How adults teach hypocrisy. *Psychology Today,* 1969, **3**, 50-52, 65. Bryan exposed a group of 9- to 11-year-olds to a set of behaviors that were inconsistent with what they had been told. Those who were exposed to a greater word-influence model still did not do what they were told when others around them were behaving differently. Bryan concluded that positive actions do speak louder than words and that exhortations evoke thoughts about a particular behavior but not the behavior itself.

Elder, G. H., Jr. Democratic parent-youth relations in cross-national perspective. *Social Science Quarterly,* 1968, **49**, 216-228. This article assesses secular trends in parent-youth patterns since the early 1900s. It was based on a sample of 1000 men and women, 17 years or older, from four nations: the United States, West Germany, Great Britain, and Mexico. The survey revealed an upward trend toward democratic parent-youth relations in the past 40 years.

Gibson, H. B. Parental attitudes and their relation to boys' behavior. *British Journal of Educational Psychology,* 1968, **38**, (part 3), 233-239. This study assessed the attitudes of the mothers and fathers of 411 urban working-class boys toward their children. Both mothers and fathers were shown to be authoritarian. Mothers also indicated some underconcern. The obtained scores were related to bad behavior in school and to subsequent delinquency.

King, K., McIntyre, J., & Axelson, L. J. Adolescents' views of maternal employment as a threat to the marital relationship. *Journal of Marriage and the Family,* 1968, **30**, 633-637. This study shows that adolescent males think female employment is a greater threat to marriage than do adolescent females. Adoles-cents belonging to a higher socioeconomic status see maternal employment as less threatening to marriage than do lower-class adolescents. The greater the father's participation in household tasks, the more accepting of mother employment are adolescent males and females.

Thomes, M. M. Children with absent fathers. *Journal of Marriage and the Family,* 1968, **30**, 89-96. Thomes' research is based on a study among children whose parents were divorced or separated and children from intact homes. The children saw the mother as the primary disciplinarian but also included the father in their description of a home. When asked what they wanted most in the home, only six children from broken homes mentioned the father. Research indicates that, although the father fits into the description of the home, children who are fatherless for two or more years learn to accept their family status and role.

five

the adolescent and school

Hurlock (1967) contends that there are three major stepping-stones to socioeconomic advancement: social mobility, schooling, and vocation. This chapter focuses on schooling. It examines the current issues in adolescent relationships with secondary education, illustrates how today's adolescent views his high school experiences, and suggests what educators can do to build a total educational program that is vital to the youths in their schools. We will also discuss the persuasiveness of peer groups, esteemed social-class values, academic and social learning, and the flexibility of school curricula and environment.

The Coleman Study

Extensive research has been conducted on the adolescent and his school, especially on whether he sees his high school as an academic or social institution. Coleman's work shows that most students regard the school as a primarily social environment. He conducted his study among 10 rural and urban Midwestern high schools with enrollments ranging from fewer than 100 up to 2000. This in-depth exploration of the high school world covered all aspects of the adolescent's own society—his unique symbols and language and his special interests and activities.

When Coleman asked what it took to get into the leading crowd at school, most adolescents agreed that academic success was not highly important. "It takes athletic prowess, knowing how to dance, owning a car, having a good reputation, or liking parties, and often not being a prude (for girls) or a sissy (for boys). Good grades and intelligence are mentioned, but not very often, and not so often as any of the other items" (Coleman, 1965, p. 19). Thus academic achievement did not count for as much as other activities.

> . . . In every school the boy named as best athlete and the boy named as most popular with the girls were far more often mentioned as members of the leading crowd, and as someone "to be like," than was the boy named as the best student. And the girl named as best dressed, and the one named as most popular with boys, were in every school far more often mentioned as being in the leading crowd and as someone "to be like," than was the girl named as the best student (1960, p. 344).

Forty-five percent of the boys wanted to be remembered as athletic stars, compared with 31 percent who wanted to be remembered as brilliant students. Among the girls, only 28 percent wanted to be remembered as brilliant students, whereas 72 percent wanted to be remembered as being most popular or leaders in activities (Coleman, 1961).

Coleman's major conclusion is that the American high school in general allows the adolescent to divert his energies and abilities into athletics and social activities. The intellectually inclined student is not socially reinforced. As a result, the academic aspect of high school suffers.

Other Investigations

Friesen conducted a comparable survey in Canadian high schools, and the first article in this chapter reports on that study. He investigated the academic-athletic-popularity syndrome among 15,000 students in 19 Canadian high schools, and his results contrasted sharply with Coleman's. Friesen also asked his students whether they preferred to be remembered for academic achievement, athletics, or popularity. He found that Canadian students are most interested in being remembered for academic achievements and place considerably less emphasis on popularity and athletics.

Other studies have examined the amount of interest adolescents have in school. The second article, by Leidy and Starry, discloses the results of a survey conducted by the Purdue Opinion Panel (Remmers & Radler,

1957) on attitudes toward school. Data collected in 1953, 1958, 1965, and 1967 indicate that most adolescents (72–75 percent) like school most of the time. Perhaps the most significant finding of the Purdue studies is the shift in students' evaluations of the educational process. In 1953 the acquisition of social skills was considered the primary educational goal; the 1966 responses ranked discipline and responsibility first. Nevertheless, today's high school student is still concerned with his social life. In fact, 59 percent of the students felt that having friends helped them to develop their personalities, and 68 percent of the sample wished they had more friends.

School Influences

The school can help a person integrate himself into his society. It can strengthen his self-concept and enhance his personality by providing the opportunity for academic success, social success, and peer and faculty acceptance. Spaulding's article discusses peer and school influences on personality and social development. For example, he suggests that a teacher's personality and behavior can affect the social development of his students. Teachers who are interested in and supportive of students have a positive effect on the personalities and social behaviors of those students. In another study, Spaulding (1963b) found high pupil self-concepts in the classes of teachers who were socially integrative or learner-supportive. A negative relationship to self-concept was found when teacher behavior was dominating, threatening, and sarcastic. Of course, the student himself represents a variable in measurements of this type. That is, regardless of how a teacher interacts with a class, he may have a positive effect on one child but a less positive or even negative effect on another child.

Unrealized Potential

In the final article in this chapter, Havighurst discusses the unrealized potentials of adolescents. He indicates three broad groups of young people whose potential for achieving adult competence is so far from being realized that they constitute social problems: (1) the socially disadvantaged and educationally maladjusted adolescent, (2) the underdeveloped and underachieving adolescent, and (3) the potentially superior but uncommitted adolescent.

The large numbers of disadvantaged and maladjusted adolescents who drop out of high school become only marginal members of the labor force and of society as a whole. They expend their energies in seeking pleasure and excitement. This group must be taught to channel their potential into more satisfying behaviors, both for themselves and for society. Havighurst suggests an educational program to separate these disadvantaged youths from the regular academic high schools. Remedial and vocational classes, some of which might involve work experiences, could help solve the dropout problem among this group.

In discussing the underachieving adolescents, Havighurst pleads for stimulation and enrichment in their school programs. These adolescents do not lack academic ability, they just seem to have an uninteresting school and home environment. The schools could help these able but unchallenged adolescents by providing motivating, thought-producing material.

Havighurst suggests that the reason why potentially superior youths often evade the tasks and issues involved in growing up is that two basic characteristics, self-esteem and social fidelity, which should have to be earned, are given freely to these students. By integrating the educational program with the larger society, high schools could provide opportunities for this group to attain self-esteem and social fidelity on their own.

Curriculum Considerations

Havighurst reports that his three categories represent about 35 percent of all adolescents. The studies by Coleman, Friesen, and Leidy and Starry all emphasize social environment rather than academic environment. Psychologists, sociologists, and educators are indicating a need for curriculum updating in today's high schools. Coleman has made an interesting observation about curriculum:

It is obvious that the content of the curriculum is a responsibility of the school, and

that it will affect the education a child receives. It is less obvious, but no less true, that the standards and values current among the students are primarily the responsibility of the school and do affect the education a child receives. The failure to incorporate an attention to student values in a formal philosophy of education means that each high school principal is on his own. If he is perceptive and imaginative and constantly alert, he can, along with his teachers, incline these peer-group standards toward educational goals. If the principal does not take interest or action, he leaves the molding of standards to the teen-agers themselves, as well as their absorption in those activities that happen to catch their attention (1965, p. 34).

A 1969 *LIFE* poll conducted among 2500 students in 100 high schools indicates that students are seeking greater participation in the policy-making processes of their schools. Tables 1 through 4 reflect student opinion, as well as contrasting parent and teacher opinion, on four specific questions. Although such a poll cannot conclusively provide school administrators with a sense of direction, it reemphasizes Coleman's comment and supports Havighurst's statements about problem students.

What alternatives to maintaining a social environment do today's educators have? Howard (1966) suggests that they develop student responsibility for learning. Previous attempts to do so have been limited to organizational innovations such as flexible scheduling, extracurricular activities, and independent study. Howard proposes a basic concept, based on psychological principles, that will give the student an option about what he will learn. Howard explains three specific subareas of his concept of student option.

1. Content Options. The student is presented with enough optional and alternative learning situations to enable him to choose the material that is most appropriate for his interests and needs.

TABLE 1. STUDENT PARTICIPATION IN POLICY MAKING*

	Students	Parents	Teachers
Want more	58%	20%	35%
Want less	2	11	4
About same	39	65	60
Not sure	1	4	1

*Harris Polls. Reprinted from *LIFE* Magazine, May 16, 1969. © 1969 Time, Inc.

TABLE 2. IMPORTANCE OF STUDENT PARTICIPATION IN POLICY MAKING*

	Students	Parents	Teachers
Very important	54%	25%	30%
Somewhat important	34	38	39
Not very important	11	33	31
Not sure	1	4	—

*Harris Polls. Reprinted from *LIFE* Magazine, May 16, 1969. © 1969 Time, Inc.

TABLE 3. SHOULD STUDENTS HAVE MORE SAY?*

	Students	Parents	Teachers
In making rules	66%	24%	40%
In deciding curriculum	63	35	47
In determining discipline of students	48	28	37
In deciding how to conduct classes	48	21	28
In determination of grades	41	14	18

*Harris Polls. Reprinted from *LIFE* Magazine, May 16, 1969. © 1969 Time, Inc.

TABLE 4. SHOULD THESE TOPICS BE DISCUSSED IN CLASS?*

	Students	Parents	Teachers
Folk rock music	35%	6%	19%
Black students' rights	52	27	36
Underground paper and films	40	17	36
Sex hygiene	52	41	62
Hair, dress, styles	37	30	28
Use of drugs	70	66	72

*Harris Polls. Reprinted from *LIFE* Magazine, May 16, 1969. © 1969 Time, Inc.

2. Time Options. Students will grow in their ability to assume responsibility if they have some control over how fast they learn. Allowing a student to set his own learning pace provides him with an incentive to pursue a topic deeply and to become interested in it.

3. Facility and Personnel Options. Students should have some opportunity to decide where they work, what materials they need, and what faculty assistance they desire.

Howard's concept is revolutionary. His appeal to reject a standard curriculum and traditional methods of instruction places a great deal of responsibility on the learner. Yet if one considers (1) the impact that socialization in school has on today's youths, (2) the deemphasis on academics in lieu of social activities, and (3) the involvement of one out of three students in Havighurst's groupings, Howard's ideas do not seem so far advanced for our society. We need to provide our adolescents with a program that emphasizes intellectual activities. Perhaps the challenge to the school can be simply stated as "the adolescent intellect deserves more respect and greater expectations" (Johnson, 1965, p. 204).

The adolescent who has negative feelings toward his education will find it difficult to adjust to policies and expected behaviors within his school system. His difficulties are often increased when the curriculum is not diversified enough to meet the range of his needs. A more adequate curriculum and increased teacher interest in students solve only part of the problem. Educators must promote an environment that lends itself to greater student thinking and responsibility. It is the school's task to stimulate the adolescent, to build self-respect and confidence through responsible freedom, and to allow him to experience degrees of success. This task was summarized by Jack P. Crowther, Superintendent of the Los Angeles City Schools, in a Special Report to the President:

> The challenge before us if we are to survive as a Nation is to assure that within the mass setting of public education each student be given the maximum individual attention possible—to the end that he will leave the school . . . able to think for himself. This is the task ahead for education (Special Report, 1968, p. 1).

david friesen

academic-athletic-popularity syndrome in the canadian high school society (1967)

One of the most readily accepted generalizations regarding adolescent society is that boys prefer athletics over academics, and girls prefer popularity. Proof of this statement has been found in a number of studies. James S. Coleman, in his large-scale study of ten mid-western high schools in the United States, found evidence to this effect (1961).

About 31 per cent of the boys wanted to be remembered as "brilliant students," compared with 45 per cent of those who wished to be remembered as "athletic stars." For the girls, 28 per cent preferred to be remembered as "brilliant students," with about 72 per cent who chose to be remembered as "leader in activities," or "most popular." On the basis of these findings, Coleman concluded that "the image of the athletic star is most attractive for boys, and the image of activities leader and most popular are more attractive to girls than brilliant student" (1961).

Coleman proceeded to probe for an explanation of this priority in values by high school students. He found evidence that the athlete who gained much status in his school did so because he had accomplished something for the school and the community in leading his team to victory. "The outstanding

student, by contrast, has few ways—if any— to bring glory to his school" (1961, p. 309).

Thus the failure of the academic image to achieve top priority in the adolescent subculture may be the result of the organization of the school itself. As a "social system," the school may not provide for the realizations of the "personality needs" of the adolescent. Does the school permit the outstanding student to bring honor to his school and his community and, more important, to his own informal peer group?

Coleman's approach may suffer limitations because of semantics. Using "high grades," "honor roll," "outstanding student," and "brilliant student" at various times to refer to the boy who represents the scholar may introduce sources of bias. Furthermore, the student who chooses to be remembered as a "brilliant student" may actually be spending most of his energy in athletics. Similarly, the one who wishes to be remembered as a "star" athlete may be spending his energy in academic work. There is at least the possibility that the outstanding student, taking his achievement for granted, may long to add another feather to his cap— and this could be in athletics. If outstanding students have never been granted much recognition for their achievement, it is entirely logical for them to aspire to recognition in some other field.

Reprinted with permission of the author and publisher from *Adolescence*, 1968, **3** (9), 39-52.

But it is not in this area that this research wishes to examine the problem. The assumption is that the students value athletics, popularity, and academic achievement in differing proportions. Why? Several reasons will be advanced.

First of all, the adolescent wishes for recognition in his own society; he wants to be accepted, respected, and applauded for his activities. This source of gratification, which is near to him and meaningful in his own terms is also immediate. How does he receive this immediate gratification? Obviously, he will derive this from activities with the high school group itself. Those who wish to be popular will be encouraged to adopt behavior leading to popularity. This could be athletics, cheerleading, dating, or even under some conditions drinking, smoking, "demonstrating" or participating in a "love-in." Such behavior depends strongly on the value held in the peer group with which the individual identifies himself.

Immediate gratification could also come out of parent-student relationship. If parents want their children to be successful in the things that count in school, and permit the peer group complete independence in determining what counts (e.g., making the basketball team), the value structure of the peer group will simply be reinforced. However, if the parents genuinely reward academic achievement with recognition, the peer group influence will be subdued or negated.

Immediate gratification can also stem from the school and society. The school, chief educating agent of society, needs to develop an organization or structure that will reward those activities most closely aligned to its major function, and use the peripheral activities to channel the energies of youth toward learning. If schools do not plan for effective education, the short-term goals of adolescents can submerge the real goals of the school.

The Academic-Athletic-Popularity Syndrome

Before stating the hypothesis of this study it may be advisable to briefly review the currently accepted position regarding the academic-athletic-popularity syndrome of the Canadian adolescent society. This belief originates mainly from American research, especially Coleman's, but also in part from that of Gordon (1957), Hollingshead (1949), Tannenbaum (1961), Goodman (1960), Riesman (1961), and Erikson (1963). Simply stated, the belief is that adolescents value *athletics, popularity,* and *academics* in that order. Lawrence W. Downey states this clearly:

> If one is to comprehend the ways of our adolescents, one must look for partial explanations of their behavior in the value system which is their own—not in the value system which characterizes the broader culture. One important question, then, is what do adolescents value?
> 1. Adolescent boys appear to value athletics and adolescent girls appear to value social success much more than they value academic achievement.
> 2. Popularity, especially with the opposite sex, is such an impelling value among adolescents that it leads to a fetish for attractiveness (Downey, 1965, pp. 140–141).

The Hypothesis

The hypothesis, then, for this study, is as follows: The priority of values of Canadian adolescents is in the order of athletics, popularity, and academic achievement.

The Sample

To examine the hypothesis, this study will briefly examine the responses of 10,019 Canadian high school students in grades 10 to 12 in one large Western Canadian city in the athletic, popularity and academic fields (Friesen, Knill, & Ratsoy, 1967). It will also draw on previous research of a similar nature in an Eastern Canadian city where two urban high schools, with a total population of 2,425 students, were studied (Friesen, 1966). Finally, it will draw evidence from a Central Canadian urban and rural high school study where eight schools of diverse nature, each with a random sample of 200 students, were examined (Friesen, 1966). All the research, now in its third year, was conducted under the same researcher and with practically the same instruments. In each case the samples included the total available school population present on the day of the survey. In all, nineteen schools and 15,000 students were involved.

Statistical Treatment of Data

Procedures similar to those used in previous sociological studies on values and attitudes of high school students were employed. Frequency distributions, percentage distributions, and chi-square analyses were used in the examination of student responses to forced-choice items. The items were constructed on the basis of the literature and recognized research in the area of the adolescent society. They were refined during three years of research. Because of the large sample size, it was found unnecessary to dwell on the statistical significance of the difference.

TABLE 1. MAJOR CHARACTERISTICS CONSIDERED NECESSARY FOR MEMBERSHIP IN LEADING CROWD

	Per Cent Responding (N = 10,019)
Friendliness	51.3
Good looks	25.4
Money	13.8
Athletic ability	7.0
Academic excellence	2.5

Findings

The Problem Examined

(a) Table 1 illustrates that the public high school students chose friendliness, good looks, money, and athletics as values which would precede academic excellence in leading toward membership in the leading crowd. The same order of preference, with very little variation, was observed in the eastern and mid-western studies.

TABLE 2. ITEMS CONSIDERED MOST IMPORTANT FOR POPULARITY

	Per Cent Responding (N = 10,019)
Being in the leading crowd	64.3
Being an athletic star	18.7
Having a nice car	12.7
High grades, honor roll	4.2

(b) Table 2 illustrates that students chose leading crowd membership, being an

athletic star, and even having a nice car as values more instrumental in gaining popularity than high grades or being on the honor roll. The variation in choices between different studies was significant, though not extensive. Rural students placed more value on cars and high grades, urban students placed more emphasis on being in the leading crowd.

TABLE 3. CHARACTERISTICS CONSIDERED MOST IMPORTANT FOR SUCCESS IN LIFE

	Per Cent Responding (N = 10,019)
Personality	57.4
Friendliness	17.7
Academic achievement	15.6
Money	8.8
Athletics	0.5

(c) Table 3 indicates what the students considered most important for success in life. Personality took precedence over academic achievement, and was preferred only slightly to friendliness. The hierarchy, though, was in the order of personality, academic achievement, friendliness, money, and last, athletics. Very slight variations occurred between the responses of students in the three regions.

These findings *suggest* that academic achievement is relegated to a very minor position in the hierarchy of values in the samples of Canadian high school students studied. In the eyes of the adolescent, academic achievement does not help him appreciably in attaining a position in the leading crowd of the high school; it does not help him in his quest for popularity—which, as we shall see, emerges as a powerful element in the adolescent society—and it does not seem to merit the highest position for the attainment of success in life.

It is relatively easy to conclude that the thesis which holds that adolescents value athletics higher than academic work because it leads to recognition in the peer group and brings satisfaction is essentially correct. But a more careful look at the findings will reveal that athletic prowess is not the most important value; it was chosen fourth as contributing towards leading crowd status, and second as leading to popularity. When viewed in its contribution to success in life, it was chosen last and by less than one per cent of the students in all three regions.

The rather nebulous concepts of "friendliness," "leading crowd membership," and "personality" were chosen as contributing most to the three goals specified. The strength of the social factors in the adolescent subculture is indicated.

What, then, about the place of athletics and academic ability? Where do they fit in the complex structure of the adolescent value system? To gain an insight into their place in the students' value system, three additional items will be analyzed briefly.

The Problem Investigated

(a) Table 4 presents the student responses to the question similar to that pursued in Coleman's study. In all three Canadian studies the students preferred to be remembered as outstanding students, with the strongest such desire expressed by the mid-western student and the weakest by the western urban students. Very little difference existed between the three studies in regard to the percentage of students who desired to be remembered as athletic stars. However, the desire for popularity took second place in the triad for the western urban students. For the total group, the order was significant: The choices for outstanding student were far ahead of those for athletic star, which were slightly ahead of those for being most popular.

TABLE 4. PER CENT OF STUDENTS CHOOSING TO BE REMEMBERED BY THREE CHARACTERISTICS

	Outstanding Student	Athletic Star	Most Popular	No Response	N
Western urban	43.5	26.0	30.5	0.0	(10,019)
Eastern urban	54.0	25.4	17.3	3.3	(2,425)
Midwest urban and rural	60.8	22.6	15.1	1.5	(1,600)

(b) Table 5 presents a summary of the findings for the western urban study by total

TABLE 5. PER CENT OF STUDENTS CHOOSING CHARACTERISTICS AS MOST SATISFYING FOR SCHOOL LIFE

	(N = 10,019)		
	Academic Achievement	Athletics	Popularity
Western urban total	43.0	12.5	44.5
Boys	42.9	16.8	40.3
Girls	43.1	8.5	48.4

and by sex. Popularity was perceived as the most satisfying for school life by the majority of these students. It was chosen slightly over academic achievement, largely on the strength of the girls' choice for popularity. Boys chose academic achievement as most important for a satisfying school life.

(c) Table 6 presents the summary of student responses to the question "Which one of the following do you regard as most important for your future: academic achievement, popularity, or athletics and cheerleading?" The choices for athletics were almost negligible; but the choices for academic achievement were preponderant.

TABLE 6. PER CENT OF STUDENTS CHOOSING CHARACTERISTICS SEEN AS MOST IMPORTANT FOR THEIR FUTURE

	(N = 10,019)		
	Academic Achievement	Athletics Cheerleading	Popularity
Western urban total	81.7	2.3	16.0
Boys	82.8	2.8	14.4
Girls	80.5	1.7	17.8

By examining each of these three characteristics in turn it can be seen that the high school student seems quite aware of what he is doing when he chooses athletic stardom as something for which he wishes to be remembered. He acknowledges that it is not the most satisfying characteristic in his school life and, furthermore, that it holds little value for his future; yet it holds strong immediate value for him, especially through his referent peer group.

The responses to the two alternatives to athletics are more ambivalent. To be remembered as an outstanding student has high priority in all centers, especially in the rural schools. Several explanations could be advanced for this unexpected phenomenon. One is the emergence of alternate courses in urban areas. Here the vocational area may receive more emphasis than the academic. The rural high schools of the mid-western study, even though fairly large, did not offer much beyond the matriculation program.

There also may be a psychological explanation. Having achieved a respectable academic performance without much reward or recognition students may desire achievement in more visible areas, and thus turn to athletic or social competencies. A third explanation is derived from viewing the school as a social system. The "organization" student in the urban setting may be reacting against the bureaucracy of the school, or he may be suffering from a dearth of social or personal satisfactions, and thus turn to the "popularity" goal as something out of his reach. It is interesting to note that 49.3 per cent (4,774) of the western urban high school students claimed that they did not participate in a single extracurricular activity in school.

No wonder that 44.5 per cent (4,261) of the students claimed that they "strive most in school to be accepted and liked by other students." Schools may have neglected to look at the adolescent society for the purpose of discovering the motivations inherent in it. The social system of the school may have to come to grips with the needs of teenagers and provide the structure for them to perform satisfactorily in school.

What is most satisfying for the adolescent? Two patterns emerged strongly. Almost 43 per cent found most satisfaction in academic work, as compared with 44.5 per cent who found popularity in social interaction. Surprisingly, boys found the academic area slightly more satisfying than girls; the difference can be attributed to the girls' greater interest in popularity.

How do these values appear to the adolescent when he views his own future? The athletic interest collapses, the interest in popularity declines, and the academic value increases greatly. Almost 82 per cent of the students claimed that academic achievement is most important for their future. Boys exceeded girls only slightly in this value area.

A broad aim of the school is to effect socially acceptable behavior in the student. Presumably this is accomplished through the activities and practices the student experiences in school. The school, as a social system, has expectations for each student as it is laid down by its bureaucratic imperatives. However, if the student achieves the desired behavior, he will also have to satisfy his major personality needs. These needs have been somewhat delineated in this brief report.

Most students need social and athletic participation beyond the academic role prescribed. A number of students seem to derive satisfaction from their academic role alone. Others need greater social and athletic satisfactions to make them function effectively in the social system. The schools have failed to provide ample satisfactions in all three areas.

1. The academic area does not receive full support from the adolescent subculture. High marks do not substantially contribute to popularity or to leading crowd membership. The school's visible honors are awarded mostly to top athletes. Academic honors are reserved only for narrowly defined matriculation students.

2. The athletic area is reserved only for a small group, especially in the large urban school. Half the students have no involvement in any extracurricular activities; they receive no satisfactions from this vital, adolescent "need" zone.

3. Popularity, which occupies a high place in the eyes of the adolescent, is desired by the majority of students. Yet only 25.7 per cent claimed to be in the leading crowd. Only 22.6 per cent had been elected to any kind of position during their last two years of school. About 28 per cent worried most about being accepted and liked by friends. Against this, about 28 per cent never went out with friends.

Conclusions

The commonly accepted position that adolescent boys value athletics, and girls social success much more than academic achievement, is not tenable in the light of the evidence.

The pattern for "enduring" values for boys emerged in the order of:

academic > athletics > popularity

For girls it was:

academic > popularity > athletics

The pattern for a most satisfying value in school for boys emerged in the order of:

academic > popularity > athletics

For girls it was:

popularity > academic > athletics

As a value of greatest importance for the future, academic achievement was chosen overwhelmingly by both boys and girls. The pattern was in the order of:

academic > popularity > athletics

This research started with the hypothesis that the Canadian adolescent society has developed a hierarchy of values in the order of athletics > popularity > academic. The research has shown that the hypothesis must be rejected.

However, the data reveal that for the satisfaction of the needs of the students in the high school social system the athletic and popularity areas are prominent, though not as overpowering as was hypothesized. Furthermore, they do not seem inexorably at variance with the goals of the school; in fact, they may provide avenues leading to the satisfaction that is needed by the students.

The research has also demonstrated the relative similarities existing in the adolescent society which indicate the presence of a subculture. Friendliness, good looks, popularity, personality, and athletics are prime values in the youth society that makes its habitat in the long corridors of our schools and on the miles of pavement in our modern cities.

These are the criteria by which youngsters judge each other and their teachers, and in turn by which they will groom their appearance and behavior. Can the school channel the energy in our adolescent subculture to make it functional in terms of the broad aims held for the school?

thomas r. leidy

allan r. starry

the american adolescent—a bewildering amalgam

How do American teen-agers look at the world around them? What are their opinions about school, about dating, about taking responsibility? How does it feel to be a teen-ager? The teacher who hopes to have a solid foundation for communicating with his students must be aware of their attitudes and ideas. This article presents some of the findings of a nation-wide survey of adolescent opinions conducted by the Purdue Opinion Panel.

American society today is characterized by internal discord and international tension, hot and cold wars, and dramatic social and technological change. Merely living in such an environment seems to require virtually all an individual's resources and skills; growing up in it is problematic indeed. It is not surprising that being an American adolescent is a difficult and demanding experience. During his seven teen-age years, an individual must acquire and perfect the techniques necessary for survival in our society (highly sophisticated skills and difficult to master) while he tries to learn about himself, his peers, and his elders and to make that painful transition from child to adult.

It is important that attempts be made to understand the teen-age subculture which constitutes such a large and complex segment of American life. Since the adolescent is a product of adult society, understanding

his behavior and motives involves understanding those of adult society also. At the same time, however, the adolescent is a member of a subculture all his own with distinct and unique values, rituals, and mores— a phenomenon worth investigating in its own right.

With this in mind, H. H. Remmers founded the Purdue Opinion Panel, a continuing series of surveys of the attitudes, beliefs, and behavior of American youth. Since its inception in 1942, the Panel has executed 80 large-scale studies, using as respondents students attending public high schools throughout the United States.

Each school year, 100 to 125 schools serve on the Panel. School personnel administer opinion questionnaires, tests, and inventories of various types to participating students and send the materials to Purdue University for processing. From total returns (usually 15,000 to 20,000 per poll) a representative sample of 2,000 students is drawn for analysis. The sample is proportionate to the total population of public high school students in terms of sex, grade level, rural-urban residence and region of residence.

In 1957, Dr. Remmers and D. H. Radler wrote *The American Teenager,* a book based on Panel data. They analyzed in great detail many aspects of American youth culture and tested several hypotheses concerning the basic determinants of normal and delinquent behavior. In the discussion which follows,

Reprinted with permission of the authors and the National Education Association from the *NEA Journal,* 1967, pp. 8-12.

data obtained more recently are compared with some of the material presented in *The American Teenager*. We will discuss two areas affecting all high school students: their views on education and attitudes toward school and their social development and relations with parents and peers.

School is a complex and constant concern of American youth. Consistently since 1953, about three-fourths of the students sampled have responded positively to the following question:

Taking everything into consideration, how do you feel about school?	1953	1958	1965	1967
I like it very much.	32%	27%	21%	16%
I like it most of the time.	43%	46%	51%	57%
I don't like it very much.	23%	24%	24%	25%
I dislike it.	2%	3%	2%	2%

Note that while the negative responses to this item have remained constant over the past 14 years, positive responses have shifted steadily away from an unqualified "I like it very much" to the more moderate "I like it most of the time." Despite the generally favorable attitude, many students are critical of their education and the manner in which schools are run.

Most students strongly favor a student government with some authority in school operation, though they do not support the notion that such a student body should have disciplinary power over students.

What do you think a student government in your school should be allowed to do?	Percent Answering "Yes"	
	1953	1965
Plan assemblies and convocations	74%	82%
Make rules about conduct in school	70%	63%
Hold court and try students who break rules	45%	33%
Have power to fine or otherwise punish students who break rules	34%	28%
Poll students on ways to improve school	86%	84%
Meet with teachers and principal to advise them on how students feel about school matters affecting them	88%	88%

A senior girl from Wisconsin writes, "The thing I like most about school is the way this school is run. It is a fifty-fifty deal. The student council is always heard and usually listened to. . . ."

School assignments and homework have an important, and usually negative, influence on students' relations with their friends. A boy living on the West Coast writes, "The thing that bothers me most about my friends is that they always want me to help them with their school work when I don't even have my own finished." A tenth grader from Georgia complains, "They don't study much and when I am around them I cannot study." A senior girl from Iowa says, "Some of my friends study too much!"

Time spent on homework has shifted significantly since this question was first asked in 1948:

How long each day, on the average, do you spend working on school assignments after school hours?	1948	1962	1967
Less than one hour	39%	21%	32%
One to two hours	54%	58%	47%
More than two hours	7%	16%	20%

Three-fourths of the students sampled are convinced that earning high grades in school is "extremely important" or "very important." Sixteen percent think it is "somewhat important." Only 3 percent of the sample feel that grades are of little or no importance.

The drive for grades often results in cheating—on homework and in tests and examinations. Since 1949, three-fourths of the students sampled consistently have stated, "Cheating is wrong; never justifiable," 20 percent feel that cheating is "sometimes justifiable," and about 5 percent think that cheating "does no harm."

In spite of strong agreement that cheating is wrong, only 5 percent say they have never cheated. . . . Teachers' emphasis on test grades is consistently the most often mentioned cause of cheating. However, the number of students who say that their cheating results from their parents' emphasis on grades, has risen substantially since 1948, from 10 to 25 percent.

High school students' view of the value education should have for them has shifted significantly over the years. In 1953, most students considered the acquisition of social skills the most important aim in education; slightly fewer favored "a sense of discipline and responsibility." By 1961, the academic area was selected as much more important than other outcomes. In 1966, discipline and responsibility ranked first (39 percent), closely followed by academic skill (35 percent).

Asked what they like about school, many students express approval of the intellectual aspects. A senior girl from Minnesota writes, "I enjoy classes in which the teachers present mature ideas and mature information to a group of adults." A tenth grade boy likes school because "You get a *chance* to learn whether you do or not." A girl from Arizona writes, "I enjoy school and I like learning new things. I find great satisfaction in discussing news, arguments, et cetera."

If high school students today tend not to perceive social development as part of their school training, it is not because interpersonal relationships and social responsibilities are unimportant to them. In some respects the student submits to rules established by adults; in others, he establishes his own rules or conforms to the codes of his peers. In all cases, he sees these relationships as both the joy and woe of his time of life.

A boy from Arkansas writes, "The thing that bothers me most about my friends is that I don't understand them at all times and they don't understand me." A girl from New York complains, "My friends get so worried about things like sororities, cheerleader tryouts, Latin, and many of them are always complaining about how dull everything is and that they don't have nothing to do."

Many students echo the fears expressed by a boy and girl from Louisiana. The boy worries about "what my friends think of me." The girl is "afraid I will do something that will make my friends mad at me."

More than half (59 percent) of the students sampled in a recent survey agree that the only way to really develop your personality is to have many friends. Although three-fourths of the sample think they are popular, 68 percent wish they had more friends.

Despite this expressed desire for friends, 65 percent say, "Most teen-agers try too hard to be well liked"; and 52 percent say, "Most teen-agers try so hard to be popular that they look foolish."

Students' responses to items concerning peer-group control of their behavior suggest that they view such influence without approval. Sixty percent of those sampled think, "Most teen-agers follow the crowd without thinking for themselves" and "Teen-agers are very unfair to those who want to act differently from the crowd." Sixty-two percent say, "Teen-agers who follow the gang often must give up what they really like to do." According to 41 percent of the students, "You sometimes have to go along with the crowd even if you don't like what they do."

Though they seem convinced that the group exercises certain sanctions on their behavior, most students question the validity and importance of those sanctions. Only 25 percent of the sample agree that "a person who doesn't like to run with a gang is pretty odd." Twenty-seven percent believe that "probably the worst thing that can happen is to be dropped by the gang."

These data point out the fundamental paradox in American youth culture. It is accepted by most adolescents that the influence the group has on their behavior is superficial and, in the long run, not particularly important. Nevertheless, the need to be popular is pervasive and requires that they accede to group demands.

Equally important and no less confusing to American youth are their relations with the opposite sex. A boy from Wisconsin complains "I am constantly searching for the 'best' or perfect girl. Whenever I find one, I feel inferior to her." A girl from New Jersey lists typical male characteristics: "immature, inattentive, obnoxious (at times) and lovable." A boy from Illinois describes girls: ". . . their feeling of superiority. They talk too much, their sloppiness about their hair and their inability to cope with reality. I like them very much."

Forty-two percent of the sample report that they date once a month or less; 35 percent date two, three, or four times a month; 21 percent report dating at least twice a week. About half the students wish they had more dates, but only 16 percent say their parents are too strict about dating. Apparently, too infrequent dating is not the result of parental restriction.

Questions concerned with dating behavior elicit widely varied responses. Asked to describe a perfect date, one high school senior would like to "go to a stage play or musical and later discuss the merits and demerits of the performance given over dinner at Traitor [sic] Vics." One tenth grade student's idea of a perfect date is to "Talk nice to the girl. Ask her if she wants a bottle of pop. Don't be dirty with her." A senior from Massachusetts says, "Go out and park, but bring her home on time." Behavior so diverse is difficult to summarize.

Fifty-seven percent of the students sampled are now going steady or have gone steady in the past. Going steady is, of course, a common source of disagreement between parents and children. It also is cause for concern among students. A girl from Arkansas complains, "Boys think they own you if you go out with them one time." A boy from Pennsylvania remarks, "If you have 1 or 2 dates with a girl, and then have 1 or 2 dates with another girl, it is highly objectionable in female circles. It seems you're a cad or playboy if you don't go steady after a few dates."

Forty-five percent of the sample agree that most teen-age romances are just puppy love, but only 16 percent feel that high school students are too young to go steady. Almost half the students surveyed believe that high school seniors are old enough to consider marriage. Girls would most like to marry when they are about 20 years old; boys prefer to wait until they are 23 or 24.

Concern about morals and sexual behavior is expressed by many students. Girls complain about boys' aggressive behavior ("They try to see how far they can go"); boys complain that girls flaunt their sexuality ("Even a nice girl can give a boy the wrong impression"). . . .

Many observers of contemporary culture have pointed out the general relaxation of American moral codes and increasing freedom of sexual behavior. High school students generally agree with these observations: 52 percent feel that in the future moral standards in the United States will be less strict; 26 percent believe that our moral standards will remain about the same; and 20 percent think that standards will be more strict. The trend toward increasing tolerance of sexual behavior is supported strikingly by students' responses to the following item:

If I learned that some friends of mine had not followed the morals or rules relating to the behavior of unmarried people:

		Total	Boy	Girl
I would not consider them good friends anymore.	1952	57%	46%	67%
	1965	30%	22%	38%
	Difference	27%	24%	29%
It would not make any difference in our friendship.	1952	43%	54%	33%
	1965	69%	77%	60%
	Difference	26%	23%	27%

In 1952, a majority of the students sampled (57 percent) chose the first alternative to this item—"I would not consider them good friends anymore." In 1965, 69 percent of the sample chose the second alternative—

"It would not make any difference in our friendship." At both times, boys were much more tolerant than girls of their friends' not conforming to established sexual mores.

While these data are not concerned with the personal morality of high school youth, they do suggest that students' moral standards and attitudes toward sexual behavior are much more liberal now than in the past.

Asked what they enjoy most about being teenagers, many students discuss the real, though limited, responsibilities they may take. A girl from Massachusetts writes, "Your basic reputation is left entirely to you and you get your first touch of real responsibility." A boy from Georgia speaks of . . . "having small problems and little responsibilities." A tenth grade student living in New Jersey says, "We are allowed to make our own decisions and accept responsibilities that were previously denied us."

Many students comment that while they are free to make many decisions for themselves, their parents and teachers are available to back them up and to help them recoup when the decisions made turn out to be the wrong ones. Adult influence, however, is both desirable ("I have my family to fall back on") and not so desirable ("Why can't they leave me alone?"), depending on the individual and the situation.

Listed below are a group of decision situations. All but one elicited the response "I decide" from the majority of students.

	My Parents or Family Decide	I Decide
How late you can stay out on a date	67%	31%
What time you go to bed at night	21%	75%
How you spend most of your money	8%	83%
What you are going to do this summer	22%	72%
Whether you go steady	19%	75%
Whether you will go to college	27%	67%
What your future occupation will be	7%	87%

Most adolescents adjust adequately (if a little noisily) to the world in which they must live. However, for many others life is quite difficult, help is hard to find, and hope is about gone. A young girl from California describes clinically her weight problem which is compounded when her parents and brother ". . . call me fatty or glut. . . ." She concludes ". . . many times I have thought seriously of committing suicide." A junior from Pennsylvania writes "I think I am an alcoholic. And I just don't know what to do about it."

This, then, is the American adolescent—a bewildering amalgam of conflicting moods and motives, habits and dreams. At times he seems all energy and innocent optimism. Then again, he is cynical and wise beyond his years. His values seem sometimes distorted, his attitudes a bit bizarre. He pays too much attention to his friends and what he sees on television and not enough attention to his parents and what he hears in school. He is aware of his many conflicts and problems (knows that adults, finally, are responsible for many of them) and realizes that he may never resolve them all.

robert l. spaulding

personality and social development: peer and school influences

Empirical research on the influence of peers and the school on personality and social development continued to be burdened with methodological difficulties during the past three years. Most investigators resorted to correlational studies, but there were notable exceptions. Those who traveled the correlational route sought to handle larger and larger numbers of variables and to depend upon the assistance of computers and data processing equipment in the monumental task of collating and relating the variables. The sifting process in many of these studies is expected to continue during the next review period, but already a number of promising variables have been identified for subsequent experimental inquiry.

Developmental Trends

Stability of social traits in young children was studied by Gellert (1961) and by Stith and Connor (1962). Gellert investigated stability of dominant, submissive, and resistant acts displayed in a series of play settings. Stable rank positions were found for most children with respect to dominance and submission, although large individual inconsis-

tencies were observed. The expression of resistance was found to vary from situation to situation.

As the preschool children in the Stith and Connor study grew older, they became less dependent upon adults, and peers were noted to increase significantly with age.

Data on the stability of ethnic attitudes in adolescents were reported by Wilson (1963). He made a cross-sectional study of 821 secondary school boys' attitudes toward and opinions of Jews, Negroes, and Southerners. The degree of prejudice was found to be approximately the same over the age 13-18 years, with the exception of attitudes toward Southerners, which became more accepting during the five-year period. Again with the exception of attitudes toward Southerners, the variance among the boys decreased from year to year until age 18. A similar pattern of stability and decreasing variance in adolescence was seen for socio-empathic ability and *expected reciprocity* (degree of correspondence between the ratings a pupil makes of others and his expectancy of the ratings made of himself by those others) in a series of related investigations with a sample of approximately 385 children in grades 5-12 (deJung & Gardner, 1962; deJung & Meyer, 1963; Meyer & deJung, 1963). Social attitudes appeared to follow a general growth curve and to reach a plateau

Reprinted with permission of the author and publisher from the *Review of Educational Research*, 1964, **34**, 588-598.

during adolescence. However, low, generally nonsignificant relationships with mental and chronological age within grade levels suggested that factors other than age, such as close association with others and availability of relevant information about others, might be responsible for the developmental curve.

Two studies on social development in middle childhood (Sutton-Smith, Rosenberg, & Morgan, 1963; Kanous, Daugherty, & Cohn, 1962) related to changes in heterosexual choice and sex role preference. Sutton-Smith, Rosenberg, and Morgan administered a play inventory to approximately 1,900 children in grades 3-6. The results showed that girls had an increasing interest in masculine games and activities during these grades and that the major increase took place during the third and fourth grades. Boys showed an increasing interest in more mature masculine games and activities. The study reported by Kanous, Daugherty, and Cohn indicated that a significant relationship existed between socioeconomic class and heterosexual choice within their sample of children in grades 2-8. Children from the lower rather than the higher socioeconomic families made significantly more cross-sex choices. Boehm's (1962) study of children at different socioeconomic levels supported this finding. She found adult role behavior earlier among children of working class families than among children of higher social status. The period of middle childhood appeared to be a source of considerable sex role confusion, especially for girls. Sociocultural discontinuities seemed to exacerbate the confusion.

Correlates of School Attendance

School attendance (as a global variable) was investigated by Photiadis and Biggar (1962). The relations of amount of formal education to church attendance, prejudice, and several personality variables in a sample of 300 South Dakota men and women were studied. Amount of formal schooling was found to be significantly negatively related to social distance—with the degree of religious orthodoxy, extrinsic religious belief, church participation, anomia, concern with status, conservatism, authoritarianism, withdrawal tendencies, and antisocial tendencies held statistically constant. Amount of formal education was the most salient factor associated with prejudice, after authoritarianism, which was positively correlated with prejudice. In another phase of the study, Photiadis (1962) obtained significant negative ninth-order partial correlations (holding the same nine variables constant) between the amount of formal education and each of the following: religious orthodoxy, concern with status, and withdrawal tendencies. Extrinsic religious belief, anomia, conservatism, authoritarianism, and antisocial tendencies were not found to be independently correlated with amount of formal education.

Attendance in secondary school was observed to be related to masculinity-femininity by Webb (1963). Good records of school attendance were found for boys and girls with high femininity scores. These data were in essential agreement with Cattell's (Cattell et al., 1962) finding that submissiveness and docility were the personality traits most highly related to school success.

Teacher Personality and Behavior

The influence of the teacher in the classroom has become the concern of an increasing number of researchers. The saliency of the teacher as a model for children to imitate in direct and indirect ways has been demonstrated in the experimental studies of Bandura and his associates (Bandura, 1962, 1963; Bandura & Huston, 1961; Bandura & McDonald, 1963; Bandura, Ross, & Ross, 1961, 1963a, 1963b, 1963c). Using nursery school children as subjects in most of these studies, Bandura and his associates have shown that adult models can be exceedingly effective in transmitting entire repertoires of behavior to young children. Models were found to be able to free children to respond, to inhibit existing response patterns, and even to stimulate novel patterns of behavior. The influence of the adult model in no-trial learning was clearly shown in these experimental studies. A number of model attributes were investigated separately for their direct influence in modifying imitation. For example, it was clearly found that imitative behavior of children can be accentuated through nurturant behavior or through the control of resources and social rewards. Verbalization of standards (in this case, the expression of a philosophy of accepting delayed rewards of greater value in place of immediate rewards of lesser value) resulted in a significant pattern of imitation in the behavior of the children.

Behavioral consistency received the attention of Heilbrun (1963, 1964). Although concerned with parents as models, Heilbrun's work, which was closely related to Bandura's, led to theoretical conclusions concerning the effects of the teacher as a model. Using Erikson's (1950) concept of ego identity—that is, a sense of consistency emerging from the responses of significant others over the lifetime of the developing individual—Heilbrun investigated the role consistency of adolescents in relation to the role behavior and nurturance of their fathers and mothers. He found that boys who had been reared by more masculine and more nurturant fathers displayed marked role consistency in adolescence. Daughters who were more consistent as adolescents reported their mothers as more feminine. For boys, the interaction between masculinity-femininity and nurturance in the father appeared to be a major determinant of ego identity in adolescence. For adolescent girls, the degree of femininity of the mother appeared to be the dominant factor.

Heilbrun's finding of an interaction effect between masculinity and nurturance in relation to role consistency in boys is reminiscent of Bandura's (Bandura, Ross, & Ross, 1963a) finding that boys exposed to a female controller of highly rewarding resources in the presence of a powerless and ignored male imitated the male more strongly than they imitated other models, whereas in every other situation tested (male dominant, female consumer; male dominant, female ignored; and female dominant, male consumer) the controller of resources was the more strongly imitated. A subsequent interview with the boys in the female dominant and male-ignored condition revealed that the rewarded boys were sympathetic toward the ignored male. Boys reared in such a wife-dominant family might well imitate the powerless, ignored father and display culturally inconsistent role behavior in adolescence.

Generalization by children of the imitative response pattern to include the dominant female teacher in the classroom setting as a model appears distinctly possible.

Correlational Research

A number of correlational studies have contributed to the growing evidence of impact of variables of teacher behavior on subsequent behavior of pupils. Most of these studies left strict cause-and-effect relationships in doubt; yet their accumulative effect supported the experimental studies reported previously.

Gold (1962) investigated relationships between dimensions of dominative-integrative ideology on the part of 30 teachers and the number of isolated pupils present in their classrooms. A significant and slightly curvilinear relationship between the percentage of isolates in each classroom and the teachers' F Scale scores was obtained, with the highest percentage of isolates associated with the highest F Scale scores. The fewest isolated children were found in the classrooms of teachers with moderately low F Scale scores.

Relationships between teacher behavior and student aspirations were studied by Rosenfeld and Zander (1961). They used a questionnaire to explore the relationships between specific teacher practices and the aspirations of tenth grade mathematics students. Students reported favorable responses to the rewarding behavior of their teachers and to the legitimate use of power in assigning grades. Indiscriminate coercion appeared to engender student resistance and to lower the aspiration levels of the students. Like for the teacher was found to be strongly correlated with an expressed desire to conform.

Punitiveness was investigated by Kounin and Gump (1961). First grade children in the classrooms of three pairs of punitive and nonpunitive teachers were asked, "What is the worst thing a child can do in school?" After their replies were recorded, a second question was asked of them: "Why is that so bad?" Children in the classrooms of punitive teachers were found to express more aggression, to have greater conflict about misbehavior, and to show less concern for school-centered tasks and school values in comparison with children in the classrooms of the nonpunitive teachers.

Two other correlational studies were focused in part upon teacher nurturance, dominance or punitiveness, and the use of rewarding or punishing resources. Sears (1963) sought to identify specific dimensions of the school's influence on the attitudes, performance, and behavior of a sample of fifth and sixth graders. She found relatively high creativity among children in classrooms of teachers who showed a high degree of personal interest and who praised the personality attributes of the child. Spending time with individual children in the classroom and listening to them attentively were also found to be associated with highly creative performance. These same teachers were found to have pupils who accepted their peers—an observation replicating to a degree the findings of Gold.

The second study (Spaulding, 1963a, 1964) was addressed to the problem of identifying dimensions of teacher behavior related to pupil self-concept. High pupil self-concepts were found in the classes of teachers who were socially integrative or learner-supportive. Negative relationships with self-concept were obtained with dominative, threatening, and sarcastic teacher behavior.

An antecedent-consequent design was employed by McNeil (1964) to study sex differences in reading performance under two conditions of instruction. He used an interview schedule with first grade children who had been taught word recognition in kindergarten by an auto-instructional method. The interview data indicated that boys received more negative comments in first grade than girls received. The boys also were given less opportunity to read. After instruction in reading in first grade by female teachers in the regular school program, the boys in the study (who had been significantly superior to the girls in word recognition after auto-instruction) were significantly inferior on a word-recognition test based on words taught in first grade.

Experimental Research

Two experimental studies were reported regarding the influence of varying degrees of teacher ability. In one of these, Burnstein, Stotland, and Zander (1961) investigated the acceptance by grade school children of adult models who had been introduced to them as having different degrees of deep-sea diving ability and as having various degrees of similarity of background to the children. The children were found to accept the preferences of the model more readily when he was introduced to them as having a very similar background or as being a very competent diver. The children also projected their own preferences onto the model when he was introduced as an expert. In the second study, Maehr, Mensing, and Nafzger (1962) employed an expert in physical development to test the hypothesis that evaluation by significant others brings about changes in the individual's self-concept. A self-report measure of physical development was administered to secondary school boys before and after a performance session in which they were rated by the expert. The boys were found to increase or to lower their self-ratings on specific items of the inventory depending upon whether they were approved or disapproved on those items by the expert. The effect of approval or disapproval spread in a diminishing fashion to related and then unrelated items on the self-rating scale.

A third experimental study (Aronfreed, Cutick, & Fagen, 1963) was concerned with the degree to which elementary school children would engage in self-criticism after being deprived of material reinforcement (candy, in this case) as punishment for aggressive acts. The children had been introduced under four conditions of cognitive structure and nurturance. Children who were given explicit cognitive standards of performance gave the greatest number of self-critical responses when a mishap occurred, regardless of the amount of nurturance by the instructor (experimenter). These results underscore the previously mentioned finding of Heilbrun that parental role consistency is a more highly related variable than nurturance.

Teaching Methods

Those effects of general teaching methods which are relevant to some degree in every classroom setting were given some attention during the reporting period. Grimes and Allinsmith (1961) tested the hypothesis that teaching method (in this study, *structured* in contrast to *unstructured*) does interact with personality characteristics in determining response to instruction. Results in their study showed that highly anxious or highly compulsive children taught primary reading by a structured method were superior in reading by the third grade to similar children taught primary reading by an unstructured approach. Compulsive children did better than did less compulsive children in the structured program; compulsivity made no difference in an unstructured setting. Although variation in anxiety level made no difference in the achievement of the children in the structured situation, a high level of anxiety in unstructured settings impeded scholastic performance. Anxiety and compulsivity which as measured variables were uncorrelated in the sample were found to interact with each other and with the teaching method. Children who were judged to be both highly anxious and highly compulsive were strikingly more competent when taught by the structured than by the unstructured method. Those who were classified as highly anxious but noncompulsive were exceptionally low in achievement in the unstructured setting, in comparison with the highly anxious but more compulsive children.

Additional data on the influence of structure in classroom practice was provided by Sears (1963). In her sample, higher self-concepts among boys of average ability were found in the classes of teachers who preferred a well-ordered, highly structured program and who were sympathetic about the effects of anxiety in children. Spaulding's (1963a) finding of a significant relationship between businesslike, orderly teacher behavior and pupil reading achievement is also consonant with the experimental findings of Grimes and Allinsmith.

An attempt to modify directly the perception of children regarding causal factors in social relations in the classroom was reported by Ojemann and Snider (1963). Fourth and fifth grade children in experimental classes were taught about the complexity of the behavior of other children but not specifically about the behavior of teachers.

Subsequently, they were asked to interpret the classroom behavior of teachers. Fifth grade children were able to generalize to some degree from their instruction, but fourth grade children were not.

Correlates of Peer Acceptance

Peer acceptance was given a great deal of attention during the period covered by the *Review of Educational Research*. Three general classes of correlates were identified: achievement, personality, and sex. Porterfield and Schlichting (1961) noted a significant relationship between peer status and reading achievement at every socioeconomic level of the school community. Hudgins, Smith, and Johnson (1962) found arithmetic ability to be significantly related to peer acceptance. Sears (1963) included general academic achievement as a significant correlate of popularity.

Among the personality variables studied, anxiety was commonly observed to be related to peer status. Hill (1963) obtained strong relationships between cross-sex sociometric status and measures of test anxiety and defensiveness. In comparison with others, anxious and defensive children more frequently reported that they wished to play with peers of the opposite sex. Results in a study by Horowitz (1962) indicated that the anxious children in her sample were less frequently chosen by either sex. In a study of delinquent boys by Rubenfeld and Stafford (1963), low status boys were found to be anxious and fearful but loyal to the high status boys.

Two investigators reported correlations of peer acceptance with self-concept scores. Reese (1961) found acceptance of others and popularity to be related curvilinearly to self-concept measures. The most popular children had moderate self-concept scores. The least popular had low self-concept scores. Sears (1963) indicated that the most popular boys and girls of average mental ability had somewhat higher than average self-concepts.

Goslin (1962) reported that adolescent children who were isolated from the peer group tended to be unable to predict how others in the group would perceive them. Accuracy of self-perception appeared to be reduced or distorted among those who were rejected by their peers.

Conclusion

Despite the extreme complexity of specific peer and school influences on personality and social development, a number of investigators during this reporting period identified promising variables for further research. For example, the study of ways in which patterns of teacher behavior interact differentially with response patterns of children of varying personality characteristics appears to be a promising line of inquiry. Children who are dependent, aggressive, withdrawn, or independently productive can be expected to respond in a different way to teachers who are highly orderly and businesslike than to those who are most permissive and less highly organized. For example, teacher support or nurturance may promote task orientation in the dependent, fearful girl, yet promote resistance and apathy in the independent, intellectually gifted boy.

Studies of the influence of teachers and peers may become more productive and more relevant to the educational task if they are addressed to the curricular antecedents of specific classroom behavior problems and to the ways in which certain teacher response patterns either reinforce or inhibit responses of specific types of children. A number of the investigations and experiments reviewed have been profitably concerned with the interaction of teacher and pupil variables. The next three years promise to be especially fruitful.

robert j. havighurst

unrealized potentials of adolescents

Everybody has unrealized potential. This is a truism. Among the many useful and interesting things a person might learn to do, he has time and energy only to do some. He might have become a good golfer, or he might have learned to read Russian, or he might have become a serious amateur student of foreign affairs, or he might have learned shorthand. I might even have become a good poker player!

When we speak of the potential of adolescent boys and girls, however, we are more likely to consider their potential for learning basic mental skills, for developing positive social attitudes, for acquiring a sense of who they are and what they want to become—in short, for building the foundations on which adult competence can rest.

Potential for adult competence may be seriously stunted or even distorted so that it damages the lives of young people and of the society around them. For example, the newspapers of a big city recently carried the following story. A group of seven boys ranging in age from 15 to 18 were loafing on a corner one evening when they decided they were thirsty, and telephoned a liquor store, ordering a dozen bottles of beer and a bottle of whiskey to be delivered to an address on a side street. The delivery man was to "bring change for ten dollars." When the delivery man came to the address, one boy hit him on the head with a metal pipe, while the others took the liquor and his money. Going into an alley they drank the beer and whiskey. Then they began to roam the district, looking for excitement. Soon they saw two young women getting out of their car and crossing the street to enter their house. Stopping the women, they commenced to insult them verbally, and then began to slap them. Just then a 50-year-old man who had been visiting friends came out of a nearby building and shouted, "Leave those girls alone!" Three of the gang went after him, knocked him down, and kicked him to death. Meanwhile the women escaped into their house, and the boys fled as the police approached. Shortly afterward they beat a man who got in their way. The police arrested them later in the night. All but one had police records. Three had spent six months each in one or another state reformatory.

These boys all had the potential to become reasonably good and law-abiding workers, at the very least. They could have become good husbands and fathers, and perhaps they may yet do so. But society has a major task to "straighten them out," and it will be a long, expensive operation, at best.

Another form of unrealized potential is to be found in young people who are not anti-social in their behavior but have either not been adequately educated to use their potential abilities, or are not motivated to develop and use their abilities. For example, many

Reprinted with permission of the author and publisher from *National Association of Secondary School Principals Bulletin,* 1966, **50,** 75-96.

children of low-income families fail to work up to their ability level as indicated by their measured IQ. This occurs most frequently when they are in schools which serve low-income families almost exclusively. Here the families do not know how to push their children in school; and the school tends to adapt its standards to a level which is tolerable to the families. Thus, Wilson's study of educational achievement in the eight high schools of a big city (1959) found that the general social-class level of a high school was related to the school grades and the college aspirations of lower-class boys. A lower-class boy attending a school with a predominance of middle-class pupils was more likely to get good grades and to plan to attend college than a lower-class boy of the same IQ level who attended a school with a predominance of lower-class pupils.

There are also boys and girls with good or very good potential and with families that have high educational aspirations, who nevertheless do not commit themselves to a program of high school and college studies that will make them into the leaders and the highly productive workers that society needs and that they could become. This "uncommitted" group are a source of concern to educators and to parents in the suburban and the middle-class city high schools.

Viewed in this sociological frame of reference, then, there are three broad groups of adolescent youth whose potential for achieving adult competence is so far from being realized that they constitute social problems. They are:

1. The Socially Disadvantaged and Educationally Maladjusted Adolescent
2. The Underdeveloped and Underachieving Adolescent
3. The Potentially Superior but Uncommitted Adolescent

My plan is to discuss each of these groups in a separate section and then go on to some more general conclusions.

The Socially Disadvantaged and Educationally Maladjusted Adolescent

Approximately one-third of adolescent youth drop out of school without completing high school. Of these about 60 per cent are boys and 40 per cent girls. They are not a homogeneous group (Havighurst, et al., 1962). Some never complete the 8th grade, while others almost finish high school. Some are from middle-class families, but the great majority are from low-income working-class families. Some are rural, most are urban.

A considerable segment of dropouts adapt to the adult society fairly well. They get work and hold steady jobs. A number of the girls get married at ages as early as 15 and make what is regarded by society as a legitimate but early start on the career of wife and mother. Even under modern conditions the fact of being a dropout is not an absolute bar to doing reasonably well.

However, about half the dropouts do not get steady work and/or do not contract a steady marriage. *These are marginal to the school, marginal to the labor force, and marginal to the adult role.* They are the ones we shall call socially disadvantaged and educationally maladjusted. In 1960, in the age group 16 through 20, 11 per cent of boys and 18 per cent of girls were in this category. The proportions of 16 and 17-year-olds are somewhat greater, since there is less likelihood of having a job or being married at these ages.

Young people, age 16 to 20, who are both marginal to the school and marginal to the labor force, have become objects of increasing concern to society because they comprise a larger group than in previous decades and because they are more visible. In an earlier time, out-of-school youth could often find work on farms, and indeed a greater number of them lived in rural or semi-rural areas than is the case today. Marginal youth today live mostly in cities and when they are idle or perhaps involved in delinquent acts, the effects of their behavior are more widely advertised.

By the mid 1950's, two forces or phenomena were becoming visible which were to have drastic effects upon the position and numbers of marginal youth: first, the large population increase of children and young people due to the "baby boom" of immediate post-war years; second, the revolution in manufacturing technology caused by automation and computers. Children born in the post-war period are now in the 16 through 20 age group. In 1960 there were

12.6 million (born 1940-44); in 1965 there were 16.1 million (born 1945-49); and in 1970 there will be 18.1 million (born 1950-54). Or putting the problem another way, 26 million young people under the age of 25 will enter the labor force during the decade of the 1960's. Of these it is estimated that 6 million or 23 per cent will have some college, and another 12 million or 46 per cent will complete high school. Eight million or 31 per cent will not complete high school. This is a larger number of dropouts than were produced during the 1950's. There is every reason to believe that the social problem of marginal youth will be even greater during the 1965-1975 decade than it has been in the last decade.

Characteristics of Boys in This Group (Ahlstrom, 1966)

When the boys in this group drop out of school, they enter a period of *aimless loafing and drifting*. Their lack of purpose permits them to be open to chance stimulations which further alienate them from the society around them. For instance, a group of six boys 15 to 17 years old were standing outside a settlement house one evening. One of the boys happened to sit down on the bumper of a small foreign car parked at the curb. It rocked slightly. Soon he was rocking it harder. Immediately the other boys became involved and they soon had the car tipped up on its side. Suddenly, although they tried to prevent it, the car went completely over on its top. The boys quickly scattered but one of them had been recognized by a neighbor and soon all were down at the police station where they were given a severe lecture and a strong warning and then released to their parents after paying for a broken aerial.

Often such youth react impulsively to apparently minor incidents which begin a series of events having serious consequences. For example, Mark and Donald, both 15 years old and considered school misfits, were suspended from school one Wednesday noon for running and yelling in the halls. They were to return with their parents on Friday to be reinstated. Both boys had been suspended before and as they walked slowly from the school they talked of the beatings they would

probably get when they got home. To kill time they went down into the railroad yard and after a while caught a slow freight which they believed would take them close to their homes. The freight picked up speed and they were afraid to jump. By Saturday morning the two boys were 200 miles from home, had stolen three cars trying to get home, had burglarized two stores for food and money, and spent one night in a city jail. Again, just a little chance! Boys like these are terribly vulnerable to chance events because they have nothing to give steady direction to their lives.

Another element in this impulsiveness is an *indiscriminate seeking for excitement and pleasure*. Stealing cars is a favorite form of this activity. The status some youth associate with possessing and driving a car seems to outweigh caution or consideration of consequences. One 16-year old boy from a large and very poor family stole a late model Lincoln and then, tooting the horn, drove it up and down the block on which he lived. Quickly arrested he explained that he had driven the car in his neighborhood so that a certain girl would see him and maybe agree to a date.

For some boys the excitement of sitting behind the wheel of a late model expensive car and driving fast appears to be the prime motive for stealing it. Tom, another 16-year old out of school and unemployed went on a car stealing binge. Following his arrest he explained that he hadn't been able to find work and buy a car so he decided to steal one and "joy ride" just to see how it would be. The first was so easy to take and so much fun that he just continued to steal them and within a week had stolen nine cars. He took each one into the country and drove it as fast as he could on country roads. During this week he let several friends in on his activities. When he finished with a car he parked it in a neighborhood adjacent to his own where his friends would then pick it up. His adventure came to an end a week after it started when he piled one of the cars up on a utility pole.

Sexual experience is another major source of excitement and pleasure for youth seeking significant experience. The 9th-grade teachers and work supervisors of one group of 200 alienated youth enrolled in a special work-study program report that most of them talk openly and with considerable sophistication about their sex life and the sex act itself, although some are quite misinformed about conception and changes in their own bodies. One 16-year-old asked his teacher if it wasn't true that a boy had to be 18 before he could give a girl a baby. The teacher's reply visibly worried him. Shaking his head he muttered, "Oh, oh, maybe she's right!" Then he explained that a girl claimed he had given her a baby, but that up till then he hadn't believed it could have been his.

In a series of interviews with 100 of these youth when they were 16 years old, about half were noncommittal to the school interviewer concerning sexual experience. Fifteen per cent acknowledged such experience but did not amplify while the remaining 35 per cent talked openly and with considerable candor about their sexual life.

Fighting and drinking are commonly observed among alienated youth. Fighting is a way of gaining status and power among peers. Drinking usually begins in the early teens for youth living in communities where alcohol in many forms is easily accessible and where habitual drinking is characteristic of many adults. Often drinking seems to provide the courage to carry out dangerous but exciting activities. Among older youth out of school and without jobs drinking may become a passive kind of substitute for success and may well lead into chronic alcoholism. Often this leads to petty crime engaged in for the purpose of buying alcohol or to a very deprived existence in which meager earnings are used to buy cheap wine or any other kind of alcoholic substance available.

The Girls in This Group

The socially disadvantaged and educationally maladjusted girl is less actively anti-social than her sociological brother, but is also an alienated person. Generally she is apathetic, uninterested if not hostile to school and almost invisible to her peers in school. On sociometric tests this kind of girl is seldom mentioned by her peers. One such girl responded as follows to an interview after she had quit school:

"Were you interested in the Girls Athletic Association or the Y Teen group?"
"No, I wasn't."
Sister: "She went down to the Y.M. for swimming."

"What did you think of the social life at junior high school, did you care at all for the dances?"
"I didn't know that they had them."
"Did you go to any of the games?"
"No."
"Do you feel that you were generally a part of the junior high school as far as the activities were concerned?"
"No, I don't. I went to one dance and stayed for ten minutes. I never went to another one."
"Do you feel like you were happy in junior high school?"
She laughed. "Just before school started and after school was out."

This girl, you see, just was not in the junior high school crowd at all. She felt uncomfortable all the time, and you can see terrible things here. You can see first that there is no reason for her to stay in school. You can also understand here why these girls marry so early and so easily as it were. (They tend to marry very quickly—at 15, 16, or 17.) Apparently what they are finding is some kind of human relationship that goes far beyond anything they have had in the home or in an organized social group in school. The first boy who offers them this kind of relationship is really meeting a starved appetite, and it is easy for the boy, not generally knowing what he is doing either, to get involved; the girl becomes pregnant, and oftentimes they get married because the boy is willing to marry and for the girl it is the best possible solution.

So then we have the girl, having quite a different history than her sociological brother, one which is more acceptable to society because she doesn't get into trouble with society very much—only a small subgroup. But her career is probably equally value-less or even positively bad for the society itself since she is obviously not going to be a very good wife and mother starting so early and with such a background.

A small number of these girls are more anti-social, and are sent eventually to a reformatory. These girls generally have family situations rife with illegitimacy, multiple marriages and unstable liaisons, and instability. They are susceptible to seduction through promises of affection or excitement. They are accustomed to relying on their wits to achieve pleasure. They are hostile toward people in authority. Like the boys of this group, they are impulsive and unrealistic in meeting the demands of everyday existence.

How about the Potential of These Boys and Girls?

There are two extreme views of the potential of this group of youth. On the one hand, there is the view that this group has the same potential as any other large group, and all that is needed is the "right" kinds of educational programs to unlock this potential. On the other hand, there is the view that the members of this group are permanently and irrevocably stunted in mental development and cannot go much above their present levels of educational achievement, no matter what educative influences are brought to bear.

I don't think either of them is true. Certainly these youngsters have been very badly hurt by living for 12 or 13 years in disadvantaged situations, and I don't think that they will ever recover fully. Whatever potential they had at birth or at an earlier age, they are going to operate much below that potential. On the other hand, I would not write them off completely. It is worth working with them at the junior high level, even if we cannot expect a whole lot, particularly because they can be so damaging in the next generation and we don't want to produce a permanent "welfare class"—and these are people who would become that. We need to do everything we can to help them inch a little bit above the present level of adjustment.

There is some evidence that the second point of view is more nearly correct than the first. For example, Bloom (1964) analyzed a number of studies of intelligence and intellectual growth and found that after the age of ten the effects of contrasting social environments on IQ were very small, compared to such effects in the first four years of life, while the effects of environment between the years of 4 and 10 were intermediate in depth.

On the other hand, there are some well-attested reports of substantial change in educational achievement through one or another form of remedial education after the age of 10 or 12.

Taking the most optimistic view of the possibilities of improvement in this group after age 12, it would seem that a successful program should have one or more of the following characteristics:

1. It should be substantially different from the program they have had in the past, in which they have failed.
2. It should contain a systematic remedial program for building mental skills, based on the best research data.
3. It should satisfy some major needs of the social type, such as excitement, challenge, money, young adult models for identification.
4. It should grow out of cooperation between the school system, the social agencies that deal with adolescents, and employers who are able to supply jobs for young people. That is, it should represent a serious and sober societal commitment to throw everything useful into the attempt to make such a program succeed. Among other things, it appears that raising the legal age for leaving school to 17 or 18 may be desirable. Doing this would require society to take formal responsibility for educative treatment of this sub-group—a responsibility not now recognized.

I think there is just no question but that our society now is going to commit itself to more systematic work with this group of socially disadvantaged and educationally maladjusted youngsters. I also think this is going to force us into something many of us don't like—I don't particularly like it—more diversity among high schools. I think the comprehensive high school as we used to know it is probably long since gone. Mr. Conant, you know, after writing so much about the comprehensive high school in *The American High School,* has since said that he never really saw one except, perhaps, in Elkhart, Indiana. It doesn't exist in the suburbs because you only get a slice of youth. It doesn't exist in the inner city because you get another slice of youth. You don't get a comprehensive high school anywhere except in a town of 10,000 or so where you have a cross-section of young people and they all go to the same high school.

But even there we may have to have some kind of sectioning off of this group of educationally maladjusted and socially disadvantaged youngsters if we are going to take responsibility to the age of 17 or 18. I think we must be very serious about thinking here of effectively separate institutions for a while, remembering that there are grave disadvantages in this, but also remembering that if a youngster comes to the age of 13 or

14 and proves that he cannot adjust to an academic high school, we may have to set up another program under other people and probably cut down the amount of interaction with the group in the academic school.

Possible Educational Programs

The most obvious type of program is a remedial one, which concentrates on reading and arithmetic skills. Students may be placed in smaller classes; remedial teachers may be used; programed texts and workbooks may be introduced; parents may be recruited in a campaign to make home conditions more conducive to school success. These things have been tried with varying reports of success and failure. For instance, Dr. Samuel Shepard of St. Louis reported that, working with 7th and 8th graders in the schools of a slum district, and holding meetings with parents to secure their understanding and cooperation, the median scores of eighth graders were raised by as much as a half-year (Programs, 1963). Programs for 7th and 8th graders have been tried in a number of big cities. For example, in Chicago, over a period of two years, seven Educational and Vocational Guidance Centers were established to serve pupils who were over age (14-1/2 or 15 years of age and over). Although actual data on improvement in educational achievement have not been published, the Chicago Public Schools report that, "This individualization of the instruction program and the personalized but firm relationship between pupil and teacher which are made possible by the reduced class size, the intensive counseling and guidance services available in the Center, and the knowledge that he may move ahead as rapidly as he develops the necessary skills have proven to be important factors in changing the attitude of the pupil, improving his motivation, accelerating his entrance to high school and increasing the probability of his graduation" *(Promising Practices,* 1964).

I must confess I am skeptical. Since I am anxious to see something work with these youngsters, I have followed every substantial claim I have been able to find. But I have not been able to get any hard data that show you can do very much on a straight remedial ba-

sis for 13- or 14-year olds of this type. You get claims that the reading level goes up and they qualify for high school; but if you follow through you often discover that 100 entered the program, 50 of them disappeared in the next two or three months, 10 of them went into high school—and the claims are based on the records of those 10. We really need some careful, controlled research on this before we make claims about existing remedial programs at junior high school age. On the other hand, I don't want us to give up, because I cannot convince myself that it is impossible to work remedially with all of these youngsters. Maybe at least a subgroup of them will succeed.

Another type of program makes use of work experience as the central agent around which the attitudes and interests of students are organized, with academic instruction related as far as possible to the work experience. Such a program is started in the junior high school and develops from simple work experience projects to part-time employment and eventually to full-time employment as the student develops the skills and attitudes and habits that are necessary to hold down a job. A dozen such programs operated by school systems are described in a casebook (Burchill, 1962).

Again I find it necessary to keep the claims modest. I have been working very closely with such a project in Kansas City, Missouri, and I can tell you that after four years of this—starting with a group of 13-year olds—the work-study program has not worked in the way we hoped it would. It has been of some value, but not nearly as successful as we expected. Actually we haven't cut the delinquency in the group at all, compared with the control group. We do have fewer dropouts. The youngsters have stayed in school—I take it because they got into something, got a relationship with a work supervisor, that meant something to them. We now think that about one-fourth of the group are all set—they have full-time jobs and are pretty stable and steady. So apparently our program has worked with about a fourth of the group as we hoped it might work for all of them. Of course, this is worthwhile; if you can get a program to work for a fourth of 15 per cent, that amounts to 4 per cent of the total group. In any sizable city this is a group worth singling out for special treatment. But no work-study program so far known is a panacea for this kind of group.

Programs designed expressly for girls of this sub-group are very few, though a good case for such programs has been made by some writers. Work-experience programs seem better fitted to boys than to girls, because the career of worker has more masculine than feminine appeal. However, certain feminine work experiences might be used, such as homemaking and baby care. This has been tried out in a few cities with special classes of pregnant girls. Such girls are usually suspended from school when their pregnancy becomes visible. But a few cities have created special classes for them, often in cooperation with a settlement house or an organization such as the YWCA. In these classes there has not been much success with home economics and child care courses. Possibly this is due to inferior planning and preparation by teachers, or perhaps it is due to a tendency among pregnant girls to reject their babies and the role of motherhood, with a desire to get the pregnancy out of the way so they can go back to school and progress in the ordinary way.

Nevertheless, I think our best chance with girls similar to the boys we have been discussing is to get them into some kind of group that concentrates on the role of the wife and the mother in terms of the kind of academic training it gives—chiefly, home economics—but combined with some kind of social group work experience. If we could find the rare combination of a home economics teacher who was also a group worker we'd have it. I'd like to turn a group of these girls over to this kind of person and say to her: "You can have as much of the time of these girls as you want from age 13 until they drop out of school. You can organize them into a club, you can meet any time you please, you can excuse them for babysitting, you can excuse them for part-time work later on if they are good enough to work in homes, etc." The only test will be whether these girls emerge then making better marriages than a control group, whether they move into the role of wife and mother somewhat better. Incidentally, experimentation on this line is something that any foundation would pay for. It's amazing to me that, with all our ingenuity in working with boys, we haven't had a number of projects for girls coming along, because any of the foundations would jump at the chance. Nobody can oppose helping girls of this type, for they pose an obvious need, etc. Probably the reason we haven't had the ingenuity and creativity to move into programs for girls is that we haven't had to, because the girls are not such an obvious threat to our society in the immediate present.

In general, it must be said that there is little or no scientific evidence for or against the experimental programs for socially disadvantaged and educationally maladjusted adolescents. Some of these projects have been acclaimed enthusiastically by their sponsors. Others have been allowed to die out. There is need of more systematic experimentation and evaluation of a variety of procedures. The problem is inherently a very difficult one.

The Underdeveloped and Underachieving Adolescent

A good way to define the group which undoubtedly has much "hidden" but realizable potential may be to describe the Demonstration Guidance Project of the New York City Public Schools *(Promising Practices,* 1964).

The Demonstration Guidance Project was begun in one junior high school, Jr. H.S. 43 Manhattan, located at the edge of the Harlem slum area. Ethnically, the pupils were 48 per cent Negro, 38 per cent Puerto Rican, and 14 per cent "others." Of the total school population of 1400, the most able 717 were selected for the project. This group, in grades 7, 8, and 9, had a median group verbal IQ score of 95, and was on the average a year and a half retarded in both reading and mathematics. As the pupils moved through the grades, and were graduated from junior high school, 365 of the original 717 went on to George Washington High School. Both in junior high school and in high school, the pupils were organized more or less as a "school within a school." The first group was graduated from high school in June 1960; the last group in June 1962.

Description

1. Cost—At the junior high school level, $100 additional per pupil per year or about 25 per cent above regular cost; at high

school level, $250 per pupil per year additional, or 50 per cent above regular cost.

2. Individual counseling—Greatly enriched program. At junior high school level, ratio increased from 1:1400 to 1:235; high school, 1:100. Supportive services included: social work, psychologist, consultative psychiatric services.

3. Group guidance—Once per week, with counselors as teachers. Stress on careers, career planning. Use of check lists, tests, questionnaires, career booklets, alumni speakers of same ethnic group, trips to colleges and places of employment, special assembly programs, Future Teacher clubs, career nights. General objective: raise self-image, aspiration level.

4. Cultural enrichment—trips to theatre, ballet, museums, laboratories, Shakespearean festivals, consulates, special movies and assembly programs, lists of "Places to Go and Things to Do"; distributed to pupils and parents.

5. Instructional services—Very small classes in math and foreign language (10-15), double period of English, individual coaching, homework rooms, special summer school remedial services in reading and math.

6. Teacher training—Emphasis on reading, test interpretation, self-image of pupils, oral work.

7. Parent education—Use of small and large group meetings; public relations campaign in community, positive approach. Objective: raise aspiration level of parents for children.

Evaluation and Outcomes

1. Dropouts: Of the 365 project admissions to George Washington H.S., 36 transferred or moved. Of the remaining, 258 (78%) were graduated—a record about 1/3 better than might normally have been anticipated.

2. Academic success: (Comparison group consists of pupils who entered George Washington H.S. from Junior H.S. 43 Manhattan in the three years preceding the project.)

	1957-1959 (control)	1960-1962 (experimental)
Academic diplomas	43	108
No failures, all terms	14	44
Average 80% or more	11	37
Average 85% or more	2	15
Best rank in class	51; 65; 226	1, 4, 6; 4; 2, 4, 9
Higher education	47	168

Of the 108 pupils receiving academic diplomas 96 went on to some form of higher education.

Of the 150 pupils receiving general and commercial diplomas, 72 went on to some form of higher education.

3. Nature of pupils succeeding in academic work in high school—A number of different studies indicate that many of these succeeding in academic courses in high school had relatively low group verbal IQ scores and achievement scores. For example, of the 108 pupils who earned academic diplomas, 38 had IQ scores below 100; 38 were 1 year or more behind in math, and 13 were 1 year or more behind in reading. However, almost invariably the students concerned had outstanding school service and character ratings.

The type of young people we are now discussing often do average work in school, in spite of an unpromising home and community environment and an uninspiring school program. What they seem chiefly to need is stimulation and enrichment in their school program. Most of them come from working-class homes. Probably 15 per cent of all boys and girls fall effectively into this group, and 30 per cent of pupils in junior high schools in working-class areas of a city.

We are getting into a number of programs for this type of youngster. The programs appear to pay off very well, and the students get a lot of satisfaction from them because they achieve relatively good success. For example, Kansas City, Missouri, has what is called the Kansas City Scholarship Program, a four-year experiment with local foundation funds. They pick youngsters who are fairly good but not good enough to get scholarships in the ordinary competition. The average IQ of the ones they have picked is around 110. They select about 100 9th graders a year, largely on the basis of teacher nominations, and they utilize a kind of seminar. They bring the parents (there is a staff for this) into several meetings a year and say in effect, "We think your youngsters are capable of good college work and if they make good in high school we will help them get scholarships. We realize that you folks are not going to be able to help them much financially if they go to college."

In the four high school years the students get great attention from guidance counselors. At the end of the 4th year they are placed in a pre-college course, a summer course usually held at some college for about two weeks. They live in a dormitory, attend college-like lectures, and get systematic training in English. The staff then grade them and they have been flunking about one-third of them—flunking them only in the sense that they do not recommend them for a scholarship.

This is a reality-based program. We know that about three-fourths of the youngsters picked in this way can make good in college. The college dropout rate of the youngsters who were in this program has been running about 8 per cent. The program provides them with adequate scholarship funds, usually in a college that will match its contribution, so that the managers of the program have been able to make the money spread pretty widely. I have spent quite a little time on this one program because it is quite clear that something like this kind of thing is going to expand and may expand very rapidly. The Higher Education bill which has just been reported out for action by the House of Representatives, with its provision for what are called "Educational Opportunity Grants," is an indicator of the great public interest in this area.

Currently there is much interest in this type of adolescent and much experimental activity looking toward the short ways of discovering him, and motivating and guiding him toward fuller realization of his potential. Negro youth from working-class and sometimes from middle-class homes are a special target group, because they have been under-motivated as a consequence of the fact that they have suffered from job discrimination in the past, and many times from doubts about their own ability.

The Potentially Superior but Uncommitted Adolescent

A third group of youth with unrealized potential consists of boys and girls with superior intellectual ability who do not achieve up to their measured ability level because they are unwilling or unable to commit themselves to achieving the tasks of growing up. This is the type which is especially troubling schoolmen in middle-class and suburban areas.

The normal child grows up to early adolescence believing in himself and in his society because his family and immediate friends believe in him and in their society. The two characteristics of *self-esteem* and *social fidelity* are bestowed upon the child by his family and friends. Because they think well of him, he thinks well of himself. Because they believe they live in a good society, he believes it. Thus the average child comes to the age of 12 or so with a reasonable amount of self-esteem and social fidelity. He has not *achieved* these qualities. He has inherited them without thinking about them.

At the coming of adolescence a person must commence to achieve his own self-esteem and his social fidelity. This is a part of his achievement of his *identity* as a person in his own right. It comes about normally as a part of his adolescent experience in school, work, play with his age-mates, and association with adult citizens and workers. The youth as he achieves identity narrows and focuses his personal, occupational, sexual and ideological commitments by getting started in one occupation, getting married and starting a family, and beginning to take part in community civic life.

Apparently this process of growth toward identity is more difficult today than it was a generation or more ago. The evidence for this statement comes from the testimony of high school counselors and teachers, from parents of intelligent and sensitive children, and from psychologists and sociologists who have studied youth culture.

Some boys and girls seem to become paralyzed in their efforts to grow up. They suffer from a diffusion of identity which makes it difficult or impossible for them to marshal their energies. They are quite sophisticated in their knowledge of the world and its complexities, as well as in their acquaintance with the seamy side of human nature. They acquire their sophistication from their schooling and from the experience of the mood of modern urban society. The mood of our society includes frankness in formerly taboo areas, self-criticism, and skepticism. Youth are exposed to this mood very directly through the mass media (television, cinema, paper-back literature, etc.). They read such books as Salinger's *Catcher in the Rye* and Golding's *Lord of the Flies,* and they are encouraged to read such literature by high school teachers of literature who represent the mood of society. These books are true portrayals of a part of human nature —an unpleasant part—but not the whole of it by any means. Perhaps they are more valid than the literature adolescents read a generation or more ago—*Rebecca of Sunnybrook Farm,* or Horatio Alger's *Strive and Succeed.* Those books only gave part of the picture, too. They enabled a youngster to grow up in a kind of fool's paradise, not recognizing that either he or his society had a bad side. But, on the whole, I would say that youngsters who grew up on that sort of thing were lucky, because at least they got the *positive* side. What we are getting now is a group of young people—and in many ways they are our *best* young people—who are sensitive enough and well enough educated to know that they also have a negative side, with a lot of depravity in it. Furthermore, the sober and realistic writing about the dangers of nuclear war and the difficulties of international control of armaments give young people an ample picture of the immorality of national policies.

Boys and girls are shown the seamy side of personal and political life and then asked to commit themselves to social loyalty.

At the same time boys and girls are confronted with the tasks of making good in school, of choosing an occupation, and of establishing themselves with the opposite sex —and these tasks are set for them a year or two earlier than they were a generation or two ago, because of the social forces making for social precocity in the middle-class part of society.

Under the circumstances it is not surprising that contemporary middle-class youth show a considerable degree of self-doubt as well as lack of confidence in the political and economic structure of modern society. It is not suprising that a *privatistic* life is preferred to one of greater social commitment. Boys find it difficult to make up their minds what occupation they will prepare for. Some of them engage in a kind of sit-down strike against the academic demands made on them by school or college. Their fathers wonder why sons are so ingrown and uncertain, as compared with the greater assurance and task-orientation they remember as normal for their generation. There is not so much concern about girls, since they are not expected to show the degree of *instrumental activism* expected of boys. With them there is more concern about their sex role, and about the place of sexual activity in the life of a teen-age girl.

I take it that the junior high period is the crucial period for these youngsters. Up to junior high there seems to be no problem of achieving identity because it is bestowed on us by our parents; that is, the Smith boy is the Smith boy, and he gets his identity from the Smith family. But some time around the age of 12 or 13 a person has to earn his own way, as it were, not economically any more, but emotionally and intellectually. And earning one's own way means that one has to be sure enough of the society to commit oneself to a career in that society. You have to have this combination of self-esteem and social fidelity, and this seems to be peculiarly difficult for intelligent and sensitive young people today. And I think we can see why. For one thing, the youngsters know that they live in a society that could easily commit suicide— and they wonder what's worth committing oneself to a society that can't control its own destiny. No sensitive, intelligent 16-year-old can read modern history or modern social science without wondering about the society in which he lives, whether it is worth his commitment. And it is understandable that he may say, "That's not for me; I'm going to live a privatistic life. My friends and I can listen to music, we can have discussions of philosophy, etc., but what's the use of working hard to become a lawyer or doctor in a society that may commit suicide before I even get my medical degree?"

That's one side of the problem. On the other side, that of self-esteem, we are so frank about human nature in our literature and mass media that a young person trying to understand himself must get the impression that he is a complex of obscene complexes—that he has all of these evil instincts boiling around inside of him, as it were; that he is a bad person. In this situation is it surprising that many of our ablest youngsters decide to refuse to commit themselves, at least for a while? They often come through after several years of worry to themselves and their teachers. But this clearly is a group that needs some kind of different secondary education—particularly at the junior high level.

It is difficult to estimate the numbers of boys and girls in this category because there is no sharp division between those who are *committed* and those who are not. It is a matter of degree. Perhaps we might estimate that 5 per cent of the new generation fall far enough short of realizing their visible potential to create a definite disadvantage for themselves and for the society that needs their best efforts.

Educational Programs for Uncommitted Youth

If the foregoing analysis is reasonably correct, the age period from about 14-16 (grades 9-11) needs an educational program designed to build self-esteem and social fidelity. The relevant characteristics of these boys and girls are the following:

Lack of self-esteem based on their own achievement in school and society
Uncertainty about vocational choice
Cognitive development more advanced than personal autonomy
Lack of naive faith in society
Discontent with school.

The educational program should be designed to build a social fidelity as well as self-confidence. It might contain the following elements:

1. Opportunity for service to society. A variety of projects during the school year and during the summer for improvement of the school, the local community, and the wider community. This will lead to a commitment to social welfare and a faith in the improvability of society.

2. Positively oriented study of society. Stress in courses in social studies on the achievement of modern society in solving problems of public health, poverty, educational and economic opportunity, and the building of an interdependent world.

3. Use of adult models who demonstrate both self-esteem and social fidelity; choice of teachers who are socially optimistic, active, and oriented toward the improvement of society. There is a greater chance in the future for the selection of teachers with appropriate personalities for certain age groups, as the teacher shortage decreases and opportunity increases to select the better ones. The use of biography in literature and the social studies could stress heroes with these positive qualities. A new set of biographical films produced by Elizabeth Drews of Michigan

State University centers around the lives of contemporary people who are making positive contributions to the life of society, who have faith in the improvability of this society, and who lead personal lives that can serve as models for youth. The eight models for the films are: Dr. Eugene Peterson, historian; Judge Mary Coleman; Robert von Neumann, artist; Dr. Barbara Redmore, radiologist; Kay Britten, folksinger active in politics; Dr. Loren Eisely, natural scientist and author; Dr. Anne Roe, social scientist; Dr. Harold Taylor, philosopher.

Dr. Drews describes the films and her use of them as follows (1966):

These models represented a development of individual potential and a kind of excellence which transcends the norm. As men and women they were creative, scholarly, and socially concerned, and none represented a sex stereotype. The men were masculine, virile, and successful, but they were also sensitive, aesthetic, and introspective. Their career engagements were in education (historical museums), writing, art, and philosophy. The women were attractive in very feminine ways with aesthetic interests and deep altruistic concerns but their careers were in such non-feminine areas as politics, law, technology, and research. Each model revealed his values and philosophy of life as the style-of-life filmed episodes unfolded. In the latter part of each film the models were interviewed about their early memories and their childhood development. In this way the students were able to see further links between their own lives and those of these unusual individuals.

Discussions followed each film and were the real bond of the course. These discussions were relatively free and unstructured, following a "conversational dialectic" pattern, and thus were vastly different from recitations. However, the freedom was not merely negative for there was positive encouragement to independence of an informed and responsible nature. For example, each student had a mimeographed copy of the sound track of each film, and could raise questions on the basis of actual statements of the models rather than fragmented memories of these statements.

For this type of student it is especially important that education should strike a balance between analysis and affirmation. The education of middle-class children in recent years has been too strong on analysis and too weak on affirmation.

Conclusion

The concept of potential ability is so general that it can be applied to all kinds of people, in the sure knowledge that all kinds of people fail to realize their potential fully. However, there are three groups of adolescent boys and girls who fail in specially significant ways to realize their potentials. Taken together, they make up about 35 per cent of all adolescents.

In this discussion we have attempted to define and describe these three diverse groups, and to show how they might be discovered and how they might be served better by secondary schools.

References

Ahlstrom, W. M. Masculine identity and career problems for boys. In W. Wattenferg (Ed.), *Social deviancy among youth.* Chicago: University of Chicago Press, 1966. Pp. 135-163.

Aronfreed, J., Cutick, R. A., & Fagen, S. A. Cognitive structure, punishment, and nurturance in the experimental induction of self-criticism. *Child Development,* 1963, **34,** 281-294.

Bandura, A. Social learning through imitation. In M. R. Jones (Ed.), *Nebraska symposium on motivation.* Lincoln: University of Nebraska Press, 1962. Pp. 211-269.

Bandura, A. The role of imitation in personality development. *Journal of Nursery Education,* 1963, **18,** 207-215.

Bandura, A., & Huston, A. C. Identification as a process of incidental learning. *Journal of Abnormal and Social Psychology,* 1961, **63,** 311-318.

Bandura, A., & McDonald, F. J. Influence of social reinforcement and the behavior of models in shaping children's moral judgments. *Journal of Abnormal and Social Psychology,* 1963, **67,** 274-281.

Bandura, A., Ross, D., & Ross, S. A. Transmission of aggression through imitation of aggressive models. *Journal of Abnormal and Social Psychology,* 1961, **63,** 575-582.

Bandura, A., Ross, D., & Ross, S. A. Imitation of film-mediated aggressive models. *Journal of Abnormal and Social Psychology,* 1963a, **66,** 3-11.

Bandura, A., Ross, D., & Ross, S. A. Comparative test of the status envy, social power, and secondary reinforcement theories of identificatory learning. *Journal of Abnormal and Social Psychology,* 1963b, **67,** 527-534.

Bandura, A., Ross, D., & Ross, S. A. Vicarious reinforcement and imitative learning. *Journal of Abnormal and Social Psychology,* 1963c, **67,** 601-607.

Bloom, B. S. *Stability and change in human characteristics.* New York: Wiley, 1964.

Boehm, L. The development of conscience: A comparison of American children of different mental and socioeconomic levels. *Child Development,* 1962, **33,** 575-590.

Burchill, G. *Work-study programs for alienated youth.* Chicago: Science Research Associates, 1962.

Burnstein, E., Stotland, E., & Zander, A. Similarity to a model and self-evaluation. *Journal of Abnormal and Social Psychology,* 1961, **62,** 257-264.

Cattell, R. B., et al. *Prediction and understanding of the effect of children's interest upon school performance.* U.S. Department of Health, Education, and Welfare, Office of Education, Cooperative Research Project No. 701 (8383). Urbana: University of Illinois, 1962.

Coleman, J. S. The adolescent subculture and academic achievement. *American Journal of Sociology,* 1960, **65,** 337-347.

Coleman, J. S. *The adolescent society.* New York: Free Press, 1961.

Coleman, J. S. *The adolescent and the schools.* New York: Basic Books, 1965.

Crisis in high schools. *LIFE,* 1969, **66** (19), 24.

deJung, J. E., & Gardner, E. F. The accuracy of self-role perception: A developmental study. *Journal of Experimental Education,* 1962, **31,** 27-41.

deJung, J. E., & Meyer, W. J. Expected reciprocity: Grade trends and correlates. *Child Development,* 1963, **34,** 127-139.

Downey, L. W. *The secondary phase of education.* New York: Blaisdell, 1965.

Drews, E. M. Self-actualization: A new focus on education. In W. B. Waetjen (Ed.), *Learning and mental health.* Washington, D.C.: Association for Supervision and Curriculum Development, National Education Association, 1966. Pp. 97-124.

Erikson, E. H. *Childhood and society.* New York: Norton, 1950.

Erikson, E. H. *The challenge of youth.* New York: Doubleday, 1963.

Friesen, D. The Ottawa study. Unpublished paper, 1966.

Friesen, D., Knill, W. D., & Ratsoy, E. The Edmonton study: Adolescent values and attitudes, 1967. Now in process.

Gellert, E. Stability and fluctuation in the power relationships of young children. *Journal of Abnormal and Social Psychology,* 1961, **62,** 8-15.

Gold, H. A. The classroom isolate: An additional dimension for consideration in the evaluation of a quality education program. *Journal of Experimental Education,* 1962, **31,** 77–80.

Goodman, P. *Growing up absurd.* New York: Vintage Books, 1960.

Gordon, W. C. *The social system of the high school.* New York: Free Press, 1957.

Goslin, D. A. Accuracy of self perception and social acceptance. *Sociometry,* 1962, **25,** 283-296.

Grimes, J. W., & Allinsmith, W. Compulsivity, anxiety, and school achievement. *Merrill-Palmer Quarterly,* 1961, **7,** 247-271.

Havighurst, R. J., et al. *Growing up in River City.* New York: Wiley, 1962.

Heilbrun, A. B., Jr. Social value–social behavior inconsistency and early signs of psychopathology in adolescence. *Child Development,* 1963, **34,** 187-194.

Heilbrun, A. B., Jr. Parental model attributes, nurturant reinforcement and consistency of behavior in adolescents. *Child Development,* 1964, **35,** 151-167.

Hill, K. T. Relation of test anxiety, defensiveness, and intelligence to sociometric status. *Child Development,* 1963, **34,** 767-776.

Hollingshead, A. B. *Elmtown's youth.* New York: Wiley, 1949.

Horowitz, F. D. The relationship of anxiety, self-concept, and sociometric status among fourth, fifth, and sixth grade children. *Journal of Abnormal and Social Psychology,* 1962, **65,** 212-214.

Howard, E. R. Developing student responsibility for learning. *National Association of Secondary School Principals Bulletin,* 1966, **50,** 235-246.

Hudgins, B. B., Smith, L. M., & Johnson, T. J. The child's perception of his classmates. *Journal of Genetic Psychology,* 1962, **101,** 401-415.

Hurlock, E. B. *Adolescent development* (3rd ed.) New York: McGraw-Hill, 1967.

Johnson, M. The adolescent intellect. *Educational Leadership,* 1965, **22,** 200-204.

Kanous, L. E., Daugherty, R. A., & Cohn, T. S. Relation between heterosexual friendship choices and socioeconomic level. *Child Development,* 1962, **33,** 251-255.

Kounin, J. S., & Gump, P. V. The comparative influence of punitive and nonpunitive teachers upon children's concepts of school misconduct. *Journal of Educational Psychology,* 1961, **52,** 44-49.

Maehr, M. L., Mensing, J., & Nafzger, S. Concept of self and the reaction of others. *Sociometry,* 1962, **25,** 353–357.

McNeil, J. D. Programed instruction versus usual classroom procedures in teaching boys to read. *American Educational Research Journal,* 1964, **1,** 113-119.

Meyer, W. J., & deJung, J. E. Consistency of pupil rating behavior over two social-psychological need situations. *Child Development,* 1963, **34,** 791-798.

Ojemann, R. H., & Snider, B. C. F. The development of the child's conception of the teacher. *Journal of Experimental Education,* 1963, **32,** 73-80.

Photiadis, J. D. Education and personality variables related to prejudice. *Journal of Social Psychology,* 1962, **58,** 269–275.

Photiadis, J. D., & Biggar, J. Religiosity, education and ethnic distance. *American Journal of Sociology,* 1962, **67,** 666-672.

Porterfield, O. V., & Schlichting, H. F. Peer status and reading achievement. *Journal of Educational Research,* 1961, **54,** 291-297.

Programs for educationally disadvantaged. *Office of Education Bulletin* No. 17. Washington, D.C.: U.S. Office of Education, 1963. Pp. 24, 42-44.

Promising practices from the projects for the culturally deprived. Chicago: Board of Education, Research Council of the Great Cities Program for School Improvement, 1964.

Reese, H. W. Relationships between self-acceptance and sociometric choices. *Journal of Abnormal and Social Psychology,* 1961, **62,** 472-474.

Remmers, H. H., & Radler, D. H. *The American teenager* New York: Bobbs-Merrill, 1957.

Riesman, D. *The lonely crowd.* New Haven, Conn: Yale University Press, 1961.

Rosenfeld, H., & Zander, A. The influence of teachers on aspirations of students. *Journal of Educational Psychology,* 1961, **52,** 1-11.

Rubenfeld, S., & Stafford, J. W. An adolescent inmate social system—a psychosocial account. *Psychiatry: Journal for the Study of Interpersonal Processes,* 1963, **26,** 241-256.

Sears, P. S. *The effect of classroom conditions on the strength of achievement motive and work output on elementary school children.* U.S. Department of Health, Education, and Welfare, Office of Education, Cooperative Research Project No. 873. Stanford, Calif.: Stanford University, 1963.

Spaulding, R. L. What teacher attributes bring out the best in gifted children? *Gifted Child Quarterly,* 1963a, **7,** 150–156.

Spaulding, R. L. *Achievement, creativity, and self-concept correlates of teacher-pupil transactions in elementary school classrooms.* U.S. Department of Health, Education, and Welfare, Office of Education, Cooperative Research Project No. 1352. Urbana: University of Illinois, 1963b.

Spaulding, R. L. Achievement, creativity, and self-concept correlates of teacher-pupil transactions in elementary schools. In C. B. Stendler (Ed.), *Readings in child behavior and development.* New York: Harcourt, 1964. Pp. 313-318.

Special Report, *American Education,* 1968, **4,** 1-3.

Stith, M., & Connor, R. Dependency and helpfulness in young children. *Child Development,* 1962, **33,** 15-20.

Sutton-Smith, B., Rosenberg, B. G., & Morgan, E. F., Jr. Development of sex differences in play choices during preadolescence. *Child Development,* 1963, **34,** 119-126.

Tannenbaum, A. J. Quoted by J. S. Coleman, *The adolescent society.* New York: Free Press, 1961.

Webb, A. P. Sex-role preferences and adjustment in early adolescents. *Child Development,* 1963, **34,** 609-618.

Wilson, A. B. Residential segregation of social classes and aspirations of high school boys. *American Sociological Review,* 1959, **24,** 836-845.

Wilson, W. C. Development of ethnic attitudes in adolescence. *Child Development,* 1963, **34,** 247-256.

Annotations

Calmes, R. E. Dissent: The teacher's role. *Arizona Teacher,* 1969, **57** (3), 10-11. This timely article discusses what a teacher can do to help regarding student dissent on campuses. A stress on democracy, on respect for mores, and on genuine interest in the student is emphasized. The author suggests that the solution to student dissent is building teacher-pupil links so that each one's role is more appropriately defined.

Combs, J., & Cooley, W. Dropouts: In high school and after high school. *American Educational Research Journal,* 1968, **5,** 343-364. This article provides an elaborate and revealing analysis of the 440,000 students participating in Project Talent. Individual abilities, interests, self-perceptions, and socioeconomic environment are analyzed. Reasons for leaving school and post-high-school activities are discussed for both males and females.

Diedrich, R. C., & Jackson, P. W. Satisfied and dissatisfied students. *Personnel and Guidance Journal,* 1969, **47,** 645-648. High school juniors were given a questionnaire that measured academic success, intellectual ability, social class, and personal values. The findings show no relationship between student evaluation of school experiences and academic success. Teacher ratings revealed a strong bias in favor of girls. Several negative adjectives—dull, restless, angry, bored, and rejected—were selected when students were asked to describe their feelings. Conclusions indicate that dissatisfied students describe school experiences in a more negative way than do satisfied students.

Glissmeyer, C. H. Which school for the sixth grader, the elementary or the middle school? *California Journal of Educational Research,* 1969, **20,** 176-185. Glissmeyer discusses the organizational basis for public schools for the sixth grader. It is conjectured that the middle school (grades 5–8 or 6–8) is a new approach based around the needs of the early adolescent. It is believed that the middle school can build the unique experiences needed by the early adolescent. In addition to mental, physical, and emotional growth factors, it provides for better interpretation of cultural forces surrounding it.

Havighurst, R. J. High schools for the future. *Kentucky School Journal,* 1969, **47** (6), 18-19. This brief article discusses the opportunities of today's high schools in a rapidly developing society. Havighurst stresses instrumental education and expressive education. Instrumental education is a kind of investment of time and energy in the expectation of future gain. Expressive education is education for a goal that lies within the act of learning or is so closely related to it that the act of learning appears to be the goal.

Sanford, N. Education for individual development. *American Journal of Orthopsychiatry,* 1968, **38,** 858-868. This article is concerned with the development of such personality characteristics as flexibility, creativity, and openness to experience. Sanford urges teachers to challenge the thinking structures of adolescent and college youths—in the interest of their growth. Emphasis is placed on self-knowledge as a prerequisite to development.

Stuckwisch, H. The dropout: Early adolescent education. *Clearing House,* 1968, **43,** 216-219. Stuckwisch interviewed school personnel and then proposed a program of minimum education to alleviate the dropout problem. His suggestions include developing problem-solving abilities, maintaining adolescent interest levels, and developing a positive self-concept.

Warner, R. W., Jr., & Hansen J. C. Alienated youth: The counselor's task. *Personnel and Guidance Journal,* 1970, **48,** 443-448. A major problem facing school counselors today is the growing number of alienated youth. Warner and Hansen suggest handling the problem by examining the educational structure, the conformity within a school, school-defined goals, and the counselor's task.

six

adolescence: peers and values

Adolescents are vitally concerned about self- and social identity and social maturation. Most behavioral scientists agree that these factors, which are essential to successful development, are worked out within one's own world—*among one's peers.*

The first article in this chapter, by Smith and Kleine, reviews the literature on adolescent development. It presents the conflicting propositions that (1) adolescents are an emphatically strong subculture, and (2) adolescent values do not differ significantly from those of their parents. In an extensive study of middle-class families, Elkin and Westley (1955) found very little difference between adult and adolescent values. Research among rural youths has reflected the same finding (Bealer, Willits, & Maida, 1964). Yet Coleman's studies (1961a) show quite distinctly that there is an adolescent subculture

that is the primary influence in adolescent social maturation. Subsequent studies support his conclusions (Strom, 1963; Cawelti, 1968; *Generations Apart,* 1969).

If adolescents do indeed constitute a subculture, it seems likely that their rebellion against parental values is no more than a natural phenomenon that would be less conflict- and anxiety-ridden if less were being said about it. Bandura's article takes this position. He maintains that most adults base their accusations of adolescent rebellion on superficial signs of nonconformity. He cogently parallels adolescent fad behaviors with adult fad behaviors. Mass media's tendency to sensationalize adolescent behaviors, especially deviant ones, also perpetuates the myth of significant adolescent-adult differences.

Some type of group interaction, such as

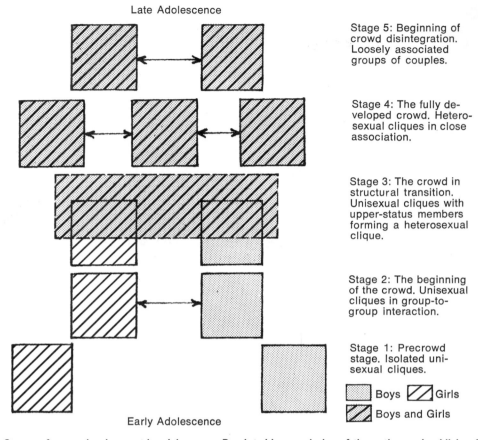

Late Adolescence

Stage 5: Beginning of crowd disintegration. Loosely associated groups of couples.

Stage 4: The fully developed crowd. Heterosexual cliques in close association.

Stage 3: The crowd in structural transition. Unisexual cliques with upper-status members forming a heterosexual clique.

Stage 2: The beginning of the crowd. Unisexual cliques in group-to-group interaction.

Stage 1: Precrowd stage. Isolated unisexual cliques.

Boys ☐   Girls ▨

Boys and Girls ▨

Early Adolescence

Figure 1. Stages of group development in adolescence. Reprinted by permission of the author and publisher from D. C. Dunphy, The social structure of urban adolescent peer groups. *Sociometry*, 1963, **26**, 236.

membership in cliques and crowds, is necessary for social maturation. Dunphy (1963; see Annotation) found that nearly 80 percent of all adolescents are involved in some form of group behavior. Figure 1 illustrates the stages of group development in adolescence.

There are several reasons why group identification is so important to developing adolescents. One such reason is that it helps them in the process of emancipation. Although Bandura suggests that emancipation from parents is more or less completed, rather than initiated, at adolescence, most writers believe that the process continues throughout adolescence and is aided by peer association (Douvan & Adelson, 1966).

Group identification also spurs competition. Healthy competition can be an aid to social maturation. However, today's society demands so many attainments for success that the method of attainment may result in

unhealthy competition and may affect the individual's overall life-style.

A third aspect of group identification is heterosexual attachments. In their formative stages, adolescents usually identify with same-sex groups; as they mature, they band into heterosexual groups (Dunphy, 1963). By 14 or 15, adolescents are comfortable around members of the opposite sex and participate in social activities with them. Many are even dating regularly. According to Dunphy, dating represents the highest stage of group development, for at this point the crowd disintegrates into loosely associated groups of couples.

One final consideration regarding group identification is conformity. Adolescent group conformity may be linked to common values, or it may stem from a need for acceptance, a fear of rejection, or a desire to escape loneliness. Whatever the cause, peers seem to exert the dominant influence on adolescent behaviors (Brittain, 1963; Cawelti, 1968; Coleman, 1961a; Friesen, 1968; Musgrove, 1966). Like adults, adolescents also manifest conformity in small social units or reference groups, which vary in activities, sentiments, and behavioral norms.

Factors Influencing Adolescent Values

Initially, interaction between parent and child provides the basis for primary value systems. Decline of parental influence usually occurs during adolescence, as Brown, Morrison, and Counc (1947) found by comparing the value structures of youths at 10 and at 16 years of age. Thus, as the adolescent matures, the sources of his value systems broaden and the family plays a less significant role.

As has already been stated, peers provide the greatest social influences outside the home. Among peers there is a sharing of differing value systems, and group behavior and identification become strong influences. Thus adolescents conform to gain acceptance. Yet adolescent values are not inflexible. With learning and maturation, the teenager changes his behaviors and attitudes when they appear inconsistent with those suggested by his environment.

Thus three factors—parents, peers, and the social-cultural milieu—contribute to the adolescent's emerging value system. The strength of each factor varies tremendously, and adolescents who feel a high level of similarity in values band together into groups.

Three Types of Peer Groups

Three distinct groups can be seen among today's adolescents: (1) high school youths, (2) noncollege youths, and (3) college youths. The groups differ in their physical and intellectual functions, their social and cultural environments, and their attitudes and values.

High School Youths

Most high school students spend their time in breaking infantile ties, developing friendships, participating in high school activities, and considering future plans. Parental, school, and peer influences assist in these processes. Although many high school youths engage in student activism, drug-taking, and premarital sex, they do so primarily to identify with some individual, clique, or gang. The primary focus at this age is the continued resolution of developmental tasks (Garrison, 1966; Havighurst, 1952; Thornburg, 1970). Sherif and Sherif have stated "Adolescents will find kicks in any activity—whether socially desirable or undesirable—that lets them act together on their own" (1966, p. 6). This interpretation may apply to many high school youths, but it is not the same type of motivation that triggers the behavior of noncollege and college adolescents.

Noncollege Youths

The majority of our youths do not go to college. In fact, recent surveys place the proportion of noncollege youths at about 80 percent (Braham, 1965). Yet little is heard of this group, and few studies have focused on this segment of the population. What are their values and attitudes? How do they differ from high school and college students and from adults?

Noncollege adolescents, compared with college students, are characterized by a more limited amount of education and a stronger work orientation. They tend to hold middle-class values, to be politically conservative, to be middle-income, blue-collar workers, and to be religiously oriented (*Generations Apart*, 1969). Their life-style is so much like that of their parents that, for this group, the Generation Gap seems to be a myth.

In April 1969, CBS News and the Daniel Yankelovich research firm undertook a study of the Generation Gap. The survey, originally the subject of a series of television shows, has since been released as *Generations Apart* (1969). It sampled the views of 2881 noncollege youths and 723 college youths

(17-23 years old) as well as 310 noncollege youths' parents and 362 college youths' parents. The following summary statements indicate differences between noncollege and college adolescents and their parents.

A. Question: Will hard work always pay off? (percentage who believe yes)

Answer: NCY* 79 CY* 56
NCY parents 85 CY parents 76

B. Question: Should everyone save as much as he can regularly and not have to lean on family and friends the minute he runs into financial problems? (percentage who believe yes)

Answer: NCY 88 CY 76
NCY parents 98 CY parents 90

C. Question: Is belonging to some organized religion important in a person's life? (percentage who believe yes)

Answer: NCY 82 CY 42
NCY parents 91 CY parents 81

D. Question: Does competition encourage excellence? (percentage who believe yes)

Answer: NCY 82 CY 72
NCY parents 91 CY parents 84

*NCY stands for noncollege youths; CY stands for college youths.

Noncollege and college adolescents were asked which of the following changes they *would welcome:*

Category	NCY	CY
A. Less emphasis on money	54%	72%
B. More emphasis on law and order	81	57
C. More emphasis on self-expression	70	84
D. More sexual freedom	22	43
E. More vigorous protests by blacks and other minority groups	9	23
F. More respect for authority	86	59

Thus the values of noncollege adolescents are more traditional and similar to parental values than are those of college students. The following responses report the attitudes of noncollege and college youths in nontraditional areas.

A. Question: Is having an abortion morally wrong? (percentage who agree)

Answer: NCY 64 CY 36
NCY parents 66 CY parents 50

B. Question: Are relations between consenting homosexuals morally wrong? (percentage who agree)

Answer: NCY 72 CY 42
NCY parents 79 CY parents 63

C. Question: Are premarital sexual relations morally wrong? (percentage who agree)

Answer: NCY 57 CY 34
NCY parents 88 CY parents 74

D. Question: Are extramarital sexual relations morally wrong? (percentage who agree)

Answer: NCY 77 CY 77
NCY parents 92 CY parents 90

Additional questions concerned acceptance of societal restraints.

Category	Accept	NCY	CY
A. Adherence to laws you don't agree with	easily	34%	15%
	reluctantly	55	74
	not at all	11	14
B. Conformity in matters of clothing and personal grooming	easily	54	33
	reluctantly	26	29
	not at all	19	38
C. Prohibition against marijuana	easily	72	48
	reluctantly	11	20
	not at all	17	31
D. Prohibition against LSD	easily	79	73
	reluctantly	7	11
	not at all	13	16
E. Power and authority of the police	easily	78	48
	reluctantly	17	42
	not at all	4	10
F. Impersonal treatment in a job	easily	21	9
	reluctantly	39	35
	not at all	39	57

The statistics shown represent less than 10 percent of the total questions asked by CBS News and do not include a political profile on the adolescents sampled. Other results of the survey showed that noncollege adolescents, as compared to college students, are (1) more conservative, (2) more prone to traditional values, (3) more religious, (4) more respectful, (5) more work oriented, (6) more money oriented, (7) more patriotic, (8) more concerned about moral living, (9) more conforming, (10) more accepting of the draft and war, (11) less activism oriented, (12) less sympathetic with activists, (13) less drug-prone, and (14) less sexually permissive (*Generations Apart,* 1969).

The behavior of noncollege adolescents is not like that of high school students. The former are more involved in social integration than in social maturation. Most of them have jobs, and many are married. The responsibility of maintaining a home and rearing a family requires making important life decisions based on what they know and what they think is most appropriate at the time.

College Youths

The most controversial group of adolescents today are college students, who are challenging the traditional, conservative structure of life. It is among this group that the Generation Gap, if any, exists.

New ideas are emerging among the college students today. Some of these ideas focus on the educational institution and maintain that college is not relevant to the needs of today's youth or society. Carry (1968) has suggested five emerging trends in attitudes about rules, education, and students:

1. The traditional view that it is the individual's responsibility to make his education relevant is being replaced by the idea that the educational institution should take that responsibility (Coleman, 1965).
2. The traditional view that every rule, right or wrong, must be obeyed is being rejected.
3. The traditional view that rules are made to ensure essential controls or to create a better educational environment is being replaced by a suspicion that many rules are made for the convenience of the educators (Goodman, 1968).
4. The traditional view that modern youth "never had it so good" is giving way to a belief that laws and processes purportedly protecting youth actually discriminate against them (Friedenberg, 1959).
5. The view that we have adequate processes available to bring about changes in laws in time to meet social pressures in a rapidly changing world is being rejected. Students believe that riots or other less violent forms of confrontation are more effective in bringing about needed changes and that the traditional methods are inadequate.

Gottlieb and Hodgkins (1963) have attempted to define the college-student subculture by categorizing students into four areas: (1) the academic subgroup, composed of students who want a good education and are willing to study to obtain it; (2) the vocational subgroup, composed of those

students pursuing primarily the same vocational choice; (3) the nonconformist subgroup, who concentrate on issues and use the university setting as an avenue for their expression; and (4) the "collegiate," or social, subgroup, who are interested mainly in social and athletic activities and sorority and fraternity functions.

The third article in this chapter, by Lewis, assesses how these four subcultures value college. Lewis questioned the students about their intellectualism, intellectual associations, autonomy, and idealism. Each subculture revealed a common set of ideals and behaviors. Students in the academic subculture showed a strong interest in education, knowledge, and understanding and spent most of their leisure in intellectual or musical activities. In contrast, those in the collegiate subculture spent most of their time in extracurricular and social activities, identified most strongly with their school, and preferred courses that provided competition with other students. Students in the vocational subculture reported that their primary reason for being in college was to obtain a degree. Extracurricular and social activities meant very little to them, and they had the lowest humanitarianism scores of any of the four subcultures. This particular subculture may closely parallel the noncollege youths in values. The nonconformist subculture was interested in intellectual association and attended college primarily to develop the resources necessary for personal autonomy.

The last article in this chapter, by Baur, discusses such student peer groups and academic development. His findings were categorized around campus life, relations with faculty, studying, the classroom, student subcultures, and honor students. Socialization was the primary objective of both dormitory and fraternity-sorority groups. Fraternity and sorority members constituted the majority (87 percent) of campuswide student leaders. Although academic pursuits were not the main activity, peer influence on academic achievement showed an interesting slant—in most cases in-group status was given to the persons with the highest grade-point averages. Baur's analysis of social and academic life gives the reader a concise picture of campus life, peer affiliations, and academic pursuits.

louis m. smith

paul f. kleine

the adolescent and his society

For purposes of this review we have considered the terms *subculture* and *subsociety* as synonyms and defined them as collections of individuals interrelated through shared experiences and possessing shared activities, beliefs, and values. We have been guided also by a concern with the several levels or areas of theory which researchers have used to attack problems in the area: sociological, social psychological, and individual psychological. We developed such a concern from shifts in language systems within arguments and the confusion which often resulted from such shifts. Finally, we have been made sensitive once again to such basic methodological problems as interpreting correlational data causally and differing operational measures of the same concept which produce conflicting data, especially when the indicators vary between such modalities as questionnaires and direct observation.* For instance, in a very complex book, *Rebellion in the High School*, Stinchcombe (1964) argued that cultural, social structural, and psychological factors produced expressive alienation and this, in turn, led to rebellious behavior. As his analysis proceeded, several problems arose. The data were all obtained from question-

naires, which raised questions of independence of measures. Some of the propositions —e.g., "girls who are low in achievement form an image of their future in marriage"— might be interpreted reversibly or in terms of third factors. Subaspects of the alienation concept became intermediary and interpretive variables in their own right. Finally, the analysis employed concepts from different theoretical systems, i.e., universalistic labor markets, negativism, etc., which were difficult to integrate with theoretical precision.

An Adolescent Society?

A question concerning the existence of an adolescent subculture was raised earlier by Elkin and Westley (1955). These authors attacked the assumptions underlying the existence of a subculture principally on two grounds: (1) their own data from 20 upper middle class teen-agers and Hollingshead's (1949) middle class subjects, who did not show differences between adult values and adolescent values, and (2) the assumption that the stress and strain of adjustment is not peculiar to the adolescent group. In a similar vein, Bealer and Willits (1961) reasoned that the existence of cultural continuity from generation to generation discounted the presence of a rebellious subculture. In direct contrast, Coleman (1961a)

Reprinted with permission of the authors and publisher from the *Review of Educational Research*, 1966, **36,** 424-436.

*While these issues were not unique to our chapter, they seemed to have enough special relevance to warrant introductory consideration.

argued emphatically that the existence of a separate subculture is beyond question. Strom (1963) tested the Coleman position regarding behavioral norm differences between high school seniors and teachers. It was assumed that the values of teachers would be representative of adults in general. He found differences in the direction of greater intensity and degree of crystallization of norms for teachers than for high school seniors. The same relationship held whether the norms were under more direct control of teachers (e.g., homework, class participation) or less direct control (e.g., dating, clique deviance). The degree of conformity did vary depending upon the type of behavior in question. Epperson (1964) questioned the wording of a key item in Coleman's questionnaire which offered the teenager a choice between "breaking with a friend" and gaining "disapproval from parents." Epperson's use of "friend's disapproval" and "parent's disapproval" resulted in only 20 percent of his subjects preferring to incur the disfavor of parents compared to Coleman's finding of 43 percent.

Bernard (1961) and Smith (1962) refused to enter the fray and simply assumed the existence of a separate subculture. Jahoda and Warren (1965), in an extended essay review, considered the question to be a "pseudo issue" and not worthy of continued debate. They reasoned that support can be gathered from any study of adolescents for either a discontinuous subculture or a continuous nonsubculture depending upon the emphasis placed by the researcher. They stated, "It follows that such a group in society can usefully be studied from the point of view of what they have in common as well as from the point of view of what they share with the major culture. Both are legitimate approaches whose ultimate value stems from what they reveal" (p.143). These brief and conflicting glimpses of research and argumentation call for a more extended analysis of the rationale underlying the various positions.

Elkin and Westley (1955) summarized the theory relevant to the genesis of an adolescent society. Western civilization provides a serious asynchronism between biological maturity in the early teens and social maturity in the late teens or early twenties; the asynchronism, besides the developmen-tal changes per se, produces "Sturm and Drang." The adolescent society arises as the individual finds peers of the same age who then cope collectively with their problems.

Dunphy (1963) found that almost all adolescents (70 to 80 percent) are involved in cliques and crowds and in pursuing heterosexual goals. However, the fact of belonging to groups does not necessarily make a society as we have defined it—a collection of individuals building a common set of beliefs and values through shared experience. As in adult society, however, the mass media and national merchandising institutions do become the principal mediating variables.

Bernard (1961) assumed an adolescent society and provided an economic explanation for its genesis in the opening sentence of her analysis: "Teen-age culture is a product of affluence; we can afford to keep a large population in school through high school" (p. 1). She presented an array of statistics which supported the commonsense notion that as bands played or singers sang and as adolescents completed the interaction through tuning radios, attending concerts of itinerant musicians, and buying records, there came to be common tastes and preferences. She characterized the society as a leisure class with money to spend on material items—clothes, cosmetics, records, cars, etc. It has a common language—"clod," "wheel," "tough," and so forth—and a journalistic literature of its own through the teen-age magazines. Brown (1961), in his analysis of the teen-type magazine, found both cultist and confessional dimensions to the literature.

A different theoretical accent occurred in the critical reaction of such social scientists as Friedenberg (1965), Henry (1963), and Musgrove (1964). Friedenberg, for instance, drew an analogy between the adolescent culture and nineteenth-century colonialism. He argued that the adult society, trying to reproduce a narrow conception of itself, controls youth and keeps them dependent through such social institutions as the public high school. He referred ironically to the high school as the "cradle of liberty," and gave descriptions of limited physical freedom, corridor passes, adult privilege, prisoner's sense of time, and lack of privacy. This environment produced an adolescent value structure characterized by superficiality, desire to make a good impression, conformity to ideals of mediocrity, and well-roundedness—qualities functional for later success in American society but alien to Friedenberg's vision of the sensitive, the cultivated, and the competent. His research focused on trends in adolescent conformity to dominant adult values, provided insights into the subtle and sometimes not-so-subtle mechanisms officials utilized to achieve "well run" schools, and offered interesting although somewhat staggering suggestions for improvement. The analysis of the value systems did not present data on the adolescent reference groups. The present reviewers take the position that Friedenberg's analysis of the value problems underlying societal goals was too simple. To condemn the values of the versatile "well adjusted" Karen Blakes represents no conceptual advance over the present condemnation of the creative and individualistic if "poorly adjusted" Johnny Adamses.

The most active research controversy concerning the existence and importance of a generalized youth culture has centered on the interrelated pressures from peers and parents. The pre-1960 literature contained important contributions by Seidler and Ravitz (1955), Rosen (1955), and Elkin and Westley (1955). More recently, the issue has been investigated by Haller and Butterworth (1960), Bealer and Willits (1961), Coleman (1961a), Simpson (1962), Brittain (1963), Alexander and Campbell (1964), Epperson (1964), and McDill and Coleman (1965). While the usual problems of sample and instrument comparability occurred, the substantive findings seemed to be these: (a) Both parents and peers exerted influences upon choices made by adolescents. (b) Among friends the closer the relationship the greater the impact. (c) When parents and peers were in agreement the behavior was most likely to occur. (d) When parents and peers disagreed or had varying relevant information, the relative influence varied with the issue; e.g., peers had more impact on courses to be taken and clothes to wear while parents had more influence on how to get selected for a school honor. Haller and Butterworth (1960), among others, remained critical of the one-way attribution of causality from correlations.

The present debate concerning the exis-

tence of an adolescent subsociety appears destined for a fate similar to that of the heredity and environment controversy: the emphatic but oversimplified "yes" and "no" answers give way to more subdued complex questions. Adolescents share some values uniquely with other adolescents on the national scale; some values are shared uniquely with specific reference groups; and some values are shared with the broader adult cultural fabric of which they represent bright, bold strands. For some research questions, phrased at varying conceptual levels (e.g., economic, sociological, or psychological), the use of the concept "subculture" may permit examination of certain discontinuous or continuous aspects; for other questions the concept will not be of help. The present reviewers concur with Epperson's (1964) social psychological position: "We still need a conceptual scheme that takes into consideration the multiple loyalties of the teen-ager and the relation of these loyalties to specific situations" (p. 96).

Locales of Adolescent Reference Groups

The settings in which adolescent groups reside have begun to receive considerable attention. The neighborhood of the delinquent gang, the high school as an institution, and college environments serve as the most frequent locales of research on adolescent groups, both those to which they belong and those to which they aspire.

Street Corner Societies

The "corner" remains the geographical setting for the nonschool youth. The researcher, backed with financing from innumerable sources and with aroused public opinion, has found it a convenient locale for the study of gangs, deviancy, and delinquency. In the course of these investigations a number of concepts and propositions regarding the adolescent society arose, for much of the exciting research (e.g., Short and Strodtbeck, 1965) had been goaded by conflicts between proponents of the continuity theory of adolescent delinquency (Miller, 1958) and the delinquent subculture as a function of inability to attain commonly held goals (Cohen, 1955; Cloward and Ohlin, 1960).

Adolescents, just as adults, form smaller social units or reference groups, and these reference groups vary in activities, sentiments, and norms. Sherif and Sherif (1964) in a poorly edited but very provocative book accented the combined field and laboratory methods, interdisciplinary orientations, processes of behavior, and the integration of the study of the individual, small group, and the environmental setting. They had young graduate students enter "naturally" into adolescent groups of varying socioeconomic levels and of varying racial and ethnic backgrounds. Their principal purpose was to explore conformity and deviation in reference groups. Among a multitude of findings they argued strongly that the peer group was exceedingly important to its members and that parents and adults usually did not have a clear idea of the behavior of youth in areas of "immorality": drinking, sexual behavior, vandalism, and theft. They stated that simple or elaborate questionnaires will not reveal these realities. The idiosyncratic nature of the particular adolescent peer group was reflected well in the Sherifs' discussion of the preferences of a group of second and third generation Mexican-American boys from a poor neighborhood in a Southwestern city: "Besides liking sports, the boys all watched games on television. They greatly preferred rock and roll to popular Mexican music, hot dogs and hamburgers to tortillas and beans, modern dance steps to traditional ones, Hollywood movies to Mexican films" (p. 26). The members of this gang wore their hair long in contrast to another which had norms for "clean cut" appearance.

Considerable disagreement existed over the stability and fluidity of group boundaries. Sherif and Sherif (1964) found that their groups tended to be stable over time and stable in membership; the boys typically knew clearly who was "in" and who was "out." Short and Strodtbeck (1965) based a large part of their group process analysis on the flux in membership and amorphous group boundaries of their gangs. Yablonsky (1963) discussed the imprecision of the word *gang*. He suggested three types of gangs as being most prevalent: (a) social, (b) delinquent, and (c) violent. The varying de-

grees of leadership structure and membership stability typically reported in the literature may be attributable to the type of gang being studied. Thus the social gang may have considerable permanence and a firm but informal leadership structure (Whyte, 1955), while a violent gang may be in a constant state of flux depending upon the emotional needs of its members. Kobrin (1961), whose data leaned toward the Sherif position, added a further note in that he found a hierarchy of gangs in the ethnic community which he studied.

In a large study of nondelinquent urban youth, Dunphy (1963) found another kind of accommodation. He made an important distinction between cliques and crowds; the former were seen as smaller, more intimate groups and the latter as larger associations of cliques. In the middle class neighborhoods of Sydney, Australia, he found these groups identifiable by members, related to residential proximity, functional for developing heterosexuality, and containing varied roles. His analysis was made especially provocative through accent on heterosexual development, the role of the clique in facilitating social development, and his attempt to span the entire adolescent period. The discussion, in contrast to that of Coleman (1961a), was carried out without reference to school-related data.

Increasing evidence (Sherif and Sherif, 1964; Short and Strodtbeck, 1965; Coleman, 1961a) suggested the generality of the proposition that as aggregates of individuals interact and become groups, differentiation of status, leadership, and "effective initiative" occurs. Sherif and Sherif (1964) cautioned that even though adolescents will often state that "we have no leader, we hang around informally together," observers reliably rated specific individuals in leadership roles. They argued, as did Short and Strodtbeck (1965), that shifts in "system requirements" often produced shifts from the incumbent leader to an individual with alternative skills. The latter investigators theorized also that much delinquent behavior results from the precarious position of the conflict gang leader who has few resources to trade for his esteem in a group that is only quasi-stable. Other roles, such as "toughs," "con artists," and "bush boys," were noted in Polsky's (1962) analysis of a naturalistic group. Also, he differentiated cliques within the larger group structure.

The High School

Barker and Gump (1964) analyzed the relationship between school size and nonacademic behavior and experience. They presented data from specimen records obtained in 13 high schools which suggested that the smaller schools evoked more varied extracurricular activities, more active rather than passive or vicarious involvement, and more chances for responsible leadership. The authors did not pursue academic settings and their variations in difficulty level, in activity, in frequency and kind of teacher-pupil interaction (e.g., questioning and discussion), and so forth.

Neill (1960), in his account of *Summerhill,* suggested that the predictions of dire consequences from drastically changing a school's authority structure did not occur in a semi-isolated environment. The youth group (ages 5-15) that was created was described as self-governing with norms for diverse and creative activity but without a strong academic emphasis.

Coleman's (1961a) study of 10 Illinois high schools continued the analysis opened by Gordon (1957) and presented the largest picture available of the social life of the teenager and its impact on education. The major data-gathering instrument was a self-report questionnaire. We have cited reviewers and investigators (Jahoda and Warren, 1965; Epperson, 1964; and Gordon, 1963) who took issue with Coleman. His description of the activity structure—cars, music, television—reflected the competition that homework received for the adolescent's time. Status dimensions ran through the culture of the high school. His findings stressed the importance of athletic competence and social skills for boys in achieving popularity and membership in the "elite" crowd. Girls achieved similar popularity but in less dramatic fashion by virtue of their beauty and participation in school activities. Being an honor student ranked consistently lower on the high school "hit parade." Differences existed between the 10 schools, but the similarities from school to school were more

striking. Coleman presented extended data on the consequences of the social system on the students' self-evaluation, e.g., desire to be someone different, academic achievement, the degree to which one specializes or generalizes (athlete, scholar, or both), and use of leisure time. The dimension of status with peers loomed large to the adolescent.

Nordstrom, Friedenberg, and Gold (1965) investigated the influence of ressentiment, an impotence or anomie, on student experience. While they found differences between high schools and relationships with social class neighborhoods, their major finding was one of pervasive ressentiment. The sociometric literature took an abrupt theoretical turn from an early concern with the psychological trait and adjustment correlates of sociometric status to a theoretical and empirical analysis of interdependent concepts. For instance, Schmuck (1963) and Epperson (1963) introduced such concepts as centrality and diffuseness of structure, potency of involvement, liking status, cognized liking status, and alienation to study interrelations of sociometric structure with attitudes and utilization of abilities. Illustratively, Schmuck found that cognized status had closer relationships with utilization of ability and attitude to self than did actual status. Goslin (1962) found low acceptance associated with inaccurate perception and self-conflict. Peck and Galliani (1962) found intelligence and ethnic background to be related to sociometric nominations for such roles as "brain" and "wheel."

The College and University

Probably the most important study of a particular adolescent society in the university locale was Newcomb's (1961) research, titled *The Acquaintance Process.* During each year of a two-year period 17 men previously unknown to each other lived for a semester in a project dormitory and reported regularly to the experimenters on the developing relationships among themselves. Newcomb conceptualized the phenomenon in terms of his "ABX model" with its components of orientation, attraction, attitude, perceived orientation of others, system strain, and so forth. A variety of data, only partially analyzed, were gathered in individual and group sessions approximating five hours per week per student. Illustrative findings included these: (a) The stronger an individual's attraction to another, the greater the likelihood that he will perceive agreement with that other person concerning objects important and relevant to him. (b) With increasing acquaintance over time pair members' attraction toward each other and their agreement about the attractiveness of other group members increased. (c) Personality variables such as authoritarianism were significantly related to accuracy in estimating orientations of others. (d) With increasing acquaintance attraction units increased in size. Newcomb drew his most far-reaching implication in his last paragraph: "The most stable of interpersonal relationships, in short, are those characterized by both system balance and high attraction—a combination that presupposes an area of mutually shared orientations of importance to system members" (p. 261). This statement has obvious relevance to the questions of group and gang stability discussed above.

The range in research on university groups varied markedly. Bonjean and McGee (1965) studied relationships of fraternity membership (among other variables) to scholastic dishonesty in universities with and without honor systems. Questionnaire data indicated less reported dishonesty in the honor school and significantly more reported cheating by those in fraternities than those not in fraternities. Gottlieb and Hodgkins (1963) attacked the assumption of homogeneous student populations in the university environment by proposing a taxonomy of subcultures: academic, vocational, collegiate, and nonconformist. They found significant correlates on a variety of variables, such as immediate career expectations: e.g., of the "vocationals" 72 percent planned career jobs and 13 percent planned for graduate training, while of the "nonconformists" only 47 percent planned for career jobs and 31 percent planned to enter graduate training. Bidwell (1963) investigated groups characterized by traditional and emergent values, roughly an individualistic versus a social ethic, and found a variety of career type differences. Illustratively, the traditionals were more professionally oriented and also more

certain of career plans while the emergents were more artistically oriented and less certain of plans. Each of these studies reflected our initial theoretical and methodological concerns: (a) the groups were statistical aggregates rather than reference groups; (b) the mechanisms of causality in moving from the independent to dependent variables were not clearly stated; and (c) most of the data were from single self-report devices.

Partial evidence for an adolescent subsociety arose with older youth who have been a part of civil rights movements, especially those seeking racial equality and freedom of speech (Fishman and Solomon, 1964; Lipset and Wolin, 1965). Lipset and Wolin's *Berkeley Student Revolt* recorded in considerable detail a social phenomenon that had broad publicity and controversy and met our definition of adolescent society: leadership, shared experiences, and common beliefs and norms. Somers (1965) quickly but carefully planned and implemented an interview study of 285 randomly sampled students from the University of California during the autumn of 1964. He suggested that dissatisfaction with academic courses and professors in the "multiversity" was not prevalent but rather that "the mainsprings of the rebellion were an optimistic idealism about the type of society . . . and an unwillingness to allow the paternalism . . . to extend its coverage . . ." (p. 534). Such findings must be positioned next to May's (1965) impressionistic data that the Berkeley student body was quite atypical of college campuses for "Berkeley has been something of a radical Mecca" (p. 456), and Selvin and Hagstrom's (1965) data that large numbers of the adolescent and adult population do not support principles and practices guaranteed by the Bill of Rights. Fishman and Solomon (1964) presented data that 75 to 80 percent of the college population had no interest in "issues" or "causes" such as the civil rights groups they studied. To the present reviewers, Fishman and Solomon's (1964) descriptions of the dynamics in the day-to-day behavior of youth in the civil rights groups were similar to the reference groups studied by Sherif and Sherif (1964) and Dunphy (1963).

Becker and others (1961) developed the concept of "perspectives," a coordinated set of ideas and actions used in problematic situations, for their extended analysis of student culture in medical school. Perhaps the most basic argument they made was that the medical school environment posed impossible demands on the time, energy, and talents of the individual student. In response to this, an informal student culture arose and gave focus to the amount and direction of the student effort. Later, perspectives were developed regarding clinical work and future practice. Orth (1963) found a similar society in the Harvard Business School.

A major review of the university scene appeared in Sanford's (1962) volume, *The American College*. Of special reference were chapters by Newcomb (1962) on "Student Peer Group Influence"; Hughes, Becker, and Geer (1962) on "Student Culture and Academic Effort"; and Bushnell (1962) on "Student Culture at Vassar."

Adult Intervention

Strategies and techniques of adult intervention with adolescent societies remained an important moral and practical issue for parents, teachers, social workers, and others who had responsibilities for adolescents. Kobrin (1961) presented a sensitive case study analysis from the detached worker perspective. He introduced such concepts as general impermeability, defensive solidarity, gang development (early and late), community resources, and adult position in local community structure. He dealt with what might be called discriminated group acceptance, an acceptance of the group except for three activities: staying in school, more conventional patterns of courtship, and knowledge of the broader community. In these areas he drew a strong line for change. His specific interaction with the boys involved "concrete problems" and "mediation of conflict." These concepts seemed viable and quantifiable.

In contrast, Meyer, Borgatta, and Jones (1965) reported extended experimental intervention into the lives of individual adolescent girls who had been identified as potential problems. Individual casework, group work, family life education, and activity groups produced no differences in the experimental and control groups on percentages of dropout, truancy, conduct marks,

court appearances, and out-of-wedlock pregnancies. The authors made little mention of the girls' reference groups as a potential determinant in the girls' behavior and also as a potential force in negating the independence of the control group. When considered in light of the Short and Strodtbeck (1965) data on motherhood in a lower class Negro street corner gang, the array of day-to-day group rewards and punishments seemed very potent to the girls. Complexities of group ties were suggested by the (a) continuity with the adult culture wherein illegitimacy and crime occurred, (b) direct teaching of how to "make suckers out of men," (c) financial aid (ADC) for living expenses and for payments to ensure continued attention from the fathers, and (d) reintegration of the bonds between mother and daughter.

Similarly, Yablonsky (1963) discussed the subtle problems involved when attempting to make activity changes in gang structure. He found the "violent gang" leadership simply went "underground" and reappeared in other activities. Schwitzgebel (1964) utilized a variety of both individual and group techniques to effect changes in delinquent behavior. Unfortunately, good follow-up information was difficult to obtain, and the effects of maturation and gang attrition due to mobility were difficult to measure except in an impressionistic sense. His discussion implicitly indicated the extreme difficulty in working with the intact gang, and yet this appeared to be the necessary route to travel.

The web of group processes as it negated the treatment attempts of adults was vividly portrayed in *Cottage Six* (Polsky, 1962). The impact of group norms, physical and verbal aggressiveness for lack of conformity, and the rewards of social rank in the group had high saliency for the individual member. As incidental comments along the way, Short and Strodtbeck (1965) indicated that the dissolution of delinquent gangs seemed to occur through aging, reduction of proximity (family moves), economic opportunity, and marriage. While these may be potent practical forces, they leave much to be desired conceptually. Their comments on adult intervention seemed similar to Kobrin's (1961) in that they described the analysis of gang leadership and status, the building of positive relationships with the leader, the elimination of threat to the indigenous leader, and direct attempts to use him to influence the gang members.

From his data on the role of athletics in the social system, Coleman (1961a, b) argued strongly that those adults who wished to influence adolescents had to make system changes rather than individual appeals. The system changes involved superordinate goals, i.e., changing the content of the games which would permit the youth to participate, to achieve competitively, and to identify.

Perhaps the most extensive analysis of adult intervention in the control of classroom deviancy involved the Wayne State University group (Kounin, Gump, and Ryan, 1961). Their experiments and correlational research clarified the implications of desist techniques, attitudes toward misconduct, internalized socialization, task focus, defiance, prestige, intensity of desire to learn, and so forth. To the reviewers, the most important general finding was that the analysis of adult or teacher style in dealing with groups of children in natural or experimental settings had been oversimplified. Each response of the teacher precipitated a number of pupil reactions, which might be judged good or bad depending on the specific purposes of the adult, the youth, or the broader society or organization. For example, a simple reprimand led to judgments of a teacher as best able to maintain order in most classes; a punitive response produced a judgment of best able to maintain order in a class of tough kids; and an ignoring response led to the teacher being rated as highest in her degree of liking for pupils. The intervention issue takes on moral complexity in the very language one uses to describe it. "Control of deviancy" and "paternalism" reflected very well the difficult and largely unanalyzed problems of goals as well as means.

A Concluding Comment

As we saw the literature, the study of the adolescent and his society had a vigorous quality. Some of the investigators were angry and their work took on the quality of a personal crusade, while others found their phenomena exciting in the sense of puzzling and resisting their best attempts to analyze and conceptualize in more dispassionate terms. Further, there were increasing attempts to eliminate issues due to methodology, as in Epperson's (1964) alteration of questionnaire items from Coleman (1961a). Several of the investigators (e.g., Friedenberg, 1965; and Brittain, 1963) have developed what seem to be quite creative measuring devices for attacking data development. Finally, more and more evidence on the more crucial problems was obtained through varied approaches, questionnaires, scales, participant observation, and their combinations in the same research (e.g., Dunphy, 1963; Short and Strodtbeck, 1965; and Sherif and Sherif, 1964).

albert bandura

the stormy decade: fact or fiction?*

If you were to walk up to the average man on the street, grab him by the arm and utter the word "adolescence," it is highly probable—assuming he refrains from punching you in the nose—that his associations to this term will include references to storm and stress, tension, rebellion, dependency conflicts, peer-group conformity, black leather jackets, and the like. If you then abandoned your informal street corner experiment, and consulted the professional and popular literature on adolescence, you would become quickly impressed with the prevalence of the belief that adolescence is, indeed, a unique and stormy developmental period (Gallagher & Harris, 1958; Hurlock, 1955; Josselyn, 1948; Mohr & Despres, 1958; Parsons, 1950; Pearson, 1958).

The adolescent presumably is engaged in a struggle to emancipate himself from his parents. He, therefore, resists any dependence upon them for their guidance, approval or company, and rebels against any restrictions and controls that they impose upon his behavior. To facilitate the process of emancipation, he transfers his dependency to the peer group whose values are typically in conflict with those of his parents.

Since his behavior is now largely under the control of peer-group members, he begins to adopt idiosyncratic clothing, mannerisms, lingo, and other forms of peer-group fad behavior. Because of the conflicting values and pressures to which the adolescent is exposed, he is ambivalent, frightened, unpredictable, and often irresponsible in his behavior. Moreover, since the adolescent finds himself in a transition stage in which he is neither child, nor adult, he is highly confused even about his own identity.

The foregoing storm and stress picture of adolescence receives little support from detailed information that Dr. Walters and I obtained in a study of middle class families of adolescent boys (Bandura & Walters, 1959). Let us compare the popular version of adolescence with our research findings.

Parental Restrictiveness

At adolescence, parents supposedly become more controlling and prohibitive. We found the very opposite to be true. By the time the boys had reached adolescence, they had internalized the parents' values and standards of behavior to a large degree; consequently, restrictions and external controls had been lightened as the boys became increasingly capable of assuming responsibility for their own behavior, and in directing their own activities. The parents were highly

Reprinted with permission of the author and publisher from *Psychology in the Schools,* 1964, 1, 224-231.

*A revised form of this paper was presented at the televised lecture series, *The World of the Teen-Ager,* sponsored by the University of Minnesota.

trustful of their boys' judgment and felt that externally imposed limits were, therefore, largely unnecessary. The following interview excerpts provide some typical parental replies to inquiries concerning the restrictions they placed on their boys:

M. (Mother). I don't have to do anything like that any more.
I think he's getting so mature now, he's sort of happy medium.
I don't have to do much with him.
I. (Interviewer). What are some of the restrictions you have for him? How about going out at night?
F. (Father). We trust the boy. We never question him.
I. Are there any things you forbid him from doing when he is with his friends?
F. At his age I would hate to keep telling him that he mustn't do this, or mustn't do that. I have very little trouble with him in that regard. Forbidding I don't think creeps into it because he ought to know at 17, right from wrong.
I. Are there any friends with whom you have discouraged him from associating?
F. No, not up to now. They are very lovely boys.
I. How about using bad language?
F. Only once, only once have I; of course I'm a little bit hard of hearing in one ear, and sometimes he gets around the wrong side and takes advantage of that.

The boys' accounts were essentially in agreement with those given by the parents. In response to our questions concerning parental demands and controls, the boys pointed out that at this stage in their development parental restraints were no longer necessary. An illustrative quotation, taken from one of the boys' interviews, is given below:

I. What sort of things does your mother forbid you to do around the house?
B. Forbid me to do? Gee, I don't think there's ever anything. The house is mine as much as theirs . . . Oh, can't whistle, can't throw paper up in the air, and can't play the radio and phonograph too loud. Rules of the house; anybody, I mean, it's not just me . . .
I. Are you expected to stay away from certain places or people?
B. She knows I do. I'm not expected; I mean, she figures I'm old enough to take care of myself now. They never tell me who to stay away from or where. Well, I mean, they don't expect me to

sleep down on Skid Row or something like that . . .

Since the boys adopted their parents' standards of conduct as their own, they did not regard their parents and other authority figures as adversaries, but more as supportive and guiding influences.

Dependence-Independence Conflicts

The view that adolescents are engaged in a struggle to emancipate themselves from their parents also receives little support from our study.

Although the boys' dependency behavior had been fostered and encouraged during their childhood, independence training had begun early and was, therefore, largely accomplished by the time of adolescence. A similar early and gradual decrease in dependency upon adults is reported by Heathers (1955), who compared the dependency behavior of two-year-old and of five-year-old children. He found that, even over this small age range, dependency on adults had declined, whereas dependency on other children had increased.

For most of the boys that we studied, the emancipation from parents had been more or less completed rather than initiated at adolescence. In fact, the development of independence presented more of a conflict for the parents, than it did for the boys. Some of the parents, particularly the fathers, regretted the inevitable loss of the rewards that their sons' company had brought them.

I. Do you feel that you spend as much time with Raymond as other fathers do with their sons, or more?
F. I would say about average, but perhaps I should spend more time with him, because as the years go by, I see that he's growing into manhood and I'm losing a lot of him every year. When he was younger, I think I was with him more than I am now. I think, as he gets older, he's had a tendency to get his pleasures from people his own age. This is fine as long as he makes home his headquarters. That's all I want.

Although the boys devoted an increasing amount of time to peer-group activities, they, nevertheless, retained close ties to their parents and readily sought out their help, advice, and support when needed.

Parent Peer-Group Conflicts

The boys' primary reference groups were not selected indiscriminately. Since the adolescents tended to choose friends who shared similar value systems and behavioral norms, membership in the peer-group did not generate familial conflicts. In fact, the peer-group often served to reinforce and to uphold the parental norms and standards of behavior that the boys had adopted. Consequently, the parents were generally pleased with their sons' associates because they served as an important source of control in situations where the parents could not be present.

An essentially similar picture of adolescence, based on an intensive study of middle class families, has been presented by Elkin and Westley (1955; see also Westley & Elkin, 1956). They summarize their findings as follows:

> Family ties are close and the degree of basic family consensus is high. The parents are interested in all the activities of their children, and the adolescents, except for the area of sex, frankly discuss their own behavior and problems with them. In many areas of life, there is joint participation between parents and children . . . In independent discussions by parents and adolescents of the latters' marriage and occupational goals, there was a remarkable level of agreement. The adolescents also acknowledged the right of the parents to guide them, for example, accepting, at least manifestly, the prerogatives of the parents to set rules for the number of dates, hours of return from dates, and types of parties. The parents express relatively little concern about the socialization problems or peer group activities of their children (1955, p. 682).

Sources of the Adolescent Mythology

What are the origins of the mythology about adolescence, and why does it persist?

Overinterpretation of Superficial Signs of Nonconformity

The view that adolescence is a period of rebellion is often supported by references to superficial signs of nonconformity, particularly adolescent fad behavior.

It is certainly true that adolescents frequently display idiosyncratic fashions and interest patterns. Such fads, however, are not confined to adolescent age groups. Several years ago, for example, coon skin caps and Davy Crockett apparel were highly fashionable among pre-adolescent boys. When Davy Crockett began to wane a new fad quickly emerged—every youngster and a sizeable proportion of the adult population were gyrating with hoola-hoops. The hoola-hoop also suffered a quick death by replacement.

If pre-adolescent children display less fad behavior than do adolescents, this difference may be primarily due to the fact that young children do not possess the economic resources with which to purchase distinctive apparel, the latest phonograph records, and discriminative ornaments, rather than a reflection of a sudden heightening of peer-group conformity pressures during adolescence. The pre-adolescent does not purchase his own clothing, he has little voice in how his hair shall be cut and, on a 15-cent a week allowance, he is hardly in a position to create new fads, or to deviate too widely from parental tastes and standards.

How about adult fad behavior? A continental gentleman conducts a fashion show in Paris and almost instantly millions of hemlines move upward or downward; the human figure is sacked, trapezed, chemised, or appareled in some other fantastic creation.

At a recent cocktail party the present writer was cornered by an inquiring lady who expressed considerable puzzlement over adolescents' fascination for unusual and bizarre styles. The lady herself was draped with a sack, wearing a preposterous object on her head, and spiked high heel shoes that are more likely to land one in an orthopedic clinic, than to transport one across the room to the olives.

Fashion-feeders determine the styles, the colors, and the amount of clothing that shall be worn. It would be rare, indeed, to find an adult who would ask a sales clerk for articles of clothing in vogue two or three years ago. As long as social groups contain a status hierarchy, and tolerance for upward mobility within the social hierarchy, one can expect imitation of fads and fashions from below which, in turn, forces inventiveness from the elite in order to preserve the status differentiations.

Mass Media Sensationalism

The storm and stress view of adolescence is also continuously reinforced by mass media sensationalism. Since the deviant adolescent excites far more interest than the typical high school student, the adolescent is usually portrayed in literature, television, and in the movies as passing through a neurotic or a semi-delinquent phase of development (Kiell, 1959). These productions, many of which are designed primarily to generate visceral reactions or to sell copy, are generally viewed as profound and sensitive portrayals of the *typical* adolescent turmoil. Holden Caulfield, the central character in *The Catcher in the Rye* (Salinger, 1951), has thus become the prototypic adolescent.

Generalization from Samples of Deviant Adolescents

Professional people in the mental health field are apt to have most contact with delinquent adolescents, and are thus prone to base their accounts of adolescence on observations of atypical samples. By and large, the description of the modal pattern of adolescent behavior fits most closely the behavior of the deviant ten per cent of the adolescent population that appears repeatedly in psychiatric clinics, juvenile probation departments, and in the newspaper headlines.

Our study of the family relationships of adolescents also included a sample of antisocially aggressive boys. In the families of these hyper-aggressive adolescents there was indeed a great deal of storm and stress for many years. The boys' belligerence and rebellion, however, were not unique products of adolescence. The defiant oppositional pattern of behavior was present all along, but because of their greater size and power the parents were able to suppress and to control, through coercive methods, their sons' belligerence during the early childhood years. By the time of adolescence, however, some of the boys had reached the stage where they were almost completely independent of the parents for the satisfaction of their social and physical needs. Moreover, they had developed physically to the point where they

were larger and more powerful than their parents. With the achievement of the power reversal and the decrease of the parents' importance as sources of desired rewards, a number of the boys exhibited a blatant indifference to their parents' wishes about which they could now do little or nothing.

I. What sort of things does your mother object to your doing when you are out with your friends?
B. She don't know what I do.
I. What about staying out late at night?
B. She says, "Be home at 11 o'clock." I'll come home at one.
I. How about using the family car?
B. No. I wrecked mine, and my father wrecked his a month before I wrecked mine, and I can't even get near his. And I got a license and everything. I'm going to hot wire it some night and cut out.
I. How honest do you feel you can be to your mother about where you've been and what things you have done?
B. I tell her where I've been, period.
I. How about what you've done?
B. No. I won't tell her what I've done. If we're going out in the hills for a beer bust, I'm not going to tell her. I'll tell her I've been to a show or something.
I. How about your father?
B. I'll tell him where I've been, period.

The heightened aggression exhibited by these boys during adolescence primarily reflected response predispositions that became more evident following the power reversal in the parent-child relationship, rather than an adolescence-induced stress.

Inappropriate Generalization from Cross-Cultural Data

It is interesting to note that many writers cite cross-cultural data as supporting evidence for the discontinuity view of child development in the American society. The reader suddenly finds himself in the Trobriand Islands, or among the Arapesh, rather than in the suburbs of Minneapolis or in the town square of Oskaloosa.

In many cultures the transition from child to adult status is very abrupt. Childhood behavior patterns are strongly reinforced, but as soon as the child reaches pubescence he is subjected to an elaborate initiation ceremony which signifies his abrupt transformation into adult status. Following the ceremonial initiation the young initiate acquires new rights and privileges, new responsibilities and, in some cultures, he is even assigned a new name and a new set of parents who undertake his subsequent social training in the skills and habits required to perform the adult role.

In our culture, on the other hand, except for the discontinuities in the socialization of sexual behavior, there is considerable continuity in social training. As was mentioned earlier, independence and responsibility training, for example, are begun in early childhood and adult-role patterns are achieved through a gradual process of successive approximations. This is equally true in the development of many other forms of social behavior.

It should be mentioned in passing, however, that cross-cultural studies have been valuable in demonstrating that stresses and conflicts are not inevitable concomitants of pubescence, but rather products of cultural conditioning. Indeed, in some societies, adolescence is one of the pleasant periods of social development (Mead, 1930).

Overemphasis of the Biological Determination of Heterosexual Behavior

With the advent of pubescence the adolescent is presumably encumbered by a powerful biologically determined sexual drive that produces a relatively sudden and marked increase in heterosexual behavior. The net result of the clash between strong physiological urges demanding release and even more substantial social prohibitions, is a high degree of conflict, frustration, anxiety and diffuse tension. In contrast to this widely-accepted biological drive theory, evidence from studies of cross-species and cross-cultural sexual behavior reveals that human sexuality is governed primarily by social conditioning, rather than endocrinal stimulation (Ford & Beach, 1951).

The cross-species data demonstrate that hormonal control of sexual behavior decreases with advancing evolutionary status. In lower mammalian species, for example, sexual activities are completely regulated by gonadal hormones; among primates sexual behavior is partially independent of physiological stimulation; while human eroticism is

exceedingly variable and essentially independent of hormonal regulation. Humans can be sexually aroused before puberty and long after natural or surgical loss of reproductive glands. Thus, one would induce sexual behavior in a rodent Don Juan by administering androgen, whereas presenting him lascivious pictures of a well-endowed mouse would have no stimulating effects whatsoever. By contrast, one would rely on sexually-valenced social stimuli, rather than on hormonal injections for producing erotic arousal in human males.

The prominent role of social learning factors in determining the timing, incidence and form of sexual activities of humans is also clearly revealed in the wide cross-cultural variability in patterns of sexual behavior. Sex-arousing properties have been conditioned to an extremely broad range of stimuli, but the cues that are sexually stimulating in one culture would, in many instances, prove sexually repulsive to members of another society. A similar diversity exists in the timing of the emergence of sexual interest and in the choice of sexual objects. In cultures that permit and encourage heterosexual behavior at earlier, or at later, periods of a child's development than is true for American youth, no marked changes in sexual behavior occur during adolescence.

It is evident from the foregoing discussion that "sexual tensions" are not an inevitable concomitant of pubescence. Furthermore, any significant increase in heterosexual activities during adolescence is due more to cultural conditioning and expectations than to endocrinal changes.

Stage Theories of Personality Development

Until recently, most of the theoretical conceptualizations of the developmental process have subscribed to some form of stage theory. According to the Freudian viewpoint (1949), for example, behavioral changes are programmed in an oral-anal-phallic sequence; Erikson (1950) characterizes personality development in terms of an eight-stage sequence; Gesell (1943) describes marked predictable cyclical changes in behavior over yearly or even shorter tem-

the stormy decade: fact or fiction?

poral intervals; and Piaget (1948, 1954), delineates numerous different stages for different classes of responses.

Although there appears to be relatively little consensus among these theories concerning the number and the content of stages considered to be crucial, they all share in common the assumption that social behavior can be categorized in terms of a relatively prefixed sequence of stages with varying degrees of continuity or discontinuity between successive developmental periods. Typically, the spontaneous emergence of these elaborate age-specific modes of behavior is attributed to ontogenetic factors. The seven-year-old, for example, is supposed to be withdrawn; the eight-year-old turns into an exuberant, expansive and buoyant child; the fifteen-year-old becomes remote and argumentative; parents are finally rewarded at sweet sixteen (Ilg & Ames, 1955). In truth, all seven-year-olds are not withdrawn, all eight-year-olds are not exuberant, expansive and buoyant, nor are all fifteen year-olds aloof and argumentative. I am also acquainted with sixteen-year-olds who are anything but sweet. The withdrawn five-year-old is likely to remain a relatively withdrawn eight, nine, and sixteen-year-old unless he undergoes social-learning experiences that are effective in fostering more expressive behavior.

Although the traditional stage theories of child development are of questionable validity (Bandura & McDonald, 1963; Bandura & Mischel, 1963; Bandura & Walters, 1963), they have nevertheless been influential in promoting the view that adolescence represents a form of stage behavior that suddenly appears at pubescence, and as suddenly disappears when adulthood is achieved.

Self-Fulfilling Prophecy

If a society labels its adolescents as "teen-agers," and expects them to be rebellious, unpredictable, sloppy, and wild in their behavior, and if this picture is repeatedly reinforced by the mass media, such cultural expectations may very well force adolescents into the role of rebel. In this way, a false expectation may serve to instigate and maintain certain role behaviors, in turn, then reinforce the originally false belief.

In discussing our research findings with parents' groups I have often been struck by the fact that most parents, who are experiencing positive and rewarding relationships with their pre-adolescent children are, nevertheless, waiting apprehensively and bracing themselves for the stormy adolescent period. Such vigilance can very easily create a small turbulence at least. When the prophesied storm fails to materialize, many parents begin to entertain doubts about the normality of their youngster's social development.

In closing, I do not wish to leave you with the impression that adolescence is a stress-or problem-free period of development. No age group is free from stress or adjustment problems. Our findings suggest, however, that the behavioral characteristics exhibited by children during the so-called adolescent stage are lawfully related to, and consistent with, pre-adolescent social behavior.

lionel s. lewis

the value of college to different subcultures*

After a careful examination of numerous studies on the influence of college on under-graduates, Philip Jacob concluded that the net effect of higher education on values is almost nil (Jacob, 1957). Considerable controversy has arisen concerning the accuracy of his assessment. Gottlieb and Hodgkins have suggested that the reason the findings of so many studies do not show changes in individuals is that student bodies are treated as monolithic entities when, in fact, there are subcultures on campuses (Gottlieb & Hodgkins, 1963). There is a suggestion that if the subcultures are considered separately, then the value of the college experience can more readily be seen.

The Four Subcultures

The most provocative delineation of student subcultures is that devised by Trow and Clark (1960). Their four subcultures emerge from an association of two variables, "the degree students are involved with ideas" and "the extent to which students identify" with their school. A combination of these two vari-

Reprinted with permission of the author and publisher from the *School Review*, 1969, **77** (1), 32-40.

*I am grateful to the Office of Institutional Research of the State University of New York at Buffalo for financial assistance which enabled me to carry out the research upon which this paper is based.

ables, after each is dichotomized, produces four possible subcultures. First, there is the *academic subculture*, composed of students who both are involved with ideas and identify with their school. Second, there is the *collegiate subculture*, composed of students who are not involved with ideas but identify with their school. Third, there is the *nonconformist subculture*, composed of students who are involved with ideas but do not identify with their school. Fourth, there is the *consumer-vocational subculture*, composed of students who neither are involved with ideas nor identify with their school.

According to Trow and Clark (1960), those in the academic subculture identify with the faculty, and the pursuit of knowledge is their overriding goal. The lives of those in the collegiate subculture revolve around campus fun; they have few vocational interests and do not usually aspire to graduate or professional school. Those in the nonconformist subculture are detached from the faculty, are seeking an identity, and are rebellious and idealistic. Finally, the consumer-vocational subculture is characterized by ambitious, mobility oriented, working class students who are in college to pursue skills and a degree.

It is the purpose of this study to isolate members of each of these subcultures and to ascertain the effects of their college experience. A sample of 646 undergraduates was obtained. Of these, it was possible to place 401 in one of the four categories, according to their responses on two questions. First, they were asked how important they believed the stimulation of new ideas was to them in college; those who believed they were of the highest importance were considered to be involved with them, and those who ranked them as less than third in importance were considered not to be involved with them. Second, those who felt close or fairly close to college were said to identify with their school, and those who felt not too close, not close at all, or indifferent about their college were said not to identify with it. The distribution of the four subcultures is as follows:

Academic	98
Collegiate	68
Nonconformist	128
Consumer-vocational	107

The university from which the questionnaires were gathered in the fall of 1966 is a large, northeastern state university. It is urban, has a full-time day school enrollment of between ten and fifteen thousand, and, like many universities in the United States, was in 1966 in the midst of rapid expansion.

An attempt was made to obtain enough questionnaires from students representing six different major fields of concentration—arts and humanities, behavioral science, business and commerce, education, engineering, and physical science—so that statistical comparisons could be carried out; the sample is thus not random. Of the respondents, 396 are male and 250 are female; 239 are underclassmen and 381 are upperclassmen; 139 have a grade average of B+ or better, 137 have a grade average of C or below, and the rest fall in between. One hundred and sixty-five come from homes in which the breadwinner is skilled, semiskilled, or unskilled, while the remainder come from white collar families.

Intellectualism

An attempt is made to help the student develop in many ways during his years in college. First, there is the process of expanding his intellectual horizons. For those who begin their higher education with little or no intellectual orientation, there is the task of cultivating one; for those who begin with a

leaning toward intellectualism, there is the task of increasing it.

Intellectualism is first of all a set of attitudes. It is the acceptance by the student of the belief that a college education is a means of cultivating the ability to use the mind, so that life experiences become more meaningful. The extent to which this belief was held by the students was ascertained through a series of questions concerning their intellectual orientation. The responses of those in the four subcultures to these questions are shown in Table 1.

TABLE 1. INTELLECTUAL FERMENT (PERCENTAGE)

Academic Subculture (N = 98)	Collegiate Subculture (N = 68)	Nonconformist Subculture (N = 128)	Consumer-Vocational Subculture (N = 107)
A. Most important reason for being in college: to obtain a degree			
15.3	33.8	14.8	48.6
B. Would like to get most out of college: education, knowledge, and understanding			
53.1	35.3	40.6	21.5
C. Intellectual values: would definitely seek information about an examination from others who had already taken it			
12.2	39.7	22.7	33.6
D. Leisure time activity: intellectual and/or musical pursuits			
74.5	39.7	100.0	51.4

An examination of Table 1, parts A and B, reveals marked differences as to what is expected from college. In Table 1, part A, it is seen that a very small percentage of those in the academic and nonconformist subcultures are in college to obtain a degree; about one-third of the collegiate subculture are there to do so; while almost half of the consumer-vocational subculture have this aim. On the other hand, in Table 1, part B, we find that slightly over one-fifth of those in the consumer-vocational subculture would like to get an education, knowledge, and understanding from their college experience, while this is true of over half of those in the academic subculture. The collegiate and nonconformist subcultures fall between these two extremes. It would not be an overstatement to say that those in the consumer-vocational subculture have almost no intellectual goals, while those in the academic subculture, particularly, and those in the nonconformist subculture, to a very large extent, have the clearest academic goals.

Table 1, part C, suggests an antecedent condition to these findings. Many of those in the consumer-vocational subculture, along with those in the collegiate subculture, hold a value that is least intellectual, namely, that they would definitely seek information about an examination from others who had already taken it. A large majority of those in the academic and nonconformist subcultures, particularly the former, hold a value that is most intellectual, namely, that they would not seek this information. Almost three times as many persons in the consumer-vocational subculture as in the academic subculture would seek information about an examination.

Finally, Table 1, part D, shows that those in the nonconformist and academic subcultures engage in activities that are more closely associated with intellectual matters than those engaged in by members of the consumer-vocational and collegiate subcultures. One hundred per cent in the nonconformist subculture and three-fourths in the academic subculture engage in intellectual and/or musical pursuits; this is true of about half in the consumer-vocational subculture and about two-fifths in the collegiate subculture.

What is thus found in Table 1 is that, more than those in any other subculture, those in the academic subculture have intellectual reasons for being in college, while this is least true of those in the consumer-vocational subculture. Those in the collegiate subculture have not internalized intellectual values to the same degree as those in the other subcultures, and this is possibly related to a lack of participation in intellectual activities.

Intellectual Associations

The way undergraduates spend their time in college naturally affects their relationship to the intellectual life of the institution. There are many extracurricular activities on American campuses, and most of these divert students from the more serious concerns of their college. It might consequently be expected that there would be an inverse relationship between involvement in extracurricular activities and intellectual pursuits.

In Table 2, parts A and B, it can be seen that those in the collegiate subculture are involved in more extracurricular activities than those in the other subcultures, and spend more time engaging in these pursuits. Those in the consumer-vocational subculture spend least time in extracurricular activities. On the other hand, it can be seen from Table 2, part C, that a larger percentage of those in the collegiate subculture spend leisure time in social activities than those in the other subcultures. Compared with the academic and nonconformist subcultures, many of those in the consumer-vocational subculture engage in social activities.

Table 2, part D, shows that those in the consumer-vocational subculture particularly, but also those in the collegiate and nonconformist subcultures, do not have the kind of associations with professors which might help them develop intellectual values. On the other hand, professors stimulate the interests of about half of those in the academic subculture. It might be assumed that if professors are not stimulating the interests of students, they are probably having little effect in changing their attitudes, values, or outlooks. If this is the case, then it would at least in part explain the lack of intellectualism found in the consumer-vocational and collegiate subcultures.

TABLE 2. INTELLECTUAL ASSOCIATIONS (PERCENTAGE)

Academic Subculture	Collegiate Subculture	Nonconformist Subculture	Consumer-Vocational Subculture
A. Number of extracurricular activities: two or more			
39.8	61.8	31.3	29.9
B. Time spent on extracurricular activities: none or very little			
56.1	47.1	67.2	75.7
C. Spend leisure time in social activities			
56.1	83.8	53.1	76.6
D. Professors stimulated interests: frequently or most of the time			
49.0	25.0	30.5	18.7

Autonomy

Besides intellectualism, adult maturity is expected of the graduating college student, partly because he is four years older than when he entered, but also because his exposure to new ideas should have broadened his horizons. A mark of this maturity is the development of autonomy. An individual who has cultivated or maintained a self-sufficiency can be said to have gained something from his college experience. Table 3 examines the degree of autonomy among persons in the four subcultures.

From Table 3, part A, it can be seen that about twice as many of those in the nonconformist and academic subcultures are in college to develop resources to become autonomous persons as those in the collegiate and consumer-vocational subcultures. About one-fifth of those in the collegiate subculture are interested in developing their resources, compared with almost half in the nonconformist subculture.

TABLE 3. AUTONOMY (PERCENTAGE)

Academic Subculture	Collegiate Subculture	Nonconformist Subculture	Consumer-Vocational Subculture
A. Important reason for being in college: to develop resources to become an autonomous person			
46.9	20.6	49.2	28.0
B. Work better in courses in which there is competition with other students for a final grade			
45.9	63.2	43.0	52.3

In addition, in Table 3, part B, an insight into the differences found among the subcultures in degree of autonomy is gained. In the collegiate subculture, a larger percentage than in any other subculture express the idea that they work better in courses in which there is competition for grades, a less than laudable motive for intellectual endeavor. This indicates that these individuals are least able to carry out their studies with self-imposed initiative. Those in the nonconformist and academic subcultures seem more able to pursue their studies for reasons other than competition.

Idealism

One of the overriding purposes of college is to help people become more civilized. Concomitant with this process is the cultivation of an idealism which enables a person to hold a view of the world as a place subject to improvement. Those who believe that the human condition can be made better usually have "a regard for the interest of mankind, benevolence, philanthropy" (Eron, 1958). In other words, they hold the value of humanitarianism.

To determine the degree to which individuals in the sample were humanitarian, a quasi-scale, using items such as "It is not right to live one's life for personal satisfaction and success alone; one must fulfill obligations to one's fellow men as well," and "We in this country should be concerned about the famines, poverty, and miserable living conditions which exist in other areas of the world," was utilized. According to the responses, ranging from "agree very much" to "disagree very much," to each of the five items, each person was rated high, medium, or low on humanitarianism. In Table 4 is the distribution of humanitarianism found for each of the subcultures.

TABLE 4. IDEALISM (PERCENTAGE)

Humanitari-anism Scores	Academic Subculture	Collegiate Subculture	Nonconformist Subculture	Consumer-Vocational Subculture
High	49.0	26.5	38.3	22.4
Medium . .	28.6	29.4	27.3	34.6
Low	17.3	38.2	28.9	40.2

It can be seen from Table 4 that those in the academic subculture manifest the most humanitarianism; over twice as many of them as those in the consumer-vocational subculture rate high. Almost 40 per cent of those in the nonconformist subculture are rated high, while this is true of a little more than 25 per cent of those in the collegiate subculture. There are apparent differences in the amount of humanitarianism, that is, idealism, exhibited by individuals in the four subcultures.

Concluding Remarks

These findings support the contentions that any study of college life should take into account the fact that various subcultures exist on campus and that the four subcultures isolated by Trow and Clark (1960) offer a fruitful approach to understanding undergraduate life. Differences among members of the four subcultures were found in intellectual ferment, intellectual activities, and individual development.

A problem now facing the researcher is to learn more about the social characteristics and the process of recruitment of members of the four subcultures. Gottlieb and Hodgkins (1963) found differences in social class, size of community of origin, and religion among members of the four subcultures. We could not replicate these findings.

On the other hand, we found a higher percentage of males than females in the collegiate and consumer-vocational subcultures. Furthermore, students studying science and arts and humanities were somewhat attracted to the nonconformist subculture and were not at all involved in the collegiate subculture, while students in business and commerce were attracted to the consumer-vocational subculture. A final pattern that emerged from the data was that twice as many freshmen (35 per cent) as seniors (17 per cent) were in the academic subculture, and a considerably higher percentage of seniors (32 per cent) than freshmen (19 per cent) were in the consumer-vocational subculture. The college experience and certainly extracurricular activities, do not appear to be adding much to the intellectual or emotional growth of many students, although longitudinal studies are needed to corroborate these observations.

It will also be necessary for the researcher to examine how the four subcultures relate to each other. It would appear that the present balance among them developed after the surge of veterans onto American campuses following World War II. At that time, many educators hoped for and expected changes in the intellectual climate of American institutions of higher learning. The decrease in importance of fraternities, sororities, and other extracurricular activities promised more intellectual ferment on campus. Yet, what happened was not a shift of students to a new-found involvement with ideas and a decrease in intellectual apathy. There was not a disappearance of the collegiate subculture and a resurgence of the academic subculture. The shift appears to have been from the dominance of the collegiate to the dominance of the consumer-vocational subculture. As centers of intellectual activity, universities did not gain much. With the recent resurgence of militant protest organizations on campus, it is likely that even fewer students are identifying with their schools. In our sample, there are 166 who identify with their school, and 235 who do not. On the other hand, it is interesting to note that there are 226 in our sample who are concerned with ideas, and 175 who are not. Student involvement with ideas is indeed not lacking, but it would be even more pronounced if fewer directed their interests to consumer-vocational activities.

By trying to cater to the wishes of almost every organized collectivity in the community, the modern university has become perilously diverse. Gottlieb and Hodgkins (1963) suggest that of the four subcultures, all but the academic have developed to reduce dissonance resulting from that part of the complex university with which they are unable to cope. In light of this, it might be necessary for universities to cease being county fairs and to take on narrower, more academic goals, if they are to foster intellectualism and autonomy in more of their students.

e. jackson baur

student peer groups and academic development*

The research reported here grew out of the need for understanding certain sociological factors affecting the educational process within a college student body. Despite the undoubted importance for higher education of large, publicly supported universities in the United States, there is scant knowledge, from a sociological point of view, of the influence of student life on the academic development of undergraduates in state universities. Penetration of this new field of inquiry must necessarily begin with description at the concrete level of human experience before valid abstract models can be constructed. The investigator must start by endeavoring to understand the situation from the perspective of the participants. Hence, this research undertakes to examine a large state university from the student's point of view. It is an exploratory, sociographic study of the effect of social and cultural factors in undergraduate student life on academic development.

Methods

The design of the study is longitudinal and comparative. A panel of students was repeatedly interviewed during their undergraduate years. Particular attention was given in the analysis to differences in the experiences of honor and regular students.

Data were collected by the techniques usually employed in community studies—interviews, autobiographies, participant-observer reports, and information in university files and publications. Field work was carried out by successive teams of student assistants who were enrolled in a seminar and compensated by research awards, college credits, or hourly earnings. The richest source of information was a systematic sample of 116 undergraduates. It was drawn from the cohort of freshmen who entered the University in the fall of 1959. Since honor and regular students were to be compared, and the former were less than one per cent of all entering freshmen, a stratified sample was used to produce 20 honor and 96 regular students. When overall statistics were computed, the influence of the honor stratum was reduced to its proper proportion by applying a weighting factor.

Reprinted with permission of the author and publisher from *College Student Survey*, 1967, 1, 22-31.

*The research reported here was supported by the Cooperative Research Program of the Office of Education, U.S. Department of Health, Education, and Welfare. Support was also received from the University of Kansas General Research Fund, Graduate School, and Computation Center, and from the Kansas City Association of Trusts and Foundation. The study is presented in greater detail in the writer's *Achievement and Role Definition of the College Student,* Report of Cooperative Research Project No. 2605 of the U.S. Office of Education (Lawrence, Kansas: Department of Sociology, University of Kansas, 1965).

Six focused interviews were held at intervals between fall, 1959, and spring, 1963, with the students in the sample who were enrolled. The completion rates for the six interview waves ranged from 68 to 94 per cent, and the overall rate was 84 per cent. Although dropouts shrank the sample to 55 per cent of its original size, it was assumed to be fairly representative of the members of the original cohort who were still enrolled. Written autobiographies of their college careers were obtained from 180 other students enrolled in introductory sociology classes, about two-thirds of whom were juniors and seniors. The autobiographies were written according to an outline of topics and questions. The content of the interviews and autobiographies was analyzed and classified by major roles, and subdivided by aspects of roles. For quantitative analysis, five persons coded the interviews according to 35 variables. Reliability was maximized by using the coding on each variable of the more reliable coders as determined by a measure of intercoder agreement (Scott, 1955). Information on 19 variables from University records and publications was also coded.

Insight into the social context of student life was obtained from participant-observer reports on groups and categories. Studies were completed of 35 organizations, housing units, cliques, and types of students. The main objective of these studies was to relate social experiences to academic development.

Findings[1]

Campus life. The state university, where the field work was conducted, is a co-educational institution in a college town near a metropolitan area. The university is the largest and most respected institution of higher education in the state. When the research was begun, about three-fourths of its many thousand students were undergraduates. They came predominantly from middle-class families for whom going to college was part of

their pattern of living. The minority, from rural and working-class backgrounds, came to the University to change or raise their class status. There was a high turnover rate among students. About one-fourth of the freshmen we sampled failed to enroll for the sophomore year, and only about half remained in school after four years; but those who left were replaced by about equal numbers of students transferring from other colleges. Most of those who withdrew failed to meet scholastic standards. The School of Letters and Sciences, which was responsible for general, liberal education, occupied a central place in the University. It enrolled one-third of all students and three-fourths of the freshmen and sophomores.

In the eyes of students, the schools and departments differed in prestige according to whether their courses were hard or easy. Departments like physics and mathematics were at the top while business and education were at the bottom. Students rated each other in a number of ways among which academic progress and success were prominent. Ranking by grade-point average cut across the seniority system of class years. The higher the grade average the greater the prestige. The gentleman's C was unknown.

Outside the academic system, the most important social units were residential— what students called "living groups." Dormitories housed 40 per cent of the sample, 30 per cent lived in fraternity and sorority houses, and 30 per cent in privately owned accommodations. Students identified one another primarily by their living groups, which were stratified into about five levels: (1) high-ranking Greek houses, (2) middle-ranked Greek houses, (3) low-ranked Greek houses and small residence halls for certain scholarship holders, (4) dormitories, and (5) rooming houses.

There was a consistent positive relationship between the prestige of residential units and the grades of their members. Published reports of grade-point averages of houses and dormitories were eagerly read and appraised by students. Other symbols of status were the number of living-group members in honor societies, positions of leadership, the quality of parties given by houses, and success in various interhouse competitions. The latter included intramural athletics, an an-

[1] The past tense is used in reporting the results of this study to emphasize that what students said about their university in the years 1959-63 may not be what they would say today. Many changes and improvements were in progress at the time of the field work, and some recent innovations have been influenced by the conclusions of this research.

nual, satirical, musical revue, numerous queen contests, house decorations for homecoming, etc.

Among the various kinds of living groups, the exclusive Greek-letter societies were dominant. The high-ranking chapters were the apex of the social pyramid. They wielded power through controlling most of the important student organizations and distributing many rewards and privileges. Although the members of fraternities and sororities were a minority, they effectively dominated undergraduate social life. The independent students, although they were a majority, found themselves handicapped in finding opportunities for full participation in student life. A sharp difference in orientation separated the Greeks from the Independents. The latter generally rejected the Greek system, and, although ambivalently emulating it in many ways, attempted to find congenial associations and opportunities for expression in groups marginal to the core of campus society.

There were over 300 student organizations, but memberships were unequally distributed, with one-fourth of the individuals holding two-thirds of the memberships, and a higher proportion of Greeks than Independents holding multiple memberships. Organizations were stratified into several prestige levels based primarily on membership exclusiveness. Control of organized activities and allocation of positions of prestige and power were largely under the informal control of the fraternities and sororities. Although Greeks were 41 per cent of the sample, 87 per cent of the campus leaders were Greeks. The effective dominance of undergraduate student life by the organized Greek minority was resented by Independents and also questioned by some Greeks. The conflict between the implicit elitism of the Greek system and belief in equalitarianism created a value dilemma.

Most friendships were made within the living groups, some emerged among members of student organizations, and a few were formed with classmates, but 15 per cent of the sample had no close friends, and the proportion was higher among transfer students.

Student values were personified in the polar social types of the "brain" and the "party boy," but the ideal was the "well-rounded" student who combined with moderation the best of both extreme types. To be highly regarded, a student had to achieve in both the academic and social spheres. Varsity athletes were assigned an ambivalent status. They were applauded for their performance in the stadium, but they occupied a low social position in campus life, and were denigrated for their generally undistinguished academic records.

Twelve per cent of undergraduates were married, and eight per cent of the sample were not dating. The others were categorized by the stage of courtship as dating, going steady or "lavaliered," "pinned," or engaged. Since peers rated one another by the prestige of the persons they dated, a certain wariness characterized the attitudes of those who held or aspired to high status. The classroom, since its members had heterogeneous backgrounds largely unknown to each other, was unfavorable for the formation of boy-girl relations. A number of customs and institutions, such as dates arranged by mutual friends and dances planned by officers of two living groups, brought together persons of similar standing and helped bridge the gap between the sexes.

Most students were financially dependent on their parents, maintained communication with them, and were strongly under their influence. Parents and children shared similar aspirations, and valued college primarily as a means for self-development. In their fourth year of college two-thirds of the members of the sample said that social development had been the most valuable part of their college experience. Intellectual development was valued most by one-fourth, and occupational preparation by nine per cent. However, when the sample was classified by attitudes toward scholarships, a majority of students found at least some pleasure in their studies, and only 14 per cent had no interest in the content of their courses. A majority had also broadened their scholastic interests while in college.

Relations with faculty. The classroom is the central feature in the academic sphere of the university. It is the scene of the public performance of the educational drama. Undergraduates learned their classroom roles primarily through direct experience with the expectations of their professors, and secondarily by observation of their classmates. The entering freshman saw his role in relation to his professors as passive, helpless, and remote. With experience, his role tended to become more active, competent, and close, but students differed greatly in the rate and amount of change. Rather than seeing the relationship as at least partially under their control, they saw it as determined by the conduct of the professor including his interest in students, enthusiasm for his subject, his teaching techniques, knowledge of the subject, and level of performance he expected.

The attitudes of freshmen and sophomores toward their academic advisors was primarily instrumental. Advisors were useful because they knew the academic rules. Only two-fifths of the sample said their advisors manifested a friendly, personal interest. Students found that their advisors made mistakes, and that they were guided by policies that sometimes conflicted with the short-run goals of their advisees. Among upperclassmen and their major advisors there was less disparity of purpose, and the relationship was more informal.

Studying. Studying was the primary activity of the student. It prepared him for his classroom performance and occupied more time than any other pursuit. He saw it as a necessary form of work with some pleasant and some unpleasant aspects. He was motivated by his own self-discipline, the expectations of others, and the enforcement of impersonal rules. Students entered the university with a tentative conception of their academic level, which was revised, usually downward, in the light of the grades received in the first semester. Once a student defined his level of competence, subsequent changes in achievement affected his feeling of self-worth. Achievement was measured by grades, and only rarely did a student reject the evaluation of the grading system. Such independence was made difficult by the use of grades for all manner of purposes other than credits required for graduation. The grade-point average was used not only for academic awards, prizes, and scholarships, but also to determine eligibility for many extracurricular groups, activities, and positions. Such rules were set up by student governing bodies as well as by the faculty and administrators. The grading system was so completely internalized by students that the grade-point average was an important basis for evaluating themselves and others.

Problems of studying were a result of the sheer bulk of the assigned work, competition from other activities, emotional problems, and uninteresting or difficult content. Studying, unlike industrial work that is typically performed under supervision, was especially vulnerable to distraction because it was done without direct supervision, and also because it often had to be done in the company of a roommate or companions having different assignments, study habits, and proclivities. In the freshman year, anxiety over status and social adjustments interfered with school work. Apathy was the greatest problem of the sophomore year, and it recurred in milder form among graduating seniors.

Students coped with the problems of studying by using disapproved and illegitimate means, as well as those provided by the university and approved by the faculty. Finding time and a place to study was virtually a universal problem. The dormitories and fraternity houses, where the majority of students lived, were noisy and, the latter particularly, were often poorly designed and equipped for studying. The efforts of individual houses to regulate studying and noise were often ineffectual. The libraries of the university were not adequate, accessible, or sufficiently free of distractions to solve the problem. Unauthorized use of classrooms was resorted to by some. The burden of work was lightened or smoothed by enrollment manipulation that often involved evasion of rules. A program could be padded with easy courses, but they were a sign of low status in the academic sphere. Students whose reputations among their peers depended on their scholastic records avoided this solution. The importance of examinations, for assigning grades, made them an object of frequent manipulation of which cramming was the most widely used technique. Files of past examinations, laboratory reports, and papers were maintained by the Greek houses and some dormitories. Cheating was almost universally condemned in principle, but widely practiced. Its use was rationalized as accidental, important to a friend, or the fault of the professor. From one-fourth to a half of the sample were estimated to have cheated at some time.

The classroom. Although the classroom was the fundamental unit within the academic sphere of student experience, it was poorly developed as a social group. For the most part classmates were strangers in competition with one another. In the freshman and sophomore years it rarely happened that the same persons were together in more than one class. Enrollment changed each semester. Students came from heterogeneous backgrounds in their home communities, and from different factions and strata of campus society. Diffidence over cultivating personal ties with classmates stemmed from concern over the consequences for dating and rating. This sensitivity to status distinctions was accentuated by the Greek system. The friendships that did exist among classmates were almost all formed in, or reinforced by, associating in living groups or other more stable relationships. Cooperation among classmates was largely confined to such pairs or cliques. Help in school work was also obtained from friends who were not classmates. Fellow members of Greek-letter societies were obligated to help one another. Pairs of students sometimes studied together on different subjects. Each one reinforced the other's efforts by acting as a conscience and model for the other.

Student subculture. Rudimentary collective action and subculture took the form of epithets applied to students who intensified competition for grades. Those who did it by ability and hard work were called "curve breakers." This invective, however, was used only when referring to an able student competing in the same classroom. The same student, in the role of fraternity brother, was respected and honored for bringing prestige to his house. The epithet functioned to release tension rather than as an instrument of social control. The "apple polisher" tried to raise his grade simply by currying favor with the instructor. The use of this term was a carry-over from high school that sanctioned social distance between students and teachers, but many students recognized that it was inappropriate in college. Attempts to collectively restrict the amount of school work were rare and usually ineffectual. Few students saw any point in even trying to control their professors.

Honor students. In the middle '50's an honors program for freshmen and sophomores was added to an existing program for seniors. About 100 entering freshmen were invited into the program on the basis of their scores on competitive examinations. They were assigned to special advisors, urged to enroll in honors sections of introductory and required courses, and some were invited to assist professors with their research. Most of the lower-division honor students quickly established friendly and even personal relationships with their advisors. In our sample, 87 per cent of the honor students thought their advisors were friendly as compared with 40 per cent of regular students. When it came to planning academic programs, on the other hand, disagreement was not uncommon. Advisees often thought they were overloaded or enrolled in courses for which they were unprepared, but they sympathetically attributed this tendency to the advisor's understandable enthusiasm for the objectives of the honors program. Eighty-six per cent of the honor students thought their special advisors were knowledgeable and helpful, while only 33 per cent of regular students had so favorable an opinion of their advisors. Outside the academic sphere, however, students found the opinions of their advisors puzzling and contradictory. Their conceptions of what was worthwhile in campus life conflicted with that of the students.

About a third of the classes taken by honor students in their first two years was in honors sections. They thought they learned more in honors than regular sections because they believed the teaching was of higher quality. They often developed gratifying personal relations with their classmates and their professors. Since they often saw one another in different classes, friendships developed, particularly among the independent students. Many honor students enjoyed the stimulation of friendly rivalry with their classmates. However, they found the level of presentation too high in some of their science and mathematics courses. In retrospection, they were more likely to speak favorably of the challenge and accomplishments of their work in honors sections than while enrolled in these courses.

Outstanding students were nominated for undergraduate research awards by individual professors. One-third of the honor students in the '59 cohort had held an award. Nearly all of them commented favorably on the experience, and, for one-third of those in the sample who received awards, it was a turning point in their careers. All were coeds who decided to become scientists. For girls, who usually entered college planning a career that would combine marriage with an occupation traditional for women, like teaching or nursing, the change to a career in a major profession, including college teaching or research, required something akin to a conversion experience. The program was more successful in scientific than in humanistic fields, perhaps because the techniques and the team approach of the sciences provided a constructive place for an apprentice. The honor student was able to take the role of scholar and researcher in a social setting that encouraged him to identify with mature workers, and to try out the role without risking his reputation or status as would happen if he took a difficult course and got a low grade. The more personal the relationship between the student and his mentors, the deeper were these influences.

The public recognition of honor students motivated their efforts through the rewards of prestige, and by arousing a sense of obligation to prove that the honor was justly conferred. The effort to perform in accordance with the expectations of the public role imposed some strain on the student. He also felt caught in the value dilemma of enjoying the recognition of his superiority over others, while subscribing to equalitarian values.

Interpretations

The undergraduate student body in the years 1958 to 1963 was a huge mass of individuals lacking firm overall structure. The formal organization of the University itself provided the only common framework and set of guidelines for all its students. However, the formal categories and groupings of students imposed by the academic system of the institution seldom provided opportunities for establishing strong interpersonal bonds. Common membership in schools, departments, classes, honor societies, etc., was too fluid, tenuous, and ephemeral for the development of friendships and commitments. Students in the typical classroom were a collection of competing strangers who were incapable of collaborating with one another in the pleasurable pursuit of scholarship. Attending class, for most students, was an unpleasant though necessary means for getting grades. The student earned grades by doing assignments, making high marks on examinations, and by writing papers. The spirit of the classroom was more like that of the marketplace than the academy. Its members were a mass of individuals rather than an integrated social group. Housing groups, on the other hand, were socially significant units. Students were primarily identified by their place of residence, and accordingly categorized in the campus prestige hierarchy. Their closest friendships were usually made with others in their living-group.

The hierarchical structure of the Greek system, and its method of membership recruitment by secret selection, gave implicit support to elitist values. The resulting conflict with the equalitarian values, dominant in American society, exposed the Greeks to criticism from Independents, and produced some doubters in their own ranks.

The fraternities and sororities were important for the University not only by providing housing for one-third of the undergraduates, and performing extracurricular rituals, but also by supporting the formal objective of academic achievement. An important status symbol was a high grade-point average. However, the full effect of this support was weakened because grades rather than scholarship were emphasized. In the Greek system, high grades were valued as symbols of status rather than signs of scholarly achievement. The grade-point average, though originally a mere accounting device for university record keeping, was transformed by the fraternities and sororities into an instrument for making invidious social distinctions between individuals and groups.

In addition to peer influences, students were affected by the opinions and beliefs of their parents. Most students had internalized their parents' values. The majority came from middle-class homes, and most of the rest were farm and working-class youth striving for a middle-class station in urban society. College provided a way of confirming or establishing a claim to middle-class status. But the students, and their parents, saw the status function of their education as an aspect of self-development. The thing they valued most in their university experience was the cultivation of social skills, and the formation of friendships. Only a small minority gave first importance to intellectual development, although it was the primary objective of the institution.

The living groups and student organizations provided meaningful and, in some cases, secure anchorage for individual students within the fluid and confusing University complex. But the dominant Greek system functioned more to serve the status aspirations of the students than their intellectual development or career preparation. The educational objectives and methods of the formal system of the University were modified to better serve the socializing needs and mobility goals of the students and their families. The fraternities and sororities, and the student organizations under their control, functioned as the mediating social structure and subculture for the dominant core of students; but the Independents, who were outside this system, lacked effective mediating agencies. They were a mass incapable of collective action and lacking a coherent subculture.

Classmates were usually strangers to one another incapable of joint action to solve their problems. The student body's demographic characteristics of large numbers, brevity of contact, turnover, and heterogeneity, interfered with group formation. There were also centrifugal forces of competition for scarce high grades, and the maintenance of social distance from peers by status conscious and vertically mobile students.

The typical freshman student's relations with his professors was characterized by helpless, distant passivity. The traditional high school denigration of apple polishers restrained him from approaching his instructors. He usually believed that it was the professor's responsibility, as a parent surrogate, to take the initiative in caring for his students. In time this gulf was bridged by most students who learned from experience that close, personal ties with professors were rewarding, and that the student himself must take some responsibility and initiative in the relationship. The relations of underclassmen with their advisors failed to provide a satisfactory personal link with the faculty. Students tended to see the advisor only as a fairly knowledgeable bureaucrat. They quickly developed a wariness over trusting his judgment when they found that his advice often conflicted with the student's own immediate goals.

In their relations with faculty, no student peer groups functioned in an adequate mediating capacity, nor was there a body of norms, traditional among the students, that provided patterns of conduct for effective interaction with professors. With few exceptions, only when students reached the upper-division years did they form close working relations with their classmates and teachers. Repeated association in smaller-sized classes helped bring this about. Even so, some students never formed personal associations within the academic sphere.

The quality of the classroom performance was measured by the grading system and, as a consequence, the satisfaction the student derived from his studying lay more in the grade he made, than in the intrinsic worth of the content. Since grades were made primarily by getting high scores on examinations, students often neglected regular study of their subjects, in favor of last-minute cramming. As a consequence, they were often ill prepared for intelligent participation in classroom discussion or for maximum grasp of the lecture.

Grades, in their quantified form of the grade-point average, were made enormously important to students by their administrative use. In addition to epitomizing a student's academic standing, minimum averages were specified by university agencies for participation and eligibility for all manner of activities and awards. The grading system, in all its ramifications, admirably suited the organizational needs of the Greek system by providing an instrument for making refined discriminations for membership qualification and relative status ranking.

Since grades were based primarily on examinations and papers, the system lent itself to manipulation by various devices more or less legitimate. The residents of organized houses gained an advantage over other students by their use of member discipline, mutual aid, and the maintenance of files of past examinations, laboratory reports, and papers. The provision of semi-legitimate means for making grades, as alternatives to legitimate scholarship, was the clearest instance of student subculture found within the academic sphere. But, rather than solving problems of studying, these subcultural means provided alternatives that were contrary to the norms of the institution and, in the case of dishonest methods, also contrary to the values of the majority of students. This part of the student subculture created more problems than it solved.

Participants in the honors program were placed in more favorable social situations for learning than regular students. They were assigned special advisors who took a personal interest in their welfare. They enrolled in more of the small honors sections, than other students, where they had an opportunity to become acquainted with one another and with their professors. Because they saw one another in more than one class, and met on other occasions, honor students had more opportunities to form meaningful social ties within the academic sphere than was true of other students. However, their interaction did not develop to the point of forming cohesive groups to serve an effective mediating function with the university as an institution.

Those few honor students who won research awards were often drawn into personal relations with faculty members through their participation in mature scholarly and scientific work. They were no longer merely playing at scholarship, but participating in actual research projects. Through close association, they often identified with their professors, and were thus able to imaginatively project themselves into the role of scholar or scientist. These occupations became realistic career choices for the student apprentices.

Students in the honors program were promptly drawn into close personal association with classmates and faculty that many other students did not experience until they began work on their specialties in the junior and senior years. The classroom was more like a group than a mass of individuals, and association in the academic enterprise was pleasurable in itself. Enjoyment of class participation motivated efficient and systematic studying. The close ties with instructors facilitated a transfer of scholarly values as well as knowledge. Scholarship became more of an end in itself instead of merely a form of work used as a means toward qualifying for a degree or preparing for a profession.

Conclusions

The poor communication, lack of understanding, and conflict of values that characterized the typical student's relations with faculty and staff of the University, can be attributed, at least in part, to the structure of student peer groups on the campus. In the academic sphere where the educational process primarily takes place, peer groups were weak. Where peer groups were strong, as some were in the spheres of housing, organized activities, and social life, their primary functions were not the transmission of knowledge, but socialization for a middle-class station in life. Undergraduate student life was dominated by the "Greek" elite and forced the majority of students into a marginal position. Thus the dominant structure of student life implicitly reinforced elitism and discrimination—values that are contrary to explicit goals of a liberal education. The strongest student peer groups operated at cross-purposes with the formal objectives of the University, and, paradoxically, some of the University's own practices and rules, such as the support of fraternities and sororities and the emphasis on the grading system, had the effect of strengthening the extra-educational objectives of students and their families, at the expense of the University's professed educational objectives.

Within this general condition of social fragmentation and cultural contradiction, however, there were some situations in which students formed close associations within the academic sphere.

When students were well along toward completing the requirements for their major subjects, some of them developed close associations with their classmates. Peer ties developed earlier among students brought together in small groups through work in laboratories and studios, and among those who enrolled in several honors sections during their freshman and sophomore years. The honor students, unlike those taking regular undergraduate courses, got to know one another and their professors. In addition to the freer interchange in smaller classes they became better acquainted because they saw one another in several different classes. For many of these students, the class meeting was an enjoyable social experience as well as a place for acquiring and demonstrating knowledge. They made friends with some of their classmates and often became personally acquainted with their professors. The pleasure of association in pursuit of knowledge tended to become transformed into a liking for the content of the course and the man who taught it. To the extent that the class became a social group, it reinforced interest in the course and the motivation to learn. It became a catalytic agent in the learning process.

These internal differences, especially the contrast between the roles of honor and regular students, point up characteristics of the social situation that affect the educational process. They suggest that (1) the level of academic achievement can be raised by close personal association in the academic setting of students with one another and with the faculty. (2) The emergence of stable, enduring groups within the academic sphere reinforces the learning process by linking it with gratifying interpersonal relationships. (3) When instructors are personally involved with their students in the learning process, there is a transfer of attitudes and values along with knowledge. Professors become more than teachers; they become role models of scholars and scientists who are emulated by many of their students. (4) When students form cohesive groups within the academic sphere, they develop collective means and· subcultural norms that reinforce the educational objectives of the university.

References

Alexander, C. N., Jr., & Campbell, E. Q. Peer influences on adolescent educational aspirations and attainments. *American Sociological Review,* 1964, **29,** 568-575.

Bandura, A., & McDonald, F. J. The influence of social reinforcement and the behavior of models in shaping children's moral judgments. *Journal of Abnormal and Social Psychology,* 1963, **67,** 274-281.

Bandura, A., & Mischel, W. The influence of models in modifying delay-of-gratification patterns. Unpublished manuscript, Stanford University, 1963.

Bandura, A., & Walters, R. H. *Adolescent aggression.* New York: Ronald, 1959.

Bandura, A., & Walters, R. H. *Social learning and personality development.* New York: Holt, 1963.

Barker, R. G., & Gump, P. V. *Big school, small school: High school size and student behavior.* Stanford, Calif.: Stanford University Press, 1964.

Bealer, R. C., & Willits, F. C. Rural youth: A case study in the rebelliousness of adolescents. *Annals of the American Academy of Political and Social Science,* 1961, **338,** 63-69.

Bealer, R. C., Willits, F. C., & Maida, P. R. The rebellious youth subculture—a myth. *Children,* 1964, **11,** 43-48.

Becker, H. S., et al. *Boys in white: Student culture in medical school.* Chicago: University of Chicago Press, 1961.

Bernard, J. Teen-age culture: An overview. *Annals of the American Academy of Political and Social Science,* 1961, **338,** 1-12.

Bidwell, C. E., et al. Undergraduates' careers: Alternatives and determinants. *School Review,* 1963, **71,** 299-316.

Bonjean, C. M., & McGee, R. Scholastic dishonesty among undergraduates in differing systems of social control. *Sociology of Education,* 1965, **38,** 127-137.

Braham, M. Peer group deterrents to intellectual development during adolescence. *Educational Theory,* 1965, **15,** 248-258.

Brittain, C. V. Adolescent choices and parent-peer cross pressures. *American Sociological Review,* 1963, **28,** 385-391.

Brown, A. W., Morrison, J., & Counc, G. B. Influence of affectional family relationships on character development. *Journal of Abnormal and Social Psychology,* 1947, **42,** 422-428.

Brown, C. H. Self-portrait: The teen-type magazine. *Annals of the American Academy of Political and Social Science,* 1961, **338,** 13-21.

Bushnell, J. H. Student culture at Vassar. In N. Sanford, (Ed.), *The American college.* New York: Wiley, 1962. Pp. 489-514.

Carry, R. W. Youth breaks the rules. *Research Resume No. 38.* Burlingame, Calif.: Proceedings of the 20th Annual State Conference on Educational Research, 1968. Pp. 124-125.

Cawelti, G. Youth assess the American high school. *PTA Magazine,* 1968, **62,** 16-19.

Cloward, R. A., & Ohlin, L. E. *Delinquency and opportunity: A theory of delinquent gangs.* Glencoe, Ill.: Free Press, 1960.

Cohen, A. K. *Delinquent boys: The culture of the gang.* Glencoe, Ill.: Free Press, 1955.

Coleman, J. S. *The adolescent society.* New York: Free Press, 1961a.

Coleman, J. S. Athletics in high school. *Annals of the American Academy of Political and Social Science,* 1961b, **338,** 33-43.

Coleman, J. S. *Adolescents and the schools.* New York: Basic Books, 1965.

Douvan, E., & Adelson, J. *The adolescent experience.* New York: Wiley, 1966.

Dunphy, D. C. The social structure of urban adolescent peer groups. *Sociometry,* 1963, **26,** 230-246.

Elkin, F., & Westley, W. A. The myth of adolescent culture. *American Sociological Review,* 1955, **20,** 680-684.

Epperson, D. C. Some interpersonal and performance correlates of classroom alienation. *School Review,* 1963, **71,** 360-376.

Epperson, D. C. A re-assessment of indices of parental influence on the adolescent society. *American Sociological Review,* 1964, **29,** 93-96.

Erikson, E. H. *Childhood and society,* New York: Norton, 1950.

Eron, L. D. The effect of medical education on attitudes: A follow-up study. In *The ecology of the medical student.* Evanston, Ill.: Association of American Medical Colleges, 1958.

Fishman, J. R., & Solomon, F. Youth and social action: An introduction. *Journal of Social Issues,* 1964, **20,** 1-27.

Ford, C. S., & Beach, F. A. *Patterns of sexual behavior.* New York: Harper, 1951.

Fort, J. Youth: How to produce drop-ins rather than drop-outs. *Research Resume No. 38.* Burlingame, Calif.: Proceedings of the 20th Annual State Conference on Educational Research, 1968. Pp. 53-64.

Freud, S. *An outline of psychoanalysis.* New York: Norton, 1949.

Friedenberg, E. Z. *The vanishing adolescent.* Boston: Beacon, 1959.

Friedenberg, E. Z. *Coming of age in America.* New York: Random House, 1965.

Friesen, D. Academic-athletic-popularity syndrome in the Canadian high school society. *Adolescence,* 1968, **3** (9), 39-52.

Gallagher, J. R., & Harris, H. I. *Emotional problems of adolescents.* New York: Oxford University Press, 1958.

Garrison, K. C. *Psychology of adolescence.* Englewood Cliffs, N. J.: Prentice-Hall, 1966.

Generations apart. New York: Columbia Broadcasting System, 1969.

Gesell, A., & Ilg, F. *Infant and child in the culture of today.* New York: Harper, 1943.

Goodman, P. Freedom and learning: The need for choice. *Saturday Review,* 1968, **51** (20), 73-75.

Gordon, C. W. *The social system of the high school: A study in the sociology of adolescence.* Glencoe, Ill.: Free Press, 1957.

Gordon, C. W. Essay review: James Coleman on "The Adolescent Society." *School Review,* 1963, **71,** 377-385.

Goslin, D. A. Accuracy of self perception and social perception. *Sociometry,* 1962, **25,** 283-296.

Gottlieb, D., & Hodgkins, B. College student subculture: Their structures and characteristics in relation to student attitude change. *School Review,* 1963, **71,** 266-289.

Haller, A. O., & Butterworth, C. E. Peer influences on levels of occupational and educational aspiration. *Social Forces,* 1960, **38,** 289-295.

Havighurst, R. L. *Developmental tasks and education.* New York: McKay, 1952.

Heathers, G. Emotional dependence and independence in nursery school play. *Journal of Genetic Psychology,* 1955, **87,** 37-57.

Henry, J. *Culture against man.* New York: Random House, 1963.

Hollingshead, A. B. *Elmtown's youth.* New York: Wiley, 1949.

Hughes, E., Becker, H., & Geer, B. Student culture and academic effort. In N. Sanford, (Ed.), *The American college.* New York: Wiley, 1962. Pp. 515-530.

Hurlock, E. B. *Adolescent development.* New York: McGraw-Hill, 1955.

Ilg, F. L., & Ames, L. B. *Child behavior.* New York: Harper, 1955.

Jacob, P. E. *Changing values in college.* New York: Harper, 1957.

Jahoda, M. & Warren, N. The myths of youth. *Sociology of Education,* 1965, **38,** 138-149.

Josselyn, I. M. *Psychosocial development of children.* New York: Family Service Association of America, 1948.

Kiell, N. *The adolescent through fiction.* New York: International University Press, 1959.

Kobrin, S. Sociological aspects of the development of a street corner group: An exploratory study. *American Journal of Orthopsychiatry,* 1961, **31,** 685-702.

Kounin, J., Gump, P. V., & Ryan, J. J. III. Explorations in classroom management. *Journal of Teacher Education,* 1961, **12,** 235-246.

Lipset, S. M., & Wolin, S. S. (Eds.) *The Berkeley student revolt.* Garden City, N. Y.: Doubleday, 1965.

May, H. The student movement at Berkeley: Some impressions. In S. M. Lipset & S. S. Wolin (Eds.), *The Berkeley student revolt.* Garden City, N. Y.: Doubleday, 1965. Pp. 453-464.

McDill, E. L., & Coleman, J. S. Family and peer influence in college plans of high school students. *Sociology of Education,* 1965, **38** (11), 112-126.

Mead, M. Adolescence in primitive and in modern society. In V. F. Calverton & S. D. Schmalhausen (Eds.), *The new generation.* New York: Macauley, 1930.

Meissner, W. W. Parental interaction of the adolescent boy. *Journal of Genetic Psychology,* 1965, **107,** 225-233.

Meyer, H. J., Borgatta, E. F., & Jones, W. C. *Girls at vocational high.* New York: Russell Sage Foundation, 1965.

Miller, W. B. Lower class culture as a generating milieu of gang delinquency. *Journal of Social Issues,* 1958, **14,** 5-19.

Mohr, G. S., & Despres, M. A. *The stormy decade: Adolescence.* New York: Random House, 1958.

Musgrove, F. *Youth and the social order.* Bloomington: Indiana University Press, 1964.

Musgrove, F. The social needs and satisfactions of some young people: Part I—At home, in youth clubs, and at work. *British Journal of Educational Psychology,* 1966, **36** (61), 71.

Neill, A. S. *Summerhill: A radical approach to child rearing.* New York: Hart, 1960.

Newcomb, T. M. *The acquaintance process.* New York: Holt, 1961.

Newcomb, T. M. Student peer-group influence. In N. Sanford, (Ed.), *The American college.* New York: Wiley, 1962. Pp. 469-488.

Nordstrom, C., Friedenberg, E. Z., & Gold, H. *Influence of ressentiment on student experience in secondary school.* U.S. Department of Health, Education, and Welfare, Office of Education, Cooperative Research Project No. 1758. Brooklyn: Brooklyn College, 1965.

Orth, C. D. III. *Social structure and learning climate.* Cambridge, Mass.: Harvard University Press, 1963.

Parsons, T. Psychoanalysis and social structure. *Psychoanalytic Quarterly,* 1950, **19,** 371-384.

Pearson, G. H. J. *Adolescence and the conflict of generations.* New York: Norton, 1958.

Peck, R. F., & Galliani, C. Intelligence, ethnicity and social roles in adolescent society. *Sociometry,* 1962, **25,** 64-72.

Piaget, J. *The moral judgment of the child.* Glencoe, Ill.: Free Press, 1948.

Piaget, J. *The construction of reality in the child.* New York: Basic Books, 1954.

Polsky, H. W. *Cottage six: The social system of delinquent boys in residential treatment.* New York: Russell Sage Foundation, 1962.

Rosen, B. C. Conflicting group membership: A study of parent-peer group cross-pressures. *American Sociological Review,* 1955, **20,** 155-161.

Salinger, J. D. *The catcher in the rye.* Boston: Little, Brown, 1951.

Sanford, N. (Ed.) *The American college.* New York: Wiley, 1962.

Schmuck, R. Some relationships of peer liking patterns in the classroom to pupil attitudes and achievement. *School Review,* 1963, **71,** 337-359.

Schwitzgebel, R. *Streetcorner research: An experimental approach to the juvenile delinquent.* Cambridge, Mass.: Harvard University Press, 1964.

Scott, W. A. Reliability of content analysis: The case of nominal scale coding. *Public Opinion Quarterly,* 1955, **19,** 321, 325.

Seidler, M. B., & Ravitz, M. J. A Jewish peer group. *American Journal of Sociology,* 1955, **61,** 11-15.

Selvin, H. C., & Hagstrom, W. O. Determinants of support for civil liberties. In S. M. Lipset & S. S. Wolin (Eds.), *The Berkeley student revolt.* Garden City, N.Y.: Doubleday, 1965. Pp. 494-518.

Sherif, M., & Sherif, C. W. *Reference groups: Exploration into conformity and deviation of adolescents.* New York: Harper, 1964.

Sherif, C., & Sherif, M. Seeking thrills with the "in" crowd. *PTA Magazine,* 1966, **60,** 5-6.

Short, J. F., Jr., & Strodtbeck, F. L. *Group process and gang delinquency.* Chicago: University of Chicago Press, 1965.

Simpson, R. L. Parental influence, anticipations, socialization, and social mobility. *American Sociological Review,* 1962, **27,** 517-522.

Smith, E. A. *American youth culture.* New York: Free Press, 1962.

Somers, R. H. The mainsprings of the rebellion: A survey of Berkeley students in November, 1964. In S. M. Lipset & S. S. Wolin (Eds.), *The Berkeley student revolt.* Garden City, N.Y.: Doubleday, 1965. Pp. 530-557.

Stinchcombe, A. L. *Rebellion in a high school.* Chicago: Quadrangle Books, 1964.

Strom, R. D. Comparison of adolescent and adult behavioral norm properties. *Journal of Educational Psychology,* 1963, **54,** 322-330.

Thornburg, H. D. Student assessment of contemporary issues. *College Student Survey,* 1969, **3** (1), 1-5, 22.

Thornburg, H. D. Adolescence: A reinterpretation. *Adolescence,* 1970, in press.

Trow, M., & Clark, B. R. Varieties and determinants of undergraduate subcultures. Paper read at the annual meeting of the American Sociological Society, New York, 1960.

Westley, W. A., & Elkin, F. The protective environment and adolescent socialization. *Social Forces,* 1956, **35,** 243-249.

Whyte, W. F. *Street corner society.* (2nd ed.) Chicago: University of Chicago Press, 1955.

Yablonsky, L. *The violent gang.* New York: Macmillan, 1963.

Annotations

Duncan, O. D., Haller, A. D., & Portes, A. Peer influences on aspirations: A reinterpretation. *American Journal of Sociology,* 1968, **74,** 119-137. This research study hypothesizes that an adolescent's best friend's educational and occupational aspirations will help form one's ego aspirations. Such aspirations were found to be reciprocal, and one's ambitions are reinforced by his friends. Ambitions correlate strongly to both educational and occupational influences.

Dunphy, D. C. The social structure of urban adolescent peer groups. *Sociometry,* 1963, **26,** 230-246. This article reports on adolescent peer groups within suburban areas. Dunphy was able to place peers into five hierarchies of groups. Initially he observed unisexual cliques, which develop at the preadolescent stage. In early adolescence these cliques became heterosexual. He then describes three stages of advanced peer activity throughout adolescence. Dunphy noted that the course of the individual's social growth is strongly influenced by his position within the peer structure.

Gordon, R. A. Social level, social disability, and gang interaction. *American Journal of Sociology,* 1967, **73,** 42-62. Gordon analyzes social life and gang activity according to social class. Findings indicate that lower-class adolescent boys are less satisfied with their social life than are upper-class boys. He provides an interesting analysis of peer commitment and peer evaluations by social class.

Hollander, E. P., & Marcia, J. E. Parental determinants of peer-orientation and self-orientations among pre-adolescents. *Developmental Psychology*, 1970, **2,** 292-302. This research was an in-depth analysis of parent and child orientation toward self or peers. The findings indicate that parents who are peer oriented have children who are peer oriented. The authors also found that, the stronger the child's peer orientation, the less self- or parent oriented he is. The study also revealed that peer orientation is strongest in father-dominated homes and in families in which the father is less academically advanced than the mother and that boys are more peer oriented than girls.

McDill, E. L., & Coleman, J. Family and peer influences in college plans of high school students. *Sociology of Education,* 1965, **38,** 112-126. Data on 612 students in six Midwestern high schools are analyzed to assess the relative effect of socioeconomic background and peer influences on college plans. The analysis reveals that by the end of the senior year of high school, status in the social system of the school contributes more to variations in college plans than does parents' education. These findings challenge the results of several studies that show the most important source of variation in educational aspirations to be the child's socioeconomic background.

Schwartz, G., & Merton, D. The language of adolescence: An anthropological approach to the youth culture. *American Journal of Sociology,* 1967, **72,** 453-468. The authors report that, to appreciate the differences between adult and adolescent orientations to social reality, we must look at the meanings that peer-group norms have for adolescence. From this perspective the youth culture is a genuinely independent subculture. The social categories inherent in the adolescent status terminology provide the members of this age grade with their own world view, life-styles, and moral standards.

Sherif, C., & Sherif, M. Seeking thrills with the "in" crowd. *PTA Magazine,* 1965, **60,** 5-6. Also in *Education Digest,* 1966, **31,** 32-33. The authors are working from the hypothesis that adolescents will find kicks in any activity, whether it is socially desirable or undesirable. The focus is on providing outlets for constructive kicks—ways in which adolescents can function without feeling that they are being imposed upon. The authors emphasize building responsibility in adolescents.

seven

adolescent delinquency

Juvenile delinquency is usually described as norm-violating behavior. Legally, a juvenile is delinquent if he commits an act that violates the law and is convicted by the court. Behaviorally, he is delinquent if he expresses aggressive, overt actions contrary to the demands of society. In either case his activity is antisocial.

Studies of delinquency generally focus on its social rather than its pathological context. The sociologist investigates the delinquent's social environment; the psychologist searches for the causative factors of delinquency; the social worker sees the delinquent as a person in need of help and tries to rehabilitate him. Delinquency is indeed a social problem, and social action, such as improving economic and educational opportunities and developing community-action programs to prevent delinquency, must be taken to solve it.

Theories of Delinquent Behavior

The theory of innate predisposition to delinquency is not regarded by most behaviorists as tenable. Yet the work of Glueck and Glueck, Harvard criminologists, indicates that body build may have some effect on delinquency. They have noted that people with mesomorphic builds show higher delinquency rates than do the endomorphic or ectomorphic types.* Glueck and Glueck have commented:

> The greater incidence among delinquents of boys of the mesomorphic constitution, and the traits frequently found associated with this muscular, well-knit, energetic physique type, should suggest to all persons and agencies intimately concerned with the wholesome guidance of youth—that special allowance and provision should be made in all major channels of self-expression for the greater energy-output and corresponding traits and interests of mesomorphic boys (1968, pp. 184-185; see also Sheldon, 1965; Glueck & Glueck, 1956).

Glueck and Glueck have suggested that delinquent behavior is a result of delayed maturation. In their longitudinal study (1968) of delinquents, 60 percent committed serious crimes during the first follow-up period (ages 17-25), and 30 percent were still offenders during the second follow-up period (ages 26-31). In the first article in this chapter they point out that "the mass impact of the external societal environment, or the general culture, is less significant in generating delinquency and extending it into criminal recidivism than are the biologic endowments of the individual and the parental influences of the formative years of early childhood." Thus evidence indicates that delinquency has a psychological-biological basis that, combined with the cultural milieu, triggers and perpetuates norm-violating behavior.

The Delinquent Subculture

Delinquent youths are said to constitute a subculture. Gordon defined a subculture as "a subdivision of the national culture, composed of a combination of factorable social situations such as class status, ethnic background, regional and rural or urban residence, and religious affiliation, but forming in their combination a functional unity which has an integrated impact on the participating individual" (1947, p. 40). The adolescent subculture in general is a tolerated form of variation from the parent culture, but delin-

---

*Mesomorphy, endomorphy, and ectomorphy are William Sheldon's three classifications of physiques. The mesomorph is characterized by a hard, rectangular build with prominent bones and muscles. The endomorph has a soft, round build. The ectomorph's physique is linear and fragile.

quent youths represent an intolerable variation.

Cloward and Ohlin (1960) described three types of delinquent subcultures: criminal, conflict, and retreatist. The criminal subculture is characterized by acts of theft, extortion, and other illegal means of securing income. The conflict subculture engages in gang activity and uses violence as a means of winning status. The retreatist subculture stresses the consumption of drugs. However, Empey (1967; see Annotation) feels that Cloward and Ohlin have defined subculture in too narrow terms:

> They see a delinquent subculture as unique and as autonomous. Organization around a specific delinquent activity, they say, distinguishes a delinquent subculture from other subcultures. Such behaviors as truancy, drunkenness, property destruction, or theft are legally delinquent activities, but these they would not include as characteristics of a delinquent subculture unless they were the focal activities around which the dominant beliefs and roles of a group were organized (p. 36).

Social Class

Delinquency has traditionally been attributed to lower-class adolescents. Cohen (1955) theorized that lower-class delinquency is a masculine protest against a female-dominated home. Kvaraceus and Ulrich (1959) maintain that delinquency stems from differences between the adolescent's lower-class goals, values, and ambitions and the middle-class goals to which he is exposed. Thus the lower-class youth finds prestige and acceptance in norm-violating gang activity. Cloward and Ohlin (1960) have proposed a differential-opportunity theory—that is, lower-class adolescents accept most middle-class goals but are unable to pursue them because of incongruity between their aspirations and their opportunities.

However, recent studies are showing that there may be a greater incidence of delinquency among middle-class adolescents than among any other class. Vaz's article in this chapter provides an excellent discussion of middle-class delinquency. He emphasizes the emergence of a youth culture in which upper- and middle-class delinquency occurs. In addition, he analyzes peer orientation, adolescent roles and rules, and "social," nonacademic activities.

Miller (1957) has found that gang delinquency among street-corner groups in lower-class communities differs from that of subcultures in which, because of a conflict between middle-class and lower-class cultures, the lower-class members deliberately violate middle-class norms. His article in this chapter is an exhaustive analysis of gang activity in a slum district of an Eastern metropolis. He focuses on violent crimes that may be results of class conflict. The article analyzes the nature and frequency of such crimes; the race, age, and social status of the offender; and the targets of violent crimes—both persons and objects. The study led him to conclude that: (1) only a small minority of gang members participated in violent crimes; (2) race had little to do with the frequency of involvement in violent crimes, but social status did; (3) violence was not a dominant activity of the gangs; and (4) violence was not motivated by sadism against the weak, the innocent, or the solitary but by the boys' need to secure and defend their honor as males—comparable to the motivation that undergirds war among nations. Miller states "When men have found a solution to this problem, they will at the same time have solved the problem of violent crimes in city gangs."

Prevention

In 1961 the Office of Juvenile Delinquency and Youth Development was established to administer the Juvenile Delinquency and Youth Offense Control Act of 1961. A new act was signed into law by President Johnson in 1968 (P. L. 90-445). The office supports community-action programs designed to (1) enable adolescents to make decisions about issues that are of direct concern to them; (2) modify the functions of institutions that affect youths; (3) develop new concepts and community competence for dealing with problems of adolescence (Project Innovation, 1966).

Government-supported approaches to delinquency emphasize resolving inequalities in our law enforcement, judicial, and correctional systems as well as in social, political, and educational areas.

Angelino (1968) has proposed three types of programs for the control and prevention of delinquency: individually oriented programs that focus around therapy and counseling sessions, group-oriented programs that emphasize extending the individual into the group as a means of modifying the behaviors and values of all individuals involved, and community-oriented programs—either federally or privately funded—that are based on the self-help approach.

In the final article of this chapter, Kvaraceus maintains that current efforts to prevent delinquency, which center around legislation, financing, and law enforcement, are essential but inadequate. He discusses nine goals that must be realized if effective delinquency control and prevention are to exist. In essence, the article stresses the importance of public awareness of the problem and suggests that lessons can be learned from the lives of juvenile delinquents.

The public school is also a vital agency in the prevention and control of delinquency. The principal and superintendent can help by selecting faculty members who offer positive goals to adolescents. The teacher should be a help and not just another critic; he should be willing to listen and not just dictate ready-made answers. Moreover, if he is aware of the student's frame of reference as well as his own, he will be able to understand and help students from different cultures and family situations. Effective, personable teachers greatly enhance teacher-student interaction.

Most adolescents who become dissatisfied with their curriculum drop out of school, and this situation compounds the problem of delinquency. Personalizing the courses of study of potential dropouts can reduce failure and boredom and meet a wider variety of needs. If a student cannot perform under the standard curriculum, he should be provided with alternative subject matter.

The school must join "with all other community youth and family agencies in coordinated effort to identify, study, and treat the troublesome student" (Kvaraceus, 1966, p. 143). This community-wide approach can help the school obtain information about a student from other perspectives. The combined efforts of all agencies involved in combating delinquency can increase the value and effectiveness of the overall endeavor.

sheldon glueck

eleanor glueck

theoretical implications

Introduction

In considerable detail and variety we have examined the past and present status of the two groups of human beings compared in this work. The descriptive analysis has indicated beyond reasonable doubt that, in all of life's activities considered in this inquiry, the men who as boys comprised our sample of juvenile delinquents have continued on a path markedly *divergent* from those who as juveniles had been included in the control group of nondelinquents. Continuing divergence, virtually always to the disadvantage of the delinquents, has been found during the long follow-up span to age 31 to exist not only in their crime records but in other significant areas of their life activity. It is revealed in the standard of academic education and vocational training ultimately achieved by the two sets of men; in their industrial record (in terms of skills, work habits, and illicit occupations); in their economic status (including the incidence of self-support, de-

pendency, debts incurred); in the various aspects of their domestic relations (including differences in the number of illegitimate children, in attitudes and practices involving assumption of family responsibilities, in family attachments); in their use of leisure (including variance in family group recreations, out-of-home recreations, unwholesome habits); in their companionships (including adherence to antisocial gangs); in their neglect of religious duties; in their conduct in the Armed Forces (including incidence of deferments and discharges for psychiatric reasons and moral unfitness, and the number discharged following general court-martial); in their ambitions and aspirations; and in other respects.

However, one aspect of the trend of consistent divergence between the delinquents and nondelinquents is worth special mention: the variance of the two groups has been shown to be most striking in the finding that, while the majority of the boys originally included in the nondelinquent control group continued, down the years, to remain essentially law-abiding, the great majority of those originally included in the delinquent group continued to commit all sorts of crimes in the 17–25 age-span. Beyond these years, the

Reprinted by permission of the publishers from Sheldon and Eleanor Glueck, *Delinquents and Nondelinquents in Perspective*. Cambridge, Mass.: Harvard University Press, 1968. Copyright 1968 by the President and Fellows of Harvard College.

phenomenon of a drop-off in the incidence of criminality, already noted in our other follow-up studies (Glueck & Glueck, 1940, 1943), suggests, as a provocative hypothesis deserving of special research by physiologists and endocrinologists, the influence of a process of *delayed maturation* (Boyer, Cormier, & Grad, 1966). We consider this in a later section of the present chapter.

Meanwhile, the fact should be emphasized that, while an appreciable proportion of the original delinquents either abandoned crime altogether or became petty nuisance offenders, it still remains true that three-fifths of them were committing serious crimes during the 17–25 age-span and three-tenths were doing so during the second follow-up period. Thus their initial divergence from the nondelinquents in *Unraveling* (Glueck & Glueck, 1950) continued with the passage of time; for in the control group only a few became serious offenders.

Significance of Findings for Etiologic Theory

The basic inference derived from the evidence of continuing and marked divergence of the original delinquent group from the nondelinquent control group in many major aspects of life's activity is this: that the *mass* impact of the external societal environment, or the general culture, is less significant in generating delinquency and extending it into criminal recidivism than are the biologic endowments of the individual and the parental influences of the formative years of early childhood.

In other words, it is not poverty that basically accounts for the original differences and continuing diversity of the two groups; for both sets of juveniles were in circumstances of poverty to begin with.[1] It is not lack of economic and sociocultural opportunity that basically and largely accounts for their original and continued divergence; for both groups were in this respect equally deprived. It is not residence in a slum that is the fundamental cause of delinquency and recidivism; for both groups lived in urban slums (Glueck, S., 1960).

In short, the generalized, unilateral, all-embracing "explanations" of delinquency and recidivism do not adequately explain because they do not *discriminate*. They do not distinguish between a differing response of various *individuals* to many of the potentially malign influences of the slum area, or "ghetto." The external, general culture with which the unilateral theories deal, while reflecting remote influences indirectly involved in the background of both delinquents and nondelinquents, are not nearly so determinative of delinquency or nondelinquency as the quality of the parents and children and the under-the-roof culture of the home.[2]

In reflecting upon the mechanisms of etiology, one must conclude that the all-embracing *constants* in the general environmental situation can contribute relatively little to an understanding of any *individual's* maladjustment to the demands of ethical norms and legal codes. The malign influences of the slum somehow do *not* produce delinquency among the great majority of those who live in such potentially evil communities. Moreover, there are numerous delinquents who reside, not in slums but in "good" neighborhoods, in city or suburb; and the "affluent society" does not always produce happy, contented, and law-abiding children (Pine, 1966). What has as yet not been adequately explored is the extent to which and in what respects parental affectional attitudes and disciplinary practices, family cohesiveness, and parental standards of ethics and behavior in *nonslum* regions vary as between families which contribute delinquent children and those which do not.

It goes without saying that a conclusion of the primary and prime importance of parent-child relations in the guidance and control of childhood and subsequent behavior in adolescence and young adulthood does not

---

[1]Long ago, E. H. Sutherland, an outstanding sociologic criminologist, recognized this fact: "The thesis of this paper is that the conception and explanations of crime which have just been described are misleading and incorrect, that crime is in fact not closely correlated with poverty or with the psychopathic and sociopathic conditions associated with poverty." "White-Collar Criminality," in L. Wilson and W. L. Kolb, *Sociological Analysis* (New York: Harcourt, Brace, 1949), p. 788. He presents the general hypothesis of differential association and social disorganization to explain both white-collar criminality and lower class criminality.

[2]The parents are not merely conveyors of the surrounding general culture, but also its selective filters and modifiers.

mean that general social programs for the reduction of poverty, improvement of slum areas, and extension of opportunity to millions of the disadvantaged and under-privileged are not needed. Strictly speaking, however, this is not the issue under discussion. The issue is rather: which influences are most frequently, potently, and selectively involved in generating delinquency in childhood.[3]

Causation in the Analysis of Delinquency

In connection with theories of delinquency causation,[4] the multidisciplinary evidence of our comparisons of delinquents with a control group of nondelinquents should be persuasive proof that, on the whole, boys having in their make-up and early home conditioning certain identifiable traits and factors which markedly differentiate delinquents from nondelinquents are very likely to turn out to be delinquents, and a substantial proportion of them are likely to continue their criminal behavior at least into adolescence and early adulthood. In this generalized sense of high probability of the origin and persistence of antisocial conduct in the presence of a syndrome of characteristics of person and *intimate milieu* that distinguishes delinquents from nondelinquents in the mass, a rough etiologic relationship has been established in *Unraveling Juvenile Delinquency* and has been confirmed in the present work with the passage of a substantial segment of time.

Thus it is clear that not all the traits and factors arrived at inductively and included in our general etiologic formulation will be found in all delinquents and not found at all in the nondelinquents. For example, the fact that twice as many delinquents as nondelinquents were originally found to be of the closely knit, muscular, energetic *meso-*

---

[3]In the most comprehensive "welfare state" in the world, Sweden, where there are no slums and where the people are "taken care of" from the cradle to the grave, there is a mounting rate of delinquency, illegitimacy, and alcoholism.

[4]We are fully aware of the pitfalls in the concept of "cause." We have always emphasized that we use the term to mean a high statistical probability of etiology rather than an inevitable one-to-one cause-and-effect linkage in each case. For an excellent discussion of the by-no-means simple concept of "cause" in criminology, see Hermann Mannheim's masterly treatise, *Comparative Criminology* (Boston: Houghton Mifflin, 1965), pp. 5-12.

morphic physique type does not mean that mesomorphy per se is inevitably related to delinquency. The very fact that 30% of the nondelinquents were also of such physique immediately contradicts any such notion. Again, such a trait as *defiance,* which one would naturally regard as closely related to delinquent behavioral tendencies, was found to exist in 50% of the delinquents; but 12% of the control group of nondelinquents were similarly characterized; and the very fact that half the delinquent group did not display this trait further reveals the inadequacy of conclusions about "causation" based on a single factor.

Even a small cluster of factors frequently involved in delinquent behavior may not, of itself, have sufficient potency in the light of the other influences involved to tip the scales in the case of boys who manage to remain nondelinquent. Thus, in any realistic sense, the cause of an effect is that *totality of conditions sufficient to produce it.* Persistent delinquency and continuing criminality are not the potential result of only one factor, or even a combination of factors, which markedly differentiates delinquents from nondelinquents, but of each of several varied combinations. Just as death, although always the same terminal event, may be the result of various preceding sequences or combinations of conditions, so the development of delinquency, or continuing criminality, may be the product of a variety of different internal and external conditions which are associated with maladapted behavior; and not all of them are indispensable to the result in any particular case. Despite the variety and complexity of etiologic involvements, however, certain combinations or syndromes of internal and external conditions tend to occur more *frequently* than others; and it is both etiologically significant and preventively and therapeutically useful to distinguish these most frequent syndromes of traits and factors. Such information is of value both in identifying *potential* delinquents at a very early age, when therapeutic-preventive intervention is likely to be most promising, and in focusing on the frequently occurring combinations of influences so that intervention can be pointed and realistic.

In emphasizing that our findings tend to confirm the view that delinquency involves both the biological make-up of the individual offender and his immediate forebears, and the family drama in which he and his parents play leading roles, especially during the first few years of life, we do not mean to ignore certain ideas which have been stressed by some sociologists. For example, we have in the past noted the influence of culture conflict in stimulating violation of social norms in some cases.[5] Again, we recognize the special influences that are involved in the recent rise of delinquency in middle-class and upper-class regions. But such influences—rapid social mobility, conflicts in values and standards, weakening of middle-class and upper-class value systems so that they no longer guide behavior as much as in the past —are two, three, or more stages removed from the immediately and intimately operative ones. For, as previously pointed out, the influences of the culture, and of exposure to rapid change from one subculture to another, are *selective*. Individuals react differently to the impact of cultural standards. That is why such general etiologic theories as the "delinquent subculture," or the working-class or middle-class subculture, or the "interstitial area," or the slum or "ghetto," or the process of "differential association" and other nondiscriminative, all-embracing general theories, do not adequately account for the operative facts in etiology.

Despite the many unwholesome and antisocial features of our culture—its excessive materialism, its stress on "success," its recent overwhelming assaults on values by various mass-communication media, its encouragement of the spread of "literature" of pornography and violence, the weakening hold of the church and formal religion—the majority of people are, in normal times, relatively law-abiding. In the research of which the present study is an extension *(Unraveling Juvenile Delinquency),* we had no difficulty in finding 500 *nondelinquent* boys living in underprivileged and high-delinquency areas of Greater Boston.

In other words, antisocial aspects of culture are only *potential* or *possible* causes of delinquency. Persons of varied innate natures and differing early parent-child relationships respond in different ways to those elements of the culture which they wish, or

are impelled, to *introject,* some of them transforming such cultural elements into antisocial motives. Environment can play no role in conduct unless and until it is, as it were, emotionally absorbed, becoming a part of the motivating force for or against the taboos and demands of the prevailing culture, its values, and its norms. For this reason it is indispensable to study individuals as well as broad social dynamics. Whatever future research may yet disclose about the causes of delinquency in the affluent segment of our society, as regards delinquency among the underprivileged, the emphases suggested by our analyses in the present and in prior works are supported by the facts.

Emphasis on Personal versus Group Influences

In recent years there has been a steadily increasing attack on what is referred to as "barren empiricism" in studies of the etiology of delinquency. There has been a correlative insistence that research into etiology must be "guided by a theory," as in the physical sciences; and it has been assumed that group, class, and cultural approaches are guided by a theory and are therefore more illuminative of etiologic relationships than the study of the traits and factors involving the individual and his intimate under-the-roof milieu. Insistence that theories which center on generalizations regarding group or cultural influences in society are *ipso facto* superior assumes without proof that such an approach is more explanatory and more revealing than the painstaking systematic comparison of delinquents and nondelinquents along many avenues of multidisciplinary exploration. Preoccupation with generalized theories in criminology has thus far yielded rather barren results (Vold, 1958; Glueck, S., 1956). The insulation of some sociologists from the discipline of biology has not helped the situation. Fortunately, there is evidence of a growing interest among social scientists in the relevancy of biological experiments and insights to the more penetrating understanding of social and societal problems. D. G. Glass, an authority in social psychology has recently said:

Contemporary social scientists no longer adhere to a simplistic environmental

---

[5]"Eleanor Glueck found that the social and economic conditions of these second generation children were not more unfavourable than those of their parents, and she concluded that their higher crime rate could, therefore, be due only to their more intense culture conflict" (1937, p. 540).

determinism, just as contemporary biologists no longer embrace a genetic determinism. In both fields the importance of an interaction between the organism and his environment is recognized. Neither the genetic parameter nor the environmental parameter alone can account for more than a portion of behavioral variability.

With the development of an interactional approach, a revitalized interest in the genetics of behavior has been witnessed (Glass, 1967).[6]

Organization of a recent conference sponsored by the Social Science Research Council's Committee on Biological Bases of Social Behavior (and by the Russell Sage Foundation and Rockefeller University) was "guided by the premise that recent advances in research on genetics portend serious social, ethical, and legal consequences in the not too distant future" (Glass, 1967). One of the speakers at the conference (William Thompson of Queen's University, Ontario, Canada) pointed out that behavioral genetic questions are relevant "particularly for patterns of social interaction and aggression. On the basis of a thorough review of animal experiments, he concluded that early in life the organism is capable of being altered in various ways, including changes in its temperament and attitude of social posture toward other members of its species. Later in development the shaping of behavior patterns becomes possible" (Glass, 1967).

Another speaker at the conference (Theodosius Dobzhansky of Rockefeller University) is cited by Glass (1967):

> The stock argument of some psychologists and sociologists is that since educators and social workers cannot do anything about people's heredity they may as well forget it. In reality they can do a lot about it; if they recognize that the human natures are not uniform but multiform, they may take steps to provide conditions in which everybody, or as nearly everybody as possible, is able to do his best.

_____

[6]See also Jacobson and Magyar: "Current knowledge of human genetics is permitting significant advances in medical, moral, and theological interpretations of genetic disease. The clinical management of congenital malformations, infertility, mental retardation, and developmental sexual abnormalities may in the next ten years undergo revolutionary changes, *if* this expanded scientific knowledge is paralleled by pragmatic innovations in the supporting medical and legal institutions of our society" (1967, p. 74).

The last observation puts one in mind of the suggestion for establishing various "therapeutic communities" or "family refuges," such as have been proposed by certain American clinicians and social workers (Tait & Hodges, 1962; Shipman, 1944).

It is indeed encouraging that certain farsighted leaders of various disciplines concerned more or less directly with human behavior are beginning to abandon their "scholarly insularity" and are taking steps to develop a "unified biosocial science" (Glass, 1967). It is in this spirit that we have long urged the indispensability of a multifaceted approach to the problems of etiology, therapy, and preventive techniques in delinquency and crime. In our experience, search for one or another supposedly unifying theory to "explain" delinquency is not only vain in the present state of knowledge, but harmful to penetrating research. G. B. Vold (1958) has expressed it well:

> It is not to be expected that criminological theory will develop wholly adequate and acceptable explanations of criminal behavior until the whole group of "the behavior sciences" reaches a corresponding adequacy of theoretical explanation of human behavior in general. The criminal will continue to be a human being, and his behavior will be only in degree and in special ways different from that of the non-criminal. Hence, criminological theory and human behavior theory in general may be expected to make relatively parallel developments.

In the meantime, it cannot seriously be contended that any unilateral theory of the etiology of delinquency, whether it is exclusively or almost exclusively sociologic or biologic, supplies the comprehensive and penetrating explanation that is needed. The research described in *Unraveling Juvenile Delinquency,* and extended in the present work, does no more than bring together in relatively integrated fashion many individual and social variables that originally differentiated the delinquents from the nondelinquents and that, in many avenues of later activity, continue through the years of early adulthood to distinguish them. There are of course certain traits and factors in which, originally and later, no statistical variance between the delinquents and the nondelinquents was found; but these are not nearly so numerous as those which clearly set off the delinquents from the control group (Glueck & Glueck, 1950, 1966).

Maturation and Recidivism

The importance of biological inquiries into criminologic problems has been discussed. A special aspect of this is one already adverted to—that is, the relation of belated maturation to the abandonment of criminal activities or to change from aggressive, serious criminalism to commission of petty "nuisance" offenses. It was pointed out that there is a significant difference in the percentages of the two sets of men judged as mature by the close of the second follow-up period. In several of our prior follow-up studies as well (Glueck & Glueck, 1937, 1940, 1943, 1945), we came to the conclusion—after ruling out many factors possibly involved (Glueck & Glueck, 1945)—that a major explanation of persistent recidivism must be sought in the lack of maturity on the part of those who, having begun their delinquencies as boys, continued their criminal behavior into adolescence and early adulthood despite all efforts of legally organized society, with its police, prisons, and parole systems, to rehabilitate them. Those men who, in their late twenties or early thirties, did abandon criminality were persons who, after an apparently delayed maturation process, finally achieved enough integration and stability to make their intelligence and emotion effective in convincing them that crime does not lead to satisfaction.

Maturation is a complex process and concept. It embraces the development of a stage of physical, intellectual, and affective capacity and stability, and a sufficient degree of integration of all major constituents of temperament and personality to be adequate to the demands and restrictions of life in organized society. Common experience indicates that, as the average person passes through the various age-spans from childhood, through puberty, into adolescence and beyond, there are certain changes in his development and in the integration of his various physical, intellectual, affective, and volitional-inhibitory powers. Normally, when he reaches chronologic adulthood, the development and consolidation of his physical and mental powers make it easier for him to achieve a capacity for self-control and foresight; to postpone immediate desires for later, less hazardous, and more rewarding ones; to profit by experience; to develop perseverance, regard for the opinion of others, self-reliance, self-respect, and other such attributes useful in adaptation to life, to the demands of society and its values, norms and religious and legal codes; and to avoid drifting into, or persisting in, crime and its frequent consequences of disgrace and punishment, often leading to a point of no return. However, individuals differ in innate biological equipment and organization, and in their early conditioning at home and in school; so that development and integration of powers sufficient to lead to "maturity" are not always achieved at the normal age-spans.

It must of course be recognized that external circumstances which occur with the passage of time contribute to the maturation process. We are beginning a correlation of the findings regarding the maturity status of the delinquents and nondelinquents with data from *Unraveling* and from the follow-up inquiry. The results should illumine the findings concerning the role of both internal and external circumstances in reducing criminal behavior with advancing years.

A psychoanalytic approach to the delayed maturation concept might emphasize that, owing to "fixation" of the "libido" at childhood levels, a clinically recognized "infantilism," or immaturity of personality, not infrequently exists in persons who might otherwise attain a degree of maturity commensurate with persons of their own age. In fact, from many angles the conduct of numerous persistent criminals may be regarded as infantile: witness their impulsiveness; their lack of forethought or clumsy planning; their unrealistic ambitions; their inability to postpone immediate desires for distant goals; their incapacity or unwillingness to profit from numerous experiences of arrest and punishment; their inability to assume marital, familial, and industrial obligations appropriate to an adult age and responsibility; and other signs of immaturity which have been indicated in prior chapters.

In *Later Criminal Careers,*[7] a systematic comparison was presented which indicated that the years from about 25 to 35 are the most crucial in the lives of offenders, since it appears that it is during this age-span that the peak of a sifting-out process occurs, differentiating those who have matured normally from those who are unlikely to reach a stage of maturity sufficient to abandon antisocial conduct and who will either end their days as criminals in jails, or in almshouses, or on the streets. In *Juvenile Delinquents Grown Up,*[8] a comparison was presented of numerous traits and social factors in the make-up and background of the ultimately reformed, as opposed to those of the persistent criminals, originally investigated as boy delinquents, who had passed through the Boston Juvenile Court and had been examined by the Judge Baker Foundation.[9] That investigation confirmed the suggestion made in *Later Criminal Careers* that, during the years which brought the delinquent boys into early manhood, a differentiation occurred between those offenders whose delinquency was probably due more to adverse environmental and educational influences than to any organic weaknesses, and those whose continuing inability or reluctance to conform to the demands of a complex society was more nearly related to innate (though partly, also, to early-conditioned) abnormalities that set limits to the capacity to achieve a socially adequate degree of maturity and adaptability. The former, sooner or later—especially in their late twenties and early thirties—acquire the requisite degree of organic integration of their innate impulsive tendencies, affect, and intelligence; the latter hardly ever achieve a stage of maturity requisite to normal adaptation in our complex, largely urban, society and culture. Despite their arrival at a high chronologic age-level, they continue to be maladapted and to be criminalistic, either seriously or in terms of persistent petty offenses and habitual vices, until they are physically and mentally "burned out," as it were. Misbehavior due in large part (though

not exclusively) to *un*integration gives way to misbehavior related to *dis*integration, until the organism runs down and finally stops (Glueck & Glueck, 1945).

To the evidence of our prior studies involving other samples of delinquents and criminals, there is now added the proof of the situation over the years with regard to the boys who had comprised the experimental delinquent group of *Unraveling.* It will be recalled that, while the original nondelinquents largely continued to be law-abiding as they grew to adulthood, the picture was different for the original delinquent group. However, the portrait was not static, but improved at certain stages. Prior to the 17th birthday, 90.4% of the 438 boys were serious offenders; between the 17th and 25th birthdays— that is, during the first follow-up span—the proportion dropped markedly to 59.6%; but, most strikingly, between the 25th and 31st birthdays, it declined to 28.9%. Thus, it is reasonable to infer that, with the passage of time, long-delayed maturation has come to this group of men, and with this belated ripening and integration of the powers of affect, intelligence, and control, there has resulted a diminuation in the commission of serious crimes. As for petty offenses, it will be recalled that while there were relatively few *persistent minor* offenders, there has been a small rise in occasional petty offenders among the former delinquents from one age-span to another (9.6%, 15.3%, 19.2%).

Since there has been relatively little change in external social conditions in the regions inhabited by the delinquents, the improvement cannot be attributed to this. Thus, it seems imperative that, in addition to the study of societal-cultural influences in delinquency and recidivism, the aid of biochemists, physiologists, endocrinologists, and psychologists be enlisted to focus attention on the *erratic maturation* phenomenon. This may or may not be related to original constitutional variations in physique type or to other findings in *Unraveling Juvenile Delinquency* not yet drawn into the picture, such as disproportion-indexes in various anthropologic measurements of different segments of the body as to which the delinquents were compared with the nonde-

---

[7]1937, Chapter x.

[8]1940, pages 107ff.

[9]Now known as the Judge Baker Guidance Center.

linquents,[10] and the striking differences between them in the pace of growth of the two sets of boys.[11] For reasons such as these, it is especially gratifying to note the recent insistence on collaboration between social scientists and biologists. The problem of *man-in-society* is much too complex to be left exclusively to the single disciplines of sociology, or psychiatry, or neurology, or biology, or biochemistry. We are certain that by systematic collaboration, meaningful advances can be made in the better understanding of delinquency and recidivism. This will mean delay in the development of theory, but the history of criminology has shown that the quest for some all-embracing, unifying theory to explain antisocial behavior has been a failure and has distracted attention from the urgent task of assembling more and more accurate, objective, and comprehensive facts, at all relevant levels.

The delay in theory construction and the imperfection of existing factual studies need

---

[10] *Unraveling Juvenile Delinquency*, pp. 335-339. Dr. Carl C. Seltzer, a highly experienced anthropologist, who was responsible for the anthropometry, concluded: "The individual analysis of the disproportions shows clearly that in seven out of the ten indices *the frequency of disproportions is substantially lower in the delinquent group than in the non-delinquent group.* In one instance the delinquents are more disproportionate than the non-delinquents, and in the two remaining disproportions there are no significant differences between the two series" (Glueck & Glueck, 1950).

[11] "At least as important as the matter of gross body *size* are the very interesting indications with regard to the *growth patterns* of the two juvenile groups." It appears that in the case of many of the measures here studied, the younger juvenile delinquents are smaller in average gross size than the nondelinquents until about the fourteenth year when the delinquents catch up to the nondelinquents, and finally in most instances surpass them as they grow older. In other words, *the delinquents exhibit a lag in physical growth until about the fourteenth year, after which time they begin to show slight superiorities in gross dimensions over the nondelinquents.*

"The really significant growth spurt of the delinquents takes place apparently between the thirteenth and fourteenth years. This is clearly indicated by the fact that in fifteen out of the sixteen measurements there is a greater difference in the delinquents than in the nondelinquents between the mean gross dimensions of the 13-year-old class and the 14-year-old group. It is thus evident from the data that the so-called 'adolescent growth spurt' takes place somewhat later among the delinquents than among the non-delinquents" (Glueck & Glueck, 1950, pp. 316-317).

not cause pessimism in experimenting with individual and social modes of prevention and therapy. It is useful to recall that in the field of medicine much good was accomplished on the basis of mere approximations to etiologic involvements. Until Edward Jenner's discovery of smallpox vaccine in 1798, smallpox took a heavy toll in disfiguration and death. Jenner's great contribution made it possible to control this disease, even though its specific etiology had not been definitely established. Similarly, the efficacy of quinine in treatment of fever was known to the Peruvian Indians for centuries before the significant connection between disease and cure was determined. Cinchona bark was introduced into Europe by the Jesuits in 1632. Soon thereafter it was used by Sydenham, enabling him to differentiate malarial from nonmalarial fevers on the basis of the therapeutic response to treatment with quinine. Yet the "cause" of malaria was not known until 1880, when the French army surgeon, Laveran, discovered and described the malarial parasites in the red blood cells. Thus, during a period of some two-and-a-half centuries, the treatment of malaria by cinchona bark and its derivatives was based exclusively upon empirical clinical evidence. To cite still another example, although the discovery by the Yellow Fever Commission of the United States Army that yellow fever is transmitted by a species of mosquito resulted in the virtual eradication of this disease, its exact etiologic agent was long unknown. The search for the real villain resulted in our day in the tragic death of the great Noguchi.

Bearing such precedents in mind, we do not hesitate, in a concluding chapter, to sketch some suggestions for prevention of delinquency gleaned from the major findings of *Unraveling* and from the present follow-up of the delinquents and nondelinquents, even though "specific causation" will long present many puzzles.

edmund w. vaz

delinquency and the youth culture: upper and middle-class boys*

The present paper explores the youth culture and its influence on private and public school middle and upper-class boys. Limited self-reported data reveal that these boys are peer oriented and are interested in "social" non-academic affairs. Proportionately more private school boys report delinquent acts. A configuration of relatively consistent attitudes towards delinquent situations is evident and suggests, perhaps, new meanings of what is proper and improper among adolescents. Discussion concentrates on the significance of roles and rules in explaining much of this behavior.

Juvenile delinquency among upper-class boys remains shrouded in mystery. So scanty is our knowledge of this group that a public image of the upper-class adolescent is non-existent, and not the barest trace nor suspicion is available of him as delinquent. Although the hard knot of delinquency (behavior that is apt to try any public tolerance) is located in the bottom levels of the working class, limited studies (using self-reported techniques) have revealed delinquency throughout the class structure (Nye, Short, & Olsen, 1958; Vaz, 1966). But nothing is known about the delinquency of boys who attend expensive private schools. Knowl-

edge of the informal handling and special treatment by officials of upper-class boys, the inaccessibility of upper-class institutions, and the absence of a socially recognized image of the upper-class youth as delinquent has, perhaps, discouraged systematic theory and research. But if knowledge is to accumulate in this area, sociological research must pinpoint these boys for study. Both their legitimate and illegitimate conduct must be uncovered and made known, the frequency of their acts, the style that it takes and the conditions under which it occurs. Are there subcultural dimensions to upper-class delinquency? To what extent are these boys peer oriented? Is their delinquency related to the system of roles and expectations among these boys and to the social status of schools (both public and private) which they attend? Are the socially approved interests and activities of these boys the source of their delinquencies? To what degree are certain kinds of delinquency institutionalized among these youths? Answers to these kinds of questions (and these are only a few) are needed if we are to understand and explain the behavior of these boys.

The major focus of this paper is on the attitudes, delinquent acts, and selected aspects of the youth culture of upper-class boys attending private and public schools. But there is considerable overlap in the atti-

Reprinted with permission of the author and publisher from the *Journal of Criminal Law, Criminology, and Police Science*, 1969, **60** (1), 33-46.

*Appreciation is expressed to Central Michigan University for a small grant covering computer services.

tudes and behavior of upper and middle-class boys, and a comparative analysis of this material is presented. Little is known about the legal and illegal behavior of these boys which is good reason for cautious speculation. Our discussion takes us beyond the data offered here; however, an effort is made to bring together and expand some of the ideas discussed in previous work (Scott & Vaz, 1963; Vaz, 1965).

As part of a larger study an anonymous questionnaire was used to gather data from boys (aged 13 to over 19) in five public schools and one upper-class boys' private school located in five Canadian communities. This group consists of all boys in the secondary grades at the time of our visits. However, this paper reports on boys aged 15-19 years only. The communities vary in size from an industrial city of over 100,000 population to residential suburbs and townships. The public schools are situated in typically middle-class areas, the private school in an upper middle-class residential area. Questionnaires were administered under similar conditions in all schools. Multiple methods were used to guarantee anonymity of respondents and necessary precautions were taken to insure honesty and reliability of responses.

Most boys who attend private schools come from the upper end of the social and economic spectrum (Porter, 1965). Today this includes boys from upper and upper-middle socioeconomic strata. Few middle-class families can afford to send their children to expensive private schools.[1] In our analysis three criteria were used for the socioeconomic classification of subjects: father's occupation, father's level of education and the size of organization in which father works. Three socioeconomic categories were established from the Blishen Occupational Scale (Blishen, Jones, Naegele, & Porter, 1961). Using father's occupation, subjects were initially classified into one of three

categories according to the Blishen Scale. Cases that were unclassifiable (where father's occupation was omitted or reported ambiguously) were reviewed and classified according to father's education level. Respondents whose father had undertaken postgraduate university training were classified into category 2; those who had completed university (*e.g.* B.A., B.Sc., etc.) without postgraduate work were grouped into category 3. No difficulty was encountered in the classification of respondents into category 1. All category 1 respondents correspond precisely with the occupations listed in the corresponding category on the Blishen Scale. In this paper categories 1 and 2 are grouped and termed "upper class"; category 3 subjects are hereafter referred to as "middle class." The private school studied in this project does not likely recruit students from the highest reaches of the upper socioeconomic strata. Very likely our private and public school "upper class" subjects come from mainly lower upper and upwardly mobile, upper middle-class socioeconomic levels.

A youth culture is not endemic to a society, but is apt to develop under special conditions. Institutional change in the social and economic spheres of Canada and the United States has made possible the emergence of a relatively prestigious youth culture. Cityward migration from rural areas and the decreasing size of families have characterized both countries (Mills, 1956; Elkin, 1964). The growth of unionization, which helps protect the semi-skilled and skilled from competition from new recruits, and the growth of professionalization which makes entry into these occupations dependent upon "educational qualifications" have helped foster the almost universal consensus that children should remain in school and be kept out of the labor market (Cohen, 1964). Thus, more children have remained in school for longer periods of time which has helped generate a youth culture.

Change has occurred also in family size, role structure (Ross, 1963; Elkin, 1964), and in the redistribution of power in the family. This has given greater individuality and freedom to family members and fostered the proliferation of peer-group contacts among young people. Furthermore, there has occurred an increasing "democratization" of family life in rural, but predominantly in urban areas with the resultant erosion of rules

[1]The private school discussed here is not to be confused with "Preparatory" or "Tutorial" private schools. Although it is not the most expensive of its kind in Canada its tuition fees run over $1,000 per year. The "highest standards" of propriety, personal appearance and "character formation" are stressed, and scholarship is strongly fostered. Discipline in school is regimented through a system of upper-grade prefects. Also a set of regulations for students is distributed to parents who are expected to adhere to its directions. Out-of-town students often live with "masters" which serves as a further control. Modelled after the British "public" school there is a quiet homogeneity about the private institution which is patently absent from the larger, heterogeneous public high school.

governing parent-child relationships in particular (Reisman, 1950), and adult-child contacts in general. Parents now experience considerable anxiety and uncertainty in the raising of children (Heise, 1961; Reuter, 1937). They turn to contemporaries for advice, to the mass media, to "experts," and ultimately, in desperation, to the children themselves (Coleman, 1961). Schools have grown increasingly "permissive" (reflecting change in educational "philosophies") and lack traditional authority. Baltzell writes, "The changes at the [private] school since the war have been far-reaching and progressive. A less puritanical and more permissive atmosphere has been consciously created in order to set a more democratic, tolerant, and possibly other-directed tone to school life" (Baltzell, 1962). In some instances power seems to have been transferred from teachers to pupils (Cohen, 1961). The vacillation in attitude and policy of teachers and high schools towards students, the continual revision of curricula and standards, and the seemingly indiscriminate experimentation with teaching "techniqes" mirror this vast social change. However, it also suggests, perhaps, not so much a commitment to "progressive" education and "scientific findings" as is often alleged, but a desperate search for purpose and stability in education.

A latent function of structural change in society has been the emergent prominence of the adolescent. As a target of exploitation adolescents have been cajoled, flattered, idealized, and have quickly become victim to the glamorizing significance of active participation in the teenage culture (Bernard, 1961). Of course this has greatly influenced the production requirements of big business. But the adaptability of corporate industry through publicity and the mass media has promoted the "needs" of adolescents, and reflects the strategic significance of sustaining the youth culture for the general economy.

Given a prominence perhaps hitherto unknown among young people, the public image of the adolescent has become his own role model. The undue attention and publicity given the fads and collective displays of teenagers and young people, besides their vociferous commentary on the "social ills" of society, serve to alert them to their own conduct and pronouncements as a growing source of power and recognition. Highly sensitive to adolescent affairs, almost any event or opportunity which conceivably might increase their publicity or improve their collective self-image seems to be legitimate prey for the teenage challenge. This has spawned a variety of groups among young people, many of which are perhaps irresponsible, often delinquent. Because standards and norms are in rapid flux, final judgment of these youths and their actions is often postponed. To be a teenager today is to be supremely valuable, and adolescents know this. The status, rights and obligations of the adolescent have become legitimized, morally valid.

The notion of a mass youth culture suggests that it cuts across social class lines and that the majority of young people are unable to escape its dominant themes, interests and values. The "world" of upper-class boys is no longer all of a single weave. For an ever increasing number of adolescents the contemporary high school has become the great leveling ground where differences become largely neutralized, students homogenized.[2] Aloofness is the shortest path to social pariahdom among teenagers. Once a boy enters high school he becomes quickly absorbed with the interests and attitudes of peers and teachers from all social strata, and peers expect enthusiastic participation in their activities.

Not even the private school can escape the mainstream of the teenage culture. Although these institutions often emphasize training in leadership and "character formation" their purpose is subverted by the prevailing youth culture. Today there is often close coordination between private and public schools in education associations, outside programs and intellectual contests. Also the private school population is becoming increasingly diverse, and upper-class "courting mores" have changed; no longer is "steady dating" considered "middle class" (Baltzell, 1962; Mays, 1965). However, all this does not deny the importance of social class for understanding adolescent behavior (Hollingshead, 1949). But class variations in teenage conduct are apt to be more a matter of emphasis than of kind (Bernard, 1961),

---

[2]It is true that under such circumstances marginal differentiation likely takes on special significance.

and in part mirror their respective adult class cultures. Typically this will be seen in the styles of teenage behavior from different classes. Nor does this preclude the emergence of adolescent subcultures, cultural pockets of values, interests and norms sufficiently distinct to set them off from their parent class culture. Although little Canadian data are available, some of these subcultures may be of a delinquent nature.

Previous studies have shown clearly that middle-class boys are often peer oriented, and that they are interested primarily in non-intellectual socially-oriented activities (Coleman, 1961; Vaz, 1965). Although our information is limited to three items it gives us a brief glimpse of these dimensions of upper-class adolescent life and allows us to compare upper and middle-class youths. The first item was used to establish the degree to which these lads were oriented to peers and parents. We asked: "Let us say that you had always wanted to belong to a special club in high school and then finally you were asked to join. But you discovered that your parents did not approve of the club. And since your best friend was not asked to join you would have to break up with your best friend. Which of these things would be hardest for you to take?" (Coleman, 1961).

TABLE 1. PEER ORIENTATION OF PRIVATE AND PUBLIC SCHOOL UPPER AND MIDDLE-CLASS BOYS

| Response Category | Percentages for Boys Aged 15 - 19 | | |
| | Upper Class | | Middle Class |
	Private	Public	Public
Breaking with your best friend	69.0	60.8	54.9
Parents disapproval	31.0	38.5	43.5
Non-responses	0.0	0.7	1.6
Total	100.0	100.0	100.0
N =	58	288	428

Table 1 makes clear that all three groups (especially private and public school upper-class boys) appear more oriented toward peers than parents. This seems to be a common characteristic among contemporary youth (Musgrove, 1964).

The next item enquired into the dating habits of these boys. Each adolescent was asked the following question: "On the average how often do you take a girl out during the week?"

These data indicate that upper-class boys (private and public school both) more often date girls than do middle-class boys.[3] Eighty-five per cent of private school upper-class boys date at least once a week; less than 53 per cent of the other groups do so. The largest percentage of each group dates once a week; proportionately about twice as many private as public school boys date this often.

TABLE 2. TIME SPENT DATING AMONG PRIVATE AND PUBLIC SCHOOL UPPER AND MIDDLE-CLASS BOYS

| Response Category | Percentages for Boys Aged 15 - 19 | | |
| | Upper Class | | Middle Class |
	Private	Public	Public
Twice or more times a week	25.4	20.1	19.2
About once a week	59.3	31.9	27.3
Hardly ever or never	15.3	47.7	53.5
Non-responses	0.0	0.3	0.0
Total	100.0	100.0	100.0
N =	59	287	428

The following item provides some indication of the general interests and youth culture orientation of these teenagers. Each boy was asked to check those items which applied "to most of the boys here at school." Table 3 presents the selected items in rank order of response frequency.

TABLE 3. ORIENTATION OF PRIVATE AND PUBLIC SCHOOL UPPER AND MIDDLE-CLASS BOYS

| Response Category | Percentages for Boys Aged 15 - 19 | | |
| | Upper Class | | Middle Class |
	Private	Public	Public
Interested in girls	77.9	74.3	77.6
Sports-minded	74.5	65.6	70.3
Cut for "fun and kicks"	57.6	49.3	50.9
Crazy about cars	52.5	59.0	65.0
Studies hard	49.1	23.3	30.2
Snobs	28.8	13.5	18.5
Not much interested in school	25.4	37.1	33.1
Non-responses	0.0	0.0	4.0
N =	59	288	428
		$\bar{P} =$ .905	

Table 3 suggests five major points: (a) each group of boys is strongly oriented to girls, sports, cars, and "fun and kicks," (b) proportionately more private than public school boys are interested in "fun and kicks," (c) cars are considerably more impor-

---

[3]Perhaps dating takes on greater significance among boys in a private school where girls are a rarity and students spend longer hours in school.

tant to public than private school boys, (d) proportionately more private than public school youths report that boys study hard in school, and (e) correlatively, public school lads are less concerned with academic matters than are private school boys.

The responses of these boys suggest a commonality of interest among them all. The evidence that considerably more private school boys report that boys "study hard" mirrors the enforced emphasis on academic matters in private school. However, this does not preclude these boys from being influenced by the youth culture. In contrast, the public high school is often the focus of youth culture events, but typically lacks a strong scholastic orientation.

Delinquency among Private and Public School Upper and Middle-Class Boys

In this paper the delinquent acts of boys are self-reported and are taken from an anonymous checklist of behavior items included in a larger questionnaire. Each item is a violation of the law or an offense which could result in official action being taken.

Table 4 indicates that of the 17 delinquency items, 14 are reported by proportionately more upper-class private school boys, two items (car theft and driving a car without a license) by upper-class public school boys, and one item (drunkenness) by middle-class boys. Two items, "serious" theft and "remained out all night without parents' permission," are disproportionately reported by upper-class private school boys. The responses of public school groups (upper and middle class) are very similar on almost each item. A few further points are noteworthy. Petty theft is reported by over 70 per cent and 64 per cent of upper and middle-class boys respectively. We suspect that this type of theft is practiced by all boys, at one time or another, irrespective of social class. Stealing for "fun" is not restricted to lower-class boys. It is more than this. The values of adventure, courage and masculinity are integral components of the male role. Notwithstanding differential class emphasis, they are taught early by all parents, and are something a youngster ought not to overlook to be accepted as a boy. Among boys courage is often an important indicator of masculinity, and petty theft and varying kinds of

vandalism usually validate a youth's claim to "manliness." In a private school where girls are absent the pressures to demonstrate one's masculinity are perhaps at a premium, and situations multiply where these kinds of behavior are encouraged, which helps explain why private school boys are more "delinquent" on most items. The data reveal that petty theft, "serious" theft, fist-fighting, and stealing money are considerably more prevalent among these boys. In the public schools the daily presence of girls very likely serves as social controls, not because girls are especially moral, but because youngsters will neither know (since theirs is a predominantly boy's "world") nor believe that girls steal, and will look upon them as virtuous. Girls define stealing as wrong, and although young boys may ridicule the femininity of girls they will likely respect their virtue and curtail their behavior accordingly.

Our data on petty theft are likely a reflection (in part) of the earlier years of these boys, but as they assume more sophisticated roles, petty theft, vandalism, fist-fighting, and stealing money decrease markedly. We note that gambling, taking a drink, driving beyond the speed limit, and driving without a license, assume more importance for older boys. This might be termed "sociable delinquency" since it tends to emerge from predominantly "social" events. Finally, the data suggest that breaking and entering, being placed on school probation, automobile theft, and purchasing liquor, are relatively unpopular delinquencies among upper and middle-class boys.

Attitudes of Private and Public School Upper and Middle-Class Boys toward Selected Youth Culture Activities

To speak of a youth culture is to refer to a relatively coherent, integrated system of attitudes, norms and values that relates to a distinguishable body of interaction. Our material has suggested that upper and middle-class boys both are peer oriented and concerned mainly with non-academic, fun-laden interests, and that their self-reported delinquencies are often "social" in quality (Barton, 1965).[4]

---

[4]Recent research reveals that both boys and girls of the middle class commit similar kinds of delinquency.

TABLE 4. SELF-REPORTED DELINQUENT BEHAVIOR OF PRIVATE AND PUBLIC SCHOOL UPPER AND MIDDLE-CLASS BOYS

Type of Offense	Upper Class		Middle Class	Upper Class		Middle Class
	Private	Public	Public	Private	Public	Public
			(15 – 19 years)			
	Per cent Admitting Offense			Per cent Admitting Offense More than Once or Twice		
Taken little things of value (between $2 and $50) which did not belong to you	37.9	15.5	15.2	8.6	4.8	2.3
Remained out all night without parents' permission	42.4	27.3	25.9	11.9	11.1	8.4
Gambled for money at cards, dice, or some other game	69.5	68.8	65.4	30.5	35.8	38.8
Taken a car without owner's knowledge	10.0	13.9	11.3	1.6	3.1	3.0
Destroyed or damaged public or private property of any kind	67.8	52.3	52.3	23.8	14.6	14.7
Taken a glass of beer, wine, or liquor at a party or elsewhere with your friends	72.9	65.0	66.4	44.1	34.6	36.2
Tried to be intimate with a member of the opposite sex	49.2	39.2	38.3	15.3	18.4	17.3
Driven a car without a driver's license	59.4	63.2	61.5	30.6	28.9	27.8
Taken little things that did not belong to you	74.5	71.5	64.7	27.1	19.8	15.4
Skipped school without a legitimate excuse	57.7	41.0	41.6	17.0	12.2	14.5
Driven beyond the speed limit	69.4	57.1	48.8	59.3	42.1	38.6
Engaged in a fist fight with another boy	63.8	53.0	58.2	13.8	8.0	9.6
Been feeling "high" from drinking beer, wine, or liquor	37.2	38.9	40.4	22.0	17.8	29.4
Broken into or tried to break and enter a building with the intention of stealing	16.8	9.0	7.7	3.3	.07	1.1
Bought or tried to buy beer, wine, or liquor from a store or adult	33.9	27.1	24.5	17.0	11.4	12.6
Taken money of any amount from someone or place which did not belong to you	45.8	36.8	29.2	11.9	10.4	4.7
Placed on school probation or expelled from school	13.6	7.3	4.7	3.5	1.0	1.1
N =	59	288	428			

$\bar{P} = .956$

The roles that individuals occupy lead them to classify objects, persons and activities in appropriate ways. Customarily the individual defines and evaluates everything in his environment in terms of the significance which it has for him and what he proposes to do with it. When attitudes are integrated about some general class of behavior or social "objects" and include an affective conception of the desirable properties of the behavior or "objects" we may legitimately refer to values (Katz & Stotland, 1959). If we think of values falling along a continuum, at one end we might have those values that are "true matters of conscience," at the other, values that deal with norms of expedience and technical efficiency (Williams, 1951). Not all values and rules that circumscribe adolescent behavior are of the former kind, nor does their violation evoke feelings of guilt. But certain kinds of conduct traditionally defined immoral such as drinking, gambling, physical intimacy and sexual intercourse remain relatively serious matters in the eyes of the community although it seems increasingly unable to control them.

We believe that during an earlier period these kinds of behavior very likely generated feelings of guilt, and provoked considerable anxiety among young people—more so than today.[5] Both the attitudes and behavior of young people have very likely undergone considerable change in these matters. We suggest that never before have these kinds of deviance been practiced on such a wide scale among middle and upper-class youths. And there is little reason to suspect that adolescents of a previous period were more adept at concealing their delinquencies. Firm family controls and the social organization of their everyday lives likely diverted these young people from extensive peer-group relationships and activities which, in turn, precluded them from engaging in widespread deviance of this nature. Discussing young people of the past the Lynds write, "[I]n 1890 a 'well-brought up' boy and girl were commonly forbidden to sit together in the dark. . . . Buggy-riding in 1890 allowed only a narrow

---

[5] Admittedly this is an hypothesis that is difficult to substantiate.

range of mobility; three to eight were generally accepted hours for riding, and being out after eight-thirty without a chaperon was largely forbidden" (Lynd & Lynd, 1937). As for sex, Frederick Allen writes, "boys and girls knew they were expected to behave with perfect propriety towards one another and only rarely did they fail to do so"; indeed, boys followed a code under whose terms "a kiss was virtually tantamount to a proposal of marriage" (Allen, 1952; Goode, 1963; Kinsey et al., 1953).[6] How odd these remarks seem when compared with accounts of the behavior and attitudes of contemporary adolescents. Indeed, the absence of anything resembling a youth culture in the past prevented adolescents from successfully claiming legitimacy for many of the behavior patterns accepted (albeit, sometimes reluctantly) by contemporary parents. Today, activities such as drinking, physical intimacy and other forms of heterosexual conduct are less often true "matters of conscience," and although adolescents are not "morally freewheeling" their attitudes towards these types of conduct point to the emergence of a morality over which they have greater control.

As the youth culture develops and acquires greater importance in the lives of adolescents, particular kinds of conduct—some delinquent—become increasingly institutionalized. The large number of boys who do not disapprove of certain types of delinquency suggests an increase in the institutionalization of this activity, although this is perhaps not yet widespread. This is not to suggest the structural collapse in our system of morals. Nor is the gradual change in morality an adventitious dimension of the youth culture, limited to a segment of especially delinquent boys. Expectedly, the attitudes and values of the youth culture tend towards greater inclusiveness. There appears a configuration of relatively consistent attitudes and sentiments towards delinquent types of situation which reflect what is proper and improper, virtuous and wicked, ugly and beautiful among these youths. This is both cause and consequence of the larger struc-

tural change taking place—an emerging general system of rules and values congruent with the increasingly permissive forms of adolescent conduct. Thus its principal function is its practicality.

The following data, gathered from a set of five items, are hardly definitive, but suggest a direction for future research. Each item is designed as a "life-situation" geared to the level of everyday reality of adolescents and assumed to be typical of the youth culture. The closer one approaches the level of interpersonal relations, the press of circumstances and the fear of consequences become more immediate conditions of conduct. Perhaps these conditions are likely to be more meaningful to the teenager and thereby elicit attitudes correspondingly valid.

Table 5 indicates that approximately 75 per cent of all groups approve of this behavior. As many as 93 per cent of the private school upper-class boys find this acceptable. "Having a couple of beers" appears so widely acceptable one suspects that it is a normative pattern among these boys.

A second item focused on "social" drinking in the company of girls. It is customary, especially among the middle classes, that masculine kinds of conduct (*e.g.* drinking liquor) will be restricted in the presence of women. Responses to the following item point in this direction.

TABLE 5. ATTITUDES OF PRIVATE AND PUBLIC SCHOOL UPPER AND MIDDLE CLASS BOYS TOWARD "SOCIAL" DRINKING

Ralph and a couple of his 12th grade classmates have nothing to do Friday evening. They decide to go for a drive together. There isn't much doing in town, so they return to Ralph's house for a couple of beers, and shoot the breeze together. Later the boys go straight home to bed. How do you feel about this? (Check one.)

	Upper Class		Middle Class
	Private	*Public*	*Public*
I do not approve that they spend an evening this way.	6.8	26.7	24.1
It is alright, I guess, to spend an evening this way.	30.5	30.6	33.9
It is OK to spend an evening this way.	62.7	42.4	41.1
Non-responses	0.0	0.3	0.9
Total	100.0	100.0	100.0
N =	59	288	428

---

[6]In discussing sexual patterns before marriage among adults Goode writes, "Cautiously stated, it seems likely that a considerable increase has occurred in the toleration of certain kinds of sexual or premarital behavior, such as petting or even sexual intercourse, before and after marriage with someone other than the marital partner." However, it is uncertain whether any change has taken place regarding sexual relations with the future spouse alone.

TABLE 6. ATTITUDES OF PRIVATE AND PUBLIC SCHOOL UPPER AND MIDDLE - CLASS BOYS TOWARD "S O C I A L" DRINKING WITH GIRLS

John, Jean, Frank, and Mary are grade 12 high school students. Saturday evening they go out driving together. Everyone is friendly, laughing and joking. Later the boys and girls begin necking in the car. Finally they all decide to return to John's house for a couple of beers and to listen to records. How do you feel about spending an evening like this? (Check one.)

	Upper Class		Middle Class
	Private	*Public*	*Public*
I do not approve that they should spend an evening this way.	23.7	42.0	43.0
It is alright, I guess, to spend an evening this way.	40.7	35.4	32.7
It is OK to spend an evening this way.	35.6	22.6	24.1
Non-responses	0.0	0.0	0.2
Total	100.0	100.0	100.0
N =	59	288	428

TABLE 7. ATTITUDES OF PRIVATE AND PUBLIC SCHOOL UPPER AND MIDDLE-CLASS BOYS TOWARD DRUNKENNESS

You are attending a party at your friend's house Saturday night. His parents are away and he is having some of the boys and girls over. Everyone is enjoying himself. There are records and dancing. Cokes and beer are available and there is food to eat. Later in the evening one of the boys appears to be feeling "high" from drinking too much beer. He is *not* behaving rudely except that he is feeling "high." How do you feel about this boy feeling "high"? (Check one.)

	Upper Class		Middle Class
	Private	*Public*	*Public*
I do not approve of his actions.	27.1	46.6	47.4
It is alright, I guess, since he is at a party.	33.9	19.4	22.9
It is OK. It happens to a lot of fellows.	39.0	34.0	29.2
Non-responses	0.0	0.0	0.5
Total	100.0	100.0	100.0
N =	59	288	428

In this instance it is clear that the major difference in responses is attributable to private school boys who disproportionately favor "spending an evening like this." Yet approval is not limited to this group; over 53 per cent of all boys (upper and middle class) approve of this activity.

Among middle and upper-class families (especially in large urban areas) light drinking in the home among older adolescents is often permitted, seldom condemned, although drunkenness is strongly disapproved. Since a relatively large percentage of boys approve of drinking we should not expect to find drunkenness among peers tabooed altogether.

If private school upper-class boys strongly approve of boys drinking in the company of girls, proportionately few (27 per cent) condemn boys who get drunk occasionally. Although there is greater similarity in the responses of the public school groups, over 50 per cent of all groups approve of this behavior. It is very likely that parties are "special" events among all adolescents during which new attitudes and sentiments are expected and special sets of rules are operative. Under these circumstances drinking and "feeling high" may fall easily within the range of acceptable behavior. At the same time events such as parties and dances are integral to the youth culture and, as the data have shown, there is continuity (with other events) in the attitudes of these boys.

Today heterosexual relationships and dating among young people are considered "healthy" activities, and are strongly encouraged (even during preteen years) by adults. Certain kinds of intimacy such as kissing and "necking" ("once it doesn't go too far") are permitted. Certainly among the upper and middle socioeconomic strata events such as parties, dances and "socials" are organized for early teenage participation. Given these conditions it would be surprising to find many boys (irrespective of social class) who disapprove of some kind of intimacy on a first date. Since boys are very likely to successfully challenge the rules of behavior, advanced kinds of intimacy (as suggested in the item) are apt to be acceptable among all groups. Table 8 shows that differences among groups are small, and that over 63 per cent of all groups approve, at least conditionally, that to "neck and pet" on a first date is acceptable.

TABLE 8. ATTITUDES OF PRIVATE AND PUBLIC SCHOOL UPPER AND MIDDLE-CLASS BOYS TOWARD SEXUAL INTIMACY ON FIRST DATE

Janet and Bob are in grade 12 in high school. They know each other because they are in the same biology class. But Saturday night will be their *first* date together. After the dance, on the way home, Bob stops the car and kisses Janet. Soon he kisses her again and they begin to neck and pet. How do you feel about this? (Check one.)

	Upper Class		Middle Class
	Private	*Public*	*Public*
I do not approve of their actions.	37.3	35.4	31.8
It is alright, I guess, how they wish to act.	40.7	40.3	46.0
It is OK.	22.0	23.6	21.5
Non-responses	0.0	0.7	0.7
Total	100.0	100.0	100.0
N =	59	288	428

TABLE 9. ATTITUDES OF PRIVATE AND PUBLIC SCHOOL UPPER AND MIDDLE-CLASS BOYS TOWARD SEXUAL INTERCOURSE

Carol is a good-looking, grade 12 student. But she has a bad reputation throughout the school. She is known to be pretty free and easy. Her classmate Robert takes her out on a date Saturday night. Before returning home Robert tries to get intimate (go the limit) with her, and *she* does *not* object. How do you feel about Robert's actions? (Check one.)

	Upper Class		Middle Class
	Private	*Public*	*Public*
I do not approve of Robert's actions.	55.9	50.3	48.1
Robert's actions are alright, I guess, since Carol did not object.	33.9	38.2	42.1
Robert's actions are OK.	10.2	11.5	9.8
Total	100.0	100.0	100.0
N =	59	288	428

We have suggested that a change in morality is emerging among these boys and much of our data points this way. But to talk of a developing youth culture and a change in morality is to imply a course of social change, a period of transition during which relatively stable values, attitudes and norms of an earlier era are being recast. It does not imply that all segments of the culture structure change at an equal rate, nor that the values, attitudes and sentiments of young people have been transformed overnight. Given our Puritan heritage some especially "sensitive" areas, such as sexual conduct (rooted in deeply felt values), are perhaps more resistant to change. But as young people gain greater license from formal adult control, and assume the management of their own affairs, they shoulder greater responsibility for their sexual conduct. In the process their sentiments and attitudes are reshaped; regulatory codes evolve, which in turn influence the conduct of sexual matters.

The data reveal that a considerable percentage of these boys approve of relatively advanced stages of physical intimacy. This is not to say that they advocate sexual promiscuity. Sexual congress remains a delicate issue for these boys even with girls of "bad reputation." Table 9 shows that the majority of upper-class boys and 48 per cent of middle-class boys disapprove of the described behavior, and that only about 10-12 per cent approve outright. Yet 34 per cent of the private school boys, and as many as 42 per cent of middle-class boys, agree that sexual intercourse is more or less acceptable.

For centuries in Western society sexual intercourse has been associated with affection (Reiss, 1961). Emergent rules governing sexual patterns among young people are influenced by both previously established and contemporary adult values and conduct. Among boys coitus continues to be associated largely with affectionate involvement. In high school, girls of "easy virtue" are apt to serve as relatively acceptable means of sexual release for a small segment of "outsiders," atypical older adolescents. Perhaps these girls have always served this service. But among adolescents generally sexual intercourse is likely associated with romantic love, and under special conditions is normatively tolerated. "Going steady" certainly legitimates sexual experimentation among teenagers. Perhaps sexual intercourse with love brings little discredit. Unlike the past when girls could "fall from virtue" today they are more apt to slip into womanhood—with confidence.

Discussion[7]

In the past the restricted home life of upper-class children precluded the proliferation of peer-group relationships, and a youth

---

[7]For the ideas in this discussion I am indebted to Albert K. Cohen, his writings and lectures. Of course he is not responsible for their present formulation.

culture as we know it did not exist. The rights and obligations of young people were confined to relatively specific age-sex roles, and the unequivocality of parental roles was well established. Having few outside contacts and associations the child was family-reared (often by a governess who over-emphasized patriarchal and class values) (Baltzell, 1962), and later in the less secular private schools which served principally to ascribe status and socialize their youthful populations. At this time sex was a matter largely hidden from children and physical intimacy among young people was tantamount to sin. Adult dictates for adolescent conduct were entrenched in Anglo-Saxon Protestant morality—a system of rules and values especially functional for a relatively stable class structure where legitimate authority resided in adult positions in the home, school and church. Goals for adolescents were relatively clear-cut and parents believed in the ideals which were taught their children and knew what direction behavior should take. Under these circumstances children were apt to be reared according to widely institutionalized rules, and parental dictates were likely meaningful to existing conditions of adolescent life.

In a fast changing technological world the upper classes have become increasingly "democratized" and heterogeneous. Today adolescent life is much less divorced from extra-class contacts, and ambiguity is evident in parent-child relationships. The "increased concern of parents with *understanding* their children" very likely reflects a desperate bid by parents to do *something* (Naegele, 1961) in the face of their moral ambiguity and the paucity of clear-cut rules for governing their offspring. In many cases schools and other organized clubs have taken over parental duties usually to the satisfaction of parents. In private schools regimentation is enforced by sets of rules for parents to follow with their teenage children. Furthermore, adult groups tend to support the values and sentiments that circumscribe "progressive" socially-oriented education and often endorse the institutionalized practices (dances, parties, dating, "socials," etc.) allegedly conducive to the development of "social competence" and adjustment of the child. In turn this helps sustain the adolescent culture.

The problem of rules is an important feature that helps explain delinquency among middle and upper-class children. Rules refer to classes of events, and as such are difficult to apply to specific situations. They can never be "legislated" (even within the family) to cover each act of the child for every occasion. Nor do we deny the need for discretion. Where uniformity characterizes adolescent roles, and where teenage activities are comparatively limited, widespread institutionalized rules may be more suitable guides for behavior. Such is not the case today. Often parental rules for contemporary adolescents seem especially inappropriate to the kinds and diversity of youth culture activities. For parents to encourage, and thereby legitimate in the child's eyes, active youth culture participation with only a blurred blueprint for behavior, is to leave uncharted a vast range of events for the child. Moreover it is risky to rely on discretion when rules are vague. Under such conditions motives become the sole criteria for establishing deviance. But motives are not always meaningful to others. Within the same social class failure to appreciate another's motives reflects a difference in socio-cultural "worlds." When a teenager explains his wrongdoing by reporting, "We were just havin' fun," adults often consider this meaningless or trivial. But fun can be serious business. What is trivial to the adult is often of consequence to the adolescent. Of course motives are often suspect as when a high school student insists on wearing his hair long for "matters of principle."

When parents rely largely on the discretion of their children there is the presumption that it will not be used towards "bad" ends. But goals often emerge from ongoing situations. Social behavior is a progression of interrelated acts which rotate about the completion of goals. But usually goals are unclear, and in social interaction goals and means are oftentimes fused; what was momentarily a goal the next moment becomes the means towards new goals. Coitus among teenagers is apt to emerge from a relatively prolonged, emotionally packed process under specific conditions. At no point need either partner orient his (or her) actions initially to that end. Oftentimes the final state of affairs is a "shock" to both partners. In such a case motives are not directed towards "bad" ends. When the teenager explains, "I don't know how it happened" he is telling the only truth he knows, that is, sexual intercourse was not his original intention. Where intermediate goals and means are fused in process they are not easily distinguished nor readily recalled. It seems that rules must set limits to discretion. Where rules are unclear, and parents are ambiguous about their roles, yet report (as one father stated) that, "We trust our daughter,"[8] this probably reflects more hope than confidence that "nothing will happen."

But unlike most children in the past, adolescents are no longer subject only to adult rules. Once a youth engages in the teen-age culture he becomes partly subject to its norms. In contrast to parental rules peer-group norms have their origin in the shared mundane experiences of teenagers, and refer to relatively specific situations. Although the youth culture is especially susceptible to fads and fashions it would be wrong to characterize it only in these terms. The normative system not only influences its content, it implies and imposes limits on what is considered proper and improper, moral and immoral, and helps regulate what form social relationships will take. It is commonplace that youths look to peers in matters of fashion, but they are also peer-oriented in academic output, sexual matters, dating and drinking patterns and other delinquent activities. These differentially institutionalized norms reflect a newly emerging morality among adolescents besides implying role expectations of those who claim "membership" in the youth culture.

A rule that is useful and appropriate at one time and for one purpose may well become useless and inappropriate at another time for the same purpose. For example, the broad prescription, "Be a good boy at the party," is apt to be much less meaningful today when applied to typical adolescent experiences. Yet these are precisely the kinds of gross indicators used by parents to guide their children. Does it mean that a boy ought not to hold hands with his girl friend, dance close, kiss good-night, practice different types of kissing and physical intimacy? Perhaps at this juncture peer-group norms become functional for youths, since they relate more precisely to their everyday "needs" and experiences, and also help relieve some

of the anxiety of social interaction. Each of the above steps possesses its own shared understandings, and is important in the dating game, but parents are apt to overlook the normative significance of these "details": rules are either nonexistent or go unspoken because parents are ambiguous about their validity.

To suggest that the freedom of today's adolescents is a result of their manifest maturity and evident sense of responsibility is false. We hold varying expectations about the ability of young people to police their own behavior and exert self-control. Responsibility and self-control are socially defined expectations and obligations of the roles that we occupy and they vary accordingly. But where uncertainty characterizes role expectations, and where the general norms governing adult-child relationships are under strain, this precludes agreed-upon criteria for evaluation. Adamant approval or disapproval of typical teenage conduct is apt to be an isolated posture among middle and upper-class parents since it mirrors role confidence and moral certainty. Parents will approve of the value of dating yet be of two minds regarding "heavy necking"; they will tolerate light beer drinking in the home yet be uncertain whether they are "doing the right thing"; they will endorse social events among young people, but reluctantly tolerate "close" dancing. At the same time no parent wishes upon his child the role of social pariah. Terms are cultural inventions and change over time. Self-control and responsibility are terms no longer easily defined. The adolescent who refuses to participate in typical teenage events because he defines them "irresponsible" is apt to be considered a case for the psychiatrist, not a model of "responsible" conduct. Since our conception of an individual's responsibility for his behavior often corresponds to his self-conception, we might wonder at the standards according to which the contemporary teenager forms his self-image. The ambiguous responses of parents are hardly conducive to the growth of the adolescent self-conception in such terms. Among young people operating criteria for self-evaluation are likely peer-centered.

The conviction in one's own sense of responsibility, "moral fibre" and self-discipline

---

[8]Conversation with a middle-class parent.

is handmaiden also to the kind of socialization that one experiences. When children are reared according to firm moral principles that highlight "character strength" and "moral fibre," as young men and women they will be expected to demonstrate self-control. Moreover, the social structure will tend to facilitate role conformity. Social distance in relationships may be highly valued, peer-group relationships will be minimal, the variety of adolescent roles restricted, and expectations will tend to overlap. Heterosexual contacts will be discouraged and physical intimacy strongly condemned. Dating in the popular sense is comparatively unknown. And behavior is likely defined in categorical terms; children will be either good or bad.

Today children are seldom reared according to clearly defined moral tenets, and the value of industry, moral integrity and "character strength" are often taught in a whisper.[9] If educational practices, rooted in fingertip awareness of moral considerations have grown wobbly, social cues have gained significantly in the socialization of children (Reisman, 1950; Seeley, Sim, & Loosley, 1956). So alien have these values become that they carry an odd ring when discussing adolescent behavior. Since they are not crucial criteria for peer evaluation, the contemporary adolescent seldom defines himself in these terms.

This does not imply that children are reared in a moral vacuum. Remnants of the Puritan ethic still comprise the hazy moral milieu of most middle and upper-class families. But in the midst of rapid social change moral principles are difficult to teach convincingly. Given the danger of being thought radical in matters of propriety, comportment, and affairs political, it is perhaps equally ill-advised to risk being different in morals. With this kind of training one's "moral fibre" becomes flexible, easily adjustable to emerging peer-group requirements. During this period of transition, when values and attitudes are still unclear in society, the majority of youths do not yet experience coitus nor do white-collar boys often engage in victimizing delinquency. We suggest that

adolescents seldom undergo traumatic experiences in moral matters; stages of physical intimacy are learned through role occupancy and are usually taken comfortably in stride according to normative expectations. Moral flexibility allows for easy adaptation to normative teenage activities and relationships, and conformity helps fortify operating norms.

None of this denies the considerable compliance of upper-class adolescents with parental demands. Indeed teenage obedience remains necessary and helps the teenager adapt to the youth culture. Recurrent compliance with parental wishes helps convince parents of the responsibility, maturity and self-control of their children.[10] The comparative absence of assaultive delinquency among middle and upper-class children or the fact that adolescents often stabilize their physical intimacy at a point prior to coitus does not, however, necessarily reflect special self-control. But generally parents are unable to explain behavior in other terms. Reluctant to admit loss of control over their children, and the felt moral confusion of their own roles, they often cling to the time-worn concepts of "character strength," "moral fibre," and self-control. More likely, however, teenage conduct reflects conformity to operating peer-group norms which cover a wide variety of situations, relationships and stages of relationship. Intense participation in peer-group events increases sensitivity to cues, behavior subtleties, and norms of action. Coitus between adolescents is neither "accident" nor loss of self-control, but behavior which falls within a range of relatively permissible acts. If coitus is not prescribed among peers, "going steady" serves to cushion condemnation should it become public knowledge—and teenagers know this. This suggests a further elasticity in the rules governing the conditions under

---

[9]We recognize that changes in "moral fibre" and "character strength" may be especially difficult to measure.

[10]Since many of the "means" and "social objects" crucial for participation in the adolescent culture are either partly or completely controlled by parents, *e.g.* the family car, a boy's clothes, pocket money, and his time, compliance with parental demands becomes necessary. Relatively recurrent obedience to parental expectations leads to predictable accessibility to such "objects" which allows adolescents to plan ahead for future social engagements. Yet it is precisely such obedience to parental wishes that often confounds middle and upper-class parents when they learn of their sons' delinquencies.

which sexual intercourse between adolescents is partially tolerated.

What happens is that the upper-class gets the delinquency that it "deserves." The cardinal values and interests of adolescents contain the seeds of delinquency. It seems to be the case for many boys that attending dances *means* late hours, dating *means* varying degrees of physical intimacy, possession of an automobile *means* speeding, "dragging" and "parking," and "hanging" with the boys *means* rough-housing and special kinds of vandalism. Conformity and deviance among these boys very likely reflect the same set of values, interests and attitudes. What tips the scales in favor of drinking, drunkenness, sexual intercourse or "raising hell" is not likely a difference in values. A boy's commitment to *respectable* adolescent activities is especially important since it includes his self-involvement and his continuing effort to support status-role claims. Equally important, it engages the adolescent in a daily round of teenage events (opportunities for status gain) in which particular kinds of delinquency are potentially possible. We have in mind events such as parties, dating, dances, "socials," sports events, motoring along the highway, "hanging" about the drive-in—almost any teenage occasion where boys and girls participate jointly. At no time are these situations likely defined delinquent nor are their consequences perceived potentially delinquent. The boys' motives are seldom predatory; the interaction is neither shocking (and thereby not inhibiting to others) nor especially serious, but unfolds as a progression of increasingly self-involving and therefore self-maintaining steps. The adolescent is seldom faced with the choice between delinquent and non-delinquent behavior and therefore seldom initiates delinquent acts to help "solve his problem." There is no "problem."[11] The bulk of delinquency among these youths is an emergent property arising from daily youth culture activities. The effort to maintain one's status serves to support the activity and increase joint participation and behavioral innovation. The perceived

risk of delinquency is minimal since the joint activity is seldom begun nor continued for ulterior motives (Lemert, 1964). The prevailing teenage vocabulary helps structure perception under these everyday circumstances.

Active participation in the youth culture helps teenagers achieve status and increases opportunities for further social participation. It also supports parental expectations that their children be "popular," and becomes a major source of motivation for future peer-group activity. The socially active youth who is caught in this normative web of events is pressured to conform or opt out. This choice is not as easy as it may seem, especially where adolescent attitudes tend to reinforce operating behavior. Reversal of behavior at this stage is both difficult and costly for the adolescent. It means the loss of social standing among peers (and is perhaps equally painful to parents), it means the loss of cherished opportunities for desired events, it means the loss of close friends and increased difficulty in dating. It means, no less, a change in "worlds" for the adolescent, and ultimately leads to a transformation in self-conception.

The choice of behavior is not willy-nilly among these boys. The conduct of youths is often their attempt to meet peer-group standards. But it is more than this. There is more than a single role available to boys in the youth culture, and much of their behavior can be seen as an effort to claim particular kinds of roles, at the same time presenting carefully selected selves, or groping behaviorally for a self, for evaluation. The "swinger," the boy with a "style," the "terrific personality," the "grind," the "sports star," and the boys with a "smooth line"— these are social roles seemingly endemic to the youth culture. To be a successful claimant to a particular role means to act in prescribed ways, to hold the correct attitudes, to display the appropriate sentiments, and to avoid the wrong moves. One cannot possess a "smooth line" without accepting the opportunities to practice one's expertise; the role of "sports star" includes both athletic participation, social activities and heterosexual relationships. The "great guy" will be expected to "go along with the boys," "skip

---

[11]By this we mean that among middle and upper-class boys generally delinquency is not a "solution" to any particular common "problem" among them.

school," and engage in a "drag." It will be difficult to be a "swinger" and not "take a drink," or perhaps smoke "pot," while the boy who has a "style" is apt to be preoccupied with the opposite sex.[12] Since peers occupy so much of a teenager's time and comprise a major source of his rewards they gradually become the lens through which he defines his self. What he is and who he is, that is, how successful he is in achieving his self-claims, depend on those sources of rewards, counsel and motivation, *i.e.,* those intimate relationships that help sustain the vital elements in his self-conception. Since the teenager wishes to be seen in as good a light as possible he will not want to jeopardize the allegiance nor provoke the antagonism of peers and thereby "risk losing himself in a total way."

We do not deny the importance of the family in the socialization of these youths, but we have recognized the obscurity of parental roles and rules, and we have seen that many middle and upper-class parents look to other institutions to "complete" the task. Parents are often defined "square" in teenage matters which means simply that their rules and counsel do not "fit" the reality of the adolescent "world." Today adults can seldom agree on what is deviant among many kinds of typical adolescent conduct in the middle and upper classes. Certain activities have become so widespread that society can do little to restrict such conduct. To increase the surveillance of teenagers or severely restrict their freedom is impossible. Given the strategic significance of the youth culture for society both men and boys would suffer. It would handcuff adolescent participation in

the youth culture and dangerously jeopardize the economic and social success of newly emerged occupations and institutions. To impose a stricter moral code on youth (if this were possible) would be to undermine seriously cherished values and beliefs concerning the education and socialization of children. The alternative seems to be to adapt to these conditions. The seriously considered proposal to lower the drinking age is one sign of this adjustment. The teaching of sex in schools is another example of society's adaptation to a situation it cannot otherwise control. The ultimate consequence of this instruction is caught neatly in the motto, "If you can't be good, be careful" (Millar, 1967).[13] Use of the category "joy-riding" as a less serious offense in handling juvenile cases in court is also to the point.

Finally, some writers have noted the sophistication of adolescents who acknowledge their own behavior as a "stage" in "growing up" (Westley & Elkin, 1957). Yet the particular role of adolescent is not apt to be a tongue-in-cheek affair for the growing boy. Strong identification occurs in recurrent interaction with close friends, and disapproval, ridicule or loss of status carries more injury among peers than among others. There is too much at stake for the teenager to "work" his peers (Berger, 1963). More likely is he to "work" one parent against the other to secure his own ends. The ambiguity of parental rules and their considerable ignorance of the adolescent "world" make this especially convenient.

[12]Interestingly, however often a middle or upper-class boy "drags," truants from school or is "expert" with girls in one or another sexual activity, and irrespective of his court appearances for this kind of conduct, he is not likely to acquire the role of "delinquent." The process and functions of acquiring the role of "delinquent" among these boys is in need of research.

[13]Dr. G. F. Millar, chairman of the provincial subcommittee with the sex education program for the province of Saskatchewan, was asked why the new course (in sex education) is being attempted in an already overcrowded school program. He replied: "I readily agree that sex education is the proper function of the home. However, for various reasons, many young people are not receiving sex education from their parents. The result of this ignorance and inadequate standard among young people is frightening. Look, for example, at the statistics for illegitimate births among teen-age girls; they have gone up about 50 per cent in the last 10 years. Then there's the increased incidence of venereal disease."

walter b. miller

violent crimes in city gangs

Abstract: The urban street gang plays a central role in the imagery of violence currently being disseminated by the mass media. Testing the reality of this image requires careful empirical studies of actual gangs. A study involving 150 gangs in "Midcity," a slum district of an eastern metropolis, and focusing on seven gangs subject to intensive field observation, reveals marked differences between the public imagery and research-derived findings. While members of slum street gangs engaged in violent crime to a greater degree than middle-class adolescents, violence was not a central preoccupation of the gangs, and most "violent" crimes were of the less serious variety. Cruel or sadistic violence was rare; violence was seldom "senseless" or irrational. Property damage was relatively uncommon. Participation in violent crimes had little to do with race, but was directly related to sex, age, and social status; most active were males of lower social status during late adolescence. The control of gang violence is seen to involve techniques for altering motivations similar to those which undergird national wars.

The 1960's have witnessed a remarkable upsurge of public concern over violence in the United States. The mass media flash before the public a vivid and multivaried kaleidoscope of images of violence. Little attention is paid to those who question the assumption that the United States is experiencing an unparalleled epidemic of violence, who point out that other periods in the past may have been equally violent or more so; that troops were required to subdue rioting farmers in 1790, rioting tax-protesters in 1794, rioting laborers in the 1870's and 1880's, and rioting railroad workers in 1877; that race riots killed fifty people in St. Louis in 1917 and erupted in twenty-six other cities soon after; that fifty-seven whites were killed in a slave uprising in 1831; that the Plug Uglies, Dead Rabbits, and other street gangs virtually ruled parts of New York for close to forty years; that rival bootleg mobs engaged in armed warfare in Chicago and elsewhere during the Capone era; and that the number killed in the 1863 draft riots in New York was estimated at up to 1,000 men. Nevertheless, however much one may question the conviction that the United States today is engulfed in unprecedented violence, one can scarcely question the ascendancy of the *belief* that it is. It is this belief that moves men to action —action whose consequences are just as real as if the validity of the belief were incontrovertible.

Close to the core of the public imagery of violence is the urban street gang. The imagery evokes tableaux of sinister adolescent wolf packs prowling the darkened streets of the city intent on evil-doing, of grinning gangs of teen-agers tormenting old ladies in

Reprinted with permission of the author and publisher from the *Annals of the American Academy of Political and Social Sciences*, 1966, **364**, 96-112.

244

wheelchairs and ganging up on hated and envied honor students, and of brutal bands of black-jacketed motorcyclists sweeping through quiet towns in orgies of terror and destruction. The substance of this image and its basic components of human cruelty, brutal sadism, and a delight in violence for its own sake have become conventionalized within the subculture of professional writers. The tradition received strong impetus in the public entertainment of the early 1950's with Marlon Brando and his black-jacketed motorcycle thugs, gathered momentum with the insolent and sadistic high-schoolers of *The Blackboard Jungle,* and achieved the status of an established ingredient of American folklore with the Sharks and Jets of the *West Side Story.*

What is the reality behind these images? Is the street gang fierce and romantic like the Sharks and Jets? Is it a tough but good-hearted bunch of rough and ready guys like the "Gang that Sang Heart of My Heart"? Or is it brutal and ruthless like the motorcyclists in *The Wild Ones?* In many instances where an area of interest engages both scholars and the public, most of the public embrace one set of conceptions and most scholars, another. This is not so in the case of the street gang; there is almost as much divergence within the ranks of scholars as there is between the scholars and the public.

One recent book on gangs contains these statements:

> Violence [is] the core spirit of the modern gang. . . . The gang boy . . . makes unprovoked violence . . . [senseless rather than premeditated] . . . the major activity or dream of his life. . . . The gang trades in violence. Brutality is basic to its system (Yablonsky, 1963).

Another recent work presents a different picture:

> The very few [gang] boys who persist in extreme aggression or other dangerous exploits are regarded generally as "crazy" by the other boys. . . . Our conservative estimate is that not more than one in five instances of potential violence actually result in serious consequences. . . . For average Negro gang boys the probability of an arrest for involvement in instances of potential violence is probably no greater than .04 (Short & Strodtbeck, 1965).

A third important work states:

> In [a] second type [of delinquent gang or subculture] violence is the keynote. . . . The immediate aim in the world of fighting gangs is to acquire a reputation for toughness and destructive violence. . . . In the world of violence such attributes as race, socioeconomic position, age, and the like, are irrelevant (Cloward & Ohlin, 1960).

What is the reality behind these differences? The question is readily raised, but is not, unfortunately, readily answered. There exists in this area of high general interest a surprising dearth of reliable information. It is quite possible that discrepancies between the statements of scholars arise from the fact that each is referring to different kinds of gangs in different kinds of neighborhoods in different kinds of cities. We simply do not know. Lacking the information necessary to make general statements as to the nature of violence in the American city gang, it becomes obvious that one major need is a series of careful empirical studies of particular gangs in a range of cities and a variety of neighborhoods. The present paper is an attempt to present such information for one inner-city neighborhood, "Midcity," in a major eastern city, "Port City."

What Are "Violent" Crimes?

The term "violence" is highly charged. Like many terms which carry strong opprobrium, it is applied with little discrimination to a wide range of things which meet with general disapproval. Included in this broad net are phenomena such as toy advertising on television, boxing, rock-and-roll music and the mannerisms of its performers, fictional private detectives, and modern art. Used in this fashion the scope of the term becomes so broad as to vitiate its utility severely. Adding the term "crimes" to the designation substantially narrows its focus. It is at once apparent that not all "violence" is criminal (warfare, football, surgery, wrecking cars for scrap), but it is less apparent to some that not all crime is violent. In fact, the great bulk of adolescent crime consists of nonviolent forms of theft and statute violations such as truancy and running away. In the present report "violent crimes" are defined as *legally proscribed acts whose primary object is the deliberate use of force to inflict injury on persons or objects, and, under some circumstances, the stated intention to engage in such acts.* While the scope of this paper prevents discussion of numerous complex issues involved in this definition, for example, the role of "threat of force" as criminally culpable, an idea of the kinds of acts included under the definition may be obtained directly by referring to Tables 3 and 4, pages 251 and 252. Table 3 delineates sixteen forms of "violent" offenses directed at persons and objects, and Table 4 delineates fourteen legal categories. It is to these forms that the term "violent crimes" will apply.

Circumstances and Methods of Study

Conclusions presented in subsequent sections are based on the research findings of an extensive study of youth gangs in "Midcity," a central-city slum district of 100,000 persons. Information was obtained on some 150 corner gangs, numbering about 4,500 males and females, aged twelve to twenty, in the middle and late 1950's. Selected for more detailed study were twenty-one of these gangs numbering about 700 members; selection was based primarily on their reputation as the "toughest" in the city. Study data of many kinds were obtained from numerous sources, but the great bulk of data was derived from the detailed field records of workers who were in direct daily contact with gang members for periods averaging two years per gang. Seven of these gangs, numbering 205 members (four white male gangs, one Negro male, one white female, one Negro female) were subject to the most intensive field observation, and are designated "intensive observation" gangs. Findings presented here are based primarily on the experience of these seven, along with that of fourteen male gangs numbering 293 members (including the five intensive-observation male gangs) whose criminal records were obtained from the state central criminal records division.

Detailed qualitative information on the daily behavior of gang members in sixty "behavioral areas" (for example, sexual behavior, family behavior, and theft) was col-

lected and analyzed; however, the bulk of the findings presented here will be quantitative in nature, due to requirements of brevity (Miller, in press). Present findings are based primarily on three kinds of data: (1) *Field-recorded behavior*—all actions and sentiments recorded for the seven intensive observation gangs which relate to assault (N = 1,600); (2) *Field-recorded crimes*—all recorded instances of illegal acts of assault and property damage engaged in by members of the same gangs (N = 228); and (3) *Court-recorded crimes*—all charges of assaultive or property damage offenses recorded by court officials for members of the fourteen male gangs between the ages of seven and twenty-seven (N = 138).

The analysis distinguishes four major characteristics of gangs: age, sex, race, and social status. Of the seven intensive-observation gangs, five were male (N = 155) and two, female (N = 50); none of the fourteen court-record gangs was female. Five of the intensive-observation gangs were white (N = 127) and two, Negro (N = 78); eight of the court-record gangs were white (N = 169) and six, Negro (N = 124). The ethnic-religious status of the white gangs was multinational Catholic (Irish-Italian, with Irish dominant, some French, and Slavic). Social status was determined by a relatively complex method based on a combination of educational, occupational, and other criteria (for example, parents' occupation, gang members' occupation, gang members' education, and families' welfare experience) (Miller, in press). On the basis of these criteria all gangs were designated "lower class." Three levels *within* the lower class were delineated and were designated, from highest to lowest, Lower Class I, II, and III. Gangs analyzed in the present paper belonged to levels II and III; the former level is designated "higher" status, and the latter, "lower." It should be kept in mind that the terms "higher" and "lower" in this context refer to the lowest and next-lowest of three intra-lower-class social-status levels.[1]

---

[1]IBM processing of court-recorded offenses and preliminary analyses of field-recorded assault behavior and illegal incidents was done by Dr. Robert Stanfield, University of Massachusetts; additional data analysis by Donald Zall, Midcity Delinquency Research Project. Some of the specific figures in the tables may be slightly altered in the larger report; such alterations will not, however, affect the substance of the findings. The research was supported under the National Institute of Health's Grant M-1414, and administered by the Boston University School of Social Work.

The Patterning of Violent Crimes in City Gangs

Study data make it possible to address a set of questions central to any consideration of the reality of violent crime in city gangs. How prevalent are violent crimes, both in absolute terms and relative to other forms of crime? What proportion of gang members engage in violent crimes? Is individual or collective participation more common? Are those most active in such crimes more likely to be younger or older? white or Negro? male or female? higher or lower in social status? What forms do violent crimes take, and which forms are most prevalent? Who and what are the targets of violent crimes? How serious are they? How does violence figure in the daily lives of gang members?

The following sections present data bearing on each of these questions, based on the experience of Midcity gangs in the 1950's. The first section bears on the last of the questions just cited: What was the role of assaultive behavior in the daily lives of gang members?

Assault-Oriented Behavior

Approximately 1,600 actions and sentiments relating to assaultive behavior were recorded by field workers during the course of their work with the seven "intensive observation" gangs—a period averaging two years per gang.[2]

This number comprised about 3 per cent of a total of about 54,000 actions and sentiments oriented to some sixty behavioral areas (for example, sexual behavior, drinking behavior, theft, and police-oriented behavior). Assault-oriented behavior was relatively common, ranking ninth among sixty behavioral areas. A substantial portion of this behavior, however, took the form of words rather than deeds; for example, while the total number of assault-oriented actions and sentiments was over two and a half times as

great as those relating to theft, the actual number of "arrestable" incidents of assault was less than half the number of theft incidents. This finding is concordant with others which depict the area of assaultive behavior as one characterized by considerably more smoke than fire.

About one half (821) of the 1,600 actions and sentiments were categorized as "approved" or "disapproved" with reference to a specified set of evaluative standards of middle-class adults;[3] the remainder were categorized as "evaluatively neutral." There were approximately thirty "disapproved" assault-oriented actions for every instance of "arrestable" assault, and five instances of arrestable assault for every court appearance on assault charges. Males engaged in assault-oriented behavior far more frequently than females (males 6.3 events per month, females 1.4), and younger males more frequently than older.

Information concerning both actions and sentiments relating to assault—data not generally available—revealed both similarities and differences in the patterning of these two levels of behavior. Expressed sentiments concerning assaultive behavior were about one and a half times as common as actual actions; in this respect, assault was unique among analyzed forms of behavior, since, in every other case, recorded actions were more common than sentiments, for example, theft behavior (actions 1.5 times sentiments) and family-oriented behavior (actions 2.2 times sentiments). The majority of actions and sentiments (70 per cent) were "disapproved" with reference to adult middle-class standards; actions and sentiments were "concordant" in this respect, in that both ran counter to middle-class standards by similar proportions (actions, 74 per cent disapproved and sentiments, 68 per cent). This concordance contrasted with other forms of behavior: in sexual behavior, the level of disapproved action was substantially higher than that of disapproved sentiment; in family-oriented behavior, the level of disapproved sentiment, substantially higher than that of action.

[2]The definition of "violent crimes" used here would call for an analysis at this point of behavior oriented to both assault and property destruction. However, the type of data-processing necessary to an integrated analysis of these two behavioral forms has not been done for "property damage," so that the present section is based almost entirely on behavior involving persons rather than persons and property. Behavior involving property damage was relatively infrequent; 265 actions and sentiments were recorded, ranking this form of behavior forty-fifth of sixty forms; vandalistic behavior was about one-sixth as common as assaultive behavior, a ratio paralleled in officially recorded data (cf. Table 4). Most subsequent sections will utilize findings based on both assault and property damage.

[3]Examples of *approved actions:* "acting to forestall threatened fighting" and "agreeing to settle disputes by means other than physical violence"; *disapproved actions:* "participating in gang-fighting" and "carrying weapons"; *approved sentiments:* "arguing against involvement in gang fighting" and "opposing the use of weapons"; *disapproved sentiments:* "defining fighting prowess as an essential virtue" and "perceiving fighting as inevitable."

TABLE 1. FREQUENCY OF VIOLENT CRIMES BY MALE GANG MEMBERS (BY RACE AND SOCIAL STATUS)

Race and Social Status	Five Intensive-Observation Gangs			Fourteen Court-Record Gangs		
	Number of Individuals	Number of Involvements[a]	Rate[b]	Number of Individuals	Number of Charges[c]	Rate[d]
White L.C. III	66	154	8.4	97	81	8.3
Negro L.C. III	—[e]	—	—	58	39	6.7
White L.C. II	50	40	1.5	72	10	1.4
Negro L.C. II	39	34	2.5	66	8	1.2
	155	228	4.7	293	138	4.7

L.C.III (8.4) = L.C.II (2.0) x *4.2*   L.C.III (7.7) = L.C.II (1.3) x *5.9*
White (5.4) = Negro (2.5) x *2.1*   White (5.4) = Negro (3.8) x *1.4*

[a] No incidents assault and property damage x number of participants.
[b] Involvements per 10 individuals per ten-month period.
[c] Charges on fourteen categories of assault and property-damage offenses (see Table 4).
[d] Charges per ten individuals ages seven through eighteen.
[e] Not included in study population.

Separate analyses were made of behavior oriented to "individual" assault (mostly fights between two persons) and "collective" assault (mostly gang fighting). With regard to individual assault, the number of actions and the number of sentiments were approximately equal (181 actions, 187 sentiments); in the case of collective assault, in contrast, there was almost twice as much talk as action (239 sentiments, 124 actions). Sentiments with respect both to individual and collective assault were supportive of disapproved behavior, but collective assault received less support than individual. Behavior *opposing* disapproved assault showed an interesting pattern; specific actions aimed to inhibit or forestall collective assault were over twice as common as actions opposing individual assault. Gang members thus appeared to be considerably more reluctant to engage in collective than in individual fighting; the former was dangerous and frightening, with uncontrolled escalation a predictable risk, while much of the latter involved relatively mild set-to's between peers within the "controlled" context of gang interaction.

Assault-oriented behavior, in summary, was relatively common, but a substantial part of this behavior entailed words rather than deeds. Both actions and sentiments ran counter to conventional middle-class adult standards, with these two levels of behavior concordant in this respect. Insofar as there did exist an element of assault-inhibiting behavior, it was manifested in connection with collective rather than individual assault. This provides evidence for the existence within the gang of a set of "natural" forces operating to control collective assault, a phenomenon to be discussed further.

Frequency of Violent Crime

The wide currency of an image of violence as a dominant occupation and preoccupation of street gangs grants special importance to the question of the actual prevalence of violent crimes. How frequently did gang members engage in illegal acts of assault and property damage? Table 1 shows that members of the five intensive-observation male gangs on the basis of field records of known offenses, were involved in violent crimes at a rate of somewhat under one offense for each two boys per ten-month period, and that the fourteen male gangs, on the basis of court-recorded offenses, were charged with "violent" crimes at a rate of somewhat under one charge for each two boys during the twelve-year period from ages seven through eighteen.[4] The 228 "violent offense" involvements comprised 24 per cent of all categories of illegal involvements

[4] Four types of "unit" figure in this and following tables. These are: (1) *Incidents:* An illegal incident is a behavioral event or sequence of events adjudged by a coder to provide a sound basis for arrest if known to authorities. Information as to most incidents was obtained from field records. In the case of assault incidents, this definition ruled out a fair number of moderately to fairly serious instances of actual or intended assault which involved members of the same gang or occurred under circumstances deemed unlikely to produce arrest even if known. (2) *Involvements:* Incidents multiplied by number of participants, for example: two gang members fight two others—one incident, four involvements. (3) *Court Appearances:* The appearance in court of a gang member on a "new" charge or charges (excluded are rehearings, appeals, and the like). (4) *Court Charges:* Appearances multiplied by number of separate charges, for example, an individual's being charged at one appearance with breaking and entering, possession of burglars' tools, and conspiracy to commit larceny counts as three "charges." The "violent crime" charges of Table 1 represent fourteen categories of offense involving actual or threatened injury to persons or objects. The fourteen offense designations appear in Table 4, and were condensed from forty categories of police-blotter designations.

(assault 17 per cent, property damage 7 per cent), with assault about one-half as common as theft, the most common offense, and property damage about one-quarter as common. The 138 court charges comprised 17 per cent of all categories of charge (assault charges 11 per cent, property damage 6 per cent) with assault charges about one-third as common as theft, the most common charge, and property damage about one-fifth as common. The total number of "violence-oriented" actions and sentiments examined in the previous section comprised something under 4 per cent of actions and sentiments oriented to sixty behavioral areas (assault-oriented behavior, 3.2 per cent; property-damage-oriented, 0.5 per cent).

These figures would indicate that violence and violent crimes did not play a dominant role in the lives of Midcity gangs. The cumulative figures taken alone—228 known offenses by 155 boys during a period of approximately two years, and 138 court charges for 293 boys during a twelve-year age span—would appear to indicate a fairly high "absolute" volume of violent crime. If, however, the volume of such crime is compared with that of other forms—with "violent" behavior, both actional and verbal, comprising less than 4 per cent of all recorded behavior, field-recorded "violent" offenses comprising less than one-quarter of all known offenses, and court charges of violent crimes less than one-fifth of all charges—violence appears neither as a dominant preoccupation of city gangs nor as a dominant form of criminal activity. Moreover, one should bear in mind that these rates apply to young people of the most "violent" sex, during the most "violent" years of their lives, during a time when they were members of the toughest gangs in the toughest section of the city.

Race and Social Status

The relative importance of race and social status is indicated in Table 1, with field-recorded and court-recorded data showing close correspondence. Of the two characteristics, social status is clearly more important. Lower-status gang members (Lower Class III) engaged in field-recorded acts of illegal violence four times as often as those of higher status (Lower Class II) and were charged in court six times as often. White and Negro rates, in contrast, differ by a factor of two or less. The finding that boys of lower educational and occupational status both engaged in and were arrested for violent crimes to a substantially greater degree than those of higher status is not particularly surprising, and conforms to much research which shows that those of lower social status are likely to be more active in criminal behavior. What is noteworthy is the fact that differences of this magnitude appear in a situation where status differences are as small, relatively, as those between Lower Class II and III. One might expect, for example, substantial differences between college boys and high school dropouts, but the existence of differences on the order of four to six times between groups *within* the lower class suggests that even relatively small social-status differences among laboring-class populations can be associated with relatively large differences in criminal behavior.

Table 1 findings relating to race run counter to those of many studies which show Negroes to be more "violent" than whites and to engage more actively in violent crimes. Comparing similar-status white and Negro gangs in Midcity shows that racial differences were relatively unimportant, and that, insofar as there were differences, it was the whites rather than the Negroes who were more likely both to engage in and to be arrested for violent crimes. White gang members engaged in field-recorded acts of illegal violence twice as often as Negro gang members and were charged in court one and a half times as often. These data, moreover, do not support a contention that Negroes who engage in crime to a degree similar to that of whites tend to be arrested to a greater degree. The one instance where Negro rates exceed those of whites is in the case of field-recorded crimes for higher status gangs (white rate 1.5, Negro 2.5).[5] Court data, however, show that the Negro boys, with a *higher* rate of field-recorded crime, have a slightly *lower* rate of court-recorded crime.

---

[5]This ratio obtains for males only; calculations which include the girls' gangs show higher rates for whites in this category as well as the others. Data on field-recorded crimes on the female gangs are not included in Table 1 for purposes of comparability with court data; there were too few court-recorded offenses for females to make analysis practicable. At the time the field data were collected (1954–1957) Negroes comprised about 35 per cent of the population of Midcity; court data cover the years up to 1964, at which time Negroes comprised about 55 per cent of the population.

TABLE 2. FREQUENCY OF VIOLENT CRIMES BY AGE: 14 MALE GANGS (N = 293): COURT CHARGES (N = 229)

Age	Number of Individuals	Number of Charges[a]	Rate[b]	Assault Charges[c]	Rate	Property Damage Charges[d]	Rate
8	293	—	—	—	—	—	—
9	293	—	—	—	—	—	—
10	293	1	0.3	1	0.3	—	—
11	293	7	2.4	2	0.7	5	1.7
12	293	—	—	—	—	—	—
13	293	6	2.0	1	0.3	5	1.7
14	293	16	5.5	12	4.1	4	1.4
15	293	19	6.5	14	4.8	5	1.7
16	293	26	8.9	21	7.2	5	1.7
17	293	25	8.5	21	7.2	5	1.7
18	293	27	9.2	23	7.8	3	1.0
19	293	21	7.2	18	6.1	3	1.0
20	293	22	7.5	21	7.2	1	0.3
21	293	20	6.8	19	6.5	1	0.3
22	292	9	3.1	8	2.7	1	0.3
23	281	10	3.5	8	2.8	2	0.7
24	247	5	2.0	4	1.6	1	0.4
25	191	7	3.7	6	3.1	1	0.5
26	155	5	3.2	5	3.2	—	—
27	95	3	3.1	3	3.2	—	—

[a] Charges on fourteen categories of offense (see Table 4).
[b] Charges per 100 individuals per year of age.
[c] Categories 1, 3, 4, 5, 6, 7, 8, 9, 13, and 14, Table 4.
[d] Categories 2, 10, 13, 12, Table 4.

An explanation of these findings cannot be undertaken here; for present purposes it is sufficient to note that carefully collected data from one major American city do not support the notion that Negroes are more violent than whites at *similar social status levels,* nor the notion that high Negro arrest rates are invariably a consequence of the discriminatory application of justice by prejudiced white policemen and judges.

Age and Violent Crime

Was there any relationship between the age of gang members and their propensity to engage in violent crimes? Table 2 shows a clear and regular relationship between age and offense-frequency. The yearly rate of charges rises quite steadily between the ages of 12 and 18, reaches a peak of about 9 charges per 100 boys at age 18, then drops off quite rapidly to age 22, leveling off thereafter to a relatively low rate of about 3 charges per 100 boys per year. The bulk of court action (82 per cent of 229 charges) involved assaultive rather than property-damage offenses. The latter were proportionately more prevalent during the 11–13 age period, after which the former constitute a clear majority.

The age-patterning of theft-connected versus nontheft-connected violence and of intended versus actual violence was also determined. Violence in connection with theft—almost invariably the threat rather than the use thereof—constituted a relatively small proportion of all charges (14 per cent), occurring primarily during the 15–21 age period. Court action based on the threat or intention to use violence rather than on its actual use comprised about one-quarter of all charges, becoming steadily more common between the ages of thirteen and twenty, and less common thereafter. At age twenty the number of charges based on the threat of violence was exactly equal to the number based on actual violence.

These data indicate quite clearly that involvement in violent crimes was a relatively transient phenomenon of adolescence, and did not presage a continuing pattern of similar involvement in adulthood. It should also be noted that these findings do not support an image of violent crimes as erratically impulsive, uncontrolled, and unpredictable. The fact that the practice of violent crime by gang members showed so regular and so predictable a relationship to age would indicate that violence was a "controlled" form of behavior —subject to a set of shared conceptions as to which forms were appropriate, and how

TABLE 3. FORMS OF VIOLENT CRIME: FIELD-RECORDED OFFENSES: SEVEN INTENSIVE-OBSERVATION GANGS (N = 205): INCIDENTS (N = 125)

Person-Directed			Object-Directed		
	Number of Incidents	% Known Forms		Number of Incidents	% All Forms
1. Collective engagement: different gangs	27	32.9	1. Damaging via body blow, other body action	10	27.0
2. Assault by individual on individual adult, same sex	9	11.0	2. Throwing of missile (stone, brick, etc.)	10	27.0
3. Two-person engagement: different gangs	6	7.3	3. Scratching, marking, defacing, object or edifice	8	21.6
4. Two-person engagement: gang member, nongang peer	6	7.3	4. Setting fire to object or edifice	4	10.8
5. Two-person engagement: intragang	5	6.1	5. Damaging via explosive	1	2.7
6. Collective assault on same sex peer, nongang member	5	6.1	6. Other	4	10.8
7. Threatened collective assault on adult	5	6.1		37	100.0
8. Assault by individual on group	4	4.9			
9. Assault by individual on female peer	4	4.9			
10. Participation in general disturbance, riot	3	3.6			
11. Collective assault on same-sex peer, member of other gang	2	2.4			
12. Other	6	7.3			
13. Form unknown	6	—			
	88	99.9			

often they were appropriate, at different age levels.

Participation in Assaultive Crime

What proportion of gang members engaged in assaultive crimes?[6] During the two-year period of field observation, 53 of the 205 intensive-contact gang members (26 per cent) were known to have engaged in illegal acts of assault—50 out of 155 males (32 per cent), and 3 out of 50 females (6 per cent). Male-participation figures ranged from 22 percent for the higher status gangs to 42 per cent for the lower. "Heavy" participants (four or more crimes) comprised only 4 per cent (six males, no females) of all gang members. During the same period nineteen gang members (all males) appeared in court on assault charges—about 12 per cent of the

male gang members. While there is little doubt that some gang members also engaged in assaultive crimes that were known neither to field workers nor officials, the fact that three-quarters of the gang members and two-thirds of the males were *not* known to have engaged in assaultive crimes during the observation period and that 88 per cent of the males and 100 per cent of the females did not appear in court on charges of assaultive crimes strengthens the previous conclusion that assault was not a dominant form of gang activity.

A related question concerns the relative prevalence of individual and collective assault. One image of gang violence depicts gang members as cowardly when alone, daring to attack others only when bolstered by a clear numerical superiority. Study data give little support to this image. Fifty-one per cent of recorded assault incidents involved either one-to-one engagements or engagements in which a single gang member confronted

[6]Findings do not include data on property damage. See footnote 2.

more than one antagonist. As will be shown in the discussion of "targets," a good proportion of the targets of collective assault were also groups rather than individuals. Some instances of the "ganging-up" phenomenon did occur, but they were relatively infrequent.

The Character of Violent Crime

What was the character of violent crime in Midcity gangs? Violent crimes, like other forms of gang behavior, consist of a multiplicity of particular events, varying considerably in form and circumstance. Any classification based on a single system does not account for the diversity of violence. The following sections use five ways of categorizing violent crimes: (1) *forms of crime directed at persons* (distinctions based on age, gang membership, and collectivity of actors and targets); (2) *forms of crime directed at objects* (distinctions based on mode of inflicting damage); (3) *forms of crime directed at persons and objects* (based on official classifications); (4) *targets of crime directed at persons* (distinctions based on age, sex, race, gang membership, collectivity); and (5) *targets of crime directed at objects* (distinctions based on identity of object).

Table 3 (column 1) shows the distribution of eleven specific forms of field-recorded assault directed at persons. In three-quarters of all incidents participants on both sides were peers of the same sex. In 60 per cent of the incidents, gang members acted in groups; in 40 per cent as individuals. Fifty-one per cent of the incidents involved collective engagements between same-sex peers. The most common form was the collective engagement between members of different gangs; it constituted one-third of all forms and was three times as common as the next most common form. Few of these engagements were full-scale massed-encounter gang fights; most were brief strike-and-fall-back forays by small guerrilla bands. Assault on male adults, the second most common form (11 per cent), involved, for the most part, the threat or use of force in connection with theft (for example, "mugging," or threatening a cab-driver with a knife) or attacks on policemen trying to make an arrest. It should be noted that those forms of gang assault which most alarm the public

were rare. No case of assault on an adult woman, either by individuals or groups, was recorded. In three of the four instances of sexual assault on a female peer, the victim was either a past or present girl friend of the attacker. Only three incidents involving general rioting were recorded; two were prison riots and the third, a riot on a Sunday excursion boat.

The character of violent crimes acted on by the courts parallels that of field-recorded crimes. Table 4 shows the distribution of fourteen categories of offense for 293 gang members during the age period from late childhood to early adulthood. Charges based on assault (187) were five and a half times as common as charges on property damage (42). About one-third of all assault charges involved the threat rather than the direct use of force. The most common charge was "assault and battery," including, primarily, various kinds of unarmed engagements such as street fighting and barroom brawls. The more "serious" forms of assaultive crime were among the less prevalent: armed assault, 8 per cent; armed robbery, 5 per cent; sexual assault, 4 per cent. Not one of the 293 gang members appeared in court on charges of either murder or manslaughter between the ages of seven and twenty-seven.

TABLE 4. FORMS OF VIOLENT CRIME: COURT-RECORDED OFFENSES: 14 MALE GANGS (N = 293): COURT CHARGES THROUGH AGE 27 (N = 229)

Offense	Number	Percentage
1. Assault and battery: no weapon	75	32.7
2. Property damage	36	15.7
3. Affray	27	11.8
4. Theft-connected threat of force: no weapon	22	9.6
5. Possession of weapon	18	7.9
6. Assault, with weapon	18	7.9
7. Theft-connected threat of force: with weapon	11	4.8
8. Assault, threat of	8	3.5
9. Sexual assault	8	3.5
10. Arson	6	2.5
11. Property damage, threat of	—	—
12. Arson, threat of	—	—
13. Manslaughter	—	—
14. Murder	—	—
	229	100.0

The use of weapons and the inflicting of injury are two indications that violent crimes are of the more serious kind. Weapons were employed in a minority of cases of assault, actual or threatened, figuring in 16 of the 88 field-recorded offenses, and about 55 of the 187 court offenses.[7] In the 16 field-recorded incidents in which weapons were used to threaten or injure, 9 involved knives, 4, an object used as a club (baseball bat, pool cue), and 3, missiles (rocks, balls). In none of the 88 incidents was a firearm of any description used. The bulk of assaultive incidents, then, involved the direct use of the unarmed body; this finding accords with others in failing to support the notion that gang members engage in assault only when fortified by superior resources.

Serious injuries consequent on assault were also relatively uncommon. There were twenty-seven known injuries to all participants in the eighty-eight incidents of assault; most of these were minor cuts, scratches, and bruises. The most serious injury was a fractured skull inflicted by a crutch wielded during a small-scale set-to between two gangs. There were also two other skull injuries, three cases of broken bones, three broken noses, and one shoulder dislocation (incurred during a fight between girls). While these injuries were serious enough for those who sustained them, it could not be said that the totality of person-directed violence by Midcity gang members incurred any serious cost in maimed bodies. The average weekend of highway driving in and around Port City produces more serious body injuries than two years of violent crimes by Midcity gangs.

Data on modes of property damage similarly reflect a pattern of involvement in the less serious forms. As shown in Table 3, in ten of the thirty-seven field-recorded incidents the body was used directly to inflict damage (punching out a window, breaking fences for slats); another ten involved common kinds of missile-throwing (brick through store window). Most of the "defacing" acts were not particularly destructive, for example, scratching the name of the gang on a store wall. Fire-setting was confined to relatively small objects, for example, trash barrels. No instance was recorded of viciously destructive forms of vandalism such as desecration of churches or cemeteries or bombing of residences. The one case where explosives were used involved the igniting of

rifle cartridge powder in a variety store. Of the forty-two cases of court-charged property-destruction, only six involved arson; the actual nature of vandalistic acts was not specified in the legal designations.

Targets of Violent Crime

While much gang violence took the form of "engagements with" rather than "attacks on" other persons, additional insight may be gained by viewing the gang members as "actors," and asking: "What categories of person were targets of gang assault, and what kinds of physical objects targets of damage?" One image of gang violence already mentioned sees the act of "ganging up" on solitary and defenseless victims as a dominant gang practice; another sees racial antagonism as a major element in gang violence. What do these data show?

Table 5 shows the distribution of 88 field-recorded incidents of assault for 13 categories of target, and 37 incidents of damage for 5 categories.[8]

Of 77 targets of assault whose identity was known, a substantial majority (73 per cent) were persons of the same age and sex category as the gang members, and a substantial majority (71 per cent), of the same race. One-half of all targets were peers of the same age, sex, and race category. On initial inspection the data seem to grant substance to the "ganging up" notion; 44 of 77 targets (57 per cent) were individuals. Reference to Table 3, however, shows that 34 of these incidents were assaults on individuals *by* individuals; of the remaining 10, 4 were adult males (police, mugging victims) and one, the female member of a couple robbed at knife point. The remaining 5 were same-sex peers, some of whom were members of rival gangs. There was no recorded instance of collective assault on a child, on old men or women, or on females by males. There was no instance of an attack on a white female by a Negro male. Partly balancing the five cases of collective assault on lone peers were three instances in which a lone gang member took on a group.

---

[7]On the basis of field-recorded data it was estimated that about one-quarter of "Affray" charges involved sticks or other weapons.

[8]Findings are based on field-recorded data only; official offense designations seldom specify targets.

TABLE 5. TARGETS OF VIOLENT CRIME: FIELD-RECORDED OFFENSES: SEVEN INTENSIVE-OBSERVATION GANGS (N = 205): INCIDENTS (N = 125)

Persons	Number of Incidents	% Known Targets	Objects	Number of Incidents	% All Targets
1. Groups of adolescents, other gangs, same sex, race	18	23.4	1. Stores, commercial facilities: premises, equipment	11	29.7
2. Groups of adolescents, other gangs, same sex, different race	12	15.5	2. Semipublic facilities: social agencies, gyms, etc.	10	27.0
3. Individual adults, same sex, same race	12	15.5	3. Automobiles	8	21.6
4. Individual adolescents, other gangs, same sex, same race	8	10.4	4. Public facilities: schools, public transportation, etc.	5	13.5
5. Individual adolescents, nongang, same sex, race	6	7.8	5. Private houses: premises, furnishings	3	8.1
6. Individual adolescents, nongang, different sex, same race	4	5.2		37	99.9
7. Individual adolescents, nongang, same sex, different race	4	5.2			
8. Individual adults, same sex, different race	4	5.2			
9. Individual adolescents, own gang	3	3.9			
10. Groups of adolescents, own gang	3	3.9			
11. Individual adolescents, nongang, same sex, different race	2	2.6			
12. Individual adults, different sex, same race	1	1.3			
13. Target unknown	11	—			
	88	99.9			

These data thus grant virtually no support to the notion that favored targets of gang attacks are the weak, the solitary, the defenseless, and the innocent; in most cases assaulters and assaultees were evenly matched; the bulk of assaultive incidents involved contests between peers in which the preservation and defense of gang honor was a central issue. Some support is given to the notion of racial friction; 30 per cent of all targets were of a different race, and racial antagonism played some part in these encounters. On the other hand, of thirty-three instances of collective assault, a majority (55 per cent) involved antagonists of the same race.

Physical objects and facilities suffering damage by gang members were largely those which they used and frequented in the course of daily life. Most damage was inflicted on public and semipublic facilities, little on private residences or other property. There was no evidence of "ideological" vandalism (stoning embassies, painting swastikas on synagogues). Most damage was deliberate, but some additional amount was a semiaccidental consequence of the profligate effusion of body energy so characteristic of male adolescents (breaking a store window in course of a scuffle). Little of the deliberately inflicted property damage represented a diffuse outpouring of accumulated hostility against arbitrary objects; in most cases the gang members injured the possession or properties of particular persons who had angered them, as a concrete expression of that anger (defacing automobile of mother responsible for having gang member committed to correctional institution; breaking windows of settlement house after ejection therefrom). There was thus little evidence of "senseless" destruction; most property damage was directed and responsive.

Gang Fighting

An important form of gang violence is the gang fight; fiction and drama often depict gang fighting or gang wars as a central feature of gang life (for example, *West Side Story*). The Midcity study conceptualized a fully developed gang fight as involving four stages: initial provocation, initial attack, strategy-planning and mobilization, and counterattack (Miller, 1957). During the study period, members of the intensive-observation gangs participated in situations involving some combination of these stages fifteen times. Despite intensive efforts by prowar agitators and elaborate preparations for war, only one of these situations eventuated in full-scale conflict; in the other fourteen, one or both sides found a way to avoid open battle. A major objective of gang members was to put themselves in the posture of fighting without actually having to fight. The gangs utilized a variety of techniques to maintain their reputation as proud men, unable to tolerate an affront to honor, without having to confront the dangerous and frightening reality of massed antagonists. Among these were the "fair fight" (two champions represent their gangs *a la* David and Goliath); clandestine informing of police by prospective combatants; *reluctantly* accepting mediation by social workers.

Despite the very low ratio of actual to threatened fighting, a short-term observer swept up in the bustle and flurry of fight-oriented activity, and ignorant of the essentially ritualistic nature of much of this activity, might gain a strong impression of a great deal of actual violence. In this area, as in others, detailed observation of gangs over extended periods revealed that gang fighting resembled other forms of gang violence in showing much more smoke than fire.

The Problem of Gang Violence

The picture of gang violence which emerges from the study of Midcity gangs differs markedly from the conventional imagery as well as from that presented by some scholars. How is this difference to be explained? The most obvious possibility is that Midcity gangs were somehow atypical of gangs in Port City, and of the "true" American street gang. In important respects the gangs were *not* representative of those in Port City, having been selected on the basis of their reputation as the "toughest" in the city, and were

thus *more* violent than the average Port City gang. The possibility remains, in the absence of information equivalent in scope and detail to that presented here, that Port City gangs were atypical of, and less violent than, gangs in other cities. I would like in this connection to offer my personal opinion, based on ten years of contact with gang workers and researchers from all parts of the country, that Midcity gangs were in fact *quite* typical of "tough" gangs in Chicago, Brooklyn, Philadelphia, Detroit, and similar cities, and represent the "reality" of gang violence much more accurately than "the Wild Ones" or the Egyptian Kings, represented as the prototypical "violent gang" in a well-known television program.

Even if one grants that actual city gangs are far less violent than those manufactured by the mass media and that the public fear of gangs has been unduly aroused by exaggerated images, the problem of gang violence is still a real one. However one may argue that all social groups need outlets for violence and that gang violence may serve to siphon off accumulated aggression in a "functional" or necessary way, the fact remains that members of Midcity gangs repeatedly violated the law in using force to effect theft, in fighting, and in inflicting damage on property as regular and routine pursuits of adolescence. *Customary* engagement in illegal violence by a substantial sector of the population, however much milder than generally pictured, constitutes an important threat to the internal order of any large urbanized society, a threat which must be coped with. What clues are offered by the research findings of the Midcity study as to the problem of gang violence and its control?

First, a brief summary of what it *was*. Violence as a concern occupied a fairly important place in the daily lives of gang members, but was distinguished among all forms of behavior in the degree to which concern took the form of talk rather than action. Violent crime as such was fairly common during middle and late adolescence, but, relative to other forms of crime, was not dominant. Most violent crimes were directed at persons, few at property. Only a small minority of gang members was active in violent crimes. Race had little to do with the frequency of involvement in violent crimes, but social status figured prominently. The practice of violent crimes was an essentially transient phenomenon of male adolescence, reaching a peak at the age when concern with attaining adult manhood was at a peak. While the nature of minor forms showed considerable variation, the large bulk of violent crime in Midcity gangs consisted in unarmed physical encounters between male antagonists—either in the classic form of combat skirmishes between small bands of warriors or the equally classic form of direct combative engagement between two males.

Next, a brief summary of what it was *not*. Violence was not a dominant activity of the gangs, nor a central reason for their existence. Violent crime was not a racial phenomenon—either in the sense that racial antagonisms played a major role in gang conflict, or that Negroes were more violent, or that resentment of racial injustice was a major incentive for violence. It was not "ganging up" by malicious sadists on the weak, the innocent, the solitary. It did not victimize adult females. With few exceptions, violent crimes fell into the "less serious" category, with the extreme or shocking crimes rare.

One way of summarizing the character of violent crime in Midcity gangs is to make a distinction between two kinds of violence—"means" violence and "end" violence. The concept of violence as a "means" involves the notion of a resort to violence when other means of attaining a desired objective have failed. Those who undertake violence in this context represent their involvement as distasteful but necessary—an attitude epitomized in the parental slogan, "It hurts me more than it does you." The concept of violence as an "end" involves the notion of eager recourse to violence for its own sake—epitomized in the mythical Irishman who says, "What a grand party! Let's start a fight!" The distinction is illustrated by concepts of two kinds of policeman—the one who with great reluctance resorts to force in order to make an arrest and the "brutal" policeman who inflicts violence unnecessarily and repeatedly for pure pleasure. It is obvious that "pure" cases of either means- or end-violence are rare or nonexistent; the "purest" means-violence may involve some personal gratification, and the "purest" end-violence can be seen as instrumental to other ends.

In the public mind, means-violence is unfortunate but sometimes necessary; it is the spectacle of end-violence which stirs deep indignation. Much of the public outrage over gang violence arises from the fact that it has been falsely represented, with great success, as pure end-violence ("senseless," "violence for its own sake") when it is largely, in fact, means-violence.

What are the "ends" toward which gang violence is a means, and how is one to evaluate the legitimacy of these ends? Most scholars of gangs agree that these ends are predominantly ideological rather than material, and revolve on the concepts of prestige and honor. Gang members fight to secure and defend their honor as males; to secure and defend the reputation of their local area and the honor of their women; to show that an affront to their pride and dignity demands retaliation.[9] Combat between males is a major means for attaining these ends.

It happens that great nations engage in national wars for almost identical reasons. It also happens, ironically, that during this period of national concern over gang violence our nation is pursuing, in the international arena, very similar ends by very similar means. At root, the solution to the problem of gang violence lies in the discovery of a way of providing for men the means of attaining cherished objectives—personal honor, prestige, defense against perceived threats to one's homeland—without resort to violence. When men have found a solution to this problem, they will at the same time have solved the problem of violent crimes in city gangs.

---

[9]The centrality of "honor" as a motive is evidenced by the fact that the "detached worker" method of working with gangs has achieved its clearest successes in preventing gang fights by the technique of furnishing would-be combatants with various means of avoiding direct conflict without sacrificing honor.

william c. kvaraceus

delinquency prevention: legislation, financing, and law enforcement are not enough

Current efforts to prevent and control juvenile delinquency are preoccupied with trying to attain improved legislation, a more adequate base of financial support, and stronger law enforcement and police protection, reflecting the myth that the panacea for reducing crime and delinquency rates is better laws, more money, and better trained police —three *necessary but insufficient* means for solving the problem. Certain underlying contingencies or conditions must exist if the combined law-fiscal-police approaches are to achieve their goals of prevention and control. These goals will be realized more effectively and readily (1) *if* the public is willing to "give up" delinquency, (2) *if* the delinquent targets are better defined and differentiated, (3) *if* the community attitude is positive and not exclusive, (4) *if* planning proceeds from a base of knowledge and facts, (5) *if* youth are involved in the solution of youth problems, (6) *if* early identification of future delinquents can be followed by systematic referral for help, (7) *if* agency aims are clearly enunciated and their activities are continuously evaluated, (8) *if* local resources can be effectively coordinated, and (9) *if* the

Reprinted with permission of the author and publisher from *Crime and Delinquency,* 1969, **15** (October), 463-470.

positive aspects of delinquency are not ignored.

If *the Public Is Willing to "Give Up" Delinquency*

The average citizen, beset with his own problems of daily life, seldom reacts to episodes and reports of delinquency with any degree of objectivity or understanding; often he becomes emotionally involved. An informed and disinterested citizenry is a prerequisite to effective social planning. It is the rare community that can achieve this.

Most middle-class citizens live staid and settled lives devoid of excitement or adventure other than what they can purchase through vicarious experience in the sports arena, in a book, or on the screen. Reports and accounts of juvenile "sex orgies," vandalism, mugging, unwed mothers, and drinking bouts can be titillating. It is no accident that the newspapers and other mass media— like the swarm of cameramen in *La Dolce Vita* —record for the adult consumer the vivid details of youth's more sensational violations of the community's norms. The adult provides a good market for such accounts—although he may complain, sometimes ruefully and sometimes bitterly, of the goings-on of today's youth. You can almost hear him smack his lips. On catching himself in this act, he reacts guiltily and frequently turns his wrath on the young rascals who were responsible in the first place for stirring in him these feelings of forbidden delights.

Nor are adults beyond direct exploitation of the delinquency phenomenon. Both political parties have been known to vie for the sponsorship of federal, state, and local conferences and programs aimed at preventing and controlling juvenile delinquency. And, of course, Hollywood has been quick to exploit the "west side story," the "rebels without a cause," and "the wild ones." Even the professional workers in the field are suspect. Note how frequently community fund drives for support of family welfare and youth services are spearheaded by the threat of increased delinquency and maladjustment if contribution goals are not reached.

The pornographic outlets, the crime-comic publishing houses, the prostitution rackets, and the drug channels are not controlled by teenage monsters; they are run by adults (Peep shows, 1969). Coming to grips with delinquency prevention will mean confronting the "responsible" and "respectable" adults who find in the social inadaptation of youth a profitable—even pleasurable—business. It will also mean broadening and intensifying efforts in informing the public of the meaning and implications of norm violation among youth.

If *the Delinquent Targets Are Better Defined and Differentiated*

The term *juvenile delinquent* is a nontechnical and pejorative label; it refers not to a specific diagnostic category but to a potpourri of many kinds of youthful offenders. Few communities bother to define delinquency or to distinguish one kind of delinquent from another. In fact, we do not yet know how many different types of offenders are to be found in the delinquency spectrum. Pure types do not exist, and there are many variants along the norm-violating continuum.

In planning preventive programs, the police and courts must differentiate more adequately among the varieties of delinquent youth. For example, they will have to spot the emotionally disturbed or sick offender for whom child guidance clinic treatment is in-

dicated. They will have to identify the culturally determined offender for whom the delinquent act may represent sportive—even acceptable—behavior when viewed in the light of the value system of the gang or neighborhood. For these youngsters community programs are needed which will change and improve the way of life that is reflected by the norms and values of their subgroups. And of course they will have to be aware of the largest group, a strong mixture of pathologically and culturally determined delinquents for whom a dual treatment program must be envisioned. The boy who steals a car to prove his manhood to his gang and the boy who steals a car to strike back at his parents operate from different motivations, which should be distinguished. Currently, most juvenile courts are prone to place most or all of their delinquents in the child guidance clinic basket.

If *the Community Attitude Is Positive and Not Exclusive*

Apart from the conscious and unconscious exploitation of delinquents, one can sense in the climate of any community five moods or attitudes—Messianic-sentimental, punitive-retaliatory, positive-humanistic, diagnostic-therapeutic, and cultural-reconstructionist—expressed by citizens who are concerned with delinquency prevention. The delinquency prevention and control programs that are "sold and sponsored" will vary considerably according to the point of view that dominates the power structure of city and state. In many state institutions and agencies, the prevailing mood swings back and forth uneasily from retaliation to rehabilitation and accounts for much friction and conflict concerning the most promising approach to solving the problems of youth. Let us take a closer look at these five positions.

The *Messianic sentimentalist* believes there is no such thing as a "bad boy" (until he meets up with two on the same day and thereafter tends to avoid them) and clings optimistically to the notion that all would be well if the youngster could only "be reached" somehow. There aren't many Messianic sentimentalists left these days.

On the other extreme, we have perhaps the most popular stance taken in dealing with delinquents, the *punitive-retaliatory* orientation—the "hard line" or "get tough" school of thought. Today many state officials and a large segment of the citizenry, fed up with the mounting rate of serious offenses and frustrated by the ineffectiveness of "scientific approaches," revert to "sterner measures," including the night stick, the curfew, and the extended sentence to institutional confinement. (This is the official FBI line.) The underlying reasoning is that the offending youngster and his family should not be tolerated or mollycoddled; rather, they should be made to suffer for the error of their ways. Having suffered, the delinquent will have learned his lesson and will sin no more. Although it is true that the delinquent often is hostile and vengeful, he also must face a hostile and vengeful community. Caught up in this mood, the state agencies find themselves playing cops-and-robbers games on a two-way street of hate and hostility.

In contrast to the punitive back-of-the-hand, the *positive humanist* extends a helping hand. Believing that "there are no problem children, merely children with severe problems," he looks for causes but often confuses them with cures. Noting, for example, the kinds of leisure-time habits that are characteristic of young offenders, the positive humanist would hasten to provide more playground space or would use recreation like a flit gun to eradicate the problem. In the meantime, the gang merely shifts its crap game to the lot behind the billboard.

If the school counselor joins with the positive humanist, the mood may swing in another direction. Plans for prevention and control would now recommend the services of the clinical team—psychiatrist, psychologist, and social worker—found in the child guidance centers. This *diagnostic-therapeutic* stance assumes that the delinquent or his parents are emotionally disturbed and require the services of the clinical team. True, some delinquents are sick (to estimate exactly what proportion is difficult) and need medical help within mental health centers, but what proportion of the delinquents seen in the juvenile courts should or could receive the services of these specialists needs to be studied carefully.

However, as indicated earlier, many delinquents are not emotionally disturbed; rather, delinquency is regarded as a normal way of life in their subculture, often representing a route to status and prestige within the youngsters' primary reference group or gang. The *cultural reconstructionist* views the neighborhood or the peer group with its value system as "the patient" to be studied and helped. In this approach, the agency or institution—school, public housing, recreation department, church, Boys' Club, Boy Scout troop, YMCA—is considered a powerful means of cultural change and renewal. In this sense, the agency sees itself as both a creation and an instrument of the culture. The cultural-reconstructionist stance is perhaps the most promising and the most neglected one at the local level.

Depending on the nature of the youthful offender, a case can be made for each of these moods. The danger is that the public and the professional worker often ride only one hobby horse, and different ones at that. There is little doubt that the popular citizen attitude leans in the direction of the punitive and retaliatory, whereas the professional power structure in state departments (mental health, welfare, education, division of youth services) leans toward the therapeutic mood. The law-enforcement agencies, police and courts, are frequently caught between two moods and leap from one to another depending on the pressure from newspaper headlines and letters to the editors. The concerned citizen should not place all his bets on one horse—there are many different kinds of delinquents, and we need different approaches. Even the punitive approach, via consequences attached to certain behavior, can help to prevent certain kinds of delinquency. What is needed is a broad program of public education using mass media (television, radio, press) to inform the citizenry of the relative merits of the various approaches. And at all times, both eyes must be focused on what the research says about the relative effectiveness of different approaches with different kinds of offenders.

If *Planning Proceeds from a Base of Knowledge and Facts*

A community or state agency that makes a commitment "to do something about delinquency" will succeed beyond merely scratching the surface only to the extent to which it becomes knowledgeable at three levels. First, at the level of theory, the worker must conceptualize and integrate a frame of reference of personality and behavior as a form of adjustment to our culture and subcultures. Second, the agency must know the local neighborhood and community situation in which youth live, go to school, play, and work. Third, the agency must come to know, via case-study methodology, the individual offender whom it is trying to help. One of the main reasons for the singular lack of success in community or agency approaches in working with delinquent and predelinquent youth can be found in the lack of knowledge at any one or all of these three levels. If the planned activities aimed at delinquency prevention and control are to be effective, they must always be relevant to the antecedents of the delinquent act. Without adequate information on any of these three levels—theory, community, and individual—workers engaged in prevention and control will run the heavy risk of program irrelevancy.

If *Youth Are Involved in the Solution of Youth Problems*

Youth can be mined as a rich community resource, but in most communities they are a surplus commodity on a glutted market. Juvenile delinquency is a youth problem and only youth can solve it. It cannot be solved by professionals working on their own. Agencies in which adults are the subject of the verb *serve* and youth the direct object will be limited in their attempts to prevent or control norm-violating behavior. Youth must become the subject of *serve,* for only when they begin to serve themselves and the community can we expect to stem the rising rate of juvenile delinquency.

Generally, youths are kept powerless in adult society. They have no vote; they are locked out of significant jobs; they are kept dependent through prolonged education; they are unorganized. Organized power movements on college campuses and some student political groups can be viewed as youthful organizations seeking a voice in decision making. Youth must be organized into a corporate structure in order to communicate and work with other corporate structures in American society, such as schools and colleges, police, labor unions, court systems, health and welfare agencies, churches, etc.

Youth involvement in the containment of delinquency is based on the following assumptions:

1. Every youth needs to feel that there is a significant place for him as an adolescent in his immediate social world.

2. Every youth needs to be able to exercise his intelligence, initiative, and growing maturity in solving problems of real concern to him and to the adult world.

3. Every youth needs to be given an opportunity to learn that his own life situation is not the only one there is.

4. Youth need to be incorporated in order to communicate and deal with the corporate structures maintained by adults in the urbanized, bureaucratic, anonymous society.

5. The emergence of an adolescent subculture characterized by self-directing community participation is not likely to occur without specific and special adult leadership. According to one study (Lukoff, Patterson, & Winick, 1956), adult leadership will be helpful only as it (a) gives supportive guidance—i.e., is responsive to adolescent problems, needs, and interests; (b) is positive and symbolic—i.e., in its behavior encourages identification with relevant values, (c) practices appropriate process manipulations—i.e., is sensitive and effective in both intervention and withdrawal tactics designed to maximize self-direction and community participation.

Youth involvement in community action programs that aim to prevent and control delinquency will be guided by the following working postulates:

1. Self-direction and initiative of youth will be maximized.

2. Participation in vital and significant community activities and operations will be encouraged.

3. The adult role will be supporting and nondirective. The adult theme will be: "You can be free and significant. Go ahead and try; you can count on us to help."

4. The first and major emphasis will be on the development of local units; later development will call for regional and state organizations.

All youths up to voting age should be eligible for participation. This may call for two major (but overlapping) groups—the younger membership, ages thirteen to eighteen and the older segment, ages eighteen to twenty-one.

Effort must be made to ensure two-way communication so that the youths will not lose linkage and identification with their own primary reference group—i.e., to avoid the fink slur.

Participants may be elected, appointed by the governor or the governor's council, the mayor, or other authority (selectman, police chief, superintendent of schools), or designated as representatives by youth organizations. Various approaches should be tried out in different situations to ensure the most representative and active leadership among neighborhood youth. For example, Boston Mayor Kevin White's promising proposal to establish decentralized city halls through a "network of neighborhood service centers" in an attempt to involve more citizens in discussion and participation in the study and solution of community problems can provide a parallel for participation of the junior citizen in the same important participatory processes. To omit the junior citizen would be to overlook a vital source of energy, imagination, and brain power.

If *Early Identification of Future Delinquents Can Be Followed by Systematic Referral for Help*

Delinquency is not a 24-hour malady; it does not develop overnight, but builds over a long period of time. The future delinquent may often give many hints of his coming explosion. Why can't the cities, working through such agencies as the schools, look for early indication of future delinquency and systematically screen out for study and treatment all those youngsters who are prone, susceptible, vulnerable, or exposed to delinquent patterns of adjustment? A number of researchers (Kvaraceus, 1966; Kvaraceus, Miller, et al., 1959) have developed some techniques for prediction, but most of these are still in the experimental stage and require further validation.

If *Agency Aims Are Clearly Enunciated and Their Activities Are Continuously Evaluated*

Many public and private community agencies and institutions, in their sincere concern for troubled youth and in their zeal to help, have tended to deflect from their special aims and unique functions. Out of this confusion of roles has emerged a never-never urban world in which parents act like their youngsters' peers, police in juvenile details are acting like probation officers or recreation leaders, probation officers conduct informal hearings as though they were judges, and juvenile court judges act in the adjudication process like psychiatrists. Other community workers, such as those in the public schools, are taking on omnibus functions, trying to be everything to every pupil. Unless agencies and institutions stop and define or redefine their unique goals and functions and begin to gather housekeeping statistics with which to evaluate their efforts, the result will be seen in a community suffering from institutional schizophrenia. The incipient stages are already visible in many metropolitan centers.

If *Local Resources Can Be Effectively Coordinated*

Implicit in any discussion of local prevention and control programs is the concept of coordination of all community resources so that any child or family requiring help can get the kind of services needed at the strategic moment of need. This assumes that public and private agencies know one another's resources and that they have developed liaison relationships and effective lines of communication. Here is where the big cities with their multiple agencies and institutions—more than 250 in the city of Boston, for example —fail most clearly.

Effective coordination will remain a vain hope or a professional fantasy until the city has established an overall community organization representing all child and family agencies, public and private, with full-time executive personnel trained to plan, coordinate, and steer the activities of this umbrella organization. It is this apparatus that should conduct local surveys and research, do local planning, and supervise continuous review of community needs and results. Youth and lay citizenry should form the core of such coordinating machinery.

If *the Positive Aspects of Delinquency Are Not Ignored*

The communication channels between the adolescent subculture and adults are seldom open and clear. Many youths subconsciously say to the adult world via their norm-violating behavior that "something is wrong" within the adolescent subculture or in the individual personal make-up. A delinquent act may serve as an SOS that the adult community cannot afford to ignore.

Delinquent behavior may also represent the youth's method of coming to grips with reality and with his problems in the best way, even the only way, he knows. The delinquent youngster often is putting up a good but losing fight against great odds. T. C. Gibbens, the British psychiatrist, in an official report to the United Nations, dared to raise the question, "Is juvenile delinquency necessary?" Even if it were possible to eliminate juvenile delinquency, we must face the question, "Is it desirable to do so?"

> There is much to indicate that delinquency is a disorder with a comparatively good prognosis and may represent a valuable safety valve. . . .
> From the wider aspect of mental health, it is arguable whether the elimination of delinquency in the present state of society would not generate more intractable disorders. . . . Where the mental hospital population is large, the prison population is small and vice versa (Gibbens, 1961).

The alternatives to juvenile delinquency may be too awesome to contemplate. However, with the lessons that can be learned from the lives of juvenile delinquents, society can do much to make the community a safer and healthier place in which to grow to maturity.

In Summary

Two major myths concerning delinquency prevention permeate the American scene—first, that "nothing can be done about it," and second, that "somewhere there is a neat and simple cure for the problem." The average citizen frequently finds himself floundering between these two extremes. However, if legislation, financial support, and law enforcement are surrounded and supported by the conditions outlined in this paper, we may have the best prognosis for reducing the steadily increasing rates of serious norm violations among the nation's youth.

References

Allen, F. L. *The big change: America transforms itself, 1900–1950.* New York: Harper, 1952.

Angelino, H. Delinquency: Control and prevention. Paper read at the Southern Regional Education Board Seminar on Crime and Correction, 1968.

Baltzell, E. D. *An American business aristocracy.* New York: Collier, 1962.

Barton. Disregarded delinquency: A study of self-reported middle-class female delinquency in a suburb. Unpublished doctoral dissertation, Indiana University, 1965.

Bealer, R. C., Willits, F. K., & Maida, P. R. The rebellious youth subculture—a myth. *Children,* 1964, **11,** 43-48.

Berger, P. L. *Invitation to sociology.* Garden City, N.Y.: Doubleday, 1963.

Bernard, J. Teen-age culture. *Annals of the American Academy of Political and Social Science,* 1961, **338.** Entire issue.

Blishen, Jones, Naegele, & Porter. *Canadian society: Sociological perspectives,* 1961, pp. 477-485.

Boyer, R., Cormier, B. M., & Grad, B. Statistics on criminal processes. *Canadian Journal of Corrections,* 1966, **8,** 104-119.

Cloward, F. A., & Ohlin, L. E. *Delinquency and opportunity: A theory of delinquent gangs.* Glencoe, Ill.: Free Press, 1960.

Cohen, A. K. *Delinquent boys: The culture of the gang.* Glencoe, Ill.: Free Press, 1955.

Cohen, A. K. Teachers vs. students: Changing power relations in the secondary schools. Public lecture given at the University of California at Berkeley, 1961.

Cohen, S. Foreward to F. Musgrove, *Youth and the social order.* New York: Humanities Press, 1964.

Coleman, J. S. *The adolescent society.* Glencoe, Ill.: Free Press, 1961.

Elkin. *The family in Canada,* 1964.

Empey, L. T. Delinquency theory and recent research. *Journal of Research in Crime and Delinquency,* 1967, **4,** 28-42.

Gibbens, T. C. *Trends in juvenile delinquency.* Public Health Paper No. 5. World Health Organization, 1961.

Glass, D. G. Genetics and social behavior. *Items,* 1967, **21,** 1-5.

Glueck, E. Culture conflict and delinquency. *Mental Hygiene,* 1937, **21,** 46-66.

Glueck, S. Theory and fact in criminology. *British Journal of Delinquency,* 1956, **7,** 92-109.

Glueck, S. Ten years of unraveling juvenile delinquency. *Journal of Criminal Law, Criminology and Police Science,* 1960, **51,** 284-287.

Glueck, S., & Glueck, E. *Later criminal careers.* New York: Commonwealth Fund, 1937; New York: Kraus Reprint, 1966.

Glueck, S., & Glueck, E. *Juvenile delinquents grown up.* New York: Commonwealth Fund, 1940; New York: Kraus Reprint, 1966.

Glueck, S., & Glueck, E. *Criminal careers in retrospect.* New York: Commonwealth Fund, 1943; New York: Kraus Reprint, 1966.

Glueck, S., & Glueck, E. *After-conduct of discharged offenders.* London: Macmillan, 1945; New York: Kraus Reprint, 1966.

Glueck, S., & Glueck, E. *Unraveling juvenile delinquency.* Cambridge, Mass.: Harvard University Press, 1950.

Glueck, S., & Glueck, E. *Physique and delinquency.* New York: Harper, 1956.

Glueck, S., & Glueck, E. Delinquents and nondelinquents in depressed areas: Some guidelines for community preventive action. *Community Mental Health Journal,* 1966, **2,** 213-218.

Glueck, S., & Glueck, E. *Delinquents and nondelinquents in perspective.* Cambridge, Mass.: Harvard University Press, 1968.

Goode, W. J. *World revolution and family patterns.* New York: Free Press, 1963.

Gordon, M. M. The concept of the sub-culture and its application. *Social Forces,* 1947, **26,** 40.

Heise, B. W. (Ed.) New horizons for Canada's children. *Proceedings of the 1st Canadian Conference on Children,* University of Toronto, 1961.

Hollingshead, A. B. *Elmtown's youth.* New York: Wiley, 1949.

Jacobson, C. B., & Magyar, V. L. Toward a better tomorrow. *American Association of University Women Journal,* 1967, **60,** 74.

Josselyn, I. Some reflections on adolescent behavior. *Children,* 1964, **11,** 122-123.

Katz, D., & Stotland, E. A preliminary statement to a theory of attitude structure and change. In S. Koch (Ed.), *Psychology: A study of a science, Vol. 3: Formulations of the person and the social context.* New York: McGraw-Hill, 1959. Pp. 423-475.

Kinsey, A. C., Pomeroy, W. B., Martin, C. E., & Gebhard, P. H. *Sexual behavior in the human female.* Philadelphia: Saunders, 1953.

Kvaraceus, W. C. *Anxious youth: Dynamics of delinquency.* Columbus, Ohio: Merrill, 1966.

Kvaraceus, W. C., Miller, W. B., et al. *Delinquent behavior: Culture and the individual.* Washington, D.C.: National Education Association, 1959.

Kvaraceus, W. C., & Ulrich, W. E. *Delinquent behavior: Principles and practices.* Washington, D.C.: National Education Association, 1959.

Lemert, E. M. Social structure, social control, and deviation. In M. Clinard (Ed.), *Anomie and deviant behavior.* New York: Free Press, 1964.

Lukoff, I., Patterson, F. K., & Winick, C. Is society the patient: Research and action implications. *Journal of Educational Sociology,* 1956, **70,** 106-107.

Lynd, R. S., & Lynd, H. M. *Middletown in transition.* New York: Harcourt, 1937.

Mays, J. B. *The young pretenders.* New York: Schocken, 1965.

Millar, G. F. *The globe and mail.* Toronto, Jan. 21, 1967.

Miller, W. B. Lower class culture as a generating milieu of gang delinquency. *Journal of Social Issues,* 1957, **14,** 5-19.

Miller, W. B. *City gangs.* New York: Wiley, in press.

Mills, C. W. *White collar.* New York: Oxford University Press, 1956.

Musgrove, F. *Youth and the social order.* New York: Humanities Press, 1964.

Naegele. Children in Canada—past and present. In B. W. Heise (Ed.), New horizons for Canada's children. *Proceedings of the 1st Canadian Conference on Children,* University of Toronto, 1961.

Nye, F. I., Short, J. F., Jr., & Olsen, V. J. Socioeconomic status and delinquent behavior. *American Journal of Sociology,* 1958, **63,** 318-329.

Ogburn, W. F. Why the family is changing. In H. L. Ross (Ed.), *Perspectives on the social order: Readings in sociology.* New York: McGraw-Hill, 1963.

Peep shows have new nude look. *New York Times,* June 9, 1969, p. 58.

Pine, G. U. The affluent delinquent. *Phi Delta Kappan,* 1966.

Porter, J. *The vertical mosaic,* Toronto: University of Toronto Press, 1965.

Project innovation: Seeking new answers to the prevention and control of juvenile delinquency. Washington, D.C.: U.S. Department of Health, Education and Welfare, 1966.

Reisman, D. *The lonely crowd.* New Haven, Conn.: Yale University Press, 1950.

Reiss, I. L. Sexual codes in teen-age culture. *Annals of the American Academy of Political and Social Science,* 1961, **338,** 53-62.

Reuter, The sociology of adolescence. *American Journal of Sociology,* 1937, **43.**

Ross, H. L. (Ed.) *Perspectives on the social order: Readings in sociology.* New York: McGraw-Hill, 1963.

Scott, J. W., & Vaz, E. W. A perspective on middle-class delinquency. *Canadian Journal of Economics and Political Science,* 1963, **29,** 324-335.

Seeley, J. R., Sim, R. A., & Loosley, E. W. *Crestwood Heights.* New York: Basic Books, 1956.

Sheldon, W. Brief communication on objectification of the somatotype and on the primary psychiatric components. Paper read at the Royal Medico-Psychological Association, London, 1965.

Shipman, G. Probation and the family. *Probation,* 1944, **23,** 106-114.

Short, J. F., & Strodtbeck, F. L. *Group process and gang delinquency.* Chicago: University of Chicago Press, 1965.

Tait, C. D., Jr., & Hodges, E. F. Delinquents, their families, and the community. Springfield, Ill.: Thomas, 1962.

Vaz, E. W. Middle-class adolescents: Self-reported delinquency and youth culture activities. *Canadian Review of Sociology and Anthropology,* 1965, **2,** 52-70.

Vaz, E. W. Self-reported juvenile delinquency and socioeconomic status. *Canadian Journal of Correction,* 1966, **8,** 20.

Vold, G. B. *Theoretical criminology.* New York: Oxford University Press, 1958.

Westley, W. A., & Elkin, F. The protection environment and adolescent socialization. *Social Forces,* 1957, **35,** 243-249.

Williams, R. M., Jr. *American society.* New York: Knopf, 1951.

Yablonsky, L. *The violent gang.* New York: Macmillan, 1963.

Annotations

Cope, W. H. Combatting juvenile delinquency. *Police,* 1969, **13,** 60-64. The author suggests, from a law enforcement perspective, ways in which the problem of juvenile delinquency can be handled. He discusses some hope for prevention in early detection of delinquency traits. He cites a need for more flexible treatment of delinquents and feels that there is shifting role for juvenile workers. He urges closer family relationships as one means of curbing delinquency. Greater education, housing, and employment opportunities may also have positive effects on combating delinquency.

Empey, L. T. Delinquency theory and recent research. *Journal of Research in Crime and Delinquency,* 1967, **4,** 28-42. Most of Empey's article is based on (1) social-class theories, (2) dimension of group delinquency theories, (3) and the delinquent subculture theory. This article is a good companion to the one reprinted in this chapter.

Gold, M. *Delinquent behavior in an American city.* Belmont, Calif.: Brooks/Cole, 1970. Gold made a large-scale study of juvenile delinquency in Flint, Michigan. The book focuses on the character and distribution of delinquent behaviors. Two other major considerations are delinquent companions and risk-taking or getting caught. Throughout each chapter Gold presents actual delinquent cases that add relevance to his points. In conclusion he discusses the dynamics of delinquency.

Gould, L. C. Juvenile entrepreneurs. *American Journal of Sociology,* 1969, **74.** This paper tested four variables: (1) delinquent associations, (2) perception of opportunity, (3) social class, and (4) achievement motivation among delinquent high school students. The author found that delinquent associations and perception of opportunity were consequences rather than causes of delinquency. Achievement motivation, which precedes delinquency, had the strongest direct effect on delinquent behavior among working-class and lower-class youths.

Kulik, J. A., Stein, K. B., & Sarbin, T. R. Dimensions and patterns of adolescent antisocial behavior. *Journal of Consulting and Clinical Psychology,* 1968, **32,** 375-382. This article is based on a self-reported checklist filled out by delinquent and nondelinquent high school boys. Findings indicate that antisocial behavior usually involves retreatist activity (drugs) and conflict patterns of behavior. Conflict with parents played an important role in provoking antisocial behavior.

Martin, J. M., Fitzpatrick, J. P., & Gould, R. E. *Analyzing delinquent behavior: A new approach.* Washington, D.C.: Government Printing Office, 1968. The authors suggest that the causes of delinquency and crime can be found in the social and political inequalities of our society. This view, explained in detail in this pamphlet, is an attempt to replace the theory that delinquency stems from individual pathology and personal failure.

Pearce, J., & Garrett, H. D. A comparison of the drinking behavior of delinquent youth versus nondelinquent youth in the states of Idaho and Utah. *Journal of School Health,* 1970, **40,** 131-135. The majority of all youths begin their drinking experiences with beer. Nondelinquents are more likely to drink at home—often with parental permission. Delinquent girls drink as often as delinquent boys. Delinquents drink earlier and more frequently than nondelinquents and are more likely to get drunk and be arrested.

Pine, G. J. The affluent delinquent. *Phi Delta Kappan,* 1966, **48,** 138-143. Delinquent behavior among the middle and upper classes tends to be hidden more than it is among the culturally and economically disadvantaged. Pine postulates ten interesting hypotheses regarding the manner and causes of affluent delinquency. Such factors as (1) bias on official reports, (2) mobility, (3) a female-based household, and (4) the "sheepskin psychosis" are possible contributors to affluent delinquency.

Polk, K., & Halferty, D. S. Adolescence, commitment, and delinquency. *Journal of Research in Crime and Delinquency,* 1966, **3,** 82-96. This article looks at the dimensions of adolescent behavior by examining the attitudes of 410 male high school students. Results show a positive relationship between delinquency and peer-group commitment. The study also confirms acceptance of peer pressure over adult pressure.

Vaz, E. W. (Ed.) *Middle-class juvenile delinquency.* New York: Harper, 1967. This compilation of 19 articles by leading researchers in the field deals with (1) the adolescent subculture, (2) the relationship between socioeconomic status and juvenile delinquency, and (3) patterns of middle-class delinquency.

Wolfgang, M. E. *The culture of youth.* Washington, D.C.: Government Printing Office, 1967. This brief pamphlet from the Office of Juvenile Delinquency and Youth Development presents an interesting theory of masculinity. Physical aggressiveness, once the manifest feature of maleness, is being reduced, and the meaning of masculinity is becoming more symbolic. If one combines this shift of emphasis in the general culture with the lack of a male model among most lower-class youth, it is not surprising that such youths act out and thus equate maleness with overt physical aggression. The boys assert their masculinity by rejecting female dominance as well as the morality they associate with women.

eight

the adolescent and drugs

The relatively new social phenomenon of drug use is imposing special problems on our society and on the behavioral scientists who work with adolescents and young adults. Many inexperienced youths, still in the trial-and-error stage of adolescence, will eat, drink, smoke, or sniff almost anything that promises to yield thrills. Some adolescents use drugs as a means of escape from our society. Still others find drugs an acceptable way of rebelling. Whatever their reason, most of them derive social reinforcement for their behavior.

Alcohol

Alcohol use in the adult society has become widely accepted and socially approved. Because alcohol is legal, few persons think of the harmful effects it can have on the consumer. Alcohol acts on the nervous system as a depressant—that is, it depresses the power of restraint. When enough alcohol has entered a person's system, he loses his inhibitions and often behaves differently than he normally does.

Alcohol has a strong addictive power and can be harmful to the body. There are 80 million alcohol users in the United States today—6 million of whom are alcoholics. Cirrhosis of the liver, a major effect of alcoholism (Keller, 1962), is the sixth leading cause of death in the United States and accounts for more than 25 percent of all liver diseases (Fort, 1968; Keller, 1962; Room, 1968). Moreover, in 1968 between 50 percent and 70 percent of all highway deaths in this country were attributed to excessive quantities of alcohol (Fort, 1968).

Much adolescent group activity is associated with drinking, most of which occurs within the homes of friends (Skolnick, 1958) or at parties and beer busts. In the first article in this chapter, Alexander indicates that teen-age drinking may constitute an expression of hostility toward the authority of society, or it may provide a means for expressing aggression against some individual who represents that authority. Alexander has expressed the fear that drinking may thus become a symbol of rebelliousness and independence.

Drug Classification

The second article in this chapter, by Strack, is an overview of all drugs currently being used by adolescents. His discussion of opiates, depressants, stimulants, hallucinogens, and solvents includes a description of the physical and psychological effects of each drug and an analysis of methods of treatment.

Smith (1969), a physician who is well known for his work in the Haight-Ashbury section of San Francisco, has classified drugs a little differently. His categories are (1) sedative-hypnotic drugs, including alcohol, barbiturates, and marijuana; (2) narcotics, such as opium, heroin, morphine, and codeine; (3) central-nervous-system stimulants, ranging from nicotine and caffeine to the amphetamines; and (4) psychedelic drugs, such as LSD, STP, PCP, and a cannabis ingredient known as THC.

TIME Magazine (Pop drugs, 1969) has listed drugs according to the danger they are most likely to produce. The hierarchy is as follows:

1. *Heroin.* This narcotic is the strongest of the opiates. The psychological effects include a physically warm and peaceful feeling, high self-esteem, and self-confidence. Users develop an addiction that demands frequent and increasing doses to maintain a high. Large doses can cause death.

2. *Barbiturates.* Their primary uses are as sleeping pills and tranquilizers. They do not produce a high but have a sedative effect. Barbiturates also have habituating properties. Users often develop strong suicidal tendencies, and overdoses can result in coma or death (Blachly, Disher, & Roduner, 1968).

3. *Amphetamines.* Because they act as stimulants to the nervous system and produce a high, adolescents and adults often become habituated to these drugs. Amphetamines can produce physical dependency, psychiatric disorders, or even brain damage.

4. *LSD (lysergic acid diethylamide).* This drug produces hallucinogenic reactions and distorts perception, thought, and sense orientation. Its psychological and physical effects are sometimes permanent. LSD does not produce physical dependence, and doses are rarely fatal. However, the psychotic effects of the drug are dangerous to the user and may lead to self-inflicted bodily harm or death.

5. *Marijuana.* This drug is also classified as a hallucinogen. It tends to lower inhibitions and often intensifies sexual pleasure, but it rarely provokes violent behavior. One of its chemical components, THC (tetrahydrocannabinols), can cause LSD-type hallucinations if taken in pure form. Marijuana is not physically addictive.

Amphetamines

Barbiturates and amphetamines are often referred to as the "softer" drugs. Fort (1968) has suggested that these drugs are used more frequently than the narcotics and hallucinogens. Amphetamines stimulate the central nervous system by sharpening physical reactions, increasing alertness, elevating mood, and reducing depression. Users usually begin by "dropping" diet pills, either for kicks or to keep awake. However, they often develop a dependence for them. When amphetamines are abused, users take doses many times those prescribed for medical purposes. It is not uncommon for a "speedster" or "pill-head" to take from 1000 to 5000 milligrams (mg) per day. The normal dosage in a prescribed diet pill is from 5 to 15 mg (Smith, 1969). Excessive dosages may result in disorganization, paranoia, or even psychosis (Johnson & Westman, 1968; Strack, 1968). Amphetamines are not usually fatal. However, they may cause the user to go through a high/depression cycle known as the *upper-downer syndrome,* which is brought on by the use of an amphetamine followed by a barbiturate. During the syndrome the user does not sleep, does not eat, and is highly excitable for a period of three to four days. When his supply runs out or when he collapses from physical exhaustion, he may sleep for 24 to 48 hours and then awake with a ravenous appetite. A period of depression, sometimes lasting for weeks, may then follow (Smith, 1969).

To gain a maximum high, many persons take amphetamines intravenously, although oral consumption is more frequent (Two doctors, 1969). Methedrine, or "speed," is also used to produce a high similar to that of the intravenous amphetamine (Johnson & Westman, 1968). Black-market speed laboratories have sprung up to synthesize and sell *methamphetamine,* which, injected into the bloodstream, provides an initial euphoric flash that has been described as a whole-body orgasm. Much methamphetamine abuse is seen in the "speedster," who repeatedly injects himself to get the sudden euphoric flashes (Smith, 1969).

LSD

The most popular of all the hallucinogenic drugs is LSD ("acid"), which is capable of producing extreme changes in perception, thought, and mood. It impairs intellectual functioning and distorts the senses (Smith, 1969; Strack, 1968).

LSD was first used medically in 1938, but its hallucinogenic effects were not discovered until 1943. There has been a general consensus that LSD does not produce physical harm, is not addictive, and, in some cases, may be used for medical or psychiatric treatment. Although research with the drug has indicated that LSD may cause a chromosomal breakdown, geneticists are still uncertain as to its direct effects (Johnson & Westman, 1968; Pop drugs, 1969; Richards, Joffe, Smith, & Spratto, 1969).

For many LSD users, "turning on" results in strong psychic disorder, which may have psychotic effects for an extended period after the drug wears off. Psychotic behaviors have been found in users who apparently had stable emotions and personalities before using the drug (Pop drugs, 1969; Strack, 1968). LSD has caused its users more severe psychological damage than has any other drug (Richards et al., 1969).

Suchman found that only 10 percent of the college students in his West Coast study had used LSD, and only 1.2 percent used it frequently. Its use is most prevalent on col-

lege campuses and in communal areas such as the Haight-Ashbury in San Francisco, Greenwich Village in New York, and Sunset Boulevard in Los Angeles. In these areas large groups of youths share in the experience of "turning on." For some adolescents turning on creates a sense of oneness that is not felt at any other time; others enjoy deep religious experiences in which they feel that they are communicating with God. Yet a few users report that an LSD trip makes them contemplative and more aware or "conscious."

If LSD is a psychedelic syndrome (Smith, 1969), its users, who are commonly rejectors of society, appear to be searching for something in their mental aberrations that will help them continue their life pursuits:

What do Vietnam, The Flying Nun, detergent and marijuana have in common? . . . Magic for one thing, and each in its own way illustrates an American return to a primitive faith in the black arts—The alchemists of the present day are the members of the drug cult. With LSD or something else exotic from the chemical retort, they believe this leaden old world can be turned into instant gold. They talk about it in terms of "expanding consciousness" or "turning on" as though their minds were light bulbs, but what they are really talking about is acquiring a love of life that will give them the strength to go on (Smith, 1968, p. 68).

Marijuana

Marijuana is also known as pot, grass, boo, tea, mary jane, broccoli, weed, charge, hemp, and gage (Pop drugs, 1969).

What is marijuana? The reefer, the joint, or the stick, whichever term you prefer for a marijuana cigarette, comes from a tall, weedy hemp plant that is a first cousin to the fig and known scientifically as *Cannabis sativa.* The flat, olive leaves, usually three times longer than wide, are found on a stalk that sometimes grows to six feet or more. When dried and pressed, the leaves, stems, and seeds are ground, sifted, and cut (diluted) for smoking. The most powerful ingredient in the plant is a resin taken from the flower of the female plant and known as hashish, the strongest and the most valuable form of marijuana (Chilnick, 1969, p. 13).

Most drug controversy centers around marijuana, because it is the most easily obtainable and frequently used drug (Suchman, 1968). Some persons maintain that marijuana is completely harmless, but others observe that most narcotic addiction begins with marijuana. A study by the American Medical Association reported that most marijuana has no addicting effects (Dependence, 1967). The National Institute of Mental Health estimates that 65 percent of all marijuana users quit within the first ten uses and that only 10 percent become habitual users (Pop drugs, 1969).

Marijuana is ordinarily inhaled through a cigarette (joint, joy stick, reefer, smoke, solid, spliff, stick). It tends to produce a delightful euphoric state in which distortion of time and space occur (Chilnick, 1969). Inhibitions are broken down, self-confidence is increased, and tensions are relieved. The effects of a single joint may last from 4 to 12 hours (Chilnick, 1969; Johnson & Westman, 1968).

The third article, by Suchman, reveals that marijuana is the most popular drug on the college campus. In his study of students on the West Coast, he found that all drug users had smoked marijuana. However, only 21 percent of his sample had ever taken drugs. Alcohol was used more frequently than marijuana or LSD. He also explored the drug user's ethical system. He found that "the more the student's self-image tends to be rebellious, cynical, anti-establishment, 'hippie,' and apathetic, the more likely he is to smoke marijuana." According to Suchman, the social use of marijuana becomes the core of the "hang-loose" subculture.

McGlothlin and West's article describes the use of marijuana, its physical and mental effects, and its relation to crime and other drug use. They feel that a reappraisal of the social and legal policies regarding marijuana is needed to resolve the crisis brought about by the current increase in the use of the drug.

Legislation and law enforcement have been the primary means of controlling marijuana use, but they have not been effective means. The legal classification of marijuana as a narcotic is an improper interpretation of the drug (Fort, 1968; Johnson & Westman, 1968; Keniston, 1969; McGlothlin & West, 1968). The following two quotes are representative of contemporary thought and are presented here as commentaries on the current dilemma.

A number of drugs are falsely and harmfully lumped together in the law with narcotics, including marijuana, in all states; in most states, cocaine; in other states, LSD; in some states, as in California, peyote, while LSD, which produces the same effect as in a different law called the "dangerous drug law" where people are subject to misdemeanor penalties while those possessing peyote are subject to felony penalties. As it has become clear that some drugs that have been called "narcotics" are not narcotics, a new concept has crept into our language: "soft narcotics." This is a beautiful term for the professional distorter because it implies that even though a drug is not a narcotic it is still a narcotic, but it is somehow "softer" than some vague but horrendous concept of "hardness" (Fort, 1968, p. 58).

Marijuana must be obtained illegally and "pot parties" ordinarily occur in marginally or frankly antisocial settings and tend to expose the user to the seduction and criminal elements and homosexuals. Marijuana is not a narcotic although it is so classified legally. Although legalizing the possession of marijuana is a controversial issue, the facts argue for new legislation to separate marijuana from the narcotics and calibrate legal action and penalties to the actual hazards and criminal behavior associated with its use (Johnson & Westman, 1968, p. 647).

Because present drug laws are not really enforceable, some reinterpretation of the 1937 Marijuana Tax Act seems necessary. Few users are ever detected, although in 1968, 80,000 marijuana arrests were made; only 1 percent were brought to trial and convicted (Pop drugs, 1969).

Although most psychologists, physicians, and law enforcement officials are disturbed by existing laws, they do not feel the solution is to legalize marijuana. The primary deterrent to its legalization is that it may hold unknown health hazards. A 1969 survey asked 27,741 physicians if they favored legalizing marijuana. Eighty-five percent said no (Modern medicine, 1969). The primary reasons given were that (1) marijuana often leads to addiction to more dangerous drugs; (2) no drug should be sold without legal restrictions; (3) marijuana use can result in irresponsible acts and deterioration of body and mind; and (4) marijuana has not been proven harmless (Modern medicine, 1969, p. 25).

Drug Education

There is a great need for drug education for adolescents today. Generally the schools, which play a major role in the socialization process, are considered the best source for such education.

Much drug education has usually focused on the medical, legal, and social aspects of the drugs themselves. Weissman (1969) has suggested that it is vital to change the emphasis from the drugs to the users. If teen-agers understood their motives for using drugs, they might be more willing to give them up.

Hollister (1969) has listed several reasons why adolescents use drugs: to rebel against parents, to hide feelings of inadequacy, to seek pleasurable thrills, to reduce boredom, to find solace for their fears and doubts, and to escape from responsibility. Smith (1969) has classified drug users into four categories: (1) experimental, (2) periodic or recreational, (3) compulsive, and (4) ritualistic. The *experimental* user is characterized by curiosity and group conformity. Since his friends are on drugs, he, too, wants to feel the experience of being high. This type of user becomes a prime target for drug education because he is often unsophisticated about drugs and will try most anything at least once.[1]

The *periodic or recreational* user may also take drugs primarily for fun and excitement. However, he has gone beyond the experimental stage by becoming a regular user; he has developed a pattern for drug use, although it is often a strictly social pattern. Smith (1969) points out that this user, like the social drinker, often overindulges.

The *compulsive* user has developed a physical or psychological dependence on a drug. This category comprises both adolescents and adults, most of whom are seeking a euphoric state that will break into the routineness or boredom of their lives. The *ritualistic* user believes that drugs provide spiritual or religious experiences (Richards et al., 1969; Smith, 1969). Contrary to common belief, these users are not drug abusers. They are cultists seeking revelation through drugs. Many of them go beyond drugs and stop taking them altogether, although they remain in a drug-oriented society.

Many scientists attribute the drug problem to our society (Fort, 1968; Keniston, 1969). Although it is important for society to reexamine some of its directions, the problem of drug abuse can be combated most effectively at the individual level. Adolescents are willing to discuss drugs and their effects; but they do not want lectures, and they do not respond to statistics on drug abuse (Weinswig, Doerr, & Weinswig, 1968). Therefore drug education must be made relevant to each individual's needs. It must combine (1) informing adolescents about drugs, (2) helping them identify social and personal factors that may contribute to drug use, and (3) integrating the discussion so that its relevance can make all individuals responsible for their behavior with drugs.

[1] A good example of the need for drug education is the new chemical drug THC (tetrahydrocannabinols), which is derived from marijuana. This drug, which is in capsule form, is a white powder and sells for about $2.50 a cap. It takes a 17-stage synthesis to manufacture THC, and it costs about $50 to synthesize a psychoactive dose. It is stable only in liquid nitrogen, its finished product is difficult to consume because of the foul taste, and it cannot be made soluble and put into a pill. Thus users are really taking something other than THC. The most common drug being sold as THC is PCP (phenylcyclohexlpiperidine), the veterinary anesthetic also known as sernyl (Smith, 1969, p. 37).

c. norman alexander, jr.

alcohol and adolescent rebellion*

Deviant Responses to Cultural Proscriptions

When people find psychologically gratifying behaviors that have potentially disruptive consequences for the social system, norms must arise to regulate activities in the area. If absolutely negative sanctions effectively eliminate widespread incidence of these behaviors, then total proscription is an efficient and simple means of maintaining social control. However, when a sizeable proportion of the population is motivated and able to deviate from the norm, then strict prohibitions may actually increase the disruption that results from these behaviors. For to "condemn and forbid" both prevents the emergence of more realistic means of achieving normative *regulations* of behaviors and, also, explicitly identifies the kinds of behaviors that can function to express rebellion against or rejection of social authority.

Societies encounter this dilemma in many areas of human behavior, but the normative regulation and social control of the use of alcoholic beverages provide a particularly striking example. In the Jewish culture norms regulate and ritualize the use of alcohol. By contrast, among Mormons, moral norms of total abstinence from alcohol preclude the societal regulation of drinking patterns, if any Mormons drink. The possible consequences of these normative differences are well illustrated by contrasting the drinking patterns in the two cultural groups.

Among Jews alcohol serves a ritual function; its use is normatively regulated, integrated into the social life of the community, and associated with activities which emphasize the social solidarity of the group. While most Jews use alcohol, problem-drinking is rare.

Among Mormons, where drinking is strongly condemned by moral sanctions, the use of alcohol is not merely a matter of individual deviance, but a threat to the maintenance of group values. The Mormon who drinks does so in a normative milieu that defines his behavior as deviant and casts him in the role of the "horrible example." Abstinence norms both preclude the integration of drinking activities with other social behaviors in the community (Straus & Bacon, 1953) and define the drinker role in terms of the very behaviors that are most conducive to individual and social disorganization (Skol-

Reprinted with permission of the author and publisher from *Social Forces*, 1967, **45**, 542-550.

*This analysis was conducted under a grant to the author from the Division of Alcohol Problems and General Welfare, General Board of Christian Social Concerns of the Methodist Church. I am indebted to Ernest Q. Campbell (principal investigator, National Institute of Mental Health Grant M-4302) for the use of these data and to the Institute for Research in Social Science, University of North Carolina for provision of facilities for the analysis.

nick, 1958). It is not surprising to find that Mormons, while less likely to use alcohol, have an extremely high rate of problem-drinking.

This interpretation implies that the relevant differences between Jews and Mormons are due to the differential normative integration of drinking behaviors within the patterned social life of the two groups and to the differences in the role defined for drinkers. If an individual in an abstinent environment begins to drink, unfortunate consequences are likely to ensue—because he is engaging in normatively unregulated, deviant behaviors oriented toward a role-image defined in terms of socially disapproved and personally dysfunctional behaviors.

Bales (1959) has suggested another possibility, one which links the dysfunctional consequences of drinking to the factors responsible for the initiation and continuance of the behavior in an abstinent environment. He has reasoned that abstinence norms may actually encourage the use of alcohol as a means of symbolic aggression against social authority.

> The breaking of the taboo becomes an ideal way of expressing dissent and aggression, especially where the original solidarity of the group is weak and aggression is strong. Thus total prohibition sometimes overshoots the mark and encourages the very thing it is designed to prevent. This situation is frequently found among individual alcoholics whose parents were firm teetotalers and absolutely forbade their sons to drink.

This hypothesis views much abstinence-oriented drinking behavior as a form of rebellion against society and those who symbolize the authority of the normative order. The dysfunctional consequences of such drinking (as seen among Mormons, for example) could be attributed to its *anti*normative and *anti*social character rather than to the *non*-nature of the social situation. Those who are frustrated by their social situation and who are provided no socially sanctioned outlets to relieve this frustration may well develop hostility toward the social order. If they drink, they may do so precisely because drinking serves both to relieve their tensions and to symbolize their aggression against society.

Unfortunately, this fascinating hypothesis, like so many other interesting hypotheses phrased at a total-societal level, is all but impossible to test empirically. More confidence in the "rebellious drinking" hypothesis would result if these behaviors could be linked explicitly to a general, social psychological theory and if, within a relatively homogeneous cultural setting, individuals could be located in social situations that roughly parallel the differences thought to be relevant between the Jewish and Mormon cultures. This paper attempts to accomplish this by exploring the rebellious use of alcohol by adolescent males in communities where abstinence norms are prevalent. The basic relationship to be considered is the adolescents' affective relationships to their fathers. First, the substantive and theoretical aspects of the situation will be discussed; then relevant data will be presented.

Adolescent Rebellion and Defiant Drinking

Drinking may represent an expression of hostility toward the normative authority of the total society; and, similarly, it may provide a means for expressing aggression against an individual who symbolizes that authority. This seems particularly likely to occur in the case of an adolescent and his parents, for the adolescent's parents—and, especially, his father—are to him the primary representatives of social authority. They are the immediate sources of reinforcement for normatively regulated behaviors and serve as the foci of his strivings for independence.

During the period of adolescence many children appear to aggress directly or indirectly against the authority of parents. While this takes many forms and usually concerns matters of privileges, proprieties, and tastes, perhaps the majority of disputes arouse more emotion than their importance would seem to justify. Even though the adolescent's hostility may be temporal, the behavioral and orientational patterns that he forms during this period may well persist beyond the conditions of their origin. Probably, most of these are unimportant. However, if orientations toward the use of alcohol are established in connection with rebellion against parental authority or with deliberate intent to defy parental proscriptions, the future consequence may be quite serious.

If rejection of parental authority includes the deliberate defiance of parentally supported abstinence norms, then the adolescent's current and future drinking patterns are likely to be affected by orientations toward alcohol as a symbol of rebelliousness and personal independence. Drinking may become a behavior that is symbolic of defiance of authority; it may become an expression of rejection of the normative demands of the social order and of those who enforce them.

Origins of the antinormative orientations toward alcohol that Bales hypothesizes may well lie in such adolescent-parent relationships. Whatever the origin, however, the antinormative orientations toward authority that constitute the essential factor in the Bales hypothesis may profitably be examined in the context of adolescent orientations toward the father as the major authority-figure in the social environment. By concentrating on individuals who symbolize the normative authority of society, rather than on the total moral order itself, we can formulate hypotheses that can be tested empirically with data on a relatively homogeneous cultural group.

These hypotheses can be derived from the social psychological theory of balance (Heider, 1958). The theory postulates relationships among "person's" affective orientations toward an "other" and their co-orientation toward an important object of common relevance. It is hypothesized that "person's" positive affect toward "other" is directly related to their agreement in attitudes toward the relevant object of co-orientation. If we take "person" to be an adolescent male, his father can serve as "other" and his drinking behavior as an object of common relevance. We may then examine the implications of balance expectations for this particular situation.

Assuming that the attitude of the adolescent's father toward his use of alcohol is prior to and independent of his behaviors, we may formulate several expectations about the relationship between the adolescent's drinking and his affect toward his father. If the father adopts a permissive attitude toward the use of alcohol, we expect the adolescent to be likely to drink to the extent that he is positively attracted toward his father; correspondingly, the adolescent drinker should be more likely than the abstainer to have positive affect toward a permissive parent. If the father adopts a negative or abstinent attitude toward his son's use of alcohol, then the likelihood of the adolescent's drinking should relate inversely to his attraction toward his father; also an abstainer should be more positively attracted to an abstinent father than a drinker.

The crucial concern of present interest involves the temporal sequence in which changes of behavior and changes in affect occur when the father has an abstinent attitude toward his son's use of alcohol. We want to know whether drinking behavior is initiated as a consequence of negative affect toward the father or whether negative affect results from the disparity between the father's attitude and his son's independently adopted drinking behaviors. In the former instance we might view the adolescent as beginning to drink for reasons essentially unrelated to parental opposition—for example, because his peers pressured him to drink. In the latter, the adolescent could be seen as beginning to drink precisely because of the opposition of a parent whose authority he rejects.

Now it is obvious that there are many reasons why an adolescent might begin to drink, and data of psychoanalytic depth would be necessary to support any claim that a particular individual began to drink in order to rebel against parental authority. Nevertheless, it is possible to compare adolescents' drinking behaviors in conditions under which they are differentially likely to be related to affective orientations toward the father. We shall assume that adolescent drinking is more likely to be related to rejection of an abstinent father if peer support for drinking is lacking (Alexander, 1964; Alexander & Campbell, in press). In other words, (1) when his best friend drinks, the drinking of an adolescent is likely to be due to this peer influence rather than to his orientations toward parental authority; but (2) when his best friend abstains, this increases the probability that his drinking is related to rejection of an abstinent father. This assumption is reasonable; and, while it provides only a crude index to assess the differential relevance of abstinent parental norms, we shall find that it serves adequately to differentiate between drinkers so classified.

Drinking Behaviors and Attitudes Toward Alcohol

If an adolescent drinks as a consequence of rebellion against parents, his drinking patterns should show all of the "unhealthy" aspects that one would expect to be associated with rebellious, antinormative behaviors, behaviors which relate to problem-drinking in later life. It is anticipated that, when drinking is most likely to be relevant to abstinent parental expectations, adolescent drinkers exhibit potential problem-drinking patterns if they reject their father. Specifically, rejection of parents should be associated with frequent drinking, extreme effects experienced from drinking, and emphasis on psychological benefits rather than social factors as reasons for drinking.

Data were gathered from 1,410 males in 30 high schools in the spring of their senior year.[1] All of the schools were located in the Eastern and Piedmont sections of North Carolina, an area in which the dominant religious groups support moral norms of total abstinence from alcohol. The independent variables of primary interest, together with their operational definitions are: (1) Parental attitudes toward the adolescent's use of alcohol: When will parents give their permission for the adolescent to drink?[2]   (2)

---

[1]These data were gathered as part of a larger study, "Normative Controls and the Social Use of Alcohol," National Institute of Mental Health Grant M-4302, Ernest Q. Campbell, Principal investigator. Questionnaires were given to 5,115 seniors of both sexes in 62 high schools selected to be representative of those in the Eastern and Piedmont sections of North Carolina. The sample in this paper includes only males in the 30 high schools that met the following criteria: (1) more than 15 males responded; (2) more than 95 percent of the males gave their names; (3) more than 90 percent of the males completed the questionnaire; (4) more than one-third of the males planned to go to college. The fourth criterion resulted in the elimination of only one school which would otherwise not have been eliminated. The criterion was included because there are certain data (in the larger study) available only for those adolescents who reported plans to attend college.

[2]The actual question asked is: "Parents sometimes tell their children that when a certain time comes they can then decide things for themselves. On *drinking alcohol,* which of the following represents the way your parents feel about it—" Permissive: I can drink if I want to while I am in high school. Nonpermissive: I can drink if I want to when I graduate from high school . . . when I am 18 . . . when I am 21 . . . after I set up a home of my own. They'd never give their permission for me to use alcohol. Only parents who would presently permit the use of alcohol are classified as permissive, since granting permission to drink only after the attainment of a certain age-related status might well encourage the adolescent to view drinking as an independence-seeking activity. Since the number of cases in these categories is too small to permit separate analysis, it was de-

Attraction-rejection of father: "How close is your relationship to your father?"[3] (3) Peer influence on drinking: Does the adolescent's best friend (his first-named choice on a "realistic" sociometric question asking for actual associations) drink or abstain—as defined by the friend's answer to the question: "Do you now (since the beginning of this school year) drink alcoholic beverages in any form?"

First, we are interested in whether or not the adolescent drinks as a function of his relationship to his father. Balance theory leads to the hypothesis that the proportion who drink will vary *directly* with positive attraction to parents who are permissive and *inversely* with positive attraction to parents who are negative toward the adolescent's use of alcohol. Table 1 presents the data relevant to this hypothesis. When fathers are opposed to the adolescent's use of alcohol, the incidence of drinking is inversely related to the closeness of the adolescent to his father ($d_{xy} = -.09$) (Somers, 1962). When the father is permissive, there is no linear relationship between attraction to him and drinking ($d_{xy} = .00$). This is contrary to expectations; but its interpretation must be somewhat equivocal, since "permissiveness" indicates only that parents do not oppose their son's drinking—i.e., a neutral rather than a positive attitude.

The small number of cases who have permissive fathers does not permit further analysis to determine the reasons for lack of confirmation of the hypothesis; and we are unable to introduce controls on the drinking behaviors of peers. Since this is a crucial

TABLE 1. PERCENT OF ADOLESCENTS WHO DRINK — BY PARENTAL PERMISSIVENESS AND CLOSENESS TO FATHER

Closeness to Father	Parental Permissiveness	
	Permissive	Nonpermissive
Closer than average	59.3 (27)	29.7 (381)
As close as average	44.8 (29)	31.9 (517)
Less close than average	60.9 (23)	39.6 (338)
$d_{xy} =$	.00	−.09

cided to equate the concepts of independence-seeking and the more genuinely rebellious defiance of absolute parental prohibitions.

[3]The father of these adolescent males was the parental figure selected because the father is the primary authority figure in the family, and at least the titular head of the family insofar as disciplinary measures are concerned.

TABLE 2. PERCENT OF ADOLESCENTS WHO LEGITIMATE DRINKING — BY CLOSENESS TO ABSTINENT FATHER, DRINKING BEHAVIOR, AND PEER SUPPORT

	Drinkers		Abstainers	
	Best Friend		Best Friend	
Closeness to Father	Drinks	Abstains	Drinks	Abstains
Closer than average	32.8 (61)	25.6 (39)	19.0 (63)	6.7 (163)
As close as average	32.6 (89)	38.7 (62)	16.0 (75)	9.8 (235)
Less close than average	40.0 (70)	42.5 (40)	13.3 (45)	13.8 (130)
d_{xy} =	+.07	+.15	−.09	+.16

variable in the analysis, we are forced to drop cases with permissive fathers and to consider in the following analyses only the behaviors of those whose fathers oppose their drinking.

To the extent that adolescents are negatively attracted to their abstinent fathers, they should legitimate the use of alcohol by their age-peers. This relationship should exist whether or not they drink, but it should increase in strength to the extent that parental factors are relevant. Thus, for both drinkers and abstainers the relationship between negative attraction to father and legitimation of drinking should be stronger when peer support for drinking is lacking.

Table 2 presents the percent legitimating drinking behaviors—by closeness to father, drinking behavior, and peer support.[4] Our prediction about the relative strengths of the relationships is confirmed: the relationships between closeness to father and legitimation of drinking are strongest in the absence of peer support (d_{xy} values of +.15 and +.16 compared to +.07 and −.09). The direction of the association is positive, as predicted, in only three of the four columns, a curious reversal occurring when the best friend of an adolescent abstainer drinks. The percent legitimating drinking actually increases with increases in attraction to an abstinent father—a finding contrary to the basic expectation that legitimation of drinking will vary inversely with attraction to one who supports abstinence norms. Before proceeding with the major analysis, then, some explanation for this unanticipated reversal must be sought.

---

[4] An adolescent is said to legitimate drinking behavior if he responded, "Yes, it's all right," to the question: "So far as moderate drinking by other people your age is concerned, do you think this is all right if they want to do it?"

In attempting to account for these data, it was reasoned that adolescents who are negative toward an abstinent father and who experience peer pressure to drink are more likely to use alcohol—unless they have some additional reasons for abstaining (such as religious commitments or internalized, negative attitudes toward alcohol use). To the extent that they continue to abstain despite pressures from peers to drink and rejection of support for abstinence from parents, then their own attitudes should constitute the source of resistance to drinking. If this line of reasoning is correct, the negative association between closeness to an abstinent father and legitimation of drinking should decrease in strength (and become positive) with increasing pressures to drink from the abstainer's peers.

This possibility was examined by an additional control on *perceived* peer pressures to drink—each nondrinker being classified by whether he reported being urged or teased to drink by his friends. Table 3 presents the percent of nondrinkers legitimating drinking —by closeness to his abstinent father, peer behavior, and experienced pressures to drink. These data support the rationale to account for the unexpected reversal of the relationship between attraction to an abstinent father and legitimating of drinking. When the abstainer does not report experiencing pressures to drink and his best friend abstains, the association between closeness to an abstinent father and legitimation of drinking is strongly negative. It remains negative, though weak, when pressures are reported and the best friend abstains and, also, when the best friend drinks and no pressures are experienced. But, when the abstainer reports pressures to drink and his best friend drinks, the relation-

TABLE 3. PERCENT OF ABSTAINERS LEGITIMATING DRINKING — BY CLOSENESS TO ABSTINENT FATHER, PEER SUPPORT, AND EXPERIENCED PRESSURES TO DRINK

	Best Friend Drinks		Best Friend Abstains	
Closeness to Father	Pressure	No Pressure	Pressure	No Pressure
Closer than average	19.5	18.2	9.6	2.9
	(41)	(22)	(94)	(69)
As close as average	17.8	13.3	9.6	10.1
	(45)	(30)	(136)	(99)
Less close than average	9.4	23.1	12.8	15.9
	(32)	(13)	(86)	(44)
d_{xy} =	−.15	+.03	+.06	+.31

ship is positive. If we may presume that these reported pressures originate with the best friend, they should be immediate and intense. In this situation in order to continue to abstain the adolescent would require strong, negative attitudes toward alcohol to the extent that he rejected parental support for his abstinence.

Drinking Patterns

Let us turn now to consideration of drinking patterns and their relationship to negative affect toward the father. The present analysis suggests that *anti*normative rebellious drinking is directly associated with negative attitudes toward the father only if the adolescent drinks without incentives to drink from his best friend. When his drinking cannot be explained in terms of his best friend's influence, then it is assumed that affect toward father is likely to be relevant to the adolescent's use of alcohol. The drinking patterns to be examined are frequency of use, effects experienced, and reasons given for using alcohol.

First, however, we shall attempt to establish a more direct connection between the behaviors of drinkers and the rejection of abstinent fathers. Ideally, we would wish for data in which the adolescent insightfully recognized and reported drinking behavior as a function of rebellion against parental norms. In lieu of such data, the plausibility of the antinormative interpretation of drinking behaviors is supported by responses to the question: "Have you ever deliberately done something you weren't supposed to do as a way of getting even with your parents?" Though it does not specifically mention drinking, the question is precisely in the spirit of the "rebellious drinking" hypothesis

and, importantly, it immediately followed the series of direct questions about drinking. Thus, it is reasonable to assume that the issue of alcohol use and its possible connection to rebelliousness was quite salient when respondents encountered this question.

TABLE 4. PERCENT OF DRINKERS WHO DELIBERATELY DEFY PARENTAL AUTHORITY — BY CLOSENESS TO ABSTINENT FATHER AND PEER SUPPORT

	Best Friend	
Closeness to Father	Drinks	Abstains
Closer than average	32.8	12.8
	(61)	(39)
As close as average	21.6	21.0
	(88)	(62)
Less close than average	37.1	42.5
	(70)	(40)
d_{xy} =	+.05	+.32

Hence, among those who drink without peer support, we expect that there will be a strong relationship between rejection of father and the frequency with which they report spiteful disobedience as a means of "getting even" with parents. Table 4 presents the percent of drinkers who report frequent wrongdoing as one means of getting back at parents—by closeness to father and peer support. The data show that, when peer support for drinking behaviors is absent, there is a striking, inverse relationship between closeness to father and the reported frequency of spiteful disobedience (d_{xy} = .32). If the drinkers have peer support, the relationship is relatively weak (d_{xy} = .05).

In order to use this measure as an independent variable in the following analyses, cell frequencies make it necessary to combine cases who report being average and above average in closeness to father. Since our major interest centers in those who indicate some degree of rejection of father, this

TABLE 5. PERCENT OF DRINKERS WHO DRANK LAST MONTH — BY CLOSENESS TO ABSTINENT FATHER, PEER SUPPORT, AND DELIBERATE DEFIANCE OF PARENTAL AUTHORITY

	Best Friend			
	Drinks		Abstains	
	Deliberately Disobeys		Deliberately Disobeys	
Closeness to Father	Frequently	Infrequently	Frequently	Infrequently
At least average	61.5	67.9	38.9	51.8
	(39)	(109)	(18)	(83)
Less close than average	61.5	75.0	76.5	78.3
	(26)	(44)	(17)	(23)
Q =	.00	+.17	+.67	+.54

TABLE 6. PERCENT OF DRINKERS EXPERIENCING SOME EFFECTS FROM DRINKING — BY CLOSENESS TO ABSTINENT FATHER, PEER SUPPORT, AND DELIBERATE DEFIANCE OF PARENTAL AUTHORITY

	Best Friend			
	Drinks		Abstains	
	Deliberately Disobeys		Deliberately Disobeys	
Closeness to Father	Frequently	Infrequently	Frequently	Infrequently
At least average	82.1	78.2	77.8	69.9
	(39)	(110)	(18)	(83)
Less close than average	80.8	77.3	82.4	78.3
	(26)	(44)	(17)	(23)
Q =	−.04	−.03	+.14	+.22

TABLE 7. PERCENT OF AFFECTED DRINKERS WHO HAVE BECOME DRUNK OR PASSED OUT — BY CLOSENESS TO ABSTINENT FATHER, PEER SUPPORT, AND DELIBERATE DEFIANCE OF PARENTAL AUTHORITY

	Best Friend			
	Drinks		Abstains	
	Deliberately Disobeys		Deliberately Disobeys	
Closeness to Father	Frequently	Infrequently	Frequently	Infrequently
At least average	31.3	20.9	14.3	10.4
	(32)	(86)	(14)	(58)
Less close than average	19.0	26.7	42.8	11.1
	(21)	(34)	(14)	(18)
Q =	−.32	+.10	+.64	+.04

TABLE 8. PERCENT GIVING SOCIAL OR PSYCHOLOGICAL REASONS FOR DRINKING — BY CLOSENESS TO ABSTINENT FATHER, PEER SUPPORT, AND DELIBERATE DEFIANCE OF PARENTAL AUTHORITY

	Best Friend			
	Drinks		Abstains	
	Deliberately Disobeys		Deliberately Disobeys	
Closeness to Father	Frequently	Infrequently	Frequently	Infrequently
Social Reasons:				
At least average	26.3	24.0	22.3	36.3
	(38)	(104)	(17)	(80)
Less close than average	34.6	27.3	13.3	34.8
	(26)	(44)	(15)	(23)
Q =	+.19	+.08	−.33	−.03
Psychological Reasons:				
At least average	42.1	31.7	41.2	32.5
Less close than average	50.0	34.1	66.7	34.8
Q =	+.16	+.05	+.48	+.05

is not especially serious. Thus, we may proceed to examine the relevant behaviors and attitudes of drinkers as they differ by closeness to abstinent fathers, support from peers for drinking, and the frequency with which parents are spitefully disobeyed.

Table 5 presents the percent of drinkers who have used alcohol at least once in the month preceding the date of their responses to the questionnaires. When they are close to their fathers, drinkers lacking peer support are less likely to use alcohol frequently than are drinkers whose best friends drink; but, when the father is rejected, drinkers lacking peer support are more likely to use alcohol frequently. The relative strengths of the relationships between frequency of use and rejection of father are shown by the values of Yule's Q. As expected, when deliberately disobedient behavior is common among drinkers without peer support, the inverse relationship between closeness to father and frequent drinking is stronger.

Table 6 examines the percent of drinkers who have experienced at least some effects ("I felt 'high' or 'gay' ") from their use of alcohol. Though differences are too slight to be very important, it is interesting to note that drinkers who reject and frequently disobey their abstinent fathers and who lack peer support are those most likely to have experienced effects from their use of alcohol. Positive relationships between effects of drinking and rejection of father exist only for drinkers without peer support; but differences between nonsupported drinkers reporting frequent and infrequent acts of spiteful disobedience are not in the expected direction. However, since "some" effect from drinking is hardly an indication of problem-drinking as a future-potential, we shall examine the percent among those reporting effects who have been drunk or passed out as a result of alcohol use.

Table 7 presents the percent of affected drinkers who have become drunk or passed out. It is clearly evident from this table that nonsupported drinkers who reject abstinent fathers and frequently disobey "to get even" with them are most likely to experience extreme effects from their use of alcohol. An association of Q = +.64 exists between the rejection of father and the likelihood of experiencing extreme effects for frequent disobeyers without peer support for drink-

ing. Finally, we shall examine the reasons given for drinking,[5] contrasting psychological benefits (i.e., drinking when unhappy, bored, or troubled; in order not to be shy) with social reasons (i.e., it's the thing to do; to be with the crowd). Table 8 presents these data. Frequently disobedient drinkers who reject abstinent fathers and lack peer support are least likely to drink for social reasons and most likely to drink for the psychological benefits provided by alcohol. Furthermore, the relationships between rejection of father and reasons for drinking are strongest among frequent disobeyers whose best friends abstain.

Summary

It has been shown that the likelihood of drinking and of legitimating the use of alcohol (in opposition to parental expectations) is inversely related to the closeness of the adolescent to an abstinent father. Furthermore, among drinkers who lack peer support for alcohol use, rejection of father is associated with frequent disobedience of parental authority in order to "get even" with them. And, when positive peer influence to drink is lacking, the rejection of parental authority (negative affect and frequent disobedience) is associated with frequent drinking, excessive drinking leading to extreme intoxication, and drinking for psychological rather than social reasons—all of these early drinking patterns being common in histories of problem-drinkers. In anticipating these results it was reasoned that drinking, when not due to positive pressures to drink, is a negative response, an expression of rebellion against the paternal authority figure.

The present data support Bales' hypothesis that drinking in a normative setting of abstinence is largely antinormative. Drinking in this type of social situation tends to become rebellious behavior when drinkers lack social support. Thus the high rates of problem-drinking and alcoholism among religious and cultural groups who promulgate abstinence norms may well be due to similar,

[5]The question asked: "Check the *one best reason* why you drink: To be with the crowd; I like the taste; When I'm unhappy, bored, or troubled; Because it's served at home; In order not to be shy; It's the thing to do."

socially aggressive drinking patterns. Other observers have examined differential rates of alcoholism, interpreting abstinence-oriented drinking behaviors as nonnormative (lacking social regulation), pronormative (adoption of the "horrible example" role-model), and antinormative (rebellious). This analysis has specified the "rebellion" hypothesis in terms of a more general social psychological theory and has subjected it to test in a relatively homogeneous cultural milieu in the context of father-son relationships. Hence, it has been possible to demonstrate that *anti*normative aspects of drinking are important in abstinence-oriented social situations and that this is certainly a significant factor in the high incidence of problem behaviors among those who drink in these social environments.

alvin e. strack

drug use and abuse among youth

To start, let us consider the following proposition: Any substance capable of altering man's mood has abuse capability. What is implied in this statement, of course, is that the specific substance abused is of less direct importance to the user than the end result, and indeed, this is frequently the case. With this as a general premise, let me cite some specific drugs and substances frequently abused in our society.

We need to define three terms about which there is considerable confusion: addiction, habituation, and dependence. Through the years "addiction" and "habituation" have been used interchangeably to describe forms or results of drug use and abuse. The resulting confusion has led to decisions by the World Health Organization to replace these terms with the more general one of "dependence." Dependence is described as "a state arising from repeated administration of a drug on a periodic or continuous basis." The use of the term dependence necessitates delineating the *exact* drug which one is discussing. Therefore, we have drug dependence of the barbiturate type, drug dependence of the opiate type, etc.

Reprinted with permission of the author and publisher from the *Journal of Health, Physical Education, and Recreation,* 1968, **39,** 26-28, 55-57.

Opiates

The opiates are among the oldest drugs known to man. They have no equal, to this day, in relieving pain. They are medically irreplaceable at the present time. When properly used in medical practice, there is little or no danger of development of dependence. When abused, they produce very serious physical and psychological dependence. Drugs in this class include morphine, codeine, and other natural opium derivatives, and also heroin, which is synthetically produced from morphine. It is heroin, of course, which is the drug of choice among opiate addicts. Given intravenously, it produces a "kick" or "high" of an almost orgasmic nature, followed by the "nod" or period of oblivion which the addict also prizes. It is perhaps this double effect which makes the opiates so attractive to individuals seeking escape from reality.

The manufacture, distribution, possession, and use of the opiates or narcotics are subject to stringent international, federal, and state regulation and control. Penalties for illicit sale are severe, and rightly so. Opiate addiction, per se, is not a crime, and yet opiate addicts have constructed a surer prison for themselves and their minds than any jailer could hope to build.

Narcotic withdrawal makes a familiar tale. Usually somewhat overdramatized, it has been portrayed on many occasions in movies, television, and other media. Withdrawal from a heavy heroin habit is indeed a painful and agonizing process. In practice today, however, and thanks to vigilant police efforts, there are few so-called "heavy" habits around, because heroin is too scarce and because the heroin bought by most addicts has been highly diluted by the seller. Hence, "cold turkey" withdrawal for most narcotic addicts is today much less formidable than it is often described.

The most prevalent form of narcotic use among young people limits itself to exempt narcotics marketed in cough syrups. The practice seems to be confined to localized areas, and the exact extent of the problem is extremely difficult to determine.

The effects of narcotic use include drowsiness and sleep; the side effects are nausea, vomiting, constipation, itching, flushing, constriction of pupils, and respiratory depression.

Depressants: Barbiturates and Tranquilizers

The barbiturate drugs have been used in medicine for half a century. They are used as sedatives, sleep producers, for epilepsy, high blood pressure, gastrointestinal disorders, and many other disease states. Used as directed, and in the doses prescribed, they are quite safe. Abused at high doses for long periods of time, they produce severe psychological dependence and a type of physical dependence which in at least one respect is more severe than that seen with narcotics. To be specific, abrupt withdrawal of barbiturates from a dependent individual can cause convulsions which can be fatal if untreated. It is this fact which has caused some investigators to say that the barbiturates are more toxic when abused than narcotics. Symptoms of barbiturate abuse include slurred speech, staggering gait, and sluggish reactions. The user is erratic and may easily be moved to tears or to laughter. Perhaps the best description of the barbiturate intoxicated individual is a reeling drunk who does not smell of alcohol.

Certain tranquilizers, notably those usually designated as minor tranquilizers and employed for the less severe mental and emotional disorders, have occasionally been abused, with the development of psychological and physical dependence. Symptoms in dependent individuals during withdrawal of these drugs closely resemble those seen with barbiturates.

Stimulants: Cocaine and Amphetamines

Cocaine is derived from the leaves of the coca tree. Although a stimulant, and not a narcotic, it is treated as a narcotic for legal control purposes. Once widely used as a local anesthetic, cocaine has disappeared from the medical scene. It is a very potent stimulant. It produces excitability, talkativeness, and a reduction in the feeling of fatigue. Cocaine may produce a sense of euphoria, increased muscular strength, and hallucinations. Its use has been associated with violent behavior.

The amphetamine derivatives have been used in medicine for about 35 years. They are very useful in the treatment of obesity, depression, hyperactivity, behavior disorders in children, and narcolepsy (a disorder characterized by excessive and sudden periods of sleep). Amphetamines increase alertness, dispel depression, mask fatigue, elevate mood, and produce a feeling of well-being. It is generally agreed that amphetamines do not produce physical dependence with abuse, but psychological dependence is common with excessive use. With abuse of amphetamines the body becomes tolerant to it, and abusers frequently use doses many times those usually employed for medical purposes. Symptoms of abuse include talkativeness, excitability, and restlessness. The abuser will suffer from insomnia, perspire profusely, have increased urinary frequency, and often exhibit tremor. Acute psychotic episodes may occur with intravenous use, or may develop with the chronic use of large doses.

Manufacture, distribution, and sale of the depressants and stimulants (except cocaine as previously mentioned) are controlled by a variety of federal and state laws, most notable of which is the recently enacted federal legislation which requires manufacturers and distributors of these drugs to register with the government and to maintain for inspection complete inventory and sales records. These laws restrict the number of times a prescription may be refilled, and place a six-month time limit on refills.

Hallucinogens

The hallucinogens, which include LSD, DMT, peyote, psilocybin, mescaline, and also marijuana, have received an inordinate amount of publicity through the news media. Only one of these agents is currently considered to have any possible medical use, and that one is LSD. When used under very carefully controlled conditions, LSD has been found to be of some value in the treatment of alcoholism and certain psychosexual disorders.

If one can judge from the publicity generated by certain enthusiastic proponents of the hallucinogens, their use is increasing by leaps and bounds. A somewhat less biased view would be that abuse of these substances has increased to worrisome proportions, especially among young people of college age.

As their name suggests, the hallucinogens produce a variety of hallucinatory effects, primarily in visual perception. When abused, these substances produce a psychological dependence which, in some individuals, amounts to an almost religious fervor. The drugs do not produce physical dependence and no physical symptoms occur on withdrawal.

LSD was synthesized in the late 1930's, but its hallucinogenic effect was not discovered for several years. Abuse of this substance has become a problem only in recent years, in part because of the articulate and persuasive devotees of "expansion of consciousness." The LSD experience is certainly memorable. It involves visual, auditory, and tactile hallucinations, changes in perception, thought, mood and activity, time sense, and comprehension. All too frequently, the LSD "trip" is a shattering psychic experience which leaves the user disoriented, in panic, or even frankly psychotic. Psychosis has developed after use of LSD in individuals who previously exhibited no signs of emotional instability. Moreover, this psychotic state may persist or recur for weeks after the drug was taken. Mescaline, psilocybin, and DMT all produce effects similar to those of LSD,

differing only quantitatively in their effects and duration of action. DMT is interestingly enough called the "businessman's trip," since its effect lasts only about as long as the ordinary business lunch. Manufacture, distribution, and sale of LSD is now restricted under the same federal laws governing stimulants and depressants.

The popular weed marijuana is also known as cannabis, pot, ghang, hashish, charas, and a variety of other names. Marijuana is an irregular stimulant of the central nervous system, and is a hallucinogen. It has no established medical use. It is used—usually smoked or eaten—for its ability to produce euphoria, a feeling of exaltation and dreaming, and hallucinations. Use of marijuana is associated with a distorted sense of time and distance. Panic and fear sometimes result, but the user is usually talkative and in good humor, or conversely sometimes drowsy and quiet.

Marijuana does not cause physical dependence or an abstinence syndrome. Tolerance does not appear to develop; in short, it causes little physical damage in the user. However, reports from areas of the world where the more potent forms of cannabis and marijuana are used indicate an association between continued intake of this substance and the development of psychosis. Psychological dependence, which is moderate to strong, can develop readily, especially in susceptible individuals.

The most serious problem associated with marijuana is pointed out in the *Bulletin of the World Health Organization:*

> Abuse of cannabis (marijuana) facilitates the association with social groups and subcultures involved with more dangerous drugs, such as opiates and barbiturates. Transition to the use of such drugs would be a consequence of this association rather than an inherent effect of cannabis. The harm to society derived from abuse of cannabis rests in the economic consequences of the impairment of the individual's social functions and his enhanced proneness to asocial and antisocial behavior (Eddy et al., 1965).

Solvents

The abuse of solvents is commonly but somewhat inaccurately labeled "glue sniffing." Inhalation of solvents contained in glues, gasoline, paint thinners, lighter fluids, and the like produces a state of excitation, exhilaration, and excitement resembling alcohol intoxication. Eventually blurred vision, slurred speech, loss of balance, and hallucinations result. Tolerance develops, but physical dependence does not occur. A strong psychological dependence develops. Reports of actual physical damage resulting from solvent abuse are rare, although the toxicity of these solvents for man is widely recognized in industry. One of the very real dangers is that of suffocation in habitues who use plastic bags to hold the glue or solvents up to the face. It is an unfortunate fact that abuse of these substances occurs to the largest extent in young adolescents.

Methods of Treatment

We are really just beginning to realize and act on the idea that abuse of drugs and other substances will require as many different methods of treatment as it has causes. Certainly, habilitation and rehabilitation will not be easy, but we must try. The comprehensive programs of California, Maryland, and New York, and the coordinated program in New York City headed by Efren Ramirez, must be given the opportunity to function effectively in this problem area. Such organizations as Daytop and Synanon must also have their chance to show what can be done. We have too few answers to turn aside any reasonable approach to cure and rehabilitation.

Legal facets of drug and substance abuse have been mentioned briefly before. I would like here to defend the role of law enforcement in preventing drug abuse. Law enforcement is primarily charged with removing one of the proximate causes of drug and substance abuse, namely, availability. There is a social need to stamp out the illicit trade in drugs and substances, and for this we are dependent in large measure on good law enforcement. They have done very well. No greater testimonial to this fact exists than the real scarcity of heroin in this country.

I would like to emphasize that it is *not* the province of law enforcement officers to be philosophical about drug addiction and abuse. They are sworn to enforce the law. It is our business to assist them whenever possible.

There are many social aspects of drug and substance abuse, but I wish to offer only a few for consideration. First, society must accept the existence of, and differentiate between, the spree or occasional drug abuser and the chronic abuser for whom abuse has become a way of life. Second, the chronic abuser is a sick individual, and however society chooses to provide care and custody for him, he should be treated as a sick man. Third, drug abuse is a symptom of some deeper, underlying disorder. It may range on the one hand from adolescent rebellion to deep-seated character disorders on the other. In all of these, loneliness and alienation play a large role.

We are left with what might be called the morality of the situation, but perhaps more precisely, the realities of the situation. One hears these days a refrain that goes something like this: "I have the right and should have the freedom to use drugs if I wish to, especially if they don't physically harm me. And even if they do harm me, they hurt only me and nobody else." This argument is frequently put forth by those who, for one reason or another, claim the right to use drugs occasionally for other than their intended medical purposes.

It is interesting that, lacking an adequate logical reason for drug abuse, these people fall back on the argument for rights and freedoms. No one, of course, wants to restrict rights or freedoms or to have to argue against them. We must recognize, though, that the "right" that these drug abusers claim is the right to be immature and uncaring about themselves and society to the point of stupidity. Society, any society, has always had the privilege of limiting individual rights and freedoms to the extent necessary to preserve the common good. This function of society extends even to protecting the individual from himself if this is necessary.

From the earliest times, man and his societies have restricted the distribution and the use of certain substances. Many early recognized the medical usefulness of certain plants and chemicals—but also their antisocial potential in terms of poisonous or intoxicant effects. Social and legal control of such substances has been accepted as a necessary limitation on individual freedom for centuries. Even the primitive societies of today have such controls in the form of a witch doctor or medicine man.

Legal controls of these substances then is not really an unnecessary, and certainly not a recent, intrusion on man's inalienable rights. They are a very real social necessity.

The delicate balance between the individual's rights, duties, and responsibilities in a society certainly enters into this picture.

Another aspect is the physical harm, or the lack of it, caused by the abuse of drugs and other substances. In this sense, physical harm means physical dependence and a withdrawal syndrome, or the toxic effect of long-term use. There is little doubt that there are substances that do *not* cause such physical harm when abused. As has already been pointed out, the real harm in these substances is their asocial or antisocial effect; their leading the abuser to association with substances which are harmful and dangerous; and the general economic impairment which they produce.

The suggestion that if drugs do harm me but no one else, then there is no reason why I should not use them, is patently ridiculous. Has the young adult gone psychotic after taking LSD harmed only himself? Who must care for him, keep him from further harming himself or others? Who has to try to put his shattered mind back together?

If you inquire of a drug abuser what he expects to get from drugs, you can expect a variety of answers:

I want to get high.
I want to get away.
I want to stay awake.
I want to go to sleep.
I want a new thrill.
I want to expand my consciousness.
I want a mystic experience.
I want to enhance my creativity.

Many users have no real reason except that "everyone was doing it," or the seldom expressed but often present need to rebel, somehow.

Many, of course, are very serious about using drugs for insight, for a mystic experience, or to enhance creativity. In the latter group one finds many of the hippies of Haight-Ashbury or Greenwich Village. They regard ingestion of drugs and other substances for these purposes as *use*, not abuse. They regard drugs as functional in this respect. They are optimistic to the point of being naive about the ability of drugs to enhance creativity or promote insights into life, love, and the things which really matter to them. They do not see abuse of drugs as dysfunctional in their lives.

Like many rebel and avant-garde groups before them, these young people have a real message to and about our society and our way of life. It is sad that most of their message is blurred and confused by being bound up with the problem of drug abuse.

Prevention is the real answer to drug abuse; the key to prevention is education. But who should educate, and what should be told about drug abuse?

The family remains of primary importance in influencing child development, and it is within the family and the home that most can be accomplished in preventing the abuse of drugs and other substances. A caring, loving, and directing home atmosphere is, and will remain, the best means of guiding youth through the difficult adolescent years. The alienation and loneliness which characterize so many abusers are much less likely to develop in a good home atmosphere. A willing ear, a kind word when needed, gentle direction, and a loving heart may be the only way to explain that most young people who are exposed to drugs do *not* abuse drugs. Most young people have no need for this kind of crutch or escape. But too many, unfortunately, must look for crutches and escapes.

To professional educators, however, will fall the role of telling young people about drugs and drug abuse. In doing this they must provide factual, clear-cut information— no horror stories, no finger-wagging. In short, they must "tell it like it is." Today's youth is quite knowledgeable concerning drugs and other substances and will quickly turn off anyone who doesn't tell a straight story about the problem. The educator, too, will often find himself in a strategic position to influence youth, either as an example setter or even in a surrogate parent role.

So what do we do for our young people? First, we listen to them as hard as we have ever listened in our lives. This shows them we care. Then tell all the facts, and in the manual for educators, *Drug Abuse: Escape to Nowhere,* I think we have the facts. It is a good starting point. But the most important message to convey to our young people is that abuse of drugs and other substances is one of the biggest "cop-outs" of all time. It is a "cop-out" on oneself.

Today's young people stress physical, material, intellectual, psychological, and spiritual self-fulfillment. I can think of very few actions that an individual can take that are more damaging to this self-fulfillment than drug abuse. Society has nothing to do with it, morality has nothing to do with it, rights and freedoms have nothing to do with it. Young people must be told: This is you— emphasis *you*. At almost any level of function you, emphasis *you*, will find yourself hung-up if you abuse drugs or substances. You will have "copped-out" on yourself. It matters little what you use—alcohol, marijuana, LSD, opiates, or whatever—it is still your "cop-out."

The total answer to the drug abuse problem lies in a judicious blend of education, legal control, more research on drugs and other substances now available, and, most important, the establishment of a dialogue across the generation gap. The latter, of course, has meaning for many social problems other than drug abuse.

edward a. suchman

the "hang-loose" ethic and the spirit of drug use

A cross-sectional, sampling survey of drug use on a college campus reveals the close association between the use of drugs (over-whelmingly marijuana) and adherence to what might be characterized as a "hang-loose" ethic. Use of drugs was more likely to occur among those students whose behavior, attitudes or values, and self-image were indicative of opposition to the traditional, established order. Such differences occurred regardless of those demographic characteristics of the students also related to drug use, such as sex, socio-economic status, and religion. For these students, marijuana was the recreational drug of choice and its use became a central core of their sub-culture.

Studies of college students made about 15 years ago found that generation of youth to be "politically disinterested, apathetic, and conservative." (Goldsen, et al., 1960, p. 199; Jacob, 1957) To an increasing degree, the college student of the current generation is striving to overcome this image of passive conformity and conservatism in order to evolve a new and more meaningful role for himself, both on campus and in the larger community. Reflecting the many social, political, and economic forces that have widened the generational gap between young people and those "over 30," this youth movement is seeking to develop new values and behavior patterns, often in defiance and

opposition to those of the established order.

Central to this new world of youth is a whole new range of recreational and psychedelic drugs. Studies of college students in the last generation found alcohol to be the major campus "vice" and alarming reports were published about the "drinking problem of college students." (Straus and Bacon, 1953) No mention was made of other drugs. In this respect, the students displayed one more sign of their conformity—drinking was also the favorite social pastime, and problem, of their parents. Almost as if rejection of the establishment also demanded the development of a different form of "high," the new generation of college students is increasingly turning to other drugs for the relaxation and "kicks" their parents found in alcohol. As described by Simmons and Winograd (1966, p. 86), "The drug scene is the central plaza of happening America . . . it is here, in the drug scene that generational change in America most vividly thrusts itself forward. . . ." And perhaps forgetting their own bouts with the law in the days of prohibition and repressing the serious threat of alcoholism as a major health problem today (Suchman, 1963a; Plaut, 1967), adults have been almost unanimous in their condemnation of this new and strange intoxicant. As one "over 30" judge recently opined, alcohol is the socially approved drug of choice for the well-adjusted, responsible, hard-working member of society seeking sociability and pleasant relaxation, while the use of marijuana represents the

Reprinted with permission of the author and the American Sociological Association from the *Journal of Health and Social Behavior*, 1968, **9**, 146-155.

neurotic and anti-social behavior of the juvenile delinquent.

Unfortunately, there is little empirical data about what is taking place in the colleges today. The present study represents an initial attempt to ascertain basic facts about the use of drugs by one college population and to examine those factors, both causes and consequences, associated with the use of drugs. The major assumption is that drug use on the campuses today is largely limited to the occasional smoking of marijuana cigarettes and represents a social form of recreation far removed in nature from the traditional problem of narcotics addiction and, for that matter, alcoholism. (McGlothlin, 1967) Furthermore, the set of hypotheses to be tested is that the use of marijuana will be highly associated with other expressions of a new breed of youth characterized by a "hang-loose" ethic. As described by Simmons and Winograd (1966, p. 12), "One of the fundamental characteristics of the hang-loose ethic is that it is irreverent. It repudiates, or at least questions, such cornerstones of conventional society as Christianity, 'my country right or wrong,' the sanctity of marriage and premarital chastity, civil disobedience, the accumulation of wealth, the right and even competence of parents, the schools, and the government to head and make decisions for everyone—in sum, the Establishment."

Method of Procedure

This study was conducted in November, 1967, at a West Coast university. A representative sample of 600 students out of a student body of 12,200 was selected at random from the registration lists of undergraduate and graduate students. A questionnaire dealing with drug use and various aspects of college life, educational and political values, and current social issues was prepared on the basis of detailed interviews of students, especially so-called "hippies," and observation of student activities, especially so-called "happenings." Interviews and observation were carried out by 125 students enrolled in a course on social research methods.

The questionnaire was administered in two parts of almost equal length. The first part was a personal interview, while the second, which sought information on more sensitive topics, such as sex, drug use and the draft, was filled out by the respondent and placed with the first part in a sealed envelope without identification. The questionnaires were thus kept anonymous to increase the probability of truthful answers. The completion rate of interviews was 81 per cent. The remaining 19 per cent were not interviewed largely because the assigned respondent could not be reached during the week allotted to field work, rather than the refusal to be interviewed (less than 5 percent). A comparison of the sample obtained with available demographic characteristics for the entire population shows no characteristic with a difference beyond what might be expected by chance.

Conceptual and Operational Model. Our dependent variable is frequency of drug use as reported by the respondent. Our major independent variable is degree of adherence to the "hang-loose" ethic as determined by a series of questions designed to tap (1) behavioral patterns, (2) attitudes and values, and (3) self-image and personality. The behavioral patterns refer to such acts as taking part in "happenings" and mass protests, and reading underground newspapers. We view such behaviors as indicative of a rejection of traditional society on the part of the student and subject to disapproval by the representatives of that society. The attitudes and values studied are drawn from the educational area (i.e., worthwhileness of college education, student power), the political area (i.e., Vietnam war, the draft), and the social area (i.e., "hippies," the law, sex and life goals). Finally, we study the student's self-image in such respects as conformity, cynicism, anti-establishment and rebellion in an effort to index his own portrait of himself vis-a-vis the established order.

In all three aspects of behavior, attitudes, and self-image, our major hypothesis is that the more the student embraces the "hang-loose" ethic (as opposed to the so-called "Protestant ethic") the more frequently will he make use of drugs.

Findings

Prevalence of Drug Use. The following proportions of students reported taking some drug (Question: "How frequently do you take drugs (marijuana, LSD, etc.)?"):

About every day	2.0
Once or twice a week	6.6
Once or twice a month	6.6
Less than once a month	6.0
Do not use drugs	78.8
Total	100.0% (N = 497)

Of the drugs used, marijuana was listed by *all* students taking drugs, with occasional use of LSD mentioned by 18 per cent of those taking drugs (2.2% of the entire population). A wide variety of other drugs (i.e. "speed," Methedrine, peyote) also was listed, none by more than 10 per cent. There can be little question concerning marijuana's being the recreational drug of choice among this college population, one of five admitting its use, despite its illegality. The word "drugs" as used in this report may therefore be equated largely with marijuana.

This figure of 21.1 per cent use is quite similar to the results of surveys at UCLA (33%) (Santa Barbara News-Press, 1967), Harvard (25%), Yale (20%), and Princeton (15%) (Time, 1967), although a Gallup Poll of 426 college campuses reports only about 6 per cent as having smoked marijuana (Reader's Digest, 1967). While this "numbers game" is largely unproductive in the absence of any reliable and valid data, it does seem apparent that marijuana use on the campus is high enough to warrant serious attention.

Most of the students using drugs began in college, 40 per cent in their freshman year, although 22 per cent had smoked marijuana before coming to college. Almost all began to use drugs through the personal influence of a friend who was already smoking marijuana (Becker, 1953). Drug use usually took place at night as a social activity with other people in the student's or a friend's room.

Overwhelmingly, the reaction of the students smoking marijuana is positive. Four out of five report that they have never gotten sick, although one out of four does mention having experienced a bad "trip." Less than 10 per cent want to stop or have ever tried to stop, although 20 per cent report being "somewhat" worried.

There is no evidence in these findings to support the claims that smoking marijuana is a predecessor to the use of other, more dangerous drugs. Marijuana users may occasionally "cross over" to try other drugs, but this is more of a search for new experiences than "progressive degeneration."

Alcohol and Marijuana. In addition to the question about their own use of drugs, the students were asked, "How frequently do most of the students you know do the following: smoke marijuana, take LSD, drink alcoholic beverages?" They were also asked in relation to these three recreational drugs, "How strongly do you approve or disapprove doing each of the following?" and "How much pressure do you feel to engage in any of the following?" A comparison of their responses to these three aspects of use, attitude, and pressure for marijuana, LSD, and alcohol is given in Table 1.

TABLE 1. COMPARISON OF DRUGS ACCORDING TO USE, ATTITUDES, AND PRESSURES

Questions	Alcoholic Beverages	Marijuana	LSD
Use[a]			
Frequently	47.2	14.1	1.2
Occasionally	36.9	24.5	8.8
Seldom	10.0	18.9	16.9
Never	2.4	30.7	53.8
Don't know	3.5	11.8	19.3
Attitude[b]			
Strongly approve	11.4	5.6	1.2
Approve	59.2	29.5	3.6
Undecided	22.2	31.5	20.9
Disapprove	5.2	20.1	25.7
Strongly disapprove	2.0	13.3	48.6
Pressure[c]			
A great deal	12.9	3.0	2.8
Some, but not much	38.2	16.5	2.0
Very little	47.0	78.1	92.6
No answer	1.9	2.4	2.6
Total per cent	100.0	100.0	100.0
Total cases	497	497	497

[a] Question: "How frequently do most of the students you know do the following:"
[b] Question: "How strongly do you approve or disapprove of students doing each of the following:"
[c] Question: "How much pressure do you feel to engage in any of the following:"

First, we note the higher perception of marijuana use as compared to actual use. While 4 out of 5 students (78.8%) report that they do not use marijuana themselves, only 1 out of 3 (30.7%) estimates that most of the students they know do not smoke marijuana. Almost 2 out of 5 (38.6%) report that most of the students they know smoke marijuana frequently or occasionally.

Second, we see that alcohol continues by far to be most frequently used, with an overwhelming majority of students (84.1%) reporting that most of the students they know drink alcohol frequently or occasionally, as compared to 38.9 per cent for marijuana and 10.0 per cent for LSD.

Third, we note that approval parallels use, with most of the students (70.6%) approving alcohol, some approving marijuana (35.4%), and few approving LSD (4.8%). The ratio of approval to disapproval is 10:1 in favor for alcohol, 1:1 for marijuana and 1:20 against LSD. It would appear that the campus is split on the use of marijuana, but overwhelmingly in favor of alcohol and against LSD.

Fourth, the pressure to use each of these drugs also parallels attitudes and practices. Most students report pressure to drink alcoholic beverages (51.1%), but only 19.5 per cent report feeling any pressure to smoke marijuana, with 4.9 per cent feeling some pressure to use LSD. These findings underscore the highly personal and voluntary nature of marijuana or LSD use. If anything, students are being more highly pressured toward possible alcoholism than drug addiction. The major recreational drug on the college campuses is still alcohol.

The relationship between pressure toward use of drugs and the actual frequency of use is quite high. An individual who reports feeling pressure to smoke marijuana is twice as likely to be a frequent user of marijuana (at least once a week) than one who reports little or no pressure (15.7% vs. 7.2%). A similar relationship exists between pressure to use LSD and actual use (16.6% vs. 8.5%). This finding is supported by the much more frequent use of marijuana among those students who report that most of the students they know also smoke marijuana. As many as 68.6 per cent of those students who report that most of the students they know smoke marijuana frequently do so themselves, as compared to only 0.7 per cent among those whose friends do not smoke marijuana.

A significant reversal between alcohol and drug use occurs in these data. The more the individual knows other students who drink alcohol, and the more pressure he feels to drink himself, the *less* likely is he to use marijuana. This finding would indicate that marijuana is more of a substitute for alcohol than a supplement. For many students it would appear that the use of marijuana represents a preference over alcohol as a source of "high."

The relationship of attitudes toward use and actual use is, not unexpectedly, extremely high. Approval is much more likely to mean use (45.7%), with only a small minority (0.6%) disapproving of smoking marijuana at the same time that they do it. This finding once again attests to the voluntary nature of this act. It is also interesting to note that half of the students who approve of smoking marijuana still do not do so themselves. Most of the students (66.6%) do not feel that "anyone smoking marijuana is foolish" although only a minority agree that "the use of psychedelic drugs should be a matter of conscience and not legal restriction" (34.7%) and that "the university should not cooperate with legal authorities in the enforcement of drug use laws" (23.2%). In all cases, those students having positive attitudes towards marijuana, either in the wisdom of its use or in its freedom from legal restrictions, are much more likely to be users of marijuana.

Demographic Comparisons. The use of drugs varies significantly by sex, social class, marital status, and religion. No differences were found by age, year in college, birthplace or current marital status of parents. Males are almost three times as likely as females to be using drugs (e.g., smoking marijuana) at least once a week (13.9% vs. 4.6%), upper income groups twice as likely as lower income groups (14.1% vs. 7.3%), single students four times as likely as married students (8.9% vs. 2.1%) (but engaged students show greatest use—10.7%), and Atheists and "other religious affiliations" reporting much more use (25.0%) than Protestants (4.9%), Catholics (4.8%), and Jews (4.0%). Similar differences occur in the category "less than once a week."

Social class differences are much more pronounced among the females than male students. Among coeds, the proportion smoking marijuana at least once a week rises rapidly from 1.5 per cent among those who come from families with annual incomes under $12,000 to 13.1 per cent from families with incomes of $20,000 or more. No statistically significant social class differences are found among the male students. In general, our analysis by demographic characteristics would support the findings of others that marijuana smoking is not, like the use of narcotics, linked to a lower income sub-culture.

The "Hang-Loose" Ethic: Behavioral Correlates. Our primary hypothesis has been that drug use is only one aspect of the more general "happening" scene and reflects a broad range of other "anti-establishment" behaviors. Support for this hypothesis comes from our finding that drug use varies considerably according to such activities as participating in "happenings" (34.3% drug users among those who participate frequently vs. 17.0% among those who do so rarely), reading "underground" newspapers (42.0% users among frequent readers vs. 3.7% among non-readers), and participating in mass protests (45.9% among those who have done so more than twice vs. 15.2% for non-participators). It appears from these results that drug use in the form of smoking marijuana is highly associated with "non-conformist" behavior.

If we look at the student's cumulative grade as an index of his academic behavior, we see that drug use is more likely to occur among the poorer than the better students. Among those with an average grade of 3.0 or higher, only 15.3 per cent report the use of drugs as compared to 31.0 per cent among those with an average of 2.5 or less. This difference in grade probably represents one more manifestation of the rejection of the "hard work-success" ethic of conventional society.

The "Hang-Loose" Ethic: Attitudinal Correlates. Similar differences in frequency of drug use are found in relation to a wide range of educational, political, and social attitudes and values indicative of a rejection of the established order. Drug use is more likely to be reported by those students who are relatively antagonistic to the educational system and who are dissatisfied with the education they are receiving. For example, among those students who disagree with the statement, "American colleges today should place more emphasis on teaching American ideals and values," more than seven times as many are frequent smokers of marijuana than among those who agree (13.8% vs. 1.8%). Simi-

larly, whereas 30.2 per cent of those students who "often" feel that what they are learning is a waste of time smoke marijuana, only 12.9 per cent of those who don't feel this way do so. However, drug use does not mean "apathy" toward academic life—more smokers of marijuana are to be found among those students who believe that students should have a more active role in making decisions about student life than among those who do not (28.4% vs. 11.1%).

On the political scene, drug use is much more likely to occur if the student is opposed to the Vietnam war (37.5% among those favoring immediate military withdrawal vs. 3.0% among those supporting President Johnson's policy). Drug users are also more frequent among those who believe that "human lives are too important to be sacrificed for any form of government" (32.0% vs. 12.6%). Opposition to the draft is another political view associated with drug use. Among those who are opposed to military service, 35.2 per cent use drugs as compared to 15.0 per cent among those who are not opposed, and, in fact, for those male students whose decision to attend college was affected by the possibility of being drafted, 41.7 per cent are drug users as compared to 25.2 per cent among those for whom this was not a consideration.

Social attitudes also reflect this "hang-loose" ethic on the part of drug users. Drug users are more likely to be found among those who feel it is all right to get around the law if you don't actually break it (34.6% vs. 13.8%) and who feel that the "hippie" way of life represents a desire for serious change as opposed to an unproductive expression of non-conformism (26.6% vs. 10.5%). The student who reports that he expects to get the most satisfaction out of life by means of his leisure time recreational activities is a much more frequent user of marijuana than the student who values participation in civic affairs or family relations (45.2% vs. 12.5% and 17.0%). An indication of possible family conflict among drug users is given by the higher proportion of drug users among those students who feel that their parents don't respect their opinions (29.2% vs. 15.3%).

One finding in regard to social attitudes appears contrary to many claims made about drug use. A series of four questions designed to index "alienation" (i.e., "These days a person does not really know whom he can count on"; "If you don't watch yourself, people will take advantage of you.") showed no statistically significant relationships to smoking marijuana, despite the claim of Halleck (Time, 1967) that "Smoking marijuana has become almost an emblem of alienation." Given the large number of significant differences found, this lack of any association between drug use and alienation is impressive. The "hang-loose" ethic, while it may represent antagonism to the conventional world, does not appear to create apathy and withdrawal. Subscribers to this ethic are not so much "anomic" in regard to society in general as critical of the existing "Establishment" in specific.

The "Hang-Loose" Ethic: Personality Correlates. The more the student's self-image tends to be rebellious, cynical, anti-establishment, "hippie," and apathetic, the more likely is he to smoke marijuana. Conversely, the more his self-image tends to be conformist, well-behaved, moral, and "square," the less likely is he to make use of marijuana. The greatest differences are to be found between those students who regard themselves as "hippies" (39% difference in favor of use) or well-behaved (37% difference against use). The smallest differences occur in relation to apathy (8% difference in favor of use) and cynicism (10% difference in favor of use).

These contrasts in self-image between users and non-users are congruent with the previous findings in relation to behavioral and attitudinal correlates. Such attitudes as disrespect for the law and skepticism about the worthwhileness of college, coupled with such behaviors as participating in mass protests and "happenings," match the self-portrait of the marijuana smoker as anti-establishment, cynical, and rebellious. If we view these traits as indicative of an underlying value system, we can quite readily see the contrast in "Protestant" vs. "hang-loose" ethic between marijuana smokers and non-smokers. These self-characterizations do lend face validity to the general public stereotyping of the marijuana smoker as "deviant" and the marijuana's own stereotyping of those who do not use marijuana as "square."

Demographic Controls. Each of the major differences in behavior, attitudes, and personality between users and non-users of marijuana was examined separately by sex, income, and religious group. Since, for example, males are more likely than females to smoke marijuana and also to subscribe to the "hang-loose" ethic, the possibility exists that both ethic and drug use are reflections of sex and are not really associated in and of themselves.

Analysis of the demographic control tables shows that this, by and large, is not the case. In almost every instance, the differences in marijuana use occur independently for both the demographic control and the behavioral, attitudinal, and personality correlates of the "hang-loose" ethic. In other words, the "hang-loose" ethic continues to be related to marijuana smoking regardless of the sub-group of the student population being studied.

This is illustrated in Table 2, which pre-

TABLE 2. RELATIONSHIP BETWEEN "HANG-LOOSE" ETHIC AND MARIJUANA USE, ACCORDING TO SEX

"Hang-loose" Ethic	(Per Cent Smoking Marijuana)	
	Male	Female
Behavioral		
Participate in mass protests		
No	9.9(141)	3.8(212)
Once to twice	12.5 (48)	5.9 (51)
More than twice	40.0 (25)	16.7 (12)
Attend a "Happening"		
Rarely	8.6(116)	2.4(168)
Occasionally	15.5 (58)	3.7 (82)
Frequently	33.3 (33)	20.8 (24)
Attitudinal		
"It is all right to get around the law, if you don't actually break it."		
Disagree	18.2 (99)	11.3(168)
Undecided	34.0 (47)	19.0 (63)
Agree	40.3 (62)	26.7 (45)
"How strongly do you approve or disapprove of students having pre-marital sexual intercourse?"		
Disapprove	0.0 (18)	1.2 (81)
Undecided	26.8 (56)	11.1 (90)
Approve	33.8(136)	33.3(102)
Personality		
"Anti-establishment"		
Not at all well	18.0(111)	12.1(182)
A little	32.4 (34)	13.2 (38)
Undecided and well	46.9 (64)	32.7 (55)
"Well-behaved"		
Very well	15.6 (32)	4.6 (65)
Fairly well	21.4(131)	17.8(185)
Undecided and not well	56.2 (48)	27.6 (29)

sents the relationship between several different indices of the "hang-loose" ethic and marijuana use separately for males and females. First, we note that males are more likely than females both to subscribe to the "hang-loose" ethic and to smoke marijuana. Second, we see that for males and females separately, the more the student adheres to the "hang-loose" ethic, either in his or her behavior, attitudes, or personality, the more likely he or she is to smoke marijuana. Thus, we conclude that both sex and ethic contribute independently to marijuana use. This same conclusion appears in general for other demographic variables and for other indices of the "hang-loose" ethic.

We can also see from Table 2, in general, that the relationship between the "hang-loose" ethic and marijuana use is somewhat higher among the males. Also, the differences due to sex are much smaller than those due to variations in behavior, attitudes, or personality. It would thus appear that one's ethic is a more important determinant of marijuana use than one's sex. For example, in all cases, those females who subscribe to the "hang-loose" ethic are much more likely to use marijuana than those males who do not.

Attitude toward Use and Frequency of Use by Other Students. In the same way that we have analyzed the student's use of marijuana according to various correlates of the "hang-loose" ethic, we can also examine his attitudes toward such use and his reports about how many of the students he knows also smoke marijuana. (Since so few students report feeling any pressure to smoke marijuana, this aspect is omitted from the following analysis.) We present the results of this analysis in a summary fashion in Table 3. With only one exception—the relationship of family income to attitudes to marijuana use —all of the variables listed are significantly related (chi square $p < .05$) to attitudes to use and frequency of use by other students in the same direction as the student's own use of marijuana. That is, the behavioral, attitudinal, and personality correlates of the "hang-loose" ethic also relate to one's attitude toward smoking marijuana and the frequency of marijuana use among the students one knows. These three aspects of attitudes toward use, use by one's friends, and use by oneself, then, all become part of the general picture of marijuana use as such use reflects adherence to the "hang-loose" ethic.

The relative size of the associations (keeping in mind the variations from question to question of the number of answer categories) can be determined in an approximate way from the size of Cramer's V, a coefficient of association (Blalock, 1960, p. 230). Self-image tends to be more highly related than either attitudes or behavior. Sex attitudes are, in general, more highly related than either political or educational values. Very high associations are to be found

TABLE 3. RELATIONSHIP BETWEEN ATTITUDE TO USE OF MARIJUANA, FREQUENCY OF USE BY OTHER STUDENTS AND SELECTED CHARACTERISTICS

Student Characteristics[a]	Attitude to Use of Marijuana[b]	Frequency of Use by Other Students[c]
Demographic		
Sex	.14[d]	.19
Income	n.s.	.14
Behavior patterns		
Attend "happening"	.17	.30
Read "underground" newspaper	.30	.26
Participate in mass protest	.16	.20
Self-image		
"Hippie"	.28	.30
Anti-establishment	.23	.19
Well-behaved	.23	.22
Educational values		
College a waste of time	.16	.16
Students active in student affairs	.14	.13
Political values		
Vietnam a mistake	.19	.20
Human lives not to be sacrificed in war	.12	.12
Conscientious objection a loophole	.19	.17
Social values		
Approval of pre-marital sex, if consent	.32	.28
Approval of abortion	.22	.20
Approval of birth control	.22	.17
Approval of law-breaking	.15	.14
Frequency of other student behaviors		
Drink alcoholic beverages	.15	.19
Smoke marijuana	.42	. . .
Take LSD	.29	.41
Have sexual intercourse	.30	.37
Attitude to student behaviors		
Drink alcoholic beverages	.25	.14
Smoke marijuana	. . .	.42
Take LSD	.33	.30
Have sexual intercourse	.42	.31

[a]See previous text for question wording used to determine student characteristics.

[b]Question: "How strongly do you approve or disapprove of students smoking marijuana?" (Strongly Approve, Approve, Undecided, Disapprove, Strongly Disapprove).

[c]Question: "How frequently do most of the students you know smoke marijuana?" (Frequently, Occasionally, Seldom, Never, Don't Know).

[d]Coefficients of association as determined by Cramer's V.

293

among attitudes and behaviors in regard to smoking marijuana, taking LSD, having sexual intercourse, and drinking alcoholic beverages, in about that order.

In summary, this table of associations underscores the interrelationships between attitudes and use, and between the various correlates of the "hang-loose" ethic and such attitudes and use. It is quite clear that the more one's behaviors, attitudes, and personality conform to the "hang-loose" ethic, the more likely one will be to approve of smoking marijuana and the more likely is it that one will associate with other students who smoke marijuana.

Finally, in Table 4, we show the mutual effects of attitude toward smoking marijuana and several aspects of the "hang-loose" ethic upon the use of marijuana. By and large, similar differences are found for all other aspects of the "hang-loose" ethic. As hypothesized, these two variables are independently related to drug use with the most frequent use occurring among those students who have both a favorable attitude toward the use of marijuana and an adherence to the "hang-loose" ethic. In general, an unfavorable attitude toward the use of marijuana will be equated with the absence of marijuana smoking. However, even among those with an unfavorable attitude, use will be higher with adherence to the "hang-loose" ethic. Similarly, given a favorable attitude toward use of marijuana, actual use is much more likely to take place among those students displaying "hang-loose" attitudes, behavior, and personality.

TABLE 4. RELATIONSHIP BETWEEN "HANG-LOOSE" ETHIC, ATTITUDE TOWARD MARIJUANA USE AND USE OF MARI-JUANA

"Hang-loose" Ethic	(Per Cent Smoking Marijuana) Attitude to Use of Marijuana	
	Favorable	Unfavorable
Attend a "Happening"		
Rarely	31.3 (83)	4.5(201)
Occasionally	51.9 (54)	11.8 (84)
Frequently	73.5 (34)	25.6 (19)
"It's all right to get around the law, if you don't actually break it"		
Disagree	37.3 (75)	4.7(191)
Undecided	42.2 (45)	14.3 (61)
Agree	60.4 (48)	14.6 (55)
"Anti-establishment"		
No	39.8(103)	6.6(260)
Yes	54.9 (71)	19.3 (47)

On the basis of these interrelationships of demographic characteristics, attitudes, behavior, and personality to drug use, the following sequence or chain of events appears quite probable (although it would require a prospective study to test it); adherence to the "hang-loose" ethic is more likely to occur among certain predisposed personality types (i.e., rebellious cynical) and in certain social sub-groups (i.e. males, non-religious); such adherence is likely to lead to a favorable attitude toward smoking marijuana both for its "high" effects and its symbolism of rebellion against authority; this favorable attitude will be supported by other students who also embrace the "hang-loose" ethic and engage in similar overt and covert expressions of rejection of the established order. Finally, given this climate of opinion and behavior, the smoking of marijuana becomes almost a "natural" act for many students far removed from the public's current efforts to define it either as a legal or a health problem.

Summary and Discussion

The data presented in this report strongly support the major hypothesis that the more the student embraces the "hang-loose" ethic, the more frequently will he make use of marijuana. Also supported is the further hypothesis that certain social sub-groups such as males will more frequently both smoke marijuana and adhere to the "hang-loose" ethic, but that regardless of group membership, the "hang-loose" ethic will be related to marijuana use. In regard to attitudes toward use, we find, as hypothesized, that the more the student subscribes to the "hang-loose" ethic, the more favorable will he be toward marijuana use; and the more favorable he is, the more will he actually use marijuana. These attitudes toward use and the "hang-loose" ethic become independent factors in marijuana smoking, reinforcing each other with the greatest use occurring among those students with a favorable attitude who also believe in the "hang-loose" ethic. Finally, the student's use of marijuana is strongly supported when his friends also smoke marijuana.

These findings have significance for both sociological theory and social action. From a theoretical point of view, they support the interpretation of drug use as part of a subcultural group way of life. Among students, this sub-culture is strongly characterized by a "hang-loose" ethic which attempts to cut itself loose from the traditional "establishment" and to develop freedom from conformity and the search for new experiences. This culture becomes expressed in such behaviors as attending "happenings," reading underground newspapers, participating in mass protests, avoiding the draft, engaging in sexual intercourse and, very much to the point of this report, smoking marijuana. Such use of marijuana constitutes an important means both of attaining "freedom" from the pressures of society and of expressing antagonism toward the "unfair" laws and restrictions of that society. For such students, marijuana serves much the same function as "social drinking" does for their parents, and their "law breaking" has the same social sanctions as drinking did during Prohibition. And just as "social drinking" is a far cry from "alcoholism," so is smoking marijuana far removed from "narcotics addiction."

The relationship of both social drinking to alcoholism and smoking marijuana to narcotics addition illustrates a significant interaction between social problems, health problems, and legal problems (Suchman, 1963b, pp. 58-64). A social act (e.g. one carried out by members of a group as part of the sub-cultural norm of that group) will be labelled a social problem when it conflicts with the accepted norms of the larger society. In this sense, marijuana smoking among students has become a social problem, whereas drinking alcohol has not. The type of corrective action "legitimatized" by the larger society to meet this problem will then determine whether it is viewed as a health or a legal problem. The more the social problem threatens the "value system" of the society, the more likely is it to be labelled a legal as opposed to a health problem and to be assigned to the police rather than the doc-

tor. Restriction and punishment become the means for handling the problem rather than understanding and treatment.

In the absence of any clear-cut evidence that (1) marijuana smoking is physiologically addictive or has serious health effects, and (2) use of marijuana leads to crime and delinquency or use of other drugs, it seems premature to view it as either a health or a legal problem. (Mayor's Committee on Marijuana, 1944) Our data would strongly suggest that use of marijuana is predominantly a social act favored by a sub-group in our society which happens to be disenchanted with the established order and for whom such use has become simply a normal preference for their own particular recreational drug. (Simmons, 1967) To crack down on these youth with all of the powerful forces of law and order and to justify such a restriction of freedom in the name of preventing crime or disease seems more an uncontrolled expression of adult moral indignation and righteousness than of human concern or social justice—and, sadly, an ineffective and destructive expression at that. (Lindesmith, 1965) While there can be little question that the "hang-loose" ethic is contrary to the Protestant ethic and the spirit of capitalism, and may be socially disapproved for that and other reasons, the issue, it seems to us, should be openly faced and debated as one of conflicting social values and not of crime or health. As formulated by Simmons (1967, p. 11), "It [the marijuana issue] seems to be the pivot around which far deeper conflicts and confrontations are raging—oldsters versus youngsters, hippies versus straight society, administered morality versus personal freedom."

Surely, it should be possible to express one's disapproval of marijuana and to seek its control without making its use a crime against society.

william h. mcglothlin

louis jolyon west

the marihuana problem: an overview*

The combination of a very rapid increase in marihuana use and the severe penalties prescribed for violation of the marihuana laws has brought about a social crisis. These two phenomena are not necessarily independent. The extreme legal penalties and the gross exaggerations of the consequences of marihuana use as fostered by the Federal Bureau of Narcotics make it an ideal target for rebellious youth to point to as an example of adult hypocrisy.

The situation is especially crucial in California. In 1967 there were 37,500 marihuana arrests in California, compared to 7,000 in 1964. Three-fourths of the cases are dismissed without trial, yet marihuana cases still accounted for 17 percent of all felony complaints issued by the Los Angeles district attorney's office during the period June through September 1967. The present rate of increase in marihuana arrests would indicate that such cases would comprise over 50 percent of the felony complaints within two years. On the other hand, in one highly publicized recent case of arrest for violation of marihuana laws, the defense collected 2,000 affidavits, the majority from persons

who stated that they used marihuana and found it harmless.

A reappraisal of the social policies controlling marihuana is clearly needed, but unfortunately there is very little recent research to provide a basis for rational decisions. Virtually all the studies done in this country were conducted some 25 to 30 years ago. The dearth of recent research and absence of long-term studies is a situation largely brought about by giving the same governmental agency control of both enforcement and research.

In assessing the current state of knowledge pertaining to the use of marihuana, probably the most important fact to keep in mind is that the range in amount used is extremely wide. Since marihuana use has been traditionally defined in legal rather than in health terms, there is a tendency to consider all users as a single group. In fact, there are no physiologically addictive qualities, and the occasional users have always far out-numbered those using it in a habitual manner.

The older studies in this country found that regular users consumed around 6 to 10 cigarettes per day (Charin and Perelman, 1946; Mayor's Committee, 1944); however, a much larger number used it on an irregular basis (Bromberg, 1934). Studies done in Eastern countries, especially India and North Africa, have concentrated on users of the highly potent hashish. Heavy users consume

Reprinted with permission of the authors and the American Psychiatric Association from the *American Journal of Psychiatry*, 1968, **125,** 126-134.

*Read at the 124th annual meeting of the American Psychiatric Association, Boston, Mass., May 13-17, 1968.

2 to 6 grams of hashish per day which is equivalent to smoking at least 20 to 60 marihuana cigarettes (Chopra & Chopra, 1939; Soueif, 1967). Moderate use of the less potent cannabis preparations in the East is not considered to be a health problem; and, in fact, bhang (the Indian equivalent of marihuana) is not even considered to fall within the definition of cannabis by Indian authorities and so is excluded from U. N. treaty control (Commission on Narcotic Drugs, 1965).

The recent increase in marihuana use in the U. S. is primarily among middle- and upper-class youth, the large majority of whom do not average more than two or three cigarettes a week. Some members of the hippie subculture and certain other individuals use marihuana in amounts comparable to that found in the older studies (6 to 10 cigarettes per day).

With this as preface, we propose to provide a brief overview of what is known about the effects of marihuana use, followed by some preliminary data from a current study.

Classification

In small amounts marihuana acts as a mild euphoriant and sedative somewhat like alcohol, although in comparable doses it is probably more disruptive of thought processes. In larger doses marihuana effects more closely resemble those of the hallucinogens than any other group of drugs. Most of the phenomena experienced with LSD, such as depersonalization, marked visual and temporal distortion, and hallucinations have been observed with sufficiently large amounts of marihuana and especially with hashish. The effects, however, are generally much milder and easier to control than those of LSD. Isbell and associates recently demonstrated a similar dose effect with tetrahydrocannabinol (THC), an active constituent of marihuana (Isbell, Gordodetzsky, Jasinski, Claussen, Spulak, & Korte, 1967).

On the other hand, there are considerable differences in users' descriptions of marihuana and LSD effects; also, marihuana acts as a sedative and tends to produce sleep, whereas the strong hallucinogens cause long periods of wakefulness. In addition, marihuana produces virtually no

tolerance, whereas very rapid tolerance accompanies use of LSD-like drugs. Isbell found no cross tolerance to THC in subjects tolerant to LSD, indicating that the two drugs probably act by different mechanisms.

Dependence

Mild irritability frequently follows withdrawal from heavy use of marihuana, but there are virtually no other symptoms of physical dependence. Psychological dependence may develop in the sense that the individual prefers the mood state resulting from marihuana use to the undrugged state. The fact that 65 percent of the hashish users in a recent Egyptian survey indicated they would like to get rid of the habit indicates appreciable psychological dependence (Soueif, 1967).

Of course, many forms of socially acceptable behavior (e.g., smoking tobacco, watching TV) may produce a form of psychic dependence. The harmfulness of such behavior should be based on the consequences of the activity rather than its existence.

Physical and Mental Effects

No long-term physical effects of marihuana use have been demonstrated in this country, although more current studies are needed before this issue can be resolved with any degree of certainty. Eastern studies of chronic users, who consume several times the amounts generally used in this country, report a variety of cannabis-induced physical ailments. Conjunctivitis is the most frequent, followed by chronic bronchitis and various digestive ailments (Chopra & Chopra, 1939). Sleep difficulties frequently occur, as is the case with opiate users in this country (Chopra & Chopra, 1939; Soueif, 1967). It is interesting to note that from 25 to 70 percent of regular hashish users in two Eastern surveys reported some impairment in physical health due to the use of the drug (Chopra & Chopra, 1939; Soueif, 1967).

There have been several cases of marihuana-induced temporary psychosis reported in this country (Bromberg, 1934;

Mayor's Committee, 1944). Panic reactions are not uncommon among inexperienced users, and such reactions occasionally develop into a psychotic episode. These very rarely last more than a day or so, and they do not usually require hospitalization. The danger of a prolonged psychosis from marihuana is very small compared to that for LSD.

On the other hand, in India and other Eastern countries, cannabis has long been regarded as an important cause of psychosis. One study reported that 25 percent of some 2,300 men admitted to psychiatric hospitals were diagnosed as having cannabis psychoses; of the total male admissions 70 percent of the patients admitted to smoking cannabis, and one-third were regular users (Benabud, 1957). Other investigators have argued that the 3 to 1 ratio of male to female hospitalized psychotics is a result of cannabis use being almost entirely restricted to males.

These studies are definitely not in agreement with the findings in this country, and many Western authorities question the adequacy of both the diagnoses made and the methodology of the studies themselves. Although part of the difference may be due to the fact that much larger amounts of the drug are used in the East, it is doubtful that this could reasonably account for the wide discrepancy in the findings.

While there is little concern about marihuana-induced psychosis in this country, there is considerable interest in the possibility of personality changes resulting from marihuana use, particularly in the development of what has been called an "amotivational" syndrome. The older studies of regular users in this country typically described them as tending to be passive and nonproductive. Eastern studies characterize heavy users in a similar manner. However, there has generally been no attempt to distinguish between preexisting personality traits and the effect of the drug use.

While systematic studies of the recent wave of young marihuana users are not yet available, clinical observations indicate that regular marihuana use may contribute to the development of more passive, inward-turning, amotivational personality characteristics. For numerous middle-class students, the subtly progressive change from conforming, achievement-oriented behavior to a state of relaxed and careless drifting has followed their use of significant amounts of marihuana.

It is difficult to parcel out social factors, as well as the occasional use of LSD, but it appears that regular use of marihuana may very well contribute to some characteristic personality changes, especially among highly impressionable young persons. Such changes include apathy, loss of effectiveness, and diminished capacity or willingness to carry out complex long-term plans, endure frustration, concentrate for long periods, follow routines, or successfully master new material. Verbal facility is often impaired, both in speaking and writing.

Such individuals exhibit greater introversion, become totally involved with the present at the expense of future goals, and demonstrate a strong tendency toward regressive, child-like magical thinking. They report a greater subjective creativity but less objective productivity; and, while seeming to suffer less from vicissitudes and frustrations of life, at the same time they seem to be subtly withdrawing from the challenge of it.

Marihuana and Crime

Enforcement agencies have long attempted to justify existing punitive marihuana laws by contending that marihuana use is criminogenic. No acceptable evidence has ever been offered to support these claims, and virtually every serious investigator who has attempted to examine the question has found no relationship between marihuana and major crime. Indeed, many feel that the characteristic passive reaction to marihuana use tends to inhibit rather than cause crime, whereas alcohol consumption is more likely to release aggressive behavior.

One recent study of drug use among juveniles reported that those who were most delinquent preferred alcohol, whereas the "pot-heads" tended to be nonaggressive and stayed away from trouble (Blumer, Sutter, Ahmed, & Smith, 1967). Moreover, a shift from alcohol to marihuana use tended to be correlated with a change toward less delinquent behavior in other respects. There apparently is some validity to the claim that professional criminals sometimes use marihuana as a means of fortifying themselves in their criminal operations; however, other drugs such as alcohol, amphetamines, and barbiturates are equally popular for this purpose.

Relation of Marihuana to Other Drug Use

A possible indirect hazard of marihuana smoking has been much debated. According to the stepping-stone theory, the use of marihuana will lead to the use of heroin in the search for greater thrills. Proponents cite the fact that most heroin users have previously used marihuana. Opponents deny that this indicates causality and cite the fact that while heroin use has remained at virtually the same level during the last few years, marihuana use has experienced a rapid rise.

Although present-day marihuana use has not been shown to predispose to heroin use, it does play a role in initiation to other potent drugs, particularly LSD. To the extent that marihuana contributes to a general disregard for the realistic consequences of behavior in young persons, its use increases the probability of the abuse of other more dangerous drugs. Thus, members of the hippie subculture frequently use methamphetamine and a host of other drugs. There is also some experimentation with heroin.

Finally, to the extent that hashish is available, its use is causally related to marihuana use. Many if not most marihuana users would welcome the opportunity to try hashish, and, if it were available, many would probably continue to use it in preference to the low-potency marihuana. Of course, the use of hashish does not necessarily lead to excess any more than does a preference for distilled liquor over beer or wine. However, the history of mind-altering drugs invariably shows that excessive indulgence increases sharply as more potent preparations of a given drug become available.

Marihuana Use among a Selected Group of Adults

Table 1 presents some characteristics of users and nonusers of marihuana among a sample of 189 persons randomly drawn

from a population of 750 who received LSD from a physician in either an experimental or psychotherapy setting during the period 1955-61. The marihuana data are incidental to an ongoing follow-up interview study of LSD effects; however, these results are of interest in two respects. First, they provide information on the use of marihuana among an older group of largely professional persons. Second, the observations of this group concerning the effects of marihuana are based on more experience and are considered to be more objective than assessments made by the less reality-oriented younger groups of marihuana users.

Forty-two percent of this group of 189 have had some experience with marihuana, although only 17 percent have used it ten or more times. One-half of the latter group were introduced to marihuana prior to 1954. About one-third of those who had not tried marihuana indicated that they might do so in the future, and a slightly higher proportion stated that they might try it if it were legal. The large majority of those who had used marihuana favored its legalization, and about one-half of those who had not tried it indicated a similar preference.

TABLE 1. CHARACTERISTICS OF USERS AND NONUSERS OF MARIHUANA AMONG A SAMPLE OF PERSONS RECEIVING LSD UNDER MEDICAL CONDITIONS, 1955-61

Characteristic	Marihuana Use		
	None (N = 110)	Less Than Ten Times (N = 47)	Ten or More Times (N = 32)
Percent of total group	58	25	17
Mean age (years)	46	40	39
Percent male	63	72	66
Education: B.A. degree or higher (percent)	56	64	44
Income: $10,000 or more (percent)	68	66	58
Used LSD under nonmedical conditions (percent)	7	19	64
Median year of initial marihuana use	—	1962	1954
Used marihuana prior to LSD (percent)	—	30	69
Use of marihuana in future:			
No (percent)	65	40	12
Yes (percent)	7	30	72
Possibly (percent)	28	30	16
Use of marihuana in future if legalized:			
No (percent)	54	32	9
Yes (percent)	15	36	84
Possibly (percent)	30	32	6
Favor removal of legal penalties against:			
Possession (percent)	54	81	97
Both possession and sale to persons over 21 (percent)	40	74	84

The remainder of the data apply to the 32 respondents who used marihuana ten or more times. Table 2 provides profession and frequency of use. Table 3 presents data on various motivations for marihuana use.

Inquiry was made concerning the effect of marihuana on driving competence. Of the 32 respondents, eight stated that they never drove under the influence of marihuana. Twenty of the remaining 24 felt that their driving competence was impaired. The reasons given were: perceptual distortion, speed distortion, slower reaction time, less alert, disoriented, poor judgment, and less careful.

TABLE 2. PROFESSION AND FREQUENCY OF USE OF MARIHUANA AMONG 32 RESPONDENTS WHO HAVE USED IT TEN OR MORE TIMES

Variable	Number
Profession	
Arts (artist, writer, actor, TV-radio, designer, etc.)	14
Physician, dentist, psychologist	7
Housewife	4
Engineer	2
Other	5
Frequency of use	
Daily	5
Two or three times per week	6
Once a week	4
Less than once a week	8
Do not use currently	9

TABLE 3. MOTIVATION FOR USE OF MARIHUANA AMONG 32 RESPONDENTS WHO HAVE USED IT TEN OR MORE TIMES

Motivation	Frequently	Occasionally
Produce "high" or euphoria	66	25
Relax	50	32
Relieve tensions or stress	38	44
Increase sociability	25	50
Increase sexual satisfaction	35	38
Increase enjoyment of plays, movies, etc.	22	44
Increase enjoyment of food	32	32
To go along with group	16	41
To cope with uncomfortable social situations	13	28
Relieve depression	16	25

Fourteen of the 32 indicated that they sometimes worked under the influence of marihuana; five stated that the effect on work was positive, four, that it was negative, and five, neutral or mixed. Fifteen of the 32 indicated that they sometimes used marihuana to enhance creative endeavors such as art, writing, music, singing, and design. Those who felt it aided in writing generally indicated that the ideas occurred to them while under the influence of marihuana, but the actual writing was done in an undrugged state.

A frequently reported advantage of marihuana over alcohol is the absence of hangover effects. Twelve of the 32 respondents reported that they sometimes experienced undesirable aftereffects the day following the use of marihuana; however, nine of the 12 indicated that such effects occurred only when large amounts were used or when it was smoked just prior to retiring. The most frequently reported symptom was lethargy, followed by inability to concentrate, irritability, and headaches.

Twenty-five of the 32 felt marihuana had resulted in no long-term effects; six reported positive long-term effects (increased insight, tolerance, spontaneity, and sexual freedom); one respondent regarded the long-term effects as mixed. It is interesting to compare these results with those of heavy hashish users in India and Egypt, where up to 70 percent report some harmful effects.

Nine of the 32 respondents were not currently using marihuana. Three said they stopped because they did not particularly like the effect, two stopped due to legal concerns, and four, due to other reasons. Of the 23 currently using marihuana, 18 indicated that they planned to continue at the same level of use and five stated they planned to decrease the frequency of use.

Four of the 32 had been arrested in connection with their marihuana use—two cases were dismissed and two received probation. Twenty of the 32 had used LSD under nonmedical conditions and 17 had used other strong hallucinogens such as peyote, mescaline, and psilocybin. Six had some experience with heroin—one had been addicted.

Social Policy

Social policy with respect to marihuana and other psychoactive drugs has many important dimensions other than those already mentioned. The most basic issue is whether or not the prohibition of behavior whose direct effects are limited to the individual is within the function of the state. Those who feel it is not argue that the state has no more right to intervene with respect to the use of harmful drugs than it does with regard to harmful overeating.

Those who take the contrary position argue that the harms are not limited to the individual but burden society in a variety of ways; hence the state is entitled to prohibit its use in the public interest. It is certainly clear that the very existence of government entails individual restraints. Whether or not individual freedoms should be curbed with respect to drug use depends on the extent of the threat to society and whether or not the sanctions against it are effective.

An objective assessment of the threat or benefit to society resulting from the non-medical use of a drug should consider: physiological effects resulting from occasional or chronic use; tendency to produce physiological or psychological dependence as a function of period of use; release of antisocial behavior; effect on motor activity, especially driving safety; and tendency to produce long-lasting personality changes. Other relevant considerations are: cost; ability to control and measure potency; convenience of mode of intake, oral vs. intravenous, for example; capacity for self-titration to control effect; protection against overdose; availability of an antidote; specific effects attainable without unpredictable side effects; predictable length of action; hangover or other short-term properties which may spill over to affect work or other activities; ability to return to normalcy on demand; and ability to detect the drug, as for monitoring drivers, etc.

One of the most neglected questions in evaluating drug effects concerns the individual benefits which motivate the user. Drug use in many instances may well be an attempt to alleviate symptoms of psychiatric illness through self-medication. In some cases, marihuana use might postpone or prevent more serious manifestations of an illness. Especially for recreational drugs, such as alcohol and marihuana, an objective assessment of user motivation should consider: effectiveness in producing pleasure, relaxation, and aesthetic appreciation; enhancement of appetite and other senses; enhancement of interpersonal rapport, warmth, and emotionality; utility of variety or newness of perception and thinking; and enhancement of enjoyment of vacations, weekends, or other periods devoted to recreation, rest, and pleasure.

Other effects of nonmedical drug use may have more far-reaching ramifications for society in general. Does the drug use provide an emotional escape-valve similar to institu-tionalized festivities employed by other cultures? What is its effect on personality, life style, aggressiveness, competitiveness, etc.? Does it affect military effectiveness through increased passivity? Would its adoption by large numbers affect the direction of society? For example, the use of peyote changed the direction of the American Indian culture by creating a pan-Indian movement—the hippies would advocate a similar cure for the ills of the present society.

In considering the effectiveness of legal sanctions against the use of a drug, three related questions must be considered at the outset: (1) How many persons would abuse the drug if legal controls were removed or not adopted? (2) Do the laws deter use, or perhaps encourage it, as has been suggested with relation to rebellious youth? (3) Is the drug abuser a sick person who, if one drug is prohibited, will find another drug or some equally destructive behavior as a substitute? More specifically, each of these questions must be examined in the context of criminal sanctions against both the user and the distributor as opposed to sanctions against sale only.

Clearly, if the law protects against a nonexisting harm, society is better off without the law. The recent elimination of all laws pertaining to written pornography in Denmark, for example, apparently resulted in no ill effects. The incidence of marihuana use as opposed to LSD use supports the position that legal penalties are by no means the overriding determiner of drug usage. The number of persons who have used marihuana is several times that for LSD and is increasing in spite of severe penalties. LSD usage is apparently declining because of concern over the hazards rather than because of any deterrent effect of the relatively moderate laws.

The argument that the drug abuser would simply find another means of escape or self-destructive behavior if the drug were not available is probably only partially correct. It is clear that persons are more vulnerable to the abuse of drugs at certain times in their lives, such as during adolescence or other highly stressful periods. If a potential drug-of-abuse is unavailable at these times, an undesirable chain of events may well be avoided. Also, it is known that alcoholism results from sociogenic as well as psychogenic causes, and marihuana abuse can undoubtedly follow a similar pattern.

Concerning the kind of drug-control laws which should be enacted and enforced, there is general agreement that the government has not only the right but also the obligation to enforce certain practices with regard to the distribution of drugs. Disagreement exists as to the point at which the advantages of restricting availability are outweighed by the harm resulting from the illicit supplying of the demand for the drug, such as occurred during the prohibition of alcohol.

Regulation, as opposed to prohibition, permits the orderly control of potency and the conditions of sale, such as age of purchaser, hours of sale, and licensing. It also permits taxation and eliminates the support of organized crime as well as the criminogenic aspects of forcing the user to deal with illegal sources. On the other hand, prohibition of sale clearly indicates social disapproval, whereas open sale does not.

Arguments for criminal sanctions against the drug user primarily stress: (1) their deterrent effect and (2) the aid such laws give to enforcement agencies in apprehending sources of supply. Major arguments against such laws stress that enforcement inevitably encourages the violation of constitutional guarantees of privacy, as well as various other practices, such as informers posing as students, hippies, or other potential drug users, which are ethically questionable though technically legal.

The social control of drug use is most difficult to handle via legal means when the drug in question permits both use and abuse: e.g., alcohol and marihuana. The problem of penalizing the majority because of the abuse by the minority was specifically dealt with by the Supreme Court at the time of the Volstead Act. The Court ruled that the state had the right to deny access to alcohol to those who would not abuse it in order to remove the temptation from those who would abuse it.

On a few occasions, exceptions have actually been carved out of the law to permit use of a drug otherwise prohibited: e.g., sacramental use of wine and religious use of peyote by the Indians. More frequently, society has informally disregarded the enforcement of the law for various groups, conditions, or in certain districts of the city. For example, during the '40s, police frequently overlooked the use of marihuana by jazz musicians because they were otherwise productive and did not cause trouble. Another means of allowing use but controlling abuse is through compulsory treatment.

Conclusion

What is especially needed is a concerted effort to produce congruence among the various drug policies and laws. What we have at present is an assortment of approaches which are not only lacking in consistency but often operate in clearly opposite directions. Much of the incongruity is based on unrecognized attitudes and fears which must be made conscious and explicit before a congruent policy can emerge. One means of forcing some of the most glaring inconsistencies into perspective is to treat alcohol abuse and drug abuse as a single problem, an approach suggested by the World Health Organization (1967).

A rational approach to reducing the harm caused to society by excessive drug use must include examination of the contributions of the massive advertising programs for alcohol and tobacco and weigh this against the economic and other costs of intervening in our free enterprise system. If public drunkenness is the manifestation of an illness to be treated rather than punished, is dependency on other drugs not also an illness?

We should critically examine the legal reasoning which concludes that being an addict is not a crime, but possessing the substance necessary to be an addict is a felony deserving a five- or ten-year sentence. The methods of controlling narcotics supply should be weighed against the expense to the victims burglarized, the increased number of prostitutes, and the large profits to organized crime, all of which accompany illegal drug traffic. The deterring effect of the current marihuana laws should be evaluated against the resulting alienation, disrespect for the law, and secondary deviance involving a sizeable portion of an entire generation.

Finally, in a somewhat speculative vein, part of the lack of congruence among drug policies in this country may be due to the fact that economic and technological factors are changing at a faster rate than are cultural attitudes and values. The drug laws in this country have always been an attempt to legislate morality, although they have been justified in terms of preventing antisocial acts. These laws and attitudes evolved at a time when the Protestant ethic and the competitive, achievement-oriented value system were very much in dominance. The freely chosen, passive withdrawal to a life of drug-induced fantasy was an extremely threatening concept.

Now we are told we are verging on an economy of abundance rather than scarcity; an age of automation will eliminate half or more of the labor force necessary for the production of goods. The concept of work will have to be redefined to include nonproductive pursuits which are now considered hobbies; a guaranteed annual income program will likely be in effect within five or ten years. The children of today's middle class have never experienced a depression or any appreciable difficulty in satisfying their material needs. They do not share the materialistic value system to the same extent as their parents because they have little fear of material deprivation.

There also appears to be an increasing acceptance of pleasure in its own right rather than as something that needs to be earned as a reward for hard work. The traditional American attitude toward pleasure was quite evident in the opinion recently given by Judge Tauro in upholding the constitutionality of the Massachusetts marihuana laws. In denying that the fundamental right to the pursuit of happiness is violated by the marihuana laws, he argues that such rights must be "essential" to continued liberty and are particularly those "closely related to some commonly acknowledged moral or legal duty and not merely to a hedonistic seeking of pleasure." In affirming that the state was justified in permitting alcohol and prohibiting marihuana, Judge Tauro argued that alcohol was used most frequently as a relaxant and "as an incident of other social activities," whereas marihuana was "used solely as a means of intoxication," i.e., pleasure.

If the age of economic abundance, automation, and greatly increased leisure time becomes a reality, it is doubtful that these viewpoints toward pleasure (hedonistic and otherwise) can survive. Excessive drug use would be seen as a threat to the individual—not as "a threat to the very moral fabric of

society." The over-all welfare of society would be much less dependent on the productivity of the individual, and a value system which demands that pleasure be earned through work would be obsolete.

In conclusion, whether or not the age of abundance arrives, social policy, with some minor reversals, will probably move in the direction of permitting greater individual freedom with respect to drug use. Society will promote the concept of allowing adults the privilege of informed decision. The crucial problem which will remain is that of protecting those who are too young to make an informed decision.

References

Alexander, C. N., Jr. Consensus and mutual attraction in natural cliques: A study of adolescent drinkers. *American Journal of Sociology*, 1964, **69**, 395-403.
Alexander, C. N., Jr., & Campbell, E. Q. Peer influences on adolescent drinking behaviors. *Quarterly Journal of Studies on Alcohol*, in press.
Bales, R. F. Cultural differences in rates of alcoholism. In R. G. McCarthy (Ed.), *Drinking and intoxication*. Glencoe, Ill.: Free Press, 1959. Pp. 263-277.
Becker, H. S. Becoming a marijuana user. *American Journal of Sociology*, 1953, **59**, 235-242.
Benabud, A. Psycho-pathological aspects of the Cannabis situation in Morocco: Statistical data for 1956. *Bulletin on Narcotics*, 1957, **9**, 1-16.
Blachly, P. H., Disher, W., & Roduner, G. Suicide by physicians. *Bulletin of Suicidology*. Washington, D.C.: Government Printing Office, 1968. Pp. 1-18.
Blalock, H. M. *Social statistics*. New York: McGraw-Hill, 1960.
Blumer, H., Sutter, A., Ahmed, S., & Smith, R. *The world of youthful drug use*. Berkeley: University of California Press, 1967.
Bromberg, W. Marijuana intoxication. *American Journal of Psychiatry*, 1934, **91**, 303-330.
Charin, S., & Perelman, L. Personality studies of marijuana addicts. *American Journal of Psychiatry*, 1946, **102**, 674-682.
Chilnick, L. Pot on the campus. *Sooner Magazine*, 1969, **41** (4), 12-13, 19-20.
Chopra, R. N., & Chopra, G. S. The present position of hemp-drug addiction in India. *Indian Journal of Medical Research Memoirs*, 1939, **31**, 1-119.
Commission on Narcotics Drugs: Report of the Twentieth Session, November 29–December 21, 1965. E/4140, E/CN. 7/488, United Nations.

Dependence on cannabis (marijuana). *Journal of the American Medical Association,* 1967, **202,** 47-50.

Eddy, N. B., et al. Drug dependence: Its significance and characteristics. *Bulletin of the World Health Organization,* 1965, **32,** 721-733.

Fort, J. Youth: How to produce drop-ins rather than drop-outs. *Research Resume No. 38.* Burlingame, Calif.: Proceedings of the 20th Annual State Conference on Educational Research, 1968. Pp. 53-64.

Goldsen, R. K., et al. *What college students think.* Princeton, N.J.: Van Nostrand, 1960.

Heider, F. *The psychology of interpersonal relations.* New York: Wiley, 1958.

Hollister, W. G. Why adolescents drink and use drugs. *PTA Magazine,* 1969, **63,** 2-5.

Isbell, H., Gordodetzsky, C. W., Jasinski, D., Claussen, U., Spulak, F., & Korte, F. Effects of (-)9-Trans-Tetrahydrocannabinol in man. *Psychopharamacologia,* 1967, **11,** 184-188.

Jacob, P. E. *Changing values in college.* New York: Harper, 1957.

Johnson, F. K., & Westman, J. C. The teenager and drug abuse. *Journal of School Health,* 1968, **38,** 646-654.

Keller, M. The definition of alcoholism and the estimation of its prevalence. In D. P. Pittman, & C. R. Snyder (Eds.), *Society, culture, and drinking patterns.* New York: Wiley, 1962. Pp. 310-329.

Keniston, K. Students, drugs and protest. *Current,* 1969, No. 104, pp. 5-25.

Lindesmith, A. R. *The addict and the law.* Bloomington: Indiana University Press, 1965.

Mayor's Committee on Marijuana. *The marijuana problem in the city of New York.* Lancaster, Pa.: Jacques Cattell Press, 1944.

McGlothlin, W. H. Toward a rational view of marijuana. In J. Simmons (Ed.), *Marijuana: Myths and realities.* North Hollywood, Calif.: Brandon House, 1967. Pp. 163-214.

McGlothlin, W. H., & West, L. J. The marijuana problem: An overview. *American Journal of Psychiatry,* 1968, **125,** 126-134.

Modern medicine poll on sociomedical issues: Abortion—homosexual practices—marijuana. *Modern Medicine,* 1969, **37** (22), 18-25.

Plaut, T. F. *Alcohol problems: A report of the nation.* New York: Oxford University Press, 1967.

Pop drugs: The high as a way of life. *TIME,* 1969, **94** (13), 68-78.

Reader's digest, November 1967.

Richards, L. G., Joffe, M. H., Smith, J. P., & Spratto, G. R. *Layman's guide to pharmacology, physiology, psychology, and sociology of LSD.* Washington, D.C.: Government Printing Office, 1969.

Room, R. Cultural contingencies of alcoholism: Variations between and within nineteenth-century urban ethnic groups in alcohol-related death-rates. *Journal of Health and Social Behavior,* 1968, **9,** 99–113.

Simmons, J. L. (Ed.) *Marijuana: Myths and realities.* North Hollywood, Calif.: Brandon House, 1967.

Simmons, J. L., & Winograd, E. *It's happening: A portrait of the youth scene today.* Santa Barbara, Calif.: Marc-Laird, 1966.

Skolnick, J. H. Religious affiliation and drinking behavior. *Quarterly Journal of Studies on Alcohol,* 1958, **19,** 452-470.

Smith, D. D. LSD and the psychedelic syndrome. *Research Resume No. 38.* Burlingame, Calif.: Proceedings, 20th Annual State Conference on Educational Research, 1968. Pp. 68-73.

Smith, D. D. The trip there and back. *Emergency Medicine,* 1969, **1,** 26-41.

Somers, R. H. A new asymmetric measure of association for ordinal variables. *American Sociological Review,* 1962, **27,** 799-811.

Soueif, M. I. Hashish consumption in Egypt with special reference to psychosocial aspects. *Bulletin on Narcotics,* 1967, **19,** 1-12.

Strack, A. E. Drug use and abuse among youth. *Journal of Health, Physical Education, and Recreation,* 1968, **39,** 26-28, 55-57.

Straus, R., & Bacon, S. D. *Drinking in college.* New Haven, Conn.: Yale University Press, 1953.

Suchman, E. A. *Sociology and the field of public health.* New York: Russell Sage Foundation, 1963a.

Suchman, E. A. The addictible diseases as socio-environmental health problems. In H. Freeman, et al. (Eds.), *Handbook of medical sociology.* Englewood Cliffs, N.J.: Prentice-Hall, 1963b. Pp. 123-143.

Suchman, E. A. The "hang-loose" ethic and the spirit of drug use. *Journal of Health and Social Behavior,* 1968, **9,** 146-155.

TIME, May 19, 1967.

Two doctors warn against the abuse of amphetamines. *U.S. News and World Report,* 1969, **57** (26), 24-25.

Weinswig, M. H., Doerr, D. W., & Weinswig, S. E. Drug abuse education. *Phi Delta Kappan,* 1968, **50,** 222-223.

Weissman, R. Teens and drugs: Monkey on our backs. *Arizona Teacher,* 1969, **57,** 10-13.

World Health Organization. *Services for the prevention and treatment of dependence on alcohol and other drugs.* WHO Technical Report Serial No. 363, 1967.

Annotations

Ball, J. C., Chambers, C. D., & Ball, M. J. The association of marihuana smoking with opiate addiction in the United States. *Journal of Criminal Law, Criminology, and Police Science,* 1968, **59,** 171-182. In this study of 2213 addicts, the researchers found a positive relationship between the use of marihuana and the opiates in 16 states, Washington, D.C., and Puerto Rico. In 12 states the opiate addicts had not used marihuana. The most positive relationships were found in the Midatlantic states, the Southwest, and in California.

Demos, G. D. Drug abuse and the new generation. *Phi Delta Kappan,* 1968, **50,** 214-217. The author offers several suggestions to educators about dealing with drug abuse: (1) know what the problem is, (2) create better communication levels with drug users, (3) offer a more flexible policy about drugs, (4) provide more constructive outlets for adolescent energy, and (5) be more attentive to the needs of youths.

Drugs. *Crime and Delinquency,* 1970, **16** (1), entire issue. The initial article, "Drugs for Kicks," is a thorough overview of the drug problem. Other discussions center on marijuana, morality, and the law; social correlates of student drug use; and slang use in addict subcultures.

Eells, K. Marijuana and LSD: A survey of one college campus. *Journal of Counseling Psychology,* 1968, **15,** 459-467. This study was conducted among 1290 men at the California Institute of Technology. About 14 percent had used marijuana and 6 percent had used LSD. Most students viewed marijuana as harmless, although they saw no value in its use. LSD was considered to be potentially harmful, with its dangers outweighing its harmlessness. Users considered the drugs less harmful than did nonusers.

Freedman, D. X. On the use and abuse of LSD. *Archives of General Psychiatry,* 1968, **18,** 330-347. Freedman presents and analyzes reasons why adolescents use LSD: to seek identity, individuality, and experience; to achieve a religious or mystic experience; or to expand one's consciousness. Although the effects of LSD are not fully understood, the drug is potentially emotionally disruptive.

Keniston, K. Students, drugs, and protest. *Current,* 1969, **104,** 5-25. Keniston distinguishes between two types of drug users: "heads," who find identity in a drug subculture that allows them to drop out of "Established America," and "seekers," who use drugs as a means of finding order within our society. Seekers often are middle- to upper-middle-class students with above-average intelligence. Keniston also analyzes the social, political, and historical factors within our society that cause unrest.

Marijuana: What it is—and isn't. *U.S. News and World Report,* 1969, **67** (15), 48-50. This report describes marijuana and its various uses. Several questions as to the legality of marijuana, its immediate effects, its addictive effects, and its association to criminality are also discussed.

Richards, L. G., Joffe, M. H., Smith, J. P., & Spratto, G. R. *LSD-25: A factual account.* Washington, D.C.: U.S. Department of Justice, 1969. This thorough analysis of LSD discusses (1) the action of LSD on the body and brain, (2) major psychological effects of the drug, (3) current research with LSD, (4) various reactions and risks of LSD, and (5) social uses being made of LSD.

Riester, A. E., & Zucker, R. A. Adolescent social structure and drinking behavior. *Personnel and Guidance Journal,* 1968, **47,** 304-312. This study considers adolescent drinking behaviors within the informal social structure of the high school. It reveals that a large percentage of students use alcohol before they legally have access to it. There are also evidences of a high incidence of social drinking by adolescents in the presence of adults.

Schonfield, J. Differences in smoking, drinking, and social behavior by race and delinquency status in adolescent males. *Adolescence,* 1967, **1,** 367-380. This interesting article compares patterns of smoking and drinking among delinquent and nondelinquent adolescent boys according to race. It shows that social and environmental variables affect individual behavior.

Smith, D. The trip: There and back. *Emergency Medicine,* 1969, **1** (11), 26-41. David Smith, M. D., is director of a drug clinic in the Haight-Ashbury section of San Francisco. He focuses on the user and indicates that exploring reasons for drug usage may be more important than information about a drug itself. Smith also discusses the diagnosis and treatment of drug abusers.

Special issue on recreational drug use. *Journal of Health and Social Behavior,* 1968, **9** (2), entire issue. This discussion ranges from beer busts to drug addiction to the social usage of the psychedelic drugs. It also comments on dissenting youths. Of special interest is an analysis of various meanings today's youths attach to alcohol and drug use.

Weissman, R. Teens and drugs: Monkey on our backs. *Arizona Teacher,* 1969, **57,** 10-13. Weissman analyzes the drug problem from the perspective of the middle-class drug user and his fight for the moral acceptance and legalization of drugs, especially marijuana. Secondly, she discusses school involvement in drug education—new approaches, the role of the teacher, and the "when and how" of such education.

nine

the adolescent and activism

Adolescent rebellion has evolved into a major social problem. The behavior of our youths, whether violent or nonviolent, has caused many people to consider adolescents irresponsible, riotous, shiftless, and unpatriotic. The fact that other periods in our history were also plagued with discontent, activism, and even violence does not lessen the significance of student unrest today.

Popular belief attributes most unrest to racial minorities or the culturally and socially disadvantaged. However, the problem is also encountered on college campuses, in hippie communities, and in several high schools.

Perhaps the most vital task of socialization is to train adolescents for responsible adulthood. Providing them with opportunities for meaningful employment could help accomplish this end. Yet the lack of such opportunities is not accidental. Automation has created a demand for technical skills that young people must spend the time to acquire before they become eligible to enter the work force (Cole & Hall, 1970).

Instead of work experiences, adolescents are given credit cards and checking accounts. Full-time financial support from parents and only part-time obligations leave much time for involvement in a variety of activities. It is no wonder that most of the New Leftists and hippies are from the middle class and are thus reacting to it. They have set out to make this generation different, and, with the financial backing of their parents, they may well succeed.

Four Phases of Activism

Modern student activism seems to have gone through four phases and may now be going through a fifth. The first phase began in about 1960 as an awareness of social inequities (Hartford, 1968). Southern black students began to try to break down the barriers of segregation in public accommodations (Flacks, 1967), and their activities were aided by the formation of the Student Nonviolent Coordinating Committee in 1960 ("New Left," 1969) and by sympathy demonstrations in many Northern universities (Flacks, 1967).

Phase two was initiated by sit-ins conducted by Southern black students. Their protests and the support rallied from white students were based on the hope that the evils of racism and segregation would be eliminated if pointed out by nonviolent demonstrations (Hartford, 1968). The sit-ins and demonstrations were the primary activities of the activists between 1960 and 1964. During this time three influential student organizations were formed: (1) the Progressive Labor Party in 1962, (2) the Students for a Democratic Society (SDS) in the same year, and (3) the Revolutionary Action Movement in 1963. Each group was to have an increasing influence on student attitudes and behavior.

The third phase of student activism began when students and minority group leaders lost their "faith in the American Dream" (Hartford, 1968). Convinced of the futility of their earlier attempts at eliminating social and political inequalities, they began to advocate the use of violence to achieve moral and patriotic ends. This phase was also characterized by the involvement of nonstudents in the struggle (Hartford, 1968). In 1964 the Free Speech Movement—a new force that was to reshape the direction of student activism—was organized on the campus of the University of California at Berkeley. After the Berkeley Rebellion, student protests became common on university campuses. From the activists' viewpoint, society was as impervi-

ous to pressure (phase three) as it was to moral persuasion (phase two). "Pressure tactics had failed to stop the war in Vietnam and had failed to deal with radical oppression. The result was to move into *resistance* and *base building* for a revolution (phase four)" (Hartford, 1968, p. 65; italics mine).

Resistance occurred on a wide scale between 1964 and 1969 on the campuses. Perhaps the most conflict was seen at Berkeley, Columbia, the University of Wisconsin, Harvard, San Francisco State, and Cornell, although activism swept over more than 200 other college and university campuses. In addition, ghetto uprisings, big-city riots, and draft resistance became major problems.

Base building was accomplished by the emergence of several student organizations designed to recruit new activists. Basically the groups were of three types: (1) the various black power movements tried to ensure more equality and less injustice for black Americans; (2) avid political groups, such as Socialists, Communists, Marxists, and New Leftists, represented political systems that were contrary to the existing system of the United States; (3) white students' organizations challenged the Establishment, conservatism, traditionalism—in effect the existing American life-style. All of these student activists were seeking a society based on justice and equality; a society in which power lies with all people, not just a few; a society that values human rights over all other rights.

Gottlieb's article in this chapter provides an overview of activism today. He notes factors in our society that have contributed to today's conflict and criticizes our method of socialization because it does not allow adolescents to become involved in the social and political issues that confront our nation.

A New Phase

It appears that the student revolt is entering a new phase, which can be labeled *constructive activism*. Many college students have begun to feel that resistance has gotten out of hand and is not accomplishing activist goals. In the fall of 1969 the Vietnam Moratorium Committee was organized to launch wide-scale peace demonstrations protesting the war in Vietnam. These protests, which were supported by many Congress-men and educators, were orderly, peaceful marches that proved students could express discontent without becoming violent. Un-doubtedly student violence is not over, but the direction of student efforts is shifting (Student revolt, 1969).

As a result of student resistance and nonviolent student peace marches, the Nixon administration developed a National Youth Policy. It consists of the following proposals:

1. Lowering the voting age to 18 in all states;
2. Reducing draft liability to one year at age 19;
3. Eventually ending the draft in favor of all-volunteer, professional armed forces;
4. Revising the criminal code to make possession of marijuana a misdemeanor instead of a felony on the first offense but providing stiffer penalties for re-peaters and for "pushers" of narcotics, other dangerous drugs, and marijuana (Nixon's efforts, 1969, p. 74).

Although all these proposals have not been effected, the policy has helped reduce stu-dent violence. In fact, many students are shifting their emphasis from Vietnam and the draft to other issues, such as pollution, mal-nutrition, and housing (Real revolution, 1970). Others are pursuing careers rather than causes (Thornburg, 1969).

However, not all student activists sympa-thize with the constructive effort. Some are employing guerrilla warfare techniques in an effort to achieve their goals. Thus the direc-tion of student activism is uncertain. Hope-fully, phase five will provide students with a realization of their aims and will engage adult interest in adolescent problems. As Gottlieb has stated, "We should respond to the needs of youth not out of fear of riots and rebellion, but because any other answer is morally unacceptable, economically incomprehensi-ble, and socially unthinkable."

The New Left Movements

Several groups have been organized with radical, New Left philosophies of open hos-tility to law and order. Their political ideolo-gies comprise elements of Communism,

Marxism, Maoism, or Castroism ("New Left," 1969).

One characteristic of all the New Left groups is inclusiveness. Keniston has stated,

> Psychologically, inclusiveness involves an effort to be open to every aspect of one's feelings, impulses and fantasies, to synthe-size and integrate rather than repress or dissociate, not to reject or exclude any part of one's personality or potential. Interper-sonally, inclusiveness means a capacity for involvement with, identification and collabo-ration with those who are superficially alien: the peasant in Vietnam, the poor in America, the nonwhite, the deprived and deformed (1968a, p. 232).

Student Nonviolent Coordinating Committee. This group was formed as a civil rights organ-ization in Atlanta, Georgia, in 1960. The pur-suit of civil rights shifted in 1966 to the goal of gaining black power through violence. Its primary spokesman was Stokely Carmichael, followed by H. Rap Brown in 1967. Both men advocated "bringing the country to its knees" by any means necessary ("New Left," 1969). The organization's current inactivity is attributed to a lack of goals in comparison to other groups.

Young Socialist Alliance. This group, formed in 1960, is pledged to replacing the existing American systems of capitalism and imperi-alism with Socialism. Members concentrate their efforts at the high school level.

Students for a Democratic Society (SDS). Formed in 1962 with only 59 students from 11 colleges, this group has become the most powerful on-campus organization and has spurred sit-ins, riots, strikes, and other mili-tant activities (Who's in charge, 1969). Yet the SDS does not limit its concern to colleges and universities, as is reflected in its stand against the draft and the U.S. military struc-ture. It also supports oppressed workers, both black and white ("New Left," 1969).

The SDS now has about 35,000 mem-bers on 350 campuses. Most members are white, middle class, highly idealistic, and very bright (Who's in charge, 1969). Politically, the SDS denounces the United States as a "capitalist, imperialist, racist state" ("New Left," 1969, p. 37). The group's aim is to effect a Marxist-Leninist revolution built around the Cuban model ("New Left," 1969; Who's in charge, 1969).

Some factions of the SDS have been quite successful in their resistance, as was seen in the Columbia University crisis of 1968 (Barton, 1968). The SDS's *Striker's Manifesto,* which was posted around the Columbia campus during the protest, advocated striking for any reason (Rampage, 1969). Although an in-depth study of the SDS may show that many of its causes seem justified, most students and faculty disapprove of its tactics (Barton, 1968).

Students' Afro-American Society. This group was organized through the recruitment of black students enrolled in predominantly white universities. Its efforts focus primarily on demands for new curricula, black housing, black athletic coaches, more black faculty, black foreign exchange programs, and scholarships for black students (New black student, 1969). Members of this organization were largely responsible for the major confrontations at Cornell University and San Francisco State University in 1969 ("New Left," 1969). Comparable organizations are the *Black Students Union* and the *Black Liberation Front.*

Black Panther Party. This group of black militants poses the greatest threat to constructive activism. When it was organized in 1966, most of its members were college students, but it has since elicited tremendous support from young black nonstudents in many major cities. Its militancy, depicted by arms, black berets, and black leather jackets, is aimed at ending oppression of the black race. The Panthers have developed a 10-point program to achieve black power.

1. We want freedom. We want power to determine the destiny of our black community.
2. We want full employment for our people.
3. We want an end to the robbery by the white man of our black people.
4. We want decent housing, fit for shelter of human beings.
5. We want education for our people that exposes the true nature of the decadent American society. We want education that teaches us our true history and our role in the present day society.
6. We want all black men to be exempt from military service.
7. We want an immediate end to police brutality and murder of black people.
8. We want freedom for all black men held in federal, state, county and city prisons and jails.
9. We want all black people when brought to trial to be tried in a court by a jury of their peer group or people from their black communities, as defined by the Constitution of the United States.
10. We want land, bread, housing, education, clothing, justice and peace (Black Panther, 1968).

Progressive Labor Party. This group was formed in 1962 by dissident Reds who had been expelled from the Communist Party–USA because they favored the political system of Communist China. Its members, working on many college campuses, claim to be waging a ceaseless struggle against the ruling class ("New Left," 1969).

Revolutionary Action Movement. This small group of black militant extremists is dedicated to the "overthrow of the capitalistic system in America and installation of a socialistic system modeled on Red China's interpretation of Marxism-Leninism" ("New Left," 1969, p. 36).

Youth International Party. This informally organized group, more commonly known as "Yippies," was founded in 1967. Spreading their anti-establishment ideas through the underground press, they have set out to destroy the present system of government, personified as "the man." As one Yippie organizer has stated, "Yippies are chipping away, blacks are chipping away, the enemy overseas is chipping away. If you keep on hitting the *man* from every side, punching him, laughing at him, ridiculing him, he will eventually collapse. That's what is going to happen in America" ("New Left," 1969, p. 37).

High School Activism

Although most discussion of activism focuses on college students, the problem is also becoming widespread on the high school level. Trump and Hunt's article in this chapter indicates that 67 percent of all urban high schools and 53 percent of all rural high schools have had problems with student activists. This article is based on an extensive study conducted by the research staff of the

National Association of Secondary School Principals (NASSP).

Many students are protesting against school regulations, especially those regarding dress and hair length (Harris, 1969). Other factors leading to activism are race relations, Vietnam, and the draft. A third major area of protest centers around the instructional program, and students are demanding greater involvement in the decision-making process (see also Chap. 5, Tables 1-4, pp. 147-148). The potential of high school students to bring about modifications in the social structure should not be overlooked.

Student Concerns

The third article in this chapter does not focus on the activist per se, but it reveals concerns and issues on campus that may tell us more about the overall university environment than does the activist himself. It illustrates that today's student is as self-oriented as he is issue oriented (Thornburg, 1969).

Thornburg surveyed students from five major universities about the problems they considered most important in their lives. Education was their greatest concern. Other significant concerns were Vietnam and the draft, occupations and economic security, sexuality, civil rights, politics, drugs, self-identity, competition, morality, and peer approval.

A Close-Up of Three Universities

The University of California at Berkeley. After the Free Speech Movement (FSM) was organized on the Berkeley campus in November 1964, several researchers began to make extensive studies of the student body at that school. Somers (1965) interviewed 285 students and found that 63 percent favored the goals and 34 percent favored the tactics of the FSM. Thirty percent supported the goals but not the tactics, and only 22 percent of the students surveyed were opposed to both the goals and the tactics.

An academic profile of the students revealed that 45 percent of those who favored both goals and tactics had a grade average of B+ or better, whereas only 10 percent of those who did not support the goals or tactics had that high a grade average (Somers,

1965). Similar findings were reported by Heist (1965) in his analysis of adolescents arrested at a sit-in.

Watts and Whittaker (1966) conducted a more systematic study of student activists on the Berkeley campus. Their work revealed two important conclusions. First, in contrast to Somers' study, Watts and Whittaker could not establish greater academic achievement on the part of FSM members as compared to other students. Second, Watts and Whittaker found that the parents of FSM members were more likely to have advanced academic degrees than were the parents of other students: 26 percent of the fathers and 16 percent of the mothers of the FSM members had either a Ph.D. or an M.A.—percentages significantly higher than those for the parents of the other students.

The University of Chicago. In May 1966, about 500 students staged a sit-in at the University of Chicago to demand that the university not cooperate with the Selective Service System in making class standings available for purposes of student deferments. Several days later Flacks began interviewing these demonstrators to determine some of their basic characteristics. His study revealed the following results (1967, pp. 65-68).

1. *Activists tend to come from upper status families.* When compared with "students who did not sit-in, and with students who signed the anti-sit-in petition, the sit-in participants reported higher family incomes, higher levels of education for both fathers and mothers, and overwhelmingly perceived themselves to be *upper-middle class.*
2. *Activists are more "radical" than their parents; but activists' parents are decidedly more liberal than others of their status.* (See Table 1.)
3. *Activism is related to a complex of values, not ostensibly political, shared by both the students and their parents.* "Whereas nonactivists and their parents tend to express conventional orientations toward achievement, material success, sexual morality, and religion, the activists and their parents tend to place greater stress or involvement in intellectual and esthetic pursuits, humanitarian concerns, opportunity for self-expression, and tend to de-emphasize or positively disvalue personal achievement, conventional morality, and conventional religiosity."

TABLE 1. STUDENTS' AND FATHERS' ATTITUDES ON CUR-
RENT ISSUES

Issue	Activists Students	Fathers	Nonactivists Students	Fathers
Percent who approve:				
Bombing of North Vietnam	9	27	73	80
American troops in Dominican Republic	6	33	65	50
Student participation in protest demonstrations	100	80	61	37
Civil disobedience in civil rights protests	97	57	28	23
Congressional investigations of "un-American activities"	3	7	73	57
Lyndon Johnson	35	77	81	83
Barry Goldwater	0	7	35	20
Full socialization of industry	62	23	5	10
Socialization of the medical profession	94	43	30	27
N	34	30	37	30

Reprinted with permission of the publisher from R. Flacks, "The Liberated Generation: An Exploration of the Roots of Student Protest." *Journal of Social Issues,* 1967, **23**, 67.

1. The great majority of students and faculty believe that the police action involved excessive police violence although opinions vary about how widespread the violence was.
2. Attitudes toward the crisis are strongly related to dissatisfaction with the educational content and impersonality of the university.
3. The crisis greatly increased communications within the university, particularly direct, face-to-face talking about university problems; both students and faculty feel that whatever else happened, faculty-student relations are better than they were.
4. Attitudes toward the demonstrations and their goals are strongly related to attitudes toward the war in Vietnam, but completely unrelated to the draft status of the individual student.

Columbia University. In the spring of 1968 a major confrontation occurred at Columbia as a protest against (1) the Vietnam War and the university's involvement with any military-affiliated group and (2) the university's plan to construct a gymnasium on land leased in the Harlem area of New York City (the students were sympathizing with local residents who would be deprived of housing). The Students for a Democratic Society (SDS) initiated the protest, which resulted in property destruction and confrontations with the police. The SDS and the Students' Afro-American Society joined forces, surrounded the Acting Dean's office, and virtually held him captive for 24 hours (Hook, 1969). Police battles, sit-ins, and class boycotts ensued, and the students called a campus-wide strike until the issues could be resolved.

Allen Barton of the Bureau of Applied Research questioned students and faculty about their support of the goals of the SDS and the tactics used during the demonstrations. Barton (1968) found that 58 percent of the students and 51 percent of the faculty were in favor of the goals, although a large majority of both students (68 percent) and faculty (77 percent) disapproved of the tactics involved. From his research Barton made the following conclusions (1968, p. 1):

Activist Ideologies

The fourth article in this chapter is an analysis of the political ideologies of 73 undergraduates at a large Northeastern state university. Kerpelman also investigated his subjects' political activities, intelligence, ego defensiveness, and social-acceptance concern. Activist ideologies were significantly different from those of nonactivists, and the more left-oriented students showed the greatest evidence of activism. Kerpelman's data also suggest that "student political activists of all ideologies are, on the whole, more intelligent than are students who are not politically active."

The Nonstudent Nonconformist

Watts and Whittaker (1968) compared nonstudent activists living on the fringe of the Berkeley campus with students enrolled at the university. Their data have yielded some interesting results. The most obvious distinguishable characteristic is personal appearance; among nonstudents 82 percent of the males and 88 percent of the females were classified as unconventional in personal appearance, compared to the university sample of 19 percent of the males and 24 percent of the females. Data on educational level, socioeconomic status, alienation from society and family, future goals, and intellectual ideas of the nonstudent reveal an interesting life-style that leads to activism and nonconformity.

Nonstudents in the Berkeley area evidently have rejected the educational system but are still strongly attracted to the university environment. Sixty-one percent of them had been dissatisfied with their schooling; only 25 percent of the students expressed such discontent. Watts and Whittaker have concluded that the large numbers of noncollege adolescents living on the fringe of university environments represent a significant nonconformist group that merits additional investigation.

Protest or Conform?

The final article in this chapter, by Flacks, is an exhaustive commentary on the components of activism. He focuses his discussion on the legitimacy of authority and what appears to be a general erosion of that legitimacy. The article also analyzes the black revolt and the personality variables that determine whether an adolescent will protest or conform. The reader can gain a valuable perspective on activism from this selection, as well as from a comment Flacks has made elsewhere (1967, p. 74):

The historical significance of the student movement of the Sixties remains to be determined. Its impact on the campus and on the larger society has already been substantial. It is clearly a product of deep discontent in certain significant and rapidly growing segments of the youth population. Whether it becomes an expression of generational discontent, or the forerunner of major political realignments—or simply disintegrates—cannot really be predicted by detached social scientists. The ultimate personal and political meaning of the student movement remains a matter to be determined by those who are involved in it— as participants, as allies, as critics, as enemies.

david gottlieb

activist youth today

The active rebelliousness of youth which seems to be so characteristic of this day and this society is unique to neither this nation nor this period of time.

In ancient history an observer of the Egyptian scene recorded: Our earth is degenerate . . . children no longer obey their parents. We also know that Socrates expressed grave concern about the young men of Athens: their long hair, their indolence, and their complete disdain for adult expressed values. The conflict was not restricted to foreign places nor to the poor: even when affluency was not a national phenomenon the gentlemen of Harvard were acting out against the establishment. "In 1776, broke out a rebellion which raged for a month. Two years later, great disturbances occurred; the Tutors windows were broken with brickbats, their lives endangered, and other outrages committed."

The next important incident at Harvard occurred in 1807 when three undergraduate classes reacted against the bad food at the Commons. Following what seems to have become an institutionalized form of protest —they did not wait for the President of Har-

vard to investigate and correct, they indulged in disorders. The troubles increased, along with faculty alarm. Even then the student response to university room and board offerings was far from enthusiastic. At the same time continuity, with regard to administrative response to student protest, appears to have been maintained through the ages. The Harvard Corporation met, and ordered the President of Harvard to attend Commons "on Sunday morning next," adding that in "consideration of the youth of the students, and hoping that their rash and illegal conduct is rather owing to want of experience and reflection rather than to malignity of temper or a spirit of defiance." Again, the view was that since they were young they were obviously immature and hence were motivated more by a lack of experience than by evil intent. More important since they were young it was assumed that they were in no position to make any kind of realistic assessment and therefore their protest could not be the result of rational, objective, or valid analysis.

With a sincere belief that boys would in fact be boys and that enlightened mental health could endorse the blowing of one's mind at an early age the Harvard Corporation appeared quite prepared to forgive and forget. After all, better that the young work rebellion out of their systems now so that as adults they would be more docile and accepting of both the written and spoken word. With

Reprinted with permission of the author and the California Teachers Association from the Proceedings of the 20th Annual State Conference on Educational Research: Educating Activist Youth–A Challenge to Research. *Research Resume No. 38,* November 1968, pp. 3-16.

this benevolent and patronizing approach the Corporation declared that the gentlemen of Harvard "make an admission of the impropriety of their conduct, their regret for it, and their determination to offend no more in that manner." Seven days were allowed for this period of confession and repentance. Although the time was extended, some of the students refused. Finally, more direct action was taken and the uprising was over. Needless to say the Corporation, not unlike some who administer our contemporary educational institutions, were quite selective in who they chose to forgive and what they chose to forget. Leader agitators were identified, charged, and dismissed from the University.

If we alter but slightly the style of the writing, and shift the focus from complaints about food to protests over university entanglements with agencies in the business of war and weapons research; with protests about the educational process; with protests over housing regulations; with protests over the treatment of the poor and minority groups—we see that protest, alienation, and rebellion on the part of the young are not new.

At the same time, it would be folly to suggest that youth alienation and rebellion have not changed dramatically in both style and scope. It would be equally inappropriate to assume that techniques utilized earlier in the easing of generational conflicts would be effective in this day and age. There are new dimensions and it is important that we recognize these changes if we are serious in our efforts to bridge the gap which does exist between the generations.

Prior to an identification and discussion of factors which appear to explain how the Now generation differs from youth of the past, I would like to make a more personal observation. I do not see all adolescents in a continuous state of social and emotional agitation. I do not view adolescence as a period of constant turmoil in which the search for self and personal identity must, by necessity, be a painful and frustrating experience. I think it is safe to say that most young people will, most of the time, fulfill most of the behavior roles which adults hold as being appropriate for the young.

At the same time and admittedly with little in the way of comparative data, I believe that the mood of discontent among the

young is far greater than ever in our past. While we can take some comfort in the fact that only in isolated instances does this discontent manifest itself in overt acts of violence, we should not be indifferent to the depth of youth unrest. A posture of "this too shall pass" will not suffice. It is clear that growing numbers of young people do not and will not accept even our most sincere explanations and apologies for who we are and what we do.

Finally, this discontent and this doubt are not limited to any single racial or socio-economic segment of the youth population. Nor are the alienation and rebellion restricted to the college campus. On the contrary, they are phenomena which can now be observed in many American high schools.

Perhaps the most vital task faced by any society, once it has established an efficient system of social control, is training the young for responsible adulthood. How the young will respond will depend, in part at least, upon how they view those who are responsible for their training and the nature of that training.

Certainly the factor of industrialization has had a great impact on both the how and where of adolescent socialization. Prior to the industrial revolution, much of what the young had to know in order to eventually function as productive adults could be taught in the home—there could be direct communication between father and son, mother and daughter. Given that a son would most likely follow in the occupational footsteps of his father, the father could teach his son the job skills required for occupational survival. Since few daughters would take on careers, a mother could, through day to day contact within the home, teach her daughter what she would need to know in order to play the wife-mother role.

With industrialization, however, a change took place in the demands and needs of our society. Our industrialized society required a wide range of technical skills and talents which could no longer be taught within the home. The son of a farmer who chose to be an engineer, a doctor, or an accountant, would be forced to obtain his training and certification outside of the home. The expanding economy did create a multitude of occupations unique to an industrialized nation. As we moved from a primarily agricultural and rural society to an industrial and urban nation, it became apparent that if we were to survive, we would have to come up with formal, highly structured educational programs which would provide the young with skills and abilities essential to the functioning of this new social system.

If the society was to survive, if the society was to resolve the problems and meet the needs of rapid industrialization, if the society was to prepare the young for entrance into the social system as productive adult citizens, it was essential that some agency or institution outside of the home take on the primary task of youth socialization. Clearly this outside institution would be the school. As we have reached new plateaus in our growth—as we have moved from one level of scientific knowledge to the next, as we have gone from primitive machines to complex and elaborate technology, so have we escalated our requirements for individual talents. So have we placed more and more value on the credentials awarded to those who survive the educational process. We should at least be willing to admit to ourselves that educational inflation has really taken hold in America. Obviously, there is no valid reason why we should insist on certain levels of formal education for certain jobs. The truth of the matter is that there are a wide range of occupations for which we demand much too much in the way of formal education. At the same time organized delay, even if it means the imposition of irrelevant hurdles and meaningless experiences, is an effective mechanism for maintaining control of the young.

The formal educational process is in fact our most effective means for keeping track of the young—it is the means by which we keep them on the sidelines until we decide whether or not they are prepared to take on adult roles. At the same time the formal educational process is but one way in which we maintain the social category adolescence. For adolescence is, in fact, a social category and not an automatic by-product of physical growth and child development. It represents the entire range of formal and informal mechanisms utilized by the society in making certain that the maximum number of young people go through the prescribed steps prior to gaining access to adult roles.

The greater the value placed on educational achievement the greater the likelihood that more and more adults will view the educational encounter as being essential for their children. The more rigid we are in demanding more and more education for the more prestigeful occupations the more likely it is that more and more of our young will be spending more and more of their time in school. Today about four out of every six young people earn a high school diploma, and approximately half of these enter college. About half of those who enter college earn the undergraduate degree . . . that is, about one of six of the age group. Since 1930 we have more than doubled the proportion completing high school, entering college and earning the baccalaureate degree— the record for professional degrees is even more impressive. One can only speculate as to the educational establishment response were we in fact to seriously pursue the task of cutting by half our current rate of high school attrition. No doubt some would propose adding a few more years to the already overextended doctoral programs.

Clearly, as more and more young people spend more and more time in school, they will be spending more time with peers and less time with parents. At the same time, school centered life leaves little opportunity for involvement in the world of work. As we have increased the time required for adult role preparation so have we delayed and frequently cut off the young from involvements with the real world. We have created agencies and institutions which have the primary purpose of preparing the young for adult roles while at the same time keeping them isolated from meaningful and significant experiences.

One result of this constant interaction between youth is the emergence of what some students of adolescent behavior refer to as an adolescent sub-culture. The physical and social separation of the ages means that both groups, younger and older, tend to develop their own rules of the game. The young appear to live by their own norms, their own values. They begin to adopt fashions which are unique to their own age group. In time the youth culture does take on the characteristics of a strange and exotic society.

In the past much of the flavor of this culture reflected overindulgence and concern with the frivolous. There was indifference to social and political issues. While some students were involved in the civil rights movement and others in political activities, the majority were concerned with gaining status and visibility within the social system of their high school or college. As Coleman noted in his study of American high schools, prestige went more to the athlete, cheerleader, and student conformist than to those who fought the system (Coleman, 1961).

Studies of college student sub-cultures conducted during the late fifties and sixties tend to show a similar pattern with, as would be anticipated, somewhat less emphasis on the non-academic aspect of student life. For the most part, in the case of both the high school and the college, the student who maintained an equal balance between studies and approved campus activities received the endorsement of his classmates.

No doubt a similar pattern still exists in our high schools and colleges. At the same time my own research and the observations of others would certainly support the proposition that the value orientation of students has changed. Many more students are concerned with the direction and purpose of their high school and university. Fewer are willing to accept the notion that they have no right to determine the nature and form of their education. More and more students are insisting that there be some obvious relevance to the educational encounter. Even the least articulate and most reserved are seeking some meaningful relationship between what goes on in the classroom and what is happening in the world beyond the classroom. The student culture which accepted and sought to make the best out of what it was given is increasingly becoming a culture of the past. The student culture of the present insists upon being involved in the determination of what is and what is not the right and responsibility of student, of faculty, and of administration.

We as adults can watch the young—we see what they are doing but frequently we fail to understand the why. We fail to comprehend the criteria the young employ in their selection of peers, of music, of dance, of popular heroes and political leaders. Despite our sensitive insights, our professional experiences, and our personal encounters with adolescents—we really fail to understand just what it is that turns them on. No matter how close we stand—we observe from a distance. The distance we keep represents our own personal hang-ups. We stand apart because we are frequently shattered by what we see and what we hear. We stand apart because somehow we lose our cool and our composure when confronted with the questions raised by the young. In truth, the young have gone us one better—adults should be neither seen nor heard. Unlike infants, adolescents do not appear overly emotionally dependent upon us. Clearly, they are difficult to coddle, and there is mutual embarrassment and awkwardness when genuine affection is expressed through physical embrace.

The lack of emotional dependency seems mutual. Both adolescent and parent find it a difficult task to maintain a continuous and deep personal alliance. At the same time there is obviously economic dependency. The young are, of course, economically dependent upon their parents, and the output of dollars goes well beyond the costs of bare subsistence. Rather from infancy through adolescence and often after marriage, the middle class parent pays the costs of education, vacations, leisure time activities, cars, clothes, dates, and records. This is the affluent generation—and the factor of affluence plays an important role in generational conflict. With the prolonging of adolescence has come a life-style for the young quite unlike that experienced by adults. The credit card and personal checking account, which were once the exclusive possession of the economic elite, are now part and parcel of the middle class adolescent's self-baggage. While many adults recall token allowances, hand-me-down clothes, after-school jobs and working one's way through college—the son and daughter of the suburban white collar worker is encouraged to enjoy. For some reason—perhaps it is some type of compensation for our own feelings of guilt—we are hell bent on giving our children not only what we never had but what we can hardly afford. At the same time our technique for socializing youth keeps the young out of the labor market. Even if they seek to work—there are few opportunities for meaningful employment. Paul Goodman has asked, "how can one learn to be a man if there is no man's work to be done?''

The lack of even marginally meaningful work for the young is not accidental. Again, a major function of the adolescent process is to delay occupational entry. The world of work belongs to adults and the status quo is maintained by controlling access to positions of authority and control. A tolerable level of unemployment (tolerable at least for those who must work and do have work) is established by preventing a run on the occupational market. Since the major source of potential workers is found among the young, it makes sense to implement legislation and social conditions which will keep the young out of the potential labor force.

At the same time there is little economic pressure on the affluent adolescent. Again, unlike his peers in poverty he need not be overly concerned about his daily bread. In many cases he has more than he needs and his parents feel that employment on his part might be interpreted by others as a sign of parental failure. For many in the middle class there is a fear of the social stigma that might come with a son or daughter who works beyond the summer vacation period. Rather there is pride and satisfaction over the fact that children need not be concerned with earning their way as they go about the business of preparing for the future.

In part the activism of students results from the fact that they need not worry about much more than the fulfillment of class requirements. Being supported on a full time basis with only part time obligations leaves time for involvement in a variety of activities. That most Hippies, New Left, and those who worked in political activities are middle class should not be too surprising. Each of these activities, if carried out on a full time basis, does require financing—and parents are most often the backers.

Parental benevolence though will come with some strings attached. In many instances adults do expect some pay-off for their investment. What is usually expected is a child who will show his gratitude by fulfilling parental expectations and aspirations—a child who will in fact prove, through performance, that the apple does not fall far from the tree. Confirmation of parental success in child rearing comes when the child is successful in gaining approval from adults—be they teachers, relatives, counselors, Scoutmasters, or neighbors. As unfortunate as it might seem, many adolescents respond to a different reference group. For them approval by peers, rather than adults, is of greater immediate importance.

Our way of socializing youth does little to encourage the young to become involved in the serious social and political issues which confront our nation. One has only to review the events of the past few years to see the conflict which occurs when the young step over the line and take on roles traditionally reserved for adults. Viet Nam is one obvious example. Berkeley and Columbia are others. The McCarthy experience is, I believe, the most illuminating. No one took McCarthy seriously except the young. Suddenly, as if in response to some mystical call, they came together to support a "straight." He was well over thirty but he could be trusted. He was a product of the establishment who was going to do his thing even if it meant banishment from the party.

The McCarthy following of Hippies, Pseudo-New Left, and squares received more coverage from the press than did the candidate himself. At first the popular media got a big kick out of the kids. Here was real proof that not all young people were hedonistic, overindulgent, and alienated. Was it not wonderful to observe how the Hippies stayed out of sight licking envelopes while the Ivy League straights made the door to door canvasses. It was indeed refreshing and wholesome. It was almost like an old fashioned July 4th picnic —with everyone having a good time—and being terribly patriotic. With few exceptions no one really took seriously the effort and commitment of this group of youth.

What the adult population failed to understand was that these were not kids playing a game. They were involved beyond the primaries—and they were not going to quit with the defeat of their candidate. Once it became apparent that they were taking their politics seriously, the tone of the media changed. According to the press the young had gone too far. They were no longer playing by the rules of the game. They were no longer behaving like happy—but well disciplined children. They were in fact no longer children. They were not minding their own business; they were no longer where they should have been; they were no longer to be excused their youthful enthusiasm or their lack of political sophistication. That youth would take themselves and their responsibilities so seriously was not anticipated. To deal with them as equals would only confirm the legitimacy of their protest and add support to those who proposed that achieved status was in fact more credible than ascribed. To accept the notion that the young were prepared to enter the adult arena prior to official confirmation could only lead to the breakdown of a system planned to keep the young under wraps—and under control—until they pass each of the tests which are required as part of the American rites of passage.

The system operates effectively and smoothly as long as the young comply with adult imposed ground rules. There will be little in the way of generational conflict if the young are willing to buy our values, our interpretations, and our methods of youth socialization. Problems can be kept at a minimum if our power to impose sanctions and controls is recognized and accepted by the young. The breakdown occurs when the young challenge, question, or no longer buy our proposed goals and our means. The conflict comes when youth either reject or are indifferent to our advice, warnings, threats, or sanctions. The rebellion comes when rejection of the system goes beyond discussion or indifference and manifests itself in active dissent.

The hang-up now lies in the fact that many youth, especially white and middle class, can't quite see why they should follow our lead. They live in a rapidly changing society. Values, like people, appear plastic and transient. The track is muddy and it is difficult to get footing. Many of the young do see a world filled with contradiction and discrepancy—discrepancy between what we say and what we do; with pronouncements of freedom on one side and social injustice on the other; declarations of peace and unending series of wars; expressed values of integrity and the realities of petty larceny and political corruption; the Sunday instruction of the church contradicted by a six day violation of the Ten Commandments. It is of importance to note that many of the most active of student rebels are following in the footsteps of their parents. In many cases, these are youth who were brought up in a politically liberal climate by parents who had been fairly active

in progressive movements. The dilemma and conflict occur when these adolescents interpret a lack of outdoor protest and involvement on the part of their parents as evidence of hypocrisy.

Your immediate response might well be: "Oh, yes, that might all be true, but there has always been evil and even now there is some good in the world." No doubt all generations have experienced some social turmoil and each of us can point to certain acts of individual goodness. This generation of youth, however, has grown up against a backdrop of violence. Violence has become part of our every day life. As we look forward to holidays and institutionalized social events so do we anticipate long hot summers, international conflict and rebellion.

This is the generation that was coming of age during Korea, the Dominican Republic, Cuba, and Viet Nam. This is the generation which could witness the final rites of a murdered young hero President and the assassination of his accused assassinator. This same group of youth were also present at the murder of Martin Luther King and Robert Kennedy—both young men who dared to challenge the system.

Through our elaborate systems of electronic communication this same generation could observe, in color or black and white, the violence and destruction of Detroit, Newark, Watts, and so many other American cities. This is the generation which saw Americans burning a peasant village in Viet Nam; the murder of Viet Cong; and the death of a young marine. Finally, this same generation was able to see itself beaten and intimidated on the streets of Chicago.

Ideally, adolescence is a period when the young make decisions about themselves: who they are and what they are to be. It is the time for the emergence of a self-identity. It is a period when one is supposed to go beyond his immediate setting and see himself within the framework of a larger society. The task, however, is made difficult and confusing in a fluid society; in a society where technology and values change on an almost daily basis; in a society where one is expected to become a man while being cut off from man's work, from man's concerns; in a society where one is expected to go through the established rites of passage without raising questions or criticizing the benefactor.

Rapid social change, affluence, and violence help to perpetuate the growing conflict between the generations and act to reinforce the suspicions of the young that perhaps the good middle class life is not really all that it is cracked up to be—that the suburban organizational man life-style is not worth the effort.

But all youth are not cut of a common cloth. It is apparent that while the rebellion of the white middle class student takes many forms and shapes, the issues raised by the black college student are clear, direct, and precise. It is also clear that they choose to go it alone. They neither seek nor particularly desire the assistance of their white peers. Separatism is one of the basic ingredients of the black student posture, no matter how bewildered or frustrated it might leave the white liberal. Black students are calling for recognition of their color. Being black is no longer accepted as a symbol of inferiority or passivity. The black adolescent, and this is most true of black youth who already are on the way to the good life, those who are college and university students, want recognition of their color. What they seek is compensation for the hundreds of years in which being black brought only humility, indignity, intimidation, physical, social and economic exploitation. The black student does not have the hang-up of some white middle class college students. He has a mission, he has a goal, he has a purpose, and he has a platform. We may be repulsed or angered by the form or method but we cannot in honesty reject the argument or the goal. Traditionally, we have had school curricula which have honored our heroes and leaders and we have not included blacks who did in fact contribute to the survival of this nation. Each ethnic group has had its day—in parades, holidays, and celebrations—with the exception of the black. We have named streets, buildings, and bridges for whites—no matter their nationality—but have somehow failed to give recognition or visibility to blacks who fought in wars, built cities, made discoveries, wrote poetry, or created musical masterpieces. When we have paid tribute, it has usually been the result of pressure and guilt—and the end product has been an act of tokenism.

I do not endorse nor do I accept racial separatism. At the same time I accept the fact that we cannot expect black youth to be responsive to our clarion calls for brotherhood and patience. One ingredient common to all adolescents is an inability to defer gratification—to just hold on—to just believe —they will not accept the idea of pie in the sky when you die.

Adolescents want action Now—they live for the present and not the future. Can we really expect black youth—based on our past and current performance—to cool it—to wait until we work things out—to wait until we resolve other problems? The answer is no— black students want and are entitled to that which we automatically offer to white students—entrance into college; representation and involvement in every phase of the college scene: faculty, administration, curriculum, social and athletic activities. This is not a radical or far-out stance. The black student demands now that which no American should have to make part of a special or dramatic plea. He demands that which is in fact the right and privilege of every American. Again, we must differentiate between the form and the content. Too often we get hung up on the how of the demand, rather than making a fair assessment of what is being demanded. If we hope to bridge racial separatism—and I do not believe this society can survive if we do not emerge as a truly racially integrated nation—we must pay less attention to the style of those who make the demands and concentrate on the development of means which will meet legitimate demands.

For poor youth there are other problems. There is less in the way of ideology, less in the way of the abstract, more in the way of a search for basic security and comfort.

I'm not out to get Whitey. I'm just out to get out. They talked about getting out. They carried signs about getting out. Now looks like you got to burn the place down and shoot your way out.

The comments are those of a 17-year-old black male who was actively involved in the Newark riots of 1967. I do not say 17-year-old teen-ager or for that matter adolescent since very little in his style and words— or those of his peers—resembles that which we normally associate with our image of the typical teen-agers or the social category Adolescence. He was not part of an organized movement. He does not believe that he has to confirm his masculinity through acts of violence and aggression. Although he has heard of Carmichael, Rap Brown, and Martin Luther King, he knows little of their ideologies nor is he overly concerned with their intentions. He seeks neither intimate contact with whites nor continued existence within a racial ghetto.

His actions and his words make one thing clear: he wants a change of status and he wants it now. He wants out of the slums. He wants out of unemployment. He wants out of a physical setting which restricts mobility and maximizes feelings of personal defeat. He realistically sees himself standing on the outside and he wants in.

His behavior, like that of many ghetto youth, would certainly place him in the slot marked Alienated. He is not abiding by the expectations of adults. He does not seem to accept the established means of goal attainment. He rejects the laws and folkways which are traditionally employed in the airing of grievances. He is not bothered by norms which are supposed to govern his behavior and his expressed attitudes. He not only goes beyond the limits set for adults but he also exceeds and goes beyond the somewhat more liberal ground rules which exist for adolescents. Clearly he is alienated—clearly he rebels.

Alienation not only takes many forms but it also touches many segments of the population. Keniston's alienated are significantly different in both background and behavior from Black urban youth (Keniston, 1965). Being a member of a racial religious minority may enhance the probability of withdrawal but it is not a necessary push variable. Yet when we talk about alienation the tendency is to include both the Harvard undergraduate who chooses the garb of the Hippie and the Harlem dropout who joins with the Black Panthers. Although both are similar in their overt rejection of traditional means and goals there are important differences.

One difference is found in the cause of the withdrawal. The middle class adolescent is likely to reject the dominant culture and chooses to remove himself from the established socialization process. No matter whether his assessment be realistic or not, the choice of involvement or estrangement is usually with him.

The middle class Hippie, Teeny Bopper, Beat, or adolescent who is not readily identifiable by some group association but adopts a life-style which we label as deviant is not usu-

ally the product of an unjust economic system. He is not the victim of a social order which blocks entry into the dominant culture. The middle class adolescent has other alternatives. No matter how painful or absurd is the business of growing up in America he can stay with it, if he chooses to do so. External pressures do not force the withdrawal. He most often has sufficient referents who have both the desire and the ability to help him attain the good life if and when he so chooses.

Keniston's alienated youth reject the American culture which they see as "trash, cheap and commercial." It is a rejection of the middle class: "I have come to experience horror at the good American way of life, namely, the comfortable middle class existence. . . . This seems to be boring me" (Keniston, 1965, p. 41).

Poor youth, and this is probably most true of Black urban males, do not initially reject involvement in the "comfortable middle class." Given the choice and a similarity in opportunities many would gladly change places with the disenchanted of Harvard, Vassar, and Yale. Although he may mock the behavior and fashions of the affluent he does not see the good life as overly phony, commercial, or cheap. His brief encounters with the middle class occur through the mass media and his own forays beyond ghetto walls. What he sees he likes. He sees the well dressed—the fat cats—with their powerful cars. He sees the ladies and gentlemen eating in fine restaurants. He knows something about the Jet Set and their ability to escape the cold and up-tightness of the city to those far-away fun and sun places. He sees people who can leave their cars for others to park. He sees these same people being waited upon and catered to by others. In most cases those being catered to are whites—while those doing the catering are blacks.

My own experience with poor youth—including several large-scale investigations of the aspirations and school behavior of low income high school students and a three year involvement with the Job Corps—leads me to believe that these people do in fact want to be middle class, but entrance is far from easy (Gottlieb, 1967). Coming of age in America may, as others have noted, be difficult for the affluent. When the workings of an unjust social and economic order are added to an educational system which is least tolerant to those most in need of its offerings, and further compounded by an unavailability of adult referents who can intervene on behalf of the child, it should not be surprising that so many poor kids either give up the game or resort to what we perceive as socially unacceptable means toward goal attainment.

What is all the more remarkable is that despite the barriers, so many have managed to survive and escape and still many more continue to play it straight in hopes that they will overcome.

Obviously if our goal is to assist youth, be they rich or poor, in the taking on of responsible and productive adult roles, it is essential that we understand something about who they are, what it is that they want, and what they see as their chances of their getting what they think they want. Further we should take a close look at what these youth may or may not have going for them as they go about the business of growing up.

Unfortunately the truth of the matter seems to be that as we have discriminated against and avoided the poor in matters of national, social, and economic policy, so have we discriminated against and avoided them in matters of scientific inquiry. With few exceptions what we do know comes from several more exotic investigations of deviant behavior. By comparison there is little in the empirical literature which relates to the vast majority of poor youth who are in school, at work, in the armed forces, or perhaps involved in some kind of catch-up educational vocational-training program. We know far more about the middle class than we do about the poor. We know much more about the attitudes, values, aspirations, and behavior of whites than we do about blacks. The poor for a variety of reasons have continued to remain the dark side of the moon. Much of what we know—or at least think we know— about adolescence comes from studies of fairly captive samples—high school and college students who have little chance of escaping research imposed from above. Much of the case-study materials provided by psychiatry deals with those who recognize that there was a problem, had both the access to helping resources, and the funds to carry on continued treatment. Our bias may even be reflected in this very conference. The theme is "Educating Activist Youth—A Challenge to

Research." "Activist Youth" most often conjures up the image of the bright, active, intellectually oriented, inquiring adolescent: the Hippie, the Teeny Bopper, the Micro Bopper, SDS, the New Left, the more affluent and visible of this nation. My comments are not meant to imply that we are not honorable, committed, and dedicated people. Nor am I proposing that the middle class is incapable of understanding the problem or of providing the resources necessary for problem solving —rather that our concern with social problems, research, and programs of intervention is part of a fairly selective process. We of the middle class, who play a part in determining educational policy and the allocation of resources, tend to be most responsive when we are most threatened. As the problem of student unrest has come closer to our own homes—residential as well as occupational— so have we become more vocal in our demands for immediate action and effective solutions.

These comments are not meant to be a plea for an understanding of the problems of poverty-stricken youth. Rather it is a call for a broader approach to the problems which confront all youth in our society. Too often we become too hung up with the more visible and the more dramatic. The Hippie, the New Left, and the SDS do represent a legitimate reason for scientific inquiry and social change. They are youth who have adopted behavior styles which are contrary to our expectations and desires. Much of what they reject and question is worthy of rejection and question. At the same time, there is a far larger group of young people who while holding serious doubts and questioning our policies and procedures are willing to seek resolution through dialogue and meaningful activities of social change.

Clearly, both rich and poor youth have a legitimate basis for protest. Although we may disagree or even be shocked by the form of their rebellion, we cannot disregard the content of their message. Both groups—poor and affluent—are demanding an open society; a social system that will not force the young to stand on the sidelines; an adult world that in fact practices what it so freely and so eloquently teaches and preaches—a society which will judge men not on the basis of ascribed status, but achievement, not on the basis of family pedigree, but on the basis of what man does and what he can do.

Affluent youth suffering disenchantment and ennui from protracted adolescence must be given earlier opportunities to experience meaningful feeling, interaction with the social problems of his times, and greater opportunity for the testing out of alternatives in the search for self.

The needs of poor youth are less prosaic and more immediate. We must pursue full scale efforts which will allow total and fair participation of poor youth in our affluent society.

We should respond to the needs of youth not out of fear of riots and rebellion, but because any other answer is morally unacceptable, economically incomprehensible, and socially unthinkable.

j. lloyd trump

jane hunt

the nature and extent of student activism

"To be a principal in times like these is not for the faint-hearted—and we're just getting started on this protest business." The principal of a large urban high school is speaking. He echoes what principals are saying across the nation, in poverty-ridden cities or prosperous suburbs—and even in rural communities where protest mainly is a word in a headline. Some believe:

> The news media and "bad" television programs such as the Smothers Brothers add to our problems. Sympathy directed to the radical minority makes it popular to join the group.

> Forces are afoot which will destroy education as it has been known here, and it is doubtful that, like the Phoenix, it could rise again from its ashes.

But others say:

> Accord respect to *responsible* protest —they might just be right.

> The students, to our utter despair, are exhibiting—at long last—the very kinds of behavior that we say we want to encourage, nourish and develop as responsible educators. The requirement for (and agonies of)

change are on our doorsteps more so than on theirs. We must change—or foster total revolution in our schools—public *or* private.

A National Survey

We sent questionnaires to a random sample of 1,982, every fifteenth principal throughout the United States. There were 1,026 responses. The principals serve in junior or senior high schools or combination schools. All different kinds of schools are included—public and private, large and small, those in major cities or small towns. The survey was not confined to principals who belong to the NASSP. The basic message is clear. Student activism is here. Three out of five principals report some form of active protest in their schools. Many who note no protest as yet add that they expect it in the near future.

Fifty-nine percent of the respondents (606 out of 1,026) reported some kind of activism or protest. We believe the respondents are typical of the entire sample, not only because of studies done elsewhere of nonrespondents to inquiry forms, but also because the responses came from every part of the country and all types of schools. The respondents were not required to identify their schools—although the vast majority did so voluntarily.

Reprinted with permission of the authors and publisher from the *National Association of Secondary School Principals Bulletin*, 1969, **53**, 150-158.

What the Data Say

Sixty-seven percent of the *city* schools we surveyed are experiencing protests. For schools in the *suburbs,* the number with protests is also 67 percent. In rural areas, it drops to 53 percent—still more than half of the respondents. One of the surprises of the survey was the fact that protest is almost as likely to occur in junior high schools as in senior high schools. Among the junior high schools, 56 percent report protest activities, as compared to 59 percent of all senior high schools so reporting.

TABLE 1. PERCENTAGE OF SCHOOLS REPORTING STUDENT ACTIVISM

	Large (over 2,000)	Medium (801-2,000)	Small (801 or less)	All
Urban	74	62	60	67
Suburban	81	72	56	67
Rural	67	67	50	53

TABLE 2. PERCENTAGES OF JUNIOR AND SENIOR HIGH SCHOOLS WITH STUDENT ACTIVISM

	Junior High	Senior High
Urban	59	63
Suburban	61	69
Rural	48	53
All	56	59

The Principals' Beliefs

The principals in our survey tell much the same story, regardless of where they live. But their tones of voice are diverse, as the previous quotations illustrate. The differences reflect variations in local situations. They also reveal profound differences in the principals themselves. The second and the last statements quoted were made by close neighbors in a major city; yet, one was in despair and the other almost elated. The variety and complexity of the principals' responses show that most are giving serious, open-minded thought to this complex problem.

Student activism is the subject of the hour. Newspaper editors, columnists, legislators—everyone has an opinion on it, whether he knows the situation firsthand or not. No wonder the principals have so much to say. Often an administrator whose students were not protesting offered as many constructive suggestions for handling situations as the principal whose students were actively objecting to something. Perhaps some principals had no activism because they had anticipated it and dealt with it before it became a problem.

How the Percentages Were Obtained

In the remainder of this report, we will use percentages based on a comparison of the number of schools reporting each kind of protest with the total number of schools that reported any protest. For example, if we say that 50 percent of the schools have protests on a certain topic, we mean 50 percent of all the respondents who reported any kind of protest. In other words, we are not counting the considerable number of schools, as indicated earlier, that reported no student protests.

Protests on School Regulations

Young people are becoming vocal on every topic from glue-sniffing to getting the vote for 18-year-olds. Except for a few issues, it is hard to discern a pattern in the unrest because so many subjects were mentioned. Many principals simply gave "society in general" or "the system" as the real target.

Dress and hair requirements head the list of complaints. One-third of all schools report objections to the dress code. One-quarter have protests on the subject of hair. Whether the community is rural, suburban, or urban makes little difference. Protests are slightly more widespread in rural and suburban localities. Perhaps this merely indicates that city administrators are more tolerant. Mini-skirted girls and long-haired boys account for most of the argument. In one area, a skirt more than two inches above the knee gets its wearer sent home, but most principals do not object until hemlines go considerably higher. Some boys want to wear bermuda shorts and sandals. Some schools forbid boots. One principal expressed a general attitude toward boys' hair when he said that anything goes, so long as the eyes, ears, and back of the neck are visible.

Who is complaining? Almost everyone. Individual students are the source of the majority of protests about appearance, but all other sources have been heard from—parents, often as individuals and occasionally through their organizations; teachers; the student council; community groups; black groups; and, where it is active, SDS. Protestors go to the principal first, as they do with every topic in the survey. Then the faculty, the student council, and even the Board of Education hear from them. Verbal complaints are most common, but the pupils use every means available from meetings and petitions, to failure to obey rules, or simply what some principals call "misbehavior."

While dress and hair account for more protests than any other single topic, the principals enumerate many other regulations which students oppose. In fact, 82 percent of the schools have protests against school regulations. In the suburban, small junior high schools, all but one school (with protests) have such complaints. Most SDS groups protest school regulations. Five percent of the schools report SDS activity of some kind.

Smoking rules and the cafeteria are the favorite targets of protest after the dress modes. Many schools report cafeteria boycotts. Issues brought up nearly as often are: assembly programs or choice of club speakers; censorship and regulation of school papers, underground papers, or pamphlets; scheduling of sporting events; and social events at the school. The suspension of pupils and "general rules of conduct" draw protests occasionally.

Other topics mentioned only a few times are: the need for new student organizations; the condition of the school's physical plant; inactivity of the student council; ROTC; rising costs; a student group's demand for more voice in rule-making; motor vehicles; open *vs.* closed campus; loss of senior privileges; cheerleader elections; lockers. Saluting the flag and standing for the national anthem were protested by one black group. It is interesting to note that laws banning the use of marijuana and other drugs are protested in only one-half of one percent of the schools.

Race Relations and Other Social or Political Issues

Only one-fourth of the schools have experienced activism in the area of race rela-

tions or other current issues such as the peace movement or the draft. Protests about these issues occur mainly in large and medium-sized senior high schools in suburban or big-city locations. Rural schools have few such protests.

Difficulties in the area of race relations—between blacks and whites, or involving other minorities—are cited by 10 percent of the schools. Racial protests occur more often in urban schools, but they happen in communities of every size. Racial problems usually concern antagonism among students. The principal of a small rural junior high school in the South describes the problem this way:

> Parents of both the white and black are our major concern. Both groups send their children to school with directions to "take nothing from the other." The children therefore get caught in the middle—they are praised by their parents and punished by the school for the same acts. . . . Every decision of the teacher and administration is questioned, regardless of how minor (this is not bad actually). There is created, however, an area of doubt, suspicion and fear. . . .

Racial tension may affect the behavior of both teachers and students. Black groups, or individual parents, or pupils complain that Negro students are not receiving fair treatment in specific instances. For example, there was criticism at one school because all the cheerleaders were white, although the school had many black pupils. This school responded by enlarging the cheerleading squad and adding several black pupils. Criticism on race relations comes from white students or parents, too. One junior high school principal reported that both CORE and the Ku Klux Klan are actively influencing the school's pupils.

In many schools, black students are asking for the inclusion of Negro history in the curriculum and for more black teachers and administrators. These suggestions come from every possible source: students and parents, Negro organizations, teachers, student councils, and community groups. Discrimination is protested verbally, in publications or through other media, and in conferences. Dramatic confrontations—boycotts, strikes, marches, sit-ins, and walkouts—are rare. One walkout was sparked by a school's failing to close when Martin Luther King was shot.

A few principals reveal their own biases about racial tensions. For example:

> About one-third of our student population is black. Most of these blacks are fine, upright, and capable citizens who get along well with all people. However, about 10 percent of the blacks come from homes or shacks where people ought not to live. . . . They are against any and all things of value. . . . I feel that the standards of any school should not be lowered in order to make a place for the small minority group which can't or won't fit into the program. There must be some other kind of a school to which these people can go.

A large number of principals think their schools are doing constructive work in this area:

> We hired a well-qualified Negro to be our consultant and add to the advice our black teachers give us. We have used some of the State Education Department films on Racial Relations and Education with the staff; we have revised courses of study to include more of the contributions of the Negro and Negro history; we have expanded our library holdings in the area of Negro History and contributions; we have made a real effort to hire qualified Negro teachers (without too much success); we have supported the organization of an Afro-American Club. . . .

> We have only 31 blacks of 1,540 students but they are organized with outside support and many of their complaints are very legitimate. We formed a school-sponsored Afro-American Club for blacks and whites. Students learn about black problems and Afro-American History—put on assemblies.

> We have a neighborhood counselor. Spends all of his time in the community. Visits parents, businesses, any and everybody—relates well—organizes parents' meetings. Relations have improved.

> Black students threatened a boycott over the inclusion of the black man in America in American History; they were aided by student teachers who were members of the Black Panther group. In response we did the following: 1. Called a meeting of the black students involved. 2. Let them "blow off steam." 3. Had them appoint a small group to meet with me. 4. Met with group and resolved issues. 5. Met with entire group again to report all outcomes of discussion and the time schedule for implementing those suggestions.

One principal of an urban junior high school with a rapid turnover in faculty, where charges of racism are directed at the staff by both black and white students, makes this point:

> Colleges are not training teachers for the urban school. We are only two miles from . . . (Here he mentioned three outstanding colleges). Yet we have never been observed by anyone from those institutions nor have they sought from us recommendations based on our experience.

Viet Nam and the draft are the next greatest source of protest, yet they are not listed often. Three percent of schools have some activity regarding Viet Nam; only 2 percent mention the draft. These topics arouse only senior high school pupils. However, activism occurs in rural areas as much as in cities and suburbs. An individual student is usually the source of protest, although parents, community groups, black organizations and SDS also speak up, according to the reports.

Other topics occur occasionally. These include the vote for 18-year-olds, centralized versus local school boards, welfare programs, the need for political activity clubs in schools, a demand for more student rights with regard to all current issues, opportunities for work experience, the police, the church, the peace movement, and criticism of "authority in general." All such issues are protested almost entirely in discussion or writing rather than in demonstrations.

The Instructional Program

Forty-five percent of our respondents report activism regarding the way the school educates its pupils. These protests hit many targets. Most often named are: teachers—their quality, where assigned; the student's freedom to choose his teachers; curriculum content; class grouping; scheduling; homework; grades; and exams. Also at issue but less frequently are study halls, ROTC, class size, religion (occasionally mentioned in responses from Catholic schools), extracurricular activities, programs for low achievers, sex education, methods of teaching foreign languages, chemistry, and other subjects, a longer school day due to time lost in a teachers' strike, freedom to choose courses, more Negro teachers, and more courses in black history and culture.

The foregoing protests come from every source, but most of all from individual students and parents. Dissatisfaction with the school program is evenly distributed throughout junior and senior high schools, large and small, wherever they are located. One category, the urban senior high school with more than 2,000 pupils, does show a much higher percentage—more than 80 percent of such schools hear protests about the instructional program.

Faculty Affairs

Teachers in 35 percent of the schools, evenly distributed through large and small communities, are protesting actively their working lives. Mostly they protest salaries and related benefits. In 12 percent of schools, teachers are asking for better pay. Suburban teachers apparently are more satisfied with their earnings: only 10 percent of suburban schools have such complaints. In one out of four rural, small junior high schools, teachers are demanding higher salaries.

Teachers also object to heavy loads, class sizes, number of preparations, staff utilization, a need for due process, extra assignments, a shortage of clerical help, lack of classroom space and equipment, and their lack of choice in curriculum and materials. They are active about academic freedom, tenure, and methods of hiring and promotion. Acting both as individuals and through their organizations, they address themselves mainly to the principal and the board of education through meetings and organized negotiations.

The Need for Better Communication

Respondents from every type of community and kind of school felt that there was a growing need for pupils, administrators, parents, and teachers to know each other better and to open new channels of communication. Many principals return to this theme when asked how they have coped with activism. They believe that getting to know each other is the heart of the matter.

Many of those who answered the survey shared with us their own experiences and their philosophies. Here are some representative statements:

School administrators need to give consideration to the paradox in the lives of today's students. Most administrators cling to the tradition that a school must open its doors to the students at 8:00 in the morning, and hold them in captivity for the remainder of the day. Since the home and community have more or less emancipated the youth, is it any wonder that they rebel at the thought of being completely regimented for six hours a day? We require our students to attend classes only, and what they do during the rest of the time is their business. . . . Bells are for animals! . . . What I'm trying to say is that our students have little to rebel against.

Teachers are a major concern. It is rough to counteract a young, militant teacher who sometimes 'uses' students. We have found no cure except firing the teacher and this seems to only multiply the problem.

Students are currently charged with directing the re-writing and updating of the student rulebook.

I feel that the press could be of greater help if they would approach activities of high school students in a more affirmative manner.

We have used a Student-Faculty Advisory Council (new this year). Their opinions are considered. The principal makes the final decision and informs the SFAC of why. . . . This role for teachers and the principal was difficult at the beginning. . . . Resentment appears to be reduced and communication improved.

Establish student court. Open press conferences with pupils and ad hoc student committees to work with faculty and parents.

It is important—almost crucial—that one anticipate what may occur. It is important that a principal build good community relations and keep the community leaders informed. The most devastating weapon a principal can employ with dissidents is the force of the community and its leaders poised against unreasonable demands.

Some areas must be handled democratically, others dictatorially. When using the democratic process, use it thoroughly. Don't try to make people believe you are democratic if you are going to make the decision.

Our school is in an area where there could be considerable stress and trouble. We don't concern ourselves with regulations about haircuts and dress, we try to operate the school on an informal relaxed basis to take the tenseness out of the building. We give second chances and third chances and just about as many as it takes; we want our pupils to like school and to feel its programs are relevant to the lives they are living.

Listen, listen, and listen some more.

This national survey on student activism has limitations, of course. It reports principals' opinions about what is happening rather than offering a set of proven facts. However, anyone who examined the replies would have been struck, as we were, by the care the principals took in composing their answers. The thoughtfulness of the responses is even more impressive in view of the fact that the questionnaire was complicated in design and four pages in length.

hershel d. thornburg

student assessment of contemporary issues

American universities and colleges, as well as American society as a whole, have strongly felt the impact of student activism within the past decade. The peak of rebellion and violence on campus came during the 1968-1969 academic year. During that year at least 669 institutions experienced disruptive protests, of which 145 were termed, by the American Council on Education, as violent (Student revolt, 1969).

Such activist groups have been identified according to cause and philosophy. One group of activists is the *New Left* movement, whose members are committed to political action. These youth want change, and their more radical elements demand revolutionary change. The involvement on university campuses includes strong political education. Many are proponents of the political philosophies of Guevara, Marcuse, and Ho Chi-Minh.

The advocates of *black power* form a second strong movement. The black power student concentrates on racial discrimination, curriculum, and black teachers and administrators. Occasionally, a liaison with white activists is formed (Barton, 1968) although most black power advocates are cautious of white influence. Most movements center on the campuses of predominantly white universities. One of the main problems

within black student conflicts has been unsuccessful dialogue interchange which mainly focuses around vernacular and imprecise meaning of words. Such words have included *integration, separatism, discrimination, racism, revolutionary, relevance, militance,* and *demand.*

Another alienated student group consists of *hippies.* They are largely apolitical. In contrast to the New Left, they have dropped out of society, separating themselves from what they consider to be a highly materialistic and competitive social order. Within their communal living, mysticism and drug usage are common.

Those who write about activism and college generally do so with reference to one or more of the groups just identified. Upon analysis, researchers have found student activism focused around (1) the American society and its multitudinous social problems, and (2) unrest within the university itself (Blocker, 1970). Upon analysis of student types that are activism-oriented they are thought to be more intelligent, more affluent, and more social conscious than the nonactivists (Bay, 1967; Flacks, 1967; Gottlieb, 1968; Halleck, 1968; Somers, 1965). One significant difference between today's activist youth as compared to previous generations of youth is the level of hostility directed toward existing institutions. However, there is still some concern as to what and

TABLE 1. MOST FREQUENT RESPONSES LISTED BY 2500 COLLEGE STUDENTS

40% or over		39.9 to 30.0%		29.9 to 20.0%		19.9 to 10.0%	
Education	45.8	Sexuality	36.6	Occupations	28.5		
Vietnam	44.1	Self-identity	32.4	Competition	27.5	Future	18.9
		Draft	30.4	Civil rights	27.4	Cultural norms	18.7
				Religion	23.8	Parental approval	18.1
				Activism	22.6	Drugs	16.5
				Politics	21.9	Marriage	15.8
				Economic stability	21.8	Individuality	13.4
				Social identity	21.7	Violence	13.3
				Morality	21.5	Generation gap	12.5
				Peer approval	21.1	Emancipation	10.6
				Social approval	21.0	World affairs	10.4

whom the "student power" movement represents. It is quite possible that what is being attended to are the demands of a small segment of youth enrolled in American colleges and universities today. Therefore, the question might be raised, "Does today's youth movement represent today's youth—their concerns about self, others, and society?"

The purpose of this study was to look at what a large cross section of youth enrolled in major universities—without such students being directly identified as student activists—think are major issues, problems, or concerns within their environment. The data reported herein are free responses from 2500 students who were asked the following question: What issues, problems, and concerns do you think are important to college youth today?

There were no hypotheses formulated for this study. The primary interest of this study was not to see what significant differences exist between nonactivists and activists, nor to see what significant differences exist between students in different geographical locations. Instead the study was undertaken to (1) listen to the concerns of a large sample of university students, (2) detect what common concerns university youth have today, and (3) ascertain what concerns might be peculiar to the geographical setting of the university within which students are enrolled.

Therefore, a sample of 2500 students, 500 each from universities located in Arizona, Florida, Illinois, Louisiana, and Oklahoma,[1] listed and commented on issues, problems, and concerns of particular impor-

tance to them. The students listed 16,235 different responses in 58 categories. Within the 58 response areas, several responses were mentioned by an appreciable number within the sample. Table 1 indicates the most frequent responses of the students.

Two issues, *education* and *Vietnam,* were mentioned by nearly 50 percent of the sample. It is not surprising that education was the most often mentioned issue. The fact that these are college students represents a sampling bias that greatly increases this issue. Also college youth today interpret societal, parental, peer, and occupational pressures in terms of education. The issue of Vietnam has long been a major concern of activists (Watts & Whittaker, 1966), and it is equally as distressing to the students in this sample. The indefiniteness of the war, and the involvement of youth which Vietnam demands, has caused much discontent among youth. In connection with Vietnam is the issue of the draft, which was mentioned by 30.4 percent of the students. Youth view the draft as a threat to interrupting their life plans and, in some cases, life-styles. Many males are using the university as a means of avoiding the draft. The most serious concern was that the draft, and subsequent involvement in Vietnam, posed enough uncertainty for youth that it significantly attributes to a lack of definiteness about more lasting things such as occupations, marriage, economic stability, and the future.[2]

Sexuality (36.6 percent) was the third most frequent response listed by the students. Basically, responses reflected concerns about how to conduct oneself as a

[1]The author is indebted to Dr. James Croake, Florida State University; Dr. Robert Karabinus, Northern Illinois University; Drs. Barbara Rothschild and O. H. Campbell, Louisiana State University; and Dr. Henry Angelino, Ohio State University for their assistance in gathering data for this study.

[2]Although the study was not designed this way, part of the sample was drawn before the 1969 draft lottery came into effect and part of it afterward. It is interesting that these youth did not consider the issue of the draft any more or less important after the lottery than before.

TABLE 2. SUMMARY OF YOUTH PROBLEMS, ISSUES, AND CONCERNS

Topic	Arizona	Florida	Illinois	Louisiana	Oklahoma	Total
Life issues	1062	1013	979	686	940	4680
Domestic/ International	873	733	880	566	765	3817
Personal identity	783	550	514	548	802	3197
Approval	430	306	407	141	553	1837
Social behaviors	437	448	275	141	231	1532
Sexuality	397	176	211	141	247	1172
Total	3982	3226	3266	2223	3538	16,235

sexual being. Specifically, 202 students mentioned premarital sex as a concern. Not included in the percentage are limited student responses in the areas of abortion, birth control, homosexuality, the double standard, and sex education.

An interesting finding in this study was that 32.4 percent of the respondents mentioned self-identity as a major problem. Its frequency of mention (fourth) indicates that it is more than a passing concern of youth. Students viewed self-identity as the process of finding one's self. Most frequently this finding of one's self meant learning enough about one's self to know and accept the self. Self-identity was also commonly mentioned in relation to social identity (21.4 percent) and the future (18.9 percent). These two terms have within them some ambiguity. However, it was not uncommon to read a student response that stressed the concern of finding oneself in relation to one's society as well as a concern for the future—that is, what it is and what it holds for the individual.

As indicated in Table 1, several other issues were stated by a significant percentage of the students. One's occupation and the competition that must be met at both the educational and occupational levels were frequently mentioned. Other prominent issues were civil rights, religion, student activism, politics, economic stability, morality, and peer and social approval.

Categorized Responses

After tabulating the data, all responses were placed into six preselected response categories in order to ascertain the interrelatedness of the responses. Table 2 presents a summary of youth problems, issues, and concerns as categorized.

1. *Life Issues (competition, education, economic stability, marriage, morality, occupations, religion, time).* This category represents factors generally considered essential to life's basic functions. The data reflect that youth are quite concerned about competition. At this point, it is most keenly felt in making the grade-point average at the university; however, several students indicated occupational competition as a concern, too. Economic stability was mentioned by 21.8 percent of the sample. This response usually referred to the ability to make money and to have money throughout life. The term *morality* was applied on a broad scale. Students referred to morality in relation to sexuality, Vietnam, the draft, civil rights, and drugs, as well as religion. However, religion was also a significant concern of youth. Most were viewing religion as a force of providing some order to life, and it was often mentioned in association with morality and values.

2. *Domestic/International (automation, civil rights, Communism, the draft, nuclear war, politics, poverty, space, Vietnam, the voting age, and world affairs).* Concerns students mentioned that were related to some type of national or international involvement are categorized here. The most common response in this category was Vietnam. Most students' responses were in opposition to American involvement in Vietnam, feeling that we should not be there and that American youths should not be demanded to "throw their life away." The draft is also included in this area. Although 44.1 percent of the respondents mentioned Vietnam and only 30.4 percent mentioned the draft, in almost all cases where the draft was viewed as a problem, Vietnam was also.

Nationally, civil rights and politics were the most common concerns. Students were quite expressive about civil rights, feeling that equal rights and opportunity were essential. Discriminatory practices were not acceptable, but students did not approve of the use of violence to obtain an end. Political expression was also strong. Interestingly, most students pointed to the "system," graft, and the aloofness of politics and politicians to the people. Little comment was made about political preference. In most cases, the concern over politics focused around (1) the vastness of the American political structure and (2) the need for an increasing number of youth to become involved politically.

Lowering the voting age was not much of a concern within this sample. Only 108 respondents (Arizona, 33; Florida, 14; Illinois, 30; Louisiana, 5; Oklahoma, 26) thought the age should be lowered, in all cases to 18 years. Other concerns such as automation, Communism, nuclear war, poverty, and the space program captured the attention of a few youth, but no issue was clearly felt by the majority.

3. *Personal Identity (cultural norms, emancipation, the future, the generation gap, individuality, self-identity, and social identity).* Responses summarized here focus around concerns related primarily to one's self. By cultural norms is meant any response that placed emphasis on accepted patterns of behavior within society. It refers to how youth typically think society wants them to behave. To some extent this response is similar to the problem of the generation gap, although this response category was mentioned considerably less frequently and more commonly dealt with a communication gap.

Self-identity and social identity were the most frequently stated concerns. Students are anxious about finding themselves and their role within society. They feel that to do this they must experience emancipation and be allowed to express individuality. It is here where the restraints of cultural norms are felt. The fear of many youth is that they may never find themselves within a computerized, impersonal social order that consistently made many youth (18.9 percent) ask "What is my future?" "What does it hold for me?"

4. *Approval (parental approval, peer approval, physical appearance, popularity, and social approval).* There has been stress placed on individuality, and many writers have alluded to a breakdown of the family

structure in lieu of individual members making up a family. Yet, the data revealed in this study indicate that parental approval (18.1 percent), peer approval (21.1 percent), and social approval (20.0 percent) are still of vital concern to today's youth. Responses emphasize the need for others to accept and approve one's actions. Youth were concerned that they be accepted by their peers and by the social groups within which they basically functioned. Although these youth were at college, they still indicated a strong need for parental acceptance. In most cases this referred to functioning within the range of their perceived parental expectations, as was most commonly reflected by academic scholarship. A limited number of students stated that physical appearance and popularity were highly important to them.

5. *Social Behaviors (alcohol, drugs, hippies, smoking, student activism, and violence).* This summary includes only those social behaviors that tend to be the form of behavior being used by youth today. The student activism movement was the single most important issue in this group. Activism was mentioned by 22.6 percent of the respondents. However, this statistic was significantly influenced by the Florida sample, which represented 44.6 percent of the total responses.

Drugs did not seem to be an overwhelming concern of most youth. Here again the statistic of 16.5 percent was greatly influenced by the Arizona sample. From this group came 42.3 percent of the responses. One other representative concern was violence, which included concern about crime and delinquency. In most cases it was deplored by youth, especially if it accompanied some phase of the student activism movement.

6. *Sexuality (birth control, the double standard, premarital sex, sexual expression, and sex education).* Within this grouping are comments involving human sexuality and sexual behavior in some form. New issues are being expressed. In addition to sexual permissiveness, students mentioned ways of birth control (4.0 percent), the need for eliminating the double standard (2.4 percent), and the concern for sex education (4.5 percent). Of most importance, however, was sexual behavior. Concerns focused around standards and expectations for one's self

TABLE 3. TEN MOST FREQUENT RESPONSES BY UNIVERSITY

Arizona		Florida		Illinois		Louisiana		Oklahoma	
Sexuality	301	Education	264	Vietnam	222	Vietnam	218	Education	232
Vietnam	240	Activism	252	Education	209	Education	204	Vietnam	226
Education	237	Vietnam	196	Civil rights	200	Self-identity	136	Self-identity	222
Self-identity	197	Occupations	163	Sexuality	169	Draft	133	Peer approval	188
Draft	192	Competition	155	Occupations	152	Sexuality	118	Sexuality	179
Drugs	175	Sexuality	147	Draft	151	Competition	112	Occupations	167
Occupations	162	Economics	145	Competition	145	Civil rights	103	Religion	143
Competition	152	Draft	145	Politics	132	Economics	96	Cultural norms	140
Civil rights	150	Politics	120	Religion	130	Social identity	95	Draft	138
Morality	147	Civil rights	120	Self-identity	126	Future	89	Politics	137

and in relation to others. Emphasis on premarital sex was noted by 23 percent of the students.

University Profiles

Each university represented in the study is in a different geographical area in the United States. On the whole, data tended to reflect a high degree of similarity in youth problems, issues, and concerns regardless of the university from which the sample was drawn. Occasionally, some concern seemed to be quite strong in one area but not in others. Table 3 indicates the ten most frequent responses from each university sample. Four response categories—the draft, education, sexuality, and Vietnam—ranked in the top ten responses of all students. Beyond that, there was some variation among universities.

1. Arizona

In contrast to all other students, the Arizona students placed considerably more emphasis on sexuality and drugs. In expressing these concerns, they placed more stress on individual behavior. Thus, they saw contemporary social behavior as highly important. These students also placed much emphasis on the civil rights issue, ranking second to Illinois students. It is interesting that these students also placed more emphasis than any other university sample on the

issue of morality. This may be somewhat reflected in their concern over drugs, sex, and civil rights.

2. Florida

The most significant issue concerning these students was student activism. Responses quite emphatically cited SDS movements on campus as a major source of contention. Since more than 50 percent of the students pointed out this problem, it is logical to assume it to be a highly important one among these students. These youth were also more concerned about economic stability than any other university sample. In stating this concern, most students focused on having assurance of financial security in their future.

3. Illinois

In addition to education and Vietnam, these students showed a strong concern for civil rights. The university sampled is within the Chicago region and, as such, students are exposed to the Chicago metropolitan papers and television, which might be attributing factors to this high concern. Another leading concern of the Illinois sample was religion. With the exception of the Oklahoma students, the Illinois youth expressed the strongest emphasis on religion. Responses focused around religion providing a guideline for decisions and influencing emerging value systems. There was an overall tendency for these youth to be issue oriented.

4. Louisiana

Because this sample was so much more nonverbal than youth from the other universities, it is more difficult to assess the particular differences in this group. In addition to the responses that were like those of the other students, reasonable emphasis was placed on self- and social identity. In contrast, the concern for approval was significantly lower than in the other university samples. Only 9 percent of the total responses regarding approval were offered by Louisiana youth. Similarly, limited emphasis was placed on social behaviors and issue-oriented statements.

5. Oklahoma

This group of students was decidedly strong on approval. Peer approval was their fourth most frequent response, cultural norms ranked eighth, parental approval eleventh, and social approval twelfth. These areas represented 30 percent of the total responses concerning approval. These students also mentioned identity statements more frequently than did other university samples. The Oklahoma students also ranked highest on the issues of religion, politics, and occupations. Concern about one's self, through identity or approval, strongly dominated the responses given by these students.

Conclusions

The results of this study were based on self-reported data that reflected the problems, issues, and concerns pertinent to the youth sampled. Although the data should not lead the reader to a set of final conclusions, it is quite likely that the information contained herein is representative of many college youth today. The frequency with which these youth expressed concern over various personal, social, national, and international problems stresses the need to listen to them as well as today's student activists. It seems incomprehensible that today's colleges and universities, designed to provide challenge and opportunity to their youth, could do any less.

larry c. kerpelman

student political activism and ideology: comparative characteristics of activists and nonactivists[1]

A more careful delineation of the characteristics associated with activism from the characteristics associated with ideology was attempted. 73 undergraduate Ss, belonging to the 6 groups that result from the combination of activism and nonactivism with left, right, and middle ideologies, were given a series of personality and intellectual questionnaires. Activists were found to be significantly ($p < .05$) more intelligent than nonactivists. There were no differences in ego-defensiveness among any of the groups. Left-oriented Ss were, to a significant degree, less concerned with social acceptance than right- or middle-oriented Ss. The results indicate the necessity of separating ideology from activism in investigations of student political activists.

Growing attention is being paid to the recent emergence of American college students from the apathy of the 1950s into the activism of the 1960s. Although the proportion of students and of universities involved in significant activism revolving around political issues is small (Peterson, 1966; Trent & Craise, 1967), it is becoming larger. Student activists are becoming more vocal and more influential in affecting educational and even political decisions. Although many studies have focused upon the personality (e.g., Trent & Craise, 1967), intellectual (e.g., Watts & Whittaker, 1966),[2] and demographic (e.g., Flacks, 1967) characteristics of student political activists, few have investigated as well all possible comparison groups (e.g., right activists, left nonactivists). This failure in primary investigations to compare activist groups with other relevant groups has led to possible errors of generalization, which are compounded as they are reported in secondary or tertiary sources. Thus, for example, a reviewer of prior research on activists comments on "the strength and richness of their intellectual, aesthetic, and emotional endowment [Katz, 1967, p. 16]." When this secondary source was reported in tertiary newspaper reports, it was headlined, "Studies Agree that Most Campus Activists Are Comparatively Intelligent, Stable and Unprejudiced [Leo, 1967]." Yet in all but two (Flacks, 1967; Westby & Braungart, 1966)

Reprinted with permission of the author and the American Psychological Association from the *Journal of Counseling Psychology*, 1969, **16**, 8-13.

[1]This investigation was supported in part by a grant from the University of Massachusetts Research Council. The author thanks Joan P. Kerpelman for her assistance in the data collection and data reduction phases of this study. An earlier version of this paper was presented at the September 1968 American Psychological Association Convention in San Francisco.

[2]It is of interest that in all the studies that have touched upon intelligence of left-oriented individuals (most of which have concluded that they were more intelligent than nonactivist, presumably middle-of-the-road, controls) none, to this investigator's knowledge, measured intelligence directly. Either reported grade-point average was used (Somers, 1965) or a measure of "intellectualism" (McClosky, 1958) or "intellectual disposition" (Trent & Craise, 1967) was used. The only investigators who even examined university records of grade-point average reported no significant difference between left activists and a student cross-section (Watts & Whittaker, 1966).

of the many studies Katz reviewed, the comparison group investigated (if any was investigated at all) was a mixed group of college students. The almost universal implication that left activists are more emotionally stable and intelligent than right activists, left nonactivists, or any specific group remains unsupported.

A closely related problem is the frequent confounding of political activism with political ideology. In an investigation of the Berkeley Free Speech Movement participants, for example, it was concluded that "few college students in general can match the positive development of those personality characteristics that distinguish student activists from their college contemporaries [Trent & Craise, 1967, p. 39]." The question arises whether these qualities are related to these students' activism or to their ideology. The confounding of ideology with activism does not allow an answer to this question.

Of the few comparative studies in the literature, Winborn and Jansen (1967) focused upon personality characteristics of campus political action leaders, and Westby and Braungart (1966) investigated only demographic characteristics of student political activists. The present research concern was with personality and intellectual characteristics of student political activist group members along the whole range of political ideologies compared with their politically nonactive counterparts. The impetus for the research reported here derived from the kinds of concerns indicated above. It used as its starting point the recent provocative papers of Bay (1967) and Katz (1967). Reviewing the literature, Bay postulated that left activists are more intelligent, less ego-defensive, and have less concern about social acceptance (career, standing in school, etc.) than, presumably, their college rightist counterparts. Katz (1967), reviewing much of the same literature, also concluded that student activists (by which he presumably meant student left activists) were more intelligent and more stable or "psychologically rich" than unspecified nonactivist groups. But what of activist rightists? Or what of nonactivist leftists? It may well be asked if the characteristics frequently attributed to student left activists may not be related to their activism per se rather than to their left ideology; yet this question cannot be answered from the existing data. The present research represents a start toward answering these questions by obtaining objective measures of intelligence, ego-defensiveness, and social acceptance concern from groups representing points along both the activism dimension and the ideology dimension.

Method

Subjects

The Ss were 73 undergraduate students at the same large northeastern state university. The political activists were selected on the basis of membership in active campus organizations that were widely recognized as engaging in political activity. Two of the three activist organizations approached for cooperation were selected on the basis of preratings by 12 political science faculty members. These faculty members were independently asked to rate several campus organizations on a scale ranging from 1 (extremely politically liberal) to 5 (extremely politically conservative). The left-oriented group received a mean prerating of 1.27, while the right-oriented group received a mean prerating of 4.52, both with 83% interrater agreement. The politically "middle" group was not prerated. The left, right, and middle politically active groups were, respectively, a campus affiliate of a national student left-oriented organization, a loosely organized group of conservative students, and the campus student government organization.

The politically nonactive middle ideology group received a mean prerating of 2.90, with 92% interrater agreement. This group did not engage in political activities—it was the campus hiking club. The politically nonactive left and right ideologists could not, of course, have been selected from extant campus organizations, for this would have been a contradiction of the term politically nonactive. These Ss were selected, rather, on the basis of their scores on a questionnaire of political ideology (to be described below) taken in introductory psychology classes earlier in the year. These latter two groups of Ss received experiment credit for participation in the study; Ss in the other four groups were paid $1.25 per hour for their participation in the research.

Procedure

The leaders of each extant organization were approached to elicit their group's cooperation in the investigation, being told in very general terms the nature of the research and the monetary reward involved. The introductory psychology Ss were sent letters requesting their participation and indicating that they could, thereby, earn required course experiment credit. After cooperation was elicited, each organization or group was met with on a separate evening, at which time the research instruments, described below, were administered. Anonymity of individual Ss and of each group was stressed and guaranteed. Names were not required on the research material; Ss instead affixed a unique code number, based on demographic variables descriptive of them, to their questionnaire material. The research instruments were compiled in a booklet. The Ss filled them out at their own rate, and, when finished, received either monetary payment or experiment participation credit. The entire procedure lasted approximately 2 hours for each of the six S groups.

TABLE 1. CHARACTERISTICS OF THE SUBSAMPLES

Group	N	Mean age	Mean year in school	Mean no. activities
Activist				
Left	14	20.4	3.0	1.9
Middle	10	19.8	2.9	4.4
Right	11	21.2	3.4	2.9
Nonactivist				
Left	14	18.9	1.1	1.2
Middle	10	19.1	2.0	2.2
Right	14	18.6	1.4	1.5

Instruments

Political ideology. To measure the criterion variable of political ideology, Levinson's (1959) 12-item revision of the Politico-Economic conservatism (PEC) scale (Adorno, Frenkel-Brunswik, Levinson, & Sanford, 1950, pp. 154-168) was used. Previous research (Kerpelman, 1968) had indicated that this 12-item form of the PEC was a valid index of political orientation. In that research, a general Liberal-Conservative factor

loaded .89 on the PEC scale in a discriminant pattern analysis. In the present study, split-half reliability of the PEC scale, corrected by the Spearman-Brown formula, was found to be .87. The 7-point PEC scale was used to confirm the relative ideological orientation of all S groups. It was also the instrument upon which the preselection of nonactivist left and right Ss was based.

Political activity. A 24-item Activism Scale (ACT) was devised for this project to obtain a quantitative confirmation of the relative level of political activity of each group.[3] It is a 5-point scale, 12 items (ACT-A) of which question Ss on their actual frequency of participation in political activity during the prior 3 years. The remaining 12 items (ACT-D) ask Ss for desired frequency of participation in the same activities during the same period had the respondent been free of all social, financial, and educational obligations. In the present study, odd-even split-half reliability of the ACT-A subscale, corrected by the Spearman-Brown formula, was found to be .93, while reliability of the ACT-D subscale was .96.

Intelligence. The Quick Word Test (QWT), Form Am, Level 2, was used to measure intelligence. This is a rapid 100-item group test of verbal ability that is highly reliable and that correlates reasonably well with other group and individual intelligence tests (Borgatta & Corsini, 1964).

Ego-defensiveness. The Gordon Personal Profile Emotional Stability Scale (GPP-E) was used as an inverse measure of ego-defensiveness. This is a forced-choice preference questionnaire that is reasonably valid, reliable, and difficult to fake (Gordon, 1963).

Social acceptance concern. To measure this variable, the Survey of Interpersonal Values Recognition Scale (SIV-R) was used. This forced-choice questionnaire is uncorrelated with intelligence, is difficult to fake, and shows good criterion validity. The Recognition Scale is defined as measuring the values of "Being looked up to and admired, being

---

[3]Copies of the ACT research instrument, constructed by Michael Weiner and the author, may be obtained from the author upon request, as may copies of the PEC scale used.

considered important, attracting favorable notice, achieving recognition [Gordon, 1960, p. 3]."

Additional instruments. The Ss also filled out a code sheet (CDS) by means of which they assigned themselves a unique code descriptive of themselves based on demographic data pertinent to them. This served not only to preserve anonymity, but also to supply relevant demographic data. The Ss also listed their campus activities (CAL). This allowed the elimination of two Ss selected for the politically nonactive dimension who belonged to a campus political organization (albeit not one studied in this research). It also provided a measure of "organization-belonging" with which to compare Ss of the various groups.

The research booklet contained the above instruments in the order: CDS, QWT, SIV, GPP, PEC, ACT, CAL.

Results

Descriptive characteristics of the S groups are given in Table 1. As can be seen, the activists tended to be older and at a higher year level in the university than were the nonactivists. This may have been due to the necessity of selecting most nonactivists from the predominantly freshman-sophomore introductory psychology classes. There seemed to be no marked differences among the groups in number of campus activities to which they belonged, although the political activists, on the average, belonged to more organizations than the politically nonactive Ss, suggesting that students who engage in political activity tend to engage in other activities as well. Additionally, the middle activist Ss, as might be expected of elected student government officials, tended to belong to more organizations than other Ss.

Group means of the various questionnaires are summarized in Table 2. A summary of the 2 X 3 (Activism X Ideology) least squares solution unequal frequency analysis of variance (Harvey, 1960) performed on each measure is given in Table 3. The acceptable level of statistical significance used throughout was $p < .05$.

TABLE 2. GROUP MEANS AND *SD*s OF THE RESEARCH INSTRUMENT SCORES

	Ideology					
	Left		Middle		Right	
Measure[a]	M	SD	M	SD	M	SD
PEC (1-7)						
Activist	2.32	0.64	3.73	1.17	5.07	1.02
Nonactivist	3.35	0.53	4.18	0.40	5.07	0.33
ACT-A (12-60)						
Activist	32.71	8.53	26.50	7.80	25.64	5.81
Nonactivist	21.36	3.62	19.20	4.19	16.43	2.43
ACT-D (12-60)						
Activist	48.71	8.34	40.00	11.41	40.82	8.31
Nonactivist	34.07	7.22	27.50	5.48	24.07	6.73
QWT (20-85)						
Activist	62.79	13.50	66.50	10.61	62.36	7.50
Nonactivist	57.86	16.56	60.40	14.50	48.00	7.81
GPP-E (6-35)						
Activist	18.64	8.17	23.40	4.78	22.27	8.14
Nonactivist	19.64	7.23	17.90	9.24	24.50	5.98
SIV-R (1-25)						
Activist	9.29	3.54	13.80	4.00	11.73	3.39
Nonactivist	9.58	3.80	11.67	4.48	12.77	4.11

[a]Numbers in parentheses following each instrument name are the possible range of scores. The higher score indicates a greater amount of the characteristic named by the scale, for example, a high GPP-E score indicates greater emotional stability.

TABLE 3. ANALYSIS OF VARIANCE OF RESEARCH INSTRUMENT SCORES

Measure	Activism	Ideology	Interaction	Within cells
ACT-A				
MS	1536.941	249.885	24.433	36.689
df	1	2	2	67
F	41.891***	6.811**	0.666	
ACT-D				
MS	3812.980	611.173	24.974	69.834
df	1	2	2	67
F	54.601***	8.752***	0.358	
QWT				
MS	1023.119	333.254	123.704	163.271
df	1	2	2	54
F	6.266*	2.041	0.758	
GPP-E				
MS	10.224	119.670	93.138	60.887
df	1	2	2	67
F	0.168	1.965	1.530	
SIV-R				
MS	1.181	75.133	14.186	16.474
df	1	2	2	63
F	0.072	4.561*	0.861	

Note.—Within cells *df* varied for different measures due to the elimination of Ss who incorrectly coded or incorrectly completed the various instruments.

*$p < .025$.
**$p < .005$.
***$p < .001$.

An analysis of variance was not done on the PEC scale. That measure was the basis for selecting nonactivist students for the left and right subgroups, artificially making the variance smaller for these two groups than would have been the case had the PEC been an uncontaminated dependent variable. Nonetheless, examination of the subgroup means for this measure suggests that all the ideology groups differed in the expected directions on this measure of political ideology.

On both subscales of the ACT the activists differed significantly in the expected direction from the nonactivists, providing further evidence that the groups were properly selected. This result also adds support for the construct validity of the ACT as an instrument for selecting political activist students. Newman-Keuls tests, modified for unequal subclass frequencies (Winer, 1962, pp. 80-84), indicated a significant difference on the ACT-A subscale between left and right ideology groups, the former being more active. The middle group did not differ significantly from either of the others. On the ACT-D subscale, left-oriented Ss were significantly more active than both right- and middle-oriented Ss. There was no significant difference between these latter two groups.

Concerning the first of three measures specific to the research questions, namely, intelligence, there was a significant Activism main effect. Activists were significantly higher on the QWT measure of intelligence than nonactivists, but there was no significant Ideology main effect nor was there an interaction effect. As regards ego-defensiveness, there were no significant differences among any of the subgroups on the GPP Emotional Stability scale. Finally, the measure of social acceptance concern, the SIV-R, revealed a significant main effect of Ideology and no main effect of Activism nor any interaction effect. A Newman-Keuls analysis of the SIV-R mean scores of the three ideology groups indicated that the mean scores of the middle- and right-oriented Ss were significantly higher than the mean score of the left-oriented Ss; middle- and right-oriented Ss did not differ significantly from each other on this scale.

Discussion

The inferences to be drawn from the present investigation depend, as in any study, in large measure upon the adequacy of the sampling procedures and the representativeness of the samples. The PEC scores suggested that the groups selected were, indeed, different in political orientation in the direction expected. The ACT scores indicated a difference in political activism between the activists and the nonactivists, also in the direction expected. Left-oriented Ss in general tended to be more politically active than the other groups, as measured by the ACT. A consequence of the selection procedure led to the nonactivists being younger and less advanced in their education than the activists, and this factor should be considered as possibly contributing to the activist-nonactivist difference in intelligence found in the present study. Finally, the representativeness of the institution sampled would also affect the generality of the findings reported here.

The data suggest that prudence must be applied to the kinds of past and future generalizations about "student activists" and about "the New Left." The main precaution is that investigators should be more precise in delineating which student group has more or less of an intellectual or personality characteristic than other student groups. The present findings on intelligence differences illustrate this point. Assuming that the QWT is a valid measure of at least verbal intelligence (and there is evidence that this is so— Borgatta & Corsini, 1964), and assuming that age was not a confounding factor, the data of this investigation suggest that student political activists of all ideologies are, on the whole, more intelligent than are students who are not politically active. Although the absolute difference among groups was small, the fact that the total sample, being university students, was already high in intelligence lends weight to the significant differences found in this study. These findings on intelligence contradict Bay's (1967) explicit conclusion and Katz's (1967) implicit conclusion that it is left activists, or leftists in general, who are more intelligent than right activists or rightists in general. It must also be cautioned that measures of "intellectualism," "intellectual predisposition," or even reported grade-point average which have been discussed as measures of intelligence in previous research are not necessarily correlated with intelligence. In the present study, there were no measured intelligence differences among ideology groups. The reason for the difference between activism groups is open to speculation. The most obvious hypothesis is that only the more intelligent students can afford the commitment of time and energy that activist group membership entails. That activists on the average belonged to more campus activities than nonactivists supports this hypothesis.

The failure in this study to find a significant difference among the subsample groups on emotional stability contradicts Bay's (1967) hypothesis that "radicals" are less ego-defensive than "conservatives," as well as Katz's (1967) suggestion that student activists approach being "psychological noblemen." In the present study, they were not. Other studies have come to similar conclusions. Trent and Craise (1967) found no significant difference in manifest anxiety between Berkeley Free Speech Movement members and a general student population sample. Winborn and Jansen's (1967) investigation leaves open the question of differences in emotional stability between student activists and others, and the present investigation, failing to find significant differences between any of the groups, must do so as well.

The significant difference between left-oriented students (activist and nonactivist alike) and middle and right students on the SIV measure of social acceptance concern is, on the whole, consistent with other research. Most of that research (e.g., Bay, 1967; Winborn & Jansen, 1967) speaks of left activists being less concerned about conventionalities than right activists. The present study would amend that conclusion to read that left-oriented students, in general, are more unconcerned about social expectancies than are nonleftist students, regardless of activism. Again, the reason is open to speculation, but it may be that the present social-political system that the left ideology seeks to change holds few values to which the left ideologist wishes to conform.

The methods of this study illustrate an approach that can be made toward more precise delineation of the characteristics of student activists of all ideological persuasions. Future research must make further and more careful delineations of the groups studied if a clear picture of the characteristics of student political activists is to emerge. Keniston (1968a) has suggested that an important element to consider is the extent of actual commitment. Thus he suggested that highly committed leaders of activist groups may have different motivations and personality characteristics than less committed follower members. It is also apparent that sampling across institutions must be done if characterizations of student activists and student ideologists are to have generality. Peterson (1966) suggested different activism "profiles" among different institutions of higher education. Not only are more individual investigations at more individual institutions needed, then, but also more individual investigations across institutions (where methodology and research instruments are more likely to be the same) are needed. If these tasks are carried out, it is quite likely that the broad brush that has heretofore been used to paint the picture of "student activist" will have to be more finely made to take account not only of the political activism, but also of the political ideology, commitment, and institutional setting of the students involved.

richard flacks

protest or conform: some social psychological perspectives on legitimacy

When John Kennedy received his discharge from the armed forces after World War II, he wrote in his notebook, "War will exist until that distant day when the conscientious objector enjoys the same reputation and prestige that the warrior does today."

In a certain sense, the "distant day" apparently hoped for by the young John Kennedy has arrived. On the American campus, the draft resister assuredly has more prestige than the willing conscript. Drs. Howard Levy and Benjamin Spock likely are more widely honored among many medical students than those in the medical profession who have dutifully served in Vietnam. National magazines have provided us with more sympathetic details concerning the exploits of Pvt. Andrew Strapp, the Fort Hood Three, the Reverend William Sloane Coffin, and David Harris than of Medal of Honor winners, ace bomber pilots, and even Green Berets. I have no doubt that a poll of attendees at this conference would show more respect for the actions of Captain Dale Noyd, a psychologist court-martialed for refusal to use his skills in support of the Vietnam war effort, than for those psychologists who continue to aid military training, psychological warfare, and counterinsurgency. In the ghetto high

schools of the country, it seems likely that the great hero of this war is Muhammed Ali. At my own university, 49 per cent of the graduate students and graduating seniors responding to a student government poll declare that they would not serve in the armed forces if drafted; Louis Harris finds that 20–30 per cent of male students nationally say they will refuse to serve. If John Kennedy's "distant day" still seems far off, it is nevertheless already here on certain campuses and in certain neighborhoods of the country (Lauter & Howe, 1968).

Current discussion of legitimacy focuses on this situation and is concerned particularly with speculation that instances of defiance, resistance, and disruption by young people, directed against established authority, represent a trend leading to the erosion and destruction of the legitimacy of military and other authority. This concern is too recent to have produced very much in the way of systematic research; instead, one is struck by the fact that whatever empirical social psychological research we have which bears directly on the problem of authority tends to dramatize the extent to which people do what they are told to do by those with authority.

There is, for example, a small tradition of rather striking experimental studies which demonstrate that persons tend to do what they perceive to be clearly expected of them

Reproduced by special permission from the *Journal of Applied Behavioral Science*, "Protest or conform: Some social psychological perspectives on legitimacy," Richard Flacks, pp. 127-150, NTL Institute for Applied Behavioral Studies.

by others whom they regard as having the right to have such expectations. Among the earliest of such studies[1] were those by Jerome Frank (1944) in which subjects were asked to perform impossible or disagreeable tasks, such as balancing a marble on a steel ball or eating dry soda crackers. In Frank's studies, subjects would continue to carry out the experimenter's instructions without overt resistance, unless explicitly informed of their right to refuse.

There are even more dramatic demonstrations of willing obedience in the recent experimental literature. Pepitone and Wallace (Gamson, 1968) encountered little resistance from subjects who were asked by experimenters to sort garbage. Martin Orne and his associates (1962; Orne & Evans, 1965) attempted to design tasks which would be refused by normal subjects so that the effects of hypnosis on subjects' willingness to accept commands could be demonstrated. In general, he found that it was extremely difficult to design a task so boring or meaningless that an unhypnotized subject would refuse an experimenter's request to continue with it. In later experiments, Orne and his associates were able to get subjects to do extremely disagreeable and harmful things by asking them to pretend that they were hypnotized. Subjects who simulated hypnosis were as fully willing as hypnotized subjects to pick up a poisonous snake, put their hands in nitric acid, and throw acid in an assistant's face. Even subjects who were told they were "normal controls" tended to show compliance with these requests. It should be added, of course, that steps were taken by the experimenters to prevent actual injury to the participants in the experiments.

There are, finally, the well-known experiments by Stanley Milgram (1965) which have demonstrated the capacity of the experimental situation to create what Milgram calls "destructive obedience." Subjects asked to deliver what they believed to be extremely dangerous electric shocks to another person, in a situation in which the administration of shocks was defined as necessary to the success of an experiment, tended to deliver the maximum voltage even when they heard or saw the victim in pain and pleading

for mercy. Even though they gave a variety of indications of stress and dislike for the situation, the majority of subjects in Milgram's basic situation continued to perceive an obligation to the experimenter to follow his orders.

Milgram's studies suggest some limits on the tendency of subjects to do what they are told to do. For instance, when commands conflict with one's personal inclinations, the latter are more likely to prevail if there is a way to evade the command without being detected or if one observes others defying the command openly. There is also the suggestion in his work that individuals who accept orders they regard as legitimate tend to believe that the primary responsibility for the consequences of such orders rests with the experimenter rather than themselves.

This small literature of experimentation on obedience is not entirely easy to interpret. Most obviously, these studies show that, at least in our culture, persons tend to be highly trusting of scientists and tend, consequently, to accept the authority of a scientist once they have committed themselves to helping him in an experiment. Although one might not wish to go very far in generalizing responses to scientific authority to other power relationships, it does seem that these experiments do constitute rather pure demonstrations of the effects of legitimacy, with other sources of motivation largely removed. These studies suggest that under conditions where authority is defined by subjects as legitimate, they appear highly ready to do what is expected of them, highly likely to delegate processes of judgment to the authority figure—even when coercion and reward are virtually absent and the consequences of obedience are likely to be negative. One concludes from these studies that it would be perilous to treat forms of compliance with national authority—such as readiness to enter military service or to pay taxes or to otherwise support war—as merely instrumental acts designed to avoid the severe negative sanctions associated with noncompliance or evasion. By the same token, obedience to national authority cannot be explained solely as positively instrumental nor as positively expressive of sentiments like patriotism or ideological commitment to the regime. What makes the experiments we have cited so striking is that they illustrate

[1]This discussion of the literature on conforming is indebted to Gamson (1968, pp. 127-135).

behavior undertaken *in spite of personal motive and without positive emotional commitment*. It is for this reason that they appear to be valid microscopic replications of such mass instances of obedience as submission to conscription or participation in bureaucratically organized genocide.

It is clear that Milgram's subjects and draft resisters stand for opposing aspects of the same culture and social system. Milgram's subjects seem to typify what C. Wright Mills called the "cheerful robot"; the prevalence of compliance in his experiments seems to support critics of modern society who fear the rise of "mass conformity." Yet the emergence of youthful opponents of militarism and of forms of protest based on civil disobedience and confrontation suggests the possibility of an opposing trend. Indeed, one of the more pressing tasks for social analysis is to attempt to understand which figure—Milgram's subject or the conscientious resister—best symbolizes the central trends in individual-authority relations in American society.

Although no coherent framework is yet available which can provide us with such systematic understanding, two lines of investigation in social psychology may be relevant for constructing such a framework. The first derives from the experiments we have cited and focuses on the way in which perceived characteristics of the authority structure influence the likelihood of obedience. Milgram's findings provide a basis for extrapolating at least three general propositions concerning those features of the authority structure which are central to the maintenance of its legitimacy.

1. Individuals tend to attribute legitimacy to authority when the exercise of that authority is perceived as beneficial to groups, institutions, or values to which the individual is committed. We have argued that explanations of compliant behavior cannot rest on notions of reward and punishment; indeed, the very definition of legitimacy involves the assumption that individuals comply with authority in spite of their personal motives. In other words, we can measure the legitimacy of a particular authority structure by the degree in which it can obtain conformity without the use of positive or negative sanctions.

Nevertheless, claims to legitimacy by authorities in modern society usually must include an argument that the exercise of this authority is instrumental to the achievement of benefits or values collectively desired by subordinates. Thus, subjects in the experiments we have cited tended to assume that the orders given them were designed to advance science; they acted against their personal inclinations, not because they were coerced or rewarded but because they perceived their actions as instrumental to the achievement of a collective goal and they perceived the experimenter as a valid representative of that goal.

All modern nation-states are "pluralist" in the sense that they govern societies consisting of diverse classes, ethnic groups, institutions, and subcultures. The legitimacy of national authority in such societies depends in part on the maintenance of the perception that common interests and values are shared by these diverse groups, transcending that which divides them, that the national authority is the authentic guarantor of those common interests, and that continued support for national authority is relatively beneficial for each such group. In such a society, legitimacy is in danger of erosion if, for example, there is a persistent pattern of inequity experienced by members of a particular class or stratum, if adherents of particular value systems or subcultures feel threatened, unrepresented, or disillusioned by the going system, if the established common values of the national culture are weakened by rapid social change and the national authorities are seen as incompetent to generate or support new values, or if members of particular institutions experience significant discontinuities between their collective goals and those of the authorities. The erosion of established authority under these conditions is probably hastened if alternative structures are perceived or envisioned by those who are disaffected.

2. Attribution of legitimacy is a function of trust; that is, the perception that those in authority are not biased against one or that the working of the system does not result in special costs for oneself or one's group. The importance of trust in the experiments we have cited is rather clear; in both the Orne and Milgram experiments, it seems likely that subjects were willing to obey commands to commit destructive acts in the belief that the experimenter knew what he was doing and was able to eliminate or control any real danger in the situation. For Orne's subjects, this perception was probably reinforced when they observed that they were prevented from actually picking up the poisonous snake by the sudden appearance of a glass screen between themselves and the snake.

At the level of national authority, trust depends on such matters as the objectivity of the authorities in mediating conflicts, the degree in which the police and the courts implement the principle of equality before the law, the openness of the political system and the media of opinion to emergent groups and dissenting views, the trustworthiness of statements made by national leaders, the degree in which officially espoused policies are actually implemented and actually have the results claimed for them, and so on.

It should be clear that trust, as we have defined it, constitutes a somewhat different basis for legitimacy than perceived benefit. Certainly, the perception that a regime or political system is biased in one's favor constitutes an important source of legitimacy; nevertheless, as Gamson (1968, p. 57) has suggested, such perceptions by some members are likely to be less stable supports for a system than a general perception of nonbias—for if one group feels particularly advantaged by the system, others are likely to feel disadvantaged and will tend to withdraw their support. Gamson argues that the optimal level of trust for maintaining legitimacy in situations of high conflict is one in which conflicting parties see the authorities as unbiased.

3. Individuals tend to attribute legitimacy to authority if they perceive a generalized consensus supporting legitimacy. This consensus may be manifested through expressions of popular opinion; it may also be manifested by the ease with which the authority in question can call upon the backing of other centers of power in the society. The Milgram experiments, in addition to suggesting the importance of trust and perceived benefit as supports for legitimacy, indicate that compliance was substantially reduced when sub-

jects perceived others disobeying. This finding is, of course, congruent with those of other experiments in conformity to group pressure which have repeatedly shown that subjects tend not to conform if they have social support for nonconformity.

No principle in social psychology is better established than the idea that individual attitudes depend on the perceived attitudes of significant others. In the case of legitimacy, the usual psychological mechanisms which bind people to accept consensual attitudes are importantly supplemented by the principle of consent of the governed. In a political democracy, the existence of general consensus about the legitimacy of a regime or a policy is a very powerful support because majority support is defined as the ultimate basis for legitimacy in the system. Thus those who are inclined to challenge legitimacy confront moral as well as psychological difficulties when they do so. These difficulties can be reduced, it appears, by the example of individuals who refuse to comply. Acts of noncompliance can have the effect of undermining the "pluralistic ignorance" which often underlies popular consensus. Many with private doubts conform because they believe others lack doubts; examples of open disobedience serve to make private doubts public. Furthermore, they can provide models of effective resistance: often, as Milgram has argued, persons tend to obey because they believe they have no alternative or because they lack the skills necessary for resistance; the overt resistant may make alternatives visible and skills available. In situations where compliance to authority entails major individual sacrifice and where obedience is demanded primarily because the commands are legitimate, public acts of individual noncompliance can be precursors of large-scale popular disaffection. This was surely the faith of Thoreau and those who have followed him.

Arthur Stinchcombe has recently argued that "power based *only* on the shifting sands of public opinion and willing obedience is inherently unstable" (1968, p. 161). In his view, it is not popular consent or the willing obedience of subordinates which is decisive for legitimatizing a power; rather "a power is legitimate to the degree that, by virtue of the doctrines and norms by which it is justified, the power-holder can call upon sufficient other centers of power, as reserves in case of need, to make his power effective" (Stinchcombe, 1968, p. 162). From a psychological point of view, we may interpret this statement to predict that individuals will tend to perceive the action of an authority as legitimate if that action has or is likely to have the support of other centers of power. We can also draw from it the prediction that popular disaffection and weakening consensus about legitimacy are less clear-cut signs of eroding legitimacy than is the failure by role-players in key institutions adequately to support the power of national authority. Finally, although Stinchcombe in his brief exercise in conceptual analysis does not deal with this point, we can expect a reciprocal relationship between popular opinion and the responsiveness of institutional leaders to the needs of national authority. In situations of growing popular disaffection, institutional authority may be decisive as a conservative force in backing up the legitimacy of the national authority; but if cracks should appear in the institutional structure, then popular disaffection may be accelerated. At any rate, Stinchcombe's strictures against overemphasizing the importance of popular consent as a basis for legitimacy are quite suggestive; they lead us to consider measuring the stability of a political system by looking at the intactness of the institutional framework rather than simply at public opinion and the distribution of attitudes.

Drawing on the Milgram and other experiments concerning obedience, we have been able to suggest some variables which seem centrally useful in describing the conditions under which persons tend to attribute legitimacy to political regimes and national authority. These variables have to do with perceived characteristics of the authority structure and with perceptions about the social context in which the authorities operate.

Another social psychological perspective on legitimacy is possible. This involves emphasis on the characteristics of subordinates rather than on the characteristics of the situation. In the Milgram studies, individual differences in the degree of compliance, in reaction time, and in eagerness to administer shock were observed. It is important to note that Milgram found that these differences

were correlated with such "personality" measures as the F scale. The existence of such individual differences and such correlations leads us quite directly to that long tradition of research on "character" which has been a distinctive contribution of psychology to political analysis.

Starting at least with Freud, there has been the hypothesis that the family constitutes a miniature political system and that attitudes toward parental authority are generalized or projected onto other political figures. Freud's view of the matter was notoriously pessimistic: the family was inherently authoritarian; in it men learned habits of submission, learned to repress or deflect their anti-authoritarian impulses, and, if well-socialized, came to idealize forms of paternal domination. But the psychoanalytic perspective does not require a view of socialization which emphasizes the repressive outcome of early childhood experience. Wilhelm Reich was among the earliest to suggest that children raised in democratic, egalitarian, and nonrepressive social settings could become adults with the capacity to resist irrational or tyrannical authority.

Speculation and investigation about the political effects of early socialization reached an important culmination with the research on the Authoritarian Personality (Adorno, Frenkel-Brunswik, Levinson, & Sanford, 1950). Whatever its methodological flaws, this research made quite credible the idea that attitudes of submission may be based on enduring personality dispositions, and that such dispositions have their origins in families characterized by highly dominant fathers, strongly hierarchical structures, rigorously differentiated sexual and generational roles, and low tolerance for free expression of impulses. Subsequent experimental studies, including Milgram's as we have noted, show positive relationships between F scores and submissive or conforming behavior.

Democratic or anti-authoritarian "personalities" have been far less well studied. Research with which I am most familiar concerns characteristics of student protestors; our own studies (Flacks, 1967), those of Brewster Smith and his associates (Block, Haan, & Smith, 1968), and of Kenneth Keniston (1968a) all provide evidence that student activists tend to come from families which are more egalitarian and democratic and less repressive than the families of students who are uninvolved in protest movements. Finally, one might call attention to case studies by Wolfenstein (1967) of "revolutionary personalities." They suggest a pattern in which paternal authority has been weak or absent at crucial stages in the development of these future revolutionaries; there is the suggestion in Wolfenstein's work that an important experience for creating the capacity for revolutionary leadership is that of having replaced one's father in the family in early adolescence. The psychoanalytic perspective contains grave and notorious dangers of psychological reductionism; still, I am convinced that the central hypotheses—that the family is a political system; that one learns within it habits of response to authority and attitudes toward appropriate behavior by authorities which can carry over to the larger political system—remain viable and fruitful ones for those who want to understand the capacities of individuals for conformity and resistance and the tendencies within cultures to facilitate or inhibit such capacities. Since political radicals and dissenters have often borne the brunt of psychoanalytic scrutiny used for *ad hominem* attack on their position, there is legitimate concern that the psychoanalytic tradition is conservative when applied to political theory. (A provocative treatment of the general problem of psychoanalysis and politics appears in Sampson, 1968.) But ever since Reich, it has been clear that psychoanalytic hypotheses on the formative role of parental authority could have radical critical functions. At any rate, we may relate our discussion of authoritarianism to the problem of legitimacy by asking such questions as: Does the persistence of authoritarian institutions and practices depend in part on the ability of these institutions to recruit appropriate character types? Is the legitimacy of, say, military authority likely to be materially affected by the emergence in the society of significant numbers of youths who are characterologically indisposed to submit to it?

The psychoanalytic tradition emphasizes the relationship between character development and political behavior, and tends to ignore explicit learning about government and politics. There is, however, a growing body of research on the latter. Briefly stated, the mass of such studies can, I believe, be summarized by saying that children tend to adopt the political beliefs and preferences of their parents, and moreover, that white children tend to be highly supportive of the American political system. In the words of Easton and Dennis (1965), summarizing their findings on children's images of government, "The small child sees a vision of holiness when he chances to glance in the direction of government—a sanctity and rightness of the demi-goddess who dispenses the milk of human kindness. The government protects us, helps us, is good, and cares for us when we are in need, answers the child." The authors believe that this early set of emotions and perceptions forms the basis for later adult attitudes toward the state. This pattern of socialization is undoubtedly crucial in maintaining the legitimacy of authority in American society.

Although no one has studied blacks or student protesters in quite the same way, we may suspect that among both groups a high proportion had somewhat different images of government in early childhood. Black respondents are far more suspicious of government authorities than whites; this undoubtedly reflects not only their actual experience but also the received experience of their parents (Marvick, 1965). Student activists' political attitudes are in large measure continuous with those of their parents; it is probable that from a very early age they were reared to be skeptical about the sanctity and benevolence of established authority (Flacks, 1967). If the white majority tends to socialize their children to support the legitimacy of the national government, it seems also to be the case that significant minority subcultures tend to rear their children rather explicitly to have doubts about that authority. If the majority of white children talk as if they were raised in the nurseries of *Brave New World,* this would seem to ensure the stability of national authority as we now know it—and this appears to be the assumption underlying much of the work on political socialization. But the existence of at least two counter-cultures, socializing their children quite differently, suggests a more dynamic, less predictable political scene.

In recent years, psychologists have displayed increasing interest in the ways in which individual conceptions of self influence the capacity for initiative, autonomy, and rationality. In a recent review Brewster Smith (1968) suggests that "competence" is a useful summary term for a variety of traits and attitudes which have been defined and measured in recent studies. The competent person, as Smith defines him, perceives the self as "causally important, as effective in the world . . . as likely to be able to bring about desired effects, and as accepting responsibility when effects do not correspond to desire. In near equivalent, the person has self-respect." Although competence is likely to be associated with favorable levels of general self-evaluation or esteem, general esteem is less important than the sense of efficacy or potency (Smith, 1968, pp. 281-282).

Although competence bears some relationship to authoritarianism, since both concepts address the capacity of individuals for independence and self-determination, it clearly is a different sort of concept. In particular, references to competence have to do with aspects of self-awareness rather than with unconscious determinants. Whereas authoritarianism as a concept asks us to focus on competence leads us to emphasize the continuing role on early socialization and enduring traits as influences on the capacity for self-determination, a focus of experience and social interaction in shaping this capacity.

If there is a generalized capacity for independence, a generalized tendency to perceive oneself as causally important and potent, then this has clear implications for political behavior and relations to authority. Indeed, there exist a considerable number of studies relating efficacy to aspects of political behavior such as voting, activism, and alienation.

With reference to legitimacy, we may hypothesize that competence is related to the individual's readiness to delegate processes of judgment and evaluation to superordinate authority, or to participate smoothly in situations where decisions which affect him are beyond his control. For persons with high competence, the legitimacy of authority depends on the degree to which they have access to the decision-making process or believe that their judgments are taken seriously by superiors, or, perhaps most importantly, have the freedom to shape their own situation without reference to higher authority. Persons with low sense of competence, on the other hand, tend to view authority as untrustworthy, but also lack trust in their own ability to affect those in authority. They are, consequently, likely to be politically apathetic, fatalistically enduring what is imposed upon them (while sometimes trying to evade the most severe consequences), unless some route to efficacy becomes manifest (as is sometimes the case).

In modern society, formal education is the socializing experience which is supposed to be most directly relevant to enhancing competence. In practice, of course, it very often has the opposite effect, particularly on children of impoverished or working class background (Kozol, 1967). Nevertheless, it seems clear that achieving high levels of education does increase the sense of competence of many individuals, particularly in the political sphere.

Alongside the rise of mass higher education in modern society has been the increasing dominance of bureaucratic forms of authority. Bureaucratic organization rewards competence, but at the same time bureaucratic hierarchy rests on the assumption that there are major differences among men in their capacity to exercise authority, and that competence in this regard ought to give a few men great legitimate power to coordinate the lives of many others who ought not to expect much voice in decisions which control them.

There is, then, a contradiction between two of the great shaping institutions of the contemporary period—mass higher education and bureaucratic authority—a contradiction which has to do with opposed definitions of competence embodied in each of these institutions. This contradiction was noted by Max Weber in his classic essay on bureaucracy. Weber felt that the tension between liberal education and bureaucracy would probably be resolved by the erosion of liberal education and its replacement by technical training. It is clear that his expectations were to a very great extent accurate. Narrow specialization, emphasis on technique, and value neutrality in higher education are widely seen as the central trend; critics continue to see these as reducing the likelihood that the highly educated person will feel himself to be competent to take part in general citizenly activity.

Still, liberal education has not been totally erased, and more and more young people, unlike their predecessors in the educated middle class, are very likely to spend much of their lives, both in the educational system and beyond it, under bureaucratic authority if they follow conventional career lines.

The heightened sense of competence produced by mass higher education and by comfortable status constitutes, I believe, one of the most important sources of instability for the legitimacy of established authority, particularly those authority structures which assume little competence and provide little autonomy for those subordinate to it.

There is one final personal characteristic which seems to deserve mention as relevant to understanding the stability of authority in American society. This is the capacity to take risks in order to defy authoritative orders. There are undoubtedly numerous determinants of this capacity, and one doubts whether there is, in fact, a generalized trait—call it courage—which predicts willingness to take risks in all spheres of life. I particularly want to emphasize the possibility that one's socioeconomic status is an important determinant of one's capacity to take risks involving disobedience. In particular, it seems likely that high status and material security, particularly if one is born into them, tend to weaken the impact of those incentives and sanctions which are usually utilized by authority to maintain conformity. Obviously, most people at the top do a great many things to stay there; still, it seems to be empirically true that they also have more objective and subjective freedom of action. This is, in part, because the status and income incentives of the society are less attractive; in part, because one has been raised to exercise rather than defer to authority; in part, because one may have a certain degree of guilt about being affluent in an egalitarian society; in part, because one discovers the limitations and psychological costs of a life-style organized around material consumption and preservation of social status. At any rate, on this analysis, one should not find it surprising

that among those most willing to be defiant of the draft; among those most prepared to face prison with some degree of equanimity; among those ready to take risks with respect to the future careers, a disproportionate number of children of affluence will be represented. Furthermore, on this analysis, one predicts that rising levels of affluence will greatly increase the number of young who are prepared to take the risks of challenging established authority.

I have formulated the foregoing propositions and hypotheses in what appears to be a deductive style; actually, however, this discussion should be read as *post hoc* argument. On the one hand, much of the previous discussion was designed to try to identify some general principles which would explain some of the data which we and others have obtained concerning the characteristics of student protesters. Second, this discussion was in large part an attempt to provide some rational grounds for the feeling, which I am sure I share with others, that present student protest movements against university administrations, against the war and the draft, are not isolated or ephemeral outbursts, but that they have major historical implications, particularly for the legitimacy of national authority in advanced industrial societies like our own.

The burden of social research which has relevance to anticipating the future of legitimacy in this society strongly suggests that the prudent observer will place his bets on continued stability. That is the implication of Milgram's studies and other experiments demonstrating the willing obedience of subjects undergoing scientific manipulation. It is the burden of research on the effects of political socialization. It is the clear implication of studies of political behavior, of voting habits and patterns, and public opinion. The main body of theory and research from diverse fields seems to say that the legitimacy of national authority in the United States rests on a broad consensus among Americans about political rules, about common values, about the trustworthiness of the system in general and the current regime in particular; and that this consensus is powerfully supported by the process of socializing the young on the one hand and by the prosperous and progressive consequences of the system on the other.

This kind of reasoning did not help social scientists to predict either the black revolt or the mass disaffection and rebelliousness of educated youth. Given the emergence of these movements, conventional social analysis leads us to expect that their effects will be neither symptomatic of, nor productive of, fundamental changes in the nature of authority and its legitimation in American society.

Such reasoning seems increasingly less credible with each passing day. And we need not rely solely on our emotional reactions to immediate turmoil to provide grounds for thinking that the legitimacy of established authority in the United States is reaching an historical turning point.

The black revolt is, of course, a primary reason for expecting a transformation of authority. The shift in its terms, from a movement for integration to a movement for colonial liberation, means that, by definition, a major portion of the black community has already decided that established authority on national and local levels is illegitimate. Current proposals for dealing with the racial crisis fall roughly into three categories: they are either proposals for the institutionalization of new forms of authority or proposals to restore the legitimacy of the political system by efforts to rapidly meet the economic needs of the black population, or they are frank appeals to recognize the collapse of legitimacy by proposing to maintain power through force.

Some of our previous discussion is helpful in understanding why legitimacy of authority has so rapidly eroded for black people. Without attempting a detailed analysis, the following points are worth mentioning:

1. Negroes have of course never felt particularly rewarded by the system nor have they been given any opportunity to see it as trustworthy. As we have previously suggested, this disaffection and mistrust is a product of direct and graphic experience; it is also a feature of the political socialization of Negro children and youth in the family.

2. The past decade has been one of increased disillusionment. Although the postwar period was expected to be one of rapid progress for Negroes, matters did not turn out this way. The gap between black and white economic position has tended to widen. Laws and government enactments which promised change were not effectively implemented. The promise of migration to the city has turned to despair. Of particular importance in intensifying distrust of and disaffection with the political system is the situation of black youth. The rising generation experiences enormous rates of unemployment and the knowledge that future opportunity will be meager; it contributes disproportionately to the casualties in Vietnam, suffers almost universal harassment at the hands of the local police—and all this in the context of an endless stream of promises and seductions. To vast numbers of black youth, it is clear that the system is strongly biased against them and that nothing is to be gained from further adherence to it.

3. The integration movement was crucial in the development of new stances toward authority. Its failure, of course, intensified disaffection. But its success in creating organization had the effect of increasing the competence and risk-taking capacity of many black people. It also transformed the consensus of the black community from one organized around accommodation and acceptance of established authority to one favoring assertiveness and independent power.

Of course, no elaborate framework of theorizing is needed to account for the emergence of deepening revolutionary sentiment in the black community. On the other hand, one need not assume that the existence of such a sentiment is particularly threatening to the long-term legitimacy of the American political system. Partial incorporation of Negro demands, it may be argued, can offset the more threatening implications of the movement; anyway, it may be said, the blacks are a special case of disaffection, with little resonance among whites.

I believe, however, that the inability of the American polity to deal effectively with Negro grievances is not the only source of erosion of its legitimacy. Indeed, the so-called youth revolt indicates that more general problems are, in fact, emerging. These, I would argue, have to do with major shifts in aspects of American culture to which I have already briefly referred. Among these changes I would emphasize the following:

1. There has been a general decline of commitment to traditional "middle class values" throughout the society. Many observers have commented on the erosion of the "Protestant Ethic"—a process which probably began with the turn of the century and which has been due largely to the impact of bureaucratization and increasing economic surplus. These processes have virtually destroyed the traditional capitalist economy; the cultural and characterological patterns associated with it have likewise lost their vitality. On the other hand, it is important to emphasize that the existing political and institutional elites continue to represent themselves in traditional ways and that large sectors of the populace still adhere to some version of the classic virtues of entrepreneurial success, self-discipline, and individualism which derive from the Protestant Ethic.

2. The rapid growth of a sector of the middle class whose status depends on high education rather than property. This group tends to be most critical of traditional values and of traditional capitalism generally, in part because of the exposure of these people to humanist values, in part because their vocations are often not tied directly to the business sector of the economy. In addition, as we have suggested, high education is likely to increase the interest of individuals in having autonomy and a voice in decision making.

3. Associated with these trends has been the transformation of the American family, especially the family of the educated middle class. This transformation involves increased equality between husband and wife, declining distinctiveness of sex roles in the family, increased opportunity for self-expression on the part of children, fewer parental demands for self-discipline, and more parental support for autonomous behavior on the part of children. Evidence from studies of student protesters suggests the existence of an increasingly distinct "humanist" subculture in the middle class, consisting primarily of highly educated and urbanized families, based in professional occupations, who encourage humanist orientations in their off-

spring as well as questioning attitudes to traditional middle class values, to arbitrary authority, and conventional politics (Flacks, 1967). Although this humanist subculture represents a small minority of the population, many of its attributes are more widely distributed; and the great increase in the number of college graduates suggests that the ranks of this subculture will rapidly grow.

4. These cultural changes inevitably generate discontent with established authority. As we have already suggested, persons raised in these "new" ways are likely to be resistant to authority which is hierarchical, bureaucratic, or symbolic of traditional capitalist and nationalist goals. On the other hand, one might imagine that authority on the national and institutional levels in America could be flexible enough to offset serious disaffection on the part of this emergent group. Change in the direction of providing greater personal autonomy and participation, elites who speak the language of modernity and change, and the adoption of public programs that fulfill the vocational and personal needs of the educated humanists might be sufficient to keep their unrest within the framework of legitimacy.

There is, however, an awesome barrier to the achievement of this kind of incorporation, namely, the commitment of American political and corporate elites to the maintenance of an international empire. This commitment has numerous internal consequences. The most central for our purposes is that it necessitates the militarization of the youth—the imposition of conscription on the one hand and the "channeling" of youth into "necessary" occupations on the other. It is this situation, more than anything else, which converts the restiveness of educated youth into direct opposition, which leads them to challenge the legitimacy of established authority, and which, incidentally, connects them to militant black youth. For both black and white humanist youth, the persistence and growth of militarism and empire building constitute a fundamental violation of central values and a severe threat to individual and collective fulfillment of central aspirations.

Militant black and humanist white youth are most directly affronted by conscription and other consequences of American imperi-

351

alism, and the result is that they come into direct and continuing conflict with authority as they try to resist its imposition. But imperialism has other consequences for political stability. For instance, continued commitment to massive military expenditures forces the postponement of domestic reform, thereby alienating, rather than incorporating, deprived minority groups and the educated middle class. Imperialist foreign policy seems to require a steady deterioration in the perceived trustworthiness of national authority: for instance, it requires the elaboration of covert, paramilitary institutions, management of information, and other practices which signify a loss of democratic control over foreign policy and an increase in direct efforts by the state to manipulate the domestic political process. The massive defense budget greatly enhances the power of the military and defense corporations, who exert powerful influence over policy without responsibility to the electorate. Those who oppose the military or who want to change foreign policy become increasingly convinced that national authority is biased against them, and legitimacy is further eroded.

One could go on in elaborating the many ways in which dissent and opposition to the Johnson Administration and its policies, or more general grievances on the part of the disadvantaged, have systematically been converted into more fundamental challenges to the legitimacy of national authority, in large part as a consequence of its imperialist character.

One might accept the above analysis and still seriously doubt whether the increasingly revolutionary mood of some sectors of the population represents an unmanageable challenge to the legitimacy of the present authority structure. The challenge is serious; the widespread use of armed force to occupy cities and protect various public installations and functions is a demonstration of this, as is the steadily rising number of jailed draft resisters, and ultimately, Lyndon Johnson's decision not to seek re-election. But its unmanageability depends on whether and in what manner the present mood spreads to other parts of the population.

If there is a potential for growing delegitimization of national authority beyond the strata who are presently disaffected, it ought to become manifest in the ranks of the armed forces. For, as we have suggested, if widespread potential discontent with legitimate authority exists, it can be catalyzed by the example of a small number of active disobedients. That small number has now begun to appear—in the form of public deserters, men who refuse orders, servicemen who participate in peace marches and love-ins. Now, a miniscule but growing movement for a union of servicemen has emerged, as well as a number of underground newspapers which are passed around army bases. Do these events represent the early stages of general disaffection among conscripts? This seems far less unlikely today than it did even a few months ago.

We have also suggested that legitimacy depends on the readiness of other centers of power to provide backing for the challenged authority. There have, it seems to me, already developed some minor, if interesting, cracks in the institutional support for American national authority. One illustration of this is the willingness of some university authorities to accede to student demands to withhold class rank information from Selective Service boards and to readmit students convicted of violating the draft laws.[2] These are rather trivial gestures; still they are symbolic of the fact that some institutional authorities —particularly university administrators and church officials—find it increasingly difficult to support the establishment in general. At the opposite pole, one observes increasingly open hostility of the police to efforts by local authorities to moderate civil disorder, resulting in increasing tension within the authority structure at least at the municipal level. Whether these actions suggest a more fundamental series of splits in the institutional framework again remains to be seen.

In short, I have been trying to say that there appears to be a fundamental incompatibility between the commitment of American national authority to the maintenance of a world empire and the continued legitimacy of the authority. The commitment to empire prevents the authorities from adequately meeting the demands of the disadvantaged.

[2] Another illustration would be the decision of Yale University officials to strip the ROTC there of its academic status. As reported in *The News American* (Baltimore, Md.) Editorial. Feb. 3, 1969. Similar actions were taken by other universities in recent months.

It necessitates forms of domination and social control which are antidemocratic and which reduce the trustworthiness of the authorities. It perpetuates forms of organization which prevent the political system from reflecting the vast cultural changes which are sweeping the society. It requires the deployment of youth for military and related purposes while cultural changes have made many youths characterologically unsuitable for such purposes.

These are some of the reasons for feeling that the draft resister and the Black Panther rather than the cheerful robot or the black bourgeois are the authentic vanguard of an emerging social and political order, and that the example of the resistant few is likely to continue to be catalytic for the ambivalent and passive many. The danger of a repressive response by beleaguered authority is quite real, as is the mobilization of popular support for the imposition of order at the expense of freedom. Yet the emergent characterological and cultural trends, and the revolutionary movements they have spawned, promise a new social system, in which militarism, racism, narrow nationalism, and imperialism have become illegitimate and where individual dignity, individual conscience, and collective participation become the primary bases for legitimate authority. This promise makes the risks worthwhile for many of us.

References

Adorno, T. W., Frenkel-Brunswik, E., Levinson, D. J., & Sanford, R. N. *The authoritarian personality,* New York: Harper, 1950.

Barton, A. H. The Columbia crisis: Campus, Vietnam, and the ghetto. New York: Columbia University, Bureau of Applied Social Research, 1968.

Bay, C. Political and apolitical students: Facts in search of theory. *Journal of Social Issues,* 1967, **23,** 76-91.

Black Panther ten-point program. *North American Review,* July 1968, pp. 16-17.

Block, J. H., Haan, N., & Smith, M. B. Students and politics. *Daedalus,* 1968.

Blocker, C. E. Dissent and the college student in revolt. *School and Society,* 1970, **98,** 20-23.

Borgatta, E. F., & Corsini, R. J. *Quick word test.* New York: Harcourt, 1964.

Cole, L., & Hall, I. N. *Psychology of adolescence* (7th ed.) New York: Holt, 1970.

Coleman, J. *The adolescent society.* New York: Free Press, 1961.

Easton, D., & Dennis, J. The child's image of government. *Annals of the American Academy of Political and Social Science,* 1965, **361,** 40-57.

Flacks, R. The liberated generation: An exploration of the roots of student protest. *Journal of Social Issues,* 1967, **23,** 52-75.

Frank, J. Experimental studies of personal pressure and resistance. *Journal of Genetic Psychology,* 1944, **30,** 23-64.

Gamson, W. *Power and discontent.* Homewood, Ill.: Dorsey Press, 1968.

Gordon, L. V. *Survey of interpersonal values.* Chicago: Science Research Associates, 1960.

Gordon, L. V. *Gordon personal profile.* New York: Harcourt, 1963.

Gottlieb, D. Poor youth do want to be middle class but it's not easy. *Personnel and Guidance Journal,* 1967, **45,** 116-122.

Gottlieb, D. Activist youth today. *Research Resume No. 38.* Burlingame, Calif.: Proceedings of the 20th Annual State Conference on Educational Research, 1968. Pp. 3-16.

Halleck, S. L. Hypotheses of student unrest. *Phi Delta Kappan,* 1968, **50,** 2-8.

Harris, L. The Life poll. *Life,* 1969, **66** (19), 22-33.

Hartford, B. Student liberation: Perspective of a political activist. *Research Resume No. 38.* Burlingame, Calif.: Proceedings of the 20th Annual State Conference on Educational Research, 1968. Pp. 102-109.

Harvey, W. R. *Least squares analysis of data with unequal subclass numbers.* Washington: U. S. Department of Agriculture, July 1960. (Publication ARS-20-8)

Heist, P. Intellect and commitment: The faces of discontent. Berkeley: Center for the Study of Higher Education, 1965. (Mimeo)

Hook, S. The war against the democratic process. *Atlantic Monthly,* 1969, **223** (2), 45-49.

Katz, J. The student activists: Rights, needs, and powers of undergraduates. Report prepared for the United States Office of Education, 1967.

Keniston, K. *The uncommitted.* New York: Harcourt, 1965.

Keniston, K. *Young radicals: Notes on committed youth.* New York: Harcourt, 1968a.

Keniston, K. Youth, change, and violence. *American Scholar,* 1968b, **37,** 227-245.

Kerpelman, L. C. Personality and attitude correlates of political candidate preference. *Journal of Social Psychology,* 1968, **76,** 219-226.

Kozol, J. *Death at an early age.* Boston: Houghton Mifflin, 1967.

Lauter, P., & Howe, F. The draft and its opposition. *New York Review of Books,* 1968, **10** (12), 25-31.

Leo, J. Studies agree that most campus activists are comparatively intelligent, stable and unprejudiced. *New York Times,* June 19, 1967, p. 29.

Levinson, D. J. T. A. P. social attitude battery. Cambridge, Mass.: Harvard University, 1959. (Mimeo.)

Marvick, D. The political socialization of the American Negro. *Annals of the American Academy of Political and Social Science,* 1965, **361,** 112-127.

McCloskey, H. Conservatism and personality. *American Political Science Review,* 1958, **52,** 27-45.

Milgram, S. Some conditions of obedience and disobedience to authority. In I. D. Steiner & M. Fishbein (Eds.), *Current studies in social psychology.* New York: Holt, 1965. Pp. 243-262.

New black student. *Sooner Magazine,* 1969, **41** (4), 8-11.

"New Left" in action. *U. S. News and World Report,* 1969, **66** (20), 35-37.

Nixon's efforts to solve problem of student unrest. *U. S. News and World Report,* 1969, **67** (20), 74-78.

Orne, M. T. On the social psychology of the psychological experiment. *American Psychologist,* 1962, **17,** 776-783.

Orne, M. T., & Evans, F. J. Social control in the psychological experiment. *Journal of Personality and Social Psychology,* 1965, **1,** 189-200.

Peterson, R. E. *The scope of organized student protest in 1964–1965.* Princeton, N. J.: Educational Testing Service, 1966.

Rampage at Fair Harbor. *Life,* 1969, **66** (16).

Real revolution on campus. *U. S. News and World Report,* 1970, **68** (2), 28-31.

Sampson, R. V. *The psychology of power.* New York: Vintage Books, 1968.

Schlesinger, A., Jr. Existential politics and the cult of violence. *Phi Delta Kappan,* 1968, **50,** 9-15.

Smith, M. B. Competence and socialization. In J. Clausen (Ed.), *Socialization and society.* Boston: Little, Brown, 1968. Pp. 270-320.

Somers, R. H. The mainsprings of the rebellion: A survey of Berkeley students in November, 1964. In S. M. Lipset & S. C. Wolin (Eds.), *The Berkeley student revolt.* New York: Doubleday, 1965. Pp. 530-557.

Stinchcombe, A. *Constructing social theories.* New York: Harcourt, 1968.

Student revolt: Where is it headed? *U. S. News and World Report,* 1969, **67** (15), 38-40.

Templeton, F. Alienation and political participation: Some research findings. *Quarterly,* 1966, **30,** 249-261.

Thornburg, H. D. Student assessment of contemporary issues. *College Student Survey,* 1969, **3,** 1-5, 22.

Trent, J. W., & Craise, J. L. Commitment and conformity in the American college. *Journal of Social Issues,* 1967, **23,** 34-51.

Watts, W., & Whittaker, D. Free speech advocates at Berkeley. *Journal of Applied Behavioral Sciences,* 1966, **2,** 41-62.

Watts, W., & Whittaker, D. Profile of a nonconformist youth culture: A study of the Berkeley non-students. *Sociology of Education,* 1968, **41,** 178–200.

Westby, D., & Braungart, R. Class and politics in the family backgrounds of student political activists. *American Sociological Review,* 1966, **31,** 690-692.

Who's in charge—IV. The students. *Sooner Magazine,* 1969, **41** (5), 10-13.

Winborn, B. B., & Jansen, D. G. Personality characteristics of campus social-political action leaders. *Journal of Counseling Psychology,* 1967, **4,** 509-513.

Winer, B. J. *Statistical principles in experimental design.* New York: McGraw-Hill, 1962.

Wolfenstein, F. V. *The revolutionary personality.* Princeton, N. J.: Princeton University Press, 1967.

Annotations

Bay, C. Political and apolitical students: Facts in search of theory. *Journal of Social Issues,* 1967, **23,** 76-91. Bay focuses on personal and political attitudes that may explain much of the activism of our youths. Most of the article is a synthesis of research that has been conducted about youths, their belief systems, and activism. Basically, Bay sees humans as potentially liberal animals who will most likely be socialized into a pliant, conforming state by those around them.

Blocker, C. E. Dissent and the college student in revolt. *School and Society,* 1970, **98,** 20-23. Blocker maintains that the student's problems stem from two sources: (1) multitudinous dilemmas within the social order and (2) the college itself. This provocative article suggests that adult authorities make a greater effort to resolve many youth-adult differences.

Carey, R. W. Student protest and the counselor. *Personnel and Guidance Journal,* 1969, **48,** 185-191. This article suggests some changing trends in attitudes about rules, education, and young people. Carey calls for a reexamination of school rules and educational policies as they affect our youth. Carey indicates some self-correcting adjustments that can be made to make the educational setting more relevant for activist youths.

Flacks, R. The liberated generation: An exploration of the roots of student protest. *Journal of Social Issues,* 1967, **23,** 52-75. The author sees most activism stemming from the young intelligentsia and advantaged youth. He also discusses themes of the protest. Most of the article is devoted to several social-psychological roots of student protest, but the author also cites research done among youth projects that gives insight into many motivations behind youth movements.

Hess, R. D. Political attitudes in children. *Psychology Today,* 1969, **2,** 24-28. This unique article is concerned with today's teaching of politics. As expressed by Hess, "The strength of current protests against social and political conditions, and the fact that they are focused on institutions, is a sign of vigor: it indicates at least a hope that remedies can be found short of full revolution. However, under the circumstances it makes very little sense to instill in children a superficial faith in the institutions under attack, to gloss over social realities, and to obscure many of the routes effective action can take. More useful would be a candid acknowledgment of political and social facts and, especially, a clear explanation of the ways that institutions can be influenced and changed."

Hook, S. The war against the Democratic process. *Atlantic Monthly,* 1969, **223** (2), 45-49. In this analysis of the riots at Columbia University, the author questions whether the students were justified in expressing resentment toward the university as they did. Hook feels that, although resentment toward university policy may have been justified, the form and extent of student action were not justified.

Keniston, K. Youth, change and violence. *American Scholar,* 1968, **37,** 227-245. Keniston asserts that many causes of youth change focus around (1) a quest for personalism, (2) nonasceticism, (3) antitechnologism, and (4) a need for greater participation in society. Keniston also traces incidences of violence throughout the post-World-War-II era and their contribution to violence in today's adolescents.

Thompson, S. D. Activism: A game for unloving critics. *National Association of Secondary School Principals Bulletin,* 1967, **52,** 142-149. Thompson identifies and describes the basic functions and philosophies of four different alienated student groups: (1) the New Left activists, (2) the advocates of black power, (3) the hippies, and (4) the Third World Liberation Front. He also discusses how each group directs hostility toward existing institutions.

the adolescent and work

Traditionally, most adolescents have selected an occupation by either following the profession of their fathers or by pursuing personal interests. Research indicates that family patterns strongly influence occupational choice and that a substantial number of adolescents do tend to enter fields either identical with or closely related to the occupation of the father (Smelzer, 1963). Personal interests generally develop in late childhood but change throughout early and middle adolescence. Interests can help a person acquire the basic habits of industry, which Havighurst (1964) categorizes as learning to organize one's time and energy to get work done and learning to put work ahead of play in appropriate situations.

Havighurst (1964) suggests that during the age-span from 15 to 25 the individual develops identity as a worker in the occupational structure. That is, the adolescent chooses and prepares for an occupation and acquires work experience as a basis for occupational choice. It is during this period that we would expect individual interest to stabilize or the father's occupational choice to emerge as the dominant factor in occupational aspirations and attainments.

Ginzberg (Ginzberg et al., 1951) has placed occupational choice into a three-phase theoretical framework. He has labeled the three psychological phases the fantasy period, the tentative period, and the realistic period.

The *fantasy period* coincides with the child's elementary school experiences and involves fantasy choice (nurse, doctor, fireman). These choices are emotional, not practical; they are made within the child's world, not in terms of the actual world in which the adolescent will eventually function.

From the ages of 11 to 17, during the *tentative period,* the individual gradually shifts toward reality. Here interest plays a vital role. On the basis of his interests, the adolescent begins to consider his aptitudes, education, personal values, and goals. If his initial interest is in a vocational area that he cannot pursue, he then modifies his choice to one more in harmony with his abilities and limitations.

During the *realistic period* the adolescent assesses his aspirational level, his motivation, and the requirements of the job he wants and then pursues his objective by educational and vocational planning.

Selecting and preparing for a vocation that will provide economic independence are quite difficult (Angelino, 1955; Garrison, 1955). Our highly industrialized and technological society has prolonged the period of adolescence. Many skilled and semiskilled jobs once held by adolescents have been eliminated by automation. The number of meaningful work experiences for adolescents is meager. Those jobs that are available are usually routine and of little usefulness to the worker.

Kuvlesky and Bealer (1966) equate occupational choices with aspirations. They have singled out several factors that contribute to the development of adolescent aspirational levels: social class of parents, aspirational urges of parents, socioemotional adjustment of the adolescent, social status of peers, school performance, and need for achievement.

Often needs affect a person's aspirations. Needs may be perceived intellectually, or they may appear only as vague interests that draw people in certain directions; in either case they influence choice. Needs and values often change. Frequently a person experiences a shift in needs or values and subsequently makes an occupational change to accommodate his new needs.

Economic factors also affect occupational choice. Usually high income is not a major factor; most adolescents prefer a modest but secure income. Yet immediate and potential earnings affect the extent to which a contemplated occupation can be expected to meet one's economic needs.

Another major influence on career choice is education, which provides an awareness of occupational opportunities. Today one in every three adolescents attends college. Of this group one in three graduates. Most educational pursuits are spurred by either parental or peer influence. Studies (Alexander & Campbell, 1964; Rehberg & Westby, 1967) indicate that student level of education is highly related to the father's educational and occupational level.

Realistically, employment opportunities for the college graduate involve only one of every six adolescents in the United States. "In February, 1963, there were 6.7 million out-of-school persons 16 to 21 years old who were not college graduates. About 45 percent of this group dropped out before completing high school, 48 completed high school and 7 percent completed 1 to 3 years of college" (Perrella & Bogan, 1964, p. 1260).

A large percentage of those who graduate from high school have no intention of furthering their education. A study by Little (1967) assessed the relationship between adolescent plans and action. The results are revealed in Table 1.

TABLE 1. EDUCATIONAL PLANS AND THEIR FULFILLMENT

	Plan	Action	Difference
To Attend College	1584 (37.8%)	1792 (42.9%)	+208
To Attend Vocational School	363 (8.7%)	666 (15.9%)	+303
To Get No Further Schooling	2239 (53.5%)	1728 (41.2%)	−511
Total	*N*=4186 (100.0%)	*N*=4186 (100.0%)	*N*= 0

It is important to make adolescents aware of the changing work world. Since the early 1900s the number of professional jobs has doubled while unskilled occupations have virtually disappeared. Wolfbein's study (1964) shows that only 5 percent of today's jobs require an unskilled worker. Moreover, many jobs that were once considered masculine and thus excluded women are now available to either sex depending on individual qualifications. Adolescents must also be prepared for occupational mobility, which usually results from job obsolescence or a desire for economic improvement. Rapid technological change may require retraining of thousands of workers in the next few years, and the adolescent who has acquired transferable work skills will be prepared to adapt to new jobs.

The first article in this chapter, by Kuvlesky and Bealer, analyzes the relevance of adolescent occupational aspirations to subsequent occupational attainments. This study, conducted over a ten-year period, indicates that aspirations play the greatest directional role in career selection.

The most commonly discussed variable in an adolescent's occupational choice is his father's occupation. Werts, in the second article, compares fathers' occupations with sons' career choices. He sampled 76,000 college freshmen preparing for careers in teaching, engineering, or medicine. Fathers' occupations were grouped as (1) low socioeconomic status, (2) semiprofessional, and (3) professional. The highest relationship between father's occupation and son's career choice occurred in the professional group. Vocational choices tend to be influenced by the family's socioeconomic level, which is most directly affected by parental occupations. Most parents encourage their children to choose vocations that are at least equivalent to parental status.

Thompson's article, reporting on his study of ninth graders, supports the idea that the characteristics of a vocation that are important to an adolescent may be internalized early in life. However, Berger (1967) has expressed concern over the pressure applied to high school seniors and college freshmen to choose occupations. Many students make premature vocational choices and then often fail in them. Berger maintains that late high school and early college choices should be tentative until the individual has an opportunity to test, confirm, or reject his choice.

Stevic and Uhlig have found that the aspirational levels of Appalachian youths are related to mobility. Students who stay in the Appalachian area tend to have lower aspirational levels than do those who migrate to urban areas or who are native to more urban non-Appalachian areas. Also, a major problem in raising the occupational aspirations of Appalachian students appears to be a lack of information and opportunity rather than a lack of ability. Rehberg (1967), Campbell & Alexander (1965), and A. B. Wilson (1959) all support the idea that upward mobility of lower-class youths is affected by their exposure to persons of higher social status. None of these researchers mentions lack of ability as a factor.

Exposure, opportunity, information—all are important to today's adolescents. Equally important are opportunities for legitimate work experiences during adolescence. Providing these experiences is indeed a challenge to education and to society.

william p. kuvlesky
robert c. bealer

the relevance of adolescents' occupational
aspirations for subsequent job attainments[1]

Abstract. Most research in recent years on the occupational aspirations of youth has characteristically evolved from the assumption that aspirations are important determinants of subsequent occupational attainment. Yet a review of the research literature indicates that the nature and extent of the relationship between aspiration and attainment is relatively unexplored. This study examines the extent and nature of this relationship existed between aspiration and attainment, and the magnitude of the relationship varied markedly by level of aspiration and type of job attainment. It was concluded that adolescent aspirations are not good predictors of long-run attainment, but that they do play a directional role.

The Problem

A great deal of research effort has been expended in recent years on the study of the occupational aspirations of youth, and the volume of such material continues to increase (Kuvlesky & Ohlendorf, 1966). Although diverse, the investigations have characteristically evolved from the assumption, often unstated, that aspirations of youth are crucial or, at least, highly important determinants of subsequent adult status attainments (Burchinal, Haller, & Taves, 1962). Most of the research has consisted of ferreting out the correlates of various aspirations. Such information is germane and wisely sought only if one presumes that the individual's preferences are causally significant to his future employment.[2]

In conceptualizing "occupational choice" researchers have argued that the job one acquires is conditioned not only by the preferences and desires of the person for a particular occupational status, but also by many factors over which the individual has little or no control (Haller & Miller, 1963; Blau et al., 1956; Burchinal, Haller, & Taves, 1962; Ginzberg et al., 1951; Tiedeman, 1961; Stephenson, 1957). The most obvious and dramatic of these factors is race. Existing conceptualizations exclude the possibility of aspirations being epiphenomenal, but they leave open the question of to just what extent aspirations influence job attainment. Most research, however, has not directly examined this question, and the nature and extent of the relationship between aspirations and occupational attainment remain

Reprinted with permission of the authors and publisher from *Rural Sociology*, 1967. **32**, 290-301.

[1] This is a revised version of a paper originally presented at the annual meeting of the Southwestern Sociological Association held in New Orleans, Louisiana, April, 1966.

[2] If aspirations are not critical in conditioning occupational attainment, information on the correlates of the former is pertinent in systematically pursuing the consequences of aspirations going awry. This matter has not been a clear focus in most aspiration studies.

relatively unexplored (Barrow, 1961). The purpose of this paper is to report the findings from a recent analysis of this relationship obtained from a longitudinal study of 1001 young males.

Review of Relevant Research

To avoid terminological confusion, it is important clearly to distinguish *aspirations* from the related but qualitatively different idea of *expectation.* An aspiration refers to a person's orientation toward a goal. An expectation refers to the individual's indication of his anticipated attainment. Expectations should not be equated with aspirations, for the object involved with the former need not be desired and, therefore, need not be a goal. Occupational aspiration will be used here to refer to a person's desires for ultimate occupational status attainment (Kuvlesky & Bealer, 1966). What is known about the relationship of this variable to future job attainment?

We have found only six studies that have explored, through the use of necessary longitudinal data, the relationship between adolescents' "occupational orientations" (*i.e.,* aspirations and/or expectations) and their subsequent attainments. Three of these were done more than twenty years ago and suffer a number of faults that seriously limit their utility; consequently, we will not examine these in detail, except to note that all three reported either "no significant relationship" or a weak, positive correlation between aspirations and attainments (Worthington, 1938; Anderson, 1944; Proctor, 1937).

Of the three more recent efforts, one by R. J. Porter in 1954 was explicitly concerned with the relationship of expectations to attainment within an extremely short time span months (1954). Porter reported that six months after graduation 79 percent of his respondents were "following the plan they had proposed or one on a comparable prestige level."

Haller and Sewell's study of rural males in Jefferson County, Wisconsin, focused directly on aspirations (Haller & Miller, 1963). In 1955 Haller restudied 431 male respondents who were first studied by Sewell in 1948 when they were juniors and seniors in high school. Index scores measuring level of

aspiration in 1948 were related to the prestige scores of 1955 occupations. A correlation coefficient of +.46 resulted and it was concluded that LOA "tends to predict behavior toward its object." Several criticisms can be raised against this study, particularly in reference to the indicator of level of aspiration used, which brings into question the validity of the correlation observed as an accurate measure of the degree of relationship between aspirations and occupational attainment.[3] But, even accepting the correlation at face value, one has to conclude that only a moderate positive relationship existed.

Kohout and Rothney, also studying a Wisconsin population, observed what appears to be a somewhat weaker correlation (1964). In this study aspirations were obtained a month before the students' high school graduation in 1951. Approximately 86 percent of their 321 male participants were *not* employed in the job category (professional, farming, skilled labor, etc.) which they had specified as their preference ten years earlier. In an earlier study of the same respondents, Rothney reported slightly higher rates of congruence between aspiration and attainment over a five-year time lapse (1964). Of particular importance, Kohout and Rothney, in the ten-year study mentioned above, found evidence to indicate that rates of congruence between aspiration and subsequent occupational placement vary by the nature of aspiration indicated—respondents desiring professions and farming more often attained their goals than respondents desiring other types of jobs.

In summary, the previous studies are divided in their evaluation of the relationship existing between occupational status orienta-

---

[3]The indicator of occupational aspiration (LOA) was an index of North-Hatt prestige scores assigned to four responses: (1) the highest prestige occupation respondents had ever considered; (2) the lowest prestige occupation they had ever considered; (3) the occupation they planned to enter; and (4) the occupation they would like to enter if they had perfect freedom of choice. The index does not appear to be unidimensional; it incorporates responses that represent different phenomena, thereby making it difficult to determine exactly what is being measured. The measure certainly ignores the distinction made previously between aspiration and expectation, since indicators of both are incorporated in the index. The selection of the highest and the lowest occupation *ever* considered is somewhat questionable in reference to the predictive quality of the index. It is not clear that the respondents were to make all their responses apply to a single point in time. This is important because the development of aspirations is generally taken to be a dynamic process.

tions of adolescents and subsequent attainments. There is an obvious need for more detailed descriptions of this relationship. Our study attempted to answer two questions about this relationship in the context of our data: (1) What level of congruence occurred between aspirations for particular levels of occupations and attainment of these? and (2) What directional role, if any, did aspirations play for subsequent attainments?

Procedures

The data for our analysis were obtained from a representative panel of Pennsylvania rural young people surveyed at two different times. The panel was selected and first contacted during the spring of 1947. The original sample consisted of 1327 males from the entire sophomore classes of 74 rural high schools scattered throughout Pennsylvania. Approximately ten years later (data were completed up to January 31, 1957) the respondents originally selected were reinterviewed (Kuvlesky, 1965). Complete data on occupational aspirations (1947) and occupational attainment (1957) were obtained for 1001 cases.[4]

The term *congruence* was used to refer to agreement between the type of occupation aspired to in 1947 and the type of occupation the respondent was employed in as of January 31, 1957. *Incongruence* refers to disagreement between these two variables. The procedure for determining congruence and incongruence was simply to cross-classify the types of occupation aspired to in 1947 by those attained in 1957. All those who were unemployed as of January 31, 1957, were classified as demonstrating incongruence. In a single word, congruence sums up the predictive relationship between aspiration and subsequent attainment.

Occupational aspiration was previously defined as a person's desire to achieve a particular type of occupation. Unfortunately, the original study obtained no information to al-

low the determination of the intensity of desire of the aspiration. Rather, it elicited simply the ultimate occupational goal-specifications of the respondents. In the 1947 questionnaire, aspiration was sought in a forthright manner by asking simply, "What occupation would you like to follow?" Three blanks for answers labeled "first choice," "second choice," and "third choice" and arranged in a single column form were offered to the respondents. Only the answers to the first-choice alternative were used. It was assumed that these responses would indicate reasonably well what occupational status the individual desired most—his *ultimate occupational goal*.[5]

The occupational classification scheme we used to group responses was a modification of the classic Census scheme (Bureau of the Census, 1950).[6] The following general categories were used:

a. *Professional* and kindred
b. *Glamour* occupation (movie star, professional sports, etc.)
c. *Managers,* proprietors, and officials
d. *White-Collar* (clerical, sales, service other than domestic)
e. *Skilled Workers*
f. *Unskilled Workers* (operatives and laborers)
g. *Farmers*

Either more specific or more inclusive categories could have been used and if so, would have influenced the rate of congru-

---

[4] Because there was attrition in the sample over the ten-year study period, efforts were made to determine whether there were any gross biasing results. Those persons who were not successfully contacted in 1957 did not differ significantly from those interviewed in terms of several important variables measured in 1947. These variables were: *occupational aspirations,* residence of origin, intelligence quotient, and personality adjustment scores.

[5] The question used is not viewed as an "ideal" stimulus for several reasons: (1) there may well have been some mixing of expectations and aspirations in answers to the question, and (2) the respondents could have been oriented toward differing goal-periods. However, we presume that the use of "would" conveyed enough indefinite futureness and "like" a personal preference connotation to generally elicit responses indicating ultimate aspirations.

[6] The usual clerical, sales and service categories were collapsed into one set called "white-collar." This was done because of the relatively low frequencies with which each category was chosen by the sample respondents. Similarly the labor grouping was not used due to its extremely low frequency of being chosen. Only one category was used for farming because of the general nature of those responses; that is, respondents did not differentiate the role of farm manager from that of farmer. The glamour category consists of occupational types normally classified as professional—movie star, pop singer, professional football player, and related jobs. Selections of enlisted military careers or police roles were placed in the white-collar category. The Census classifies such choices as craftsmen and operatives, respectively. The few who wanted to be laborers (three persons) and farm laborers (one person) were grouped with individuals desiring to "hunt, fish, and/or trap" (six people), and were then placed with the operatives or semiskilled and labeled "unskilled workers."

ence observed between goals and attainment.[7]

The source of information on occupational attainment was a complete work history of the respondents that was part of the 1957 schedule. The same classificatory scheme was used for attainment as for aspirations, with one exception—a category titled *Unemployed* was added.[8]

The Findings

Among the aspirations held in 1947, the most frequently desired occupational goal was to be a professional (Table 1). This was closely followed by aspirations to become a farmer or a skilled worker. Over 70 percent of the respondents desired one of these three occupational statuses. All the other types of jobs were desired by only small proportions of the sample: less than ten percent in each case. There was a marked preference for relatively high-status employment and a general inclination for aspirations to exceed the opportunities likely to be readily available for attainment. The general distribution of aspirations appeared to be quite similar to that for other similar samples (Burchinal, Haller, & Taves, 1962; Cowhig et al., 1960; Sperry & Kivett, 1964). The proportion of this sample desiring to farm is naturally much higher than that for urban youth.[9]

In general, whereas almost three-fourths of the respondents wanted to become professionals, farmers, or skilled workers, over half the respondents were classified as

having attained either unskilled blue-collar jobs or low-prestige white-collar jobs by 1957 (Table 1). The greatest deflection was away from the two highly desired occupations of farming and the professions and towards two of the less desired occupational types, low-prestige white-collar and blue-collar work. A more detailed analysis follows.

TABLE 1. DISTRIBUTIONS OF OCCUPATIONS DESIRED IN 1947 AND OCCUPATIONS ATTAINED IN 1957 FOR 1001 MALE RESPONDENTS

Occupational Type	Aspiration—1947		Attainment—1957	
	Number	Percent	Number	Percent
Professional	294	29	147	15
Glamour	81	8	0	0
Managerial	51	5	40	4
White-collar	72	7	181	18
Skilled worker	196	20	163	16
Unskilled worker	93	9	350	35
Farmer	214	22	72	7
Unemployed	–	–	48	5
Total	1001	100	1001	100

Congruence between Goals and Attainments

Table 2 shows that the vast majority of the respondents did not attain by 1957 the type of occupation they desired as high school sophomores in 1947. Over three-fourths of the boys had not reached their professed occupational goals ten years after having stated them. In the same time period, almost half those aspiring to unskilled work attained this type of occupation and more than a third of those aspiring to white-collar jobs were successful in fulfilling their aspirations. The least successful was the glamour grouping, where not one of the aspirants was congruent. In brief, in the sample as a whole, occupational aspirations were not very good predictors of future occupational attainment. However, there was marked variability in the degree of congruence experienced among the aspiration groupings.

In other words, although the average incongruence rate for the sample was 77 per-

[7]This is a good demonstration of how methodological decisions can color the findings of an analysis. However, any level of congruence may be influenced by the classification system used. The more inclusive the categories used, the higher will be the probable rate of congruence. Those cases found to be incongruent using the selected scheme would probably have demonstrated incongruence using a scheme that incorporates finer distinctions. If broader, more inclusive categories were used, the probability rate of congruence would increase. A desire to preserve as much qualitative differentiation as possible led to the acceptance of the scheme described above rather than a simpler one.

[8]Those defined as unemployed met the two following criteria: (1) not employed full-time as of January 31, 1957, and (2) not following a full-time educational program as of January 31, 1957. We decided to consider the 54 respondents meeting the first standard but not the second as employed. The bulk of these (52) were classified as professionals and were pursuing higher education.

[9] If one recognizes the large capital outlays, managerial responsibilities, and business acumen necessary to handle successfully the typical, modern farm operation as rightfully placing

the average commercial farmer in a middle-level managerial position, then it can be shown that the occupational goal-levels of American rural and urban youth are generally similar. For elaboration of this proposition, see William P. Kuvlesky, "Occupational Aspirations and Expectations of Rural Youth: Some Suggestions for Action Programs," Paper presented at the Association of Southern Agricultural Workers' meeting, Jackson, Mississippi, February, 1966. A limited number of copies are available upon request.

TABLE 2. COMPARISON AMONG THE ASPIRATIONAL GROUPINGS OF RESPONDENTS ON LEVELS OF CONGRUENCE AND IN-CONGRUENCE

| | Occupational Aspirations | | | | | | | |
	Professional (294)	Glamour (81)	Managerial (51)	White Collar (72)	Skilled Worker (196)	Unskilled Worker (93)	Farmer (214)	Total (1001)
				percent				
Congruent	26	0	10	29	20	48	21	23
Incongruent	74	100	90	71	80	52	79	77
Total	100	100	100	100	100	100	100	100

$X^2 = 66.88$ D.F. = 6 $P < .001$

cent, this figure was not an accurate reflection for *all* the aspiration groupings. A chi-square test clearly showed that a null hypothesis of no differences among aspirational groupings on congruence rates must be rejected under conventional decision rules (Table 2). Therefore, we examined more closely each of the aspiration groupings with regard to nature of the occupational attainments associated with them.

Table 3 shows that, however much deflection occurred, those persons aspiring to particular occupations attained this type of job with greater frequency than those aspiring to any other occupational goal. For instance, even though the managerial aspirants had a very low rate of congruence (10 percent), they attained managerial jobs at more than twice the proportional rate of the total sample. An even more dramatic instance is observed in reference to farming: a ratio of more than three to one between aspirants to farming and the total sample. Therefore, it appears that an aspiration for a particular occupational status does tend to increase the probability of attaining that status, even though aspiration is generally not a good predictor of attainment.

This idea can be approached differently. Table 4 cross-classifies 1947 aspiration classes with 1957 attainment groupings. It is obvious that every aspirant type has had a significant number of respondents deflected into nearly every type of attainment category. The number of aspiration-attainment sets were many, not few. However, this does not mean that aspirations lack any directional influence on attainment. Rather, it suggests that progression from desire to realization is characteristically influenced by many intervening factors which in some instances may push attainment beyond one's initial aspira-

tions or, what appears to occur more often, curtail it. Unfortunately, our data do not permit a rigorous examination of this matter.

TABLE 3. COMPARISON ON PROPORTIONAL RATES OF ATTAINMENT BETWEEN ASPIRANTS FOR EACH OCCUPATIONAL TYPE AND THE TOTAL SAMPLE

| | Percent Attainment | |
Type of Attainment	Respondents Aspiring to This Occupation	Total Sample
Professional	26	15
Glamour	0	0
Managerial	10	4
White-collar	29	18
Skilled	20	16
Unskilled	48	35
Farmer	22	7

that even if aspiration to farm is no guarantee of attainment, without it a farm occupation will probably not be achieved. In other words, aspiration to farm may be one of the necessary conditions for attaining agricultural employment.

However, a closer examination of the data shows not only that for every aspiration grouping the greatest proportion of the members actually attained unskilled blue-collar jobs, but that the proportional rate of attaining unskilled jobs increases consistently with decreases in the relative prestige value of the original occupational goal. A converse trend can be observed in reference to the attainment of professional type jobs. These two observations seem to indicate a tendency for the goal level of adolescent aspirations to influence at least extreme levels of attainment. This reveals the weakness in using only rate of congruence as an indicator of the possible influence of occupational goals in attainments.

Very small proportions of each aspiration grouping, except those aspiring to farm, became involved in farming. This indicates

TABLE 4. CROSS-CLASSIFICATION OF 1947 OCCUPATIONAL ASPIRATIONS AND 1957 OCCUPATIONAL ATTAINMENTS FOR 1001 ORIGINALLY RURAL RESPONDENTS FROM PENNSYLVANIA

Attainment	1947 Aspirations							
	Professional (294)	Glamour (81)	Managerial (51)	White Collar (72)	Skilled (196)	Unskilled (93)	Farmer (214)	Total (1001)
	— — — — — — — — — — — — — percent — — — — — — — — — — — — —							
Professional	26	16	14	11	11	5	8	15
Glamour	0	0	0	0	0	0	0	0
Managerial	5	2	10	4	2	0	6	4
White-collar	17	22	21	29	18	14	15	18
Skilled	18	14	4	17	20	17	14	16
Unskilled	25	35	35	38	45	49	32	35
Farmer	3	5	6	0	2	6	21	7
Unemployed	6	6	10	1	2	9	4	5
Total	100	100	100	100	100	100	100	100

TABLE 5. COMPARISON AMONG SIX ATTAINMENT GROUPINGS ON LEVELS OF CONGRUENCE AND INCONGRUENCE

Goal, Attainment Relationship	Type of Occupation Attained							
	Professional (147)	Managerial (40)	White Collar (181)	Skilled Workers (163)	Unskilled Workers (350)	Farmers (72)	Unemployed (48)	Total (1001)
	— — — — — — — — — — — — — percent — — — — — — — — — — — — —							
Congruent	52	12	12	24	13	64	0	23
Incongruent	48	88	88	76	87	36	100	77
Total	100	100	100	100	100	100	100	100

that even if aspiration to farm is no guarantee of attainment, without it a farm occupation will probably not be achieved. In other words, aspiration to farm may be one of the necessary conditions for attaining agricultural employment.

By reversing the procedure used up to this point, we can examine the level of congruence from the perspective of attainment groupings. The attainment groupings of professionals and farmers demonstrate a relatively high level of congruence: approximately two-thirds of each aspired to their respective type of jobs in 1947 (Table 5). All other attainment categories demonstrated much lower levels of congruence. These figures indicate that aspirations for farming and professional status jobs may strongly influence their actual attainment. For other types of occupational attainment, aspirations are not so important.

These findings are not surprising when one considers that professional and farming types of occupations are probably the most difficult to attain because of the nature of prerequisites required for both. For professional and kindred type of jobs, a relatively high level of specialized education is characteristically involved. In order to farm, one

normally must have access to a large amount of capital. A stated preference for a professional work role can certainly trigger, through anticipatory socialization, the beginning of the right kinds of educational programs. Similarly, a desire to farm can set the stage within the kinship structure for the generational transfer or inheritance of land and equipment, which is the most usual way for farming capital to be "raised." In both cases aspirations could be a highly facilitating quality.[10]

Conclusions

Overall, we found that adolescent aspirations were related to subsequent occupational attainments in a positive manner. The association was never overwhelmingly strong

---

[10]One might ask, what about the cases where individuals become professionals or farmers without indicating aspirations for these types of attainment? Since the indicator of aspiration utilized here was procured from the respondents as high school sophomores, their aspirations may have changed during the ten-year span of the study. In both cases, but particularly with regard to farming, some individuals who attained the occupation may never in fact have desired it, but found it the easiest course of employment to follow. For example, because of the family investment in a farm, parental encouragement and pressures may have been aimed at involving the boy in farming and capitulation was easiest.

and it varied considerably, ranging between the absolute attainment failure of those who aspired to glamour positions to the one person in two who achieved by 1957 the unskilled job aspired to in 1947.

One general conclusion is that aspirations do not seem to be a good predictive device for long-run occupational attainments. However, some caution is called for in making this statement. It is entirely possible that with the development of more sensitive and efficient indicators, a greater association might be found to exist between aspirations and attainment. Also, a longitudinal record of occupational aspirations through young adulthood might show a patterned change that would increase the positive nature of their association to attainment. Extending the period of time in which attainment is measured might also produce an increase in the relationship. However, it seems unwise to develop a predictive device for occupational attainment that utilizes only goal-specification.[11]

Our findings indicate that differences exist in the predictive power for attainment associated with different types or levels of occupational aspirations. Although this supports the general findings observed by Kohout and Rothney in their Wisconsin study, the specific nature of the differentials of congruence observed in the two studies appears to be in direct contradiction. Whereas our findings indicate that aspirants to unskilled jobs, particularly blue-collar ones, had by far the highest rate of congruence, their findings showed that respondents aspiring to the professions and farming had the highest rates of attainment success. This marked discrepancy in results indicates a need for more detailed studies aimed at discovering what factors influence the probability of attainment success for particular types or levels of occupational aspiration.

[11] One of the major elements left out of most examinations of aspirations, including this study, that might increase predictive ability is an indicator of the individual's attachment to his goal-specification—either measured in isolation or, better yet, relative to his desire for goal-specifications in other goal areas.

Whatever the intensity of relationships between aspirations and attainment that might be demonstrated through possible refinements, the fact of correlation, and in turn predictive quality, does not establish any necessary causal linkage between aspiration and attainment. Just exactly what part does aspiration play? Unfortunately, the answer is not available in the current data, although we have suggested that aspirations probably play at least some directional role and that the magnitude of influence may vary by the level or type of aspiration held. The exact dimensions of this influence represent an important area for future research.

Whatever causal significance aspirations have for attainment, differentiating types of incongruity still seems reasonable. Past research has shown that there are important behavioral differences resulting from the job a person holds. For example, even when two persons are unskilled laborers, the fact that one started with an aspiration to be a doctor and the other desired to be a carpenter is probably an important difference. Similarly, going in the opposite direction, if two persons aspired to a managerial status with one attaining a high-prestige professional position and the other a low-prestige labor job, significant consequential behavior will occur.

The most obvious way where these differences in kind of incongruity might be manifest is in the degree of frustration or deprivation felt in the work role. The dream of a great number of Americans is to be socially mobile (in a vertical sense) and high occupational achievement is normally an integral part of the former. The degree or extent of failure may influence the extent and/or nature of possible adjustment problems. Our own data indicate a marked positive association between deflection from occupational aspirations to undesired subsequent attainments and degree of negative self-evaluation (Kuvlesky, 1965). It is in this area that the apparently unabated interest in the study of aspirations may yield the greatest insight.

charles e. werts

paternal influence on career choice[1]

Fathers' occupations were compared with sons' career choices for a sample of 76,015 male college freshmen. The results indicated that for sons of professionals, the occupational groupings on the Strong Vocational Interest Blank are useful in describing broad types of "inherited" occupations.

The literature on the relationship between a father's occupation and that of his son has shown that *(a)* the social class (SES) level of a father's occupation is strongly associated with the level of his son's occupation (Blau, 1965; Duncan, 1965; Jenson & Kirchner, 1955) and *(b)* the son is more likely than others of equivalent class background to choose the same occupation as that of his father (Nelson, 1939; Werts, 1966b). These studies raise the question: Are sons also more inclined than others of comparable class background to choose occupations "similar" to those of their fathers? The difficulty here is in defining "similar," since we do not know if any of the common procedures (e.g., Roe, 1956, Part III; Strong,

1964) for classifying occupations are useful in describing types of "occupational inheritance." Furthermore, "level" of occupation must be clearly distinguished from "type," which refers to the varieties of occupations within a level. The research design therefore must control occupational level in order to study types, and vice versa. Fathers' occupations were compared with sons' career choices in the quest for an empirical answer to whether occupational inheritance follows broad types.

Method

The subjects were 76,015 males entering 246 4-year colleges and universities in the fall of 1961. The sample, with few exceptions, included all of the male freshmen at each institution. The colleges were heterogeneous in size, type (coeducational, public, private, nondenominational, denominational, etc.), quality (PhD productivity, prestige), geographic region, and SES level of entering students (see Astin, 1965). The absence of 2-year and some overrepresentation of "elite" institutions probably has resulted in some restriction on social class variability in the sample. The disadvantages of studying college freshmen are: *(a)* it cannot be ascertained if low-SES sons choose occupations

Reprinted with permission of the author and the American Psychological Association from the *Journal of Counseling Psychology*, 1968, **15,** 48-52.

[1]This study is part of the National Merit Scholarship Corporation's research program, which is supported by grants from the Ford Foundation, the National Science Foundation, and the Carnegie Corporation of New York. The author is indebted to Bruce K. Eckland, John K. Folger, and Robert C. Nichols for reviewing the manuscript.

like their fathers, since college students rarely plan careers in low-SES occupations; and *(b)* the effects of social class background (as indicated by level of father's occupation) on career choice apply only to sons who actually enter college, thereby restricting the range of career choices studied to the semiprofessional and professional levels. One considerable advantage of this sample is that career-choice differences as related to fathers' occupations cannot be attributed to ability differences. Werts (1966a) has shown that among college students, SES background is only slightly related to academic ability.

At the time of registration each freshman was required to fill out a short information form which included the following questions:

1. Probable future occupation:
2. Circle one: Male   Female
3. Father's occupation:

Probable future occupation and father's occupation were coded into the categories shown in Tables 1, 2, and 3. The percentage of sons in each career-choice category was computed for each father's occupation.

Results

Teaching

Table 1 shows for each father's occupation the percentage of sons, ordered from high to low, who indicated a career choice of teacher (primary and secondary level only). A larger percentage of low- than high-SES students chose teaching; the range was from 21.1% for laborers' sons to 2.8% for architects' sons. For the most part, the percentage of sons choosing teacher ordered fathers' occupations along a social class scale: low-SES, semiprofessional, and professional. Some notable exceptions to this ordering were the sons of teachers, school administrators (mainly principals), college administrators, clergymen, and social workers, who chose teaching at a rate similar to that of low-SES students rather than at a rate appropriate to their class level. In our society these occupations are assigned the role of guiding people's lives—of molding and teaching. The percentage of psychologists'

and college professors' sons who chose teaching also tended to be higher than that of sons of men with equivalent education, such as lawyers, physicians, and physicists. All these occupations, except for psychologist, conform to the SVIB Social Sciences group, and this Social Scientist designation will be used in the rest of the discussion.

TABLE 1. PERCENTAGE OF SONS WITH THE CAREER CHOICE OF TEACHER FOR VARIOUS FATHERS' OCCUPATIONS

Percentage choosing teacher	Father's occupation	Exception
Group 1—low SES		
21.14	Laborer	
18.34		Teacher
16.67	Semiskilled worker	
16.22		School administrator
15.53	Service worker	
15.29	Farmer	
14.94	Skilled worker	
14.38		College administrator
14.16		Clergyman
13.82	Clerical worker	
13.17	Foreman	
10.87		Social worker
Group 2—semiprofessional		
9.41	Artist, interior decorator	
9.01	Technical worker	
8.25	Businessman	
7.99	Salesman	
7.77	Actor, musician, entertainer	
7.26	Elected official	
7.22	Accountant	
6.82		Psychologist
6.70		College professor
6.31	Writer	
Group 3—professional		
5.76	Military officer	
5.04	Engineer	
5.00	Scientist[a]	
4.76	Biologist	
4.67	Paramedical professions[b]	
3.96	Dentist	
3.76	Physician	
3.72	Chemist	
3.63	Lawyer	
2.82	Physicist	
2.79	Architect	

Note.—The sample consisted of 76,015 male college freshmen. Fathers' occupations were ranked by the percentage of sons choosing teacher. This procedure showed that the higher the class background, the lower the percentage of sons choosing teacher, with the exception of fathers' occupations noted. These exceptions suggest that when fathers are in social science occupations, their sons are more likely than other sons of similar class background to choose teacher.

[a]Not elsewhere classified.

[b]Paramedical professions: pharmacist, optometrist, osteopath, chiropractor.

Engineering

Table 2 shows fathers' occupations ordered within each SES group by the percentage of sons indicating a career choice of engineer. A modest class trend appeared, in that 16.5% of Group 1 (low-SES) sons chose engineer, in contrast to 12.3% of Group 3 (professional) sons. Within the professional group, an expected high percentage (24.8%) of engineers' sons chose engineering, followed by sons of military officers (many of whom may have technical degrees and interests), scientists, architects, biologists, and physicists. Since, with the exception of military officer and biologist, these occupations fall into the SVIB Physical Science group, the SVIB designation will be used here.

Medicine

Table 3 shows the percentage of sons who indicated a career choice of physician for various fathers' occupations, grouped as in Table 2. The percentage of sons choosing medicine correlated positively with SES level: that is, Group 1, 4.4%; Group 2, 8.8%; and Group 3, 15.4%. At the low end of Group 3, sons of physicists and psychologists chose physician at a rate similar to that of low-SES sons, while sons of physicians (41.1%), dentists (24.3%), and paramedical profession-

TABLE 2. PERCENTAGE OF SONS WITH THE CAREER CHOICE OF ENGINEER FOR VARIOUS FATHERS' OCCUPATIONS

Percentage choosing engineer	Father's occupation
Group 1—low SES	
19.21	Foreman
19.09	Skilled worker
18.19	Service worker
17.69	Semiskilled worker
16.63	Clerical worker
14.59	Farmer
13.88	Laborer
16.51	Group 1 average
Group 2—semiprofessional	
18.58	Technical worker
15.64	Elected official
14.77	Businessman
14.71	Artist, interior decorator
14.09	Accountant
11.64	Salesman
9.71	Actor, musician, entertainer
9.61	Writer
14.07	Group 2 average
Group 3—professional	
24.82	Engineer [a]
19.06	Military officer [a]
16.92	Scientist [a,b]
15.09	Architect [a]
14.29	Biologist [a]
12.68	Physicist [a]
12.31	Teacher
12.03	Chemist
11.36	Psychologist
10.40	School administrator
9.34	Paramedical professions [c]
7.58	Clergyman
7.44	College professor
7.19	College administrator
6.52	Social worker
6.00	Lawyer
4.95	Dentist
4.90	Physician
12.33	Group 3 average

Note.—Fathers' occupations were ranked by the percentage of sons choosing engineer. This procedure showed that the higher the class background, the lower the percentage of sons choosing engineer. The percentage of sons making this career choice for fathers in scientific professions was high.

[a] Scientific professions.

[b] Not elsewhere classified.

[c] Paramedical professions: pharmacist, optometrist, osteopath, chiropractor.

TABLE 3. PERCENTAGE OF SONS WITH THE CAREER CHOICE OF PHYSICIAN FOR VARIOUS FATHERS' OCCUPATIONS

Percentage choosing physician	Father's occupation
Group 1—low SES	
6.21	Clerical worker
5.74	Service worker
5.04	Foreman
4.93	Semiskilled worker
4.72	Skilled worker
4.39	Laborer
2.39	Farmer
4.38	Group 1 average
Group 2—semiprofessional	
9.38	Businessman
9.36	Accountant
7.76	Salesman
6.84	Technical worker
6.70	Elected official
6.61	Writer
6.18	Artist, interior decorator
5.83	Actor, musician, entertainer
8.82	Group 2 average
Group 3—professional	
41.05	Physician [a]
24.26	Dentist [a]
19.03	Paramedical professions [a,b]
12.42	College administrator
12.06	School administrator
11.75	Chemist
11.65	Lawyer
10.87	Social worker
9.52	Biologist
9.23	Scientist [c]
8.46	Engineer
8.45	Clergyman
8.30	Teacher
8.04	College professor
7.26	Architect
6.83	Military officer
4.55	Psychologist
4.23	Physicist
15.38	Group 3 average

Note.—Fathers' occupations were ranked by the percentage of sons choosing physician. This procedure showed that the higher the class background, the higher the percentage of sons choosing physician. The percentage of sons making this career choice for fathers in medical professions was exceptionally high.

[a] Medical professions.

[b] Paramedical professions: pharmacist, optometrist, osteopath, chiropractor.

[c] Not elsewhere classified.

als (19.0%) had exceptionally high choice rates as noted. These sons of medical men were the only ones exceeding the average Group 3 rate of 15.38%. The present medical occupations, with the exception of pharmacist, fall into the SVIB Biological Sciences group; thus, the SVIB label was rejected in favor of the narrower "medical" label, since it fit the data better.

Other Career Choices

Because sample sizes were insufficient for separate analysis by father's occupation, other career choices were studied differently. For each combination of father's occupation and son's career choice, an expected cell frequency was computed by multiplying the total number of sons in a given father's occupation category by the total number of students with that same career choice, and dividing the product by the total sample size. This resulted in the frequency that would be expected if there were no relationship between father's occupation and student's choice. Each combination of occupation and career choice then was tested to determine if the observed cell frequency was significantly higher (at the .05 level) than the expected frequency. The chi-square statistic was used when the expected frequency was equal to or greater than five and Poisson distribution analysis when this value was less than five. This technique is not as powerful as the one used for teacher, engineer, and physician, because each cell frequency is compared against an expected value derived from the whole sample rather than against an expected frequency for persons of similar class background. The term, "overchose," will be used in the discussion to refer to cases in which the number of sons with a particular career choice was significantly higher than expected.[2]

Werts (1966b) reported earlier that in every case sons overchoose the same occupations as their fathers. This finding was confirmed, and some additional relevant findings were:

1. For fathers' occupations in the social sciences: teachers' sons overchose college professor; clergymen's sons overchose college professor, social worker, and missionary; and school administrators' sons overchose missionary.

2. For fathers' occupations in the physical sciences: chemists' sons overchose mathematician and physicist; biologists' sons overchose architect; scientists' sons overchose mathematician, physicist, and geologist; and physicists' sons overchose mathematician.

3. For medical fathers' occupations: physicians' sons overchose only physician; dentists' sons overchose dentist and physician; and sons of men in the paramedical professions overchose veterinarian, pharmacist, dentist, and physician.

When only professional occupations were considered, 30%–40% of sons of men in the physical sciences chose scientific careers (e.g., engineer, chemist, physicist, architect, mathematician, biologist, and college scientist), compared with 10% of sons of medical men and 14% of sons of men in the social sciences. Of sons of social scientists, 20%–30% chose related careers (e.g., teacher, clergyman, college professor, social worker, and missionary), compared with 7% of sons of physical scientists and 6% of sons of men in medical fields. Of sons of medical men, 35%–45% chose medical careers (e.g., veterinarian, pharmacist, dentist, and physician), compared with 10%–15% of sons of men in the physical and the social sciences. Because large numbers of students were "undecided" or "not elsewhere classified," these comparisons should be interpreted cautiously.

Discussion

At least three broad types of occupations appear to be passed from father to son. The first two types correspond closely to the SVIB Physical Sciences and Social Sciences groups; the third includes only medical occupations and, thus, is slightly less comprehensive than the SVIB Biological Sciences group (which also includes psychologist and biologist). Unfortunately, the data shed no light on why there is an association between the type of father's occupation and the type of son's career choice. Perhaps the father directly and indirectly encourages his son to have the same interests: For example, fathers in the

---

[2]Although the complete results are not presented here because of space limitations, all statistically significant cases of overchoice were recorded. The author will furnish additional information on request.

physical sciences may encourage an interest in the why and how of things (i.e., Super & Crites', 1962, "scientific factor"), while social scientists may further an interest in people per se (i.e., Super & Crites' "social welfare" factor).

Among the many interpretative pitfalls in this type of research, some are worth mentioning. For example, the results suffer to an unknown degree from unreliability in the student's report of his father's occupation and of his own anticipated career choice. Further-more, it is difficult to discern how the original coding of father's occupation and son's career choice may have affected the results. Although data on freshman career choice may reflect the father's influence on early interests, it remains to be shown whether the same broad occupational types would be found if father's occupation were compared with son's actual occupation. Likewise, it remains to be shown whether the same types apply to occupations below the professional level.

o. e. thompson

occupational values of high school students

Responses of high school students as freshmen and later as sophomores in this study support the belief that the characteristics of a vocation that are important to students may be internalized relatively early in life. There were differences between what girls and boys thought was important in an occupation; however, little difference was found between the group means of these students when freshmen and a year later when sophomores. Most students did not change occupational preference between the freshman and sophomore year. Students in the study as freshmen, but transferring out or withdrawing a year later, differed little in occupational values or in occupational choice from the sophomores. These findings agree only in part with work of other researchers in this field.

This study was designed to explore Super's (1960) belief that the ninth-grader is in the vocational exploration stage, i.e., he is exploring himself to determine what features of a vocation will help him gain personal satisfaction and he is exploring the world of work to find how these features appear in reality. An occupational value scale, adapted from Centers' (1949) study, was used to determine how important certain features of a vocation are to students. This scale includes 10 job characteristics hereinafter called occupa-

tional values. The scale, plus a personal information survey, was administered to 2,287 ninth-graders in 10 California high schools during the fall semester of 1962. It was read-ministered the following fall to 1,790 of the original sample, then sophomores. Following is a summary of the findings of this test-retest. Whenever differences between groups are mentioned, these are significant at the five per cent level or lower.

Findings

Certain occupational values are accepted almost universally as very important by students, others are of moderate importance, and the remainder are generally rejected (Table 1). Judged important by over 80 per cent of the students were the occupational characteristics of an interesting job, the opportunity for self-expression, a secure position, and the opportunity to help others. Characteristics of moderate importance (important to 50 to 70 per cent) were the opportunity to gain self-esteem, to obtain prominence and recognition, to be relatively independent, and to receive high pay. The remaining two values were practically rejected: a job where one could be a leader and a job where one could be the boss were important to less than one-third of the students.

Reprinted with permission of the author and publisher from *Personnel and Guidance Journal*, 1966, **44**, 850-853.

TABLE 1. OCCUPATIONAL VALUES OF FRESHMEN AND SOPHOMORES

| | Percent Rating Value Important | | | | | |
| | Men | | | Women | | |
Occupational Value	Freshmen* n = 895	Sophomore* n = 895	Transfer† n = 238	Freshmen n = 893	Sophomore n = 893	Transfer n = 261
A very interesting job	93.94	93.38	91.60	96.32	95.39	96.54
A job you are sure of keeping	90.03	87.91	89.92	85.12	85.45	86.58
A job where you could express own ideas	88.13	89.58	87.82	91.28	92.60	91.56
A job where you could help other people	82.43	74.84	83.20	93.74	90.25	93.09
A job where you would gain esteem	62.66	62.89	67.65	57.45	58.75	64.36
A job where you could make a name for self	59.76	65.57	59.66	51.86	59.20	60.91
A highly paid job	58.54	57.75	65.55	43.46	37.08	46.35
A job where you could work on your own	55.85	52.50	56.30	54.54	49.59	57.46
A job where you could become a leader	41.21	41.21	39.08	21.95	23.01	22.98
A job where you could be boss	27.14	27.70	22.69	9.07	7.71	11.10

*Students in study both years.

†Students in study as freshmen only.

TABLE 2. RESPONSES OF STUDENTS IN THE FRESHMAN YEAR AND THE SOPHOMORE YEAR TO IMPORTANCE OF AN OC-CUPATIONAL VALUE

Occupational Value	Same Response %	Different Response %
A very interesting job	91.06	8.94
A job where you could express own ideas	86.19	13.81
A job you are sure of keeping	84.24	15.76
A job where you could help other people	81.05	18.95
A job where you could be boss	79.82	20.18
A job where you could become a leader	69.31	30.69
A highly paid job	68.92	31.08
A job where you would gain esteem	65.51	34.49
A job where you could make a name for self	64.50	35.50
A job where you could work on your own	60.51	39.49

These findings agree with a study by Thompson (1961) of a sample of 400 California high school students.

There is practically no difference in importance placed upon each occupational value between the freshmen in the total sample, the sophomores (those who were in as freshmen and remained as sophomores), and those studied as freshmen but not included in the sample of sophomores. Tests of significance between the responses of the 1,788 in the test-retest group to each value failed to demonstrate significant differences in responses between the freshmen and the sophomores when treated as groups. Likewise, no difference in responses on any value could be demonstrated between the group who dropped out of the study and those who remained.

A comparison of how the students rated each occupational value as freshmen and as sophomores showed that chances were about three in four that the same response was given the second time as the first (Table 2). Note that the four occupational values considered most important by the group also had the highest percentage of repeat responses. Only 160, or less than 10 per cent, changed their rating of the importance to them of a job that was interesting. The greatest change in importance was in a job where you could work on your own. About half of the students thought this was important to them each year. However, when sophomores, nearly 37 per cent switched their responses from important to not important, while 34 per cent changed from not important to important.

When the data were stratified by sex, some differences were found in rating occupational values. Since there was so little difference between the responses of freshmen and sophomores, only those of the sophomores are tabled (Table 3). Women place significantly less emphasis than do men upon the importance of a job where one would be a leader or the boss, where high pay was involved, and one where recognition was possible. In contrast, men placed significantly less importance than did the women on a job that would permit an expression of one's own ideas and one where the individual

TABLE 3. COMPARISON OF OCCUPATIONAL VALUES HELD IMPORTANT BY SOPHOMORE HIGH SCHOOL STUDENTS

Occupational Value	Rated Value as Important	
	Men n = 895	Women n = 893
Having an interesting job	836	854
Opportunity to express own ideas	802	829
Having security	787	765
Helping other people	670	808
Being recognized	587	530
Gaining esteem	563	526
Obtaining a high salary	517	332
Having independence	470	444
Being a leader	369	206
Being a boss	248	69

could help other people. No differences were found between the sexes in the importance placed on the remaining four values.

Relationships were found between certain occupational values and socio-psychological factors. The importance that students placed upon leadership in the occupation was related to the socio-economic level of the student's family as measured by the father's occupation. Students whose fathers had high-prestige vocations placed significantly more importance on a job where one could be leader than did students whose fathers were in the manual or skilled trades. This finding was also reflected in the occupation the student thought he might pursue: those choosing a high-status vocation placed more importance on being a leader than did those choosing a vocation in the low white- or blue-collar classes. As one might expect, leadership through one's vocation was significantly more important to the student in the college-preparatory curriculum and to the high-achieving student.

The desire for an interesting job was associated with scholastic ability. Students in the college-preparatory curriculum, those who were high achievers, and those with above-average capacity placed significantly more importance on an occupation that was interesting and challenging.

What others would think about you because of your occupation was highly important to students who lived in urban areas and those whose mothers worked outside the home for pay.

Having a vocation in which one would gain power through being the boss was considered important by less than one-fifth of the students. Students interested in power tended to be from rural areas, had received low grades, and seldom attended church.

Job security is much more important to students whose fathers are in the low-prestige occupations than to those whose fathers are in the professions, and students who elect occupations in the low-prestige area are more security-conscious than those choosing the professions. Rural students also place higher importance on security than their urban cousins. Students whose mothers worked outside the home also deemed security exceedingly important. Security was less vital to college-preparatory students, to high-achieving students, and high-ability students than to other students.

The opportunity to have a vocation which encourages individuality was important to over 90 per cent of the students, but more so to those in college-preparatory majors than those in other majors, to high achievers than to low achievers, and to high-ability students than to low-ability students.

Surprisingly, students place extreme importance on security yet only moderate importance on high pay. High pay was more important to students whose fathers were in low-prestige occupations than to those whose fathers were in the professions. High salary was less important to college-preparatory students than to others, to high achievers than to low achievers, and to high-ability than to low-ability students.

The occupational values of recognition, altruism, and independence, although moderately to highly important to the students as a group, failed to be more important to one stratification of students than to another.

Summary

Super's (1960) hypothesis that ninth-graders are ready to consider problems of pre-vocational and vocational choice is borne out in this study. Freshman students were very definite in what was important to them in a vocation, and in their sophomore year over three-fourths still rated the importance of these occupational values just as they had a year previously. Super studied just boys, whereas this study includes both boys and girls. While there were some significant differences between boys and girls when considered as groups in the importance placed upon certain values, there was no significant difference between how the boys, as a group, responded as freshmen and as sophomores. The same was true for girls. Thus, how ninth- and tenth-graders view their vocational choice may be well established upon entering high school and may not change readily.

Are these young people in the decision-making stage? Perhaps so. One can scarcely quarrel with Super's (1960) belief that the years of the ninth and tenth grades may be too early to start preparation for a specific vocation. However, our educational system is so structured that decisions relative to preparation for a community of occupations or an occupational area must be made early in the high school years if any preparation for it is to be done while in school.

It must be further considered that up to one-fourth of the students in this study will have to enter the world of work without the benefit of completing high school, and another third will not receive education after high school. For these young people an early vocational choice, even though tentative, provides some direction to what otherwise might be aimless wandering through high school.

richard stevic

george uhlig

occupational aspirations of selected appalachian youth

This study examines the concepts that Appalachian youth have concerning their probable life work. After comparing and contrasting these students with a group of native and Appalachian migrant students in an Ohio city, the following results were noted: (a) Appalachian youth who stay in the geographic area have a significantly lower aspirational level than do those students who are native to a rurban area; (b) the Appalachian youth have different personal role models and characteristics for success than those students who have migrated from the Appalachian area; (c) one of the major problems in raising the occupational aspirations of Appalachian students appears to be lack of information and opportunity rather than lack of ability.

In many areas of the nation, transition in employment and change of occupations has been fairly constant and accepted. We have become accustomed to the fact that certain jobs will not continue to exist and that new jobs will be created. Those who lose the old jobs will retrain or redirect themselves to the newly created jobs. These job changes have been facilitated by positive action by such agencies as the state employment service, the school, and most importantly, by the the individual members of society. These groups have cooperated to establish a situation where the prospective employee can seek new possibilities for employment, learn any new skills which might be necessary, and thus adjust to change.

In the Appalachian area, acceptance of change has not been the usual case for several reasons. First, as long as coal was "king," there was little need to seek new occupational areas. Father and son went together to the coal mine because the supply of workers never quite kept up with the demand for skilled miners. Second, since one could live fairly well under the "protection" of the coal mine owner-operator, there was no need or desire on the part of the miner to look elsewhere. The owner-operator provided housing, food, clothing, work, schools, church, and social life. Third, the owner may not have always wanted the miner to know about other occupational opportunities. The owner needed the miner and his strong-bodied sons. He also needed the fertile women of Appalachia to bear sons and daughters to perpetuate his supply of laborers. It is the staggering dependency relationship, fostered by the company store concept, accepted by the miners, and promoted by the owners, that has brought about many of the present occupational problems in Appalachia.

The research described in this paper is intended to provide insight into one part of the occupational problem of Appalachia, namely, the self-concept of students con-

Reprinted with permission of the authors and publisher from *Personnel and Guidance Journal*, 1967, **45**, 435-439.

cerning their probable life work. If an inadequate self-concept is part of the trouble, we may be able to assist school officials and other public officials to provide the assistance to change this concept.

Procedures

The Occupational Aspiration Scale (OAS) (Miller & Haller, 1963) was administered to selected students in a high school of Appalachia. This school, located in southeastern Kentucky, is in the midst of the Kentucky Appalachia area. It is a county school located near the edge of the largest city in the county. The feeder elementary schools are located in highly disadvantaged areas where many persons have spent a significant portion of their lives on some sort of welfare. The high school includes grades nine through twelve and has one certificated counselor for 965 students.

Five homeroom classes were chosen to complete the scale. Each class, freshman through senior, was represented by one homeroom, and the fifth class was composed of those students who were unable to attend one of the regular homeroom classes due to scheduling conflicts.

The groups that were used for comparison were located in a rurban[1] area of Ohio and represented those persons who had spent their lives in this community and those who migrated into the area from Appalachia during the last three years (Riccio, 1965). Thus students in the school represent both the rural and urban portions of the culture. The point that should be considered most important in the present study is that the school population normally includes many newly arrived Appalachian youth whose parents chose the area for the rural atmosphere and the nearness to occupational opportunities.

In addition to the OAS, the students were asked to complete two open-ended questions. The first of these, intended to identify a role model that the students held, was: "Which people in this world would you most want to be like?" The responses to this question were classified into the following cate-

gories: Aesthetic, Athletic, Conforming, Economic, Political, Religious, Social, and Theoretical.

This list includes six types of men that are included in the Allport-Vernon-Lindzey (1960) study of values. It also includes two new types, athletic and conforming. The athletic man is best represented by a professional athlete of the Mantle, Mays, or Unitas type. The conforming man is best represented by Dad or Charlie Smith, the guy next door.

The second question that was asked attempted to elicit the perceptions of characteristics necessary for success in one's vocation: "What must a person do or what must he be like to become a success in this world?" The responses on this question were classified as follows: Adaptability, Ambition, Character, Education, Effort, Influence, Intelligence, Opportunity, Patriotism, and Physical Appearance.

Findings

Aspiration Level

The data for aspiration level are found in Table 1. The mean of the Appalachian group is significantly lower than the mean of the migrant and native groups at the .001 level. The migrant and native groups do not differ significantly.

TABLE 1. VALUES OF "t" BETWEEN KENTUCKY APPALACHIA GROUP, OHIO MIGRANT GROUP AND OHIO NATIVE GROUP ON THE OCCUPATIONAL ASPIRATION SCALE

	X	SD	N	t value
Kentucky Appalachia	35.51	11.2	144	
				5.1581*
Ohio natives	43.34	11.7	97	
Kentucky Appalachia	35.51	11.2	144	
				4.2095*
Ohio migrants	41.90	11.7	97	
Ohio natives	43.34	11.7	97	
				0.853
Ohio migrants	41.90	11.7	97	

*Significant at .001 level.

The next step was to examine the occupations most desired and least desired by the Appalachian group (Table 2). The number in parentheses represents the scale value as determined by the OAS of the occupation listed. This value indicates the relative posi-

---

[1]Rurban is used in this paper to indicate a residential area located near an urban area but which also is in close proximity to a predominantly rural section.

tion of the occupation in terms of the other nine listed in each question of the scale. The interpretation is zero (lowest ranking item) through nine (highest ranking item). The ranking throughout the scale corresponds to the North-Hatt system (Hatt & North, 1962).

In five of the questions the most popular choice was a low-ranking job. It is of some interest, however, that for questions 5, 6, and 8 the students chose the third-best occupation most often. There was a large amount of highway and bridge construction going on in the area and thus a large number of students at least knew about civil engineers. This circumstance may explain the responses to Question 5 since knowledge of the more attractive aspects of the job is perhaps the real reason for this choice. When one examines the pattern for choice-made-least-often, some interesting results can be noted. For example, no student wanted to be a coal miner although this was once the most important job in the area and even today offers a few people relatively stable employment. Practically no students wanted to accept the jobs of garbage collector, street sweeper, or shoe shiner. This finding may reflect a belief that the person really can do better than these occupations or may be an indication that being unemployed and on relief is more desirable and perhaps more profitable than these three menial positions.

TABLE 2. OCCUPATIONAL CHOICES OF APPALACHIAN STUDENTS

Question	Most Desired	Least Desired
1.	Filling station attendant (1)	Supreme court justice (9)
2.	Machine operator in factory (2)	Singer in night club (1)
3.	Farm hand (1)	County judge (8)
4.	Carpenter (3)	Coal miner (1)
5.	Civil engineer (7)	Minister or priest (8)
6.	Airline pilot (7)	Garbage collector (0)
7.	Truck driver (2)	Street sweeper (0)
8.	Owner of a factory (7)	Shoe shiner (0)

Role Models

The Appalachian group responded to the question concerning "the kind of person they would most want to be like" as shown in Table 3. In order to determine the classification of these responses, the two researchers judged each questionnaire independently. Where differences of opinion occurred, a determination was made cooperatively as to which of the categories was more appropri-

ate. It should be noted that the responses given by the students were most often very easy to classify because the exact name or title of the person was given. In relatively few cases was there a need for researchers to reexamine responses.

TABLE 3. PREFERRED ROLE MODELS

	Kentucky Appalachia	Ohio Migrants	Ohio Natives
Aesthetic	1	2	1
Athletic	15	13	5
Conforming	39	13	23
Economic	17	22	23
Political	29	8	9
Religious	1	2	0
Social	5	10	20
Theoretical	0	4	8
No response	37	23	8

A chi-square was applied to the three groups of role model data, i.e., native, migrant, and the group from Appalachia. The "No response" category was dropped from all three groups so that the total group included only those who actually indicated a type of person he wanted to be like. Table 4 includes the chi-square data for the role model distribution.

TABLE 4. CHI-SQUARE VALUES FOR THE ROLE MODEL DATA

Group	df	X	p
Kentucky Appalachia/Ohio migrants	7	27.69	.001
Kentucky Appalachia/Ohio natives	7	37.13	.001

Kentucky Appalachia = 107. Ohio natives = 89. Ohio migrants = 74.

The distribution obtained in the Kentucky Appalachian group was significantly different from the distribution of the Ohio migrant and Ohio native group. In terms of frequency of choice, the Kentucky Appalachian group tends toward the conforming man while the Ohio migrant selects the economic man and the Ohio native selects both of these with equal frequency. The theoretical man was not chosen by the Kentucky Appalachian group and the religious model was not selected by the Ohio native. The migrant group chose the aesthetic and religious man less frequently than other models.

When the chi-square computation for the Kentucky Appalachian/Ohio migrant group is examined, the greatest difference between observed and expected frequencies occurs in the conforming model, with the Kentucky Appalachian choosing this model more frequently than predicted. The least difference between the two groups was for the athletic man, where observed and expected frequencies were almost equal. Between the Kentucky Appalachian and the Ohio native, the greatest difference occurred in the social category which the Kentucky Appalachian chose much less frequently than expected. Similarity of observed and expected frequencies was noted for the aesthetic man.

Characteristics for Success

The responses of the three groups for the last question of the scale are shown in Table 5.

TABLE 5. PERCEPTIONS OF CHARACTERISTICS REQUIRED FOR SUCCESS

	Kentucky Appalachia	Ohio Migrants	Ohio Natives
Adaptability	8	17	21
Ambition	17	10	10
Character	7	17	19
Education	47	36	54
Effort-commitment	14	31	42
Influence	2	2	1
Intelligence	2	8	6
Opportunity	3	1	0
Patriotism	1	0	2
Physical appearance	0	3	4
No response	42	20	2

The classification of the responses on this question was more difficult than on the role model question covered earlier. The same procedure was used, with any disagreement on classification examined cooperatively and resolved by the researchers.

Chi-square was applied to each of the six characteristics that had frequencies of sufficient magnitude to make this technique appropriate—Adaptability, Ambition, Character, Education, Effort-Commitment and Intelligence. Inspection of the data suggests no apparent differences in the remaining four categories. Of the six categories analyzed, only Effort-Commitment displayed a significantly different distribution, with the Kentucky Appalachian group choosing it least often. While the Ohio natives and migrants appear to perceive Effort-Commitment as important, the Kentucky Appalachian group does not. It is difficult to ascertain the cause of such a finding. Do individuals in the Appalachian area who have faith in the Effort-

Commitment approach leave the area, possibly becoming the Ohio migrants of the study? Do individuals who remain in Appalachia, with its frustrations and welfare programs, lose sight of the importance of Effort-Commitment? These are questions that seemingly must be answered before meaningful habilitation programs can be developed.

Discussion

Evidently there is a relationship between moving out of the Appalachian area and occupational aspiration. Since the migrant group had been in the rurban area a relatively short time, a portion of the difference in aspiration must have developed while still in Appalachia. Family conversations about moving to new employment possibilities, information about new occupations that would be available, or the factor of needing to find out about the new location may affect the level of aspiration and increase it to the significantly higher level that was indicated. This may mean that we might predict that some of the higher scoring Appalachian subjects are destined to leave the area.

The data support the hypothesis that the group remaining in Appalachia have different role models and conceptions of success characteristics than do those moving out and those who are native to the rurban area. Whether this finding is due to faulty interpretation of society or to a realistic appraisal of the "facts of life" in Appalachia remains to be determined. It is true, however, that the Appalachian youth values the conforming man more than does the migrant youth in the urban area. In the area of characteristics, the Appalachian youth perceives effort and commitment as having less significance than expected.

A problem may exist in terms of knowledge of occupations. The students in Appalachia seem to select and reject familiar occupations. Not choosing an occupation when one does not know very much about the occupation fits most vocational theories and the intent of the Occupational Aspiration Scale. If the only limiting factor in striving for a higher occupational level is lack of knowledge, it becomes society's job, through the school, to provide more information. In Appalachia this process will be facilitated by providing those experiences, academic and vocational, that will assist the youth to make full use of whatever abilities he has. The Appalachian youth in a rurban society does not appear to be a great deal different from the native rurban youth. Predetermination of occupation because of geographic origin is to be deplored. Each youth, no matter where he lives, needs the opportunity to go as far as his abilities will take him regardless of his present cultural, economic and social setting.

References

Alexander, C. N., Jr., & Campbell, E. Q. Peer influences on adolescent educational aspirations and attainments. *American Sociological Review,* 1964, **29,** 568-575.

Allport, G. W., Vernon, P. E., & Lindzey, G. *Study of values.* (3rd ed.) Boston: Houghton Mifflin, 1960.

Anderson, C. S. *Young men ten years after leaving Pennsylvania rural high school.* University Park: Pennsylvania Agricultural Experimental Station Bulletin 468, 1944.

Angelino, H. Developmental tasks and problems of the middle adolescent period. *Education,* 1955, **76,** 226-231.

Astin, A. W. *Who goes where to college?* Chicago: Science Research Associates, 1965.

Barrow, H. Vocational development research: Some problems of logical and experimental form. *Personnel and Guidance Journal,* 1961, **40,** 24.

Berger, E. M. Vocational choices in college. *Personnel and Guidance Journal,* 1967, **45,** 888-894.

Blau, P. M. The flow of occupational supply and recruitment. *American Sociological Review,* 1965, **30,** 475-490.

Blau, P. M., et al. Occupational choice: A conceptual framework. *Industrial and Labor Relations Review,* 1956, **9,** 531-543.

Burchinal, L. G., Haller, A. O., & Taves, M. J. *Career choices of rural youth in a changing society.* St. Paul: Minnesota Agricultural Experimental Station Bulletin 458, 1962.

Bureau of the Census. *Classified index of occupations and industries.* Washington, D. C.: Government Printing Office, 1950.

Campbell, E. Q., & Alexander, C. N. Structural effects and interpersonal relationships. *American Journal of Sociology,* 1965, **71,** 284-289.

Centers, R. *The psychology of social classes.* Princeton, N. J.: Princeton University Press, 1949.

Cowhig, J. D., et al. *Orientations toward occupation and residence.* East Lansing: Michigan Experimental Station Special Bulletin 428, 1960.

Duncan, O. D. The trend of occupational mobility in the United States. *American Sociological Review,* 1965, **30,** 491-498.

Garrison, K. C. Developmental tasks and problems of the late adolescent period. *Education,* 1955, **76,** 232-235.

Ginzberg, E., et al. *Occupational choice: An approach to a general theory.* New York: Columbia University Press, 1951.

Haller, A. O., & Miller, I. W. *The occupational aspiration scale: Theory, structure and correlates.* East Lansing: Michigan Agricultural Experimental Station Technological Bulletin 288, 1963.

Hatt, P. K., & North, C. C. Prestige ratings of occupations. In S. Noscow & W. H. Form (Eds.), *Man, work and society.* New York: Basic Books, 1962. Pp. 277-283.

Havighurst, R. J. Youth in exploration and man emergent. In H. Borow (Ed.), *Man in a world at work.* Boston: Houghton Mifflin, 1964.

Jenson, P. G., & Kirchner, W. K. A national answer to the question, "Do sons follow their fathers' occupations?" *Journal of Applied Psychology,* 1955, **39,** 419-421.

Kohout, V. A., & Rothney, W. M. A longitudinal study of consistency of vocational preferences. *American Educational Research Journal,* 1964, **1,** 10-21.

Kuvlesky, W. P. The non-attainment of adolescents' occupational aspirations: A longitudinal study of rural Pennsylvania males. Unpublished doctoral dissertation, University of Pennsylvania, 1965.

Kuvlesky, W. P., & Bealer, R. C. A clarification of the concept "occupational choice." *Rural Sociology,* 1966, **31,** 265-276.

Kuvlesky, W. P., & Ohlendorf, G. W. *Occupational aspirations and expectations: A bibliography of research literature.* College Station: Texas A and M University, 1966.

Little, J. K. The occupations of non-college youth. *American Educational Research Journal,* 1967, **4,** 147-154.

Miller, I. W., & Haller, A. O. *The occupational aspirations scale: Theory, structure and correlates.* East Lansing, Mich.: State University Press, 1963.

Nelson, E. Fathers' occupations and student vocational choices. *School and Society,* 1939, **50,** 572-576.

Perrella, V. C., & Bogan, F. A. Out-of-school youth, February 1963. *Monthly Labor Review,* 1964, **87,** 1260-1268.

Porter, R. J. Predicting vocational plans of high school senior boys. *Personnel and Guidance Journal,* 1954, **33,** 215-218.

Proctor, W. M. A 13-year follow-up of high school pupils. *Occupations,* 1937, **15,** 306-310.

Rehberg, R. A. Adolescent career aspirations and expectations: Evaluation of two contrary stratification hypotheses. *Pacific Sociological Review,* 1967, **10** (2), 81-90.

Rehberg, R. A., & Westby, D. L. Parental encouragement, occupation, education and family size: Artificial or independent determinants of adolescent educational expectations? *Social Forces,* 1967, **45,** 362-374.

Riccio, A. C. Occupational aspirations of migrant adolescents from the Appalachian South. *Vocational Guidance Quarterly,* 1965, **14,** 26-30.

Roe, A. *The psychology of occupations.* New York: Wiley, 1956.

Smelzer, W. J. Adolescent and adult occupational choice as a function of family socioeconomic history. *Sociometry,* 1963, **26,** 493-513.

Sperry, I. V., & Kivett, V. R. *Educational and vocational goals of rural youth in North Carolina.* Greensboro: North Carolina Agriculture Experimental Station Bulletin 163, 1964.

Stephenson, R. M. Realism of vocational choice: A critique and an example. *Personnel and Guidance Journal,* 1957, **35,** 482-488.

Strong, E. K., Jr. *Vocational interests of men and women.* Stanford, Calif.: Stanford University Press, 1964.

Super, D. E. The critical ninth grade—vocational choice or vocational explorations. *Personnel and Guidance Journal,* 1960, **39,** 106.

Super, D. E., & Crites, J. O. *Appraising vocational fitness.* (Rev. ed.) New York: Harper, 1962.

Thompson, O. E. What is the high school student of today like? *Journal of Secondary Education,* 1961, **36,** 210-219.

Tiedeman, D. V. Decisions and vocational development: A paradigm and its implications. *Personnel and Guidance Journal,* 1961, **40,** 15-21.

Werts, C. E. Career choice patterns: Ability and social class. *NMSC Research Reports,* 1966a, **2** (3).

Werts, C. E. Social class and initial career choice of college freshmen. *Sociology of Education,* 1966b, **39,** 74-85.

Wilson, A. B. Residential segregation of social classes and aspirations of high school boys. *American Sociological Review,* 1959, **24,** 836-845.

Wilson, W. C. Value differences between public and private school graduates. *Journal of Educational Psychology,* 1959, **50,** 213.

Wolfbein, S. L. Labor trends, manpower, and automation. In H. Borow (Ed.), *Man in a world at work.* Boston: Houghton Mifflin, 1964.

Worthington, E. H. *Vocational and educational choices of high school pupils.* Philadelphia: University Press, 1938.

Annotations

Idea forum: IV. *National Association of Secondary School Principals Bulletin,* 1969, **53** (334), entire issue. This issue is devoted to the problem of occupations and vocational education. Four especially significant topics are (1) the potential of vocational education, (2) the secondary school and occupational preparation, (3) an economic analysis of youth employment, (4) characteristics of high-ability dropouts.

Little, J. K. The occupations of non-college youth. *American Educational Research Journal,* 1967, **4,** 147-154. About 75 to 80 percent of American adolescents enter the work force without a college education. This article concerns their occupational aspirations, occupational attainments, and the factors that facilitate their occupational attainment. It also proposes a realistic and practical program for educating youths from mid-high school to midcollege.

Perrella, V. C., & Bogan, F. A. Out-of-school youth: February, 1963. *Monthly Labor Review,* 1964, **87,** 1260-1268. This article analyzed the work status of a group of youths from 16 to 21 who were not in any type of educational setting. The authors elaborate on reasons why adolescents leave school and on family characteristics that influence youths in their educational decisions. An excellent description of employment and unemployment patterns of youths is presented.

Rehberg, R. A., & Westby, D. L. Parental encouragement, occupation, education and family size: Artificial or independent determinants of adolescent educational expectations? *Social Forces,* 1967, **45,** 362-374. Data from 2852 male high school sophomores revealed that (1) the father's education helps determine son's occupation, (2) the father's education and occupation influence the adolescent's educational expectations, and (3) the greater the family size, the less encouragement of education from the father.

Tobias, J. J. Work activities and future goals of the affluent suburban male delinquent. *Vocational Guidance Quarterly,* 1969, **17,** 293-299. One hundred white male delinquents and 100 white male nondelinquents were interviewed about family and peer relationships. Both groups agreed that friends influence participation in delinquent behaviors. Boredom and parental influence are other causative factors. In addition, the author found that nondelinquents (1) had a closer family relationship, (2) participate in more activities, (3) hold more part-time jobs than does the delinquent.

Venn, G. Occupational education for everyone. *National Association of Secondary School Principals Bulletin,* 1968, **52,** 112-122. Venn advocates vocational-education programs to help prepare our one million annual dropouts for a place in the work force. He claims that adolescents are plagued by a lack of realistic work goals. Schools are urged to (1) give occupational orientation and guidance to youths and (2) to cooperate with business and industry to provide work-experience programs.

eleven

adolescent personality

An adolescent's personality may be defined as the pattern of interrelationships between his cognitive-emotional systems and his environment. Most adolescent behaviors are interpersonal and oriented toward other adolescents. Through such interactions emerges a greater awareness of self and others. The adolescent's environmental experiences are interpreted and accommodated in terms of the self. Thus he either strengthens or modifies his cognitive (mental) system. In turn, the effect his experiences have on his affective (emotional) system strengthens or modifies his self-concept.

Mouly (1968) has described the self-concept as a system of attitudes about oneself. Presumably the self-concept emerges from the "self," which Jersild (1952, p. 9) has described as follows:

> A person's self is the sum-total of all that he can call his. The self includes, among other things, a system of ideas, attitudes, values, and commitments. The self is a person's total subjective environment; it is the distinctive center of experience and significance. The self constitutes a person's inner world as distinguished from the outer world consisting of all other people and things.

Throughout adolescence the individual learns to differentiate, and his self-concept becomes clearer as he finds order in his interrelationships with peers, parents, the school, and other adults. Good peer affiliations, strong adult identification, and social status at school all enhance the adolescent's self-concept (Mouly, 1968; Williams & Cole, 1968). Maintaining harmony within oneself and within one's environment builds stability into the adolescent personality.

A theory of personality is a scientific attempt to explain personality structure. Such a theory takes into account all factors within a person and his environment that affect the emerging self. Three important theories of personality are discussed in this chapter: (1) the trait theory, (2) the type theory, and (3) the psychoanalytic theory.

Trait Theory

A dimension of personality that manifests itself consistently is termed a personality trait. Personality traits tend to be abstract, since they are inferences or general statements of observed behavior. Moreover, they may change as the individual adapts to new situations. By definition, personality traits represent a developed constitutional potentiality (Crow & Crow, 1965).

One major trait theorist was Gordon Allport, who proposed that individuals have *common traits* and *personal dispositions* (1961). Common traits are comparable among many persons. Personal dispositions are unique to each individual and thus cannot be used in comparing people.

Allport maintains, in contrast to other theories, that the individual personality is unique. Because the individual is always changing, there is no fixed ego or self that regulates man throughout life. Allport sees normal personality development as a conscious process. Thus the adolescent personality emerges as a complex entity but with awareness (1964).

A second major trait theorist was Raymond B. Cattell. Allport and Odbert (1936) had found nearly 18,000 words in the English language to describe behavior. Cattell (1946) eliminated synonyms and reduced the list to 171 words that describe the "personality sphere" of any individual. Through factor analysis he isolated 12 traits that he believed would describe an individual's personality characteristics (1946, 1957). The

following traits apply to the age range from 10 to 16 years (Cattell et al., 1953):

Emotional sensitivity	Toughness
Nervous tension	Autonomic relaxation
Neurotic fear	Stability of ego strength
Will control	Relaxed casualness
Impatient dominance, cyclothymia (emotional expression)	Schizothymia (withdrawal)
Socialized morale	Dislike of education
Independent dominance, energetic conformity	Quiet eccentricity
Surgency (cheerfulness)	Desurgency (depression), intelligence

Cattell made a distinction between *surface traits*, which are obvious to others as characteristic of a person's behavior, and source traits, which are less observable and mostly theoretical but which nevertheless influence an individual's behavior (Deese, 1967; Hilgard & Atkinson, 1967).

Many psychologists do not feel that trait theory is the best explanation of personality. Because an individual's traits represent his ways of behaving within his environment, and because their existence depends on interaction (Hilgard & Atkinson, 1967), these traits are flexible and may not be truly characteristic of the person.

Type Theory

Body constitution, physical attractiveness, and general health have been thought to have strong effects on the development of personality, and theorists have attempted to describe man's personality by his body type, or physique. One prominent theory based on body type was formulated by Sheldon and his colleagues (Sheldon, Stevens, & Tucker, 1940) and categorizes physiques as (1) endomorphic, (2) ectomorphic, or (3) mesomorphic.

The *endomorphic* type refers to the short, flabby build that results from a predominance of the abdominal section. The endomorphic person's corresponding temperament is that of one who likes to eat, likes bodily comforts, and is sociable (Hilgard & Atkinson, 1967).

The *ectomorphic* type refers to a long, thin physique characterized by a predominance of the nervous system. Temperamentally, the ectomorph is sensitive, worries, fears groups, and needs solitude (Hilgard & Atkinson, 1967). Research by Sanford (Sanford, Adkins, Miller, Cobb, et al., 1943) on the structured personality (characterized by orderliness, self-sufficiency, quiet dignity, cooperativeness, and strong conscience) indicated that more ectomorphs than any other type fit the structured description.

Sheldon's third body type, the *mesomorph,* is characterized by a predominant development of the bones and muscles. The mesomorph's body is muscular, well proportioned, and athletic in appearance. Temperamentally, he is energetic, likes exercise, and is direct in manner (Hilgard & Atkinson, 1967). Sanford et al. (1943) classified mesomorphs as social beings—popular, assured, uninhibited, and able to express themselves in a variety of ways. Moreover, they are generally assertive and involved in many activities, and many are highly athletic and competitive—traits that are strongly reinforced within our society.

A theory of personality based on body type warrants some consideration. Since body types are determined genetically and formed in the embryonic stage, heredity may play an important role in personality development. The ectomorphic individual is not too inclined to participate in athletic and physical tasks; his thinner, less muscular body does not allow him the success in these areas that a mesomorph enjoys. Therefore the ectomorph is likely to withdraw from his peers and may perhaps expend his energy in academic pursuits. Although body build does not thoroughly explain personality, it does modify a person's learning and behavior, thus influencing his personality development.

Psychoanalytic Theory

Sigmund Freud (1856-1939), one of the first and possibly the most influential personality theorist, presented a systematic and dynamic approach to personality. His system is complex; in fact, Freud himself modified parts of his theory as new research provided additional information. As a result, many of his followers (Jung, Adler) disagreed with some of his earlier statements, which compounded the difficulty of understanding psychoanalytic theory. However, since much of the literature has been influenced by this point of view, a brief but simplified discussion of Freudian theory will be presented.

Freud held that the important elements of personality are fixed within the first three years of a person's life (Alexander, 1963). Although shaping experiences may be forgotten, individual reactions are built into the person and become influential forces in personality development.

The basic theoretical constructs that represent the components of personality structure are the id, the ego, and the superego. *Individual personality, then, is made up of the dynamic interactions of the id, ego, and superego.*

The id is the instinctive, pleasure-seeking, impulsive element of man. It is the reservoir of libidinal (sexual) energy. The id is unconscious, amoral, biological, and illogical. It is dominated by the pleasure principle.

The ego represents conscious rational man and attempts to reconcile the conflicting forces of the id and superego as well as the demands of man's outer world. The ego keeps man in touch with reality. It organizes the mind and maintains cognitive control of the external environment. Freud's construct of ego is otherwise described as the "self," the "I," and the "conscious self."

The superego, man's conscience, prescribes culturally, ethically, and morally acceptable behaviors. Thompson (1962, p. 568) has described the superego as follows:

> The superego is an outgrowth of the ego. Its principal function is to serve as a model for and a censor over the ego's transactions. It constitutes a permanent expression of parental influence from which it was largely derived. One of its functions is similar to the popular notion of conscience. It is responsible for much of man's socially conforming, moral behavior. Its influence often creates feelings of anxiety and guilt in the ego. Another of its functions is the setting of standards of exemplary conduct and human aspirations.

Freud hypothesized that every person is born with a predetermined amount of libidinal energy that causes him to seek pleasure, especially sexual pleasure. Such energy is expressed at three psychosexual stages. During the infantile period (birth to 6 years) the child passes through the oral, anal, and genital (phallic) stages, in which libidinal energy is expressed and satisfied through pleasures gained from the various erogenous zones. During the latency period (7 to 11 years) no interest in new erogenous zones develops. Rather, the child's sexual energy and narcissism (self-love) seem to diminish. The third stage is the pubertal period (12–19 years), in which libidinal energy is revived and reaches its peak during adolescence.

Freud bases personality on a biological model; that is, he maintains that different personality characteristics emerge in each stage of development. The ability of the ego and superego to control the id throughout these stages is highly contributory to the type of personality that develops. Although Freud's theory has been highly criticized, it must still be recognized for the profound effect it has had on the study of personality.

Factors Affecting Personality

During adolescence several factors affect personality. One such factor is personal appearance. If an adolescent has unusual or abnormal physical characteristics, he may feel self-conscious and inferior. If these differences are repeatedly called to his attention, his self-concept will suffer (Schneiderman, 1956).

Another factor affecting personality is one's family. Many adolescent personality characteristics are adopted from family members. The adolescent tends to identify strongly with one parent—usually the parent of the same sex—and tends to acquire, through identification, many similar personality traits. The degree of influence parents have is generally determined by the type of relationship the adolescent has with the same-sex parent (Miller, Campbell, Twedt, & O'Connell, 1966).

A third factor is peers. Their influence is usually strong because the adolescent's self-concept is a reflection of his peers' concept of him and because peer social pressures influence the development of traits approved by the group. Some peer groups are close knit. Research has indicated that the more solid the structure of the group, the greater its influence on individual members' personality (Baker & Mandell, 1965; Thompson, 1968).

One further consideration is level of aspiration. It is not unusual for adolescents to set unrealistic goals while they are in the process of assessing their capabilities. The frustration of not being able to achieve these goals has a negative influence on the self-concept. However, when they attain their goals, the self-concept is strengthened and personality patterns become more set.

The first article in this chapter, by Thompson, is related to values and aspirations. He studied a group of students over their four-year high school period and found that their values changed very little during that time. The high achiever, the college-bound student, and the regular church attender all held traditional values, which were highly similar to parental values. These students emphasized planning for the future, work success, and individual initiative. In contrast, the low achiever tended to be present oriented, conforming, and highly dependent on others. Thompson's survey indicates that value systems and peer acceptance are highly significant in one's emerging life-style and self-concept.

Personality Development

One of the most astute writers on personality was the late Gordon Allport. His article in this chapter describes some of the crises of adolescence. Allport defines a crisis as a situation of emotional and mental stress that requires significant alterations of outlook within a short period of time. He reports the following crisis areas: (1) intellectual inferiority, (2) physical inferiority, (3) minority group membership, (4) religious conflict, (5) sexual conflict, and (6) family conflict. Allport also suggests that apathy and anxiety evolving from an unchallenging environment can affect personality growth.

The third article in this chapter, by Berdie, is an analysis of personality change

from ninth-grade entrance to college entrance. Using the Minnesota Counseling Inventory, Berdie detected several significant
shifts, most of which indicated self-improve-
ment. The changes were measured according
to social relations, emotional responsibility,
approach to life, contact with reality, mood,
and leadership attitudes. Berdie found that,
although his subjects were better adjusted as
college freshmen than as high school freshmen, they suffered greater family strains
during college than they did during high
school. In addition, girls showed fewer
changes throughout high school than did
boys.

The Self in Perspective

In the final article in this chapter, Otto
and Otto allege that society has not given due
consideration to its adolescents. Unfair publicity and derogatory labels distort the public
image and even the self-image of adolescents. Otto and Otto present a new perspective of the adolescent—one that they hope
will create a better image of our youth and
will strengthen them in their identity-striving
process. The values, habits, and ideas of society, as they are transmitted through word
or action, are important aspects of encultura-
tion for adolescents, who indeed are in the
process of "becoming."

o. e. thompson

student values in transition

Throughout history, society has been concerned with transmitting to the younger generation the values approved by the culture and maintaining these values in adults. Today, many adults believe that time-honored values are being eroded. Youth of today are vocal in confronting time-cherished moral and social value standards; and, as stated over twenty years ago by Linton (1945), "Under the necessity of reorganizing our social structure to meet the needs of a new technology and of a spatial mobility unparalleled in human history, our inherited system of statuses and roles is breaking down, while a new system, compatible with the actual conditions of modern life, has not yet emerged."

Even though values are discussed copiously and many studies have attempted to measure values, surprisingly little is actually known about when and how youth gains its values. Contributing to this dilemma is the disagreement among authorities about the precise definition of values. Yet no one questions the extreme importance of values in the psychological and emotional makeup of the individual.

The definition of values used as the basis of this study comes from works by Getzels (1958), who divided personal values into

Reprinted with permission of the author and publisher from the *California Journal of Educational Research*, 1968, **19**, 77-86.

two major categories, social and secular, and from Spindler (1955), who further refined secular values into four categories based upon tradition and four which characterize the emerging society.

Problem

This study was designed to provide information on the personal and occupational values of high school students and their teachers. Students were involved as freshmen, sophomores, and seniors to test the hypothesis that there would be no change in personal and/or occupational value scores during high school. Their teachers were also tested to determine if the ability of teachers and students to communicate with each other is related to their value patterns. Other objectives of the study were to determine whether friendship patterns within high school classes are related to personal values of students, and to determine whether value patterns of students are influenced by certain socio-economic and psychological factors.

Procedure

Ten high schools were selected from central California communities representative of the various socio-economic areas within the state, and representative of small, medium, and large schools. Of the 2,287 freshmen (1,133 boys, 1,154 girls) in the sample in 1962, 1,791 (897 boys, 894 girls) were available for testing again as sophomores. By the senior year, the sample had decreased to 1,365 (701 boys, 664 girls). Complete data were obtained for 371, or approximately 90 percent, of the teachers of these students.

The instrument used to measure personal values was the *Differential Values Inventory*, developed by Prince (1957). This forced-choice questionnaire contains 64 pairs of items, with each item including a traditional- and an emergent-value statement. The instrument contains four traditional-value subscales (Puritan morality, individualism, work success, and future-time orientation) and four emergent-value subscales (sociability, conformity, moral relativism, and present-time orientation). The subscales were totaled to obtain an emergent- and a traditional-value score for each individual. The basic intent of this instrument is to attempt to assess the individual's true internal feelings regardless of what he actually does. This sense of obligation, preferential feeling, is then considered to be what the individual truly cherishes and, as such, is interpreted to be his true values.

Reliability of the instrument was measured by the split-half method and by two test-retest procedures. Correlations were computed on test-retest of the entire instrument after a one-year time lapse. A second method was through personal interview. About three months after completion of the paper pencil test a random sample of 100 students was interviewed using a schedule which contained twenty-two sets of the original 64 pairs of statements. Correlations ranged from 0.78 upward for the latter procedure and 0.951 for the split-half formula procedure using the Kuder Richardson formula. Test validity was determined by the test designer through use of a panel of experts and by a system of graphic analysis, which considers both item difficulty and discrimination among groups of known characteristics. Further confidence in the instrument was obtained by a factor analysis of the response on 1790 tests. Seven unique factors were identified with an eighth which was less pronounced. It is assumed these eight factors are the personal value subscales which the test designer built into the instrument.

The occupational-value scale was adapted from Centers (1949). Ten characteristics of jobs were to be rated by the respondent as being important or not important to him in deciding the job or occupation he planned for his life's work.

Occupational Choice and Values

The students in this sample were tested at a time in their lives during which many important decisions are being made. Over 90 percent of the freshmen identified a vocation which they hoped to enter eventually. Indecision about future vocations increased to about 20 percent by the senior year. The students appeared quite realistic in the selection of an occupation: high-achieving students tended to select occupational areas which have high academic demands, while average achievers tended to select vocations with less demanding requirements. Further evidence of the ability of the high school student to plan his future and the persistence of the decision made as a freshman was shown in his post-high-school plans: over three-fourths of those freshmen who planned for college still had college as their goal as seniors; only one-fifth who were undecided about their future plans as freshmen were still undecided as seniors. Although the 80 percent who gave post-high-school education as their goal would have been considered an extremely high percentage several years ago, and still is in some states today, it is not unrealistic in California.

Significantly (1 percent level) more men than women rated as important these occupational values: the opportunity to be a leader, to be boss, to receive high pay, or to gain fame. Female students placed significantly (5 percent level) more importance on having jobs which offer the chance to express one's abilities and to help other people. Between the freshmen and senior years, for both males and females, the importance of security in one's occupation, high pay, and helping others through their occupations decreased significantly. Group averages in the other six occupational values remained relatively constant in importance, strengthening

TABLE 1. COMPARISON OF TEACHER AND STUDENT OCCUPATIONAL VALUES (PERCENT STATING THAT THIS VALUE WAS IMPORTANT TO THEM)

Occupational value	Males		Females		Total	
	Teacher	Senior	Teacher	Senior	Teacher	Senior
Leadership	61.3	46.2	47.7	24.0	55.5	35.4
Interesting experience	99.1	94.6	97.9	95.8	98.1	95.2
Esteem	64.4	61.9	55.0	57.9	60.1	60.0
Power	22.5	31.5	16.8	7.6	20.2	19.9
Security	30.2	84.4	36.9	80.0	32.6	82.3
Self-expression	99.5	89.7	99.3	94.3	98.9	91.9
High pay	15.8	55.2	16.8	35.9	16.2	45.8
Fame	59.9	63.2	49.7	52.6	55.5	58.0
Social service	97.3	70.8	96.6	91.7	96.5	81.0
Independence	75.2	53.2	81.9	48.0	77.4	50.7

the hypothesis that many of the criteria a person uses in selecting his vocation may be reasonably fixed before high school.

Occupational values of teachers provided a good yardstick with which to compare student values. Since teachers are established in the labor force, their rating of the ten occupational values presumably represents mature judgment and true feelings gained through experience. When teacher values were compared with student occupational values, a surprising similarity appeared.

Teachers placed extremely high importance on having their vocation provide them interesting experiences, the opportunity for self-expression, and the opportunity to help others—three of the four values to which students gave top priority. Teachers placed less emphasis upon security and high pay than did students, and this is explicable: teachers have jobs, tenure, salary schedules, and other benefits which lead to economic security. Teachers also were more interested in being leaders and in being independent in their vocation, which may be symbols of maturity.

Personal Values

The nature of the *Differential Values Inventory* made the standard analysis of variance inappropriate for that part of the study. Since this inventory yields ipsative data (by the forced-choice items), it was necessary to use a procedure for analysis of profile data formulated by Greenhouse and Geisser (1959), which gives a conservative *F*-test. Comparison among groups on each scale

was made by Duncan's multiple-range test with Kramer's (1956) procedure used for extending this test to groups of unequal size.

Freshmen vs. Seniors

When the *Differential Values Inventory* profile of freshman males (n=701) was compared with that of all senior males, freshmen were significantly higher on Puritan morality and conformity and lower on moral relativism and hedonism.

Senior females (n=664) had significantly higher scores than freshman females on individualism and work success and significantly lower scores on sociability and conformity. When the value profiles of all students tested as freshmen and again as seniors (n=1,365) were compared, freshmen were significantly higher in Puritan morality and conformity, and significantly lower on individualism, work success, and moral relativism.

Students were stratified by school, and comparisons were made between freshman and senior testing. For the males, a significant difference in value profiles occurred in only one school out of the ten, and this significance was attributed to the Puritan morality subscale. That score average was lower for seniors. Personal values of females were less stable: significant differences in value profiles were found in four of the ten schools, and these differences included most of the eight subscales. In three of the schools the females tended to change from an emergent-value orientation as freshmen to a traditional-value orientation as seniors. The fourth school, a parochial school, showed a de-

TABLE 2. MEAN VALUE SCORES BY SEX AND YEAR

Year and sex	PM	IND	WS	FTO	Value Subscale SOC	CONF	MR	PTO	F-value
1963 male	6.98*	8.18	8.94	8.62	8.12	5.99*	8.60	8.55	8.1712*
1966 male	6.23	8.45	8.94	8.35	8.31	5.64	9.19*	8.90*	
1963 female	7.12	8.19	7.79	8.42	9.04*	5.89*	8.97	8.56	17.8511*
1966 female	7.25	9.13*	8.24*	8.69	8.69	4.66	8.93	8.39	
1963 male	6.98	8.18	8.94*	8.62	8.12	5.99	8.60	8.55	15.1894*
1963 female	7.12	8.19	7.79	8.42	9.04*	5.89	8.97*	8.57	
1966 male	6.23	8.45	8.94*	8.35	8.31	5.64*	9.19	8.90	21.5756*
1966 female	7.25*	9.13*	8.24	8.69	8.69*	4.66	8.93	8.39	
1963 total	7.05*	8.19	8.38	8.52	8.57	5.94*	8.78	8.56	14.6901*
1966 total	6.73	8.78*	8.59*	8.52	8.49	5.16	9.06*	8.65	

*Significant 5 percent level or beyond.

PM — Puritan morality
IND — Individualism
WS — Work success
FTO — Future-time orientation

SOC — Sociability
CONF — Conformity
MR — Moral relativism
PTO — Present-time orientation

crease in mean traditional scores. Thus, when testing by school and according to sex, the hypothesis that there is no difference between personal values as freshmen and seniors becomes difficult to reject, especially when one considers only males. Demonstrable differences occurred in only five of twenty possible profile comparisons, and four of these were females.

Values, Achievement and Aspirations

A very distinct relationship was found between personal values and student achievement as measured by grades. High-achieving students had high scores on individualism, work success, and future-time orientation. By comparison, students who had significantly higher scores on conformity, moral relativism, and present-time orientation were consistently "C" students or lower. When the subscale scores were totaled, the result further emphasized that the tradition-oriented student, whether male or female, freshman or senior, was also the high-achiever. For example, the mean traditional score for freshman students increased progressively from 30.60 for "D" students to 35.30 for "A" students. (The mean traditional score for all freshmen was 32.14.) As would be expected, students in the college-preparatory curriculum, regardless of year or sex, also had higher mean traditional scores than did students in other curricula.

Values and Church Attendance

Scores on the traditional scales (Puritan morality, individualism, work success, future-time orientation) were significantly higher (32.83 to 34.42) for those students who attended church at least every other week than for those who attended less often. Students who seldom or never attended church had significantly higher scores on conformity, moral relativism and present time orientation. Only the sociability subscale was not related to frequency of church attendance.

The student who planned to attend college had significantly high scores on all traditional subscales with a mean traditional score of 33.36. The student who planned to take any job available was high on conformity. The undecided student was high on all the emergent subscales (sociability, conformity, moral relativism, and present-time orientation), with a mean traditional score of 29.07.

Values and Socio-Economic Factors

The socio-economic level of the family as measured by the occupation of the father

TABLE 3.   COMPARISON OF VALUE PROFILES OF 311 ACCEPTED AND 264 REJECTED STUDENTS

Status of Student	PM	IND	WS	FTO	Value Subscale SOC	CONF	MR	PTO	F-value
Accepted	7.10	8.04	8.23	8.14	8.66	6.00	9.02	8.71*	2.846*
Rejected	7.17	8.29	8.66	8.72*	8.38	5.96	8.62	8.20	

*Significant 5 percent level or beyond.

PM — Puritan morality
IND — Individualism
WS — Work Success
FTO — Future-time orientation

SOC — Sociability
CONF — Conformity
MR — Moral relativism
PTO — Present-time orientation

was highly related to the value patterns of freshmen. Students whose fathers were manually-skilled workers had significantly low scores on individualism and work success (traditional values) and significantly high scores on sociability, conformity, and moral relativism (emergent values). Students with fathers in the professions had high scores on individualism and work success, and they were significantly lower than others on sociability, conformity, and moral relativism. No significant differences could be found between seniors' value profiles and socio-economic level of the family. The impact of the family as a source of values may decrease between the freshman and senior years, giving way to things in the immediate environment, such as friends, academic studies, and vocational plans.

The desired socio-economic level of students as measured by their occupational choice shows that those students selecting the professions or white-collar occupations had higher mean traditional scores (33.80 and 33.22) than those selecting manually-skilled occupations, self-employed occupations, or those undecided about a future vocation (mean traditional scores, 29.75, 31.23, 31.30).

Values, Peer Acceptance and Friendship Patterns

Profile analyses were made to determine the relationship between personal values and student popularity—peer acceptance or rejection (determined by asking each student to identify his three best friends). The value-profile comparison produced an F-value of 2.85, significant at the 5 percent level.

The accepted students were significantly higher on the present-time-orientation sub-scale and significantly lower on future-time orientation than were the rejected students. The generalization can be made, for this sample at least, that time orientation is related to acceptance or rejection by peers. The more popular students had a mean emergent score of 32.40, compared with 31.38 for the entire sample of 1,365 students.

Student friendship patterns were identified by comparison of students who listed each other as best friends. When all pairs of freshman mutual friends were compared, significant correlations were obtained on all subscales except Puritan morality; as seniors, significant correlations were obtained on all subscales except moral relativism.

The effort to relate personal values with friendship patterns was only partially successful. Relationships were not nearly as clear-cut as anticipated. The primary fault may lie either in the lack of precision of the measurement instrument or in the validity of the means used to identify friendship.

Values of Teachers

The teachers in the sample completed the *Differential Values Inventory* and identified students with whom they felt they could communicate easily. Comparisons were made between the personal-value subscales of the teacher and the student he identified. The resultant correlations were not of sufficient magnitude to be significant.

Students were asked to identify the teachers whom they best understood in class. An arbitrary decision was made to divide the listed teachers into two groups (by numbers of students listing them) and to test the extremes, which were labeled as accepted and rejected teachers. The personal-value profiles of these two groups of teachers, when compared by analysis of variance, yielded an *F*-value of 1.40 with 3 and 133 degrees of freedom—too small to be significant at the 5 percent level. Thus, it was not possible to demonstrate that personal values were related to the ability of the teacher to be understood by his students.

Summary

Previous research concludes that college experience has little impact upon student values. This study, which deals with a sample of 1,365 high school students over a four-year period arrives at the following conclusions:

1. Whether one accepts or rejects the null hypothesis (i.e., that there will be no difference in personal values between students as freshmen and the same students as seniors) depends upon the groupings one chooses to use. When stratified by school, significant differences were found between value scores of boys as freshmen and as seniors in only one school, and then on only one sub-scale (Puritan morality). Profile analysis of value scores of freshman and senior girls showed differences in four schools but on only 19 of 80 sub-scale comparisons. Thus there were significant differences in freshman and senior scores in only 5 of the 20 school comparisons and on only 20 of 160 sub-scale comparisons, hardly a large enough proportion to conclude that personal values of students changed during the high school years. This would appear to be particularly true for boys.

2. Little evidence was found to confirm that there was any relationship between personal values and the ability of teachers and students to communicate with each other. Nor was it possible to demonstrate conclusively that personal values were related to friendship patterns among students.

3. There was a significant relationship between personal values and peer acceptance. Those students determined to be the most popular were hedonistic, while those defined as rejected had significantly higher scores on the future-time-orientation sub-scale. Perhaps this helps explain the popularity of the "now generation" attitude.

4. Personal values were definitely related to level of achievement, frequency of church attendance and future plans. The high achiever, the college-bound and the regular church attender held what was defined as traditional values. They placed high importance on future-time planning, work success, and on individual initiative. Their opposite, the low achievers, tended to be present-time oriented, conformists, and tended to rely heavily upon others for their success.

5. The characteristics which students sought in their future occupations were revealing, and for the most part these didn't change drastically during the high school years. They wanted their future occupations to be interesting, to permit self-expression, to provide security, and to permit them to help others. They rejected characteristics of leadership and being the boss.

gordon w. allport

crises in normal personality development

There is one trick every teacher knows: When trapped in a state of ignorance throw the question back to the class. Without suspecting the teacher's predicament, bright students will often rescue him.

This is the strategy I employed to learn something about crises in normal personality development. I passed along the assignment to my class of 100 captive undergraduates, and they obligingly provided me, through their own autobiographical writing, with the insights that I articulate now. Parenthetically, let me say that in my opinion no teacher or counselor has the right to require intimate autobiographical documents from students. Yet when given a completely free choice, the large majority will choose to write in the autobiographical vein. For the few who would find the experience too threatening, it should not be prescribed.

Influence of Teachers

First I shall report a minor investigation related to our main topic. I asked the hundred students, mostly sophomores and juniors, four questions with the results reported here. My first question was "Approximately

Reprinted from *Teachers College Record*, 1964, **66**, 235-241. Permission granted by Mrs. Ada Allport. This article is now in *The Person in Psychology: Selected Essays*. New York: Beacon Press, 1968.

how many different teachers at school and college have you had up to the present stage of your education?" The 100 respondents mentioned a total of 4,632 teachers. The three remaining queries were concerned with varying degrees of influence exercised by the teachers on the development of these students. With the percentages indicated as having played formative roles in student lives, the questions and their answers were as follows:

> How many teachers had a very strong or powerful influence on your intellectual or personal development? (8.5 per cent)
> How many others would you say had a reasonably strong, well-remembered influence? (14.8 per cent)
> How many do you remember only vaguely, or who seem to have had no substantial influence on your development? (76.7 per cent)

We are immediately struck by the fact that more than three-quarters of the teachers are remembered only vaguely and credited with no appreciable influence, whether intellectual or personal. As teachers, we all know the shock of discovery how little impact we had. A former student of mine brightened my day by remarking, "Years ago I took a course with you, but all I can remember about it is that the textbook had a blue cover." He grinned pleasantly while I shuddered inwardly.

Only about eight per cent of teachers are reported as having a very strong influence, and about 15 per cent are credited with a less strong but well-remembered influence. Another way of stating this finding is to say that the average teacher (assuming all teachers are equally effective) "gets through" to less than a quarter of the class, and exerts a really strong influence on not more than one student in ten.

Varieties of Influence

Asked to tell when and in what way they were influenced the students give us three facts of special interest. First, about half of all their examples deal with experiences of intellectual awakening. For example,

> She encouraged me to read poetry and drama beyond the class assignment.
> In chemistry the instructor asked us why bubbles appeared overnight in a water glass. When we said we had never wondered about that, he told us that everyone must question even the most common and seemingly trivial things.

And about half of the examples deal with personal development:

> She made me see that others did not judge me as harshly as I was judging myself.
> He had so much warmth and humanity that I wanted to be like him.
> She seemed tough and disagreeable, but was so kind and helpful to me that I realized I must think twice before passing judgment on anyone.

A second insight, based on the large array of illustrative incidents, reveals the remarkably *casual* nature of the influence. In hardly any case could the teacher or counselor have known that what he was saying at a given moment would make a lasting impression upon the growing mind and character of the student. Elsewhere (Allport, 1961) I have argued that in teaching values and attitudes it is not the deliberately adopted curriculum that is effective; it is rather the *obiter dicta,* the parenthetical remark, the "little true things," and above all the example of the teacher that count. And what holds for teachers no doubt holds for the counselor, too.

Finally, and most relevant to my topic, is the finding that in elementary school there are few remembered influences of special strength. Apparently development is gradual at this time, and the teacher does not often bring a sudden and traumatic experience of "dawn" to the pupil. Only 12 per cent report any strong or even appreciable teacher influence in elementary school. Fully 88 per cent of the reports date the occurrences in high school (58 per cent) or in college (30 per cent, with the college years still incomplete).

So it is in middle and late adolescence where the role of the teacher is most vivid to the student. It is in this period, according to Erikson (1950), that the identity crisis is in the ascendance. The young person seems to be moving from past childhood into present adulthood in a jerky manner. Development is not continuous like a hill; rather, it is episodic like a flight of stairs. It is this episodic or crisis character of development that brings both challenge and opportunity to the guidance officer.

Nature of Crisis

What precisely is a "crisis"? It is a situation of emotional and mental stress requiring significant alterations of outlook within a short period of time. These alterations of outlook frequently involve changes in the structure of personality. The resulting changes may be progressive in the life or they may be regressive. By definition, a person in crisis cannot stand still; that is to say, he cannot redact his present traumatic experience into familiar and routine categories or employ simple habitual modes of adjustment. He must either separate himself further from childhood and move toward adulthood, or else move backward to earlier levels of adjustment which may mean becoming disorganized, dropping out of school, escaping from the field, developing hostilities and defenses, and in general becoming a thorn in the flesh of the teacher, the parent, the counselor, the dean, and occasionally of the police. Sometimes, following a crisis, the adolescent will become stabilized anew after four or five weeks of severe disorganization; but in many cases the trauma retards development for a year or more, and may even leave a life-long scar.

Turning now to my data, drawn from college undergraduates, we ask first about the phenomenology of crisis. What does it "feel" like to the student? Common is a sense of numbness and apathy. Upon entering college, the youth finds fewer strict role-prescriptions than at home. He is no longer tied to his domestic filial role, to the highly structured routine of high school, to his siblings, to his church connections, to his teen-age sub-cultures. He has left his possessions behind—his stamp collection, his television, his girl friends, his boy friends. All his familiar roles are in suspension. As one student writes,

> The complete freedom of college is itself a crisis. For the first time I live in close contact with people who are not members of my family. They don't even resemble people I have known before. They have different opinions, different origins, and different emotions. I feel numbed by it all.

Interestingly enough, this sense of hollowness does not necessarily have its maximum effect during the freshman year. The excitement of new scenes and especially frequent correspondence with and visits back to the home town keep the silver cord intact. The student feels that he should prove to his parents, teachers, friends, that he can master the college environment and thus please them and win their approval as he has done in the past. The impending crisis has not yet overwhelmed him (or her—for what I am saying is as true for college girls as for boys).

It is the sophomore year that seems (from my data) to be the year of crisis *par excellence.* Suddenly it becomes no longer tolerable to live one's life for the edification of people "back home." The time has come for the child of the past to be separated once and for all from the adult of the present. Here are typical phenomenological statements of this stage of the crisis:

> I feel I have been dragged into something against my will.
> I feel like a rat in a maze.
> I want to be a law unto myself, but cannot.
> It seems suddenly that the decisions I make must be valid for the rest of my life.
> To shake off parental norms and values seems to me the most important thing I must do.

The life of the past and the life of the future seem suddenly to be at cross purposes. There is often an intolerable feeling of suspended animation. Recrystallization is not yet possible. The youth is waiting still to make a choice of careers, a suitable marriage, and to find an integrative philosophy of life which his diverse college courses are too discordant to supply.

Apathy and Anxiety

It is small wonder that apathy and a paralysis of will often occur. But apathy is only a mask for anxiety. The whole framework of life is disturbed. Whereas the majority of students contrive gradually to build a new framework in spite of, or perhaps because of, the goals of anxiety, yet a large minority cannot cope with the situation unaided.

From my data, I would estimate that three-quarters are able to take the progressive road in creating their new frame of existence. About one-quarter cannot immediately do so. Proof of this point is that the dropout rate during undergraduate years is surprisingly high—over 20 per cent at Harvard, about three-quarters of the cases representing voluntary withdrawals (Blaine & McArthur, 1961). The dropouts present a special problem of guidance. Blaine and McArthur write,

> The drop-outs as a group ultimately do quite well if properly handled. We attempt to establish a relationship, however brief or tenuous, with these students, not so much to prevent their leaving school, but rather in the hope of giving them some insight into the determinants of their difficulties so that their dropping out can be ultimately converted into a meaningful constructive experience instead of mere failure.

After a year or two of constructive work elsewhere, the majority of voluntary dropouts return to college and graduate. But they could not have met their crisis by remaining in the environment that was the context of their conflict.

The regressive road is surprisingly common. Among eventual dropouts, but also among other students, we find such self-destroying behavior as quitting classes, a compulsion to do trivial things, playing bridge until four AM, drinking bouts, feelings of unreality, fugues, and general debauchery. The candid documents received startle me a bit by the extent of plain juvenile delinquency among my innocent-appearing students:

One student finding himself unable to handle his conflicts over choice of career and over friction with his roommate, indulged in plagiarism on a term paper in such a way that he would be caught and forcibly separated from college. In this case a wise instructor, catching him in the transgression, turned the occasion into constructive counseling, forgave the deed, and put the lad onto the progressive rather than regressive road.

Here I venture a theoretical digression. The problem, as I see it, is one of interiorizing motivation. To put it in a student's words: "I am fed up with having everybody else cheer me on. I want to work to please myself rather than others, but I don't know how to do it." This plaintive statement points to a serious dilemma in our educational process. In school, the child is rewarded and punished by good grades and bad grades. Even in college, As and Bs are pats on the back, Ds and Fs are punishments. To gain love, the student must read books and toe the academic line. Finally, he obtains his degree (which is a symbol of academic love) and is freed from this external form of motivation. What then happens?

We know that a shockingly high percentage of college graduates rarely or never read another book after receiving their bachelor's degree. Why should they? Their love now comes from their employer, their wife, their children, not from the approval of parents and teachers. For them, intellectual curiosity never became a motive in its own right. External rewards are appropriate props in early childhood. But we educators, being limited by current inadequate theories of learning, do not know how to help the student free himself from the props of reward and develop a functionally autonomous zeal for learning. With our slavish dependence on reinforcement theory, I think it surprising that we arouse as much internal motivation as we do. In any event, we cannot be proud of the many educational cripples who after graduation, lacking the routine incentive of college, sink into intellectual apathy.

Crisis Areas

The counselor or teacher, of course, cannot wait for better theories of learning. He is confronted here and now with crises in the concrete. Four areas of conflict, judging from my data, are especially common.

Intellectual Crises. First, there are students whose problem is one of intellectual malplacement. Among my cases, a large number report that in primary and secondary school they were too bright for their class. The penalty is one of boredom lasting down into college work, which they still do not find challenging enough for their abilities. At the same time, double promotions in elementary and high school are not a solution. To be placed with older children often creates social difficulties far more serious than boredom. In fact, the evil consequences reported from double promotion are so numerous that we should challenge this particular solution of the bright child's dilemma.

The opposite type of intellectual crisis is also common. It is the deep disturbance that often results in college from intensified competition. It is statistically impossible for most students to maintain the same relative superiority in college that they enjoyed in high school. While this fact does not trouble the majority, it is a critical experience for those who depend on scholarship aid or who frame their self-image almost entirely in terms of scholarly pre-eminence. They are suffering a severe narcissistic wound.

Specific Inferiorities. A second area of crisis is the old, familiar "inferiority complex." Besides the sense of intellectual inferiority just described, we encounter deep disturbance due to physical handicaps or to plain physical appearance, with resulting shyness, loneliness, and misery. To be poor at athletics creates a crisis for males, probably more acute in high school than in college. To be a member of a minority group likewise creates an inevitable crisis somewhere along the line. Here again I suspect the major adjustments and defenses are prepared before the college age. Occasionally, the inferiority concerns guilt due to moral lapses. One student is still haunted by her dishonesty which enabled her to pass a certain course three years ago. She has felt miserable ever since about this critical experience and badly needs a means of expiation.

In this connection we may speak of religious crises. While they are uncommon in my sample, Havens (1963) estimates that at any given time 12 per cent of college students have a critical concern, and sometimes acute crises, due to their religious conflicts. I suspect the concern is even more widespread, but since it pertains to one's whole ground of being, it is seldom configured as a specific crisis at a given moment of time.

Another area, seldom mentioned but surely important, is the ideological crisis of modern society as a whole. Youth is inevitably worried, as are adults, by our uncertain future. Elsewhere I have discussed the withdrawal of American youth from their social and political context (Gillespie & Allport, 1955). Both the earlier and present data show an almost exclusive concern among American youth with their own lives. Compared with autobiographies of youth in other cultures, the American documents are far more self-centered, more privatistic. They are too baffled to articulate their distress, and so take refuge in their private concerns.

Sex and Family

Sex Conflicts

Needless to say, our candid discussions of crises frequently, in fact usually, report acute sex conflicts. Extremely common are breakups in boy-girl relationships which are usually taken as a disaster only slightly less fatal than the end of the world. Such breakups are so recently experienced that college students do not realize that they will, in spite of their present feelings, eventually make a good recovery.

We should face the fact that at least in the early years of college life crises in the sexual sphere are for the most part frankly genital in their reference. The biological drive is so powerful that the youth is concerned with it almost by itself. Its integration into mature love, into marriage, into career plans, into an embracing philosophy of life, exceeds his present capacity. He is likely to think that genitality by itself is maturity. Sexual gratification is frankly the aim, often with devastating consequences. At this stage of development, the students have much to say about sex and little to say about mature love.

Family Conflicts

I have left until last the most pervasive area of conflict and crisis. I am referring, of course, to the situation that exists between every adolescent and his parents. It is not enough to say that adolescent rebellion against the parents is the rule. Of course it is; but my documents show that the whole history of the relationships from the time of earliest memories is important. Almost any irregularity in normal family life is felt bitterly and may trouble a student even into adulthood. A mother who is neglectful or self-centered, or perhaps overpossessive and neurotic, leaves traumatic traces in the child's life. A father who is ineffectual and weak, or cruel, or absent (if only for wartime service) leaves the child with a lasting feeling of protest.

One document of unusual maturity notes that many college students seem to need their parents as scapegoats. They find it comfortable to blame parents for their own shortcomings. Perceiving that their parents are not all-powerful, all-wise, and all-perfect, they can say, "Well, no wonder I am having a hard time growing up; they didn't raise me right." Thus, an adolescent, having no genuine ground for complaint, may yet soak himself in self pity, not being mature enough to relate his restricted image of his parents to the totality of human nature—not yet ready to appreciate the fact that his parents, considering human limitations, may have done a good job. Even if the job was not especially good, the adolescent seems not yet able to appreciate his parents' good intentions as an important value in their own right. From talking with many parents, I hazard the hypothesis that normally it is not until the age of 23 that a child encounters his parents on a mature, adult-to-adult basis.

This brief account of crises emanating from the parent-child relationship leads me to a final point. My students were required to discuss their crises from the point of view of personality theory. They were free to employ any of the theories they were studying in my course. Most of them took Freud. (I may add that the reason was not because Freud was their instructor's favorite author.)

The Conditions of Theory

Now my observation is this: Their Freudian interpretations seemed to fit well if and when the family situation in early life was disturbed. When the father was absent or ineffectual, when the mother was notably aggressive, when there was deliberate sex stimulation within the family—in such cases, it seems that the Oedipal formula provides a good fit, together with all its theoretical accoutrements of identification, superego conflict, defense mechanisms, castration threats, and all the rest.

When, on the other hand, the family life is reasonably normal and secure, a Freudian conceptualization seems forced and artificial. If we say, by way of rough estimate, that 60 per cent of the students try a Freudian conceptualization of their own cases, about 10 per cent turn out to be wholly convincing and theoretically appropriate. The remaining 50 per cent appear to be somehow contrived and badly strained.

I am wondering whether the same ratio might be applicable to cases that come to counselors. If a counselor or a therapist approaches every client or patient with the preconceived belief that his life must fit a Freudian frame of conceptualization, he may win in a minority of the cases, but lose in the majority.

Even where a Freudian approach is clearly justified, exclusive adherence to it may distract the counselor from many significant developments within the life—for example, from the present functional significance of religious and aesthetic values, from the competence and interests that extend beyond the neurotic core, from the client's conscious plans for the future, and from his "will to meaning" and existential concern with life as a whole.

Every person concerned with guidance, or for that matter with teaching, needs as background some general theory of the nature of human personality (Allport, 1962). Our tendency, I fear, is to draw our theories from the realm of illness and deviance. It is somehow tempting to apply psychiatric rubrics to all personalities, for psychiatric rubrics are vivid, incisive, dramatic, and easy. Our conceptual banners bear such sloganized concepts as Oedipal complex, character disorder, identity diffusion, schizoid, acting out, and maybe an array of dimensions drawn from the Minnesota Multiphasic Personality Inventory. All such concepts, of course, have their proper place. But personality theory for guidance and teaching needs also to be woven of less lurid fabrics.

Youth, whatever neurotic threads may lie in his nature, is busy with his realistic perceptions, with his gradual learning and quiet coping, with the slow extension of selfhood, with noncritical failures and successes, with developing a generic conscience and a personal style of life. Even in the throes of crisis, he seeks in undramatic ways to consolidate his gains and continue on the path of becoming. A theory of personality adequate to undergird the art of guidance will keep such nondramatic facts in mind. Crises in normal personality development are important, but so too is the slow growth of each youth's unique style of life.

ralph f. berdie

personality changes from high school entrance
to college matriculation*

In order to determine the extent of personality changes occurring between the 1st
yr. of high school and the 1st yr. of college,
comparisons were made of the scores on
the Minnesota Counseling Inventory of a
group of 259 students tested when they
entered high school and again when they
entered college. Of the 9 comparisons of
mean scores, 7 were statistically significant
for the men and 4 for the women. In each
instance but 1, changes in the mean scores
reflected improved psychological status.
Correlations between 9th and 13th grade
scores ranged .34–.71 and the social and
family attitudes of women appeared more
predictable than those for men. To an appreciable extent, the way a student responds to a personality inventory in Grade
9 is related to the way he will respond 4 yr.
later.

The adolescent, as he evolves into the young
adult, undergoes considerable personality
change, but relatively little systematic information is available concerning these changes
as they occur between the ages of 14 and
18. Developmental studies have given more
attention to changes occurring from birth to
adolescence or from adolescence to later
maturity. Often the variables with which

Reprinted with permission of the author and the American
Psychological Association from the *Journal of Counseling Psychology*, 1968, **15**, 376-380.

*The author expresses his appreciation to Ellis Sage for his
efforts in identifying *S*s included in this study.

these studies have been concerned are of
greater significance to the psychologist or
case worker than to the counselor, parent, or
teacher. Two of the reasons for this paucity
of information are the difficulty of following
the development of a selected group of persons over an extended period of time and the
dearth of adequate observational methods.

The purpose of this study was to observe
changes in measurable aspects of personality occurring between the ninth and thirteenth grades. Systematic information
regarding these changes has been reported
by Hathaway and Monachesi (1953), in their
follow-up study of Minnesota Multiphasic
Personality Inventory (MMPI) scores of ninth
graders. The orientation of the MMPI, however, is essentially medical and clinical, and
the information derived from it sometimes is
difficult to interpret relevantly to those working with typical adolescents. The Minnesota
Counseling Inventory (MCI), which contains
some of the scales of the MMPI, was developed by Berdie and Layton in 1957 to
provide a less clinically-oriented inventory
than the MMPI that could be used in schools
for purposes of counseling and research. The
personality dimensions included in the MCI
were selected following considerable discussion with counselors and teachers of personality variables significant in the student's
school behavior. The inventory provides a

means for appraising the status of a student's personality in terms of these variables.

The Family Relationships (FR) scale reflects the adjustment of the student to his family. The Social Relationships (SR) scale refers to the nature of the student's relation with other persons. The Emotional Stability (ES) scale tends to reflect the extent to which students worry, are self-conscious, are calm and relaxed, are fearful and timid, and are emotionally stable or unstable. The Conformity (C) scale indicates the type of adjustment a student makes in situations requiring conforming or responsible behavior. The Adjustment to Reality (R) scale refers to a student's way of dealing with reality—how he approaches threatening situations in order to master them or withdraws from them in order to avoid them. The Mood (M) scale indicates a student's mood or emotional state. The Leadership (L) scale is related to personality characteristics reflected in leadership behavior. The Validity (V) scale represents the degree of defensiveness of the student. The first three scales were derived from the Minnesota Personality Scale, the remainder of the scales from the MMPI.

High scores on all of the original scales suggest characteristics usually considered undesirable; low scores suggest desirable behaviors.

Evidence for the validity of the inventory is found in the standardization procedure, in a restandardization for college students performed by Brown (1960b), in a validity analysis of the original scales and factorial scales performed by Crewe (1967), and in studies that have reported relationships of MCI scores to smoking (Berger, 1967), to college persistence (Brown, 1960a), and to success or failure in a hospital treatment program (Davis, 1959). Other studies have reported characteristics of students who are and who are not disciplinary problems (Lesar, 1964), relationships of MCI scores and accident involvement (Schwenk, 1966), characteristics of students with various high school activities patterns (Smith, 1964), and persistence of Institute of Technology students (Watley, 1965). Evidence from these studies suggests that an observable relationship often is found between MCI scores and other meaningful and relevant behaviors of high school and college students.

Method

The present study consists of a comparison of the MCI scores obtained by a group of Minnesota high school students tested in ninth grade and the scores of these same students retested as college freshmen.

In the fall of 1963, 1964, and 1965, 148 men and 111 women entering the University of Minnesota as freshmen were identified who had taken the MCI as ninth grade students in 43 Minnesota high schools in the fall of 1959, 1960, and 1961. The students tested came from relatively small noncity high schools in Minnesota which at that time were administering the MCI to all of their ninth grade students as part of the Minnesota State-Wide Testing Program. These students, along with most other entering freshmen at the university, were again given the MCI during the advanced registration and orientation program. Of the 259 freshmen, 161 were entering the arts college; 51, the Institute of Technology; 46, the College of Agriculture, Forestry, and Home Economics; and 1, the School of Mortuary Science; 177 came from rural schools, 82 from suburban schools. The mean scores of these students on the college aptitude tests used by the university were slightly higher than the means for the entire university, but the differences were not large.

The mean MCI scores of the students tested in the ninth grade were plotted on the profiles for ninth and tenth grade students and the mean scores obtained by college freshmen were plotted on the college freshmen profile. These comparisons indicated that the ninth grade scores for both men and women were extremely close to the scores obtained by the norm groups, and the college freshmen scores closely resembled the scores of the college norm groups. The group studied here did not seem to be different in terms of either their ninth or thirteenth grade scores when compared to available norm groups.

On each MCI scale the mean and standard deviation were calculated for each sex and correlation coefficients calculated between scores of ninth grade and college tests. The significance of differences between means and variances was calculated using appropriate tests for correlated measures.

TABLE 1. MINNESOTA COUNSELING INVENTORY *M*s, *SD*s AND CORRELATIONS OF MINNESOTA STUDENTS TESTED IN GRADE 9 AND LATER AS COLLEGE FRESHMEN

| Scale | Men[a] | | | | | Women[b] | | | | |
| | Grade 9 | | College freshmen | | *r* | Grade 7 | | College freshmen | | *r* |
	M	*SD*	*M*	*SD*		*M*	*SD*	*M*	*SD*	
Validity	3.63	2.31	3.41	2.36	.62	3.77	2.27	3.66	2.01	.34
Family Relations	7.12	5.28	7.56	5.84	.50	8.50	6.73	8.46	6.08	.59
Social Relations	22.12	11.00	20.04	14.31	.56	19.23	10.86	17.59	11.50	.71
Emotional Stability	13.13	6.52	10.49	6.54	.55	15.85	6.58	13.43	6.90	.48
Conformity	11.90	3.93	10.84	3.87	.46	12.64	3.36	11.41	3.50	.38
Reality	10.90	6.86	7.41	6.14	.52	11.75	7.57	8.47	6.85	.60
Mood	11.93	3.41	10.71	3.79	.40	12.93	4.15	12.62	4.41	.46
Leadership	11.95	4.40	11.18	5.71	.49	12.65	4.89	12.15	4.90	.65
Developmental	19.34	6.45	11.15	4.77	.35	16.28	4.11	10.73	4.28	.43

[a]*N* = 147.
[b]*N* = 110.

Included in the analysis was the developmental or age scale developed by Sage (1966). Sage, using this same sample of students and a double cross-validation design, identified 51 items for men and 31 items for women that showed differential responses from Grade 9 to Grade 13. Scores on the men's scale correlated −.73 with age and on the women's scale −.71 with age. A high score on this scale was characteristic of the younger age group. The results presented here on the developmental scale must be interpreted in light of the fact that this was the validation group used in standardization of the scale, although the original research using the cross-validation method showed little shrinkage.

Results

The results of the analyses are presented in Table 1. For the women, in each instance the mean score obtained in Grade 13 is lower than the mean score obtained in Grade 9. For the men, on each scale but FR the mean score drops from Grade 9 to Grade 13, and on the FR scale there is a slight increase.

For the men, the differences between means are statistically significant at or beyond the .01 level for the FR, ES, C, R, M, L, and developmental scales, between the .01 and .05 level for the SR scale, and not significant for the V and L scales. Among the women, differences are significant at or beyond the .01 level for the ES, C, R, and developmental scales, between the .01 and

.05 level for the SR scale, and not significant for the V, FR, M, and L scales.

The changes reflect a slight improvement in the social relations of students, a slight increase in emotional stability, a more responsible approach to life, better contact with reality, better mood, and a somewhat more extroverted or leadership attitude. The women show about the same family attitudes in Grade 13 that they demonstrated in Grade 9, but the men show slightly more negative family attitudes.

Most ninth grade boys have not progressed very far into the adolescent rebellion against the family and this rebellion is perhaps at its height around the time of graduation from high school or entrance to college. Many fathers will agree that the relationship the 18-year-old boy has with his family is not quite as satisfactory as that he had when he was 14. Perhaps a larger proportion of girls by the time they have graduated from high school have resolved many family conflicts and this may be reflected by the slightly lower thirteenth grade score on FR.

Not only did the mean scores change over the 4-year period, but so did some of the variances for the men. Changes in variance were statistically significant among the men for the SR, L, and developmental scales, all significant at the .01 level. On the first two scales, which are highly intercorrelated, the men became increasingly variable, on the developmental scale less so. The average boy, as he matures, may become increasingly socialized, but a broader range of social behaviors and preferences may typify an older group more than a younger group of teen-age boys. The variances did not change for the women.

All of the correlation coefficients in Table 1 are significant beyond the .01 level of probability. These correlations between ninth and twelfth grade tests reveal a degree of personality stability somewhat surprising, in light of the relatively low reliabilities of most personality inventories, including the MCI. The test-retest correlations after a period of 3 months for high school seniors described in the test manual ranged .56–.86 and the odd-even reliabilities ranged .57–.94. The M scale tends to have the lowest reliability, and it also is the scale in this study that, at least for the men, has the lowest test-retest correlation. The scale with the highest reliability tends to be the SR scale and in this study it tends to be the scale with the highest test-retest correlations. The size of these test-retest correlations suggests that considerable change takes place in personality, that these changes are not consistent from person to person, but that nevertheless some consistency can be claimed for these personality variables over a 4-year period.

On the FR scale the correlation between ninth and thirteenth grade for the men is .50, for women .59, and for the SR scale .56 for men and .71 for women. The L scale, which is related with the SR scale, provides test-retest correlations of .49 and .65. Except for the V scale these tend to be the largest differences between men and women.

These differences suggest that the attitudes toward family and social relations for women are more fully developed in Grade 9 and persist unchanged to a greater extent than they do for men during the following few years. One might say that for ninth grade boys it is quite difficult to predict what they will be like in terms of their family or social attitudes 4 years later, but for women this is done with greater accuracy. The age scale provides a lower test-retest reliability than do most of the other scales. Apparently if the scale is used in Grade 9 to assess the developmental level of a student's personality, this cannot be used to predict what his developmental level will be 4 years later.

The interscale correlations were compared for the ninth grade tests and for the thirteenth grade tests, and inspection suggested that the relationships between the scales did not change during the 4-year period. For example, the correlation for men between FR and ES was .48 in Grade 9 and .56 in Grade 13, between SR and L, .75 in Grade 9 and .86 in Grade 13. Slightly more of the correlations increased than decreased during the 4-year period, but a number of them decreased, and no pattern could be observed suggesting that there were systematic changes in relationships between scales during the interval.

Correlations available but not reported here between the developmental scale and other MCI scales suggest that the age scale is most closely related to the R scale. For a sample of 100 arts college women this correlation was .55, and for a sample of 100 arts college men, .82. Consistently the R scale has been the most difficult MCI scale for which to observe validity relationships. It is closely similar to the schizophrenic scale of the MMPI and the correlations suggest that a person who obtains a high score on the schizophrenic scale may be responding in many ways similar to persons in a much younger age group. The changes over time in the R scale closely resembled those in the developmental scale.

Conclusions

The results reveal that considerable change occurs in the personality of typical students from Grades 9 through 13, but for the variables considered here there is some order in these changes. To some extent, the way a student responds to a personality inventory in Grade 9 is related to the way he will respond 4 years later. In general, the changes suggest that the person as a college freshman is somewhat better adjusted personally than he was as a high school freshman, but that men as college freshmen perhaps are experiencing greater family strain than they were 4 years earlier. The results also suggest that in so far as social and family attitudes are concerned, less change occurs among women from Grades 9 to 13 than among men. Finally, the results suggest that personality inventories such as the one used here may be useful in charting personality growth and development during adolescence and early maturity.

herbert a. otto

sarah t. otto

a new perspective of the adolescent

In a society which is "image-conscious" the image of the adolescent has become succeedingly less favorable over the years. The words "adolescent" and "teenager" are increasingly associated with "juvenile delinquent" and "trouble-maker." The public media of communication have contributed materially to the shaping of a traumatized or deformed image of the teenager. To cite but one example which could be duplicated on a national scale many times: a recent dance in Salt Lake City attended by over 3,000 adolescents resulted in fights, which police estimated involved about sixty persons. Approximately two per cent of those attending were therefore involved in what the newspapers subsequently headlined as a "Full-Scale Teenage Riot." The (sometimes) unwitting but consistent shaping of a distorted image of the teenager by the media of communications raises a number of questions: (a) Does the distorted image of the teenager fostered by the public media affect the self-system and self-image of our young people? (b) Does the adult perception of the adolescent erect a barrier between him and the adult world? and (c) Does this barrier impede the development of both the adolescents' and adults' potential? A new perspective of the adolescent is long overdue.

Reprinted with permission of the authors and publisher from *Psychology in the Schools*, 1967, **4,** 76-81.

As a part of the Human Potentialities Research Project at the University of Utah, a number of studies (Healy, 1965; Souba, 1965) have been conducted to determine the nature of the adolescent's strengths and personality resources. One outcome of these studies was the gradual emergence of a new perspective of the adolescent.

The role of the adolescent in contemporary culture has been both misunderstood and distorted. *We can speak of a cultural conspiracy in the sense that major "culture carriers," the adults, appear to enter into a tacit agreement to stereotype and label the adolescent. The adolescent keeps his part of the agreement by conforming to the label.* A vicious cycle is thus set in motion. Our lack of understanding of what the adolescent *can* contribute denies him his true function in relation to society and social institutions. We have closed our eyes to the fact that the adolescent has a vital function in relation to our institutions. Equally important, by not understanding the essential nature of the adolescent's role, *the adult denies himself a substantial measure of growth which is possible through his relationship to the adolescent.*

The image of the teenager combined with the culture conspiracy operate to suppress the development of human potential both in the adolescent as well as the adult. The following New Perspective of the adolescent is suggested as a means of regenerating the image of the teenager and as an opening wedge toward breaching the cultural conspiracy.

The adolescent is fully engaged in the process of clarifying and developing his identity—he issues the challenge that identity formation is a life-long undertaking.

There is a growing awareness in professional and lay circles that identity formation is an integral part of adult existence and does not cease until death. This process is often referred to as "the search for identity." It would be more correct to call it *"the ongoing development of identity."* This ongoing development of identity involves the searching out of latent and unrealized aspects and fragments of the self, thus bringing greater wholeness to the total self structure.

Closely related to this process is the concept of the open-self system. The open-self system is characterized by an attitude toward self and life which has the qualities of open-endedness and flexibility. Flexibility and being accessible to new ideas, new experiences, new viewpoints is an index to the individual's psychological health.

> The measure of health is flexibility, the freedom to learn through experience, the freedom to change with changing internal and external circumstances, to be influenced by reasonable argument, admonitions, exhortation and the appeal to emotions; the freedom to respond appropriately to the stimulus of reward and punishment, and especially the freedom to cease when sated. The essence of normality is flexibility in all of these vital ways. The essence of illness is the freezing of behavior into unalterable and insatiable patterns (Kubie, 1958, pp. 20-21).

The self of the teenager particularly has the elements of an open-ended system. Many aspects of his functioning have not as yet become frozen and are highly labile. Much of what appears to be erratic functioning is actually *purposive and developmental,* a manifestation of the open-self system in an accelerated state of growth. If we accept the view that identity formation (the ongoing un-

foldment of our uniquely individual abilities and powers) is a life-long process, *then the adolescent becomes the highly visible symbol of a challenge.* He challenges us to enter more fully into the searching out of that which is latent and unfulfilled; he challenges us to enter more fully into this process which brings wholeness to the structure of the self and which is a means of developing our identity.

As a part of developing his identity, the adolescent is engaged in an ongoing search for truth, for the meaning of life and death.[1] The adolescent is involved in searching out the meaning of existence. In contradistinction, for many adults the search for the meaning of existence is frozen into systems and certainties, *whereas it is the quality of search which lends vitality and joy to life.* The adolescent's quality of search can, for the adult, become a source of stimulation and inspiration.

The adolescent is at a point of major impetus in self-actualization and unfoldment—he symbolizes the human potential actively committed to self-realization.

Many well-known behavioral scientists (Gordon Allport, 1955; Carl Rogers, 1961; Abraham Maslow, 1962; Margaret Mead, 1966; and Gardner Murphy, 1958, to name only a few) subscribe to the hypothesis that the average healthy human being is functioning at a fraction of his potential. This recognition is not restricted to this country. There is a clear awareness by Russian scientists of the importance of the human potential. In an official publication of the U.S.S.R dated November, 1964 reporting the work by Vasili Davydov of the Moscow Institute of Psychology, we find the following under the heading of "Inexhaustible Brain Potential":

> The latest findings in anthropology, psychology, logic and physiology show that the potential of the human mind is very great indeed. "As soon as modern science gave us some understanding of the structure and

[1] In 1954 suicide was the fifth-ranking cause of death in the age brackets fifteen to nineteen. By 1962 it was the third most common killer of youth.

work of the human brain, we were struck by its enormous reserve capacity," writes Yefremov. (Ivan Yefremov, eminent Soviet scholar and writer.) "Man, under average conditions of work and life, uses only a small part of his thinking equipment . . .

"If we were able to force our brain to work at only half its capacity, we could, without any difficulty whatever, learn 40 languages, memorize the Large Soviet Encyclopedia from cover to cover, and complete the required courses of dozens of colleges."

The statement is hardly an exaggeration. It is the generally accepted theoretical view of man's mental potentialities.

How can we tap this gigantic potential? It is a big and very complex problem with many ramifications. (*U.S.S.R.,* 1964, pp. 42-43).

The recognition that healthy humanity is operating at 10 to 15 per cent of its potential represents the major challenge of this age. Yet very few people consciously select the development of their potential as a life goal and then systematically and planfully proceed to actualize this potential.

The adolescent is, for the most part, clearly aware that a great deal is potential within him and that the realization of this potential will determine the course of his future. He is at the same time instrumentally engaged in self-actualization and in becoming what he can be. He represents to everyone the human potential energetically engaged in self-realization, self-actualization and unfoldment.

The adolescent is a growth catalyst.

The teenager extends an invitation to adults to participate in growth. If this invitation is accepted and the adult is able to open himself, the teenager by the quality of his being and the nature of his interaction can trigger growth in adults. Since the essence of his being is growth and *becoming,* the adolescent offers both a challenge and opportunity to grow with and through him.

If we grant that the matrix of interpersonal relationships is the major medium of personality growth and if we acknowledge that the multiple and complex relationships between family members are for both parents and children a means of development and fulfillment, then it becomes clear that what the adolescent brings to the family is of

a high order of quality. He offers parents an opportunity to break established and restricted habit patterns, habitual modes of perception and habitual modes of relating. By the keen and discerning nature of his observations and the honesty of his confrontations ("Mother, you are often afraid of life," "Father, you are too much of a stick-in-the-mud.") he brings into existence a moment which can be grasped for insight and self-understanding—an opportunity to root out cherished yet destructive stereotypes one has about oneself.

The teenager in the home through the quality of his relationships presents to his parents the chance to regain the spontaneity, freshness and vitality so often buried beneath the cares and routines of adult existence. This, for the parents, usually comes at a time of life when it is most needed.

Unless the adult acquires the perspective or recognition that the adolescent functions as a catalyst, minimal change in the adult can be expected. *Outlook inevitably determines outcomes.* The very same principle also holds for the professional. His perceptions and emotional meanings (how he sees the adolescent and what he means to him) determine whether in the course of the professional relationship with the adolescent the professional will open himself to growth.

The adolescent by the nature of his qualities, his fundamental honesty, idealism and by virtue of his capacity to ask searching questions of life and experience creates multiple occasions for the examination, reassessment and regeneration of adult and familial values. Finally, the ideational flow or wealth of ideas of the adolescent (if allowed to proceed unimpeded) can lead to creative exchange and better communication between all family members. If understood and allowed to function in his natural role, the adolescent becomes a growth catalyst par excellence for parents and for the family as a whole.

The adolescent represents a force for social and institutional regeneration.

It has long been recognized that the teenager is a very astute critic of our social and institutional structures and is able to ask penetrating questions and raise fundamental issues. Unfortunately, this ability has largely been dismissed as a manifestation of "rebellion" and "revolt against authority." This is the equivalent of throwing out the baby with the bath water.

The adolescent brings to the social scene an idealism, integrity and commitment to values which penetrate to the very heart of dysfunctional institutions and social structures. He contributes a fresh viewpoint and often shows a keen ability for organizational analysis. If an institution shows lack of soundness in its functioning, the teenager will not accept this as the status quo but will ask "Why?" and call for change and reform. Perhaps more than the adult, the teenager recognizes the extent to which personality is indebted for its functioning to the social structures and inputs which form its environment. *The rebellion of the adolescent against institutions may stem from an awareness that social disorganization is related to personal disorganization and that a healthy self demands a healthy society.*

The adolescent represents a vital resource which has never been adequately tapped for institutional regeneration and renewal. There appears to be a partial awareness that the adolescent *can* make a contribution toward our institutional structures. In recent times a growing number of mayors of municipalities (and even governors and legislative bodies of states) have voluntarily relinquished their offices for a day to teenagers. Many of these officials have found it profitable to listen to the comments and suggestions of teenagers following their "term" in office. In the process of institutional evaluation and renewal, the adolescent represents a much neglected resource: he can make a significant contribution as co-investigator and partner, in efforts directed toward the study, improvement and the regeneration of our institutions.

The adolescent's healthy body sense and capacity for sensory awareness is an indicator of Individual Potential.

The adolescent is noted for a *healthy narcissism,* a healthy pride in his growing, developing body. He is also noted for his ability to enjoy fully the sights, sounds, and smells of the wonderful world which surrounds him.

This heightened sensory awareness, *joie de vivre,* and life-affirmative outlook need not be restricted to the period of adolescence. There is every indication that adults whose physical systems suffer from lack of proper exercise (with a consequent dulling of sensory capacities) can regain healthy body tonicity and body sense and experience an increase in sensory function by entering into a regime of physical conditioning and sensory awareness training. For the adult, the regaining of a healthy body sense usually brings with it not only an increased enjoyment of life and living, but also increased energy, drive and interest—qualities for which the teenager is noted.

It has been a finding from the Human Potentialities Research Project (Otto, 1964) that the development of a healthy body sense via a physical conditioning regime appears to have a markedly positive affect on the self-image and self-concept as well as the self-confidence of adults. The adolescent through his healthy body sense and quality of sensory functioning, issues an invitation to the adult to regain a soundness of physical well-being, pride in the body and increased enjoyment of living which is the potential of every man and woman.

The adolescent represents the wave of the future.

In many ways the adolescent is a cultural innovator. For example, the widespread acceptance by the adult world of the "new sound" and the plethora of new dances (the frug, the watusi) had their origin in an extended period of teenage enthusiasm and support of these forms of expression and communication. Certain styles of apparel and popular sports (surfing, for example) have first found favor with the teenager and then been adopted by the adult world. The innovative contribution of the adolescent to the cultural mainstream is much more pervasive than suspected—and largely ignored.

Ignoring the contribution of the adolescent is but another subtle manifestation of the conformity pressures which are exerted on youth with special care. Among the institutions our educational system plays a dominant role in delimiting the development of the individual's unique capacities. This fact is repeatedly rediscovered by investigators, most recently by Friedenberg's research (1963) which makes clear that "through pressures both direct and indirect the schools encourage or demand that the student relinquish his autonomy, sacrifice his personal desires and often reject his particular excellence on behalf of institutional and social considerations which themselves are often trivial." One step in the right direction is the recognition by some professionals that *adolescenthood* just as *adulthood* is a distinct entity rather than a period of transition. "As long as adolescence is conceptualized as an in-between stage, the adolescent has no status in his own right" (Maier, 1965). And we might add, we attach minimal worth and dignity to an in-between stage.

The adolescent symbolizes and is the wave of the future. The nature of his being and *the quality of his developing self* foreshadow the man of tomorrow. He is the citizen and leader of the years to come and should be the pride and hope of the generation which is moving into his shadows. The tragedy of this generation is that through its distorted view of the teenager it is both shaping him and inviting the anger and contempt which will be an inevitable harvest.

True understanding of the close *interrelationship between all members of the family called man must lead to the development of a new perspective of the teenager* which more accurately reflects his real function and contribution. The adolescent is the living symbol of man's unfolding possibilities—of the human potential actively engaged in the process of self-realization.

References

Alexander, F. *Fundamentals of psychoanalysis.* New York: Norton, 1963.

Allport, G. W. *Becoming: Basic considerations for a psychology of personality.* New Haven, Conn.: Yale University Press, 1955.

Allport, G. W. Values and our youth. *Teachers College Record,* 1961, pp. 211-219.

Allport, G. W. Psychological models for guidance. *Harvard Educational Review,* 1962, **32,** 373-381.

Allport, G. W. Crises in normal personality development. *Teachers College Record,* 1964.

Allport, G. W., & Odbert, H. S. Trait-names: A psycho-lexical study. *Psychological Monographs,* 1936, No. 211.

Baker, R. W., & Mandell, T. O. Susceptibility to distraction in academically underachieving and achieving male college students. *Journal of Consulting Psychology,* 1965, **29,** 173-177.

Berdie, R. F., & Layton, W. L. *Minnesota Counseling Inventory.* New York: Psychological Corporation, 1957.

Berger, E. M. MMPI item and MCI scale difference between smoker and nonsmoker college freshmen males. Unpublished paper. University of Minnesota, 1967.

Blaine, G. B., & McArthur, C. C. *Emotional problems of the student.* New York: Appleton-Century-Crofts, 1961.

Brown, F. G. Identifying the college dropouts with the Minnesota Counseling Inventory. *Personnel and Guidance Journal,* 1960a, **39,** 280-282.

Brown, F. G. The validity of the Minnesota Counseling Inventory in a college population. *Journal of Applied Psychology,* 1960b, **44,** 132-136.

Cattell, R. B. *Description and measurement of personality.* Yonkers, N. Y.: World, 1946.

Cattell, R. B. *Personality and motivation structure and measurement.* Yonkers, N. Y.: World, 1957.

Cattell, R. B., et al. *Handbook for the junior personality quiz.* Champaign, Ill.: Institute for Personality and Ability Testing, 1953.

Centers, R. *The psychology of social classes.* Princeton, N. J.: Princeton University Press, 1949.

Crewe, N. M. Comparison of factor analytic and empirical scales. *Proceedings of the 75th Annual Convention of the American Psychological Association,* 1967, **2,** 367-368.

Crow, L. D., & Crow, A. *Adolescent development and adjustment.* New York: McGraw-Hill, 1965.

Davis, H. G. Probability of success or failure among adolescents in a hospital treatment program as predicted by the Minnesota Counseling Inventory. Unpublished paper, Big Spring State Hospital, Big Spring, Texas, 1959.

Deese, J. *General psychology.* Boston: Allyn and Bacon, 1967.

Erikson, E. *Childhood and society.* New York: Norton, 1950.

Friedenberg, E. Z. *Coming of age in America.* New York: Random House, 1963.

Getzels, W. The acquisition of values in school and society. In F. W. Chase & H. A. Anderson (Eds.), *The high school in a new era.* Chicago: University of Chicago Press, 1958. Pp. 146-161.

Gillespie, J. M., & Allport, G. W. *Youth's outlook on the future.* New York: Doubleday, 1955.

Greenhouse, S. W., & Geisser, S. On methods in the analysis of profile data. *Psychometrika,* 1959, **24,** 95-112.

Hathaway, S. R., & Monachesi, E. D. *Analyzing and predicting juveniles with the MMPI.* Minneapolis: University of Minnesota Press, 1953.

Havens, J. A study of religious conflict in college students. *Journal for the Scientific Study of Religion,* 1963, **3,** 52-69.

Healy, S. L. Adolescent strengths: Strength concepts of adolescents. Unpublished master's thesis, Graduate School of Social Work, University of Utah, 1965.

Hilgard, E. R., & Atkinson, R. C. *Introduction to psychology.* (4th ed.) New York: Harcourt, 1967.

Jersild, A. T. *In search of self.* New York: Bureau of Publications, Teachers College, Columbia University, 1952.

Kramer, C. Y. Extension of multiple range tests to group means with unequal numbers of replications. *Biometrics,* 1956, **12,** 307-310.

Kubie, L. S. *Neurotic distortion of the creative process.* Lawrence, Kans.: University of Kansas Press, Porter Lectures, Series 22, 1958.

Lesar, D. J. Personality characteristics of high school disciplinary and nondisciplinary students. Unpublished paper, University of Missouri, 1964.

Linton, R. *The cultural background of personality.* New York: Appleton-Century-Crofts, 1945.

Maier, H. W. Adolescenthood. *Social Casework,* 1965, **46,** 3-6.

Maslow, A. H. *Toward a psychology of being.* New York: Van Nostrand, 1962.

Mead, M. Culture and personality development: Human capacities. In H. A. Otto (Ed.), *Explorations in human potentialities.* Springfield, Ill.: Thomas, 1966.

Miller, N., Campbell, D. T., Twedt, H., & O'Connell, E. J. Similarity, contrast, and complementarity in friendship choice. *Journal of Personality and Social Psychology,* 1966, **3,** 3-12.

Mouly, G. J. *Psychology for effective teaching.* (2nd ed.) New York: Holt, 1968.

Murphy, G. *Human potentialities.* New York: Basic Books, 1958.

Otto, H. A. The personal and family strength research projects—some implications for the therapist. *Mental Hygiene,* 1964, **48,** 447-450.

Prince, R. H. A study of the relationship between individual values and administrative effectiveness in the school situation. Unpublished doctoral dissertation, University of Chicago, 1957.

Rogers, C. R. *On becoming a person.* Boston: Houghton Mifflin, 1961.

Sage, E. H. An empirical approach to a developmental scale for college freshmen age differences on the Minnesota Counseling Inventory. Unpublished paper, University of Rochester, 1966.

Sanford, R. N., Adkins, N. M., Miller, R. B., Cobb, E. A., et al. Physique, personality, and scholarship: A cooperative study of school children. *Monograph of Social Research and Child Development,* 1943, **8** (1).

Schneiderman, L. The estimation of one's own bodily traits. *Journal of Social Psychology,* 1956, **44,** 89-100.

Schwenk, L. C. Personality correlates of accident involvement among young male drivers. Unpublished doctoral dissertation, Iowa State University, 1966.

Sheldon, W. H., Stevens, S. S., & Tucker, W. E. *The varieties of human physique.* New York: Harper, 1940.

Smith, A. T. Differential personality characteristics associated with participation in high school student activities. Unpublished doctoral dissertation, University of Minnesota, 1964.

Souba, C. E. Revision of inventory of personal resources from "A." Unpublished master's thesis, Graduate School of Social Work, University of Utah, 1965.

Spindler, G. D. Education in a transforming American culture. *Harvard Educational Review,* 1955, **25,** 145-156.

Thompson, G. G. *Child psychology.* (2nd ed.) Boston: Houghton Mifflin, 1962.

Thompson, O. E. Student values in transition. *California Journal of Educational Research,* 1968, **19,** 77-86.

USSR *Soviet life today.* Pedagogical quests, November 1964, pp. 42-45.

Watley, D. J. The Minnesota Counseling Inventory and persistence in an institute of technology. *Journal of Counseling Psychology,* 1965, **12,** 94-97.

Williams, R. L., & Cole, S. Self concept and school adjustment. *Personnel and Guidance Journal,* 1968, **46,** 478-481.

Annotations

Carlson, R. Stability and change in the adolescent's self-image. *Child Development,* 1965, **36,** 659-666. This article reports a longitudinal study of changes in self-image from sixth grade to twelfth grade. Self-esteem was found to be a rather stable characteristic and was not associated with one's sex. The study did indicate that boys and girls learned appropriate sex roles. Throughout the six-year period girls showed an increasing social orientation while boys showed an increasing personal orientation.

Chabassol, D. J., & Thomas, D. C. Sex and age differences in problems and interests of adolescents. *Journal of Experimental Education,* 1969, **38,** 16-23. This study surveyed 1366 adolescents. Major problems expressed by the youths were money, mental hygiene, study habits, personal attractiveness, family relationships, and personal and moral qualities. Money was the prime concern of boys and personal attractiveness was the prime concern of girls. Both ranked sex adjustments as the second most important problem by the eleventh grade.

Constantinople, A. An Eriksonian measure of personality development in college students. *Developmental Psychology,* 1969, **1** (4), 357-372. Students at each grade level in college were questioned about self-concept in a study based on Erikson's theory of personality development in late adolescence. The author observed some shifts in self-concept between freshmen and seniors, but many learning processes involving the self were still going on. Data also indicated a greater degree of male than female maturity over a four-year period. The article gives some insight into the unfolding self-concept.

Kurtzman, K. A. A study of school attitudes, peer acceptance and personality of creative adolescents. *Exceptional Children,* 1967, **34,** 157-162. This study relates creativity to other adolescent characteristics. The researcher found that more creative students tend to be more intelligent, adventurous, extroverted, and self-confident. They are not so acceptant of school as are noncreative adolescents. Also, creative adolescents are less popular among peers, although boys had a higher amount of peer acceptance than girls.

Nichols, R. C. Personality change and the college. *American Educational Research Journal,* 1967, **4,** 173-190. This four-year study of 432 boys and 204 girls indicates that during college the students became more specific and differentiated in their motives and interests, more aware of their own shortcomings and negative feelings, and less dependent on external standards for behavior.

Perez, J. F., & Cohen, A. I. *Mom and dad are me.* Belmont, Calif.: Brooks/Cole, 1969. This book represents a case study of a high school boy who was having difficulty in school and in developing his self-concept. It focuses around dialogue between a psychiatrist and the boy, his mother, and his father. Throughout the book one is able to see various influences that each parent had on the youth's development.

Rosenkrantz, P., Vogel, S., Bea, H., Broverman, I., & Broverman, D. M. Sex-role stereotypes and self-concept in college students. *Journal of Consulting and Counseling Psychology,* 1968, **32,** 287-295. Despite changes in the legal status of females, this article indicates that the double standard is still a dominant part of our society. Analyzing the opinions of individuals in their late teens to early 20s, the authors found that male behaviors are more socially acceptable than female behaviors. They also found that females held negative values of their worth relative to men. The authors hypothesize that stereotypes persist because of the cultural lag.

Sherif, C. W. Adolescence: Motivational, attitudinal, and personality factors. *Review of Educational Research,* 1966, **36,** 437-449. Sherif analyzes cross-cultural differences in personality and attitudes. She cites research articles indicating that the theoretical view of self as an organized system of attitudes toward others is consistent with behavior. The article also reports on studies relating self-other attitudes to sociocultural factors. Sherif emphasizes the importance of self-values.

index